COMBINED TRANSPORT DOCUMENTS

LLOYD'S PRACTICAL SHIPPING GUIDES

Other titles in this series are:

Chartering Documents
4th edition
by Harvey Williams

Hague & Hague-Visby Rules
4th edition
by John Richardson

Introduction to P&I
2nd edition
by Chris Hill,
Bill Robertson
and Steven Hazelwood

ISM Code: A guide to the legal and insurance implications
by Philip Anderson

Laytime and Demurrage in the Oil Industry
by Malcolm Edkins

Marine Claims
2nd edition
by Christof Luddeke

Maritime Law
5th edition
by Chris Hill

Multimodal Transport: Avoiding Legal Problems
edited by Diana Faber

Neil Cockett on Bunkers
by Neil Cockett

COMBINED TRANSPORT DOCUMENTS

A

Handbook of Contracts for the
Combined Transport Industry

by

JOHN RICHARDSON, FCII

LLP

LONDON HONG KONG
2000

LLP Professional Publishing
a trading division of Informa Publishing Group Ltd
69–77 Paul Street
London EC2A 4LQ

EAST ASIA
LLP Asia
Sixth Floor, Hollywood Centre
233 Hollywood Road
Hong Kong

British Library Cataloguing in Publication Data
A catalogue record
for this book is available
from the British Library

ISBN 185978 578 6

Text set in 10/12 Plantin by
Interactive Sciences Ltd
Gloucester
Printed in Great Britain by
MPG Books Limited
Bodmin, Cornwall

ABOUT THE AUTHOR

JOHN RICHARDSON retired from full-time employment with P&O Nedlloyd in April 1999 after a lifetime career in the shipping industry, firstly with the New Zealand Shipping Company Ltd/Federal Steam Navigation Company Ltd, and then with Overseas Containers Ltd (now P&O Nedlloyd Ltd), who he joined at the commencement of containerised combined transport operations in 1969. He has always been involved in the marine law and insurance area of operations and is a Fellow of the Chartered Insurance Institute (Chartered Insurance Practitioner) as well as having qualified for membership of the Chartered Institute of Transport (MCIT).

Having been in the combined transport industry since day one, John has been closely involved with the development of:

- combined transport bills of lading
- consortium operating agreements
- slot charter parties
- time charter parties or containerships
- various ancillary contracts in the combined transport industry
- various indemnities

which have required him to make an in-depth study of the chain of indemnity necessary in a complicated consortium operation, such as applies in the major containerised trades today. He is the author of Lloyd's of London's Press's publication "The Hague and Hague-Visby Rules" (now in its fourth edition). He prepared the first draft of the BOXTIME standard time charter party for containerships and was a member of the BIMCO working party that produced the final contract. He was also involved with the drafting of BIMCO's SLOTHIRE and GENTIME contracts and was a member of their working party considering the problem of delivery of cargo without production of a bill of lading. Until his retirement he was a member of the UK Chamber of Shipping Marine Law Policy Committee and the British Maritime Law Association Standing Committee on the Carriage of Goods and General Average. He is a frequent lecturer and author of articles on his subjects and has been particularly associated with efforts to develop the use of the waybill as an alternative to the bill of lading. John also produced the very successful P&O Nedlloyd brochure "The Merchant's Guide", which has become a standard work of reference in the industry.

In retirement John continues to maintain his interest in his subject and has associated himself with an organisation seeking to develop an internet based paperless documentary credit procedure using his electronic waybill idea. This continues to occupy his time and keep him in touch with developments within the industry, which he supplements by maintaining contact with his worldwide network of friends and contacts within the industry.

ACKNOWLEDGEMENTS

The author gratefully acknowledges the permission of Baltic and International Maritime Council (BIMCO) to reproduce the BOXTIME and SLOTHIRE charter parties and the CONLEASE Container Lease Agreement, together with their explanatory notes on SLOTHIRE and CONLEASE. He also acknowledges the co-operation of P&O Nedlloyd in allowing him to reproduce their bill of lading and waybill forms and quote extensively from their standard contracts.

The publishers and the author would like to thank P&O Nedlloyd for permission to reproduce the picture of the containership on the front cover.

CONTENTS

TABLE OF CASES

LIST OF FIGURES

PREFACE

I retired from full time employment in April 1992, after 42 years' experience in the shipping industry, broken only by two years' national service in air traffic control RAF Transport Command. Before national service I spent three and a half years with the Port of London Authority as a ledger clerk, learning the intricacies of documentation for imports. On demobilisation I joined the New Zealand Shipping Company's Insurance and Claims Department, where I was introduced to the legalities of the carriage of goods by sea and learnt that truism that, whilst shipping is international, law is national and, whilst there are many similarities, mainly thanks to various international conventions, interpretation in the UK may differ from that in America, China, Saudi Arabia, France or Belgium.

In December 1968 I followed my NZS Co. manager, who had moved over a couple of years earlier, into the embryonic consortium: Overseas Containers Ltd., which represented the container shipping interests of the major British public shipping companies: P&O (of which NZS Co. was a subsidiary), Ocean (Blue Funnel), Cayzer Irvine (Union Castle) and Furness Withy (Shaw, Savill & Albion) whilst the private companies: Blue Star/Port Line, Ben Line, Ellermans and Harrisons, formed ACT.

I soon discovered that we were involved in an entirely new ball game and had to start with a blank sheet of paper, from square one. For example, the O, S and D (over, short and damage) report, prepared on the outturn of each traditional break-bulk vessel at each port (which formed the basis of all cargo claims settlements, as it was a record of the tally and condition of cargo as it crossed the ship's rail, the traditional point at which the carrier's liability commenced and ceased) was useless in a combined transport service. Here liability commenced and ceased at a myriad of different places inland, where marine surveyors were not always conveniently to hand. Thus a whole new system had to be drafted to provide the claims clerk with the necessary data to process claims.

Contracts of carriage needed to cover land as well as sea transport and the consortium arrangements, whereby companies formed groups to swap slots to carry each other's cargo, created a minefield, particularly in the chain of liability area.

I soon became involved in international meetings with our international consortium partners from Europe, Australia, Japan etc. to draft the intricate documents to control the activities and inter-line relationships developed within the consortia. These were frequently highly complex, as the accountants insisted that activities were run in the most cost-effective way, regardless of the liability problems which they created. They then looked to the risk management team to achieve this contractually, in such a way as to protect the company from unwanted liability and ensure that any residual liability was adequately insured, in accordance with the company policy on such matters. Thus preparing such contracts required knowledge of the nature of the operation, the law on such matters, in all areas where a court might decide that it was entitled to hear a case involving that contract, and a knowledge of marine insurance, particularly protection and indemnity insurance.

Over the years I had many complex but enjoyable discussions on these matters as consortia formed, split and reformed with different members. These meetings involved experienced combined transport operators, who had been through the formative processes and understood the problems inherent in this type of operation, and new entrants, who thought it would all be just like break-bulk, port-to-port operations. Meetings with lawyers, insurers and sub-contractors invariably followed, in the quest to convince all concerned of the need for certain liability requirements to be followed in everybody's interest, requirements which were complex and not easily explained to one whose mother tongue was English, let alone many for whom it was not!

Upon hearing of my pending retirement I was urged by many to set down the benefit of my experience for those who follow. It was pointed out that, as one of the last of the original parties who drafted the initial combined transport contracts, I was in a position to know why things were drafted the way they were and, perhaps even more importantly, why they were not drafted in some alternative way. Now that I have a little more time to do so and after dealing with the pressure of a number of requirements following on from retirement, I have settled down to do just that. As a glance at the contents shows, I have tried to do this in some logical order, starting from a decision to become a Combined Transport (or Multi-Modal) Operator and then examining the contracts that follow from that decision in some sort of chronological order.

I trust that readers will find useful guidance in this book.

CHAPTER 1

PROCURING TONNAGE

INTRODUCTION

It will never actually happen like this but, for the purpose of placing things in chronological order, let us suppose that someone, with no existing assets, decides to become a combined transport operator. The first decision he must take is whether or not he is going to operate containerships or be an NVOCC (Non-Vessel Owning Common Carrier), procuring space for the cargo, for which he acts as a contracting carrier, by means of slot purchase agreements or cover bills of lading from carriers who do operate tonnage (of which more later).

If he decides to operate containerships, his options are as follows:

(1) He can purchase new or second-hand tonnage (in which case he will need a building contract or purchase agreement, both of which are outside the scope of this book).

(2) He can demise charter tonnage (in which case he will need to crew, manage and operate the vessels—an unlikely scenario for a newcomer). Or

(3) He can time charter tonnage.

The third is the most likely scenario for a new entrant into the business, as the time-consuming business of crewing and managing a vessel is undertaken by the owner (or his ship managers) and all the charterer has to do is give orders and supply bunkers. This leaves him free to concentrate on managing the trade interfaces with other sub-contractors and customers. It also means that he can "test the water" in a trade without putting too much capital at risk, as he can charter for a short period and hope to meet the charter hire payments out of freights collected from customers. The first contract needed, therefore, is a time charter for containerships.

BOXTIME

The remainder of this chapter is adapted from the author's previous publication "A Guide to the 'BOXTIME' Charter Party" published by LLP in 1990, with indications of likely amendments to be considered by BIMCO in the near future.

When containerisation first came upon the scene in the late 1960s, the only charter parties that needed consideration were "in house" arrangements (often demise charters) between related lines for taxation purposes, followed in 1968–69 by the birth of the cross or slot charter party, by means of which lines, who were parties to the consortia that were formed, swopped slots with each other on mutually acceptable terms (*see* Chapter 3).

It was some years before there was need to consider an "arm's length" time charter party for a containership and, when the time came, there was no suitable document available.

"Well of course containerships are only another form of dry cargo vessel, so the New York Produce Exchange (NYPE), Baltime, Linertime or some other dry cargo time charter party can easily be converted", went the reasoning at the time. Those who took this view were clearly unfamiliar with the combined transport operation which had been born on the back of containerisation. How, for example, can an NYPE Inter-Club Agreement operate in a situation where shortage and loss is established away from the vessel's side? Who is responsible for stowage and lashing? Just what should the respective liabilities of the owners and the charterers of a containership be?

For some years I watched with fascination and increasing frustration as containership time chartering was carried on using manifestly unsuitable documents as a starting base, which then suffered the indignity of having most of their terms and conditions deleted and were then swamped with a plethora of additional clauses that were frequently, and rather obviously, not drafted by professional draftsmen. In support of my chartering manager I argued long and loud with the owners, or the charterers (according to our position), brokers and P & I clubs to try and remove some of the more onerous or manifestly unsuitable provisions and replace them with something better. A long, arduous, uphill battle that was not always successful.

As containerships started to be built for chartering in the late 1970s, I felt sure that a custom drafted document for containerships must emerge, as the requirements are so different from those of breakbulk dry cargo vessels, but none made its appearance. Finally, in desperation, I raised the matter with the Documentary Committee of the General Council of British Shipping (GCBS) in 1982 and, for my troubles, I was invited to prepare a suggested draft working document.

Due to pressure of work and the need for research, it was nearly five years before I submitted my suggested draft to GCBS for consideration. GCBS referred my draft to the Baltic and International Maritime Council (BIMCO), who decided to sponsor the project and appointed a small working party (of which I was invited to be a member) to develop the idea to fruition. Hereafter the project became the joint venture of the working party, who were responsible for producing a recommended draft for presentation to BIMCO's

Documentary Committee for approval and implementation. This approval was granted in May 1990 at the meeting of the Committee in Leningrad.

Section I: Philosophy and aims

When I was invited to prepare a draft for discussion of time charter party designed specifically for containerships, I started by reminding myself of the aims which I hoped to achieve in such a document before proceeding to decide on the philosophy of the document which would achieve those aims.

(1) Simple, readable and well signposted

I was heartily sick of ploughing my way through acres of unsignposted, incomprehensible print (otherwise known as "NYPE amended") only to find conflicting provisions spread randomly throughout the text without cross-referencing. To me these equated to the conventional bills of lading over 30 years ago in which clauses like the following were common:

"(g) In the event of the imminence or existence of any of the following:—War between any nations or civil war: prohibition, restriction or control by any Government of intercourse, commercial or otherwise, with any country from at or to which the vessel normally proceeds or calls: control or direction by any Government or other Authority of the use or movements of the vessel or the insulated or other space in the vessel: the Carrier and/or his Agents and/or the Master, if he or they consider that the vessel or her Master, Officers, Crew, Passengers or any of them or cargo or any part thereof will be subject to loss, damage, injury, detention or delay in consequence of the said war, civil war, prohibition, restriction, control or direction, may at any time before or after the commencement of the voyage alter or vary or depart from the proposed or advertised or agreed or customary route or voyage and/or delay or detain the vessel and/or discharge the cargo (for delivery or storage or transhipment) at or off any port or ports, place or places without being liable for any loss or damage whatsoever directly or indirectly sustained by the Owner of the goods. If and when the goods are so discharged at such port or ports, place or places, they shall be landed or put into craft or vessels at the expense and risk of the Owner of the goods and the Carrier's responsibility shall cease on discharge, the Carrier, Master or Agents giving notice of such discharge to the Consignee of the goods so far as he is known. The vessel, in addition to any liberties expressed or implied herein, shall have liberty to comply with any orders or directions as to departure, arrival, route, voyage, ports of call, delay, detention, discharge (for delivery or storage or transhipment), or otherwise howsover, given by any Government or any Department thereof, or any person acting or purporting to act with the authority of any Government or of any Department thereof, or by any Committee or person having under the terms of the War Risks Insurance on the vessel the right to give such orders or directions, and if by reason of or in compliance with any such orders or directions or by reason of the exercise by the Carrier of any other liberty mentioned in this clause anything is done or is not done the same shall be within this contract. Discharge under any liberty mentioned in this clause shall, notwithstanding anything contained in the Bill of Lading, constitute due delivery of the goods under this Bill of Lading and the Owner and/or Consignee of the goods shall bear and pay all charges and expenses resulting from such discharge, and the full freight stipulated herein, if not prepaid, shall on such discharge become immediately due and payable by the Owner and/or Consignee of the goods, and if freight has been prepaid the Carrier shall be entitled to retain the same. The vessel is free to carry contraband, explosives, munitions or warlike stores, and may sail armed or unarmed."

This sub-clause, taken from a conventional liner bill of lading over 30 years ago, almost defies comment. It reads like a masticated dictionary regurgitated at random. To read and understand it requires the memory of an elephant, the breathing of an opera singer and the logical interpretation of a QC. In short it is a disgrace to the draftsman's art.

I longed to see something more resembling the approach in my company's bills of lading, where all clauses have headings and sub-headings and every opportunity is taken to present data in tabulated form to improve readability (*see* Chapter 6 for details).

(2) Logically organised

Logic, like beauty, is in the eye of the beholder and one man's logic is another man's random confusion. Nevertheless, a charter party, like any other contract, ought to impart its information to its reader in some sort of logical sequence. In short, it ought to tell a story in such a way that its user can easily find what he is looking for without the need to have to search through the entire text.

Inevitably some provisions are relevant in more than one place. Where this occurs the detailed provision is set out in the clause considered to be of closest relevance and reference is made to it in the other clause(s) by way of cross-reference. Not all the headings in the index are clauses. Some are merely cross-references (e.g. clauses 5(a) and (g), 6(c), (d), (g) and (j) etc.).

(3) Clear, unequivocal and unambiguous

I have read more gibberish in charter party clauses than I care to remember. Clauses that would guarantee a court case or arbitration if an incident, to which the clause even vaguely applied and involving a sufficiently high sum of money, arose during the period of the charter party. I have seen so many such clauses that I am forced to the conclusion that there are parties involved in chartering who operate, not on the basis of clarity to avoid dispute, but on the basis of "if I cannot get my wording I want something sufficiently vague to give me something to argue over if the subject of the clause becomes the cause of a dispute so I can at least force a compromise". Hopefully such persons will find little to attract them in "BOXTIME", which is designed with the unachievable idea of creating redundancy in the ranks of maritime arbitrators.

(4) Consistent language

Part of the discipline I have learned as a contract draftsman of operational transport contracts is the use of consistent language. This is really a branch of (3) above and makes a very important contribution to clarity, particularly in court where a judge is likely to say that different words mean different things and go looking for an alternative meaning where none is intended. One does not have to read many transcripts of commercial judgments to discover just how skilled the judiciary can be in splitting hairs when they have a mind so to do.

A good example of this type of slapdash inconsistency is reference variously throughout a contract to "containership", "vessel" and "ship" when referring to one and the same subject.

(5) Comprehensive

This is quite a tall order given the plethora of matters requiring attention in the operation of a time chartered containership and, in reality, total comprehensiveness is an impossibility as, whatever and however many points you cover, something which you have overlooked will turn up or something will happen in a way not envisaged. Nevertheless, comprehensiveness is an important goal after which to strive, if the intention is to avoid disputes. If a contract is left silent on any point deliberately after identification and consideration, this should only be on the basis of acceptance of the common law solution which will be applied in the absence of contract.

(6) Unbiased

Bias, like logic, depends on your point of view! This draft has been criticised as being an owners' charter by some and a charterers' charter by others, which perhaps indicates that it has found the middle path that has been sought. I genuinely feel that I have no axe to grind. Furthermore, as most containership charter parties are contracts between two carriers and not a carrier and a merchant, I consider that both parties ought to be prepared to accept an equitable document clearly delineating carriers' responsibilities.

Clearly biases of varying natures will be built into the contract as amendments are made in negotiation according to the slant of the market. However, if these are made to a contract starting from an unbiased base, there is less chance of either party inadvertently assuming unintended obligations, but the fewer the alterations the better. Ideally the charter party should be used unamended with the state of the market reflected in the rate and not in the clauses. If alterations must be made, then use of the correct language of the charter party and care not to leave cross-references to deleted clauses is recommended.

Looking back over these aims, it is clear to me that what I was looking for was a time charter party with the equivalent characteristics which my consortium colleagues and I had evolved over the past 20 years in operating agreements, slot charter parties and combined transport bills of lading. We had put our own house in order, so the time was now ripe to try and extend our consortium and combined transport philosophy into the procuring of additional tonnage to supplement the owned tonnage in our liner services and the chartering out of surplus tonnage to colleagues in other trades.

Laudable as these aims appear, the question is: to what extent have they been achieved? Only time will tell and I believe that we can claim a substantial degree of success, but to claim total success would be to delude oneself. Readers may be familiar with the definition of a camel as a horse designed by a committee and this spectre hangs over all committees attempting to achieve acceptable compromises between parties with different vested interests, as is clearly the case with time charter parties and the sometimes conflicting interests of the owners and the charterers. The working party, so far as was possible, attempted to meet all the reasonable requirements and objections of all factions in their deliberations and this often led to shuffling of clauses and amendments to wordings.

Fortunately such occasions were few and far between but it is on just such occasions that compromise wordings are produced which are sometimes not as clear as is desirable. (After all, compromise is sometimes defined as the process by which nobody gets what they want.) Such problems did not arise when drafting consortium slot charter parties as no one had a vested interest, each party in his turn being both the owners and the charterers, thereby making the drafting of a contract acceptable to all much easier.

I recall reading somewhere an article by a shipping journalist with a sense of humour (it could have been Chris Hewer in *Fairplay*) that all marine lawyers and arbitrators should subscribe to raise a monument to the drafter of the NYPE charter party, who has kept them comfortably in employment for so many years. Personally I think the suggestion erroneous. The monument should be to the thousands of amateur draftsmen whose incomprehensible, contradictory and obscure additional clauses made such a nonsense of the original document in trying to apply it in circumstances it was never meant to cover. Anyway, I sincerely hope that I and my colleagues on the BIMCO working party do not achieve immortality (or notoriety) in the manner suggested for the draftsman of the NYPE charter party. The bid for immortality of amateur draftsmen is something outside our control.

Section II: Problems

The problem in any contract of carriage for international transport is always that, whilst transport is international, law is very much a national matter. Quite apart from the differences between the laws of different states, the fact that such laws are written in and interpreted in the local language, whilst the charter party is in that "commercial Esperanto": English can also cause problems, as many words and phrases are incapable of precise direct translation.

Also, even when using the English language, words carry different interpretations in different areas. We quickly discovered that certain continental owners were unprepared to "warrant" certain things. However, they were prepared to "undertake" to do those things or that certain data was accurate even though, in English law at least, there is little or no difference. In either case the remedy for breach is provable damages, subject to all the legal doctrines of English law, particularly remoteness/foreseeability. So use of the right language became important in the deliberations of the working party.

The next problem was balance. Balance between the requirements of the owners and the charterers. Given a free hand the owners would have one responsibility only: collecting their charter hire and exercising their lien to secure it, whilst the charterers would seek a totally free hand in the operation of the vessel, with no liability for vessel damage and full recourse for all loss or damage to goods and containers. Somewhere in between these two polarised views lay the equitable solution we had to seek. The owners' attempts to base the charter party on "Baltime" had to be resisted, whilst the charterers' attempts to incorporate the more "charterer-friendly" aspects of consortium slot charter parties also needed toning down.

Another problem arose because many owners can only obtain finance to build a new vessel on the back of a long-term charter party covering the period of the loan. Financiers, it seems, are easily frightened by references in charter parties to the charterers' right to terminate the contract. So, even though this remedy naturally flowed from certain breaches, direct reference to cancelling the charter party had to be avoided "pour viter effrayant les chevaux". Again, no change in the effect of the charter party, merely a change in wording to accommodate the requirements of one of the parties to the contract.

At times during the deliberations of the working party I began to feel decidedly naïve. I had put forward several suggested clauses designed to offer formulae solutions to difficulties that frequently caused problems. The problems arose because these suggestions invariably called for a degree of co-operation on the part of both parties. More than once I was informed that, in dealing with owners or charterers like P&O, such provisions would be readily acceptable; however, there are owners/charterers who will abuse such provisions so that, whilst it is a good idea, we cannot agree to it. Some of my best ideas were knocked down in this manner and highlighted the degree of mistrust which can exist between certain owners and charterers.

The aim of consistent language also proved a most elusive one and, whilst I hope that readers will be hard pushed to find examples of inconsistency of wording, I know that one or two exist. For example, note that whereas the approach is to refer to sub-clauses as, for example, "clause 10(a)", in sub-clause 16(f) reference is made to "sub-clause 16(a)" instead of clause 16(a), which is the pattern elsewhere in the charter party. Also I now note that in clause 17(c)(i) bill of lading is referred to in the same paragraph with capital and then small letters. The same goes for arbitrator(s) in clause 20(a). Yes, total consistency is a most elusive goal.

These were just a few of the problems, over and above those inherent in agreeing a basic form of wording, which faced the working party and made the task of producing a totally new standard charter party a far from easy one.

Section III: Style

The BIMCO format of a Part I memorandum with a Part II contract is by far the best approach. A clear gathering together, in a position separated from the prose of the contract, of all the essential variable data to which the owners, the charterers and brokers need to make frequent reference, is clearly to be preferred (*see* page 9). Thus the BIMCO memorandum Part I format was adopted to display the operational detail of the charter party.

As the main contract in Part II is a relatively long one, an index is provided (*see* page 334) to assist in rapid identification of the required data. It is hoped that this innovation proves useful and meets with approval.

More so than for most other types of vessel, operating containerships calls for a particularly large amount of technical data upon which reliance can be placed. This is gathered together in Part III and its accuracy is undertaken by the owners. This is important: consider, for example, the House of Lords decision in the case *Tor Line AB* v. *Alltrans Group of Canada Ltd.* [1984] 1 Lloyd's Rep. 123 where, according to the charter party, the deck height was 6.10 metres but where it was, in fact, only 6.05 metres. That 5 centimetres made sufficient difference to prevent double height stowage of containers on a Mafi trailer.

As a quick glance at the index to Part II shows (*see* page 334), the major part of the charter party is grouped into six clauses: the Owners' and the Charterers' Obligations, Requirements and Responsibilities/Liabilities, with separate clauses to cover other matters of mutual concern or which are important enough to warrant separate clauses on their own. During the deliberations of the working party, many clauses were shuffled around to try to ensure that provisions appeared in their logical position. In many cases both parties had requirements/obligations etc. relating to a certain matter which also had reference made to it elsewhere. To avoid spreading clauses around too much, such data was usually grouped together into one clause with liberal cross-referencing made to it in the other areas. A good example of this is Lashings and Stevedoring, to which cross-references may be found in both Owners' and Charterers' Obligations and in Owners' Responsibilities/Liabilities.

Section IV: "BOXTIME" Part I

There is little that can be said about Part I that is not self-evident. It closely follows the approach and format so successfully adopted by BIMCO as its standard approach.

One thing worthy of note is that, unlike other BIMCO charter parties, which come in two parts, "BOXTIME" comes in three with a degree of duplication likely between Parts I and III. This is because I is designed to provide that data needed in the operation of the *charter party* whilst III is designed to provide that which is needed in the operation of the *vessel* and certain data is likely to be needed in both cases. Part I is the shipbroker's/

Issued by
The Documentary Committee of
The Baltic and International Maritime Council (BIMCO), Copenhagen

THE BALTIC AND INTERNATIONAL MARITIME COUNCIL (BIMCO)
UNIFORM TIME CHARTER PARTY FOR CONTAINER VESSELS
CODE NAME: "BOXTIME"

PART I

1 Shipbroker	2 Place and Date
3 Owners/Disponent Owners & Place of Business, Telephone, Telex and Telefax Number	4 Charterers & Place of Business, Telephone, Telex and Telefax Number
5 Vessel's Name	6 Call Sign/Telex Number
7. GRT/NRT / 8 DWT on Summer Freeboard	9 TEU Capacity (Maximum)
10. Class (Cl. 5) / 11 Flag	12. Service Speed (See Part III) / 13 Fuel Consumption (See Part III)
14. Type(s) of Fuel(s) (Cl 12 (d))	15. Maximum Bunker Capacity
16. Bunkers/Price on Delivery (Min -Max) (Cl. 12 (a) and (c))	17 Bunkers/Price on Redelivery (Min -Max) (Cl 12 (a) and (c))
18 Place of Delivery (Cl. 1 (b))	19 Earliest Date of Delivery (local time) (Cl 1 (b))
20. Latest Date of Delivery (local time) (Cl. 1 (b))	21. Place of Redelivery (Cl. 6 (m))
22 Trading Limits (Cl. 3 and Cl 5 (c))	
23. Period of Charter and Options if any (Cl 1 (a), Cl. 6 (m) and Cl 7 (f))	24 State number of Days Options have to be declared after commencement of Charter Period (Cl. 1 (a))
25. Rate of Hire per Day and to whom payable (Cl 1 (a), Cl. 7 (a) and (b))	26 Quantity of Hazardous Goods allowed (Cl 4 (b))
27. Insured Value of Vessel (Cl 18 (a))	28 Daily Rate for Supercargo (Cl. 13 (h)) / 29. Victualling Rate per Meal for other Charterers' Servants etc (Cl. 13 (j))
30. Name of Owners' P & I Club (Cl 18 (b))	31 Name of Charterers' P & I Club (Cl. 18 (b))
32. Charterers' maximum Claim settlement authority (Cl 16 (h))	33 General Average to be adjusted at (Cl. 14 (c))
34. Law and Arbitration (state a, b, or c of Cl. 20, as agreed, if c agreed also state Place of Arbitration) (Cl. 20)	35 Brokerage Commission and to whom payable (Cl 21)
36 Number of Additional Clauses covering special Provisions	

It is mutually agreed between the party mentioned in Box 3 (hereinafter referred to as "the Owners") and the Party mentioned in Box 4 (hereinafter referred to as "the Charterers") that this Contract shall be performed in accordance with the conditions contained in Part I including additional clauses, if any agreed and stated in Box 36, and Part II as well as Part III In the event of a conflict of conditions, the provisions of Part I and Part III shall prevail over those of Part II to the extent of such conflict but no further

Signature (Owners)	Signature (Chaterers)

Printed and sold by Fr G Knudtzons Bogtrykkeri A/S, 55 Toldbodgade, DK-1253 Copenhagen K. Telefax +45 33 93 11 84,
by authority of The Baltic and International Maritime Council (BIMCO), Copenhagen

Figure 1: BIMCO Uniform Time Charter Party for Container Vessels: "BOXTIME"

chartering manager's document. Part III is for the operations manager and stowage planner (*see* Part I and Part III in Appendix 1).

Note that the times in boxes 19 and 20 are local. Obviously these need to be converted to universal time co-ordinated (UTC) (*see* clause 7(a)) for the purpose of hire calculations, but it was felt that local times were less confusing in Part I.

Note also that, in the event of conflict between the provisions of Parts I or III and Part II, Parts I or III prevail over Part II; the standard contract.

BIMCO have it in mind to add "Fax Number" to box 6 and amend "GRT/NRT" to "GT/NT" in box 7.

Section V: "BOXTIME" Part III

Whilst "BOXTIME" provides a suggested format for this part, many owners already have the operational data that this part is designed to provide pre-printed for circulation to the charterers' operational staff to enable them to operate the vessel and attach a copy of such data to charter parties. It is likely that they will continue to do this with "BOXTIME", thereby replacing Part III with a list of details in their own format. In such cases two points are important:

(1) Check to make sure that the details provided include ALL the details you require (indeed the suggested format of Part I is not guaranteed as exhaustive and you may find that in any given circumstance you need different or additional data to that suggested).

(2) Ensure that the details provided are clearly headed "Part III' and are attached to and form part of the "BOXTIME" charter party so that the warranty in clause 2 can operate. THIS COULD BE VITAL.

If you fail to do this and then, for example, find the vessel's reefer plugs for power are incompatible with those on your containers, you may have a costly delay on your hands.

Section VI: "BOXTIME" Part II

This is a long and fairly comprehensive contract and represents a fairly radical departure from the type of contract in general use for chartering for dry cargo liner trades, in which field it is the first totally new document of its type for some time. For this reason close study of the text is recommended, as much of it is of a type which many in the commercial chartering markets may find unfamiliar. Those familiar with consortium operations in containerised liner shipping may find the text rather more familiar, as in several places it owes much to the draftsmen of slot charter parties and consortium operating agreements.

The charter party endeavours to be consistent in its language throughout and users would be well advised to follow this approach in any additional clauses.

"the Vessel"	(not vessel, ship or containership)
"the Owners"	(plural, not singular and with the definite article)
"the Charterers"	(likewise)
"Charter Party"	(with capitals and as two words)
"goods and containers"	rather than cargo (except where cargo is obviously the right word—*see* heading Clause 4).

Preamble

An opening introduction.

"It is agreed on the date shown in Box 2 between the party named in Box 3 as 1
the Owners of the Vessel named in Box 5 and the party named in Box 4 as 2
the Charterers as follows: 3"

Clause 1: Period of Charter Party and Delivery

"(a) In consideration of the hire detailed in Box 25 the Owners let and the 5
Charterers hire the Vessel for the period together with any optional exten- 6
sion(s) thereto as indicated in Box 23. Such options, always at the Charter- 7
ers' discretion, must be declared to the Owners within the period as indi- 8
cated in Box 24. 9"

This sub-clause has three purposes:

(1) To establish clearly the existence of the necessary three factors for a valid contract: Offer, Acceptance and Consideration.

(2) Provide for the period of the charter party by reference to box 23, and

(3) Provide for the mechanism for the charterers to declare any options written into the charter party in box 24.

"(b) The Owners shall deliver the Vessel to the Charterers at the Place of De- 10
livery as indicated in Box 18. Unless agreed by the Charterers to the contra- 11
ry, delivery shall take place no earlier than the time/date as indicated in Box 12
19 and no later than the time/date as indicated in Box 20. 13

If prior to delivery the Owners give notice to the Charterers that the Vessel 14
will not be ready for delivery by the time/date as indicated in Box 20, the 15
Charterers shall declare within 48 hours after receiving notice thereof from 16
the Owners whether they cancel or will take delivery of the Vessel but 17
without prejudice to the Charterers' right to claim proved damages. 18"

Paragraph 1 of this sub-clause merely provides, by reference to the appropriate boxes in Part I, for the place of delivery of the vessel on hire and the dates within which delivery must be effected, if the charterers are not to have the option to cancel the charter party. Note that the times stated in Part I are local times and not universal time co-ordinated (UTC)/GMT.

"Place of Delivery" is preferred to "Port of Delivery" as many charter parties commence either outside a port (crossing a meridian or parallel) or more specifically within a port than by mere reference to the port (e.g. the charterers' nominated berth Hamburg).

Paragraph 2 is an attempt to forestall disputes if the owners can predict in advance that the vessel will fail to meet her laydays cancelling (laycans) and will not be available for delivery by the date shown in box 20. Charter parties are sometimes made to commence some time ahead and may involve quite lengthy positioning voyages, sometimes in ballast. If the charter party is quite a long one, such voyages are clearly economical. However, it may happen that the previous employment delays the vessel in commencing its positioning voyage (for example: off hire time on account of engine breakdown added on to end of expiring charter party).

In such circumstances the charterers clearly have a right to cancel, which should not be denied them as, whether or not through any fault on their part, the owners are clearly in breach and the delay may be critical to the charterers. What this paragraph seeks to prevent is a situation in which the owners undertake a long positioning voyage without any indication from the charterers as to whether or not they will accept a late delivery. This is done by giving the charterers 48 hours within which to make up their minds whether to cancel or accept late delivery, if the owners advise their inability to meet the originally contracted dates. No doubt agreement to accept late delivery of the vessel will be qualified by setting revised laydays cancelling so that, if the vessel is delayed further, the charterers again have an option to cancel.

In either case the charterers' rights to claim any proved damages arising from the owners' failure to deliver on time are unaffected, so this provision is a sensible economical provision which could avoid an acrimonious situation arising if the charterers let the owners make their delivery voyage and then, out of spite, cancelled.

"(c) If the Owners are unable to deliver the Vessel at the Place of Delivery as indicated in Box 18 for any reason beyond the control of the Owners, delivery shall be made at the nearest point to the nominated Place of Delivery to which the Vessel may safely and reasonably proceed.

The Owners to give notice of readiness to deliver to the Charterers and/or the Charterers' local agents when in position to come on hire."

Paragraph 1—Effective delivery on hire features high on the list of subjects for charter party disputes, so this is something to which it is worth giving close attention. The problem is that disputes invariably revolve around the interpretation of a standard general wording in the light of infinitely variable facts of the case, which will always be different. It is impossible to draft a standard clause which obviates the need to make this interpretation: just what is "*beyond the control of the Owners*"? Clearly the unavailability of a nominated berth due to it being occupied by another vessel is, but what of weather? Some is a justifiable reason and some is not. If the weather is such as to make it dangerous to enter a port with a dangerous entrance, weather would probably qualify, but not in most other circumstances.

Accordingly, after much deliberation, it was felt that any attempt to provide guidance as to what was and what was not beyond the control of the owners would likely create as many problems as it solved and it was decided to produce a general unspecific clause, which left the interpretation to the arbitrator if the parties concerned could not agree.

Paragraph 2 covers the giving of notice of readiness to deliver. Note *readiness to deliver*, not to load, as delivery can take place in open water. Note also the *and/or* so that the owners discharge their responsibility by giving notice to the charterers OR their local agents but are expected to give notice to both if so requested.

Note also that notice cannot be given until the vessel is *in position to come on hire*. A master proceeding up the Elbe and passing Blankenese cannot radio ahead for the charterers' local agent: "Expect to berth at Burchardkai in the Waltershoferhafen at 1800 hours local. Please accept this as notice of readiness to deliver" (assuming that Burchardkai is the required place of delivery) and expect this to discharge his responsibility under this clause. He must wait until he is at Burchardkai before he can effectively give such notice, but that is not to say that he should not inform the charterers of his expectation to be in position to give notice at that time so that they can be ready to accept delivery. In any event, the owners will always give plenty of notice to the charterers of a vessel about to come on hire in order to secure payment of the first instalment of hire, which is due prior to delivery of the vessel. Contrast the delivery provisions with those for redelivery in clause 6(m), where much more forward notice must be given.

"(d) Delivery shall be effected at any time, day or night, Saturdays, Sundays 25
and holidays included. 26"

A sub-clause which surely leaves no room for doubt and needs no interpretation. With hire adjustable on a pro-rata basis (see clause 7(a)) the owners clearly wish to get their vessel on hire as soon as they have complied with sub-clause (c), even if circumstances are such that the charterers cannot make use of it (port not working night shifts) until some time later.

"(e) At the time of delivery the Vessel shall be clean and in all respects fit to 27
receive goods and ISO containers. 28"

If the owners are to be allowed to deliver in accordance with sub-clause (d) then the charterers are clearly entitled to expect to be able to commence working immediately. So the vessel must be ready before she can deliver. This means clean and fit to receive goods and containers that comply with ISO (International Standards Organisation) specifications. This means containers of 8 foot width and 20 or 40 foot length. A vessel set to carry bastard size American containers would not meet with the requirements of this sub-clause.

"(f) The Charterers' acceptance of delivery of the Vessel shall not prejudice 29
their rights against the Owners under this Charter Party. 30"

It often happens that a vessel is in some way deficient and in breach of the charter party at the time of tendering for delivery. If this deficiency is minor, does not affect the working of the vessel and is capable of rectification within an acceptable timescale, the charterers often agree to overlook this and accept delivery, so that the charter party can commence without delay. Unscrupulous owners have been known to claim that such acceptance of delivery amounts to a waiver of their need to comply with the requirement of the charter party, whereas the charterers intend it only as a temporary indulgence on their part to give the owners time to rectify a deficiency which may not be needed until later (e.g. charts not needed until later on in the charter or certificates required in accordance with clause 5(h)). This sub-clause makes the charterers' position in accepting delivery in such circumstances absolutely clear.

Clause 2: Owners' Undertaking

"The Owners undertake that, at delivery, the Vessel shall be of the description set out in Parts I and III hereof."

A clause which was the subject of much debate within the working party. Adopting a cautious approach, some owners' representatives were hesitant at the idea of guaranteeing all details of a vessel, particularly if it be data of a vessel still being built. However, certain facts and statistics are fundamental to the charterers in deciding whether or not they will charter a vessel and if so what they are prepared to pay and, in container operations above all, a small error can make a lot of difference. This was never more clearly illustrated than in the House of Lords decision in *Tor Line AB* v. *Alltrans Group of Canada Ltd.* [1984] 1 Lloyd's Rep. 123, in which the owners quoted a deck height as 6.10 metres. It was in fact 6.05 metres. Those 5 centimetres precluded the loading of a Mafi trailer with a two high stack of containers, thereby substantially reducing the payload available to the charterers.

In such circumstances accuracy of data is vital to the charterers and the only source of such data is the owners. It is not unreasonable therefore that the owners should be asked to be responsible for the accuracy of the data they provide as part of their promotion of their vessel.

Of course the immediate retort of the owners is that, if they undertake the accuracy of such details, the charterers will go round with a fine tooth comb looking for discrepancies if they wish to abort the charter party or claim damages to reduce charter hire and if you look hard enough you can always find something. The trading truism, that unless you have a willing buyer and a willing seller you will always have trouble, is as valid in chartering as elsewhere so, to prevent this, I suggested a second paragraph to this clause to restrict the opportunity of the charterers to abuse this benefit. It read as follows:

"Should any of these details be shown at any time prior to the commencement of the Charter Party, or during the currency of the Charter Party, to be inaccurate then, provided the Charterers can prove that the inaccuracy was instrumental in prejudicing their operation of the Vessel as planned prior to the discovery of such inaccuracy, the Charterers shall have the option to cancel this Charter Party, upon notice to the Owners and without prejudice to the Charterers' right to damages for breach of warranty. If the Charterers elect not to cancel this Charter Party, the Owners shall reimburse the Charterers for any proved loss, expense or claim attributable to said inaccuracy which the Charterers incur throughout the period of this Charter Party."

Without prejudice to the charterers' right to damages for breach of warranty it gives the charterers two options:

(1) To cancel the charter party, OR

(2) Claim against the owners for any "PROVED loss, expense or claim attributable to said inaccuracy".

BUT ONLY if they can "PROVE that the inaccuracy was INSTRUMENTAL in prejudicing their operation of the Vessel AS PLANNED PRIOR to the discovery of such inaccuracy".

This clearly restricts the opportunity of the charterers to abuse this benefit but recognises that a small inaccuracy could make a lot of difference to them.

However, after much debate, the working party unanimously decided that this additional paragraph should not be adopted in a standard charter party, even though it gave the owners some protection from the charterers' abuse of this clause. They recognised the owners' concern at going to their mortgagee bankers (whose knowledge of charter party law is often somewhat restricted) with too many overt references to the charterers' right to cancel the charter party. This is, of course, the common law position which prevails in the absence of the paragraph.

So, even though the paragraph does give protection to the owners, it appears that most owners prefer to do without it in case it alarms their bankers. However, for those owners without a mortgagee banker to consider (do any exist?), or with a "knowledgeable, understanding one" (even more rare), this may be an additional clause worth considering.

It is important to differentiate between this "undertaking", which is an absolute warranty, and the responsibility of the owners in the operation of the vessel (detailed later), which is subject to the "due diligence" provision (*see* clause 17).

Clause 3: Trading Limits

"The Vessel shall be employed in lawful trades within Institute Warranty Limits (IWL) and within the Trading Limits as indicated in Box 22 for the carriage of lawful goods between safe ports or places where she can safely lie always afloat. The Vessel shall not be obliged to force ice nor to follow icebreakers.

The Owners warrant that, at the time of signing this Charter Party, the Vessel has not traded to any countries which would make the Vessel unacceptable for calls at ports within the Trading Limits indicated in Box 22. The Charterers shall provide a list of such countries."

This clause started life with a heading "Trading Limits and Safe Port" and included extensive efforts to define "safe port" and provide for "blacklisting", of which more later once the clause as finalised is explained.

By means of the first paragraph the employment of the vessel is subject to ALL of the following restrictions:

(1) "*lawful trades*": i.e. not smuggling (passengers or goods), trading with the enemy, etc.

(2) "*within Institute Warranty Limits*": That is to say within those limits defined by the International Underwriting Association as being the normal trading limits imposed on vessels for Hull and Machinery purposes without payment of additional premium. The IWL exclude trading to the following:

"1. *Warranted no*:
  (a) Atlantic Coast of North America, its rivers or adjacent islands,
    (i) north of 52° N Lat and west of 50° West Long;
    (ii) south of 52° 10′ N Lat in the area bounded by lines drawn between Battle Harbour/Pistolet Bay; Cape Ray/Cape North; Port Hawkesbury/Port Mulgrave and Baie Comeau/Matane, between 21st December and 30th April both days inclusive.
    (iii) west of Baie Comeau/Matane (but not west of Montreal) between 1st December and 30th April both days inclusive.
  (b) Great Lakes or St Lawrence Seaway west of Montreal.
  (c) Greenland Waters.
  (d) Pacific Coast of North America its rivers or adjacent islands north of 54° 30′ N Lat, or west of 130° 50′ W Long.

2. Warranted no Baltic Sea or adjacent waters east of 15° E Long
  (a) North of a line between Mo (64° 24′ N Lat) and Vasa (63° 06′ N Lat) between 10th December and 25th May b.d.i.
  (b) East of a line between Viipuri (Vyborg) (28° 47′ E Long) and Narva (28° 12′ E Long) between 15th December and 15th May b.d.i.
  (c) North of a line between Stockholm (59° 20′ N Lat) and Tallinn (59° 24′ N Lat) between 8th January and 5th May b.d.i.
  (d) East of 22° E Long and south of 59° N Lat between 28th December and 5th May b.d.i.

3. Warranted not North of 70° N Lat other than voyages direct to or from any port or place in Norway or Kola Bay.

4. Warranted no Behring Sea, no East Asian waters north of 46° N Lat and not to enter or sail from any port or place in Siberia except Nakhodka and/or Vladivostock.

5. Warranted not to proceed to Kerguelen and/or Croset Islands or south of 50° S Lat, except to ports and/or places in Patagonia and/or Chile and/or Falkland Islands, but liberty is given to enter waters south of 50° S Lat, if en route to or from ports and/or places not excluded by this warranty.

6. Warranted not to sail with Indian Coal as cargo:
  (a) between 1st March and 30th June, b.d.i.
  (b) between 1st July and 30th September b.d.i. except to ports in Asia, not West of Aden or East of or beyond Singapore."

(3) "*within the Trading Limits as indicated in Box 22*": A further restriction by reference to the trading limits listed in Part I.

(4) "*lawful goods*": i.e. not contraband, banned goods (military goods from USA to communist countries, pornography to Saudi Arabia etc.), or unathorised hazardous goods.

(5) "*safe ports or places*": What is safe? See discussion below. To clarify that, in relation to ice, safe means the absence of ice rather than a port or place where navigation is kept open by icebreakers, it is specifically provided that the vessel shall not be obliged to follow icebreakers.

(6) "*always afloat*": A usual charter party clause to preclude the Vessel from being obliged to risk bottom damage by sitting on the bottom at low water at tidal berths.

Within these parameters the charterers may operate the vessel, subject, of course, to the other terms and conditions of the charter party.

The second paragraph addresses the problem of blacklisting/boycotts whereby, for example, vessels that have traded to Israel are barred by certain Arab authorities and those that have traded to certain communist countries are barred from USA ports. Clearly the charterers wish to ensure that the past employment of the vessel will not affect their employment of it in the trade(s) envisaged.

Initially I sought to define a safe port and cover this well-chewed bone of contention in a way to minimise disputes and produce an equitable solution. The clause I proposed read:

"(c) *Safe Port*: A safe port or place is one which, at the time of the Charterers ordering the Vessel to said port or place, or 24 hours before the expected arrival of the Vessel at said port or place (whichever is the later), vessels of similar size and draught are able freely and safely to arrive at, use and depart from said port or place without, in the absence of abnormal occurrence, being exposed to dangers which cannot be avoided by good navigation and seamanship.

Should the Master or the Owners acquire information after the time limit above has expired which leads them to the conclusion that the port or place has become unsafe, or is likely to become unsafe whilst the Vessel is at such port or place, the Owners may defer entry into the port or place nominated by the Charterers and may (if necessary) proceed to a place of safety (if the environs of the port have also become unsafe). If the Owners act under the provisions of this clause they shall give immediate advice of same to the Charterers together with their reasons for so doing and consult with the Charterers to determine the future movements of the Vessel.

If the Master and the Owners act prudently and reasonably in the light of all prevailing circumstances, the Vessel shall continue to remain on-hire and the actions of Master and the Owners shall be considered to be in accordance with the requirements of this Charter Party."

This proposal also attracted much comment and debate. It is quite a long clause which more or less states the position that would obtain in the absence of it, based on decisions about this matter, the leading one being *The Eastern City* [1958] 2 Lloyd's Rep. 127 in which Lord Justice Sellers opined:

"... if it were said that a port will not be safe unless, in the relevant period of time, the particular ship can reach it, use it, and return from it without in the absence of some abnormal occurrence being exposed to danger which cannot be avoided by good navigation and seamanship it would probably meet all circumstances as a broad statement of the law."

Furthermore, it leaves the parties very little further forward, as most safe port disputes turn on the facts, which are different on each occasion and cannot be comprehensively anticipated in a contract. Accordingly it was unanimously decided to leave "safe port" to be defined by reference to past precedents.

Clause 4: Permitted Cargoes

"Except as provided below, the Vessel shall be used exclusively for the carriage of goods in ISO standard containers complying with the International Convention for Safe Containers."

This introduction to the clause provides that the primary purpose of the vessel is to carry goods in containers, but not just any old containers. Unless the owners agree to the contrary, they must be containers:

(a) of ISO (International Standards Organisation) dimensions (that is to say 20 foot or 40 foot long, 8 foot wide, and 4 foot 3 inches, 8 foot or 8 foot 6 inches or 9 foot 6 inches high), and

(b) complying with the International Convention for Safe Containers (CSC), that is to say they must be "plated", i.e. bear an inspection plate stamped to indicate that they are "in date" between inspections, rather like an MOT inspection for a motor vehicle.

Except for the containers of a few American trade operators, almost all containers are of ISO width and length dimensions and the use of "high cube" (9 foot 6 ins) containers is growing, particularly in the transpacific and transatlantic trades to/from the USA. These containers can create problems in vessels not designed to carry them. For example, they often have to be carried on deck because carriage below would reduce the numbers of containers carried, as the below deck stack height with the normal number would exceed the hold height and the top of the stack would come above the hatch. Then on deck the charterers may tend to put these "high cube" boxes on top stow so as to avoid the need to supply special lashings, which could be needed if they were carried lower down on many vessels. Although they are designed as "high cube" boxes, i.e. boxes for low weight/high volume goods, they are not always used as such and, giving them automatic top stow, often means stowing "heavies" over "lights" (*see* clause 10(c)) contrary to the classification society requirements for the approval of the stowage and lashing pattern for the deck stack.

For this reason it is common to find the charterers, seeking to achieve the highest possible loading, either pressurising the owners to accept such deviations from the charter party, or loading in this manner without telling the master, who only finds out what is going on when he gets a copy of the stowage plan five minutes before sailing, when he is under pressure to sail and it is too late to do anything about it. These are the "tricks of the trade" of the less scrupulous charterers. Clauses 6(a) and 10(c) are attempts to control this malpractice.

When 9 foot 6 ins containers are carried the owners will need to watch these points and possibly control the freedom of the charterers to tender "high cube" boxes with an appropriate additional clause.

"(a) *Uncontainerised Goods*: Uncontainerised goods may be carried only with the prior consent of the Owners and the Master provided that they are suitably prepared for carriage."

This sub-clause gives the owners and the master the necessary control over the carriage of non standard items that are not containerised. If such items are to be carried on containerships, they usually require special preparation and the provision of special lashings. These are all for the charterers' account.

Note that the consent of BOTH the owners AND the master is necessary before "*Uncontainerised Goods*" may be carried.

"(b) *Hazardous Goods*: The Owners agree that the Charterers may carry the maximum quantity indicated in Box 26 of hazardous goods in containers, provided same are loaded, stowed, discharged and documented in accordance with IMO regulations, any mandatory local requirements and regulations of the flag state."

The carriage of hazardous goods is necessarily always a matter for concern to both the owners and the charterers. The owners need to keep a strict control over the types, amounts and stowages of such goods and to ensure that all necessary documentation is available to facilitate carriage and compliance with the requirements of various authorities at ports of call, canals etc. as well as the authorities of the country whose flag the vessel flies. On the other hand, the charterers need a degree of flexibility in their operation of the vessel, so that they can book consignments of commonplace hazardous goods in the normal way. This is done by allowing the charterers to load hazardous goods up to a quantity allowed in Part I box 26 provided they are:

"(1) *loaded*
(2) *stowed*
(3) *discharged and*
(4) *documented*"

in accordance with regulations of:

(1) IMO
(2) local authorities through whose area goods pass
(3) flag state of vessel

"(c) *Live Animals*: Live animals may be carried only with the prior consent of the Owners and the Master."

The feasibility of carrying live animals will vary from vessel to vessel, the voyage to be undertaken and the animals involved. At one end of the spectrum it may not be possible for a small vessel to carry any animals at all, whilst a very large one may be able to transport, *inter alia*, a whole circus, subject to the charterers providing livestock handlers, for whom the vessel is able to offer accommodation.

It is possible to carry quite a wide variety of animals in special custom built or adapted containers and in some trades there is quite a regular shipment of such goods. This clause gives control to the owners and the master (BOTH of whom must consent before shipment can be effected) over such shipments, putting them in a position to apply special conditions for their carriage (e.g. payment to a crew member to look after them or carriage of a stock-handler as a supernumary at supernumary rates).

"(d) *Radioactive Goods*: Radioactive goods other than isotopes shall be excluded. Radioactive isotopes may be carried only with the prior consent of the Owners and the Master and provided that they are of such a category as not to invalidate the Vessel's P & I cover."

Radioactivity is an emotive subject, even though many radioactive substances or products are innocuous if handled properly. For example, monazite sand, which is shipped in substantial quantities from Brazil and Australia, is slightly radioactive, as are luminous watch dials. The main concern of the owners in relation to the carriage of radioactive goods is not to breach their P & I cover, so control over the carriage of these types of goods is exercised by reference to the owners' P & I cover. If carriage does not breach P & I cover then, with the prior consent of the owners and the master (BOTH of whom must consent before shipment can be effected) they may be carried. If carriage does breach P & I cover, then it is barred absolutely.

"(e) *Arms and Ammunition*: Arms and ammunition may be carried only with the prior consent of the Owners and the Master."

The carriage of arms and ammunition always has political and military overtones, even if designed for non belligerent sporting use, and features high on reasons for vessels being arrested. Note that BOTH the owners and the master must consent before shipment can be effected.

Clause 5: Owners' Obligations

Without in any way detracting from the importance of the earlier clauses, it is fair to say that they are introductory clauses and it is here in clause 5 that we start to get to the main provisions of the charter party.

"Except as provided elsewhere in this Charter Party, the Owners shall, at their expense, maintain the Vessel in the Class as indicated in Box 10, in a thoroughly efficient state of hull and machinery and in every way fitted for the service throughout the currency of this Charter Party."

Early drafts of this charter party went into detail about master, officers, crew, charts, handbooks, deck and engine room stores and provisions, lubricants and water as well as maintaining class and an efficient state of hull and machinery and fitted for the service but the working party decided that all of this could more simply and efficiently be conveyed by the above clause which is based on a time-honoured provision found in many other charter parties.

Clause 6(j) provides for the charterers to provide the bunker fuel but nowhere else is provision made for lubricants and water so the obligation to supply these commodities falls on the owners.

Thus the owners' obligation is, except as elsewhere provided:

(1) "*At their expense*",

(2) to "*maintain the Class indicated in Box 10*",

(3) to maintain the vessel "*in a thoroughly efficient state of Hull and Machinery*",

(4) to maintain the vessel "IN EVERY WAY *fitted for the service*" to which the charter party commits the vessel.

Note A. This obligation is absolute and not subject to the "due diligence" qualification.

Note B. The obligation operates "*throughout the currency of this Charter Party*" and not just at the time of delivery on hire.

Having made the opening sweeping statement about providing and maintaining an efficient classed vessel, this clause now addresses itself to more specific matters which are the responsibility of the owners to

(1) provide AND

(2) pay for,

starting with a preamble to that effect:

"The Owners shall, inter alia, provide and pay the cost of the following: 69"

Inter alia means "amongst other things" and is used to signify that clause 5 is not exhaustive in chronicling those matters for the provision of which and the payment for which the owners are responsible.

"(a) *Container Lashings*: (See Clause 10(a)). 70"

This is the first of many occasions when, although the matter is clearly one to which reference relevantly needs to be made in this sub-clause (container lashings being an owners' obligation), there is another more specific clause elsewhere where the matter is dealt with, so that this sub-clause contents itself with a cross-reference to the detail elsewhere.

"(b) *Crew Assistance* with inter alia: 71
(i) preparing the Vessel's cranes, derricks, winches and/or cargo handling gear for use, 72–73
(ii) opening and closing any hatches (other than pontoon type hatches), ramps and other means of access to goods and containers, 74–75
(iii) docking, undocking and shifting operations in port, 76
(iv) bunkering, 77
(v) maintaining power during loading and discharging operations, 78
(vi) instructing crane drivers and winchmen in use of Vessel's gear, 79
(vii) supervising stevedores lashing and unlashing goods and containers and the regular checking of lashings at sea when weather conditions 80–81

permit (See Clause 10(d)(ii)),

(viii) monitoring, recording performances and, when available, supplying labour for the repairing of the Charterers' refrigeration machinery, weather permitting (See Clause 17(b)).

The above services shall be rendered by the crew if required, provided port and local labour regulations permit, and, except when repairing the Charterers refrigeration machinery, any overtime incurred shall be for the account of the Owners."

This sub-clause sets out those tasks for which the charterers are entitled to look to the owners for crew assistance, "PROVIDED *port and local labour regulations permit*". If the owners incur any overtime costs meeting this obligation, these are for their own account, "*except when repairing the Charterers' refrigeration machinery*".

(i) Not all containerships have gear, many are gearless and rely entirely on shore-based cranes for working the goods and containers, but those that have should present themselves for working with their gear rigged and ready for use, unless this is not possible for some reason.

(ii) Some vessels have automatic winch-operated hatches that crew can operate, in which case the crew are expected to do so. However, some larger vessels have huge pontoon-type hatches that are only movable by shore-based portainer cranes.

(iii) Clearly any movement of the vessel must be a crew responsibility.

(iv) By "bunkering" is meant assisting with the receipt on board and connection of bunkering hoses from a bunkering barge or shore-based installation. It does not extend to requiring crew to leave the vessel to assist with such operations ashore or on board the bunkering barge.

(v) Clearly power must be maintained at all times in port to allow winches, cranes, lighting and other necessary facilities to function.

(vi) If stevedores are unfamiliar with the controls of any cranes or winches aboard, the crew are expected to instruct them in the use of such equipment.

Note the clause covers instruction only and not supervision or even taking over the driving of cranes or winches themselves. If the charterers require this, they must come to a separate arrangement for it with the parties concerned outside of the charter party.

(vii) This is a most important paragraph. Whilst the stevedoring is contracted and paid for by the charterers (this is after all a Free In, Out and Stow Charter), it is the responsibility of the master to ensure that this is done in the correct fashion, so that the vessel proceeds to sea in a seaworthy condition. It can be likened to the responsibility placed upon a lorry driver under the Road Traffic Act to ensure the safety and roadworthiness of the loading of his vehicle even though he, himself, did not load it.

This paragraph puts the responsibility on the owners to employ the crew to supervise the lashing and unlashing of goods and containers. Clause 10(d)(ii) expands upon this by putting responsibility on the master for ensuring that this is done properly. Crew must also check lashings whilst at sea, weather permitting, to ensure that twistlocks are properly locked and the bottle-screw connections of lashing rods are tight and have not worked loose with the movement of the vessel. Clause 10(d)(ii) puts the responsibility on the master for ensuring that this is done properly. Do not confuse the owners' responsibility for correct lashing (covered here) with responsibility for correct stowage, which is upon the charterers to accomplish under supervision of the master (*see* clause 10(d)(ii)).

(viii) Providing for the carriage of refrigerated goods is one of the most difficult matters, particularly where the provision of refrigeration is by means of the charterers' equipment, as is usually the case, most refrigerated containerised goods carried on containerships being carried in the charterers' integral refrigerated containers with their own machinery or in insulated containers with a charterers' "Clip-On Unit" attached.

Drastic reduction in crew numbers means that, even if weather conditions are such as to allow working on an integral refrigerated container's machinery (such containers usually being carried on deck), it does not necessarily follow that a complicated repair is immediately possible, even if the necessary spares and equipment are aboard, because the appropriately qualified crew may be fully employed elsewhere at that time on a more urgent task. Hence this sub-clause only provides for the supplying of labour "*when available*" and clause 17(b), to which cross-reference is made here, provides for a "reasonable endeavours without responsibility" approach to repairing refrigeration machinery.

Nevertheless, weather permitting, the crew are expected to monitor and record the performance of refrigerated containers and, when available, supply labour so that reasonable endeavours to repair broken down machinery in accordance with clause 17(b) are possible.

Note that "*repairing the Charterers' refrigeration machinery*" is specifically excluded from the occasions when the owners must pay the cost of overtime incurred in carrying out their obligations under this clause, thereby avoiding conflict with clause 17(b), which clearly provides for all additional costs incurred in repairing the charterers' refrigeration machinery to be for the charterers' account.

BIMCO suggest adding "connecting and disconnecting" before "monitoring" in line 83.

"(c) *Documentation*: Any documentation relating to the Vessel that may be re- 90
quired to permit the Vessel to trade within the limits as indicated in Box 22, 91
including, but not limited to, certificates of financial responsibility for oil pol- 92
lution (provided such oil pollution certificates are obtainable from the Own- 93
ers' P & I Club or some other available source), valid international tonnage 94
certificate, Suez and Panama tonnage certificates, valid certificate of regis- 95
try and certificates relating to the strength and/or serviceability of the Ves- 96
sel's gear (See Clause 11(a)). 97"

Any foreign traveller these days will not get far without documentation: passport, visa, bail bonds, etc. Similarly any vessel expecting to trade internationally needs a substantial amount of documentation if it is to proceed and operate without hindrance. Provision of documentation relating to the vessel is the responsibility of the owners, whilst that relating to goods and containers is the responsibility of the charterers.

Documents required by the vessel may, depending upon the areas traded to, include:

(1) "*certificates of financial responsibility for oil pollution*": The certificates in mind here are the Certificates of Financial Responsibility (Water Pollution) issued by the US Coastguard upon receipt of confirmation from the vessel's P & I club that the vessel is entered for pollution risks with that club and payment of a small fee. Such certificates have a lifespan of three years, provided that the vessel is not renamed in the interim, in which case a new certificate is required.

However, the requirement in the clause as drafted is not just for the US Coastguard certificate but any certificate of this nature worldwide. Thus it is necessary to restrict the certificates which the owner must produce to those which are reasonably available to him, as otherwise he would be required to produce something which is unobtainable and could be put off hire as a result, quite unfairly. This restriction is particularly necessary in view of current US federal legislation on this subject, much pending state legislation and the P & I clubs' declared intention not to provide any further undertakings than those already provided for the current US Coastguard certificates.

BIMCO suggests adding "at no higher cost from" before "some other available source" in line 94. This clearly arises from the American requirement for direct action against a guarantor in the event of pollution, which P & I clubs will not provide and which is met by third party cover, the cost of which, under this alteration, would be for the account of charterers directing the vessel to American waters.

(2) "*international tonnage certificate*": This is a certificate issued by the government of the country where the vessel is registered and certifies the tonnages of the vessel.

(3) "*Suez and Panama tonnage certificates*": As readers will be aware, some vessels' "tonnages" are measurement rather than weight based and are reached by measuring the vessel and then making certain allowances/deductions, according to the tonnage being measured. The Suez and Panama Canals have their own formulae to arrive at vessels' tonnages upon which canal dues are based and, if the vessel is not to be delayed when attempting to transit these canals, it must have an appropriate valid tonnage certificate.

(4) "*certificate of registry*": This is the vessel's passport issued by the government of the country where the vessel is registered and certifies where the vessel is registered and thus what nationality of flag it is entitled to fly.

(5) "*gear certificates*": In certain areas of the world (Saudi Arabia and Australia spring readily to mind), vessels are required to produce certificates to attest to the recent survey and good working order of their gear. This can cause problems if the regulation says such a certificate is a prerequisite of entry into the port and the vessel cannot produce anything because it is gearless!

This list is by no means exhaustive and, in the same way as it is the responsibility of the owners to ensure that the vessel has the correct up-to-date charts to transit the areas through which it must pass under the charterers' orders (within the parameters of the trading limits in box 22), so must the owners ensure that the vessel is equipped with the necessary documentation to enable the vessel to pass through all authorised trading areas and enter all ports therein. Any failure on their part in this respect will lead to the vessel being placed off hire in accordance with clause 8(a)(iv) for any delay thereby caused.

"(d) *Insurance of the Vessel*: (See Clause 18)."

Another occasion where the owners' obligation is incorporated by reference only and dealt with in detail elsewhere.

"(e) *Fumigation and/or Deratisation*: The provision of certificates thereof at the commencement of the Charter Party and the renewal thereof throughout the Charter Party, except if this is required as a result of the Charterers' goods and containers carried under this Charter Party, in which case these expenses shall be for the account of the Charterers."

This is a sub-clause which is not quite so important with containerships (where goods are contained within containers so that the vessel remains clean), as it is in a charter party for a vessel to carry bulk cargoes, particularly those that might attract infestation.

Nevertheless it is important that the vessel is both free from vermin and certificated to be so, as such evidence may be called for as a pre-requisite of allowing entry into a port or as evidence to assist in repudiating a cargo claim for infestation. Accordingly the owners are required to maintain the necessary fumigation and deratisation certificates throughout the period of the charter party, bearing the costs thereof, unless the vessel becomes infested by the charterers' goods, in which case the expense is theirs.

> "(f) *Smuggling*: In the event of smuggling by the Master, Officers and/or crew, the Owners shall bear the cost of any fines, taxes or imposts levied and the Vessel shall be off hire for any time lost as a result thereof (See Clause 6(p))."

This is another important sub-clause and one which was the subject of substantial debate within the working party, who were particularly concerned in the light of recent developments in trading with the USA and the Sea Carrier Initiative scheme initiated by the US Customs. It was suggested that a specific Sea Carrier Initiative sub-clause be included but, after debate, it was agreed that this was too specific and a broader based sub-clause, such as that above, which had international application was required.

The sub-clause needs to be read in conjunction with clause 6(p), to which cross-reference is made and which outlines the charterers' obligations relating to "Contraband", if a full picture is to be obtained, as this sub-clause covers the owners' obligations only. Between them the two sub-clauses attempt to address the very difficult subject of what happens if contraband is found aboard (especially drugs, to which specific reference is made in clause 6(p)).

The working party recognised the difficulties which usually arise in such circumstances, of proving who is at fault and where the onus of proof should lie. They therefore decided that, if contraband were found in the goods and containers on board, there should be a rebuttable *prima facie* assumption that they were loaded as part of the goods, the charterers should bear any fines, etc., and the vessel should stay on hire. (Of course the charterers could then seek recourse through their bill of lading indemnities to their customers but, as between the owners and the charterers, the charter party is the only contract, so such considerations are of no consequence here.)

How might the charterers seek to rebut the assumption that they are responsible for contraband found in goods and containers and that the owners are responsible? One way might be if the seal has been tampered with or if the container is sealed by a seal other than the one which the charterers' records show being on the container concerned at the time of loading.

If contraband is found elsewhere in the vessel, other than in the goods and containers, the owners bear the brunt of fines etc. and the vessel is put off hire.

In the former case the charterers must put up security if the vessel is arrested, in the latter security is the responsibility of the owners.

In my original draft I attempted to address the thorny subject of who puts up security when the vessel is arrested, for smuggling, security for a cargo claim or any other reason whatsoever. Such arrests invariably occur on a Friday night and both the owners and the charterers are reluctant to put up security, so the vessel remains under arrest whilst this dispute is sorted out and an unnecessary off hire dispute arises as a result of it. I suggested an additional sub-clause to clause 5 which would read:

"*Arrest or Restraint*: In the event of arrest or restraint of the Vessel by whomsoever and for whatsoever reason, the Owners shall initially provide the necessary security to secure the prompt release of the Vessel to continue her voyage, without prejudice to the Owners' right to be indemnified by the Charterers for all damages, costs and expenses thereby incurred if the cause of arrest is a matter which is the Charterers' responsibility under the terms of this Charter Party. If the Charterers are clearly identified as the responsible party prior to the arrest, the Charterers to provide the initial security and if they are identified as the responsible party after the arrest the Charterers to provide counter security or substitute security at the Owners' option."

After careful consideration the working party unanimously agreed that this sub-clause was unsuitable for a standard charter party and that the problem should be left to be resolved on each occasion according to the facts. However, in individual charter parties, subject to the views of the parties involved, it may be that such a sub-clause is worth considering as a basis of avoiding problems in relation to security if the vessel is arrested.

Clause 6: Charterers' Obligations

Preamble:

"Except as provided elsewhere in this Charter Party, the Charterers shall 108
provide and pay the costs of the following throughout the currency of this 109
Charter Party. 110"

By introducing this clause "*Except as provided elsewhere*" ensures that, in the event of conflict between this clause and any other provision in this charter party, the provision elsewhere is paramount and overrules.

The charterers' obligation is to:

(1) *provide AND*

(2) *pay the costs of*

and this requirement applies "*throughout the currency of this Charter Party*".

"(a) *Provision of Details*: The provision of full and accurate details of goods 111
and containers (including any documentation required at any ports of call), 112
their weights and stowage positions to the Master as early as possible but 113
not later than upon arrival at the port of loading, with regular updating 114
thereof and the provision of a full and accurate plan of the stowage of all 115
goods and containers actually loaded prior to sailing. Such details shall in- 116
clude: 117
(i) gross weights of containers, 118
(ii) any feature of the goods requiring attention by the crew during the voy- 119
age, including, but not limited to, any hazardous or other dangerous 120
feature and/or the need for carriage within a specified temperature 121
range. 122"

This is an area in which many charterers are frequently sadly remiss. Many a master of a containership under charter has received details of the goods and containers loaded five minutes before he is due to sail, with the labour all gone home, only to find that he has "heavies over lights", torsional moment problems and hazardous goods stowed in undesirable (if not illegal) places. On the one side the charterers are pressing him to sail, whilst on the other he has a responsibility to ensure that the vessel is seaworthy before he does so and, whilst the charterers may have effected the stowage, the seaworthiness of the vessel and the care of the goods and containers are quite clearly his responsibility (*see* clause 10(d)(ii)). In short he often finds himself on the horns of a dilemma.

This sub-clause attempts to give the master the power to redress this problem by giving him the right to demand to be provided with initial details on arrival, to be kept informed of all changes made during loading as they occur and to be provided with a full and accurate plan prior to sailing. Along with other responsibilities placed upon the charterers, particularly in clause 10, this puts the master of a containership in a much more equitable position than he would have been under most other standard dry-cargo charter parties.

The "*full and accurate details of the goods and containers*" mentioned in this sub-clause are not exhaustively defined but examples are given in (i) and (ii) of what these might include. It is up to the charterers and the master to decide what details additional to those outlined are required by the master to carry out the owners' obligations. Such details will not include a full manifest of all the goods on board in the containers, as this is sensitive detail rightly restricted on a "need to know" basis and the master does not need to know, unless anything needs special attention or is dangerous. The anonymity that a container bestows upon goods is their best protection against theft and the one thing potential thieves need to know most is "what is in the box?" Waste paper or scotch? China clay or video recorders? Manifests are very confidential documents in container shipping.

Let us examine firstly what detail the master needs and why:

(1) *Gross weight of containers*: Whilst not always needing details of the nature of the contents, the master must have details of the weights of each container and where they are stowed so that he can calculate his ballasting requirements to eliminate (or reduce) torsional moment problems in the vessel. This information is usually provided by means of a series of "Bay Plans" showing container numbers and weights in appropriate positions.

(2) *Hazardous goods*: Details of hazardous goods are necessary to ensure that IMO stowage requirements (and charter party limits) have been observed. Additionally, should any casualty occur, it is imperative that the master is aware of the amount, nature and position of any hazardous goods he may be carrying so that speedy appropriate action can be taken. This should be provided by means of a detailed list of all hazardous goods and their stowages.

(3) *Goods requiring special attention*: Clearly if the cargo includes containers with refrigerated goods, which require plugging in and monitoring, fantainers with goods requiring forced ventilation, which also require plugging into the vessel's power supply, or any other goods and/or containers requiring any action whatsoever by the crew (other than checking lashings), the charterers must provide adequate instructions to the master. The charterers usually provide such detail to the master in a set of instructions identifying such goods, their stowage and their special requirements.

The sub-clause covers not only the provision of detail but also the timing of it, which is all important to a master attempting to prepare his vessel for sea. Note that detail has to be provided:

(1) "*as early as possible but no later than upon arrival at the port of loading*", with

(2) "*regular updating*", and

(3) "*a full and accurate plan of the stowage of all goods and containers actually loaded PRIOR TO SAILING*".

"(b) *Instructions to the Master*: The Master, although appointed by the Owners, shall at all times during the currency of this Charter Party be under the orders and directions of the Charterers as regards employment and agency. The Charterers shall be obliged at all times to furnish the Master with full and timely instructions."

This sub-clause gives the charterers the right to give direct instructions to the master and not have to address him via the owners on:

"(1) *employment AND*

(2) *agency*".

It then puts the responsibility on the charterers to furnish the master with instructions that are:

"(1) *full AND*

(2) *timely*".

Note that this sub-clause does not include any confusing provision that the master shall be regarded as the servant of the charterers, which is designed to cast doubt on the responsibility of the owners for the actions of their employee: the master in case any claims arise. In this sub-clause the subject of liability is not raised and is left for attention in clauses 16 and 17.

"(c) *Stevedoring*: (See Clause 10(d)(i)).
(d) *Charterers' Lashings*: (See Clause 10(b))."

Two more provisions incorporated into the clause by cross-reference only and dealt with in detail later.

"(e) *Condition of Containers*: The Charterers warrant that all containers carried pursuant to this Charter Party have been constructed to a design approved by a Classification Society and are properly maintained."

Unlike vessels, which are built under inspection by a classification society surveyor, containers are too numerous to be constructed in this way. Instead they are built to a design approved by a classification society.

Clause 4 already requires that containers comply with the International Convention for Safe Containers (CSC), which requires them to be plated as evidence of regular inspection. In pursuit of improved container safety, the working party considered it desirable to require the charterers to warrant that containers have been "*constructed to a design approved by a Classification Society*". They also added a warranty of "*properly maintained*" to prevent the CSC plating being misused as evidence of proper maintenance, by providing for an absolute warranty of proper maintenance.

(f) *Stowage in Containers*: The correct stowage and safe securing of all 133
goods within containers (including securing to flat rack containers) to with- 134
stand the rigours of the voyage. 135"

A most important sub-clause in containership charter parties. Whilst the owners have the responsibility for ensuring the safe and correct stowage and securing of the containers on the vessel, clearly the responsibility for ensuring the safe and correct stowage and securing of goods in containers must fall upon the charterers. In the case of an enclosed container this is vital because the owners have no opportunity to inspect the stowage and securing of the goods in the containers.

Note that the sub-clause goes further than this and puts upon the charterers the responsibility for stowage and securing of goods on flat rack containers (i.e. open-sided and open-topped containers), where the stowage is inspectable by the owners. Thus there is a clear delineation of responsibility as between the owners and the charterers for stowage and securing, regardless of who actually accomplishes it:

(1) The owners are responsible for the stowage and securing of the containers on the vessel.
(2) The charterers are responsible for the stowage and securing of the goods in the containers.

"(g) *Stowage Planning*: (See Clause 10(c)). 136"

Incorporated by cross-reference only. Dealt with later.

"(h) *Operating Expenses*: All port charges, light and canal dues, pilotage, 137
towage, consular charges and all other charges and expenses relating to 138
the operation of the Vessel not otherwise provided for in this Charter Party, 139
other than charges or expenses relating to the crew. 140"

This charter party follows the usual division of responsibility as between the owners and the charterers on operating expenses which, broadly speaking, is that the owners bear the costs of offering a vessel ready to provide normal service (*see* clause 5) whilst the charterers bear the costs of trading it wherever they wish to despatch it.

"(j) *Bunker Fuel*: (See Clause 12)."

Incorporated by cross-reference only. Dealt with later.

"(k) *Agency Costs*: All agency fees and expenses for normal ship's husbandry at all ports or places of call."

Note that the sub-clause says "NORMAL *ship's husbandry*" only. Anything out of the ordinary (repairs, crew hospitalisation, embarkation or repatriation etc.) does not count as normal ship's husbandry and, in such cases, the owners must pay the additional fees and expenses thereby incurred or appoint their own agent.

Initially the sub-clause was longer, incorporating a second sentence:

"In cases of services beyond normal ship's husbandry (such cases to include, inter alia, repairs to the Vessel and crew hospitalisation, embarkation or repatriation), the Owners to pay additional agency fees and expenses thereby incurred or appoint their own agents."

but during a "pruning session" (the charter party is rather a long one) this sentence was deemed not to add anything that did not follow automatically and was deleted.

"(l) *Damage to Vessel*: Any damage to the Vessel or loss or damage to its equipment caused by stevedores during the currency of this Charter Party shall be reported by the Master to the Charterers or their agents, in writing, within 24 hours of the occurrence or as soon as possible thereafter but latest when the loss or damage could have been discovered by the exercise of due diligence. The Master shall endeavour to obtain written acknowledgment by the party causing loss or damage unless it is made good in the meantime. The Charterers shall pay for stevedore damage whether or not payment has been made by stevedores to the Charterers.

Damage for which the Charterers are responsible affecting seaworthiness, or the proper working of the Vessel and/or her equipment, shall be repaired without delay to the Vessel after each occurrence in the Charterers' time and shall be paid for by the Charterers. Other repairs to damage for which the Charterers are responsible shall also be carried out in the Charterers' time but, if this is not possible, such repairs shall be carried out whilst the Vessel is in drydock in the Owners' time provided this does not interfere with the Owners' repair work, or by the Vessel's crew at the Owners' convenience. All costs of such repairs shall be for the Charterers' account."

Note that paragraph 1 covers stevedore damage to the vessel whilst paragraph 2 covers all damage to the vessel for which the charterers are responsible.

Paragraph 1: Without in any way detracting from the charterers' responsibility to be vicariously liable to the owners for damage to the vessel done by their servants—the stevedores—this paragraph of this sub-clause seeks to enlist maximum assistance from the owners to put the charterers in a position to make an appropriate recovery from the negligent party for the claim which he must pay to the owners.

Thus the MASTER must:

(1) Report damage to the charterers or their agents:
  (a) within 24 hours if discovered immediately, OR
  (b) when damage is discoverable by the exercise of due diligence, AND
(2) Endeavour to obtain written acknowledgment from the negligent party, unless they repair damage there and then.

This latter requirement is frequently less than easy to accomplish and, if the master cannot get an acknowledgment of liability, he should at least attempt to secure an inspection by the guilty party and an acknowledgment of the nature and degree of damage incurred.

Obviously the degree of damage sustained will influence the master in the degree of pressure he brings to bear upon the stevedores to acknowledge liability. If the damage is serious, he should liaise with the charterers' agent to approach the stevedores and arrange a joint survey, which will probably establish, *inter alia*, that damage is of recent origin, thereby providing valuable evidence against stevedores.

Paragraph 2: This paragraph seeks to minimise claimable costs of damage repairs by particular reference to whose time in which they are repaired. It starts by dividing damage into two categories:

(1) Damage affecting seaworthiness or the proper working of the vessel and/or her equipment.
(2) Damage not affecting seaworthiness.

(1) is repaired without delay, with the vessel remaining on hire during repairs. These repairs may be temporary or permanent. If they are temporary, subsequent permanent repairs come into category (2); (2) is repaired:

(a) whilst on hire if possible, if not
(b) during drydocking in the owners' time (off hire), provided same does not interfere with the owners' repair work, or
(c) by the vessel's crew at the owners' convenience, failing which
(d) in the charterers' time after the end of the charter party.

Thus, for damages to the vessel falling in category (2), which are still in existence at the end of the charter party, repairs are effected either:

(a) during drydocking in the owners' time, provided it does not interfere with the owners' repair work; or
(b) during the charterers' time, which means that the vessel nominally returns on hire to have the charterers' repairs done (unless repairs are done by the vessel's crew at the owners' convenience).

In any event the charterers must pay the costs of such repairs, the only benefit they may gain from this paragraph being in respect of hire payment, if repairs are done in the owners' time in accordance with the provisions of the paragraph.

"(m) *Redelivery*: Redelivery of the Vessel at the Place of Redelivery as indicated in Box 21, unless agreed by the Owners or provided elsewhere to the contrary, in the same condition to that pertaining when the Vessel was delivered, fair wear and tear excepted, at the end of the period as indicated in Box 23. The Charterers shall give the Owners one month's notice of expected date and Place of Redelivery, which advice shall be updated 10, 5 and 2 days prior to expected redelivery.

At the time of redelivery the Vessel shall be clean and fit to load goods and ISO standard containers. If the Charterers have changed the configuration of the Vessel to carry different size ISO standard containers or non ISO standard containers, they shall, in their time and at their cost, prior to redelivery, return the Vessel to its previous configuration, unless the Owners agree to waive this requirement, in which case the Charterers shall return the Vessel to its previous configuration, at their cost, after redelivery at such time and place stipulated by the Owners but in the Owners' time. Without prejudice to any other claim the Owners may have under this Charter Party the Owners shall not be obliged to accept redelivery of the Vessel before it is returned to its previous configuration."

Paragraph 1: Note that, whereas with delivery the owners are not obliged to communicate with the charterers until they are in position to come on hire within the period of laydays as provided in clause 1(b), the charterers are required to give the owners one month's notice of expected redelivery and the actual place of redelivery (redelivery is commonly provided for one of a range of ports in the charterers' option), with updates at 10, 5 and 2 days prior to the expected date of redelivery. (Of course any prudent charterers will be in constant contact with the owners or their agents as laydays approach, so that they know precisely when to expect delivery on hire and can arrange to accept delivery and commence utilisation of the vessel immediately hire is commenced, but the onus is upon the charterers to enquire and not upon the owners to inform.)

At the time of redelivery the vessel must be "*in the same condition to that pertaining when the Vessel was delivered, fair wear and tear excepted*". If the period of the charter party has been short, little dispute is likely to arise as to what constitutes fair wear and tear but, at the end of a long charter party, a dispute might arise over the definition of this phrase.

Paragraph 2: As this standard charter party provides in clause 1(e) for the vessel to be delivered fit to receive ISO containers and clause 2 undertakes that the details in Part III, which includes details of the vessel's configuration, are accurate, it is reasonable that the owners should expect the vessel to be redelivered in the same format.

Cleaning is not usually too much of a problem with containerships in the way that it is with bulk and dry cargo vessels, where cargo residues and unwanted dunnage must be disposed of before a new cargo can be loaded, although spillages and leakages from containers do occasionally need cleaning up. Thus the usual provision that the vessel must be redelivered in the same condition and format as that in which it was accepted at delivery is made in the first sentence of paragraph 2.

The paragraph then addresses itself to the problems that may arise if the configuration of the vessel has been changed during the charter party by the charterers pursuant to the liberty in clause 13(b). It envisages two scenarios.

(1) Because the next employment of the vessel requires the vessel to be returned to its original configuration, the owners may refuse to accept redelivery until the charterers have changed the configuration back to its original format.

(2) Because the next employment of the vessel can utilise the configuration which the charterers have arranged, or the next employment is not yet fixed, so that the owners do not know what configuration is required next, the owners may agree to accept the vessel in its present configuration. However the charterers must pay to have it changed back at a later date, but in the owners' time.

This way both sides gain:

(1) The charterers save hire as they can redeliver earlier, not having to expend time reconverting the vessel.

(2) The owners save the cost of converting the vessel for its next employment but retain the recourse to the charterers for the cost of reconversion at a later date.

Of course, if the owners intend to trade the vessel in its converted configuration permanently thereafter, there is nothing to stop them releasing the charterers from their obligation to pay for reconversion at a later date.

The paragraph concludes with a reminder of the owners' right to refuse to accept redelivery of the vessel before it is returned to its previous configuration, should they so choose.

"(n) *Additional Premiums*: All additional premiums for hull and machinery, war risks, including blocking and trapping, or protection and indemnity insurance incurred by the Owners over and above the premiums payable by the Owners. The Owners shall allow the Charterers to arrange these additional covers on their behalf if the Charterers so request and if the proposed insurers and terms are acceptable to the Owners. If the Charterers arrange such insurance the Charterers' insurers shall confirm cover latest 24 hours before the Vessel is due to be exposed to the risk so insured (See Clause 18)."

The owners are responsible for insuring the vessel for normal trading for hull and machinery, war risks and P & I at their expense but, if the charterers wish to trade the vessel into a restricted or additional premium area, which is within the trading limits, they are responsible for paying the additional premiums levied (*see* clauses 5(d) and 18). The question then arises as to who places such additional insurances. Both parties have a vested interest, the charterers to obtain the cover at the most advantageous rates, as they are paying the premiums, and the owners to ensure that cover does not contain any unacceptable exclusions and is placed with reputable insurers.

This sub-clause provides a solution designed to meet both parties' requirements: it provides for the charterers to be allowed to place the cover, if they so wish PROVIDED:

(a) the proposed insurers are acceptable to the owners;
(b) the terms of the cover are acceptable to the owners; and
(c) the insurers confirm the existence of cover to the owners at least 24 hours before the vessel is due (scheduled) to be exposed to the risk insured (i.e. enter the additional premium zone).

The most likely occasions when this sub-clause will be invoked is when entering war zones or breaching Institute Warranty Limits (IWL).

"(o) *Advances to Master*: The Charterers shall procure that their local agents at all ports of call shall, upon request by the Master, make funds available to him for disbursements, which advances the Charterers may recoup from the Owners by deduction from the hire payments in accordance with Clause 7(e)."

Despite modern methods of remitting funds across the world, there still appears to be a requirement for the charterers, through their local agents, to make advances of funds to the master to meet disbursements in foreign ports, which they then recoup by deduction from the next payment of hire.

"(p) *Contraband*: In the event that contraband and/or unmanifested drugs and/or goods are found to have been shipped as part of the goods and/or in containers on board, any fines, taxes or imposts levied shall be for the Charterers' account and the Vessel shall remain on hire during any time lost as a result thereof, unless it can be established that the Master, Officers and/or crew are involved in smuggling (see Clause 5). In this event any security required shall be provided by the [Charterers.]"

This is the complementary sub-clause to clause 5(f) and the two sub-clauses are considered together in the commentary on clause 5(f).

General: Looking back over the clause after it had been finalised and had been involved in several switching of sub-clauses between clauses, it is possible to see that the fluency of the clause as a whole has suffered somewhat.

The clause was designed for each sub-clause to read on from the preamble. This is the case in (a), (c), (d), (f), (g), (h), (j), (k), (m) and (n) but not in (b), (e), (l), (o) and (p), which are freestanding and do not require the preamble to apply. Nevertheless, the provisions of the clause are clear, although the amendments seem to have led to an INADVERTENT ERROR WHICH *MUST* BE RECTIFIED. The word "Charterers" in line 200 (around which

I have put square brackets) must be changed to "Owners". BIMCO have this in line for rectification at the first review.

Clause 7: Hire

The owners' favourite clause but one which differs little from the provisions of many other charter parties on this point.

"(a) *Rate*: The Charterers shall pay hire at the rate stated in Box 25, per day or pro rata for part of a day, from the time the Vessel is delivered to the Charterers until her redelivery to the Owners. All calculation of hire shall be made by reference to Universal Time Co-ordinated (UTC)."

This sub-clause merely incorporates into the contract the obligation of the charterers to pay hire at the daily rate provided in box 25 or pro-rata for any part of a day. On large vessels, where hire often exceeds US$1,000 per hour, pro-rata will probably be calculated most precisely.

As the vessel may be delivered in one time zone and redelivered in another, the local times of delivery and redelivery have to be converted to UTC to facilitate accurate calculation of the total time on hire for hire payment purposes. UTC means Universal Time Co-ordinated and is a non-nationalistic way of expressing what most of us still know and refer to as Greenwich Mean Time (GMT).

"(b) *Payment*: Payment of hire shall be made in cash in full and without discount, semi-monthly in advance. If hire or any instalment thereof is not paid as aforesaid, the Charterers shall pay interest at the rate of 0.1 per cent per day on the amount outstanding from and including the due date until the date of payment."

Payment (or rather non-payment) of hire features high on the list of potential grounds for dispute between the parties to a charter party. This sub-clause and the next two are based on clause 10 of "GASTIME" and this particular sub-clause may appear to be a little imprecise but this is purely illusory. "*Semi monthly*" would appear to be variable according to the number of days in the month but, fortunately, it is accepted within the industry that "semi-monthly" means the anniversary date of when the first payment was due and fifteen (15) days after that date and subsequent anniversary dates.

Being payable "*in advance*" means that the first hire payment must be made prior to delivery. "*Cash*" means immediately usable funds, such as a banker's draft or telegraphic transfer, as opposed to a cheque which takes time to clear. "*In full and without discount*" means precisely that, i.e. no discount for prompt payment. Do not confuse "discount" with "deductions" which can be made in accordance with clause 7(e). Note that the sub-clause says nothing about commissions, which are dealt with in clause 21.

Some owners have preferred to delete "and including" in line 209 and add "both dates inclusive" at the end of line 210.

"(c) *Default*: In default of punctual and regular payment as herein specified, the Owners may require the Charterers to make payment of the amount due within 96 running hours of receipt of notification from the Owners, failing which the Owners will have the right to withdraw the Vessel without prejudice to any claim the Owners may have against the Charterers under this Charter Party. Further, so long as the hire remains unpaid, the Owners shall be entitled to suspend the performance of any and all of their obligations hereunder and shall have no responsibility whatsoever for any consequences thereof in respect of which the Charterers hereby indemnify the Owners. Hire shall continue to accrue and any extra expenses resulting from such suspension shall be for the Charterers' account."

The sub-clause tries to prevent disputes caused by inadvertent non- or late-payment of hire and gives protection to the charterers against the owners seeking to terminate a charter party (probably because the market has gone up and they can get better rates now).

If the charterers fail to meet a regular hire payment, the following procedures apply:

(1) The owners give notice of non-payment to the charterers.

(2) The charterers now have 96 running hours (4 consecutive days Saturdays Sundays and Bank Holidays included) from receipt of notice from the owners in which to rectify this omission and pay hire due in accordance with the requirements of this charter party. Note time runs from receipt of notice, not from when payment due.

(3) If 96 hours after the owners gave notice of non-payment to the charterers hire has still not been paid, then the owners may withdraw the vessel.

(4) If the hire is paid within the 96 hour period, the vessel remains on hire but the charterers remain responsible for payment of interest in accordance with sub-clause (b).

(5) Whilst hire is unpaid the owners may, if they choose, "*suspend performance of any and all of their obligations*" under the charter party but the vessel remains on hire so far as the charterers' responsibility to pay hire is concerned. If this suspension of performance causes any consequential loss, or cost, it shall be for the charterers' account who shall indemnify the owners accordingly.

"(d) *Redelivery Adjustment*: Should the Vessel be on her voyage towards the Place of Redelivery at the time payment of hire becomes due, said payment shall be made for the estimated time necessary to complete the voyage, less disbursements made by the Charterers for the Owners' account, including the estimated value of bunker fuel on board at redelivery. When the Vessel is redelivered to the Owners any difference shall be refunded to or paid by the Charterers as appropriate, but not later than three months after redelivery of the Vessel."

This is another familiar clause covering the last payment of hire at the end of a charter party, if it is anticipated that the vessel will be redelivered before the next payment of hire is due. In such cases the payment to be made is calculated as follows:

Hire due to estimated date of redelivery, minus:

(1) Disbursements made by the charterers for the owners' account and recoverable from hire payments.

(2) Estimated value of the estimated bunkers remaining on board at redelivery which will be purchased by the owners in accordance with clause 12(c).

Once the vessel is redelivered and accurate calculations can be made, an adjusting payment must be made by the relevant party to the other party no later than three months after the date of redelivery of the vessel.

"(e) *Deductions*: On production of supporting vouchers the Charterers shall be entitled to deduct from payments of hire any expenditure incurred on behalf of the Owners which may be payable by the Owners under this Charter Party. If such expenditure is incurred in a currency other than that in which hire is payable, conversion into such currency for the purpose of deduction shall be effected at the rate of exchange at the place of the bank where hire is paid prevailing on the date when the expenditure was incurred."

This sub-clause has two important provisions:

(1) The charterers must produce supporting vouchers for any deductions they make from hire and all such deductions must be in respect of expenditure incurred on behalf of the owners which is payable by the owners under the terms of this charter party.

(2) If the expenditure is in a currency other than that in which hire is paid, it shall be converted into the currency of the hire payment at the rate of exchange prevailing on the date when the expenditure was incurred, at the place where hire is paid.

The currency in which the charterers incur expenditure is their own domestic currency, which they use to buy foreign currencies to reimburse agents who incur expenditure on their behalf. Thus the rate of exchange to which this clause refers is that between the charterers' domestic currency and the currency of the charter party, into which expenses are converted for deduction from hire.

"(f) *Extension*: The Charterers shall arrange the Vessel's trading so as to permit redelivery at the place and in the period as indicated in Boxes 21 and 23, respectively. If the Vessel is not chartered for a minimum/maximum period and the Vessel is sent on a final voyage reasonably calculated to allow redelivery within such period at a Place of Redelivery as provided under this Charter Party, and the voyage is prolonged for reasons beyond the Charterers' control, the Charterers shall have the use of the Vessel at the rate and on the conditions of this Charter Party for such extended time as may be required for completion of said voyage and redelivery as aforesaid."

The charterers are obviously expected to arrange their trading of the vessel so that they can redeliver in accordance with the terms of the charter party but even the best laid plans can be thwarted and this sub-clause attempts to provide for this eventuality. Provided the charter party is not specifically arranged for a minimum and/or maximum period (in which case the only latitude allowed to the charterers, beyond that provided in Part I, is any additional time added on for off hire periods—*see* clause 8 last provision) and the charterers act reasonably in commencing a last voyage calculated to bring the vessel to the place of redelivery within the time allowed in the charter party then, if the voyage is prolonged for reasons beyond the control of the charterers, the charter party is extended, at the same rate and on the same conditions, to cover this additional period and no breach of charter party is thereby incurred.

This is an important concession to the charterers, who have this extension plus the ability to extend the charter party to make up for any time lost off hire (*see* clause 8) which they can add on at the end of the charter party. All of this does not assist the owners in obtaining their next employment and trying to calculate realistic laydays cancelling.

In practice modern communications mean that close liaison is maintained between the owners and the charterers, either directly or through their representatives and, with the master in radio contact with the owners to supply updates of the progress of the vessel, not too many problems occur in this area.

Clause 8: Off Hire

"After delivery in accordance with Clause 1 hereof, the Vessel shall remain on hire until redelivered in accordance with Clause 6(m), except for the following periods:"

This clause contains details of some of the various reasons which may lead to the vessel being placed off hire and thus must qualify as the owners' least favourite clause.

"(a) *Unable to Comply with Instructions*: If the Vessel is unable to comply with the instructions of the Charterers on account of:-

(i) any damage, defect, breakdown, or deficiency of the Vessel's hull, machinery, equipment or repairs or maintenance thereto, including dry-docking, excepting those occasions when Clause 6(1) applies,

(ii) any deficiency of the Master, Officers and/or crew, including the failure, refusal or inability of the Master, Officers and/or crew to perform service immediately required, whether or not within the control of the Owners,

(iii) arrest of the Vessel at the suit of a party where a claim is not caused by the Charterers, their servants, agents or sub-contractors (See Clause 5(f)),

(iv) any delay occasioned by any breach by the Owners of any obligation or warranty in this Charter Party.

If any of the above incidents affect the full use of the Vessel, it shall be off hire. If they partially affect the use of the Vessel, it shall be off hire to the extent such incidents affect the Charterers' use of the Vessel (see also Clause 11(b))."

Sub-clause (a) lists a series of reasons for which the vessel may be unable to comply fully with the instructions of the charterers, which will lead to the vessel being put off hire, either partially or totally. If they affect the full use of the vessel and prevent it from complying with the charterers' instructions at all, then the vessel is totally off hire but, if they only partially affect the ability of the vessel to comply with the charterers' instructions, then the off hire/loss of hire is in direct proportion (pro-rata) to the degree of effect that the reason has on preventing the vessel's full compliance with the charterers' instructions.

One of the principal reasons for a vessel being placed off hire pro-rata is defective gear affecting the speed of working of a vessel in port. This particular matter is dealt with in detail in clause 11(b), so cross-reference is made to that clause in this sub-clause.

Paragraph (i): The first reason listed is time lost on account of any repairs to damage or maintenance, except repairs to damage for which the charterers are responsible in accordance with clause 6(1), to which reference is made.

Examples of damage for which the charterers may be liable, apart from the obvious stevedores' damage are:

(1) Ordering the vessel to an unsafe berth.
(2) Cargo causing damage to the vessel (leakage of brine from containers of wet salted hides stripping paint from the hold is an obvious example).

Examples of damage for which the owners are responsible and which may cause the vessel to be put off hire are:

(1) Collision or contact damage.
(2) Grounding due to negligent navigation or defective charts but not if the vessel is ordered to an unsafe berth.
(3) Heavy weather damage.

BIMCO suggests in line 252 to delete "or" and replace it with a comma, then add "or other accident" after "deficiency". Some charterers have already done so and additionally added "or detention" after "arrest" in line 259.

Paragraph (ii): If the master, officers or crew are the reason that the vessel is unable to respond to the charterers' instructions, the vessel goes off hire, whether the reasons behind their inability to give service IMMEDIATELY are within the control of the owners or not. Thus whether it be:

(1) striking crew;
(2) illness or injury of crew reducing numbers of qualified crew below that which are required safely to operate the vessel;
(3) inadequate crew due to desertion, arrest or any other reason,

the vessel is put off hire.

Paragraph (iii): I have already discussed in detail the responsibility for the arrest of the vessel for smuggling when considering clause 5(f)—to which cross-reference is made here. In this paragraph it is provided that the vessel goes off hire if the vessel is arrested, except if the arrest is caused by the charterers, their servants, agents or sub-contractors. Note that putting the division of responsibility this way round leaves the responsibility for the middle ground with the owners if there is any doubt or dispute as to whose responsibility is involved.

Paragraph (iv): This paragraph is rather a catch-all to cover DELAY which is caused by BREACH by the owners or any OBLIGATION or WARRANTY in this charter party. As a warranty can be implied as well as expressed, any failure on the part of the owners to do or provide something which they have undertaken to do or provide will, if it causes delay, cause this paragraph to be implemented as well as any breach of obligation.

There is a degree of duplication between this paragraph and clause 8(e), which covers loss of time arising from any circumstances for which the owners are responsible.

"(b) *Deviation*: In the event of the Vessel deviating (which expression includes putting back, or putting into any port or place other than that to which she is bound under the instructions of the Charterers) other than to save life or property, hire shall cease to be payable from the commencement of such deviation until the time when the Vessel is again ready to resume her service from a position not less favourable to the Charterers than that at which the deviation commenced, provided always that due allowance shall be given for any distance made good towards the Vessel's destination and any bunkers saved. However, should the Vessel alter course to avoid bad weather or be driven into port or anchorage by stress of weather, the Vessel shall remain on hire and all costs thereby incurred shall be for the Charterers' account."

The deviation covered by this sub-clause is the physical deviation of the vessel only and thus is narrower than the term as used in the Hague and Hague-Visby Rules, where it covers contractual deviation, which includes such things as unauthorised deck stowage of uncontainerised goods, as well as physical deviation of the vessel.

The sub-clause provides that any deviation from the voyage ordered by the charterers leads to the vessel being put off hire for the time thereby lost, unless it be to save life or property at risk, in which case expenses are dealt with as provided in clause 14(d). Not only does the vessel go off hire in the case of such deviation but the owners become responsible for the costs of extra bunkers consumed.

There is one area of slight ambiguity in this sub-clause and that is in the interpretation of "*to save life or property*". As drafted, life or property on board the vessel are not excluded, so there can be little doubt that deviation to land or seek assistance for an injured or sick crew member would not lead to the vessel being placed off hire under the present wording. This ambiguity could be removed if "*(including the Vessel's crew)*" or "*(excluding the Vessel's* crew)", according to how it is intended to resolve this ambiguity, were added after the word "*life*" and property were qualified by adding "*all*" or "*third party*" before this word.

The sub-clause seeks to aid interpretation by specifically providing that deviation caused by bad weather is not a breach and, if this leads to the vessel seeking shelter at a port or anchorage, the charterers are responsible for all costs thereby incurred, just as if that place had been a port of call under the charterers' orders. The vessel also remains on hire.

If after a deviation the vessel does not pass the point at which deviation commenced, as will likely be the case unless the vessel puts back, the voyage for the account of the charterers recommences when the vessel is at a point equally favourable to the charterers to that from which deviation started. If a vessel from A to B deviates to C at 500 miles from B, hire recommences when the vessel is 500 miles from B on the voyage from C to B. The charterers' responsibility for bunker consumption recommences at the same time.

"(c) *Blocking and Trapping*: If during the currency of this Charter Party the 280
Vessel is blocked or trapped in circumstances where Clause 19(b) applies, 281
the Vessel shall be off hire for the period blocked or trapped. If the Vessel is 282
blocked or trapped for a period of 365 days this Charter Party shall be termi- 283
nated. 284"

Blocking and trapping is a risk to which attention was forcibly drawn by the trapping of vessels in the Suez Canal in the Egyptian/Israeli war. Vessels that were undamaged were unable to gain access to the open sea and thus became constructive total losses, along with their cargoes.

The provisions of this sub-clause are inextricably bound up with clause 19(b), to which cross-reference is made here, and will be explained in detail later, when considering that clause.

"(d) *Requisitions*: Should the Vessel be requisitioned by any government or 285
governmental authority during the period of this Charter Party, it shall be off 286
hire during the period of such requisition and any hire or other compensa- 287
tion paid by any government or governmental authority in respect of such 288
requisition shall be paid to the Owners. However, the Charterers shall have 289
the option of cancelling the balance period of this Charter Party, provided 290
this option is exercised within 14 days of receipt of notice of requisition. 291"

Most states maintain the right to requisition (i.e. to require the use on non-negotiable terms, rather than to charter) of tonnage registered under their flag, usually in time of war but not necessarily only on this occasion. If this happens to the vessel in the middle of the charter party, it has the effect of frustrating the balance of the charter party, at the option of the charterers, provided they exercise that option within 14 days of being advised of the requisition of the vessel.

If the requisition looks likely to be a short one and charter rates appear likely to rise, the charterers may choose not to cancel the balance period but rather to implement the final paragraph of this clause 8, allowing them to extend the period of the charter party to make up for the period off hire.

"(e) *Loss of Time*: In the event of loss of time for which the Owners are res- 292
ponsible, including but not limited to terms of employment of Master, Offic- 293
ers and/or crew, the Vessel shall be off hire for the time thereby lost. 294"

As has already been pointed out when considering sub-clause (a)(iv) of this clause, this sub-clause has a degree of duplication with that sub-clause. Sub-clause (a)(iv) covers delay, whereas this sub-clause covers loss of time, surely two words with an almost identical meaning. However, this sub-clause is wider in application than the earlier one, as it covers loss of time arising from anything "*for which the Owners are responsible*" (under this charter party), whereas the earlier sub-clause covers only a "*breach by the Owners of any obligation or warranty in this Charter Party*".

It is in the example of what the owners are responsible for in this sub-clause that one gets the true flavour of it. It is a boycott clause, designed to cover International Transport Workers Federation (ITF) boycott of vessels, usually flying flags of convenience, which pay, what they consider to be, unacceptably low wages to crew, mostly recruited in third world countries. The wording of the sub-clause is carefully designed to avoid mention of politically sensitive words like "boycott" and to avoid giving any tacit recognition to the ITF but to provide for the vessel to go off hire if time is lost through the activities of this organisation.

"Any time during which the Vessel is off hire under this Charter Party may be 295
added to the charter period, at the option of the Charterers. Such option 296
shall be declared not less than two months before expected redelivery, or 297
latest two weeks after the event if less than two months before expected re- 298
delivery. 299"

The clause finishes with what is an important option to the charterers, to which reference has already been made when considering clause 7(f). Because this option arises at the end of a charter party, when the owners are trying to forecast with as much accuracy as possible when their vessel will be redelivered so that they can agree realistic laydays cancelling for the vessel's next employment, there necessarily has to be a strict time limit on exercising it. Thus any option to extend for any off hire which occurred more than two months before expected redelivery must be declared two months before expected redelivery, or two weeks after the off hire commenced if it commences within the period of two months before expected redelivery.

This sub-clause should be read with clause 6(m).

I did consider whether or not a sub-clause should be added providing for a minimum period of failure to comply with this clause before a vessel is placed off hire but this seemed impractical, as it would vary greatly according to a variety of factors including:

- length of charter
- state of market
- rate of hire etc.

Accordingly no such sub-clause is offered but it is something which the owners may consider attempting to negotiate in individual instances, particularly for longer charter parties. The minimum period could be expressed on the basis that no individual period of under a set period (1 hour?) would count and/or an allowance of X hours per Y month period before deductions are made.

Clause 9: Loss of Vessel

"Should the Vessel be lost, or become a constructive total loss, hire shall cease at noon on the day of her loss or constructive total loss, and if missing, from noon on the date when last heard of, and any hire paid in advance and not earned shall be returned to the Charterers and payment of any hire due shall be suspended until the Vessel is reported safe."

Whilst clause 9 is really a continuation of clause 8 as a list of occasions when the vessel is placed off hire, it was felt that, being of such a drastic nature, loss of the vessel warranted a separate clause on its own. The clause covers three possible eventualities:

(1) Total loss.
(2) Constructive total loss.
(3) Missing.

In the event of the first two eventualities hire ceases at noon on the day of loss or constructive total loss. The only problem here is "when did loss or constructive total loss" occur? Loss is not likely to cause much of a problem, a vessel is either a loss or it is not in most cases, but when does constructive total loss occur? This can be more difficult to define and one has to refer to section 60 of the 1906 Marine Insurance Act for the only satisfactory definition. This reads:

> 1 . . . there is a constructive total loss where the subject-matter insured is reasonably abandoned on account of its actual total loss appearing to be unavoidable, or because it could not be preserved from actual total loss without an expenditure which would exceed its value when the expenditure had been incurred.
>
> 2. In particular, there is a constructive total loss:-
>
> (i) Where the assured is deprived of the possession of his ship or goods by a peril insured against, and (a) it is unlikely that he can recover the ship or goods, as the case may be, or (b) the cost of recovering the ship or goods, as the case may be, would exceed their value when recovered; or
>
> (ii) In the case of damage to a ship, where she is so damaged by a peril insured against that the cost of repairing the damage would exceed the value of the ship when repaired.
>
> In estimating the cost of repairs, no deduction is to be made in respect of general average contributions to those repairs payable by other interests, but account is to be taken of the expense of future salvage operations and of any future general average contributions to which the ship would be liable if repaired; . . .

As can be seen from the above definition, the timing of a constructive total loss turns on the interpretation of the facts of individual cases, which will be different every time. However, where marine or war perils are involved, the vessel will already have gone off hire under clause 8(a)(i) or, if the vessel is blocked or trapped, under clause 8(c).

If a vessel goes missing without trace hire is suspended from noon on the day when she was last heard of until:

(1) "*the Vessel is reported safe*",

in which case hire continues from when it was suspended and, if any hire payment dates have passed whilst the vessel was posted as missing, such hire is immediately payable, or:

(2) the vessel is accepted as lost,

in which case the vessel is off hire from the date of suspension.

In the case of loss, constructive total loss or missing presumed lost, any hire paid in advance, beyond the date when the vessel is put off hire, must be returned to the charterers.

Clause 10: Lashings and Stevedoring

Whilst most of the sub-clauses in this clause would fit quite happily in clauses 5 or 6 (Owners'/Charterers' Obligations), this is such an important aspect of containership chartering that it warrants a clause all to itself. It is a clause which must be clear if disputes are to be avoided.

"(a) *Owners' Lashings*: The Owners shall supply and maintain in good working order throughout the currency of this Charter Party sufficient lashing and securing equipment to facilitate the proper lashing and securing in accordance with the plan supplied by the Owners of the maximum number of ISO standard containers which may be carried in accordance with the details provided in Part III hereto. The Owners further warrant that both the strength of the lashings and the design of the lashing pattern are adequate for the stowage in accordance with Part III hereto and that these have been approved by the Vessel's Classification Society."

Sub-clause (a) puts a clear responsibility upon the Owners to:

1. *Supply* AND
2. *Maintain in good working order throughout the currency of this Charter Party*

sufficient lashing and securing equipment" as is required to lash and secure properly "*the maximum number of ISO standard containers*" which the vessel may carry ("*in accordance with the details provided in Part III*" according to the container stowage plan provided in accordance with clause 13(a)).

Note that the lashings and securing equipment to be supplied relate to ISO containers only, which include the 9 foot 6 inch "high cube" boxes. As use of these types of container is increasing, the owners must ensure that they have lashings and securing equipment to cope with a maximum number of 9 foot 6 inch containers as well as the 8 foot 6 inch and 8 foot types or alternatively control the number of "high cube" boxes they offer to carry with a suitable clause.

Whilst the first sentence covers supply and maintenance, the second covers responsibility for:

(1) "*strength of lashings*", and

(2) "*design of lashing pattern*"

and WARRANTS to the charterers that both are:

(1) "*adequate for the stowage in accordance with Part III*", and

(2) "*approved by the Vessel's Classification Society*".

These are two very onerous warranties by the owners. If the deck stack collapses in heavy weather, the owners will need to demonstrate compliance with the requirements of this sub-clause if they are to have any chance of avoiding liability for loss and damage sustained by the charterers as a result thereof. Accordingly, the owners of any vessel trading under this charter party would be well advised to ensure that their compliance with the terms of this sub-clause is well documented, in case they need to produce evidence of it. Sub-clause (e), which is discussed later, only serves to reinforce this.

"(b) *Charterers' Lashings*: Should any additional or alternative lashings to those supplied by the Owners be required, these shall be supplied by the Charterers at their expense. Should the Charterers supply gear, equipment or stores, the Master shall keep a record of it and care for it. Such gear, equipment or stores shall be redelivered to the Charterers at the time required by the Charterers in the same condition as supplied fair wear and tear excepted."

This sub-clause provides that, if the charterers need any additional lashings to those for which they are entitled to look to the owners to supply under sub-clause (a), they must supply these themselves. This covers lashings for non-ISO containers as well as lashings for uncontainerised goods and any other abnormal loads.

Having supplied these non-standard lashings, or any other gear, equipment or stores, the charterers are entitled to expect the master to care for them and redeliver them on demand in the same condition as supplied, fair wear and tear excepted and subject to sub-clause (e), which is discussed later. Although not specifically provided here, by implication the owners must reimburse the charterers for any lost or damaged lashings, gear, equipment or stores for which they cannot account by fair wear and tear.

"(c) *Stowage Planning*: The Charterers shall ensure that stowage is effected in accordance with the requirements of this Charter Party and of the Vessel's stability including, inter alia, ensuring that stack and tier weights are not exceeded and that heavy containers are not stowed over light containers on or under deck, except with the Master's prior approval."

Having clearly provided for the owners to be responsible for the strength of lashings and design of the lashing pattern in sub-clause (a), sub-clause (c) puts upon the charterers the responsibility for the correct practical accomplishment of a safe stowage.

Whilst it is appreciated that the charterers may be reliant upon a third party: their shipper for accurate data relating to the nature of the goods in containers and their weights, it is up to the charterers, as carriers under bills of lading, to protect themselves, by providing in their bill of lading terms and conditions for recourse to their customers for misdeclaration. As between the charterers and the owners, the charterers must be strictly liable for the accuracy of the data relating to the goods and containers (*see* clause 6(a)) and then for arranging the stowage of containers so that it complies with the requirements of the charter party in practice as well as in theory. In particular stack/tier weights must not be exceeded and heavies must not be stowed over lights.

Stack weight and tier weights are one and the same thing, namely, the maximum weight of goods and containers that may be placed in a vertical column on the area thus rated. In preparing a stowage, consideration has to be given to the maximum weight that the corner castings of the bottom container can bear as well as the stack weight rating of the tank-top or hatch-lid.

Stowage of heavies over lights is of particular concern on deck, where too much weight too high may have a very deleterious effect on stability. If the vessel with too much top weight sets up a rolling motion in heavy weather the result can be catastrophic. Below deck other considerations apply as the stowage planner, with his load computer and containers generally divided into lights, mediums and heavies, tries to achieve a stowage that meets the stability requirements of the vessel and its itinerary without making it too stiff. The better he does his job the better chance the charterers' goods have of a smooth damage-free voyage.

However, any departure from the lights over heavies requirement, whether on or under deck, requires the master's prior approval and, in practice, his cargo officer will operate closely with the stevedore/stowage planner, checking the calculations so that the vessel can be ballasted properly to reduce torsional moments as part of the owners' responsibility to exercise due diligence to provide a seaworthy vessel (*see* clause 17(a)(i)).

Purpose built cellular containerships (as opposed to multi-purpose con-bulkers designed to carry bulk cargo or containers secured by means of under-deck lashing systems) have massive ballasting capacity, as they are double sided as well as double bottomed. As containers cannot be moved sideways once placed under deck, the space below deck level between the vessel's side and the hatch coaming is unavailable for carrying containers. Therefore, most large cellular containerships use this space as an underdeck walkway and wing tanks to carry fuel or ballast. This facility, plus an ability to pump ballast quickly from one side of the vessel to the other, is necessary to ensure that the vessel is kept upright at the quay during loading/unloading, so that containers do not become jammed in the cell guides and it enables the vessel's cargo officer to switch ballast to reduce torsional moments on the vessel and prepare the vessel for seagoing in a stable seaworthy condition, even if the distribution of weight throughout the vessel is imperfect.

The added bonus of this arrangement is that it makes the vessel double sided as well as double bottomed so that, if the vessel is in collision, the other vessel must penetrate two skins before the vessel and its goods and containers are threatened. Several cellular containerships have had good reason to be thankful for this method of construction, which must make cellular container-ships amongst the safest vessels afloat.

"(d) *Stevedoring*:

(i) The Charterers shall provide and pay for the cost of all stevedoring operations during the currency of this Charter Party including, inter alia, receipt, loading, handling, stowing, lashing, securing, unsecuring, unlashing, unstowing, discharging, tallying and delivering of all uncontainnerised goods and containers and shall be liable to the Owners for all loss or damage caused to the Vessel by the improper or careless performance of such operations.

(ii) The Master shall supervise stevedores undertaking the tasks outlined in Clause 10(d)(i) to ensure that these are done correctly and to his satisfaction. The Master shall ensure that all lashings are regularly checked whilst at sea, weather permitting."

(i) This being an FIOS (free in out and stow) charter party, the cost of stevedoring falls on the charterers and stevedores are the servants of the charterers, so that all costs relating to stevedoring activities are for the charterers' account. As the stevedores are the servants of the charterers, the latter have a vicarious liability to the owners for the actions of the former (*see* clause 6(1) also).

(ii) Whilst the charterers are responsible for meeting the costs of stevedoring, it is up to the master to supervise this activity and ensure that it is accomplished to his satisfaction (*see* also comment on clause 5(b)(vii) in relation to lashing and unlashing). The master also has to ensure that, weather permitting, lashings are checked regularly whilst at sea, as they sometimes have a tendency to slacken as the vessel and stowage "work" in reaction to the seas encountered.

"(e) *Liability*: Except in respect of the failure of any lashing supplied by the Charterers, the Owners shall be responsible, subject to the provisions of Clause 17, for the consequences of the failure of any lashings or lashing pattern design or execution or the failure to properly service lashings during the voyage."

If there is a breakdown of stowage during a voyage the chances are that substantial damage will be incurred by the vessel, goods and containers. The causes may include the following, which are the responsibility of the party indicated:

Neither party

(1) Heavy weather (perils of the sea).

The owners

(2) Failure of the owners' lashings.
(3) Faulty design of vessel's lashing plan.
(4) Failure of the stevedores to lash properly.
(5) Failure to tighten lashings during voyage.

The charterers

(6) Failure of the charterers' containers.
(7) Failure of the charterers' lashings.
(8) Failure of the stowage or securing of the goods in the containers.
(9) Overweight containers (actual weight in excess of declared weight).

It is quite likely that investigations after such an incident will show that several of the above causes contributed to the breakdown of stowage.

In the case of (4) there will likely be a dispute between the owners and the charterers, as the charterers or their servants were responsible for effecting the defective stow. However, sub-clause (d)(ii) above clearly provides for the master to supervise and ensure that this is done to his satisfaction so in the final analysis the responsibility is with the owners.

So much for responsibility. This sub-clause covers LIABILITY and provides that the owners can seek protection in the provisions of clause 17, so that they are only liable for loss or damage to the extent that this is due to failure on their part to comply with clause 17(a), once responsibility is attributable to them in accordance with the above allocation.

Thus, subject to clause 17, the owners are liable for the consequences of failure of the:

(1) Lashings (other than the charterers' lashings).
(2) Lashing pattern design.
(3) Pattern of lashings used on voyage in question.
(4) Master to service the lashings properly during the voyage.

Clause 11: Vessel's Gear

"(a) *Regulations*: The Vessel's cargo gear, if any, and any other equipment shall comply with the regulations of the countries to which the Vessel will be employed and the Owners shall ensure that the Vessel is at all times during the currency of this Charter Party in possession of valid certificates of efficiency to comply with such regulations. If stevedores are not permitted to work due to failure of the Master and/or the Owners and/or the Owners' agents to comply with the aforementioned regulations or because the Vessel is not in possession of such valid certificates of efficiency, then the Charterers may suspend hire for the time lost thereby and the Owners shall pay all expenses incurred incidental to and resulting from such failure (see Clause 5(c))."

In a world where people are increasingly becoming aware of their rights and thus litigiously minded, there is an increasing tendency to look to profit from any mishap. Injuries at work, that would once have been accepted as part of the job or due to the victim's own fault, now precipitate claims on employers. Upon being injured, the first thought of a victim these days is: who can I sue?

This being the case, it is unsurprising that port employers produce bye-laws and governments, under social pressures, produce legislation detailing minimum requirements in respect of the gear of vessels calling at their ports, which often require the production of valid certificates, certifying regular inspection of that gear, which is found to be maintained in good working order, as a prerequisite of allowing entry of that vessel into port. Such bye-laws and legislation commonly cover a whole range of the vessel's equipment: cranes and winches, chains and tackle, access to the vessel from the quay and to the holds from the deck and so on.

Such regulations are often rigidly enforced and work may be stopped on any vessel found to be in contravention of them. Accordingly, it is most important for the owners to ensure that they are familiar with the regulations of the ports at which they are required to call, that all necessary gear is up to scratch and all necessary certificates in date before they call there (*see* clause 5(c)). Failure to do so will lead to the vessel being placed off hire if work on the vessel is stopped. In addition the owners are liable to the charterers for "*all expenses incurred incidental to and resulting from such failure*". This could include, *inter alia*, paying the cost of stevedores ordered but unable to work because of the breach of the regulations.

"(b) *Condition*: All cargo handling gear, including derrick(s), crane(s) and winch(es) if any, shall be kept in good working order and the owners shall maintain, repair and/or replace such gear whenever necessary. In the event of loss of time due to a breakdown of derrick(s), crane(s) or winch(es) for any period by reason of disablement or insufficient power, hire shall be reduced pro rata for the period of such inefficiency in relation to the number of hatches affected, unless caused by mishandling by the Charterers or their servants. If the Charterers continue working by using shore-crane(s) the Owners shall pay such cranage but not exceeding the hire payable for such period, in which case the Vessel shall not be off hire pro-rata as stipulated above. The Vessel shall, however, be pro-rata off hire if shore-cranes are not available during stoppages of derrick(s), crane(s) or winch(es) and all other unavoidable expenses thereby incurred shall be for the Owners' account."

This sub-clause follows on from sub-clause (a) above to provide that, in any event, whether there is a need for certification or not, the vessel's cargo handling gear must be maintained in good working order, a more specific reinforcement of the obligation put upon the owners in the opening paragraph of clause 5. Then, whereas sub-clause (a) above covers non-working of the vessel because of non-availability of valid certification, sub-clause (b) provides for off hiring if the vessel is unable to work because of "*breakdown of derrick(s), crane(s) or winch(es)*" or the non-availability of the necessary power to operate them (perhaps a generator breakdown), "*unless caused by mishandling by the Charterers or their servants*" (e.g. stevedores damage crane by mishandling).

Recognising that such inability to work may only be partial, this sub-clause provides for pro rata off hire for pro rata inability to work. Similarly, unserviceability of the vessel's lifting gear may be made good, either wholly or in part, by shore crane(s), with the owners paying the cost of hiring the shore crane(s) as an alternative to being placed off hire, provided that such cost does not exceed hire payable for that period. As with sub-clause (a) above, "*all* other unavoidable expenses . . . incurred" following breach of this sub-clause are payable by the owners in addition to being placed off hire, partially or totally.

Note that the way in which this sub-clause is drafted gives the Charterers the option whether to use shore crane(s) or not ("*IF the charterers continue working by using shore-crane(s)*") so they have an option, subject to the restrictions of this sub-clause, to expedite matters by engaging shore crane(s) or put the vessel off hire. According to their requirements at the time they may choose either course.

"(c) *Suez and Panama Canal*: The Vessel shall be maintained during the cur- 371
rency of this Charter Party with all necessary fittings for Suez and Panama 372
Canal transit in good working order. 373"

The regulations of both canals contain requirements for vessels transiting designed to enhance safe transit. These include, *inter alia*, requirements regarding fairleads, lighting, davits for line handling boatmen's craft etc. This sub-clause requires the vessel to be maintained throughout the currency of the charter party with all the necessary fittings to allow transit of these waterways.

"(d) *Refrigeration*: The Owners shall ensure that all refrigeration facilities as 374
described in PART III are maintained in good working order throughout the 375
currency of this Charter Party. 376"

Most carriage of refrigerated goods on chartered vessels is effected in integral refrigeration containers in which the container has its own built-in machinery and relies upon the vessel solely for a supply of power. Some are carried in insulated containers with "porthole" air delivery and return ducts with a "Clip-on-Unit" attached to supply the cold air and this arrangement also relies upon the vessel for a supply of power. The third arrangement, which is found in the chartering market, albeit rarely, is the insulated container that is carried below deck and linked up to the vessel's refrigeration system via pneumatically operated couplings to provide cold air from the vessel's machinery. (This system is encountered mostly in liner owned and operated vessels in the Europe-Australia/New Zealand and Europe-South Africa trades at present but generally seems to be losing ground to the integral machinery approach.)

This sub-clause provides for the charterers to have the use of all refrigeration facilities described in Part III: Vessel's Specification, and for these facilities to be maintained in good working order throughout the currency of the charter party. Part of the description which should appear in Part III should be the type of connection with which the vessel is fitted to supply power via the outlet sockets to the containers. Alas these are not all standard, so it is important when chartering a vessel to carry refrigerated containers to ensure that the vessel's power supply is delivered via outlets compatible with the plugs on the refrigerated containers' leads, otherwise adapters may be needed.

"(e) *Lighting*: The Owners shall ensure that the Vessel will supply sufficient lighting to deck and holds to permit 24 hour working free of expense to the Charterers and that such lighting will comply with the port regulations at all ports of call throughout the currency of this Charter Party."

Many major container terminals operate on a 24-hour shift basis and they turn vessels round in a matter of hours rather than days, thereby enabling the vessel operator to make maximum use of his capital equipment, which is earning only whilst it is moving. Thus there is a need to ensure that the vessel has sufficient lighting to facilitate 24-hour working that complies with the regulations of the ports of call. This sub-clause provides for the owners to supply this, free of expense to the charterers throughout the currency of the charter party.

Although not specified here, should a vessel be prevented from working because the lighting is inadequate or does not comply with port regulations, the vessel would be put off hire as the owners would be in breach of this sub-clause and clause 8(a)(i).

Clause 12: Bunker Fuel

Encouraged by the first energy crisis, which caused a rapid escalation in the price of fuel, major advancements have been made in marine engines in the past 20 years. At the time when the first containerships were ordered, fuel was relatively cheap and was a minor consideration when ordering a new vessel, as compared to the need for speed.

Thus the first containerships were mostly turbine steamers with a high fuel consumption. One American operator even had jet turbine driven vessels operating across the Atlantic at speeds in excess of 30 knots. Such of those vessels that survive today, unre-engined, and operate in the charter market, find employment difficult to come by and, when they can get it, rates of hire very low to compensate for the excessive fuel bill.

The sudden increase in the cost of oil had two effects: the search for a fuel efficient engine rather than a fast one (although speeds of about 20 knots were still required) and the efforts by the refiners to extract the maximum refined product from the raw crude to maximise product efficiency. The former led to the development of diesel engines able to operate on filtered boiler fuel on a fraction of the tons per day (tpd) consumption of their turbine powered forebears. The latter produced a bunker fuel (always what is left after everyone else has taken their bit) of decreasing quality and increasing viscosity that needed substantial heating before it could be pumped, let alone burnt. Designing fuel efficient engines to cope with this worsening quality fuel is the achievement of marine engine designers, who have produced the modern marine diesel engine capable of burning a fuel that is unpourable and more like road tar at ambient temperatures and consuming less of it than its forebears did of a much higher grade fuel.

Fuel is now a substantial proportion of voyage costs. Under the terms of the charter party it is supplied by the charterers to be burnt in the owners' engine(s). Thus the charterers want a vessel with a low consumption that burns a cheap bunker fuel whilst the owners want a fuel of a specification that meets their engine's needs, which are not always consistent requirements. Hence bunker fuel is another regular subject of dispute between the owners and the charterers, so that this is clearly a subject warranting a clause of its own, which gives close consideration to matters likely to cause problems.

"(a) *Quantity at Delivery/Redelivery*: The Vessel shall be delivered with ap- 382
proximately the quantity of fuel as indicated in Box 16, and unless indicated 383
to the contrary in Box 17, the Vessel shall be redelivered with an approxima- 384
tely similar quantity, provided that the quantity of fuel at redelivery is at least 385
sufficient to allow the Vessel to reach safely the nearest port at which fuel of 386
the required type is available. 387"

In a time charter party fuel provision is always the responsibility of the charterers but, of course, no vessel is ever delivered or redelivered with full or empty tanks. Thus at delivery the charterers buy the bunker fuel in the vessel from the owners and the reverse process applies at redelivery.

This sub-clause provides for this arrangement by reference to estimates in Part I, with the one proviso that the amount of bunker fuel on board at redelivery must be "*at least sufficient to allow the Vessel to reach safely the nearest port at which fuel of the required type is available*".

"(b) *Pre and Post Charter Bunkering*: Provided that it can be accomplished 388
without hindrance to the operation of the Vessel, the Owners shall allow the 389
Charterers to bunker for the account of the Charterers prior to delivery and 390
the Charterers shall allow the Owners to bunker for the account of the Ow- 391
ners prior to redelivery, in both cases by prior arrangement between the 392
parties. 393"

It often happens that, towards the end of a previous charter party and/or the end of the charter party in question, the vessel calls at a port where bunker fuel can be obtained at advantageous rates. This being the case it is natural that the party about to accept delivery or redelivery of the vessel should want to take advantage of this opportunity to obtain bunker fuel for their account ahead of the time when the provision of bunker fuel becomes their responsibility.

This sub-clause provides for the parties to agree to this arrangement, "*provided that it can be accomplished without hindrance to the operation of the Vessel*".

"(c) *Purchase Price*: Unless otherwise stated in Boxes 16 and 17, the Char- 394
terers shall purchase the fuel on board at delivery and the Owners shall pur- 395
chase the fuel on board at redelivery at the Platts Oil Gram mean prices at 396
the ports and dates of delivery and redelivery, respectively, or the nearest 397
bunkering port thereto. 398"

Having provided for the taking over of existing supplies of bunker fuel on board at delivery and redelivery in sub-clause (a), this sub-clause provides for the price to be paid. It is necessary for this to be most precise as prices can fluctuate quite dramatically in a short time and there can be different prices from different suppliers in the same port. Thus this sub-clause provides for the price to be by reference to the indicative prices advised in the *Platts Oil Gram* (an informative publication) for the ports and dates of delivery and redelivery. A mean is taken of the range advised and applied.

If there are no prices supplied for the port concerned, the prices for the nearest bunkering port to that port are used.

"(d) *Specification*: The Charterers shall supply fuel of the BSMA 100:1989 specification or any amendment thereto as indicated in Box 14."

Sophisticated engines to burn a low grade bunker fuel need to have that bunker fuel rigidly controlled within acceptable parameters if they are to operate to maximum efficiency and not be damaged by "bad fuel". BSMA 100: 1989 is a specification which some owners find acceptable but others require an even more highly controlled specification. If this is the case the owners will need to delete this sub-clause and replace it with an additional clause setting out their specification or incorporating it into the contract from the Part III specification, where it is frequently listed.

Damage to the vessel's engines by "bad fuel" supplied by the charterers' suppliers is a common cause of charter party disputes, so specification is an important feature to watch if disputes are to be avoided. If disputes arise the samples taken during bunkering (*see* (f) *below*) become important.

"(e) *Consumption*: The Vessel's fuel consumption in port and at sea shall not exceed the amounts shown in Part III, at all times for port consumption and in smooth water with winds not exceeding Beaufort Scale 4 for consumption at sea."

In view of the high cost of fuel the charterers look carefully at consumption figures and take these into account when fixing the charter party. Obviously consumption will vary according to speed (when under way) or if in port and the charterers require some undertaking from the owners as to the vessel's maximum fuel consumption in normal circumstances, which is defined as "*smooth water with winds not exceeding Beaufort Scale 4*".

In order to meet these requirements it is necessary for the owners to ensure that machinery is in good order and the hull not fouled by marine growth because, if the fuel consumption of the vessel exceeds the indicated levels, the owners may well face a claim from the charterers for reimbursement of the excess of fuel consumed over that indicated in the charter party, unless it can be explained by bad weather as provided in this sub-clause.

It is a feature of this charter party that the charterers pay for ALL bunker fuel, including that used to meet the domestic needs of the vessel. No allowance is made for cooking, hot water etc. as the former is often electric and the latter a by-product from an economiser or some other source, which makes it difficult to determine how much bunker fuel is used for the crew's needs and how much for propulsion. So, unlike many other charter parties, no attempt is made and the charterers supply all the bunker fuel, whilst the owners supply all the lubricating oil and water (*see* Preamble to clause 5).

"(f) *Bunkering*: the Chief Engineer shall co-operate with the Charterers' bunkering agents and fuel suppliers and comply with their requirements during bunkering, including, but not limited to, checking, verifying and acknowledging readings or soundings, meters etc. before, during and/or after delivery of fuel.

Three (3) samples of all fuel shall be taken during delivery, sealed and signed by suppliers, Chief Engineer and the Charterers' agent, each of whom should retain one sample. If any claim should arise in respect of the quality or specification of the fuel supplied, the Owners and the Charterers agree to have samples of the fuel analysed by a mutually agreed qualified analyst."

Paragraph 1 provides for the co-operation of the chief engineer with the charterers' bunkering agents and fuel suppliers during bunkering operations. In the light of the above comments relating to the price and quality of bunker fuel, it is clearly vital to have this undertaking to co-operate in checking the fuel being supplied and acknowledging the quantity received.

Paragraph 2 provides for a situation as envisaged in considering sub-clause (d) above, namely a dispute arises over the specification or quality of fuel supplied. If this happens resort is made to sealed and signed samples taken at bunkering and held, one each, by the owners, via the chief engineer, the charterers, via their agents and the supplier. These are analysed by a mutually agreed qualified analyst. This will resolve any dispute as to whether or not the correct fuel has been supplied but there is still scope for dispute over the degree of damage caused by the deficient fuel, which no clause can avoid.

Other clauses to consider

The following additional clauses, which are unsuitable for a standard charter party that needs to cover all types and sizes of containership, may be appropriate in individual charter parties.

(1) *Bunkering into empty tanks only*: If the vessel is a large one with many tanks it should be possible for the vessel to prepare itself for bunkering in such a way as to allow the charterers to bunker into empty tanks only. This is desirable as it avoids mixing different fuels which, although they may be of similar specification, do not mix and thus cause problems.

Such a clause might read:

"The Charterers may only bunker into empty tanks to avoid mixing potentially incompatible fuels. The Owners will co-operate in making maximum bunkering capacity available commensurate with stability and trim requirements. Bunker fuel supplied by the Charterers at each bunkering to be kept separate from bunker fuel on board at delivery and bunker fuel taken at previous bunkerings."

Such a clause is inappropriate for a standard charter party that may be used with small containerships, that do not have the number of fuel tanks to make this requirement viable. Thus this is a potential additional clause for charter parties for large containerships.

(2) *Blending*: Bunker fuel is often a blend to produce the required specification. As has been pointed out earlier, the viscosity of bunker fuel is such that it does not readily mix of its own volition. Thus it needs mechanical mixing in a blender to produce the right blend. This cannot be done on the vessel. Thus a clause requiring any blended fuel to be blended ashore is worth considering. Something along the lines of:

> "If bunker fuel is a blend, such bunker fuel to be blended by a shore installation or blending machine approved by the Owners."

(3) *Bunker fuel on total loss vessel.* I have always believed that carriers (owners and charterers) should organise their affairs in such a way as to minimise costs vis-à-vis a third party, particularly insurers. Reasoning that the owners, in insuring their vessel, must take account of a full stem of bunker fuel, it seemed illogical that the charterers should need to insure their bunker fuel in the owners' vessel against total loss, thereby giving insurers two premia for the same risk.

If it were contractually provided that bunkers were deemed redelivered to the owners as the vessel sank, the owners' cover would operate and the charterers would be relieved of the need to insure bunkers. After all, why should insurers (corporately) get two premia for the same risk from carriers (corporately)?

Such a clause might read:

> "In the event of the Vessel becoming an actual or constructive total loss, the estimated bunker fuel on board shall be deemed redelivered to the Owners at the time when the actual total loss occurs or the constructive total loss is accepted by hull insurers."

Bunker fuel is a relatively short clause but a very important one. It warrants careful consideration.

BIMCO proposed to review the bunker clause at the next opportunity to bring its provisions into line with their FUELCON standard contract.

Clause 13: Charterers' Requirements

There is a thin line between a *Charterers' Requirement* and an *Owners' Obligation* (clause 5) and in the end it all turned on the view of the working party as to which clause the various matters were allocated. By and large obligations are matters involving costs and physical tasks that are an essential part of almost every charter party, whilst the requirements are primarily rights to receive or do things that are necessary in the operation of the charter party or at some stage in a charter party's life.

To have put the two together would have created a clause of unmanageable proportions, so some division was necessary and, once this process is started, it becomes a matter of opinion as to what best fits where. Readers and users may disagree with the allocation but at least they have an index to speed their search for the relevant provision.

"(a) *Plans*: On signing this Charter Party the Owners shall, if the Charterers so request, furnish the Charterers with the following documents in English:

(i) General Arrangement Plan
(ii) Capacity Plan
(iii) Container Stowage Plan
(iv) Plan of Deck and (where the Vessel not cellular) Under-Deck Container Lashing Plan approved by the Vessel's Classification Society.
(v) Trim and Stability Book
(vi) Hydrostatic Curves Plan
(vii) Loading Scale
(viii) Tank Plan

and any other operational documents that the Charterers may reasonably request and which are necessary for the safe and efficient operation of the Vessel. All documents received by the Charterers shall be returned to the Owners on redelivery."

Containerships are sophisticated vessels and their safe operation depends upon detailed calculations to ensure that stowage of containers and lashings is effected within defined parameters. In most cases these calculations are made by specialised computers, either ashore or on the vessels themselves, often both with the latter checking the calculations of the former. Thus, to plan a safe correct stow, a planner needs details of the vessel and accurate data relating to the weight of the containers and their destinations. This sub-clause provides for the owners to supply the former of these requirements.

Note the timing of the requirement: "*on signing this Charter Party*", not on delivery, as the charterers need to have these documents as soon as possible. This is so that they can start planning the stow for the first voyage in conjunction with the data provided by their operational or commercial departments relating to the expected number, weights and destinations of containers for shipment.

Note the requirement for the documents to be in English and that the list (i) to (vi) is not exhaustive and may be supplemented by "*any other operational documents that the Charterers may reasonably request and which are necessary for the safe and efficient operation of the Vessel*".

In a standard charter party, such as this, it is impossible to envisage all of the different types of containership. So each individual charter party needs to be negotiated for the owners to provide what is necessary for the operation of that particular vessel. As it is in the mutual interest of both parties that the charterers should have this information, there is usually little problem in arranging for its production by the owners.

Plans etc. of this nature are expensive to produce, so the sub-clause provides for their return to the owners on redelivery.

"(b) *Flag, Funnel, Name and Configuration*: The Charterers, if required, shall be allowed to fly their house flag, paint the funnel in the Charterers' colours and/or the name of the Line on the Vessel's side, change the Vessel's name, subject to the authorities' approval, and/or change the Vessel's container stowage configuration to carry different sized containers, all during the currency of this Charter Party. If the Charterers elect to exercise any or all of these options all alterations necessary shall be effected during the Charterers' time and at the Charterers' expense. Unless the Owners elect to waive this requirement or enter into an alternative agreement with the Charterers, the Vessel shall be returned to its condition prior to the commencement of the Charter Party at the Charterers' expense before redelivery."

Flag in this sub-clause means the charterers' house flag, which has no legal significance, only marketing effect, the matter of the flag of the vessel's country of registry being dealt with in sub-clause (m)(i) below.

Containership chartering is effected almost exclusively by charterers operating liner services and thus relatively high profile operations seeking to establish a regular market profile. The ports to which they trade are frequently close to the areas they serve or alternatively they have to pass within sight of such areas proceeding to/from their ports. Part of this profile is to use the vessel as a floating billboard to advertise the charterers' name and, particularly if the charter party is a relatively long one, the cost of time and materials incurred in painting the vessel's funnel in their colours and/or their name on the side of the vessel, flying their flag on the vessel and changing the vessel's name to one in the charterer's naming sequence is often considered worthwhile.

Even if the customer never sees the vessel, the change of name means that he sees a familiar name on his bill of lading instead of some unknown name that he may mistrust. In PR there is a lot in a name. Image is important. It costs a lot to build up and it is worthwhile spending a little to preserve it.

Accordingly this sub-clause provides for the charterers to be allowed to:

(a) *fly their house flag*;
(b) *paint the funnel in the Charterers' colours*;
(c) *paint the name of the Line on the Vessel's side*;
(d) *change the Vessel's name*;

subject to the following provisos that:

(a) the authorities concerned approve of the name change;
(b) it is done in the charterers' time;
(c) it is done at the charterers' expense;
(d) it is all returned to its original state before redelivery in the charterers' time and at the charterers' expense.

Additionally the sub-clause provides for the charterers to be allowed to change the container stowage arrangements of the vessel, something already extensively discussed in considering paragraph 2 of clause 6(m). The vessel may be set up to carry 20 foot containers and the charterers may wish to carry more 40 foot containers. Below deck, if the vessel is cellular, this entails rearrangement of the guides. If it is a conbulker or where deck stowage is concerned, it may involve welding more stools and pad eyes to the deck to accommodate the larger containers.

In the case of stools and pad eyes, it is quite likely that the owners can make further use of them after the end of the charter party and will waive the right to insist on the charterers removing them and returning the stowage arrangements to their original form prior to redelivery. However, in the case of cellguides, everything depends upon the owners' requirements for his next employment.

Of course the liberty to change the stowage configuration for containers also carries the requirement that it be done in the charterers' time and at the charterers' expense and must be reconverted on similar terms prior to redelivery, "*unless the Owners elect to waive this requirement or enter into an alternative agreement with the Charterers*".

Some owners prefer "original livery, name and configuration" to "condition" in line 441.

"(c) *Ballast Warranty*: The Owners warrant that the Vessel is capable of operating under this Charter Party in ballast without requiring any solid ballast and using fuel and water ballast only."

In case it is necessary for the vessel to undertake a voyage in ballast, the charterers wish to avoid the cost of having to spend time and money providing solid ballast and wish to be assured that the vessel has sufficient capacity in its ballast tanks for this purpose. This is rarely a problem with containerships, particularly larger cellular ones with wing tank capacity. Note that this is a warranty!

"(d) *Weather Routing*: The Charterers may supply the Master with weather routing information during the currency of this Charter Party. In this event the Master shall comply with the reporting procedure of the charterers' weather routing service."

Weather routing services sell their services to operators on the basis of savings in time and fuel and reduced exposure to damage. The efficiency of such a service depends heavily upon the accuracy of the local weather information it receives. It is not unknown in some areas where there are not too many weather reporting vessels (like certain places in the Pacific Ocean) for a vessel to be reporting weather as part of the weather reporting service and then to be getting back its own weather from the weather routing service. The problem here is the advice it gets back is hours old and the situation has since changed dramatically (as it can in the North Pacific Ocean).

Not surprisingly, therefore, weather reporting services are not universally popular with masters. They are often not seen as indispensable aids but rather as interfering busy-bodies living off their backs.

This sub-clause takes these views into account. It allows the charterers to supply weather routing information to the master and requires him to comply with the reporting procedure of that service but it stops short of requiring the master to follow the weather routing advice given and leaves the master, as master under God and not under the weather fax chart, to make his own decision. However, the master does have to take notice of the weather routing information provided because, if he does not follow it, he may have to justify his actions if he goes another way and runs into bad weather causing cargo damage or consumes more fuel than the charterers calculate that he would have done following the advice.

So the position of the weather routing service is rather like that of a pilot: the master ignores him at his peril but he always remains in charge and ultimately responsible for the decision regarding route.

"(e) *Communications Facilities*: The Owners shall permit the Charterers use of the Vessel's communication facilities at cost during the currency of this Charter Party."

This is a rather infrequently used facility, usually only exercised on those few occasions when a charterers' supercargo is carried and/or the vessel is operating through a small remote port with poor communications. As most containerships usually operate to substantial facilities this happens rather infrequently.

"(f) *Logs and Witnesses*: The Owners shall maintain full deck, engine room and, where appropriate, refrigeration logs during the currency of this Charter Party and the Charterers shall have full access to all the Vessel's logs, rough and official, covering this period. The Owners undertake to produce all such documentation promptly upon request of the Charterers.

The Owners also undertake to endeavour to assist the Charterers by producing or assisting the Charterers to trace the Vessel's witnesses as may be requested by the Charterers to give testimony in connection with matters arising in relating to this Charter Party and such expenses as may be incurred shall be for the Charterers' account."

This sub-clause provides for the owners to co-operate with the charterers to provide for the charterers' access to the necessary documentary information needed to handle claims. Information from the vessel has to be supplied to the charterers at the owners' expense.

Additionally, the owners undertake to try and help the charterers if they need to trace witnesses amongst crew members, who may be required to give statements or testimony in relation to such claims, but in this case at the expense of the charterers.

"(g) *Replacement of Master and Officers*: If the Charterers shall have reason to be dissatisfied with the conduct of the Master or Officers, the Owners shall, on receiving particulars of the complaint, investigate same and, if confirmed, replace the offending party(ies) at the Owners' expense."

In reading clauses and sub-clauses it is important to note what is not there as well as what is there. This sub-clause covers the master and officers, not the master, officers and crew.

If, for any reason, the charterers are dissatisfied with the conduct of the master or officers (refusal to co-operate with the charterers' local agents, suppliers or sub-contractors etc.), the charterers may complain to the owners.

If the charterers complain to the owners, then the owners are obliged to investigate the complaint and, if they find the complaint justified, they must replace the offending person(s) at their expense.

Crew are excluded from this provision because it is not anticipated that they have any direct interface with the charterers, their agents, suppliers or sub-contractors and it is expected that the master and officers will control them. A drunken seaman is unlikely to threaten the charterers' operation, a drunken master or officer may.

> "(h) *Supercargo*: The Owners shall provide and maintain a clean and adequate room for the Charterers' supercargo if any, furnished to the same standard as officers' accommodation. Supercargo shall be victualled with the Vessel's officers. The Charterers shall pay for accommodation and victualling of any supercargo at the daily rate as indicated in Box 28."

A supercargo is the charterers' representative travelling with the vessel. Because charterers operating a container service are usually liner operators calling regularly at their ports of call, they will usually have competent agents at those ports, so supercargoes are only carried infrequently but charterers like to preserve the right to require the vessel to carry one just in case.

This sub-clause provides for one to be carried and for his accommodation and victualling at the rate provided in box 28.

> "(j) *Victualling*: The Owners, when requested and authorised by the Charterers or their agents, shall victual other officials and servants of the Charterers at the rate per person per meal as indicated in Box 29."

Shipping has a language all its own, often still using words which were commonplace centuries ago but which have been largely replaced in normal use today. Victualling is one such word (meaning to feed).

Container terminals are often miles away from habitation and hostelries, so it is sometimes necessary for the vessel to provide food for the charterers' servants or certain port officials. This sub-clause provides for this to be done at the charterers' expense at the rate provided in box 29.

> "(k) *Sub-Letting*: The Charterers shall have the right to sub-let all or part of the Vessel with the prior consent of the Owners, which shall not be unreasonably withheld, whilst still remaining responsible to the Owners for the performance of this Charter Party."

This can be a most important provision. The vessel may be chartered for a number of years in anticipation of being used in a certain trade and suddenly something unforeseen occurs to prevent that trade. Thus the charterers will always want a right to sub-let (sub-charter) to guard against such changes in demand necessitating changes in operation.

However, the owners want a say in this to make sure that they are not sub-chartered to charterers that they would not be prepared to operate under and with whom they may have refused to do business in the past. Thus they have a power of veto over sub-chartering, provided that their reasons for refusing are reasonable.

Sub-letting may be of the whole of the vessel or just part of it. The latter provision is necessary if the vessel is to be used in a consortium operation, where the charterers will swap slots on the vessel with their consortium partners.

Whilst the owners may be prepared to allow sub-chartering of the vessel (in full or in part), they insist that the charterers are the party with whom they made the contract and that they are the party to whom they look for the performance of it, any sub-chartering terms being the concern of the charterers only. So, if the charterers sub-charter, they cannot operate the cesser/demise clause approach and attempt to drop out of the arrangement and leave the contract between the owners and the sub-charterers.

"(l) *Inspections*: The Owners shall co-operate with the Charterers to facilitate the Charterers' inspection of the Vessel at any time, upon receipt of reasonable notice, in the Charterers' time."

The charterers like to retain powers of inspection over the vessel, although they rarely exercise this power. However, if the charterers received a series of similar claims which they suspected to have arisen on the vessel, they might call for such an inspection to investigate. They cannot just turn up and demand to go aboard but may inspect at any time, provided they give reasonable notice to the owners and inspect in their time (which suggests that they lose the right of inspection under this sub-clause once the vessel is redelivered).

"(m) *Substitution and Sub-Contracting*: Unless the Charterers' prior consent be obtained in writing, which shall not be unreasonably withheld, the Owners may not:

(i) substitute any other Vessel for that named herein, even though it might be of identical specification, before, at the beginning of or throughout the currency of this Charter Party or,

(ii) sub-contract any of their obligations, including the management of the Vessel. In the event of any sub-contracting the Owners shall remain responsible for the performance of this Charter Party or,

(iii) change the flag of the Vessel."

When the charterers charter the vessel they do so on the basis of the vessel as it is then, including by whom it is managed and according to what regulations it is run. They, therefore, like to exercise control over any changes that the owners may seek to make during the life of the charter party which, in their view, might bring about some deterioration in the quality of service from the vessel.

This sub-clause gives them a veto over the owners doing any of the following without their prior permission but that permission must not be unreasonably withheld. In other words if they say no they must have a good reason.

(i) Substitute another vessel for the one chartered (even though it be of identical specification) at any time.

(ii) Sub-contract any of their obligations, in particular those relating to the management of the vessel: the quality of ship management is a substantial factor in determining the quality of service that the charterers receive from the vessel. These days all owners are looking to reduce costs and may seek to change the management of their vessels from their own in-house arrangements to an outside ship management company or from one ship management company to another. If the owners seek to do this in the middle of a charter party, the charterers will wish to be assured that the change will not affect the quality of service from the vessel before they agree.

Note that, as with the case of sub-letting by the charterers (but reciprocally in this case), even if the charterers agree to any sub-contracting by the owners, the charterers continue to look to the owners direct as being responsible for the performance of their obligations under the charter party.

(iii) Change the flag of the vessel: This is allied to paragraph (ii) above, in that it is included to protect the charterers from a deterioration in the service for which they have contracted, in this case by reason of the owners "flagging out" their vessel, often to a "flag of convenience" which may have less strict standards regarding the manning and running of the vessel. (Classification, like MOT on a car, covers the state of the vessel only. Flag of registry applies rules and regulations regarding the operation of the vessel.)

"(n) *Laid-Up Returns*: The Charterers shall have the right to order the laying-up of the Vessel at any time and for any period of time at a safe berth or place and in the event of such laying-up the Owners shall promptly take steps to effect all the economies in operating costs, including insurance, which may be possible and give prompt credit to the Charterers in respect of all such economies. At the request of the Charterers, the Owners shall at any time provide an estimate of the economies which would be possible in the event of the laying-up of the Vessel. The laying-up port or place shall be at the Charterers' option but shall always be safe and acceptable to the Owners' insurers. Should the Charterers in liaison with the Owners decide that the Master, Officers and crew should be paid off, then the costs of repatriation and, later, cost of rejoining, including laying-up preparation and reactivation cost, and all expenses incurred shall be for the Charterers' account. The Charterers shall give sufficient notice of their intention in this respect to enable the Owners to make necessary arrangements for decommissioning and recommissioning.

Any returns of premium or calls payable to the Owners by reason of the Vessel remaining within the confines of any port area in excess of any minimum period provided for in the Owners' insurance policies shall be remitted to the Charterers upon receipt by the Owners, provided the Vessel was on hire for the full period, otherwise such return shall be shared pro rata between the Owners and the Charterers according to the proportion of qualifying time on and off hire."

This sub-clause provides the ultimate backstop if the envisaged use of the vessel on a long term-time charter changes so radically as to make employment of the vessel uneconomical, no alternative employment can be found and all this happens in circumstances which fall short of creating a situation in which the charter party may be terminated by frustration or some other cause.

Paragraph 1. As hire is still payable and the vessel is continuing to incur costs for the charterers' account with nothing being earned, it can be appreciated that any charterers will be most loath to invoke this sub-clause except as a last resort. It provides for the full co-operation of the owners in making maximum reductions to running costs, should such a situation arise, by reducing/repatriation of crew whilst the vessel is laid up, at a place of the charterers' choosing but safe and acceptable to the owners' insurers, provided the charterers meet the cost of decommissioning and later recommissioning when the vessel comes out of lay-up.

The owners' co-operation starts with providing the charterers, on request, with estimates of the economies that are possible if the vessel is laid up in a place nominated by the charterers.

The charterers have the right to order the vessel to be laid up and later recommissioned but must give the owners sufficient notice of their intentions to enable the owners to make the necessary arrangements.

Paragraph 2. One of the economies possible, if a vessel remains within the same port area for a substantial length of time, is that returns may become payable from hull and machinery and P & I insurers, according to whether or not there are crew on board, cargo is on board and whether or not the vessel is under repair. Such returns are paid in recognition of the reduced exposures to loss/damage and liability respectively and, as the owners are still getting their hire and these returns are solely on account of the trading (or lack of it) by the charterers, it is only equitable that the charterers should have the benefit of them.

Accordingly this sub-clause provides for the owners to pay them to the charterers when they receive them from the insurers (which will not be until the end of the policy year). If the vessel goes off hire whilst in lay-up (e.g. repairs) such returns must be shared between the charterers and the owners in proportion to the proportion of qualifying time on and off hire.

"(o) *Signing Bills of Lading*: If required, the Master shall sign bills of lading as presented by the Charterers. If required, the Charterers and/or their agents are hereby authorised by the Owners to sign bills of lading on the Owners' and/or the Master's behalf (See Clause 16(a), (b) and (c)). The Charterers shall indemnify the Owners and the Master against all consequences or liabilities arising therefrom."

This sub-clause gives the charterers considerable freedom of action in relation to the production and signature of bills of lading for their customers but this freedom is only in relation to document production and signature and not in relation to liability, as what is given at the beginning of this sub-clause is more than adequately clawed back in the last sentence and later in clauses 16(a), (b) and (c).

(1) The master may be required to sign bills of lading as presented by the charterers: this covers the situation if, for some incomprehensible reason, the bill of lading must be signed by the master and not by the charterers, as agents, on his behalf. Most first class combined transport operators have no need of such a right as they sign bills of lading as the contracting carrier on their own behalf and do not involve the vessel in the contract with their customer at all.

(2) The charterers and/or their agents can sign bills of lading on the owners' and/or the master's behalf: The implication here is that the charterers are not the contracting carrier but merely an agent for the owners, who are the real contracting carrier, and the party in contract with the owner of the goods. For a container operator running a combined transport service on a door-to-door basis, this approach does not fit in with his operation. How can he, in a door-to-door contract, purport to act as agent of someone who, in reality, is his sub-contractor for only part of that contract? It doesn't fit.

Whilst it is not immediately obvious from the wording of the sub-clause, the implications of the charterers being able to sign bills of lading on behalf of the owners are that the charterers may include a demise clause in their bill of lading terms and conditions. Such a clause might read:

"If the Ocean Vessel is not owned or chartered by demise to the Carrier issuing this Bill of Lading (as may be the case notwithstanding anything that appears to the contrary), then this Bill of Lading shall take effect only as a contract of carriage between the Merchant and the owner or demise charterer (as the case may be) as principal through the agency of the named Carrier, who acts as agent only and shall be under no personal liability whatsoever in respect thereof."

(As may be observed, demise clauses in bills of lading are comparable to cesser clauses in voyage charter parties.)

Demise (or identity of carrier) clauses are generally valid in English common law based jurisdictions (i.e. Commonwealth countries) but not in civil code law countries (Continent of Europe) so reliance upon them can be dangerous. For this reason continental members of the working party understandably would have preferred not to allow demise clauses but, in any event, did not wish to make specific reference to them in a standard charter party.

Demise clauses used to be used for a variety of reasons, most of which are now outdated, some of which benefited the owners and some the charterers. Amongst these reasons are:

A. To give the owners the protection of the bill of lading contract, vis-à-vis the owner of the goods shipped, to prevent claims by the owner of the goods against the owners in tort: This is now dealt with in most consortium lines' bills of lading by a circular indemnity: the combined transport operators' adaptation of the "Himalaya" clause, which usually reads along the following lines (*see* Chapter 6, clause 4, reproduced here for ease of reference).

"SUB CONTRACTING AND INDEMNITY

(1) The Carrier shall be entitled to sub-contract the Carriage of any terms whatsoever.

(2) The Merchant undertakes that no claim or allegation shall be made against any Person whomsoever by whom the Carriage is performed or undertaken (including all Sub-Contractors of the Carrier), other than the Carrier, which imposes or attempts to impose upon any such Person, or any vessel owned by any such Person, any liability whatsoever in connection with the Goods or the Carriage of the Goods, whether or not arising out of negligence on the part of such Person and, if any such claims or allegation should nevertheless be made, to indemnify the Carrier against all consequences thereof. Without prejudice of the foregoing every such Person shall have the benefit of every right, defence, limitation and liberty of whatsoever nature herein contained or otherwise available to the Carrier (including, but not limited to, Clause 24 hereof) as if such provisions were expressly for his benefit and in entering into this contract, the Carrier, to the extent of these provisions, does so not only on his own behalf but also as agent and trustee for such Persons or vessel.

(3) The provisions of sub-clause (2), including but not limited to the undertakings of the Merchant contained therein, shall extend to claims or allegations of whatsoever nature against other Persons chartering space on the carrying vessel.

(4) The Merchant further undertakes that no claim or allegation in respect of the Goods shall be made against the Carrier by any Person other than in accordance with the terms and conditions of this Bill of Lading which imposes or attempts to impose upon the Carrier any liability whatsoever in connection with the Goods or the Carriage of the Goods, whether or not arising out of negligence on the part of the Carrier and, if any such claim or allegation should nevertheless be made, to indemnify the Carrier against all consequences thereof."

This clause thus:

(1) Gives the carrier the right to sub-contract.

(2) Is the circular indemnity under which the merchant undertakes that only he will claim in respect of the subject goods and to claim only against the carrier under bill of lading terms and conditions. He indemnifies the carrier for liabilities incurred under his sub-contracts with third parties if this undertaking is breached. Ratified by decisions in English and Australian courts. In particular *see NYK* v. *International Import and Export Company Ltd. (The Elbe Maru)* [1984] 1 Lloyd's Rep. 206.

(3) Extends (2) to cover fellow co-charterers/consortium partners whose goods are carried on the same vessel as the subject goods.

(4) Is an indemnity from the merchant to the carrier against any claims being brought against the carrier outside the terms of the bill of lading contract by a party to whom the merchant has sold all or part of the goods but who is not a party to the bill of lading and who tries to sue the carrier in tort to avoid limitation. Such claims would be invalid in an English court following the *Aliakmon* decision (*Leigh & Sillivan Ltd.* v. *Aliakmon Shipping Company Ltd.* [1986] 2 Lloyd's Rep. 1) but, in the absence of a clause like this, might succeed elsewhere.

Such clauses are then backed up by clauses in the carrier's sub-contracts with his contractors giving similar benefits to them as those extracted by him from the owner of the goods. The clauses in "BOXTIME" giving these benefits to the owners are in clauses 16(a), (b), (c) and (f), which gives a limited agency appointment to the charterers so they contract for the owners to give them the required benefits.

So, if anyone claims against the vessel outside of the contract of carriage in the bill of lading, clauses 16(a), (b) and (c) give the necessary protection if there is no identity of carrier clause in the bill of lading. If there is, clause 13(o) provides the protection required. Thus the owners are protected either way against claims by cargo interests.

B. To enable the owners to plead the Merchant Shipping Act limitation in the event of a catastrophe in a court where only vessels' owners are entitled to limit. (The 1976 LLMC (Limitation of Liability for Maritime Claims) Convention allows charterers to limit and there are now few places left where limitation would be denied to charterers.)

C. Operators of vessels, particularly if they are not also liner operators themselves, are often much more difficult to communicate with than chartering liner operators: this means that the task of recovery agents is made more difficult.

The final sentence of this sub-clause claws back all the apparent liberties granted to the charterers earlier in the sub-clause by providing for the charterers to give the owners a full indemnity against all consequences or liabilities arising from the earlier granted liberties. This, plus the provisions of clause 16(a), (b) and (c), to which cross-reference is made, redress the balance as between the owners and the charterers.

Where a vessel is to be used in consortium operation, in which each principal carrier signs bills of lading in his own right as the contracting carrier, this sub-clause is superfluous and is often deleted.

Clause 14: Owners' Requirements

In the same way as there is little difference between an *Owners' Obligation* and a *Charterers' Requirement* (*see* opening comments on clause 13) so there is not much to choose between an *Owners' Requirement* and a *Charterers' Obligation* (clause 6).

"(a) *Maintenance*: The Owners shall have the right to take the Vessel out of service for emergency repairs at any time and for routine maintenance by prior arrangement with the Charterers. The Owners shall endeavour to accommodate the Charterers' requirements in determining the timing of such maintenance and the Charterers shall endeavour to accommodate the Owners' choice of location for maintenance (See Clause 8(a) (i))."

Clearly the owners must have the right to take the vessel out of service for maintenance and repairs. In the case of emergency repairs, this must be immediately but for maintenance and less urgent matters the charterers naturally wish to be consulted.

The owners naturally wish to repair where it is cheapest for them to do so, commensurate with the standard of repair required, and the charterers wish to have the repairs arranged so as to cause minimum disruption to their schedule and to be given adequate notice, so that they can arrange accordingly to minimise the disruption. This sub-clause provides for consultation to solve this problem in a mutually acceptable manner.

As the cross-reference to clause 8(a)(i) indicates, the vessel will go off hire during repairs (unless it is for damage covered by clause 6(l)).

"(b) *Bills of Lading*: The Charterers warrant that bills of lading issued in respect of the carriage of goods and containers under this Charter Party shall contain the following clauses:

(i) A clause paramount applying the Hague or Hague-Visby Rules or a carriage of goods by sea statute making either of these mandatorily applicable, in either case according to the practice prevalent at the port(s) of loading.

(ii) A 'New Jason' clause.

(iii) A 'General Average' clause providing for adjustment at a port or place at the option of the Carrier according to the York-Antwerp Rules 1974 or any amendment thereto.

(iv) A 'Himalaya' or 'Circular Indemnity' clause giving the Owners the benefit of the bill of lading terms and conditions and/or protection from tortious claims by third parties.

(v) A 'Sister Ship Salvage' clause.

(vi) A 'Both-to-Blame Collision' clause"

(With the growth in the use of waybills and with electronic commerce "around the corner", BIMCO propose to change the title of this sub-clause to "Contracts of Carriage" and to add the words "and other contracts of carriage" after "bills of lading" in line 528 and to replace "bill of lading" in line 540 with "contract of carriage".)

As they are not the party making contracts of carriage with the owners of goods, the owners wish to be assured that the terms and conditions of the charterers' bills of lading contain certain provisions in case they are needed. They, therefore, require the charterers to WARRANT that their bill of lading terms and conditions contain these provisions. If the charterers sign a charter party including these provisions and then fail to include them in their bill of lading terms and conditions, the charterers will be liable for breach of contract and must indemnify the owners for any loss or expense which they may incur as a result thereof. This may not always be as onerous as it sounds as is explained below in considering the individual requirements.

(i) Note that the clause paramount must make either the Hague or Hague-Visby Rules applicable according to the practice at the port of loading. Few bills of lading are likely to fail to do this but, if the bill incorporates a circular indemnity clause (*see* paragraph (iv)) and, in any event, in view of the provisions of clauses 16(a), (b) and (c), it is unlikely that such an omission would have a deleterious effect upon the owners. It would be the charterers that might suffer from such an omission.

(ii) The "New Jason" clause is a supplementary general average clause relevant only when GA is adjusted according to US law so, unless a vessel is trading through America or the bill of lading has a clause providing for GA to be adjusted in America, such a clause (or the absence of it) is unlikely to be of any significance. A "New Jason" clause might read:

"In the event of accident, danger, damage or disaster before or after the commencement of the voyage, resulting from any cause whatsoever, due to negligence or not, for which, or the consequence of which, the Carrier is not responsible, by statute, contract or otherwise, the Merchant shall contribute with the Carrier in General Average to the payment of any sacrifices, losses or expenses of a general average nature that may be made or incurred and shall pay salvage and special charges incurred in respect of the Goods."

(iii) The GA clause is important to ensure that GA is adjusted at the place required by the owners according to the York Antwerp Rules and not some obscure alternative.

(iv) Particularly in the absence of a demise clause, an effective "Himalaya" or circular indemnity clause is essential to prevent direct tortious actions by the owners of goods against the owners (*see* commentary on clause 13(o) for details of such a clause).

(v) A "Sister Ship Salvage" clause is desirable to overcome the inability to indulge in the incestuous action of suing oneself for salvage (if salvage services are rendered by a sister ship) in order to secure salvage contribution from the owners of goods on board who, in the absence of such a clause, might seek to use this omission to avoid contribution.

(iv) The "Both-to-Blame Collision" clause ought, by now, to have followed the Dodo into extinction. It has been ruled ineffective in the USA by the decision in the *Esso Belgium* v. *Nathaniel Bacon* case (*USA* v. *Atlantic Mutual Insurance Company* [1952] A.M.C. 659) and is only designed to apply in the courts of countries that do not apply the 1910 Collision Convention. Even if parties to a collision were foolish enough to elect to arbitrate a collision in the court of such a country, it is likely that court would follow the US line and reject this highly technical and complicated attempt to avoid circumvention of the errors of navigation exception in Article IV, Rule 2(a) of the Hague Rules.

But P & I clubs insist on its retention as a condition of cover, so the clause frequently survives, if only by reference to the standard BIMCO version, to avoid taking up space with what is quite a long clause.

Given the unlikelihood of it being applied it is not likely that failure by the charterers to incorporate such a clause in their bill of lading terms and conditions would have any deleterious effect. A "Both-to-Blame Collision" clause might read:

"If the carrying vessel comes into collision with another vessel as a result of the negligence of the other vessel and any act, neglect or default in the navigation or the management of the carrying vessel, the Merchant undertakes to pay the Carrier, or, if the Carrier is not the owner and in possession of the carrying vessel, to pay to the Carrier as trustee for the owner and/or demise charterer of the carrying vessel a sum sufficient to indemnify the Carrier and/or the owner and/or demise charterer of the carrying vessel against all loss or liability to the other non-carrying vessel or her owners insofar as such loss or liability represents loss of or damage to, or any claim whatsoever of the Merchant, paid or payable by the other or non-carrying vessel or her owners to the Merchant and set-off, recouped or recovered by the other or non-carrying vessel or her owners as part of their claim against the carrying vessel or her owners or demise charterer or the Carrier. The foregoing provisions shall also apply if the owners, operators, or those in charge of any vessel or vessels or objects, other than, or in addition to the colliding vessels or objects, are at fault in respect of a collision, contact, stranding or other accident."

Of course, now that York-Antwerp Rules 1994 have replaced the 1974 version, "1994" should be used instead of "1974" in lines 537, 545 and 657.

"(c) *General Average*: General average shall be adjusted at the place indi- 544
cated in Box 33 according to the York-Antwerp Rules 1974 or any amend- 545
ment thereto by an adjuster appointed by the Owners. In the event of general 546
average or salvage, the Charterers to provide an acceptable temporary 547
security covering all goods and containers to avoid delay and secure their 548
release so that transit/delivery may continue. The Owners agree that the 549
Charterers' temporary guarantee may be exchanged in due course for a full 550
set of securities from the appropriate interested parties covering all goods 551
and containers. The Charterers agree to co-operate with the Owners and 552
the Owners' appointed adjusters to assist by supplying manifest and other 553
information and, where required, to endeavour to secure the assistance of 554
the Charterers' local agents in the collection of security, at the Owners' ex- 555
pense. 556

All goods and containers shall contribute in general average, whether ship- 557
ped on or under deck. Charter hire shall not contribute. 558

General average shall be adjusted in any currency at the sole option of the 559
Owners. Exchange into the currency of adjustment shall be calculated at the 560
rate prevailing on the date of payment for disbursements and on the date of 561
completion of discharge of the Vessel for allowances, contributory values 562
etc. 563"

This is quite an extensive sub-clause and warrants a close sentence-by-sentence consideration. The first sentence provides:

(1) For GA to be adjusted at the place named in box 33,
(2) according to the York-Antwerp Rules or any amendment thereto (the present draft is "York-Antwerp Rules 1994"),
(3) by an adjuster appointed by the owners.

Owners are, almost invariably, the party who declares GA, but there is nothing to stop any other interested party from doing so, hence the need to provide clearly in the charter party (between the owners and the charterers) and the bill of lading (between the charterers and the owner of the goods), where, by whom and according to what rules GA will be adjusted, in case of maverick declarations by other interests.

The second sentence covers GA AND SALVAGE and provides for the charterers to provide "*temporary security covering all goods and containers to avoid delay and secure their release so that transit/delivery may continue*".

This needs to be read with the third sentence providing for the "*temporary guarantee*" to "*be exchanged . . . for a full set of securities from the appropriate interested parties covering all goods and containers*".

Because of the invariable multiplicity of interests involved in the event of GA or salvage on a containership, it is necessary to consider ways of overcoming the problems of the security required by the owners and/or salvors before the goods can be released to their consignees. This is particularly desirable as, if any delay is caused, arguments may arise about responsibility and off hire.

Whereas the discharge and retention of break-bulk goods is dependent upon the availability of adequate warehouse space, which is expensive, with containers discharge and storage is easier and cheaper. Furthermore, many containers will not be delivered at the port but inland at the end of a combined transport contract. Thus an arrangement such as this benefits both parties; the owners and/or salvors are spared the nightmare of trying to obtain security from a multiplicity of parties, with whom they are not in contract, and the charterers are allowed to retain control of the goods and to continue to forward them to destination, whilst they obtain the necessary security which will release them from the temporary security they have provided.

The sub-clause calls for the charterers to provide security but is not specific as to whether or not this is personal or backed by their P & I club, leaving it to the two parties to determine what is acceptable. One would hope that, if the charterers are a sufficiently substantial company, personal security would suffice, particularly as the charterers are taking a lot of problems off the owners' and/or salvors' hands by agreeing to this arrangement but, if club-backed security is insisted upon, this will have to be provided, as the sub-clause says "*acceptable*" and this implies acceptable to the party asked to accept it, namely, the owners in the case of GA and the salvors in the case of salvage. In this case, if the club charge the charterers for providing this security, the charge is admissible as an item in the adjustment.

The fourth sentence provides for the charterers' co-operation with the owners and their average adjusters by:

(1) Supplying manifest and other information.
(2) Endeavouring to secure the assistance of their local agents in the collection of security, at the owners' expense.

(1) *Manifest.* Manifest information is a commercially sensitive commodity supplied only on a "need to know" basis to parties who can be trusted not to impart such information to competitors and criminals. For example, if (as can happen) the owners and the charterers are both competitors in a liner service when a GA and/or salvage incident occurs, there is no way that the charterers will allow the owners to have access to their manifest. Alternatively consider a GA and/or salvage on a vessel in consortium operation, owned by A in a

consortium in which he trades with B, C, D and E. B, C, D and E will not let A see their manifests.

So how can the average adjuster acquire the necessary data to prepare his adjustment? The answer is that the charterers supply their manifests directly to the average adjuster against a promise of confidentiality and the adjuster produces an adjustment in which the charterers only receive a statement of contributions, in respect of goods for which they are principal carrier, set out in detail. The adjustments sent to the owners and their hull insurers show goods' contributions as a summary only, thus preserving the charterers' confidentiality of their commercially sensitive data. In the case of consortium operation, each member receives a detailed summary of his own customers' contributions but a summary only of the contributions of his consortium colleagues' customers.

(2) As they are usually liner operators, the charterers are most likely to have an extensive network of agents at the ports of discharge/places of delivery, whereas neither the owners and/or the salvors, nor their average adjusters may have representation there. Thus the owners and/or the salvors need the charterers' co-operation to persuade their local agents to assist, by acting as agents of the owners and/or the salvors' average adjusters in collecting the necessary security prior to delivery. The local agent's fees have to be met in the first instance by the owners and/or the salvors but are later recovered as an allowable expense in the adjustment.

The first sentence of the second paragraph provides for all goods and containers to contribute in GA, whether shipped on or under deck. This means all goods, whether in containers or not, whether on deck or not.

Care must be taken not to confuse the obligation to contribute in GA, which falls upon all goods and containers on board, with the right to contribution in the event of sacrifice, which is denied to certain interests by Rule 1 of the York-Antwerp Rules, which reads:

Jettison of Cargo:—No jettison of cargo shall be made good as general average, unless such cargo is carried in accordance with the recognised custom of the trade.

This means that, whilst containers carried on deck on vessels properly fitted to carry them thus, together with large uncontainerised loads usually carried on deck, can expect to be recompensed in GA if they are jettisoned (as opposed to washed overboard), any small parcels not normally carried on deck will probably be denied contribution.

The second sentence of the second paragraph provides for charter hire not to contribute in GA. This endeavours to preserve the same situation between the owners and the charterers as the "Freight earned on Shipment" clause in the bill of lading provides between the charterers (as the principal carrier) and their customer, namely, that charter hire/freight is not at risk in a GA situation (of course this is where the simile ends as voyage rated freight in a bill of lading is otherwise not comparable with daily rated time charter hire in a time charter party).

The third paragraph of this sub-clause addresses the problems arising on account of the different currencies that are inevitably involved in a GA. It gives the owners the advantage of being able to choose the currency of adjustment and then provides a formula for determining exchange rates into that currency. This formula is in accordance with usual practice:

Disbursements–Rate prevailing on date of payment.
Allowances and contributory values etc.–Rate prevailing on the date of completion of discharge.

"(d) *Salvage*. All time lost and all legal and other expenses (excluding any damage to the Vessel) incurred in saving or attempting to save life or property shall be borne equally by the Owners and the Charterers. All salvage and proceeds from derelicts shall be divided equally between the Owners and the Charterers after deducting the Master's, Officers' and crew's share. The Charterers shall be bound by all measures taken by the Owners in order to secure payment of salvage and to settle its amount."

This sub-clause addresses the situation which arises if the vessel renders salvage services to a third party, as opposed to seeks salvage services itself from a third party, which situation is covered in sub-clause (c) above. Although no cross-reference is made between this sub-clause and clause 8(b) there is a clear link, and a greater understanding of this sub-clause will be achieved if the remarks made against clause 8(b) are read in conjunction with those made here.

As in clause 8(b), this sub-clause recognises, not only the obligation of the master to honour the unwritten law of the sea to go to the aid of other vessels in distress to save life, but also that whatever is done to attempt to save life is often indistinguishable from efforts to salve property. This means that justifiable deviations can lead to salvage awards being gained.

The charter party takes the view that these are joint ventures involving both the owners and the charterers. Therefore it provides for an equitable distribution of costs and benefits on a 50/50 basis. The following clarifies the situation:

Charter hire: the charterers pay 50% of the normal charter hire during salvage operations.

Legal and other expenses: 50/50 payment by both parties.

Damage to the vessel: borne by the owners, who can recover from their hull and machinery insurers but who are out of pocket 100% on any deductible.

Salvage awards: 50/50 to both parties, after deducting amounts due to the master, officers and crew.

The owners have control of all negotiations with the salved vessel/property to agree the amount and secure the payment of salvage. This means that it is the owners who decide on what terms to offer salvage, what security is acceptable, whether to arrest, whether an offer of settlement is adequate or to proceed to arbitration, etc.

> "(e) *Liens*: The Charterers warrant that they will not suffer, nor permit to be continued, any lien or encumbrance incurred by them or their agents, which might have priority over the title and interest of the Owners in the Vessel. In no event shall the Charterers procure, nor permit to be procured, for the Vessel any supplies, necessaries or services without previously obtaining a statement, signed by an authorised representative of the furnisher thereof, acknowledging that such supplies, necessaries or services are being furnished on the credit of the Charterers and not on the credit of the Vessel or of the Owners and that the furnisher claims no maritime lien on the Vessel therefor.
>
> The Owners shall have a lien on the Charterers' goods and containers and upon all sub-freights and/or sub-hire for unpaid charter hire, unreimbursed Charterers' expenses initially paid by the Owners and contributions in general average properly due."

A lien is a right to retain property belonging to a debtor pending settlement of a debt and is a process often used in maritime commerce. A lien may be specific (i.e. only exercisable on goods and chattels in respect of charges etc. due on those specific goods and chattels) or general (i.e. exercisable on goods and chattels in respect of all monies owed to the party exercising the lien by the owner of the goods and chattels).

This sub-clause starts with a warranty by the charterers that they will protect the owners from any lien being exercised on the vessel for debts of the charterers. If the charterers fail to meet their obligation under this sub-clause and the vessel is arrested or impounded for their debts (e.g. unpaid port and stevedores charges, bunker fuel bills etc.) it remains on hire and the charterers must continue to pay charter hire, as the cause of arrest is not covered by clause 8(a)(i), so the preamble to clause 8 provides for the vessel to remain on hire. In addition the charterers must pay provable damages (e.g. other costs incurred on account of the arrest of the vessel).

The second sentence requires a little more explanation and is aimed at defeating a quirk of American law, designed to protect American maritime suppliers, regardless of its equity vis-à-vis innocent third parties. Under American law any supplier of goods and services to a vessel can arrest that vessel for payment, even though the parties responsible for payment were not the owners of that vessel. This came to light a few years ago when, following a spate of bankruptcies of some charterers, bunker fuel suppliers, stevedores, port authorities and ships' chandlers successfully arrested several vessels for payment of their bills in full by the vessels instead of proving in the bankruptcy of the charterers for a percentage only, even though the fuel etc. was ordered by and for the account of the charterers. It seems that, only by getting him to acknowledge that he would not claim against the vessel in advance, could the supplier's lien be defeated and P & I clubs recommended suitable clauses which the owners should require the charterers to put on all requisitions for supplies and services from American suppliers.

Of course, not too many suppliers are willing to sign such undertakings, but it is not unreasonable for the owners to seek to protect themselves in this way, although the true worth of such a provision is questionable. If the charterers sign a charter party with such a clause and fail to secure the required acknowledgement from their suppliers, the only effect is that they are liable if the vessel is arrested for their debts (which they would have been anyway—*see* first sentence of this sub-clause). If they become bankrupt, the owners' recourse against them is affected accordingly. Thus the sentence has little legal effect and is more in the nature of an attempt by the owners to encourage the charterers to take appropriate steps.

In the final analysis there is no substitute for owners ensuring that they contract with reputable and solvent charterers and vice versa, but commercial pressures mean that this is not always possible. Nevertheless, in the light of the above, owners need to be particularly careful in their choice of charterers if trading to the USA is involved.

The second paragraph of this sub-clause seeks to put the owners in the best possible position if the worst happens and the charterers became difficult or insolvent. It gives the owners a lien on:

(1) "*the Charterers' goods*": The problem here is that they are usually not the charterers' goods but those of his customers. If the customers hold bills of lading with demise clauses in them, the owners are the contracting carrier as far as the customers are concerned and, if the customers hold freight paid bills of lading, the owners hold on to the goods at their peril. If there is no demise clause in the bill, the owners are rather better off and may probably be able to exercise their lien on the goods, leaving the charterers, as the contracting carrier, to resolve the problem;

(2) "*and containers*": Again the problem is often that they are not the charterers' containers but those of a big leasing company. Whilst this may cause problems, it should not defeat the lien of the owners;

(3) "*sub-freight and sub-hire*": The problem here is for the owners to get their hands on monies usually paid directly to the charterers by bill of lading holders and sub-charterers. This means speedy action to give appropriate notice to the parties concerned to intercept these monies before they are paid to the charterers, should need arise, always assuming that they can obtain the identity of the parties concerned to approach them.

These liens can be exercised to recover:

(1) "*unpaid charter hire*";

(2) "*unreimbursed Charterers' expenses initially paid by the Owners*";

(3) "*contributions in general average properly due*".

Clause 15: Sundry Matters

As the name suggests, this clause provides a home for those provisions that do not happily belong anywhere else, mostly because they cover matters where responsibilities are split between the owners and the charterers.

> "(a) *Pilotage/Towage*: Although engaged by the Charterers or their agents 586
> and paid by the Charterers, all pilotage, towage and other such services to 587
> the Vessel to assist with navigation shall be engaged as agents of the Ow- 588
> ners who, for the purposes of this Charter Party, shall remain responsible for 589
> the due performance thereof. Nothing contained in this Charter Party shall 590
> be construed as a demise of the Vessel to the Charterers and the Owners re- 591
> main responsible for the navigation thereof at all times. 592"

As the charterers have control of the vessel's movements, subject to the terms of the charter party, it follows that they pay the costs incurred pursuant to the vessel being required to transit any waters or call at any ports. However, the navigation and management of the vessel remains with the owners at all times and they are thus responsible, subject to the terms of the charter party, for any losses, damages or expenses arising therefrom. Pilotage, towage and other services to assist the vessel's navigation are, outside American waters, almost invariably provided on no liability/full indemnity terms, so that the consequences of any negligence or omission by pilot or tugmaster etc. are usually borne by the employing vessel.

In the light of the above, this sub-clause makes it clear that, whilst the fees for these services are paid by the charterers, the pilot and tugmaster are the servants of the owners and the charterers act as the owners' agents only in procuring their services. This clearly leaves the responsibility for the navigation of the vessel with the owners whilst under pilotage or towage etc., so that any claims arising as a result of the use of such sub-contractors must be met by the owners, even though the charterers pay the cost of employing such sub-contractors. As these services are provided directly to the vessel, it is the responsibility of the master to control them and be responsible for making sure that they accomplish their tasks according to his orders and satisfaction to achieve the required objective.

The sub-clause finishes with a statement to make it quite clear that this is not a demise charter party (under which the actions of the crew would be the responsibility of the charterers) and that the navigation of the vessel remains the responsibility of the owners at all times.

> "(b) *Watchmen*: The cost of compulsory shore gangway watchmen shall be 593
> borne equally between the Owners and the Charterers throughout the cur- 594
> rency of this Charter Party. 595"

Note that this sub-clause covers the employment of COMPULSORY shore gangway watchmen only and provides for the cost of this unavoidable expense to be borne 50/50 by the owners and the charterers. Other than in the case of compulsory shore gangway watchmen, all costs of watchmen are borne by the party requiring them.

Some owners, feeling that, as they are in any port on charterers' instructions, consider that charterers should pay all of these costs and delete "equally between the Owners and" in line 594 and replace these words with "by".

"(c) *Stowaways*: Any costs incurred in respect of stowaways shall be for the Owners' account, unless it can be established that the means by which the stowaway gained access to the Vessel was by secreting away in the Charterers' goods and containers prior to loading, in which case all such costs shall be for the Charterers' account."

Most charter parties understandably provide for the expense of stowaways to be borne by the owners, as stowaways can usually only gain access to the vessel by reason of some lapse of the vessel's security. However, where containers are involved, it is not unknown for stowaways to secrete themselves away in containers prior to loading to gain access to the vessel. Thus, in this charter party for containerships, it is felt equitable to make provision for the charterers to bear this expense, if it can be proved that the stowaway gained access to the vessel via the charterers' containers (or in some large uncontainerised load). For the expense to fall on the charterers, the owners must discharge the onus of proof of showing that the stowaway gained access to the vessel via the charterers' goods and containers rather than merely hid in them after gaining access to the vessel.

"(d) *On/Off Hire Surveys*: Joint on and off hire surveys shall be conducted by mutually acceptable surveyors at the Place of Delivery and Redelivery, respectively. The on hire survey shall be conducted in the Owners' time unless the Vessel has commenced loading. The off hire survey shall be conducted in the Charterers' time.

Both surveys shall cover condition of the Vessel and amounts of fuel on board and the Owners shall procure that the Master, Chief Engineer, Officers and crew shall co-operate with the surveyors in conducting such surveys."

The cost of surveys is high so it is usual practice for both parties to agree a mutually acceptable surveyor to act on their joint behalves rather than have two surveyors conduct a parallel survey. As the surveyor acts on joint behalves, his fee is paid 50/50 by the two parties, both at delivery and redelivery. The sub-clause does not specifically mention costs but it is clear enough that, as the survey is joint, the costs are joint and borne equally by the parties.

Whilst the charter party provides for the on hire survey to be done in the owners' time, it is often the case that the charterers are anxious to accept the vessel on hire as quickly as possible so that they can commence loading. Thus most on hire surveys are done in the charterer's time, as he has already accepted the vessel on hire, relying on clauses 1(f) and 8(a) to protect him if any defects are found.

When it comes to redelivery, although the sub-clause provides for this to be done in the charterers' time, in practice this is usually done whilst the vessel is completing discharge prior to redelivery, so that time is not lost awaiting survey prior to redelivery.

The sub-clause provides for the surveys to cover the amounts of fuel on board as well as the condition of the vessel and for the co-operation of the master, chief engineer, officers and crew with the surveyors in conducting the surveys.

"(e) *Sub-Contractors*: In this Charter Party the term 'sub-contractor' shall include sub-contractors and their respective servants, agents and sub-contractors."

This is just a short definition clause to ensure that references throughout the charter party to "sub-contractor" get the widest interpretation to include servants, and agents of sub-contractors and sub-sub-contractors, etc.

Clause 16: Charterers' Responsibilities/Liabilities

We now come to two very long and very important clauses, to which reference will probably be made most frequently, if not during the currency of the charter party, then long afterwards when any disputes are negotiated.

"(a) *Charterers' Responsibilities*: Except as elsewhere provided in this Charter Party and without prejudice to the Charterers' right to initiate recovery against the Owners under Clause 17, the Charterers shall be responsible for all claims in respect of any liability or expense whatsoever or howsoever arising in connection with the goods and containers carried pursuant to this Charter Party or their carriage (even if such liability arises wholly or in part by reason of the act, neglect or default of the Owners or of such servant, agent or sub-contractor)."

The first sub-clause is a sweep-up clause providing for the charterers to be primarily liable for any claims arising in connection with their goods and containers or their carriage, except as provided elsewhere in the charter party and without prejudice to the charterers' right to later claim against the owners under the terms of the charter party. Although no cross-references are made here, this sub-clause is clearly inextricably bound up with clause 13(o) and sub-clauses (b) and (c) below.

The words in brackets provide for this liability to be unaffected by the act of neglect or default of the owners, their servants, agents or sub-contractors. This is to satisfy the requirement identified in the case *Smith and Anor.* v. *South Wales Switchgear Company Ltd.* [1978] 1 W.L.R. 165, where it was held that an indemnity could only operate in the absence of negligence by the person indemnified, unless the indemnity made clear that it would operate notwithstanding such negligence being responsible, wholly or in part, for the subject of the claim.

"(b) *Claims Handling*: If any such claim or allegation as described in Clause 16(a) shall be made against the Owners or against any vessel owned by any of them, the Charterers will:—

(i) take over the conduct and defence of such claim or allegation and settle same at their own expense obtaining, where appropriate, releases in joint names or, should the Owners so request,

(ii) put the Owners in funds to meet legal fees, witness and third party expenses and settlement funds, excluding the Owners' own office expenses, to deal with such claim or allegation themselves."

Whilst it is possible in the charter party to govern the relationship between the owners and the charterers, it is not possible for the owners to govern the actions of any third parties (such as the charterers' customers) directly. This can only be done by the owners requiring the charterers to do so via their contracts with these parties and to indemnify the owners for any failure so to do. All of this is closely linked to the circular indemnity provision, which the charterers are required to have in their bill of lading terms and conditions by clause 14(b)(iv) and which the charterers would be well advised to incorporate (*see* comment on clause 13(o) for details).

This sub-clause recognises that, despite contractual provisions to the contrary in sub-clause (a) above, claims may well be made against the vessel by the charterers' customers. Indeed, in the USA the owner of goods has a right to proceed against the vessel as well as the contracting carrier, so such a provision is necessary. If such a claim is made against the owners, this sub-clause gives the owners a choice of two options:

(1) The owners can require the charterers to take over the conduct etc. of the claim and "*settle same at their own expense, obtaining where appropriate releases in*" the "*joint names*" of the owners and the charterers.

(2) Alternatively, if for some reason the owners prefer to handle the claim themselves, they can require the charterers to put them in funds to do so, such funds to include "*legal fees, witness and third party expenses*" as well as "*settlement funds, but excluding the Owners' own office expenses*".

Note that this sub-clause refers only to "*such claim or allegation as described in Clause 16(a)*" so that nothing in it precludes the charterers from later initiating recovery against the owners under the terms of the charter party.

"(c) *General Indemnity*: If in spite of Clause 16(a) any claims as therein described are nevertheless made, the Charterers shall indemnify the Owners and such servant, agent or sub-contractor against all consequences whatsoever thereof, without prejudice to the Charterers' right subsequently to initiate action against the Owners."

This sub-clause provides the indemnity from the charterers to the owners to back up the obligations undertaken in sub-clauses (a) and (b) above. When viewed alongside that in the final sentence of clause 13(o) it provides a comprehensive protection for the owners, their servants, agents and subcontractors against tortious claims from third parties.

"(d) *Fines etc. Indemnity*: The Charterers shall indemnify the Owners against 636
any expenses, fines, liabilities, losses, damages, claims or demands which 637
the Owners may incur or suffer by reason of any failure of the goods or con- 638
tainers or the documentation relating thereto to comply with any relevant 639
laws, regulations, directions or notices of customs, port and other authori- 640
ties, or by reason of any infestation, contamination or condemnation of 641
goods or containers or infestation, damage or contamination of the Vessel 642
by the Charterers' goods or containers. 643"

This sub-clause provides an indemnity to the owners against:

"*any*
   expenses,
   fines,
   liabilities,
   losses,
   damages,
   claims or
   demands
which the Owners may incur or suffer by reason of any failure of
   the goods,
   containers or
   the documentation relation thereto
to comply with any relevant
   laws,
   regulations,
   directions or
   notices
of
   customs,
   port and
   other authorities
OR by reasons of any
   infestations
   contamination or
   condemnation
of goods or containers
OR by reason of any
   infestation,
   damage or
   contamination
of the Vessel by the Charterers goods or containers".

A step-by-step analysis of this sub-clause aids understanding of what is otherwise a sentence packed with lists, that makes divining the full meaning less than easy. In brief it provides that, if the charterers' goods and containers, or any inaccurate or incomplete documentation relating to them, result in any fines or costs etc. to the owners, then the charterers must bear those fines or costs. Similarly, if the goods or containers damage the vessel, the charterers pay (e.g. brine from wet salted hides can be a very effective paint stripper if it leaks out of containers into the hold). This latter provision is really a duplication of the requirement in clause 6(m) (to redeliver in same condition as delivered, fair wear and tear excepted).

"(e) *Time Limit*: The Charterers shall be discharged from all liability under 644
this Charter Party unless notice of arbitration in accordance with Clause 20 645
is given within 15 months of redelivery. 646"

Whilst it is common to find clauses in charter parties applying time bars in respect of the claims by the charterers against the owners, it is not so common to find time bars applied to claims the other way about, so that often the charterers have only the six-year Statute of Limitations to protect them. This sub-clause provides a *quid pro quo* for the more usual time bar in favour of the owners, found in clause 17(d), to make the owners progress any claims they may have against the charterers promptly and to have issued notice of arbitration if the dispute is not resolved within 15 months of redelivery.

Note that the time bar is made by reference to redelivery, not the occurrence of the incident giving rise to the dispute.

"(f) *Agency*: Without prejudice to sub-clause 16(a) the Owners authorise and 647
empower the Charterers to act as the Owners' agents and/or trustees to sti- 648
pulate for the Owners to have as against other persons the benefit of any im- 649
munities, exemptions or liberties regarding the goods and containers the 650
subject of this Charter Party or their carriage but the Charterers shall have 651
no authority to make any contracts imposing any obligations upon the Ow- 652
ners in connection with the goods and containers of their carriage. 653"

This sub-clause is the agency appointment provision, by which the owners appoint the charterers as their agent, so that they may stipulate for the owners the benefits of the immunities, exceptions or liberties in their bill of lading terms and conditions and thus complete the chain of indemnity in the "Himalaya" or circular indemnity clause, to which reference is made in clause 14(b)(iv).

This appointment of agency is, however, severely restricted to this purpose only and it is specifically provided that the charterers have no authority to act as the agent of the owners to commit them to any obligations.

(BIMCO propose to add ", except to the extent provided in Clause 13(o)," before "Charterers" in line 651.)

"(g) *General Average Exclusion*: Nothing in this Clause 16 shall apply to pre- 654
clude any claim made by the owners of any property on board the Vessel for 655
general average contribution in accordance with the York-Antwerp Rules 656
1974 or any amendment thereto. 657"

As much of clause 16 is aimed at protecting the owners from claims by the charterers' customers, it is necessary to insert this exclusion clause to allow the owners of goods to make claims for GA contribution, provided that these are made in accordance with the requirements of clause 14(c), without the owners being able to invoke the indemnities incorporated earlier on in this clause.

"(h) *Claims Authority*: The Charterers shall make no payment in excess of the amount as stated in Box 32 in settlement of a claim for which they intend to seek recovery from the Owners without prior consultation with the Owners. The Owners authorise the Charterers to grant extensions of time in respect of such claims provided the Charterers give the Owners immediate notice thereof."

In a liner service operation, where a multiplicity of small claims can arise, the charterers need a degree of flexibility in handling claims arising from their customers. At the same time, the owners need to keep a close watch on such matters and ensure that they get the earliest advice of claims so that they can advise their P & I clubs, who take an increasingly strict approach to prompt claims reporting. This sub-clause seeks to satisfy the requirements of both parties in this respect in a reasonable compromise.

First, the owners give the charterers authority to settle small claims for which they intend to seek reimbursement from the owners, up to a level stipulated in box 32 without the prior approval of the owners. However, if any claims, for which recovery is intended, run beyond the time bar period (12 months), the charterers may only give extensions of time provided they give the owners immediate notice, whether the claims exceed the amount in box 32 or not. (The amount in box 32 will usually be regulated by the deductible applied to the owners' P & I entry.)

For claims in excess of the amount stated in box 32, the charterers, if they wish to make a subsequent recovery from the owners under the terms of the charter party, must consult the owners prior to effecting settlement. It is difficult to imagine that any charterers would not do this, as they would almost certainly need to obtain any evidence the owners may have to process or defend the claim but, if they do not consult, they cannot recover. They must also give the owners immediate notice on granting time extensions on such claims.

Clause 17: Owners' Responsibilities/Liabilities

Whilst the owners' liabilities for goods and containers, as set out in this clause, are generally Hague Rules to create a back-to-back recourse situation between the charterers' liability to their customer, under their bill of lading terms and conditions, and their recourse to the owners, under the charter party, no specific reference is made to the Hague Rules as such for international political reasons. Nevertheless, it is the intention that this clause should provide the charterers with equivalent recourse to the owners for the liability they incur to their customers under their bill of lading terms and conditions, if loss or damage is identified as having occurred in the care of the vessel, in circumstances for which the owners would be liable under the Hague Rules.

"Except as elsewhere provided in this Charter Party, the responsibilities and liabilities of the Owners shall be as follows:"

The preamble gives precedence to any provisions elsewhere regarding the owners' responsibilities and liabilities by providing that this clause operates only in the absence of provision elsewhere.

"(a) *For Goods and Containers*: The Owners shall be liable for loss, damage or expense in respect of goods and containers arising or resulting from:—

(i) lack of due diligence on their part before and at the beginning of each voyage to make the Vessel seaworthy and to properly man, equip and supply it and make all parts of the Vessel in which goods and containers are carried fit and safe for their reception, carriage and preservation, unless the Charterers consent to load containers in parts of the Vessel which the Master considers to be unfit, in which case the Charterers shall indemnify the Owners.

(ii) failure on their part properly and carefully to carry, keep and care for the goods and containers while on board, or

(iii) unreasonable deviation from the voyage ordered or approved by the Charterers."

The first sub-clause in this clause covers:

loss,
damage or
expense,

in respect of both goods and containers resulting from the following causes:

Paragraph (i). A study of the wording of this paragraph quickly reveals that it consists of the relevant provisions of Article III, Rule 1, of the Hague Rules, with the added proviso that this responsibility does not operate if the master initially refuses to load containers in parts of the vessel which the master considers to be unfit, but the charterers request that, notwithstanding the master's advice, goods and containers should nevertheless be loaded into those parts of the vessel. In this case the charterers have to indemnify the owners. In this context it should be noted that this charter party does not have the provision, found in many other charter parties, that the charterers shall have the full use of all cargo spaces throughout the vessel at all times and contents itself with the clause 2 undertaking that the details of the vessel provided in Part III (which include hold and deck stowage capacity and arrangements) are accurate.

Paragraph (ii). This paragraph paraphrases those parts of Article III, Rule 2, of the Hague Rules that are the responsibility of the owners. (Load, handle, stow and discharge are the responsibility of the charterers.)

Paragraph (iii). The Hague Rules equivalent of this paragraph is Article IV, Rule 4, but, whereas the Hague Rules merely legislate against "*unreasonable deviation*", this paragraph forbids "*unreasonable deviation from the voyage ordered or approved by the Charterers*". Somewhat different criteria.

"(b) *For Refrigerated Goods*: In respect of blown-air containers, the Owners shall be responsible only to maintain the supply of air at the required temperature to the containers, provided proper instructions are given to the Master by the Charterers and the containers are presented at the carriage temperatures.

In respect of integral refrigerated containers or blown-air containers with a marine refrigeration clip-on unit attached or any containers with any machinery for temperature/atmosphere control containing goods, the Owners shall be responsible for the provision of electrical power only. The Owners shall endeavour to monitor and record the performance of all such units whilst on board in accordance with the Charterers' instructions and to repair and rectify any breakdown, fault or deficiency which may occur in respect of such units, using the resources on board the Vessel. If repair works are performed, all additional expenses incurred by the Owners, including spare parts, shall be for the account of the Charterers and the Vessel's crew shall always be considered the Charterers' servants. If such resources are insufficient, the Owners shall immediately notify the Charterers so they may take action to obtain any required spares or specialised repair facilities.

Except as provided above, the Owners shall not be liable for malfunctioning of integral refrigerated containers and power packs put on board by the Charterers.

The Owners shall be entitled to reject and require the Charterers to discharge any container loaded at a temperature not within the required carriage temperature range. If, at the Charterers' request, the Owners consent to receive and carry such container(s), the Charterers shall indemnify the Owners against all consequences thereof."

This is quite a long sub-clause to deal with a rather complicated matter, to which reference has already been made during comment on clause 5(b)(viii). The problem arises primarily by reason of the fact that most refrigerated goods carried on chartered containerships are carried in containers of which the charterers are either the actual or disponent owners. The question then arises as to what extent the charterers can look to the owners to effect repairs if any refrigeration machinery in those containers malfunctions, particularly in these days of depleted crews, which means that skilled manpower is often more urgently needed elsewhere at the critical time. Furthermore, as most integral refrigerated containers are carried on deck, the state of weather and size of vessel may also make it impossible for immediate attention to be given to a container with malfunctioning machinery, always assuming that the weather is not so bad as to preclude inspection and monitoring of the performance of those containers (unless the vessel has remote monitoring facilities).

The first paragraph covers the simple situation, analogous to that which would apply when chartering a refrigerated conventional vessel, in that the machinery that provides the cold air to refrigerate the goods belongs to the owners, so any breakdown of refrigeration machinery is the responsibility of the owners. In this case the charterers' containers are insulated only and have two porthole apertures at the front that are connected by a pneumatic coupling on the vessel to the vessel's cold air supply. Thus, where "blown-air containers" are carried, the owners are responsible for supplying cold air at the correct temperature to the containers PROVIDED:

(1) the charterers give proper instructions to the master regarding the carrying temperatures required, and
(2) the containers are presented to the vessel at the correct carriage temperature.

Point (2) means that there either has to be refrigeration facilities at the port of loading (refrigeration towers, clip-on units or a refrigeration stack that is really a replica of the vessel's hold) or the containers are sent straight from loading at a nearby cold store and shipped on board immediately. Too many shippers of refrigerated goods expect vessels to REDUCE the temperature of their goods whereas the machinery is designed to MAINTAIN temperatures obtaining at loading. Thus the requirement to present containers at carriage temperature is a very necessary one for the owners. "Hot boxes" can affect a whole series of containers on the same air supply trunking system with consequent deleterious effect upon the goods in the other containers connected to the same system.

The second and longest paragraph deals with the more usual situation: refrigeration supplied by the charterers' machinery relying upon a power supply from sockets on the owners' vessel. This type of refrigeration can be of two types:

(1) Integral refrigerated containers, where the machinery is built into the container, or
(2) blown-air insulated containers with a marine clip-on unit attached.

Both systems operate identically, only the arrangement is different and, with the second type, the addition of the marine clip-on unit means that the container length exceeds the ISO length by some 50–60cm, because the clip-on unit width is additional to the normal length, whereas the integral unit is included within the ISO dimensions.

Note that the sub-clause provides for the carriage of "*containers with any machinery for temperature/atmosphere control containing goods*". This means that, in addition to refrigerated containers, the sub-clause could cover:

- mechanically ventilated containers (e.g. onion boxes)
- tanks with heating coils
- containers with atmosphere control machinery (e.g. Transfresh type machinery)

and all containers where there is mechanical control of temperature and atmosphere in the container.

In relation to the carriage of such containers, the responsibility of the owners, in addition to those outlined in clause 5(b)(vi), is to supply electrical power. If there is any deterioration of the goods, traceable to a failure in the vessel's power supply, then the owners are liable, subject to the other provisions of the charter party.

The second sentence reinforces the provisions of clause 5(b)(vi) requiring the owners "*to endeavour to monitor and record the performance of all such units whilst on board*". As bad weather may restrict the ability to do this (*see* clause 5(b)(vi)), the responsibility of the owners is to endeavour and there is no penalty for justifiable failure. Such monitoring and recording is to be "*in accordance with the charterers' instructions*", so clearly the charterers must ensure that adequate instructions are given (*see* clause 6(a)(ii)).

Now comes the difficult part: if the machinery malfunctions. The sub-clause requires the owners only "*to endeavour . . . to repair or rectify . . . using the resources on board the Vessel*", so it would be prudent of the charterers to put a selection of spares, gas and lubricant on board to facilitate this. Note that the obligation of the owners here is "*to endeavour*" and in clause 5(b)(vi) is to supply labour "*when available*". With today's small crew, such a provision is necessary, as it cannot be guaranteed that an engineer will be available when required. He may be urgently employed elsewhere on the vessel.

The third sentence provides for repair of the charterers' containers to be an extraordinary task, so that the charterers are responsible for all ADDITIONAL expenses incurred by the owners. Furthermore, the vessel's crew are considered the charterers' servants during such repairs, so the charterers have no recourse to the owners if they feel that repairs were not done properly or that something which could have been repaired wasn't repaired.

Thus, if a defect in the temperature/atmosphere control machinery in a container is repaired by the vessel's crew, the charterers pay for:

(1) Spares, lubrication and gas,
(2) Any overtime payable to crew for working on container machinery (*see* clause 5(b)(vi)),

whilst the owners provide crew assistance free of charge during normal duty hours, when available.

The fourth and last sentence addresses the problem if the repair is beyond the resources of the vessel. In this case it is the duty of the owners immediately to notify the charterers, so that they may take appropriate steps, usually by arranging for an engineering contractor with the necessary spares and equipment to meet the vessel at its next port of call to carry out the necessary work.

Note that all the owners must do is to advise the charterers IMMEDIATELY. Thereafter it is the charterers' responsibility to make the necessary arrangements.

The third, single sentence, paragraph merely emphasises that, except as provided in this sub-clause, the owners have no liability for malfunctioning of the charterers' equipment. Thus the owners' only unavoidable responsibility with such containers is to supply power. Everything else is on a reasonable endeavours without responsibility basis.

The sub-clause closes with an important provision, applying to all controlled temperature containers, which reiterates and reinforces the point made at the end of paragraph 1 in relation to blown-air containers and provides an indemnity to the owners if "hot boxes" are shipped. It gives the owners the right to reject "hot boxes" that are not proffered for shipment at the required carriage temperature or, if they are already loaded, for them to be discharged.

The threat of such action frequently precipitates a request from the charterers to the owners to accept the container anyway (as the temperature will stabilise at the required temperature in a short while). The second sentence of the last paragraph enables the owners to agree to such requests without prejudicing their position, if there is a bad outturn at destination, by providing for an indemnity to the owners "*against all consequences thereof*".

The paragraph provides for the owners' consent but, in practice, it will invariably be the master who takes such decisions on his owners' behalf.

To ensure that the benefit of this sub-clause accrues, any master being asked to receive "hot boxes" would be well advised to record the fact in a notice to the charterers' local agent as well as in the vessels' records.

BIMCO suggest adding the words "connect, disconnect and" before "maintain" in line 681 and similarly to add "connecting, disconnecting and" before "provision" in line 688.

"(c) *Limitation of Liability*: The liability of the Owners to the Charterers for loss, damage or expense in respect of goods and containers as herein provided shall be limited as follows:-

(i) In respect of goods liability shall be on the same basis as applicable under mandatory law between the Charterers and a third party by reason of the Charterers having issued a bill of lading or similar contract of carriage, provided that such Bill of Lading contains no declaration of value. Where no mandatory law so applies, liability shall be limited to GB Pounds 100 per package.

(ii) In respect of containers, liability shall be the reasonable cost of repair or the value of the container at the time of such loss or damage, whichever is the lesser. The value of a leased container is the value stated in the lease agreement and for an owned container it is its market value. For the purpose of this Charter Party containers not owned or leased by the Charterers shall be regarded as goods for liability purposes."

A subject dear to any owner's heart! This sub-clause only addresses itself to the subject of limitation in relation to "*loss, damage or expense in respect of goods and containers*". This is because limitation is not possible on personal injury claims, which are made by third parties in tort. Also it was not felt necessary to make any reference to the ability to apply global limitation, under an appropriate limitation of liability for maritime claims convention, as the appropriate limitation would automatically apply, according to the forum chosen to establish the limitation fund. (*See* sub-clause (f) below regarding control of limitation proceedings.)

The sub-clause deals with limitation in relation to goods and containers separately although, as between the owners and the charterers, both could be regarded as the charterers' cargo and a common approach taken to determining limitation of liability, similar to that adopted earlier on in clause 17(a) to determine the owners' liability for goods and containers.

Paragraph (i). In relation to goods, the approach is to provide a full indemnity to the charterers for any claims they have to pay to their customers, which are attributable to the responsibility of the owners in accordance with the terms and conditions of the charter party. No attempt is made to provide that, so far as the owners are concerned, each container is a package and the owners only accept liability for £100 per container.

So, if the goods are LCL (Less than Container Load) as between the charterers and their customers and the charterers acknowledge a tally in packages and must settle claims on that tally, the owners reimburse the charterers on the same basis. If the charterers, having issued a bill of lading to their customers, are obliged to settle claims on the basis of Hague-Visby rather than Hague Rules, *because of the application of mandatory law*, then the owners must reimburse the charterers on the basis of Hague-Visby limits. Two exceptions are provided to this rule:

(1) If the charterers issue an "Ad Valorem" bill of lading, that is to say one where the value of the goods is shown on the face of the bill, thereby making that value the limitation figure. In such cases the charterers will need to buy separate SOL (Ship Owners Liability) cover, as normal P & I cover excludes liability in excess of Hague/Hague-Visby limits.

(2) Where the shipment is from a nation that has no mandatory legislation applying either the Hague or Hague-Visby Rules and the bill of lading applies Hague Rules contractually. In this case, in the absence of mandatory law, the charterers have freedom of contract and can control limitation.

Article IX of the Hague Rules is known as the "Gold Clause" and provides that the limit of £100 per package set in Article IV Rule 5 is to be gold value. Litigation has indicated that the value of this was around £6,630 in 1988—*The Rosa S* [1988] 2 Lloyd's Rep. 574. This must be in the £8–9,000 range now.

With careful drafting this pitfall can be avoided. If, instead of merely incorporating the Hague Rules into the bill of lading to apply contractually whenever there is no mandatory law, a more selective incorporation is made—i.e. Hague Rules, Articles I—VIII only (carefully leaving out the dangerous Article IX—Gold Clause) and then a contractual limit of £100 sterling is provided, the effect of the Gold Clause is nullified.

If the charterers choose to be incautious in their bill of lading terms and conditions, they can hardly expect the owners to give them back-to-back cover. Thus, if the limit of liability during sea carriage applied by the charterers to their customers is a contractual one, the sub-clause provides for the limit, as between the owners and the charterers, to be "*GB Pounds 100 per package*". Only where there is mandatory application of the Rules, to determine limitation where a bill of lading is issued, is the mandatory limitation applicable as between the owners and the charterers.

Paragraph (ii). Limitation in respect of containers is calculated differently and is set at:

(1) reasonable cost of repair, or

(2) value of the container at the time of such loss or damage.

which provides full indemnity.

However, problems will always arise, in the event of total loss of a container, in determining value, so the sub-clause gives some assistance. If the containers are leased, value is determined by the liability of the charterers under their lease agreement with the container lessor. If the containers are the charterers' own property, liability is determined by market value.

The final sentence of the sub-clause provides for containers neither owned nor leased by the charterers to be regarded as goods. This is in line with the approach adopted in most combined transport operators' bills of lading, where merchants' own containers are treated as goods.

"(d) *Time Limit*: Except as provided in Clause 16(h), the Owners shall be dis- 721
charged from all liability under this Charter Party in respect of claims for 722
which extensions of time have not been sought and obtained by the Charter- 723
ers unless notice of arbitration in accordance with Clause 20 is given within 724
15 months of the delivery of goods, if the claim relates to goods, or the date 725
when the Charterers become aware of the incident giving rise to the claim 726
for all other claims. 727"

This sub-clause is the owners' equivalent of clause 16(e). It starts by giving recognition to the practice of granting time extensions, as provided for in clause 16(h), which will overrule the provisions of this sub-clause. Note that, to overrule, it is not sufficient just to seek an extension within time, as the extensions must be acknowledged and granted by the owners to defeat the timebar.

Subject to this proviso, if the claim is in respect of goods, unless notice of arbitration in accordance with clause 20 is given within 15 months of the delivery of the goods, the claim is time barred. Note that time bar here is by the reference to "*the delivery of the goods*" and not the redelivery of the vessel, as in clause 16(e). Delivery in a contract between the owners and the charterers can only mean delivery by the owners to the charterers and not delivery by the charterers to their customers.

If the claim is other than in respect of goods, the time limitation period starts to run from "*when the charterers become aware of the incident giving rise to the claim*".

"(e) *For Personal Injury*: The Owners shall indemnify the Charterers against any claims for personal injury incurred on or about the Vessel unless caused by the negligence of the Charterers, their servants, agents or sub-contractors or any defect in the Charterers' goods and/or containers."

This is the usual indemnity by the owners to the charterers in respect of claims for injury "*on or about the vessel*". It contains two logical exclusions:

(1) "*negligence of the Charterers, their servants, agents or sub-contractors*", and

(2) "*any defect in the Charterers' goods and/or containers*".

"(f) *Limitation Proceedings*: The Owners shall have the control and conduct of any limitation proceedings on the joint behalf of the Owners and the Charterers. If successful, any recovered costs of such proceedings shall be borne equally between the Owners and the Charterers. If unsuccessful, the costs shall be borne by the party responsible under the terms of this Charter Party for the factor which caused the proceedings to fail. If more than one factor contributed and the Owners and the Charterers were each responsible for at least one factor the costs shall be borne equally."

The limitation proceedings referred to in this sub-clause are those in accordance with a Limitation of Liability for Maritime Claims Convention under which, in the event of a catastrophe, a vessel may limit its total liability by reference to its tonnage or residual value by reference to a stipulated formula. Separate limits are usually set for loss of life/injury claims and property claims. In some countries only the owners can limit, so it pays the charterers to allow the owners to lead if this is the case. Furthermore, denial or right to limit may occur in some areas if there has been fault and privity on the part of the owners.

Thus it may be seen that, in the event of a limitation action being required, it is much better that the owners should have control, as they are the party under seige and the party with the evidence to fight the case. It is therefore provided in this sub-clause that, although the conduct of normal claims is in the hands of the charterers, if there is a limitation action the owners act on joint behalves.

The costs of such proceedings may be considerable, so it is necessary to provide for who pays for them, whether the proceedings are successful or not. If the proceedings are successful, most of the costs will be recoverable from the unsuccessful plaintiffs, but any surplus left after costs are taxed is borne 50/50 between the parties. If the proceedings are unsuccessful, one must look to see whose negligence caused them to fail and that party bears the costs. Frequently there is fault on both sides and, if that is the case, regardless of whether it is 50/50 or 80/20, both parties contribute equally to meet the costs.

Note that the costs referred to in this sub-clause relate to limitation proceedings only.

"(g) *Consequential Loss*: Under no circumstances shall the Owners be responsible for any indirect or consequential loss arising from loss, damage or delay to goods and containers, howsoever caused."

Consequential losses have always been an anathema to carriers and are a frequent cause of dispute. Even if the English law doctrine of remoteness/foreseeability is overcome, such claims are usually fought tooth and nail with much rancour. Their exclusion from the relationship between the owners and the charterers is, in my view, a wise decision, whether or not the cause of the consequential loss be "*loss, damage or delay to the goods and containers, howsoever caused*".

Clause 18: Insurances

"(a) *Hull and Machinery*: The Owners warrant that the Vessel is insured under Institute Time Clauses or similar clauses for IWL trading against loss, damage and collision liabilities for the value as indicated in Box 27 which cover will be maintained throughout the currency of this Charter Party. Upon 10 days notice to the Charterers, the Owners shall be entitled to effect any reasonable change to this value. The Owners agree that their insured value for the purpose of this Clause shall represent the Charterers maximum liability to the Owners for damage to the Vessel in accordance with Clause 6(i), including time spent on repairs."

The first sentence of this sub-clause is a warranty by the owners that, throughout the currency of the charter party, the vessel will be insured on the usual terms for worldwide trading within the limits provided for in the Institute of London Underwriters' Institute Warranty Limits (IWL) (*see* comments on clause 3 for details), at the expense of the owners. Cover must include:

> "*loss,*
> *damage and*
> *collision liabilities*"

and the insured value of the vessel must be as provided in box 27. However, the owners may amend this value on giving 10 days' notice to the charterers, provided the change is reasonable.

The third sentence links this sub-clause with clause 6(l) to provide that the charterers' maximum liability for loss or damage to the vessel (which in the absence of specific provision in the charter party would be market value) shall be the insured value as shown in box 27. This is quite an important clause for the charterers, as market value of vessels can fluctuate substantially in quite a short period of time if trading conditions alter. In the absence of such a provision as this, the charterers would have great difficulty in quantifying their exposure to risk under clause 6(l) and therefore what value they should place upon the vessel when insuring Charterers' Liability for Ship Damage under their Ship Owners' Liability (SOL) Cover.

This uncertainty is removed by this sentence, agreeing to deem the insured value to be the maximum liability of the charterers for damage to the vessel, thereby putting the onus on the owners to review and update their insured value as necessary, if they wish to be covered in the charter party for market value.

Note that the valuation shown in box 27 covers not only the cost of repairs, but also hire payments during time under repair.

"(b) *Protection and Indemnity (P & I)*: The Owners and the Charterers warrant that the Vessel is entered on full terms with their respective P & I Clubs as indicated in Boxes 30 and 31 and that such entries will be maintained with all calls paid up to date throughout the currency of this Charter Party."

Both parties have a vested interest in knowing that the liabilities of the other are fully insured in a P & I club with calls paid up to date throughout the currency of the charter party and the identity of the other party's club. The latter information is provided in boxes 30 and 31 and the former undertakings are warranted by the respective parties in this sub-clause.

"(c) *War Risks*: The Owners warrant that the Vessel is insured against loss of the Vessel by War Risks and War P & I Risks for IWL trading excluding additional premium/restricted/prohibited areas, which cover will be maintained throughout the currency of this Charter Party."

The subject of war is dealt with in much greater detail in clause 19. This sub-clause is the equivalent warranty from the owners in respect of War Risks insurance as is provided in sub-clauses (a) and (b) in relation to Navigation Risks and P & I.

Note that both Hull and Machinery and P & I covers normally exclude War Risks so that War Risks insurance covers both the Hull and Machinery of the vessel and liabilities of a P & I nature if the proximate cause is a war risk.

The warranty given here covers trading within the normal IWL limits EXCLUDING additional premium/restricted/prohibited areas. If the charterers wish to trade in any such areas, they must first secure the agreement of the owners under clause 19(a) and bear the cost of additional insurance necessary (clause 6(n)).

Clause 19: War

This is a clause to which usually insufficient attention is given until it is too late. Only when war flares up somewhere, in an area to or through which the vessel is likely to trade, do many owners and charterers accord this important clause the attention it warrants. Unlike other sub-clauses in this charter party, those in this clause do not have headings.

"(a) Unless the consent of the Owners be first obtained, the Vessel shall not be ordered to nor obliged to:-

(i) remain in or pass through any area which is dangerous or is likely to become dangerous as a result of war, hostilities, warlike action or piracy, actual or threatened, nor

(ii) call at any port where there is any revolution, civil war, civil commotion or any threat thereof, nor

(iii) carry any goods that may in any way expose her to any risk of seizure, capture or detention."

The first sub-clause gives the owners the necessary rights to refuse to take the vessel into or through a war zone, which is defined in paragraphs (i) and (ii). Note that likelihood or threat is sufficient to enable the owners to invoke this sub-clause and refuse to take the vessel into or through the area in question, they do not have to wait for bullets to fly and bombs to fall.

Whether or not a decision to refuse to enter a zone is justifiable is a subjective decision, which will vary according to infinitely variable circumstances, so it is not possible to provide a more clearly defined sub-clause indicating when such refusals are justified. One must look at the current jurisprudence for such guidance in the light of individual circumstances but clearly this has to be based upon the situation as it appeared to the master and the owners at the time they took the decision to refuse to enter the zone. Anyone can be wise with the benefit of hindsight, so that what eventually happened is no guidance whatsoever.

Paragraph (iii) relates to goods carried rather than areas traded to or through and appears quite wide. Clause 4(e) already controls shipment of arms and ammunition, which are the goods most likely to fall foul of this provision. However, the United Nations operated an embargo on all trade to/from Iraq following the war there, so apparently innocuous goods could come into this category, if they are to or from prohibited areas.

"(b) However, should the Owners consent to allowing the Vessel to proceed, 771
notwithstanding the existence or threat of the danger(s) outlined in Clause 772
19(a), the Owners agree that the Vessel proceeds at their own risk in con- 773
consideration of the Charterers agreeing that the Owners may effect the follow- 774
ing insurances for which the Charterers will reimburse the Owners the net 775
cost of premium/calls therefor: (See Clause 6(n)). 776

(i) Reinstatement of the War Risks cover on Hull and P & I for trading to the 777
required area. 778

(ii) Any further additional premia necessary to maintain Hull cover whilst 779
blocked or trapped pending release of the Vessel, acceptance of con- 780
structive total loss by insurers or trapped for 365 consecutive days, 781
whichever shall first occur. 782

(iii) Insurance of hire on the Vessel for not exceeding 365 days. 783"

Sub-clause (b) starts from the assumption that the owners have consented to allow the vessel to proceed, after being consulted by the charterers in accordance with sub-clause (a). It provides for the vessel to proceed AT THE OWNERS' RISK, in consideration of which the charterers agree that the owners may place the following insurances at the expense of the charterers.

(i) Reinsurance of the War Risks insurance (*see* clause 18(c)) to the extent that the normal war risks insurers have withdrawn normal cover for vessels trading in that area by invoking the cancellation clause in the policy.

(ii) If a vessel becomes blocked or trapped in a war zone and remains thus trapped for 365 days, under the terms of the policy the insurers will pay out on that vessel as a constructive total loss. However, the trapped vessel remains exposed to physical loss or damage by war risks throughout that 365-day period and the reinstatement of cover under paragraph (i) will have been arranged for a short finite period (e.g. seven days). Thus the owners need to continue payment of reinstatement premiums under paragraph (i) throughout the period of blocking and trapping to maintain the cover for physical loss or damage whilst the 365 day period elapses or until the vessel is released, whichever occurs first. If the vessel is blocked and trapped for 365 days, the charter party is automatically terminated in accordance with clause 8(c).

(iii) As under clause 8(c) a blocked or trapped vessel is placed off hire, the owners must necessarily be allowed to insure their exposure to loss of hire for the maximum period that they may be deprived of the use of their vessel before they receive payment as a constructive total loss.

The cost of the above insurances could be considerable. Those payable under paragraph (ii) on a blocked or trapped vessel in a dangerous war zone could, over the period, exceed the value of the vessel. Thus the charterers need to think carefully before asking the owners to allow the vessel to proceed into a war zone.

"(c) In the event of the wages of the Master, Officers and/or crew and/or other of the Vessel's operating expenses are affected by any of the factors mentioned in (a) above, the amount of any increase shall be added to the hire due upon production of the Owners' account therefor together with appropriate receipts and paid by the Charterers to the Owners with the next hire payment."

When vessels enter war zones it is common practice for the crews to seek "War Bonuses" for the increased danger to which they are exposed.

A vessel will probably find the cost of purchasing necessary stores in a war zone substantially higher than elsewhere, so that the owners' operating expenses may be increased by reason of a vessel proceeding into a war zone.

This sub-clause provides for the charterers to reimburse the owners for such enhanced costs, which the owners may add to the next bill for hire, provided that they substantiate the amounts claimed with appropriate receipts.

"(d) The Vessel shall have the liberty to comply with any orders or directions of whatsoever nature given by the government of the nation where the Owners are domiciled or whose flag the Vessel flies or any other government or person or body acting, or purporting to act, with the authority of such government or by any party having, under the terms of the war risk insurance on the Vessel, the right to give such orders or directions."

This sub-clause allows the owners to accept instructions from the following without being put off hire:

(1) government where the owners are domiciled;
(2) government whose flag the vessel flies (usually the same as 1);
(3) any other government;

(4) any person or body acting or purporting to act with the authority of such government;

(5) any party having, under the terms of the War Risks insurance on the vessel, the right to give such orders or directions.

(1)–(2) In addition to requisitioning (*see* clause 8(d)), the government where the owners are domiciled or whose flag the vessel flies may issue mandatory instructions which the owners must obey (e.g. no trade with Iraq).

(3)–(4) For example a warship belonging to a country that is part of the multi-national force enforcing the embargo on Iraq might order the vessel to stop or might redirect it.

(5) War Risks insurers might give notice of withdrawal of cover under the cancellation clause so that the vessel needs to depart from the area quickly.

The owners have no option but to comply with these instructions so it is reasonable that they should be allowed to do so without being prejudiced by being placed off hire, particularly as they are only there under the directions of the charterers.

"(e) In the event of the outbreak of war, whether there be a declaration of war 796
or not, between any two or more of the following countries or involving the 797
nation where the Owners are domiciled or whose flag the Vessel flies: 798

People's Republic of China, France, Federal Republic of Germany, United 799
States of America, United Kingdom, Union of Soviet Socialist Republics, 800
either the Owners or the Charterers may cancel this Charter Party and, un- 801
less otherwise agreed, the Vessel shall be redelivered to the Owners at the 802
port of destination or, if debarred under this Clause from reaching or enter- 803
ing it, at a near open and safe port at the Owners' option after discharge of 804
any goods and containers on board. 805"

The Armageddon clause! In as much as, if the need arises to invoke this sub-clause, charter party disputes will be the least of worries. One might almost suggest that in most circumstances it is superfluous.

In the event of war between two of the powers named (often referred to as the Superpowers) "*or involving the nation where the Owners are domiciled or whose flag the Vessel flies*", the sub-clause provides a formula for the cancellation of the charter party, recognising that a conflict between Superpowers would have worldwide repercussions and one involving the Flag nation would likely lead to massive requisitioning.

Is the list of "Superpowers" up to date? (It is the list usually used and the clause has been taken from earlier charter parties.) Should not "Federal Republic of Germany" now be just "Germany"? Should not, "Japan" be added? The USSR is disbanded. This is something more likely to be decided by war risks insurers in the drafting of their clauses.

"(f) If in compliance with the provisions of this Clause anything is done or is 806
not done, such shall not be deemed a deviation. 807"

This sub-clause, which closes clause 19, merely emphasises, for the sake of clarity, that compliance with the provisions of this clause does not cause a deviation and therefore cause the vessel to go off hire.

BIMCO intend to replace this entire clause with their standard war clause "Conwartime" at the next opportunity.

Clause 20: Law and Arbitration

We are now into the usual closing clauses found in all charter parties, which hold few surprises for anyone, starting with law and arbitration.

Provision is made to give a choice between London and New York arbitration or allow a choice of some other forum.

> "(a) *London*: This Charter Party shall be governed by English law and any dispute arising out of this Charter Party shall be referred to arbitration in London, one arbitrator being appointed by each party, in accordance with the Arbitration Acts 1950 and 1979 or any statutory modification or re-enactment thereof for the time being in force. On the receipt by one party of the nomination in writing of the other party's arbitrator, that party shall appoint their arbitrator within fourteen days, failing which the decision of the single Arbitrator appointed shall apply. If two Arbitrators properly appointed shall not agree they shall appoint an umpire whose decision shall be final."

The London arbitration provision applies English law and the provisions of the Arbitration Acts 1950 and 1979 or any statutory modification etc.

Each party appoints an arbitrator and, if they cannot agree, they appoint an umpire, whose decision is final. Once one party nominates an arbitrator and advises the other party, then the other party has 14 days in which to nominate their arbitrator. If they fail to do so, the decision of the first party's nominated arbitrator is applicable.

> "(b) *New York*: Should any dispute arise out of this Charter Party, the matter in dispute shall be referred to three persons in New York, one to be appointed by each of the parties hereto, and the third by the two so chosen; their decision or that of any two of them shall be final, and for the purpose of enforcing any award, this agreement may be made a rule of the Court. The arbitrators shall be members of the Society of Maritime Arbitrators, Inc. of New York and the proceedings shall be conducted in accordance with the rules of the Society."

The New York arbitration provision does not specifically apply US law but provides for the rules of the Society of Maritime Arbitrators Inc. of New York to apply and these use US law interpretation.

The sub-clause provides for three arbitrators, one appointed by each of the parties and the third by the other two, with no provision in the sub-clause as to what happens if either party is dilatory in their appointment, this being left to the governing rules.

The decision of the arbitrators is final and a majority decision is acceptable.

The successful party may apply to the Court to enforce the arbitrators' award.

"(c) *Alternative*: Any dispute arising out of this Charter Party shall be referred to arbitration at the place indicated in Box 34, subject to the law and procedures applicable there."

The parties are free to opt for an alternative forum of arbitration in box 34. If they do arbitration shall be "*subject to the law and procedures applicable there*" (unless agreed to the contrary in an additional clause).

"If Box 34 in Part 1 is not filled in, sub-clause (a) of this Clause shall apply. (a), (b) and (c) are alternatives; indicate alternative agreed in Box 34."

If box 34 is left blank London arbitration is automatically applied in accordance with sub-clause (a) above.

BIMCO intends to replace this entire clause with their "Standard Law and Arbitration Clause" at the next opportunity.

Clause 21: Commission

"The Owners shall pay a commission at the rate stated in Box 35 to the party mentioned in Box 35 on any hire paid under this Charter Party but in no case less than is necessary to cover the actual expenses of the Brokers. If the full hire is not paid owing to breach of Charter Party by either of the parties the party liable therefor shall indemnify the Brokers against their loss of commission.

Should the parties agree to cancel this Charter Party, the Owners shall indemnify the Brokers against any loss of commission but in such case the commission shall not exceed the brokerage on one year's hire."

The shipbrokers' favourite clause!

The owners are responsible for paying commission at the rate and to the party indicated in box 35, with the proviso that this must be at least sufficient to cover the brokers' actual expenses.

If the charter party is breached by either party so that full hire is not paid, the party responsible for the breach indemnifies the brokers against their loss of commission. If the parties agree to cancel the charter party, the owners must indemnify the broker against any loss of commission up to commission on one year's hire.

Clause 22: Notices

"Any notice to the Owners shall be sent to the address as indicated in Box 3. Any notice to the Charterers shall be sent to the address as indicated in Box 4."

The section of standard clauses (before the inevitable additional clauses always added to meet specific individual requirements) ends with this clause, providing for notices to be sent to the addresses in boxes 3 and 4, respectively.

Section VII: Additional clauses

It is only realistic to expect additional clauses to be added to tailor the charter party to meet individual requirements. Indeed box 36 provides for the number of clauses to be recorded and incorporated into the contract.

One such clause which charterers may require, in the light of developments since BOXTIME was first drafted, is one dealing with the ISM Code and Port State Control Authorities. Now that the ISM Code is operative for some vessels and will soon be so for all, the requirement that the vessel's management be ISM compliant is likely to be encountered. In truth such a clause is mostly superfluous and most of its requirements are already covered elsewhere. Care is needed in responding to such requests and the BIMCO clause is recommended as being fair to both parties. It reads as follows:

> "From the date of coming into force of the International Safety Management (ISM) Code in relation to the Vessel and thereafter during the currency of this Charter Party, the Owners shall procure that both the Vessel and 'the Company' (as defined by the ISM Code) shall comply with the requirements of the ISM Code. Upon request the Owners shall provide a copy of the relevant Document of Compliance (DOC) and Safety Management Certificate (SMC) to the Charterers.
>
> Except as otherwise provided in this Charter Party, loss, damage, expense or delay caused by failure on the part of the Owners or 'the Company' to comply with the ISM Code shall be for the Owners' account."

When drafting such clauses great care should be taken to ensure that the following points are given attention:

(1) Use the correct language of the charter party (*see* comment at the beginning of the commentary on Part II) to ensure that the additional clause blends in. Do not just transplant a favoured clause from elsewhere willy nilly without checking the language in it and amending as necessary to bring it into line.

(2) Do not create conflict with any unamended provisions in the standard charter party.

(3) If the additional clause has any bearing on a standard charter party clause, cross-reference it to the standard clause.

(4) Give the additional clause a heading.

(5) Give it a number, starting from 23. (I was tempted to suggest that additional clauses should be numbered in sequence with the standard charter party so that, for example, an additional clause on bunker fuel would be 12(g), but this would not fit in with the need to put the number of additional clauses in box 36. Instead the same desired effect can be produced by liberal cross-referencing.)

And finally please take care to be clear when drafting such clauses. Let us see if we can reduce the ranks of maritime aribtrators not swell them. I sometimes think that for every claim that goes to arbitration the shipbroker that drafted the clause should pay the costs. That would create a flourishing industry in shipbrokers' professional indemnity cover but at the same time I am sure we would see greater care taken in drafting charter party clauses than is the case at present.

But then is it the shipbroker who is at fault or is it the owners and the charterers that want the ambiguous clauses to have something to argue about? No doubt each will blame the other and tell me that my purist view is uncommercial. All I know is that neither the owners, the charterers nor the shipbrokers gain from slack drafting. They merely contrive to support the ever growing ranks of maritime lawyers.

Section VIII: Conclusion

Some owners and charterers will doubtless object to responsibilities and liabilities placed upon them over which they have little or no control, such as the charterers being responsible for the effect of bad packing of goods in containers by FCL customers. Should not they be able to limit their liability to what they can recover from the customer? The charterers may think so but, looked at from the owners' point of view, why should they allow such a restriction? So far as they are concerned all goods and containers belong to the charterers, who must answer for any shortcoming in them. It is then up to the charterers to protect themselves vis-à-vis their customers by appropriate bill of lading indemnities.

Conversely the owners may dislike having the master responsible for a stowage effected by the charterers' stevedores. However, as was explained when considering this point, it is analogous to the position of the driver of a lorry under the Road Traffic Act to ensure that his vehicle is roadworthy. The stevedores do the work but nothing can remove from the master his overriding responsibility to ensure that stowage is done properly, so that the vessel goes to sea in a seaworthy condition.

In a charter party there is no third person to pick up the tabs for any accident other than the owners or the charterers. Thus, the effect of any accident must inure to the detriment of one of these two parties. Therefore, ask not whether it is fair that the owners (or the charterers) should be responsible for the effect of any accident, ask rather whether it is fairer that it inures to the detriment of the other party, because it must inure to one of them. If this charter party is viewed in this way, I feel sure that it will be seen to provide a fair division between the two parties.

POSTSCRIPT

Over a period of time other charters have been prepared with containerships in mind, amongst other things! The NYPE (New York Produce Exchange) charter has been made more container friendly and the NYPE Inter-Club Agreement has finally been amended to recognise that, in its previous form, it was a nonsense, so far as combined transport/containers were concerned.

BIMCO's new "GENTIME" has been drafted with containers in the back of the draftsmen's minds but it is primarily, as its name suggests, a general charter. It might be suitable to charter a small hub feeder containership but not a large deep-sea vessel destined for consortium operation. So, whilst I would never suggest that BOXTIME is the only basis upon which to charter a containership (many large operators have prepared their own forms which, being for long-term charters and because of the size of the operators, they are able to enforce), it is the only standard charter designed solely for use with containerships. It is the only standard charter in which all of the idiosyncracies of container carriage are addressed without the need to resort to wholesale additional clauses. For this reason any substantial containership operator would be strongly advised to use it as the best basis upon which to prepare a charter for a containership, whether that operator be chartering in or chartering out.

When drafting such clauses great care should be taken to ensure that the following points are given attention:

CHAPTER 2

OPERATING AGREEMENTS

INTRODUCTION

When a number of carriers decide to co-operate to form a consortium in order to rationalise their services in a trade by sharing space on each other's vessels, they need to consider carefully not only the operational aspects of such co-operation, but also the liability matters, as such arrangements create quite complicated chains of indemnity. These chains arise out of the numerous and varied contracts involved in the operation and need to take into account the absence of contract in many cases. Here, unless suitable arrangements are made, parties can find themselves exposed to liabilities to third parties without the protection of a contract.

Let us demonstrate this by a simple example: Carriers A, B and C, who swap slots in a consortium, issue contracts of carriage (bills of lading) respectively to Merchants 1, 2 and 3, so that A is in contract with 1, B with 2 and C with 3. A has a slot charter contract with B and, when this operates on B's vessel, C is a co-charterer, with a slot charter with B but no chartering contract with A. (You begin to see the complications developing even in a simple example like this!) So if A's cargo (1) damages C's cargo (3) in B's vessel, where is the contract to protect A from direct action by C's cargo (3) in tort to avoid any defence or limitation in the contract of carriage issued by C to 3?

In a situation where only two lines swap slots the problem does not arise, because one of the two parties is always the (disponent) owner and the other the charterer, so that suitable indemnity clauses in a mutual slot charter will cover the matter. However, once more than two carriers enter into a slot swap situation, the problems of slot co-charterers arise. This means that, in addition to a slot charter party to operate between the vessel provider and each individual slot charterer, there is also need for an operating agreement, signed by all the lines involved, governing the operation of the consortium and its inter-line liabilities outside the slot charter governing the (disponent) owner/slot charterer relationship.

Even this sort of complication is relatively simple, compared to the situation where one consortium enters into a slot swap arrangement with another line or consortium and sells slots to another line or consortium, either on the basis of individual lines chartering out or on the basis of the consortium as a whole chartering out. The questions that must be borne in mind throughout when concocting such arrangements are:

(1) Who could be liable?
(2) To whom?
(3) Under what contract? (or if none where is the liability protection?)
(4) Has the liable party got adequate insurance cover? (P & I usually)
(5) Is the chain of indemnity to protect all other parties intact?

In consortium operations it is often agreed to depart from the usual risk management principle of: he who damages must pay in order to create an incentive to care, in the interest of reducing insurance costs. Usually this is done only where there is mutuality and reciprocity. That is to say, in slot swapping one line agrees to put its policy at risk for a consortium partner in consideration of the consortium partner doing likewise when the roles are reversed. Provided that the number of slots chartered roughly equates to the number of slots provided to consortium partners, this principle has equity on the "swings and roundabouts" basis. Concessions like this are rarely made where the slot charterer is purchasing slots, because of the absence of equity, but are quite common in slot swapping arrangements. This principle is usually referred to as the mutual waiver principle.

MUTUAL WAIVER CLAUSE

Because we are dealing with a chain of indemnity in a complicated series of contracts, if the chain is to be effective, every link must be in position and effective. A chain is as strong as its weakest link and this is as true of chains of indemnity as it is of anchor chains. In equity the construction of such indemnity clauses must be such that, if any link fails, the effect of the breach is imposed upon the party whose contract failed or on a party with adequate appropriate insurance.

The principle involved starts from the assumption that all parties are carriers with the usual Protection and Indemnity (P & I) cover, either on the basis of an owner's or a charterer's entry. It then sets out to negate (or at least minimise) the need for any additional cover arising out of a slot chartering operation. The principal cover involved is the Charterer's Liability for Ship Damage cover but it extends further than that as study of the clause demonstrates.

Just on the basis of Charterer's Liability for Ship Damage, consider the usual situation in a consortium of say three carriers: A (three vessels), B (four vessels) and C (five vessels) in a service of twelve vessels. Each carrier is considered as the (disponent) owner of the vessels that he supplies to the consortium operation and so is assumed to have cover for ship damage, either through a Hull and Machinery (H & M) policy, if owned or demise chartered, or through a Charterers Liability for Ship Damage policy (SOL) if time or voyage chartered. In this example, in the normal way, A would have cover on his three vessels and would need to purchase SOL cover on B and C's nine vessels in case his cargo damaged their vessels and he could not recover from a third party. B would need to buy cover on eight vessels and C on seven vessels, giving insurance premium for cover on 24 vessels over and above the normal cover on the twelve vessels!

To avoid this the mutual waiver principle is invoked and each slot charterer is only liable to the (disponent) owner to the extent of any recovery from a third party. The need for additional SOL cover is consequently avoided. Of course this arrangement has to be declared by all owners to their H & M/SOL insurers, as these insurers' rights of recourse under subrogation are affected and this is a factor "which might influence a prudent underwriter in setting the rate".

Mutual waiver agreements have always to be total and unqualified if they are to achieve their objective of avoiding the need for additional insurance. If there is any qualification, then there is a potential exposure and thus a potential need for insurance.

Since inception this clause has passed through three stages of development:

Stage 1: Limit to recovery

Initially, after considerable discussion with lawyers (including opinions and drafting assistance from a QC), the approach adopted was that, in the situations covered by the mutual waiver, the liability of the charterer would be limited to whatever he could recover from a third party. This preserved the right of recourse to parties outside the agreement but put no direct liability upon those within it, so that there was no exposure needing insurance.

Stage 2: Control and enforcement

Stage 1 was the form in which the mutual waiver was first introduced and operated. However, when negotiating a new consortium agreement, the point was raised that some third party might respond to a claim by drawing attention to the clause and refusing to pay on the grounds that, "if I do not pay you, you are not out of pocket and thus have no chose in action against me". This would defeat one of the main objects of the clause, which was to preserve actions against third parties in order to minimise costs and losses to consortium members.

In order to overcome this point, the agreement was changed, so that the defendant would continue to have a liability but there was agreement between the parties that, whilst action could in theory proceed as far as a court action against the defendant, a victorious plaintiff would only enforce that judgment to the extent that the defendant could recover from a third party. In this way the chose in action of the defendant against any third party would be preserved but he would have an assurance that no award would be enforced against him by a consortium colleague, except to the extent that he could recover from a third party.

Stage 3: Assignment

Stage 2 applied for a while, until a particularly cautious and astute operator, extrapolating potential situations of multi-million dollar disasters, that are the real test of such clauses, saw a potential exposure in some court if a plaintiff ignored such an undertaking and sought to enforce an award, which situation might arise if a sufficiently high sum of money was involved.

This led to further considerations of the clause and the situations which might arise causing difficulties in its application. For example, the third party might be a very good customer of the charterer, who might therefore pursue a claim with less than reasonable vigour, secure in the knowledge that, if he didn't collect, he needn't pay (consortium partners might co-operate for mutual benefit but, at times, there could be a singular lack of trust between some parties who were, after all, only co-operating for part of the service (the sea leg) and were still competing furiously for shares of trade on a door-to-door basis for the land leg and in other service areas, like documentation etc.). How could these problems be best addressed, whilst at the same time minimising actions between members of consortia, which actions were usually fought most fiercely (as a matter of honour) and which could create conflict within a consortium, which requires a degree of trust and co-operation to function smoothly?

A new formula was devised in which the main criteria were:

(1) The charterer would exercise reasonable endeavours to recover from the third party and account to the owner therefor.
(2) If the charterer advised that he could not recover, the owner could ask for an assignment of the right of action and demand the co-operation of the charterer in pursuing the action.
(3) If the charterer refused he would lose his right of indemnity.

This is the present approach adopted by the clause, which needs to appear in each "link" in the "chain of indemnity". The precise format in each will be considered as each contract is examined.

This is one rule in the operating agreement where I will provide a text and (hopefully!) explain it. Before commencing I would just reiterate that this is the link in the chain of indemnity in the operating agreement, which governs the general relationship between all of the members of the consortium where these number three or more. Liabilities as between individual owners and slot charterers are governed elsewhere in the slot charterparty, which is a two party agreement, whereas the operating agreement is a multi (three plus) party contract. In the following notes I readily acknowledge that I have drawn heavily on an explanatory note produced many years ago by my good friend Volker Zumbeck of Hapag Lloyd, with whom I was one of the co-authors of the liability provisions in the various consortium contracts back in the late 1960s/early 1970s. Having read the clause and notes you may find your eyes revolving like a fruit machine and your brains concentrated into a knot! However, I defy anyone, given the complicated set of circumstances (with chains of indemnity disappearing in all directions like wires from a telephone exchange), to produce something simpler and shorter but equally comprehensive, as comprehensive it must be in view of the potential multi-million dollar exposures to which it might be applied. We must ensure that all liabilities are channelled according to our wishes to a party with adequate insurance, the cost of which must be minimised, and even then provide for a back-up situation if first choice solutions are overturned in some foreign court.

"(1) Each line agrees that, except as otherwise specifically provided to the contrary in this Agreement:

- in respect of loss or damage to any of its Containerships or Containers used in the service, and/or
- in respect of any liability it has as owner or disponent owner of any Containership or as owner or user of Containers to a third party (which expression shall, where used in this clause, exclude any line) for loss, damage or delay of whatsoever nature and howsoever arising in connection with the service, other than claims covered by sub-clauses (2) or (3),

for which another line (other line) would otherwise be liable to that line (owning line) by reason of the utilisation of space on board a Containership used in the service, the liability of that other line to the owning line shall be limited to the amount, if any, recoverable by it from any third party (which expression for this purpose shall not include that other line's insurers) in respect of such loss or damage (even if such liability arises wholly or in part by reason of the act, neglect or default of that other line or of its servants, agents or sub-contractors), provided that the other line shall take all reasonable steps (short of court action) to recover such amount.

The other line shall, upon receipt of a written request from the owning line, allow the owning line to take over all conduct of any enforcement of any rights which the other line may have against any third party to enable the owning line to exercise such rights in the name of the other line but at the expense of the owning line. The other line shall co-operate as much as is reasonably possible to assist the owning line to exercise such rights which the other line may have against the third party.

If the other line should not be willing to transfer to the owning line all conduct of any enforcement of rights and to co-operate as required above in assisting the owning line, the provisions of this sub-clause shall be null and void. The other line shall be deemed to have shown unwillingness to transfer if it has not given the necessary authority in writing to the owning line to proceed within 30 days of receipt of a written request from the owning line so to do.

(2) If any claim or allegation is made by a third party against the principal carrier for loss, damage or delay to Goods, the principal carrier shall settle such claim or allegation directly with the claimant and any recovery by the principal carrier against any other line, not being the owner or disponent owner of the Containership, shall be limited to the amount, if any, recoverable by that other line from any third party (which expression for this purpose shall not include that other line's insurers) in respect of such loss, damage or delay (even if that other line's liability arises wholly or in part by

reason of the act, neglect or default of that other line or of its servants, agents or sub-contractors), and the other line shall take all reasonable steps (short of court action) to recover such amount.

The other line shall, upon receipt of a written request from the principal carrier, allow the principal carrier to take over all conduct of any enforcement of any rights which the other line may have against any third party to enable the principal carrier to exercise such rights in the other line's name but at the principal carrier's expense. The other line shall co-operate as much as is reasonably possible to assist the principal carrier to exercise such rights which the other line may have against the third party.

If the other line should not be willing to transfer to the principal carrier all conduct of any enforcement of rights and to co-operate as required above in assisting the principal carrier, the provisions of this sub-clause shall be null and void. The other line shall be deemed to have shown unwillingness to transfer if it has not given the necessary authority in writing to the principal carrier to proceed within 30 days of receipt of a written request from the principal carrier so to do.

(3) If, nevertheless, a claim or allegation for loss, damage or delay to Goods is made against any other line, not being the owner or disponent owner of the Containership, or against any of its servants or agents or sub-contractors, then the principal carrier shall indemnify that other line or its servants, agents or sub-contractors in respect of that claim or allegation, notwithstanding that such liability arises wholly or in part by reason of the act neglect or default of that other line or its servants, agents or sub-contractors.

The indemnity referred to in this sub-clause shall be unlimited except where there is a responsible line (including the indemnified line but excluding the principal carrier), in which case the indemnity shall be limited to the amount recoverable by the principal carrier from any third party (which expression for this purpose shall not include the principal carrier's insurers) in connection with such claim or allegation and the principal carrier shall take all reasonable steps (short of court action) to recover such amount.

The principal carrier shall, upon receipt of a written request from a responsible line, allow the responsible line to take over all conduct of any enforcement of any rights which the principal carrier may have against any third party to enable the responsible line to exercise such rights in the principal carrier's name but at the responsible line's expense. The principal carrier shall co-operate as much as is reasonably possible to assist the responsible line to exercise such rights which the principal carrier may have against the third party.

If the principal carrier should not be willing to transfer to the responsible line all conduct of any enforcement of rights and to co-operate as required above in assisting the responsible line, the obligations of the principal carrier to indemnify the responsible line shall be unlimited. The principal carrier shall be deemed to have shown unwillingness to transfer if the principal carrier has not given the necessary authority in writing to the responsible line to proceed within 30 days of receipt of a written request from the responsible line so to do.

(4) Except for loss, damage, delay or liabilities falling under sub-clauses (1) or (2) above (whether or not fully recoverable thereunder), where there is a responsible line, liability to third parties, including cargo interests, for loss, damage or delay, of whatsoever nature and howsoever arising in connection with the service, shall, to the extent not indemnified by the principal carrier under sub-clause (3) above, be borne by the responsible line and the responsible line shall indemnify the other lines in respect of any claim or allegation made against them for such loss or damage.

(5) If any claim or allegation of the nature set out in sub-clause (4) is made against any line, resulting in it being held jointly liable with the other lines, and it is impossible to identify a responsible line or, to the extent that recovery from a responsible line is impossible under that sub-clause (4), liability for such loss, damage or delay shall be

shared by the lines in proportion to their trade shares and any line held jointly liable shall be indemnified by the other lines accordingly in respect of any such claim or allegation.

(6) For the purposes of sub-clauses (3)–(5) "responsible line" shall mean the line which is determined as being responsible for loss, damage or delay in accordance with the following order of priorities:

(1) First, the line which causes the loss, damage or delay by its act, neglect or default or that of its servants, agents or sub-contractors (not being another line), or if none

(2) Second, the line which is the owner of the Containership, Container or equipment or has hired or leased from a third party, other than a line, the Containership, Container or other equipment, from the condition of which the loss, damage or delay originated, or if none

(3) Third, the line which is the principal carrier in respect of the Goods, from which the loss or damage originated."

In the normal course of events, in a conventional shipping operation, the issuer of the bill of lading and the shipowner are one and the same person. In the circumstances, the issuer of the bill of lading can rely both on the Hague or Hague-Visby Rules (which will be incorporated by the bill of lading) and to the overall tonnage limitation of liability imposed by the various conventions. However, in a container operation run by a consortium, each line charters space on each other's vessels and, moreover, certain additional services related to the carriage (for instance the provision of containers, terminal services, marketing services and land haulage) may be sub-contracted to companies which are subsidiaries of consortium members, although not necessarily of the member which is issuing the bill of lading.

The intention of the liability clause and chain of indemnity is, first to minimise insurance costs by mutual waiver of recourse, thus limiting the area of double insurance, second to give the various consortium lines (and their associated companies, where appropriate) the protection which they would have had if the entire carriage had been carried out by the line which issued the bill of lading and third to regulate between them who bears the liability if those protections fail.

One of the major potential areas of double insurance is in the case of charterer's liability. By virtue of mutual waivers contained in this clause, any liability of charterers to the owners of a containership or container and, in respect of cargo claims, to co-charterers that have issued bills of lading (as principal carriers) is excluded, except to the extent that the co-charterer can recover from a third party. Thus the need for charterer's liability insurance covering loss of or damage to a containership and containers is effectively removed; the same applies in relation to liability for goods carried by co-charterers as principal carriers.

In view of the fact that basically the same standard of operation is maintained by each line and because of the mutual nature of this provision, the insurers involved (i.e. H & M underwriters and P & I clubs) are usually prepared to accept these waivers without extra charge.

In the past, attempts to extend the protection of the bill of lading contract to sub-contractors and employees have been made by way of the "Himalaya" clause or in some cases a demise clause. Some form of agency arrangement based on an expanded Himalaya clause can, in certain circumstances, be effective. Provision is made for this as a "second string" in the liabilities clause. (A demise clause approach is inconsistent with the chain of indemnities concept.)

The solution which has been adopted in a large number of consortia is to apply the so-called "chain of indemnities" approach. Under this arrangement, when the line issuing the bill of lading enters into a sub-contract with, for instance, the shipowner under the slot charter party, it agrees to indemnify the shipowner and its servants, agents and sub-contractors against any claims which may be made against them, other than by the issuer of the bill of lading itself. In the bill of lading the issuer takes a similar indemnity from the shipper. Thus, to take a simple example, if shipper A enters into a bill of lading contract with line B in respect of cargo which is in fact carried under a slot charter party on a vessel belonging to line C and, during the sea leg, cargo damage occurs, it remains open to A to bring an action directly against C in tort, without the protection of the limitations imposed by the bill of lading. However, if such an action is brought, C is able to claim against B under its indemnity in the slot charter and B in turn can claim against A under the indemnity in the bill of lading. The net effect will be that A will receive nothing.

It is hoped that, in most jurisdictions, the courts would agree to hear all three actions together, such that it would immediately become clear that the initial action should not proceed. In both England and Australia successful defences based on these clauses have been mounted and in each case the court has ordered that the proceedings be stayed.

Over the years further improvements and amendments have been made to the clause so as to restrict the liability of one line to another (in most cases) to the amount which that line can recover from third parties, so as to minimise the need for double insurance. Thus, for instance, in the example set out above, C's recovery from B under the indemnity would be limited to what B could recover from A and, additionally, any claim by C for damage to the vessel caused by B or B's cargo, for which it was liable, would be limited to what B could recover from third parties, thus removing the need for charterers liability insurance.

The clause is intended to extend the concept of the chain of indemnities still further, so as also to protect the other lines of the consortium utilising space as co-charterers together with the principal carrier, without being the servant, agent or sub-contractor of that principal carrier, on board a containership.

As a fall-back, arrangements are also included in the clause to cover the possibility of the indemnities failing to operate effectively in some jurisdictions or the risk that a claim may be brought by a third party against one line solely on the basis that, in the jurisdiction in question, the relationship between the lines gives rise to a partnership or similar relationship and therefore to joint and several liability. These operate by allocating the liability in such circumstances, first to the line which is likely to have the protection of the bill of lading (the principal carrier), next to the responsible line (which is defined in the clause) and finally according to trade shares. In summary therefore, the purpose of the clause is to prevent, so far as is possible, lines within a consortium (and their subsidiaries) incurring liabilities, or the need for additional insurance, which they would not have incurred as a non-consortium independent operator. The clause has, in its basic form, been in existence for many years and has appeared to work effectively. It is explained in more detail below.

Sub-clause (1) covers two aspects, namely:

- loss or damage suffered by a line to its property due to the fault of another line as co-charterer of space on a containership, and
- liability of a line as owner etc. of a containership or container arising due to the fault of another line as co-charterer of space on a containership.

In each case the liability of the line which is at fault is limited to what it can recover from third parties. The implications of this sub-clause can best be illustrated on the basis of an example involving a fictitious consortium consisting of four lines which are hereinafter identified as lines A, B, C and D.

Suppose line A and line B are co-charterers of space on a containership belonging to line C. A's goods leak, due to improper packaging by A's customer, damaging B's cargo whilst on board the containership, making it unstable so that it explodes, whilst the containership is berthed at a terminal, damaging the containership, third party property and a container belonging to line B itself. Lines B and C can only recover from A:

(a) in respect of the damage to the containership and the container; and

(b) in respect of any liability of line B or C to third parties;

to the extent that line A can recover from its customer.

If the explosion occurs after unloading whilst the container is in a terminal stack, causing damage to equipment belonging to a third party, then line B can only recover from line A, in respect of line B's liability to the owner of the damaged equipment, to the extent of line A's recovery from its customer.

It will be noted that this clause only covers matters arising from co-chartering (it does not, in consequence, cover hiring of space in a container which is covered in the containerspace hiring agreement). Therefore it applies to accidents occurring on board the containership or during loading or discharging operations. Additionally the waiver of recourse provision will include accidents occurring ashore, provided the causes of such events were set on board the containership.

However, this clause will not cover such cases where the accident occurred and the causes of which were set on land and thus outside the sphere of the containership. The reason for this distinction follows from the characteristics of the joint trade being restricted to the joint utilisation of the containership, whereas land activities are carried out by each line on an independent basis outside the operational scope of the consortium.

Sub-clauses (2) and (3) relate to cargo claims and incorporate the same waiver of recourse provisions in respect of such claims as sub-clause (1) does in respect of the charterer's liability. It also incorporates the chain of indemnities, which extends to lines the protection already given to servants, agents and sub-contractors of the principal carrier, against claims by customers, which they might initiate against any line not being the principal carrier, in order to circumvent exemptions from, and limitations of liability available to the principal carrier under his bill of lading.

This indemnity is unlimited, unless a responsible line (*see* sub-clauses (4), (5) and (6)) can be identified and that responsible line is not also the principal carrier (in which case the principal carrier's obligation to indemnify the other line shall be limited to what the principal carrier can recover from his customer). The intention of this qualification is that, if the chain of indemnities fails to operate, an innocent line being sued by a customer in tort shall have the chance of full recovery from the responsible line under sub-clause (4). However, if no responsible line can be found, it is felt to be appropriate that financial responsibility be borne by the principal carrier, as the party who is most closely connected (albeit innocently) with the damage and who is, in any event, properly insured, otherwise there is a risk that an innocent line, faced with a claim from cargo interests, would not be able to obtain full recourse if the chain of indemnities was for any reason ineffective.

In the example set out in explaining sub-clause (1) above, the owner of the goods being carried by line B as principal carrier is supposed only to sue line B and, if in practice he sues line A, line B must indemnify line A against that claim. Considering that the damage originated from line A's goods, A falls under the definition of a responsible line as per sub-clause (6)(3) (determined in accordance with the order of priorities set out in that sub-clause (6)). Consequently line B's obligation to indemnify A is subject to the qualification to the extent that line B can recover from his customer. If such recovery actions fail, the responsible line A has to bear the loss alone.

The same result would be achieved if the customer decided to sue the innocent line D on the basis of joint and several liability. In the first instance line D would seek indemnification from the principal carrier B. This indemnification, however, would again be subject to line B being able to recover from his customer. In case line B would not recover from his customer, line D could claim against line A as the responsible line under sub-clause (4).

The objective behind sub-clauses (1), (2) and (3) is to reduce the need for the lines to carry double insurance and in particular charterers liability insurance. Additionally it extends the scope of the chain of indemnities to all lines utilising space on board the containership. This objective has been explained earlier.

Sub-clauses (4) and (5) provide a "fall-back" position for all third party claims (including cargo claims) not covered by sub-clauses (1)–(3).

As explained above, the waiver of recourse provisions contained in sub-clause (1) are inapplicable in relation to accidents occurring and having been caused ashore. Thus, if in the example referred to above, where the explosion was assumed to have arisen on land, the leak had also occurred ashore, the responsible line A would have been liable with the resulting obligation to indemnify line D for the third party claims by the owners of the damaged equipment.

In connection with cargo claims this sub-clause is intended to channel the ultimate liability to the responsible line if the mechanism of the indemnity under sub-clause (3), as explained above, fails to operate. Thus, if, for instance, the innocent line D could not recover from the principal carrier B under the indemnity set out in (3), it could then fall back upon the responsible line A and recover from the latter in full under sub-clause (4).

Sub-clauses (4) and (5) are also designed to prevent a line, which has no real connection with a claim, suffering the effect of that claim simply because, in a particular jurisdiction, the liability of the line is considered to be joint and several because of the relationship being considered to be akin to a partnership and the claimant, for some reason (perhaps because that line has its head office in the country concerned), elects to sue that line alone. If in such event the owner of the damaged equipment should decide to sue the innocent line D, then the responsible line A would be under an obligation to indemnify line D. In case the responsible line A would be unable to pay the claim, it would be borne by all lines according to their trade shares. The same applies if, in a given case, no responsible line can be identified.

In the example quoted above it is clear which is the "responsible line". However, it may not always be so clear and accordingly it is necessary to provide a mechanism for determining which line is "responsible" and sub-clause (6) sets out such a mechanism in the order of priorities. Paragraph (2) of this sub-clause may not be appropriate if, for example, a line introduces containers into a pool for the benefit of all lines and then has no further maintenance obligations in respect of such containers.

Reference in the clause to (even if such liability arises wholly or in part by reason of the act, neglect or default of that line or its servants, agents or sub-contractors) arises from a need identified in the English decision in *Smith and Anor.* v. *South Wales Switchgear* [1978] 1 W.L.R. 165, in which it was held that, unless by its terms it is clearly applicable even in the event of negligence, an indemnity applies only in the absence thereof (the *contra proferentem* principle).

Whilst the mutual waiver clause attempts to provide a formula applicable in all situations and to leave little room for manoeuvre, drafters found that a total formula was impossible, hence the use of the word "reasonable" in the clause. Readers will appreciate that interpretation of "reasonable" is very subjective but no clearer approach appeared to be available.

It is vital to the effective operation of the Mutual Waiver clause that all the lines have suitable clauses to link with it in all their other contracts, thereby preserving the chain of indemnities.

Having outlined the approach and thinking behind this major liability component in consortium operation, it is now time to move on and consider the other potential contents of a typical operating agreement.

OPERATING AGREEMENTS: GENERAL

There is no such thing as a standard operating agreement. Each one varies according to the requirements of the parties. However, they frequently follow a pattern of topics, even if how they deal with those topics differs.

Some call them "Operating Agreement" whilst others prefer "Vessel Sharing Agreement" or some other similar name. Some prefer to roll the operating agreement and slot charter party into one contract. It can be done, but it complicates matters to deal with bi-party matters in the same contract as multi-party matters. As the two contract approach is recommended, this book will concentrate on that form of presentation.

Preamble

Most agreements start with a preamble, in which the parties and their intentions are outlined: a "vision statement" as it is called in one agreement I have seen.

Definitions

As in the bill of lading contract (*see* Chapter 7), carriers find it convenient to define certain key words to carry a wider than usual meaning (when used with (say) the first letter as a capital) and certain jargon. This avoids a listing in clauses, which often detracts from the ease of understanding when reading the contract.

Period of Agreement

If one thing is certain these days, it is that change is continual and proceeds in different directions at different speeds for different companies. Specialist multi-million dollar vessels (which have a lifespan of 25–30 years) are ordered on the basis of agreements for their employment, so it is important that lines agree on a period for the consortium contract to run, after which it can be reviewed and renewed, with or without changes in the light of developments since the last agreement was signed, or terminated, with the constituent lines going off to form new consortia with other operators.

There are also usually provisions to cover the situation where a consortium member gets taken over by another line, who may not be a member of the consortium and may even be a member of a rival consortium.

Trading Areas/Scope

It is important that the scope of the agreement is carefully defined to ensure a common view and interpretation of it by all parties. For example, some members of a consortium may operate in several adjacent (or even overlapping) trades and the scope of the consortium operation may be only one of those trades. It may be that a line continues to operate passenger or break-bulk services in an area covered by the consortium.

It is common to have an undertaking by all lines that all their cargoes/containers carried within a defined trade area shall be carried only on vessels operating in the consortium.

It is also common to have a provision that the consortium operation starts upon disengaging twistlocks as a container is lifted into stow and finishes upon engaging twistlocks ready for discharge, as most consortium operations are FIOS (free in, out and stow) based. This means that, so far as terminal contracts are concerned, the owner contracts with the terminals to berth the vessel and handle any hatch moves, whilst each principal carrier (one who has issued a contract of carriage as a principal to the owner of the goods) or slot charterer contracts with the terminal for the handling (receipt, packing, checking, storage, loading, stowing, unstowing, moving, unpacking, delivery, cleaning etc.) of all containers and goods for which he is the principal carrier. If (as happens in some ports) a terminal operator will deal only with one party per vessel, the agreement will usually provide that, in engaging with the terminal for the handling of the slot charterer's containers and cargo, the owner acts as agent only without liability.

Sometimes a topic is considered so important, but likely to need changes to cope with changing circumstances, that parts of it are shown as an appendix at the end, rather than entered in detail in the main contract. As such it is more easily amended. Trading areas and scope may well be just such a topic. For example, details of the ports of call and the frequency of the service can change as requirements change within the trade. For this reason, they are often shown as an appendix at the end to facilitate alteration as a trade develops (or declines), without the need to change the main body of the agreement.

Conference

Some agreements provide for all members of the consortium to be members of the relevant conference to prevent competition on the basis of sea freight costs. It would be unusual (but not unheard of) to encounter a consortium with a mixture of conference and non-conference members. They are usually all one or the other.

Service Details

Service details is another topic which is frequently partly dealt with as a separate appendix, because of the likelihood of the need for change. Few trades remain static, they grow, shrink, change and develop in ways requiring reaction by the carriers in that trade. Trade is affected by a myriad of matters: politics, good/bad harvests, competition from other trades in the same commodity, competition from newcomer carriers in the trade etc. Representatives of the members, who come together to operate the consortium, have to consult regularly, look into their crystal balls and guess what is going to happen in the near future. They then have to ensure that the consortium is in a position to deal with/profit from it. If they guess wrong, urgent last minute changes have to be agreed, which may be expensive and difficult, particularly if all members are not similarly affected, so that their best interests are represented by different courses of action, an urgent decision is required and agreement is difficult.

Tonnage

One of the most important areas of discussion in any consortium centres around the ideal specification of tonnage for the trade and the number of vessels needed in order to provide the frequency of service required. Having considered the ideal situation, a compromise then has to be made in the light of what is available by way of tonnage owned by the members or available in the chartering market. It then has to be decided how many vessels each member of the consortium will provide to cover his share of the trade and whether or not he has vessels available which meet the required specification (capacity, speed, reefer facilities, gear/ungeared etc.) or which are acceptable to the consortium in lieu thereof. Tonnage is usually provided by members in accordance with their share of the trade but, of course, this can never bring about a precise provision and there will always be situations where members are either over-providers or under-providers. This is compensated for in financial adjustment.

If a member with a commitment to provide tonnage does not have suitable tonnage he must charter to meet his obligation to provide tonnage. It is not unknown for this to be done by chartering from another consortium partner, who has spare tonnage. This can considerably complicate the chain of indemnity situation and it may be worthwhile providing a short basic demonstration of what can happen in such circumstances.

Consider line A charters vessel X from its consortium colleague line B to meet its commitment to provide tonnage to the consortium. The charter is an "arms'-length" time charter under which all cargo on the vessel is deemed to be charterers' cargo, so far as the owner is concerned and, of course, it would be most unusual for an arms'-length time charter to incorporate any mutual waiver. Line A then makes space available on vessel X to line B (i.e. line B slot charters space on his own vessel). Cargo from a line B container leaks and contaminates vessel X and all cargo/containers on board. Line B sues line A under the time charter for ship damage (even though it is his cargo which has caused the damage). Additionally other member lines sue line A for cargo/container damage under the slot charter party. Line A holds line B liable for damage under the slot charter party, which is subject to a mutual waiver clause, and line B genuinely cannot recover from a third party. The result is that line A's P & I and SOL covers take a hammering as line A has to meet all of the claims! (The actual case was even more complicated than this, on account of a late discovery of the pollution in the vessel's hold, so that there was damage to a part of the homeward cargo. Also line B's P & I cover as owner and as slot charterer were with different P & I clubs. Detailed discussion of how this affects matters is too mind blowing to set out here!)

Provision may also be made for changes in the required fleet by replacement, increase or decrease in tonnage to meet changing trade requirements. Old ships need to be replaced (perhaps with larger and faster as well as newer models) and agreement needs to be reached on the approach if the fleet size changes. Are vessels committed to the consortium long term and thus chartered out by it if withdrawn from service (so that owners receive remuneration as per operating agreement and the consortium receives the hire from the chartering out) or is there a formula to ascertain who must withdraw their vessel if requirement decreases and to provide the additional vessel (as owner or disponent owner) if it increases. In the latter case (particularly if the increase is for a short period) one line may contract as agent for all consortium members in entering into a joint charter on behalf of all lines.

The clause also addresses the subject of off hire in the event of breakdown/repairs, planned maintenance/dry docking, blocking and trapping, failure to maintain schedule etc. according to the diktat of the trade.

As can be appreciated, this clause is frequently a long and detailed one addressing, as it has to, a long list of potential situations for which provision needs to be made.

Trade Shares

There is usually a clear link between trade shares and the provision of tonnage but this link can never be precise, so that there will always be a financial adjustment to be made for over-/underprovision of space. Provision needs to be made as to how much space/how many slots/how much deadweight (or any combination of all three) is to be available on each vessel to each principal carrier/slot charterer. On any one voyage there may be a general overdemand for space, in which case every line gets only its allocation. There may be a general underdemand, in which case every line gets all of its cargo and containers carried but gets no credit for space unused and must pay for all slots to which it is entitled, even though it has not used them all. If some lines need extra space and others have spare space, there needs to be a formula as to how spare space is allocated out, who pays what and who gets what. Like many other complicated clauses, this one may be supported by a detailed appendix.

Financial Arrangements

Like most companies these days, carriers are mostly run by accountants, so that the financial arrangements tend to be of the variety that would give Einstein a headache and make the average person's eyes revolve like a fruit machine! For these reasons I have quite deliberately stayed well away from this aspect of any contract in which I have been involved. Suffice it to say that such arrangements are detailed and complicated and usually take up a substantial amount of space in the contract and appendices and usually contain a variety of formulae to calculate inter-line indebtedness.

Containers

There is usually a clause to control the specification of containers which slot charterers may present to owners for carriage under the terms of the operating agreement. It frequently reads as follows and its terms are self-explanatory.

"The lines shall only introduce into or use in the service Containers which are:

(1) of a specification approved by ISO standards;
(2) physically compatible with the Containerships;
(3) properly maintained;
(4) in compliance with relevant port and other safety regulations (including quarantine regulations, Container Safety Convention);
(5) constructed of taint free materials; and
(6) free from defect in construction.

The Containership Operator may refuse to carry any Container which does not comply with the above requirements.

In the interests of economy and efficiency lines will liaise on Container requirements and, wherever possible, assist each other by a line with surplus Containers at any location hiring the same to another line with a local shortage. Whenever such hiring shall take place, it shall be effected upon the terms of the Container Hiring Agreement attached hereto."

Break-bulk, Oversize and Dangerous Cargoes

This is essentially a slot charter party item but mention is often made of it in the operating agreement as a matter of policy.

Whilst the service is primarily for the carriage of containerised goods, it is usual to carry large oversize/uncontainerable items, which are, in practice, usually lashed to a, or a series of, flat tracks on deck. They count as the number of slots into which their bulk impinges, sideways and upwards and, frequently being very heavy items, they have to be stowed on the hatch and not at the top of the deck stack (stowing heavies over lights is forbidden for stability reasons) so that overstowage is not possible, thereby losing space above. Such cargoes are frequently stowed in the centre of the stack for stability reasons and because the containers stowed around them offer protection from the elements. Clearly such items create problems for ship stowage planners and require adequate prior notice and acceptance from the owner's planner before they can be offered for shipment.

Similar considerations apply to dangerous goods as the ship planner must ensure that dangerous goods from all of the slot charterers and his own company are co-ordinated in stow so as to comply with the IMO IMDG Code.

Animals may also be carried on converted flat racks, subject to such requirements as the owner may determine, which will inevitably cover the handling services required by the animal(s). These may be provided by the crew (for a consideration) or by a supernumerary handler provided by the shipper.

Administration

According to its size and complexity, a consortium may be administered by a separate COU (Central Operating Unit) which keeps the records to determine who owes what to who, plans the stowage and programming of all consortium vessels and generally provides a back-up service to consortium members. COU's were quite common in the early days but nowadays it is more common to find such matters handled "in-house", with each carrier planning his own stow and various committees from the member lines meeting regularly to thrash out the problems over financial matters, programming of the vessels/voyages etc.

Terminals

Whilst it is not essential, it is clearly highly desirable that all lines in a consortium should berth their containerships at the same terminal in any given port. If more than one terminal is used, merchants/hauliers etc. would not know which one to go to collect or deliver cargo and confusion would reign.

Some carriers have interests in certain terminals in their home (and sometimes some other) ports and would naturally prefer to use them. It is usual to provide that this is allowed, provided that the preferred terminal's services and rates are competitive with its rivals in the port concerned and any nearby port serving the same area.

Speed of working, rates and a berth guarantee to ensure that the berth is available to the containership when it arrives are all important. Containerships cannot afford to waste time at a berth with poor turnaround times that cannot guarantee an available berth and adequate labour when required.

Additional Parties

Sometimes a philosophy on whether or not (and if so on what terms) additional lines may be admitted to the consortium is included in the operating agreement.

Non-assignment/Confidentiality

It is also usual to preclude assignment of rights and/or obligations under the agreement to anyone (sometimes excluding subsidiaries and parent companies) without the prior approval of the other members (sometimes not to be unreasonably withheld). In these days where rationalisation and takeover are common, this is yet another attempt to preserve the integrity and confidentiality of the consortium's operations from competitors. This is often reinforced by a confidentiality clause.

Relationships with Outside Consortia/Lines

This might cover the policy of selling spare space to outsiders. Is it allowed by individual lines or must it be done on a consortium basis, even though the contract of carriage has to be issued by an individual line for insurance purposes? (Only an owner has P & I cover for a contract of carriage (other than as a principal carrier in a bill of lading) and one line has to issue a contract of carriage as a consortium is usually not a legal entity and has no cover or capacity to contract independently of its members. It can merely bind them jointly and severally.)

Conversely, what happens if there is a shortage of space on any sailing? Can individual lines, or the consortium as a whole, buy space from a competitor with space available on a timely sailing, if the gap to the next consortium sailing is too long (end of month "shipped on board" requirement by shippers may feature in such decisions)?

Force Majeure

The definition of force majeure, like beauty, is in the eye of the beholder, so operating agreements frequently attempt to define the circumstances in which this defence is applicable and to control its application by providing a formula for when force majeure becomes frustration of contract.

Language

English being the commercial Esperanto, most international trade contracts are in English and provision is often made for all notices, communications and other writings relevant to the agreement to be in English. As consortia are frequently constructed from carriers of differing nationalities, it can be important to provide for the official medium for communication.

Law and Arbitration

For the same reason, most agreements are interpreted according to English law and provision is made for arbitration in London, often in accordance with the terms of the LMAA (London Maritime Arbitration Association). Sometimes New York Arbitration is preferred but US jurisdiction is not popular, on account of the arrangement of the judiciary there, so that maritime/commercial matters can often be heard by judges with little or no maritime/commercial expertise. In contrast, in the UK, courts are divided into divisions so that commercial matters are heard in a Commercial Court and maritime matters in an Admiralty Court.

Sundry Clauses

In addition to the above, operating agreements will inevitably have a sprinkling of other clauses, covering minor matters or matters specific to that agreement which fall outside the main headings. Minor matters often covered include, *inter alia*:

- Notices: how to give them and when they are deemed served.
- Enforceability: only any invalid part not enforceable, the rest of the contract stands.
- Disclaimer of partnership: this is not necessarily effective in all jurisdictions, where it is the method of operation rather than any statement which determines how the law interprets this.
- Interpretation: in the event of conflict between the agreement and any appendix, which one prevails.

CHAPTER 3

SLOT CHARTERS

INTRODUCTION

There are various types of slot charter, according to the nature of usage intended:

- *Cross Charter Parties*: These are charters, primarily designed to cover liability matters, but including brief reference to operational matters to allow them to be a free-standing contract, which form an appendix to an operating agreement in a consortium operation. They usually incorporate a mutual waiver provision.
- *Slot Sales Charter Parties:* These may vary in approach according to the circumstances.
  - (1) Where a disponent owner has procured space via a cross charter party which permits him to sub-contract, he may sub-contract on identical terms to those under which he obtained space (minus the mutual waiver provision) to create a back-to-back situation.
  - (2) A non-consortium operator may make space available to an NVOCC on the standard SLOTHIRE terms.
  - (3) A consortium operator, seeking to ensure that he has the benefit of global limitation in the event of a catastrophe on a feeder vessel, may seek to introduce a feeder slot charter party into his relationship with his feeder operators.

CROSS CHARTER PARTIES

This form of charter party is used within a consortium operation to govern the relationship between the (disponent) owner and slot charterer but not relationships between co-charterers. Its essential feature is mutuality, in that each party to it knows that he will be in the other position as often as he is in the position in which he currently finds himself. Thus, in negotiating such a charter, there is no point in trying to achieve a charterer-favourable or an owner-favourable position, because the party concerned will be on the other side of the fence on other occasions. Accordingly, parties can concentrate on producing a fair contract which minimises insurance costs and inter-line claims, which might create bad feeling.

A typical cross charter party may contain the following provisions. After an introduction to identify the owners, charterers and containership the first clause is usually:

1. Space Allocation and Period

"The Owners let and the Charterers hire for the carriage of goods and containers _____ per cent of the container carrying capacity of the Containership by reference to TEU capacity and deadweight, whichever is reached first, (or more or less as may be agreed for each voyage) from _______________ until _______________ and thereafter unless and until terminated by either party giving _____ months' notice in writing."

This clause is fairly self-explanatory. Note that this particular clause gives the charterers a percentage of the space by TEU or deadweight. It might do so by reference to a number of TEUs with a maximum deadweight (draft can sometimes be a problem) instead. In this form the slot charter is of the time variety but it could equally be for voyage or a number of voyages.

2. Employment

"2.1 The Containership shall be employed only in lawful trades within the Institute Warranty Limits for the carriage of lawful goods, properly packed and stowed in seaworthy containers of standard sizes and specifications, as may be mutually agreed, between good and safe ports, where it can safely lie always afloat, save that uncontainerised and out of gauge goods may be carried, but only with the prior consent of the Owners. If accepted, such items shall be carried under the terms of this Charter party but subject to such additional conditions as the Owners may require.

Goods which are of a dangerous, inflammable, radio-active, obnoxious or damaging nature shall not be shipped unless:

(a) prior written notice of their nature has been given to the Owners by or on behalf of the Charterers (including particulars of the characteristics of the goods, the flash point (if any), the type of packing of the goods and any other information which the Owners may reasonably require); and
(b) the Owners have consented, after receipt of such notice, to accept those goods for shipment; and
(c) all the relevant requirements and recommendations of the International Maritime Organisation and the law and regulations in force in the country of registration of the Containership, the port of shipment, the port of discharge, any area through which the Containership may pass and any scheduled port of call have been complied with; and
(d) the goods shall have been packed, labelled and stowed within the containers and the containers have been labelled in accordance with such law, regulations, requirements or recommendations and, in any event, so as to avoid such goods causing damage, injury or material discomfort to the Containership, crew and other goods and to any other property or person.

Live animals shall not be shipped, except by special arrangement with the Owners and then on no liability terms.

2.2 If the requirements of sub-clause 2.1 are not complied with, the Charterers shall, to the extent provided in sub-clause 10.9, indemnify the Owners against all loss, damage or expense arising out of the goods being tendered for shipment or being handled or carried by the Owners.

2.3 Goods which, in the opinion of the Owners, are or may at any time become dangerous, inflammable, radio-active, obnoxious, damaging or injurious may, at any time or place, be unloaded, destroyed, or rendered harmless, without compensation to the Charterers and without liability to make any general average contribution in respect of such goods."

Sub-paragraph 2.1 is a typical charter party clause, found in most charter parties, that starts to lay out the ground rules as to what cargoes can be carried and the trading parameters of the containership. In short, the charterers have minimal control over the containership's movements, so that there is need only for the most superficial references to trading area and ship movement here, these being matters dealt with in more detail in the operating agreement, where the route, speed, scheduling of the containership etc. are controlled.

Trading is restricted to Institute Warranty Limits (IWL), so as not to compromise merchants' cargo insurance, and cargo is generally restricted to carriage in ISO compliant containers.

By and large the charterers may, within their allocation of space (TEUs) and weight, carry any containerised cargo they choose except for:

- out of gauge goods;
- dangerous, inflammable, radio-active, obnoxious or goods of a damaging nature (note this clearly goes well beyond the IMO IMDG dangerous goods category);
- live animals (note if accepted, carried on no liability terms as allowed in the Hague/Hague-Visby Rules).

Out of gauge goods are awkward and cause problems to ship planners. Dangerous etc. goods may need special stowage, so as to comply with regulations and declarations at ports or canals etc. en route. Live animals are always unpredictable and vulnerable. Accordingly, owners are entitled to prior notice if such cargoes are to be offered and entitled to refuse them if they so choose.

Note that in 2.1(d) (dangerous goods) packing has to be such "as to avoid such goods causing damage, injury or material discomfort to the Containership, crew and other goods and to any other property or person", quite a wide coverage.

Sub-paragraph 2.2: failure to obtain the prior approval, as required in 2.1, results in the charterers having to indemnify the owners, but only to the extent provided in the mutual waiver in clause 10.9. This is because (as explained under this heading in Chapter 2), unless a waiver is total, there is a residual liability, so that the object of minimising insurance costs is defeated.

Sub-paragraph 2.3: this is a usual right retained by owners over goods which preserves to them the option to decide if goods are or are likely to become dangerous etc. and to take such steps as they consider appropriate.

3. Remuneration

"The Owners shall be remunerated in accordance with the provisions from time to time separately agreed or, in default of agreement, shall receive such remuneration as shall be fair and reasonable."

This is not a matter dealt with in the cross charter party and this clause is included merely to ensure that all the necessary constituents of a contract are present: offer, acceptance and consideration.

4. Owners' Expenses

"Save as provided in sub-clause 10.7, the Owners shall pay all wages, insurance premiums, charges, dues, taxes, agencies, commissions, fees and all other expenses whatsoever incurred in connection with the operation of the Containership."

A cross charter party is an FIOS (free in, out and stow) contract, so that all the costs of operating the containership are borne by the owners. In this context it is more like a voyage than a time charter. As can be seen by referring to the comment on sub-clause 10.7, which is excluded, the cargo/container handling costs at the terminals are for the charterers' account.

5. Voyage and Destination

"5.1 The itinerary of each voyage shall be mutually agreed between the Owners and the Charterers.
5.2 The Owners shall be entitled to exercise the liberties to deviate provided in the Hague Rules at any time without prior notice to the Charterers. However, if during the course of a voyage the Owners should deviate in circumstances which under English law does not permit the Charterers to deviate under the Hague Rules, the Owners shall indemnify the Charterers for any liability thereby incurred, unless the Owners shall have obtained the prior consent of the Charterers to such deviation, in which case this indemnity shall not operate. Any deviation agreed by the line's representatives in the Operating Committee shall be deemed to have the prior consent of the Charterers.
5.3 Subject as may be otherwise agreed, the Owners shall have the liberty to take the Containership out of service for maintenance and repairs. In arranging such periods the Owners will take account of the Charterers' requirements so far as is possible."

Sub-paragraph 5.1: This is the extent of the charterers' control over the operation of the containership which is covered in greater detail in the operating agreement.

Sub-paragraph 5.2: This is the deviation clause. As the deviation provisions in both the Hague and Hague-Visby Rules are identical, reference to just the Hague Rules suffices.

It is possible for the provisions of this sub-clause to be expressed in two ways, according to whether it is wished to give the ultimate control to the owners or to the charterers. The clause shown here gives it to the charterers by putting the owners in breach unless they get the charterers' prior approval to any deviation. An alternative, which would give the owners the ultimate control, would provide instead for the owners merely to give (say) 24/48 hours' prior notice to the charterers.

The purpose of requiring the obtaining of approval or the giving of notice is to give charterers the opportunity to decide whether or not they consider the deviation being undertaken puts them in breach of their contract of carriage with their customers and thus their P & I cover, thereby necessitating SOL cover, so that a declaration may need to be made against their annual SOL policy. Such decisions are difficult, because most deviation decisions in the courts are BC (before containers) and thus, what was a deviation in a conventional service, where changes of voyage and transhipment were rare, is not necessarily so in a containerised "hub and spoke" style of operation, where changes are so much more common and a "custom of the trade". Different countries' laws view this differently, so different charterers may take a different view of any particular deviation.

Decisions to deviate are frequently taken by the operating committee of the consortium (e.g. miss a port to get back on schedule and tranship cargo for the omitted port) in the mutual interest. If such deviations are agreed in discussion with the other lines, they are deemed to have those lines' prior consent (although the operating agreement may penalise owners by putting them "off hire" if the reason for the containership being behind schedule is their fault, according to the formula in the operating agreement).

Sub-paragraph 5.3: Again, a point usually covered in greater detail in the operating agreement but briefly referred to here so as to make this a free-standing contract.

6. Opening Containers

"The Owners shall be entitled, at any time (but under no obligation), to open any container or package and to inspect the contents at the Owners' expense and shall promptly notify the Charterers if they do so.
Containers opened must be properly closed and sealed and records maintained, which must be available to the Charterers. The Owners must advise the Charterers promptly in writing of the replacement seal number."

As the safety of the vessel must always be the master's primary consideration, he must always have the right to inspect any cargo, in case he suspects that something is wrong. Equally, from a liability point of view, charterers have to deliver containers with the seal intact or account therefor to the customer. This clause is designed to meet the requirements of both parties in a mutually satisfactory fashion.

7. Access to Logs

"The Master and Engineer shall keep full and correct logs and adequate records concerning the care and condition of the containers and the goods and all the logs and records relevant to the voyage, the containers and the goods shall be accessible to the Charterers.
The Owners will co-operate with the Charterers to assist them to identify witnesses and obtain statements in respect of any incident during the currency of this Charterparty which gives rise to a claim against the Charterers."

In dealing with cargo claims for damage (and sometimes loss) of cargo in containers (or even perhaps loss of whole containers overboard!), charterers are always going to need access to the containership's records and sometimes also to the crew for statements. This clause provides for the owners to facilitate this but makes no mention of timescale. If a containership berthed after suffering a heavy casualty, it is unlikely that the owners would allow the charterers to have immediate access to records and crew until they had finished their own investigations (although in some states, like the US, they may not be able to prevent it).

8. Charterers Obligations

"8.1 The Charterers shall provide such information in relation to any goods shipped under this Charterparty as the Owners may reasonably require in connection with this Charterparty, and the Charterers warrant such information shall be complete and accurate.
8.2 The Charterers shall comply with the directions of the Master or other persons responsible for the stowage on behalf of the Owners as to when and where containers are to be stowed. The Charterers shall, in their capacity as such, be under no liability in respect of the consequences of complying with such directions, notwithstanding the provisions of sub-clause 10.7, and the Owners shall indemnify the Charterers against the same.
8.3 Any liability of the Charterers arising from their obligations under this clause 8 shall be subject to sub-clause 10.9."

Sub-paragraph 8.1: As members of a consortium compete for business amongst themselves, as well as with members of other consortia, manifest data is a highly sensitive matter and jealously guarded. However, the owners have need of certain information and this clause provides for the charterers to provide it. This information usually includes:

- any information required under clause 2;
- any special stowage requirement (on/under deck);
- container weight (to facilitate draft, trim and torsional moment calculations); and sometimes
- a brief description of cargo.

The charterers have to warrant the completeness and accuracy of this information but, in 8.3, this warranty is subject to the mutual waiver.

Sub-paragraph 8.2: Being an FIOS charter, the charterers are responsible for the loading, discharge and handling of their containers and cargo. (The containership's responsibility starts at disengaging twistlocks on loading and finishes upon engaging twistlocks on discharge.)

Despite the provisions of sub-clause 10.7, the charterers are not under any liability arising from the consequences of following the owners' instructions regarding stowage and the owners indemnify the charterers accordingly.

Sub-paragraph 8.3: This subjects charterers' liabilities to owners (but not owners' liabilities to charterers) throughout the clause to the mutual waiver provision in sub-clause 10.9.

9. Indemnity and Agency

"9.1 The Charterers undertake that no claim or allegation shall be made against the Owners or any servant, agent or sub-contractor of the Owners by any person whomsoever, other than the Charterers, which imposes or attempts to impose upon the Owners, or any such servant, agent or sub-contractor or any Containership owned by any of them, any liability whatsoever in connection with the goods and containers the subject of this Charterparty (even if such liability arises wholly or in part by reason of the act, neglect or default of the Owners or of such servant, agent or sub-contractor) and, in the event of any such claim or allegation nevertheless being made, the Charterers shall (to the extent provided in sub-clause 10.9) indemnify the Owners and such servant, agent and sub-contractor against all consequences whatsoever thereof.
9.2 The Charterers shall not make any claim or allegation against any servant, agent or sub-contractor of the Owners which imposes or attempts to impose on any such servant, agent or sub-contractor any liability whatsoever in connection with the goods and containers the subject of this Charterparty (even if such liability arises wholly or in part by reason of the act, neglect or default of the Owners or such servant, agent or sub-contractor) and, in the event of any such claim or allegation nevertheless being made, the provisions of sub-clause 9.1 shall apply as if such claim or allegation had been made by a person other than the Charterers.
9.3 Without prejudice to sub-clause 9.1, the Owners authorise and empower the Charterers to act as the Owners' agent and/or trustees to stipulate for the Owners to have, as against other persons, the benefit of any immunities, exemptions or liberties regarding the goods and containers the subject of this Charterparty or their carriage, but the Charterers shall have no authority to make any contracts imposing any obligations upon the Owners in connection with the goods and containers or their carriage."

We now start to come to the all important liability and indemnity provisions that are the principal raison d'être of this contract. In short, sub-clause 9.1 says charterers undertake that no claims will be made against owners or their servants, agents or sub-contractors by anyone other than themselves. In sub-clause 9.2 they undertake not to claim against owners' servants, agents or sub-contractors (thus leaving the only course of action as by charterers against owners under the cross charter party contract), whilst in 9.3 owners appoint charterers as their agents, with the restricted right to give owners the benefit of the protection in their contract of carriage (Himalaya/circular indemnity clause in the bill of lading forms the link in the chain of indemnity in that contract) and specifically excludes them from any right of agency to enter into any contract imposing any obligations upon the owners.

This is an indemnity clause, so the references, in brackets, to (even if such liability arises) an agent or a sub-contractor are necessary to overcome the decision in *Smith and Anor.* v. *South Wales Switchgear* [1978] 1 W.L.R. 165 in which it was held that indemnities apply only in the absence of negligence, unless they make it absolutely clear that they apply even in the event of negligence. However, the indemnity is subject to the mutual waiver and the charterers are liable only to the extent that they can recover from a third party.

"9.4 Sub-clauses 9.1 and 9.2 shall not apply to or preclude any claim made by the owners of any property on board the Containership for a General Average contribution in accordance with the York-Antwerp Rules 1994, unless any subsequent modification

thereto is approved by the CMI, in which case the latter shall apply.
9.5 If the Owners are not the actual owners of the Containership, the provisions of sub-clauses 9.1, 9.2 and 9.3 shall also apply to the actual owners of the Containership, their servants, agents and sub-contractors in the same manner as they apply to the Owners, their servants, agents and sub-contractors."

Sub-clause 9.4 places general average outside the protection given in sub-clauses 9.1 and 9.2.

Sub-clause 9.5 covers the situation where the owners are disponent owners only and extends the protection of the clause to the actual owners as well. Without this charterers could proceed in tort against the actual owners, who may then have a counterclaim against the owners under a time charter, thereby circumventing the indemnity. The charterers do warrant no claims "by any person whomsoever" in 9.1, but 9.5 reinforces this point.

10. Responsibilities, Liabilities and Exemptions

"Without prejudice to the provisions of clauses 2, 8 and 9 hereof, as between the Owners and the Charterers, the responsibilities arising out of and in connection with this Charterparty shall be borne and divided as follows:"

Instead of trying to divide it into owners'/charterers' liabilities, as in BOXTIME, the cross charter party prefers to deal with them all together in one clause.

"10.1 The Owners will be responsible for the seaworthiness of the Containership in accordance with Article III, Rule 1 and Article IV, Rule 1 of the Hague Rules as scheduled to the Carriage of Goods by Sea Act 1924 and for all purposes in connection with this Charterparty shall be entitled to the rights and immunities set out in Article IV, Rules 2, 4 and 6 of said Hague Rules."

The general approach to liability in the cross charter party is that, to the extent that loss, damage or delay occurs and can be shown to have occurred during the currency of the cross charter party, the liability of the owners to the charterers should be identical to the liability of the charterers to their customers under their contracts of carriage. However, as not all consortium members' bill of lading contracts are identical and some provide more protection than others, it was not felt equitable to make this provision in the cross charter party in as many words. Rather, it was felt, the cross charter party should provide a reasonable level of recourse and then, if any charterers' contract provided for something more generous or was in any way defective, the cost of that generosity/defect would fall upon the charterers and not upon the owners. This is in line with the philosophy that, if there is any defect in a contract or series of contracts, the effect of the defect should fall upon the party in whose contract the defect arises.

Sub-clause 10.1 applies the Hague Rules to determine the responsibilities of the owners regarding seaworthiness (Article III, Rule 1 and Article IV, Rule 1) and gives the owners the protection of Article IV, Rules 2 (Exemptions), 4 (Deviation) and 6 (Dangerous Goods). The Hague-Visby Rules made no changes in any of these rules, so reference to the Hague Rules is equally applicable where the Hague-Visby Rules apply.

"10.2 Subject to sub-clause 10.1, the Owners will be responsible for the proper and careful carriage, custody and care of the containers and goods whilst on board the Containership, and for discharging, handling and storing containers and goods discharged solely in order to be reloaded or in order to load or discharge other containers and goods, and for reloading and restowing the same."

This sub-clause repeats those parts of Article II that are relevant to the owners' responsibility under an FIOS contract, where loading, handling, stowage and discharge are the charterers' responsibilities. These responsibilities are then added back to apply in those situations where the owners land and reship containers as part of their stowage planning.

"10.3 Subject to sub-clause 10.1, the Owners shall be responsible for the provision of:
(a) electrical power;
(b) a supply of refrigerant gas; and
(c) a supply of the recommended lubricating oil;
(d) plugging in or unplugging
to integral refrigerated containers, insulated containers with marine clip-on units fitted and ventilated containers (hereinafter in this clause 'mechanical containers') containing goods shipped on the Containership.
The Owners shall use all reasonable endeavours to monitor and record the performance of all such units whilst on board and to repair and rectify any breakdown, fault or deficiency which may occur in respect of such units, using the resources on board the Containership. If such resources are insufficient the Owners, at the expense of the Charterers, shall use all reasonable endeavours promptly to obtain any required spares or specialised repair facilities. The Owners shall be liable for any loss of or damage to a mechanical container or the goods therein arising out of any breakdown, fault or deficiency of its machinery, only to the extent that such loss or damage was caused by the failure of the Owners to comply with the terms of this sub-clause. Save as expressly provided, nothing in the sub-clause shall reduce or limit the liability of the Owners to the Charterers under this Charter party."

The growing amount of refrigerated cargo moving these days makes this an area of growing concern, particularly as such carriage includes the carriage of chilled cargoes within very fine tolerances and the carriage of "controlled atmosphere" containers, in which the constitution of the atmosphere in the container is controlled to retard ripening processes. It is particularly difficult to cover this in a satisfactory way, because in most cases the container is maintained by integral machinery (i.e. the machinery maintaining temperature belongs to the charterers). Reefer containers are frequently carried on deck (sometimes not even in bottom stow) where bad weather may preclude any inspection/repairs etc. (even assuming appropriate spares are on board) and, with modern reduced manning, it cannot always be guaranteed that an engineer will be free to repair a container, even if not prevented from doing so by one of the above factors.

For these reasons great care is needed in deciding upon the terms of such a clause and, remember, each party deciding upon its terms knows full well that he will be the owners on one occasion and the charterers on another, so that there cannot be a "vested interest" approach. This is a subject which must be addressed in any charter party where reefer containers may be carried and the above is, perhaps, the most popular formula.

It lists the items that the owners must supply and undertake so that the remainder (including spares) are the responsibility of the charterers (who may put a supply of spares on board the containership). Thereafter everything is on a "reasonable endeavours" basis to take account of the various difficulties outlined above, but the owners are left with the usual Hague Rules responsibilities. However, as the machinery belongs to the charterers, these are not very onerous, beyond the responsibility to supply power and plug in.

The need for a clause like this is entirely due to the fact that the machinery is the charterers' and this situation is not envisaged by and therefore not satisfactorily covered in the Hague Rules. Note that there is no mention of insulated port-hole containers, where the containership supplies cold air. This situation is more akin to the refrigerated hold in a conventional vessel and such a situation is adequately covered in the Hague Rules and therefore dealt with elsewhere in the charter party.

"10.4 The liabilities of the Owners under sub-clauses 10.1, 10.2 and 10.3 shall be time barred absolutely 18 months after discharge of the goods from the Containership. If the Charterers receive a claim for which they intend to pursue recourse against the Owners, the Charterers shall give prompt notice thereof with full details to the Owners. Requests for extensions of time shall not be unreasonably refused."

Claims arising during the currency of the charter party may be made up to twelve months after delivery to the cargo owner against the charterers under the Hague or Hague-Visby Rules and, if such a claim is made at the last minute, the charterers need time to investigate, identify the point at which damage occurred and claim against the owners if it happened at sea. Accordingly eighteen months from discharge is allowed.

Provision is made for prompt notice and extensions of time.

This clause makes no provision for the Hamburg Rules, where the limit is two years. For this reason it might be preferable to apply the time extension by reference to "six months after the Charterers have settled (or received) the claim concerned with (from) the merchant". This would allow the same six month leeway and the prompt notice requirement would ensure that the owners were given earliest notice to investigate the claim if the "settled" rather than "received" approach was adopted.

"10.5 The liability of the Owners for any loss, damage or delay to or in connection with the goods, including containers not owned or hired by the Charterers, shall be subject to Article IV Rule 5 of the said Hague Rules, but as if no declaration as to value is made, provided always that:

(a) the liability of the Owners to the Charterers as aforesaid shall in no event exceed the liability (if any) of the Charterers to the persons interested in such goods in respect of such loss or damage;
(b) where the liability of the Owners to the Charterers and the liability of the Charterers to any other person(s) in respect of such goods are both subject to Article IV

Rule 5 of the said Hague Rules, those goods shall be deemed, as between that the Owners and the Charterers and for the purposes of the said Rule 5, to consist of the number of packages or units which is applicable for the purposes of the said Rule 5 as between the Charterers and such other person(s).

(c) where, by operation of law, the liability of the Charterers to any other person is subject to Article IV Rule 5 of the Hague Rules as amended by the Carriage of Goods by Sea Act 1971 or similar legislation (the Hague-Visby Rules), the Owners' liability to the Charterers shall be subject to Article IV Rule 5 as so amended.

(d) notwithstanding the provisions of this Charterparty elsewhere, if the liability of the Charterers to any other party for loss, damage, delay or expense to the goods and containers is governed by some other mandatory law, then the liability of the Owners to the Charterers shall be determined according to that mandatory law.

(e) in addition to liability for the claim in accordance with the provisions of this sub-clause, the Owners shall be liable for and shall reimburse the Charterers for reasonable legal and other expenses incurred by the Charterers in defending/settling claims for which the Owners are liable under the terms of this Charter party.
Except in cases of emergency, the Charterers shall consult with and obtain the Owners' prior approval to expenses which will form a part of a claim against the Owners under the provisions of this sub-clause.

(f) the Charterers do not contractually incorporate Article IX of the 1924 Hague Rules into their contracts of carriage with their cargo interests and, where such Rules are contractually applied, they limit liability to GBP 100 Sterling per package or equivalent national Hague Rules limit."

This is the quantum clause in the contract in which the amount of the owners' potential liability to the charterers is explained. The preamble makes it clear that containers owned by the charterers' customers are regarded as cargo for the purposes of this charter party and not regarded separately as containers, as is the case with the charterers' owned or hired containers. The preamble then goes on to apply the GBP100 per package limit in the Hague Rules, subject to the following provisos:

(a) Clearly the charterers can never make a profit out of a claim and only have a chose in action against the owners for whatever they have paid to their customer.

(b) This sub-clause provides that the owners will treat the charterers' LCL containers as LCLs when it comes to calculating limitation. Bearing in mind that this is a charter party and not a bill of lading, where Hague/Hague-Visby Rules may be mandatorily applied, there is freedom of contract, so that Hague Rules can be applied in an amended form by the use of appropriate wording. In an arm's-length arrangement the owners may take advantage of this to say that, as far as they are concerned, all the charterers' containers are FCLs to them and they regard the container as a package and their limit of liability is £100 per container! Accordingly this clause makes it clear that the liability of the owners to the charterers is intended to be back-to-back with the liability of the charterers to their customers when it comes to the tally upon which limitation is to be based.

(c) This sub-clause applies Hague-Visby Rules limits instead of Hague Rules limits where the liability of the charterers to their customer is mandatorily (by the operation of law) subject to the Hague-Visby Rules. Note that it must be mandatorily applicable by law. If the charterers' contract of carriage with his customer contractually applies Hague-Visby Rules, where there is no legal compulsion so to do, the charterers could not claim the benefit of this clause.

(d) To many carriers "Hamburg Rules" is a dirty word that they cannot bring themselves to utter and certainly they will do everything they can to deny such rules the "oxygen of recognition and publicity". Nevertheless they do have to recognise that, in some obscure areas, they may be subject to liability as determined by these rules. This sub-clause makes provision for just such a situation without overtly identifying the rules and preserves the back-to-back situation between the charterers and the owners if the Hamburg Rules are mandatorily applicable. Whether the wording is sufficient to cover time limits as well as defences and limits is unclear, hence my suggested alternative wording in 10.4 above.

(e) As legal fees can be expensive, this sub-clause makes it clear that they form part of the charterers' claim against the owners. So that the owners can have some degree of control over such costs, provision is made for prior consultation by the charterers with the owners whenever possible.

(f) The purpose of this sub-clause is to ensure that, if the charterers want a back-to-back recovery from the Owners, they must take all reasonable steps to protect their liability position in their contract of carriage. Article IX of the Hague Rules is known as the "gold clause" and reads: "the monetary units mentioned in these rules are to be taken to be gold value". These rules were drafted when the UK was on the gold standard and £1 = one gold sovereign. So £100 equalled 100 gold sovereigns. Today 100 gold sovereigns are worth in excess of £8,000 sterling giving a liability of +£8,000 per package!

In those countries where the 1924 Hague Rules are still in force, the legislation usually makes provision for the package limit, often in local currency. However, it is the custom of many carriers contractually to apply the Hague Rules to cover carriage from those countries with no mandatory law. If this is done merely by applying the Hague Rules (full stop), case law has shown that a liability of +£7,000 per package is applied. This can be avoided with judicious wording by incorporating the Hague Rules Articles I to VIII only and making a separate provision for the package limitation (*see* Chapter 7). Hence the requirement that, if the Charterers want back-to-back recourse, they must ensure that their contract of carriage with their customer does not in any way contractually incorporate Article IX (the gold clause of the Hague Rules) and instead provides for GBP100 Sterling or an equivalent national Hague Rules limit.

"10.6 The liability of the Owners and the Containership for any loss of or damage to or in connection with a container owned or hired by the Charterers shall not in any event exceed the cost of repair or the market value of the container at the time of such loss or damage, whichever is the lesser, and the Owners and the Containership shall not in any event be liable for any damage to a container which does not exceed US$500 on any one voyage."

The charterers' containers are part of the property for which the owners are responsible but, whilst the basis of liability is identical to that for cargo, containers are treated separately for calculating quantum in addition to the quantum for cargo.

As inter-line claims are an anathema the mutual waiver principle is partially applied to cut out claims below US$500 per container on any one voyage (franchise not deductible), on the grounds that minor damages will equal out over a period of time and high cost administration is unwarranted chasing small claims anyway.

"10.7 Subject as aforesaid and subject to sub-clause 10.9, the Charterers will be responsible for the proper and careful receipt, loading, handling, stowage/securing of goods inside containers, discharge and delivery of the goods and containers and shall pay all sums relating to such operations and shall be liable for all loss, damage (including loss of or damage to the Containership) or expense caused to the Owners by the improper or careless performance of such operations."

This clause needs to be considered in conjunction with clause 10.2, which covers the owners' part of the responsibilities put upon the carrier in Article II of the Hague Rules. These are the charterers' share of those responsibilities by reason of this being an FIOS contract.

The liability at the end of the clause (which is subject to the mutual waiver provision) links in with clause 8.

"10.8 The Charterers shall, to the extent provided in sub-clause 10.9, indemnify the Owners against any expenses, liabilities, losses, damages, claims or demands which the Owners may incur or suffer by reason of any failure to comply with any relevant laws, regulations, directions or notices of Customs, port and any other authorities, or by reason of any infestation, contamination or condemnation or damage or loss arising from any act, neglect or default of the consignors or consignees of any goods or containers, the subject of this Charterparty, their servants or agents.
The indemnity provided in this sub-clause shall extend to any loss suffered by the Owners in procuring, by whatever means the Owners consider appropriate, the release of the Containership where the Containership has been arrested either:
(a) by virtue of any act done or omitted to be done by the Charterers, or
(b) in circumstances where, but for the fact that the Containership was chartered to the Charterers, such arrest would not have occurred.
Unless the arrest follows from an event for which the Owners are responsible under this Charter party or otherwise."

This is an indemnity by the charterers to the owners (subject to the mutual waiver provision) for any expenses etc. which the owners may incur by reason of any failure on the part of the charterers and their customers.

It includes the right of the owners to take whatever steps they consider necessary to secure the release of a containership arrested by virtue of any act or omission of the charterers or in circumstances where, but for the fact that the charterers chartered space on that containership, the vessel would not have been arrested. It naturally excludes situations where the owners are at fault. In the absence of definitions sub-clause (a) is somewhat of a mouthful, rather like a conventional bill of lading clause with several lengthy lists of nouns in an effort to be all-inclusive.

"10.9

(a) The liability of the Charterers for loss, damage or delay of whatsoever nature and howsoever arising in connection with this Charter party (even if such liability arises wholly or in part by reason of the act, neglect, or default of the Charterers or their servants, agents or sub-contractors) shall not in any event exceed the amount (if any) recoverable by the Charterers from any third party in connection with such liability, but the Charterers shall take all reasonable steps (short of court action) to recover such amount and shall account therefor to the Owners. For this purpose the Charterers' insurers shall not be considered as third parties.

(b) The Charterers shall, upon the written request from the Owners, allow the Owners to take over all conduct of any enforcement of any rights which the Charterers may have against any third party to enable the Owners to exercise such rights in the Charterer's name but at the Owner's expense. The Charterers shall co-operate as much as is reasonably possible to assist the Owners to exercise such rights which the Charterers may have against the third party.

(c) If the Charterers should not be willing to transfer to the Owners all conduct of any enforcement of rights and to co-operate as required above in assisting the Owners, the provisions of sub-clause (a) shall be null and void. The Charterers shall be deemed to have shown unwillingness to transfer if they have not given the necessary authority in writing to the Owners to proceed within 30 days of receipt of a written request so to do.

Notwithstanding the above, the provisions of this sub-clause shall not operate in respect of the indemnities under sub-clause 9.1 and 10.8 where fines or other penalties have been imposed by any Customs, port or other authorities in respect of a failure to comply with the regulations relating to declaration of goods or documentation of cargo or other infringement of the law or regulations of any Customs, port or other authority. The provisions of this sub-clause shall also not operate in respect of the indemnity in sub-clause 10.8 relating to the arrest of the Containership."

This is the slot charter party version of the mutual waiver clause explained exhaustively in Chapter 2. Whilst it is still quite a long clause, it is much shorter and simpler than the operating agreement version, as it only involves two parties and does not have any co-chartering problems to consider, these having been accommodated in the operating agreement. However, the principle remains the same.

(a) The charterers' liability to the owners is limited to what the charterers can recover from any third party (usually their customers or sub-contractors), provided that they take all reasonable steps (short of court action) to recover from such third party and account to the owners therefor.

The reference in brackets to "(even if such liability . . . or sub-contractors)" is needed on account of the principle of "*contra proferentem*" as decided in *Smith and Anor.* v. *South Wales Switchgear* [1978] 1 W.L.R. 165, in which it was decided that, unless it is made clear that it applies even in the event of negligence, an indemnity would apply only in the absence of negligence. It is also made clear that the charterers' insurers do not come within the definition of third parties.

(b) This paragraph allows the owners to take over the claim if they feel that the charterers are not pressing the claim vigorously enough for any reason (valuable customer involved etc.) or if they feel that they can do better but, if they do so, it is at their expense, even though in the charterers' name, and they are entitled to look to the charterers for full co-operation.

(c) As an incentive to the charterers to co-operate as required in sub-clause 10.9(b), this paragraph provides for the charterers to lose the benefit of the waiver unless they co-operate within the timescale laid down.

The waiver clause specifically exempts:

(a) penalties arising from misdeclaration or documentation;
(b) costs incurred freeing a vessel from arrest.

This is because, if innocent, the charterers would have cover via their P & I club for such costs and, if not innocent, it is right that such costs should fall on the guilty head. Negligence is one thing, deliberate wrongdoing is another.

As explained in Chapter 2, waivers such as this can only operate where there is mutuality and the conceding party is compensated by benefiting from an equivalent concession when the roles are reversed. Also there has to be a basic equality between the degree and frequency of exposure which any line concedes and that which it receives.

"10.10 The Owners undertake that no claim or allegation shall be made against the Charterers by any person other than the Owners which imposes or attempts to impose upon the Charterers any liability whatsoever arising from loss or damage to the Containership, whether for actual loss or consequential loss and whether or not arising as a result of negligence on the part of the Charterers, their servants, agents or subcontractors and, if any such claim or allegation should nevertheless be made, to indemnify the Charterers, their servants, agents or sub-contractors against all consequences thereof."

This is the *quid pro quo* by the owners to the charterers for the indemnity by the charterers to the owners in clause 9. It is necessary if the containership concerned is chartered by the owners (so that they are only disponent owners), in which case the actual owner may have an action in tort against the charterers if the latter damage the containership, thereby defeating the mutual waiver. This indemnity plugs that gap.

"10.11 Nothing in this Charter party shall prejudice or deprive the Owners of their rights of limitation or exclusion of liability under any applicable or relevant law."

This clause makes it clear that the owners may avail themselves of global limitation (under the LLMC or some equivalent local legislation) in the event of a major casualty. In this case they can limit on the basis of the tonnage of the vessel rather than the limits set out earlier in this contract.

Global limitation creates problems for consortium operators and this will be discussed below when considering "feeder slot charter parties".

"10.12 The Owner shall maintain the Containership's class and container carrying capacity throughout the period of this Charterparty, unless otherwise mutually agreed."

A self-explanatory clause found in most containership charters, time as well as slot charters.

11. Bill of Lading, etc.

"11.1 The Charterers shall issue bills of lading and other contracts of carriage in their own regular forms for all goods occupying slots (space) hereby chartered. All such contracts shall contain the Paramount Clause incorporating Hague or Hague-Visby Rules legislation for the sea transportation period, the New Jason Clause, the Both-to-Blame Collision Clause and a full Circular Indemnity/Himalaya Clause in favour of both the Owners and Co-charterers.
11.2 Such contracts shall provide for General Average to be adjusted and settled at any port or place in the option of the Owners according to York-Antwerp Rules 1994 (unless any subsequent modification thereto is approved by the CMI, in which case the latter shall apply). All such contracts shall mention that the rules governing responsibility and provision for General Average apply to containers and goods loaded either on deck or under deck.
11.3 It is hereby agreed that no such contracts of carriage will be issued by the Charterers whereby a contractual relationship is established between cargo interests and the Master or Owners respectively.
11.4 Issuers of such contracts of carriage are to process all claims lodged under their respective contracts/bills of lading."

11.1: The charterers are to issue their own contracts of carriage (for cargoes carried under the cross charter party) to their customers. Under the cross charter party the charterers contract should include certain clauses in order to give protection to the owners. However, it sometimes happens that not all such clauses are included. If the charterers consider that the clause does not warrant the space that it occupies on the back of their contract, they may not use it. However, if they do not do so, they are in breach of the cross charter party contract and must bear any consequent cost/claim, without the benefit of any waiver.

The clauses are:

(a) paramount clause: applying Hague or Hague-Visby Rules for the sea transit period;
(b) new Jason clause: only needed in the event of GA adjusted in the US;
(c) both-to-blame collision clause: a clause proved ineffective in practice and thus, in the views of many, useless. P & I cover is subject to its retention but many carriers, confident that it is a waste of space, leave it out.
(d) circular indemnity: the contract of carriage link in the chain of indemnity. This must be wide enough to cover owners and co-charterers.

11.2: Contracts of carriage are to provide for GA to be adjusted according to York-Antwerp Rules 1994 with containers and cargo contributing, whether stowed on or under deck.

With owned vessels there is no problem here but with chartered vessels, care must be taken to ensure that the time charter under which the containership is procured calls for York-Antwerp Rules 1994, otherwise the disponent owners cannot comply with the requirements of this clause.

11.3: This clause prohibits demise clauses. If any consortium member uses such a clause he is in breach of the contract and must indemnify the owners in full for any consequences, without the benefit of any waiver.

11.4: It follows from 11.3 that each principal carrier is responsible for handling all cargo claims arising in respect of cargo for which he has issued contracts of carriage (bills of lading, waybills etc.), so that this clause could be said to be a statement of the obvious. It does, however, make for clarity.

Despite the provisions of this clause, in the event of a major casualty the owners may agree to handle all claims in order to consolidate all actions into the hands of one party. This is subject to the concurrence of the charterers, who may not wish consortium partners, who are also competitors, to handle sensitive claims with their blue-chip customers.

12. Sub-contractors

"In this Charter party the expression 'sub-contractor' shall include direct and indirect sub-contractors and their respective servants and agents."

It is the essence of a combined transport/multimodal contract that a series of services and contracts come together into one contract. Accordingly such contracts invariably involve numerous sub-contracts, sub-sub-contracts and even sub-sub-sub-contracts. It is necessary that the chain of indemnity reaches right down to the end of such arrangements and the purpose of this clause is to achieve that aim.

13. General Average and Salvage Services Received

"13.1 General Average shall be settled according to the York-Antwerp Rules 1994 (unless any subsequent modification thereto is approved by the CMI, in which case the latter shall apply). The Owners remuneration shall not contribute to General Average. The Owners authorise and empower the Charterers to act as the agents of the Owners in the collection of General Average securities. The Charterers shall guarantee the contributions properly due to the Owners in respect of:

(a) goods for which the Charterers are principal carrier under a Bill of Lading or contract of carriage unless delivered to the consignees prior to notice being given by the Owners to the Charterers that General Average security is required; and
(b) containers owned or hired by the Charterers.

13.2 In the event of the Containership needing to engage salvage services and, in order to secure the release of goods and containers for on-carriage, the Owners are required to give any undertaking to salvors to assist in the collection of security and not to release goods and containers until acceptable salvage security has been provided, the Charterers shall guarantee to the Owners that the requirements of such undertaking will be met in respect of the goods for which the Charterers are the contracting carrier and containers owned, hired or operated by the Charterers, provided that these requirements are notified to the Charterers prior to the delivery of the goods and containers to the Charterers.

13.3

(a) The Owners undertake not to declare General Average or seek contribution in salvage from the Charterers unless they are also doing so from their own cargo interests, to whom they have issued Bills of Lading, Waybills or similar contracts of carriage, provided always that, where the Owners are prepared to absorb cargoes' proportion of General Average or salvage for goods for which they are principal carrier, the Charterers are willing to do likewise in respect of goods for which they are principal carrier.

(b) The Owners undertake that their demands for General Average security and counter security for salvage (where sub-clause 13.2 applies) shall be reasonable in the light of what is readily available at the destination port/place of delivery. If the Owners are unprepared to accept security offered, they will accept any storage costs which the Charterers, despite best endeavours, are unable to recover from their cargo interests.

(c) In the event of a General Average situation arising at a port of refuge, the Owners and the Charterers shall consult on the desirability and practicability of on-carriage under a non-separation agreement. Unless agreed to the contrary, the arrangement and cost of on-carriage shall be for the account of the Charterers."

One of the prime objectives of combined transport operators is the speedy movement of cargo and anything that causes hold-up and delay is an anathema to be avoided or overcome by the most expedient means possible. Casualties, general average and salvage are potential causes of delay that need consideration to reduce their effect.

Combined transport operators avoid general average whenever possible and cargo insurers are campaigning for its total abolition (but that is another story!). Many Owners have GA waiver clauses in their hull and machinery policies, under which hull underwriters pay all GA expenses up to an agreed figure, provided that they are not principally cargo sacrifice and no interest is added to the adjustment. It is also not unknown for carriers to absorb excess GA costs for marketing reasons, to avoid troubling customers. At least one operator has a separate insurance (up to US$3 million) to cover cargoes' proportion of GA for this very reason.

With the number of potential contributing interest on a large containership running into thousands (if not tens of thousands), a GA on a containership, if fully adjusted, represents a massive task for the average adjuster and, with costs which usually exceed US$100 per contract of carriage, the expense of preparing the adjustment can be colossal. There can be little surprise, therefore, that GA is avoided whenever possible and that, where adjusted, adjustments are often truncated, as collecting from some smaller lower valued consignments would involve cost in excess of their contribution and thus benefit nobody (except the adjuster!).

In some consortia there is a provision in either the operating agreement or the cross charter party (in which case it would appear as part of this clause on GA) under which:

"The Owners undertake to attempt to arrange their Hull and Machinery insurance on the Containership on terms which enables them to elect, in case of any incident where

a General Average is estimated not to exceed US$X and the General Average does not consist mainly of cargo expenses or sacrifice, to claim the whole of the General Average from Hull and Machinery underwriters, subject to any excess or other policy restriction. The Owners will, if possible, exercise such option whenever General Average arises on the Containership.
Additionally, even if the General Average expense and sacrifice exceeds US$X, if the Owners' average adjusters certify that involving cargo interests would be uneconomical for the Hull and Machinery underwriters, the Owners will approach their underwriters requesting that recovery of the whole General Average should nevertheless be made from them and, if such request is successful, the Owners shall claim such recovery. In any event the Owners will not declare a General Average below an estimated US$X without prior consultation with the Charterers."

This is more often an operating agreement clause but, wherever it appears, its purpose is clear: to reduce general average. Pursuant to the last sentence of the clause, members of a consortium often agree to absorb any excess general average, once maximum recovery has been made from the owners' Hull and Machinery underwriters, amongst themselves in proportion to the amount of cargo on board at the time for which each was a principal carrier.

The purpose of this clause is to keep cargo moving following a GA or salvage and use each slot charterers' network of agents to collect the necessary security, exercising their lien so to do wherever necessary.

13.1:

- The adjustment is prepared in accordance with York-Antwerp Rules 1994.
- Owners' hire does not contribute.
- Owners appoint the charterers as their agent to collect security. This enables the owner to deliver the cargo and containers to the charterers for oncarriage to destination, so as to be ready for delivery once security is obtained.
- In return for the early release, the charterers guarantee contribution to the owners:
  - (i) for cargo for which they are principal carrier, provided the owners declared GA to them before they delivered the goods to their customers;
  - (ii) for their containers.

13.2: The purpose of this clause is to enable the owners to react promptly in the event of a lien being exercised on a containership, its containers and cargo for salvage security. The salvor wants security from all parties before he will allow anything beyond the place of safety, where he redelivers a containership and its cargo to the owners. At the same time he needs the co-operation of the owners and the charterers to assist in the collection of contribution. For this reason, where the owners are a reputable company, he is often persuaded to accept a personal "blanket" guarantee from the owners in return for redelivery.

In this unsupported undertaking the owners agree not to release cargo at destination without firstly collecting security, acceptable to the salvor, from the consignees or, if they do so, to be personally responsible to the salvor for the contribution on that consignment. The "blanket" guarantee gradually reduces as security from the consignees is passed to the adjusters acting for the salvor, until the guarantee covers only the containership, containers and any remaining cargo for which counter security has not been provided.

If the owners are going to do this and then allow the charterers immediate delivery, they naturally need a back-to-back undertaking from the charterers, to that which they have given to the salvor in respect of the charterers' cargo and containers.

13.3(a): This sub-clause is to prevent the owners from declaring GA to the charterers to reduce their overall costs but not declaring GA to their own customers, whose contribution they absorb for marketing reasons. This clearly links with the GA waiver requirements outlined above.

13.3(b): This is another clause to prevent the owners from requiring the charterers to do something which they are unprepared to do. In some countries, particularly in Africa and South America, the currency is so unstable that it may be unwise to accept security in local currency, as it may devalue massively whilst the adjustment is being prepared and become worthless. In such countries there are frequently draconian rules preventing the exportation of foreign exchange, so that to ask for security in dollars puts a local importer into an impossible position, unless he or his insurers have access to such funds abroad. This clause effectively prevents the owners from requiring the charterers to secure contribution in hard currency unless they are requiring their customers to do the same. This requirement, designed to make the owners reasonable regarding what security is acceptable, is reinforced by a requirement that storage charges, incurred on account of delays in delivery whilst alternative security is arranged, must be paid by the owners and included in the adjustment, unless the charterers can recover same from their customers.

13.3(c): When a GA incident occurs short of destination and the containership is in a port of refuge, the question arises whether the cargo awaits the repair of the containership to complete its voyage or, with the pressure to avoid delay, whether it is forwarded on the next available containership under a non-separation agreement. This clause provides for the owners and the charterers to consult on such occasions and, unless agreement to the contrary is reached, the arrangement and cost of oncarriage is for the account of the individual slot charterers.

If this were not so, the containership, once in a fit state to continue its voyage, may have little or no cargo and be condemned to a ballast or semi-ballast voyage to reposition. It may be, however, that consortium members agree that, in order to regain schedule, cargo should be transhipped to some ports, which are omitted, so that the containership can regain schedule, which is all important in these days when a reliable, regular, timeous service is required by importers, many of whom operate on a JIT (just in time) basis. Such importers maintain minimal stock levels to reduce the amount of capital tied up in warehoused goods and rely instead on regular supplies arriving on time.

14. Salvage

"The Charterers shall be entitled to the percentage, as agreed for the voyage under Clause 1, of all Salvage and assistance to other vessels, after deducting the Master's and crew's proportion and all legal and other expenses, including a reasonable sum for the time lost in salvage and the cost of repairing damage incurred in the salvage, to the extent not recoverable from Hull insurers. The Charterers shall be bound by all measures taken by the Owners in order to secure payment of salvage and to fix its amount."

This clause covers the situation where the containership is the salvor and provides for the charterers to receive a share of any salvage.

Containerships are the "ocean greyhounds" for whom any form of delay is to be avoided. Therefore, whilst always obeying the unwritten law of the sea in going to the aid of any vessel in distress or to save life, containerships will always look to allow any other vessel in the area to take on such a task to avoid delay and because a fully laden containership with a large deck load is not an ideal candidate as a tug (although it provides an admirable lee in which someone else can effect a rescue!). Accordingly this is not a frequently applied clause.

15. Stowaways

"Any fines, costs and losses incurred in respect of stowaways shall be for the Owners' account, unless it can be proved that the means by which the stowaway gained access to the Containership was by hiding in the Charterers' goods and/or containers prior to loading, in which case all such fines, costs and losses shall be for the Charterers' account, except to the extent that such fines, costs and losses have arisen as a result of unlawful conduct by the Master officers or crew."

This subject is dealt with in the cross charter party in a similar fashion to that in the BOXTIME time charter. Because containers offer a means of boarding a vessel as a stowaway, it is clearly equitable that, if it can be proved that the stowaway got on board by means of the container (and did not merely enter the container to hide once having boarded the containership in some other way), the charterers should be liable for the resultant cost etc. For this reason it is prudent to consider sealing even empty containers to preclude their illegal use as a means of stowing away.

16. Deck Carriage

"Goods and containers may be carried on deck and shall contribute in General Average whether carried on or under deck.
Goods not in containers and goods stowed on flat tracks may be carried on deck only with the prior approval of the Charterers."

As the Hague Rules apply mandatorily to cargo shipped under a bill of lading unless that bill of lading is claused to indicate that goods are carried on deck (Article I(c)) and deck carriage, contrary to the custom of the trade, is a breach of contract, it is necessary that this matter is properly addressed in the cross charter party. Carriage of containers on deck is now an accepted custom of the trade, so it is not necessary to clause bills for such cargo. This is equitable as the carrier offers the same recourse whether stowage is on or under deck. For this reason there should be no difference when it comes to GA contribution.

Because any cargo not shipped in covered containers is exposed to the elements if shipped on deck, the owners are not entitled to stow cargo in this way without the charterers' prior approval, so that the charterers can judge whether or not their liability cover is adequate and, if not, take appropriate steps to rectify it.

17. Non-Assignment

"The Charterers shall not assign this Charter party. The Charterers shall not sub-let any space or part thereof unless otherwise agreed."

This is a simple clause to preserve the owners' control over the charterers' use of their right to space in the containership.

18. Law and Arbitration

"18.1 This Cross Charterparty shall be governed by and construed in accordance with the laws of England and each line hereby submits to the jurisdiction of the English courts.
18.2 All disputes or differences arising under this Cross Charterparty, which cannot be amicably resolved, shall be referred to arbitration in England in accordance with the Arbitration Act 1996, together with the LMAA (London Maritime Arbitration Association) terms.
18.3 The lines agree to appoint a single/sole arbitrator, having appropriate commercial and consortia experience, within 21 days of any line seeking an appointment. If any line should so request, a panel of three arbitrators shall be appointed. Should there be no agreement on the appointment within the said 21 days, then the LMAA president will appoint a single/sole arbitrator (or a panel of three arbitrators as appropriate) at the request of any line.
18.4 The lines further agree that, where the amount in dispute is US$200,000 or less, the arbitration will proceed on a document and written submission basis only. However, oral evidence will be allowed exceptionally and at the discretion of the arbitrator(s)."

There is nothing magic or exclusive about this law and arbitration clause, which is merely an example of one of many which could be used, according to wishes of the parties. Only two points are really worth comment. Firstly, that the contract is usually subject to English law and jurisdiction and secondly, that the law clause here should mirror that in the operating agreement, to which this cross charter party is an appendix, in case the dispute requires reference to both contracts, which would make different law clauses an unnecessary complication.

Cross charter parties are rarely signed for each containership operating between each (disponent) owner and each charterer because this would be a waste of paper (there would need to be a large number of identical contracts printed, calculated as the number of containerships X (number of consortium members minus one) which, in a consortium of, say, four members operating twelve containerships would be 36!). Instead the contract is usually an appendix to the operating agreement and, in the operating agreement, consortium members undertake that, if called upon to do so by another member, they will sign a contract in the agreed format, dated as per the date of the operating agreement, as owners or charterers as the case may be.

SLOT SALE CHARTER PARTIES

(1) Slot charter parties

Charter parties for the sale of slots can take on a variety of forms, according to the requirements of the parties. It may occur that a recognised carrier (perhaps with whom one or more consortium members trade elsewhere) has an insufficient share of the consortium trade to warrant supplying tonnage to the trade but wishes to purchase regular space to service his share of the trade. On account of lack of mutuality he is not entitled to any mutual waiver consideration but, that apart, there is no reason why the terms under which he purchases space should not be the same as those in the cross charter party, minus sub-clause 10.9 and all cross-references thereto.

It may be that a small trade is served by a consortium using all chartered tonnage but, because of local law, owners' insistence on chartering to one charterer only, rather than joint chartering to a group of charterers, or some other reason, all members of the consortium are chartering tonnage on different terms and wish to slot charter to each other on the basis of back-to-back with the terms of their time charters with the actual owners. In this case a sub slot charter party is required.

With the underlying contract being in the main (time) charter with the actual owner, such charter parties can be admirably brief and will probably cover the following points.

(2) Sub slot charter parties

Whereas A is disponent owner of vessel X operating in the Y trade and B wishes to charter space therein on all sailings, A, being entitled by the terms of his charter with the actual owner to let space, agrees to sub-charter space to B as follows:

(1) *Slot allocation*: number of slots and price.
(2) *Terms*: back-to-back with head charter (FIOS).

(3) *Ports of call/voyages/schedules*: as notified to charterers from time to time.
(4) *Period of charter*: tied into equivalent provisions in head charter.
(5) *Law and jurisdiction*: preferably the same as the head charter but to cover disputes under this sub-charter as well as the head charter.
(6) *Liability of owner*: waiver (recoverable from actual owner or other third party).
(7) *Liability of charterer*: According to the relationship between the disponent owner and the sub-charterer, this can be a waiver, putting the disponent owner's SOL cover for ship damage at risk for the vessel but possibly leaving the sub-charterer open to claims by co-charterers (unless there is an operating agreement to cover this). Alternatively just back-to-back with the head charter.
(8) *Sundry liability matters*: agency appointment (*see* sub-clause 9.3 of cross charter party) and GA provision.

This is FIOS. If the sub-charterer wants a stack/stack or gate/gate contract and the disponent owner is prepared to oblige, a further clause, providing for the disponent owner to act as agent only either side of the FIOS contract in arranging receipt, storage, loading, unloading, storage, delivery etc. with the terminal companies, is required.

(3) "SLOTHIRE"

BIMCO created a standard format for slot chartering in 1993, following closely the approach adopted when preparing BOXTIME in 1990. As the explanatory notes prepared by BIMCO in 1993 at the time of publication of SLOTHIRE are exhaustive, I do not think that I can improve upon them. Accordingly, with BIMCO's kind permission, I repeat those notes here with minimum editing and my grateful acknowledgement.

In the wake of the development of the "BOXTIME" Charter, the Documentary Committee of BIMCO decided that BIMCO should also engage in the development of a standard slot charter party. The task to develop a standard slot charter was entrusted to a drafting committee composed of individuals (some of whom had also been involved in the drafting of the "BOXTIME" Charter) with expert knowledge in the business of slot chartering representing the various interests involved, i.e. shipowners, operators, charterers, brokers and club representatives.

Slot charter parties, or space charter agreements, as they are also called, were first introduced in the very late 1960s by major container operators in consortia on the basis of exchanging slots on each other's vessels. Usually, each operator's entitlement to space on other operators' vessels would be in relation to the tonnage entered into the consortia by that particular vessel operator. Even though financial adjustments were made to match the number of slots being exchanged, the essence of the arrangement was exchange rather than sale. Therefore, terms and conditions reflecting this form of slot chartering were often provided in what could be referred to as a cross charter party.

However, whilst the above practice of slot exchange was predominant in the early days of slot chartering, another form of slot chartering developed whereby non-vessel owners or individual shipowners, who may from time to time not be in a position to provide tonnage to meet their trading requirements, enter into an agreement with container vessel operators to hire slots on their vessels in a given trade. Terms and conditions of this form of slot chartering would often be established in what could be called a slot sale charter party.

The main characteristic of a cross charter party, in particular when used in consortia operation, is that it is rarely used as a free standing document. On the contrary it is usually attached to an operating agreement which contains the essential details of the slot charter arrangement such as number of slots to be exchanged, financial arrangements, the specified voyages, and other operational details, leaving the cross charter party primarily as the liability document.

The drafting committee involved in this matter realised, however, that it would serve little purpose to develop a standard slot charter party which could not be used as a self-contained document, as such document would stand little chance of becoming a standard within the industry.

It was therefore decided that, as the rapid development of containerisation during the 1970s and 80s had made slot sale arrangements increasingly important and as the major container consortia, who are the predominant parties in the practice of slot chartering already, had their specific trade requirements in place, BIMCO should embark upon the development of a slot charter party which could be used in its own right by non-vessel owners or by individual shipowners not operating within the established consortia, both when they are selling and buying slots.

General background

The feature of a slot charter party as a contract of carriage is unique in the sense that, whereas the slot charter party is not a time charter party nor a voyage charter party, it bears some similarity to both types of contract. As such, a slot charter party can be said to be a "hybrid" type of contract. It may be mentioned that, as distinct from a time charter party when the entire vessel is being chartered, the slot charterers are only hiring space on a vessel and they are therefore not acting as operators as under a time charter party and usually have no control over the operation of the vessel.

This has been recognised by the drafting committee in developing the "SLOTHIRE" charter party as a complete new charter party.

The standard slot charter party, code name "SLOTHIRE", is the final result of the work of the drafting committee after consultation with trade interests.

The "SLOTHIRE" charter party was officially adopted by the Documentary Committee of BIMCO at its meeting held in Singapore in May 1993.

Special observations

The "SLOTHIRE" charter party follows the usual pattern used by BIMCO for a number of years in the preparation of modern charter parties for various trades, i.e. the "Box Layout" system with a separate Part I and Part II.

The main idea behind this division is to have a charter party where the filling-in and all amendments and special provisions are made by the parties in Part I, leaving the printed text of Part II unaltered. In this context it may be useful to emphasize that a standard charter party constitutes an integrated whole and that a change or changes to some of the printed clauses may destroy the overall balance of the charter party, a fact which should never be overlooked when attempting to introduce changes or amendments to standard clauses. In particular, it is important that any additional clauses should not conflict with the terms and conditions of Part II and that they should be in the same terminology as that used in Part II.

Part I

As far as Part I is concerned, all items to be agreed for the particular fixture and to be filled in by typewriter or computer have been arranged in boxes in Part I. The boxes contain a brief description of the particular item and a reference to the relevant clauses in the printed body of Part II.

Additional clauses covering special provisions, if necessary and agreed for a particular fixture, may be added as a rider to the charter party and the clauses should be referred to in box 24 in Part I.

Some of the boxes to be completed in Part I may call for special observations; however, in view of the fact that the details to be written into the boxes should be considered against the background of the provisions in the corresponding clauses in Part II, it has been considered more practical to make these observations together with the comments on the standard clauses in Part II.

Part II

The following is a brief description of the standard clauses contained in Part II, to give some background explanation to the clauses so as to assist owners, slot charterers and other interested parties in the practical use of the charter party.

Part II: "SLOTHIRE" Standard Slot Charter Party

"It is agreed on the date as indicated in Box 2 between the party named in Box 3 (hereinafter referred to as "the Owners") of the Vessel named in Box 5 and

1 Shipbroker	THE BALTIC AND INTERNATIONAL MARITIME COUNCIL (BIMCO) STANDARD SLOT CHARTER PARTY CODE NAME: "SLOTHIRE" PART I 2 Place and date
3 Owners/Address	4 Charterers/Address
5 Vessel	6 Call Sign
7 Slot Allocation (state no. of TEUs) (Cl. 1)	8 Weight Allocation (state maximum total weight of Containers) (Cl. 1)
9 State no. of Containers to be connected to Vessel's refrigerating machinery/ power supply (Cl. 1)	10 Vessel's Itinerary (Cl. 6)
11. Commencement Date and Place (Cl. 2)	
12 Termination (state period of notice of termination) (Cl. 2)	
13. Notice (state earliest date on which notice of termination may be given) (Cl. 2)	
14 State port and date, or scheduled period (Cl. 2)	
15 Slot Charter Hire (FIOS) per voyage (Cl. 5)	16 Additional amount (per day) payable for each Container receiving a supply of power from the Vessel (Cl. 5)
	17 Place of payment, also state beneficiary and bank account (Cl. 5)
18. Latest payment date (Cl. 5)	19 Interest rate per annum (Cl. 5)
20 Charterers' maximum claim settlement authority (Cl. 15(d))	
21. General Average to be adjusted at (Cl. 19)	22 Brokerage commission and to whom payable
23 Law and Arbitration (state (a), (b) or (c) of Cl. 23; if (c) agreed also state Place of Arbitration) (Cl. 23)	24 Number of additional clauses covering special provisions

Issued by
The Documentary Committee of
The Baltic and International Maritime Council (BIMCO), Copenhagen

It is mutually agreed that this Contract shall be performed in accordance with the conditions in PART I including additional clauses, if any agreed and stated in Box 23, and PART II. In the event of a conflict of conditions, the provisions of PART I shall prevail over those of PART II to the extent of such conflict but no further.

Signature (Owners)	Signature (Charterers)

Printed and sold by Fr. G. Knudtzons Bogtrykkeri A/S, 55 Toldbodgade, DK-1253 Copenhagen K, Telefax +45 33 93 11 84, by authority of The Baltic and International Maritime Council (BIMCO), Copenhagen

Figure 2: BIMCO Standard Slot Charter Party: "SLOTHIRE"

with the call sign as stated in Box 6, and the party named in Box 4 (hereinafter referred to as "the Charterers") as follows:

Definitions

In this Slot Charter Party, the following words shall have the meanings hereby assigned to them:
"TEU" means a Twenty Foot Equivalent Unit.
"Slot" means the space on board the Vessel necessary to accommodate one TEU.
"Container" means any Standard ISO Container.
"Goods" means the whole or any part of the cargo received from the Charterers and includes any Container not owned or hired by the Charterers.
"Sub-contractor" shall include direct and/or indirect sub-contractors and/or their respective servants and agents."

In line with other recent BIMCO standard documents the "SLOTHIRE" charter contains a set of definitions.

Clause 1: Slot and Weight Allocation

"(a) The Owners shall let and the Charterers shall hire the number of Slots as agreed in Box 7 for the carriage of Goods and Containers, of which the number of Containers as indicated in Box 9 may be connected to the Vessel's refrigerating machinery and/or power supply, provided that the total weight of said Goods and Containers does not exceed the weight shown in Box 8.

(b) Slots shall be available to the Charterers on a voyage basis as specified in Box 15 and may be used by the Charterers for the carriage of Goods and Containers between all the specified ports.

(c) The Owners shall have free use of any Slot or weight allocation unused by the Charterers on any voyage leg, provided that such Slot or weight allocation is available to the Charterers at the next port at which the Charterers are entitled to load."

Careful consideration must be given by the slot charterers to the weight allocation provided by the owners. It is often the weight allocation and not the number of slots hired which determines the ultimate limit of the number of containers to be shipped on board the vessel if some of the containers are heavy. Therefore, in the event the total weight allocation as stated in box 8 has been reached without full use having been made of all the slots hired by the slot charterers, such slots will have to remain unused by the charterers. In this connection it may be useful to recall that slots, whether or not used, shall be paid for by the slot charterers.

Sub-clause (b) reflects the practice within slot chartering, i.e. that slots may be hired for use between two ports only or that slots may be hired continuously for a round voyage. Box 15 should show the voyage legs contracted for and the relevant slot charter hire per leg.

Sub-clause (c) permits the owners to make free use of any slot or weight allocation unused by the slot charterers. Accordingly, if the owners know long enough in advance of the departure of the vessel that the slot charterers are not going to make full use of their slot allocation, the owners may hire out such slots to other customers or they may wish to make use of the slots for the transportation of their own goods and containers, provided that such slot allocation is available to the slot charterers at the next port of call at which the slot charterers are entitled to load. Again, this reflects common practice within slot chartering.

Clause 2: Period

> "This Slot Charter Party shall commence on the date and at the place shown in Box 11 and shall terminate upon either party giving notice in writing as agreed in Box 12, which notice shall not be given before the date agreed in Box 13. Alternatively, the parties may agree that the termination of this Slot Charter Party shall be effected upon discharge at a port and on a scheduled date or within a scheduled period as agreed in Box. 14."

According to the provisions of this clause, the owners and the slot charterers may agree that the period of the slot charter party shall run for an indefinite period of time until terminated by either party giving notice of termination as per box 12.

However, to reflect the fact that the parties may agree that slots shall be hired on a voyage-related basis, i.e. for one round voyage, alternatively for a single voyage only, or that slots may be hired on a time charter-related basis, alternative provisions of this Clause provide that the termination of the slot charter party shall be effected upon discharge at a port and on a scheduled date or within a scheduled period as agreed in box 14.

Clause 3: Trading Limits

> "The Vessel shall be employed in lawful trades within the Institute Warranty Limits for the carriage of lawful merchandise."

According to this clause the employment of the vessel is subject to the following restrictions:

(i) Lawful Trades, i.e. the vessel must not be engaged in smuggling of passengers or goods, trading with the enemy etc.

(ii) Within Institute Warranty Limits, i.e. the vessel must only trade within the limits defined by the Institute of London Underwriters (now the International Underwriting Association—IUA) as being the normal trading limits imposed on vessels for hull insurance purposes without the payment of additional premium.

Clause 4: Permitted Cargoes

"Except as provided below, the Slots shall be used exclusively for the carriage of Goods properly packed and stowed in Containers complying with the International Convention for Safe Containers. The following items may only be shipped with the prior approval of the Owners (see also Clause 12):

(a) Uncontainerised Goods
(b) Containers of Non-Standard Sizes and Specifications
(c) Live Animals
(d) Hazardous Goods, provided also that such Goods are loaded, stowed, discharged and documented in accordance with IMO Regulations
(e) Radioactive Materials

provided that

(i) previous written full particulars of such Goods have been given to the Owners by or on behalf of the Charterers and;
(ii) all the relevant requirements and recommendations and the law in force in the port of loading and discharge and any intermediate scheduled port of call as well as the law of the country in which the Vessel is registered, have been complied with
(iii) the carriage of such Goods is not excluded under the Owners' P&I cover."

The preamble of this clause suggests that the primary purpose of vessels engaged in the container trade is to carry goods in containers which comply with the International Convention for Safe Containers.

However, recognising that the container trade can be quite diversified and that container vessels are not always used exclusively for the carriage of goods in containers of standard specifications, this clause provides that, subject to the owners' approval, items such as uncontainerised goods, containers of non-standard specifications, live animals etc., may also be carried.

It is, however, important to note that the approval which may be given by the owners to ship such items as listed in (a) to (e) of this clause is, again, subject to the conditions established in sub-sections (i) to (iii) being complied with. An increasing number of regulations to enhance the safe handling and carriage of goods enter into force and it is therefore of utmost importance for the slot charterers to ensure that all relevant requirements related to the carriage of such goods are met before tendering them for carriage.

Clause 5: Slot Charter Hire

"Slot Charter Hire at the rate shown in Box 15 and an additional amount (per day) indicated in Box 16 for each Container receiving a supply of power from the Vessel, if any, shall be payable at the place indicated in Box 17, within the number of days shown in Box 18 after commencement of the voyage. Such

Slot Charter Hire and additional amount, if any, shall be deemed earned upon the commencement of the voyage, irrespective of the number of Slots used, and shall be non-returnable in any event.

Late payment shall entitle the Owners to an interest rate per annum as agreed in Box 19. If Box 19 has not been filled in, the official discount rate on bills of exchange as valid at the place of payment indicated in Box 17, increased by 3 per cent., shall apply."

Slot charter hire may be expressed either as a daily rate per slot or as a lump sum rate per slot, the latter being common in the case of port-to-port movements. The additional rate for the use of refrigerating machinery or power supply is usually given as an amount per day, but can also be expressed as a surcharge on the basic rate.

As will be seen, and again in accordance with common practice within slot chartering, slot charter hire shall be deemed earned upon the commencement of the voyage and shall be non-returnable in any event.

In the event of late payment of slot charter hire and if the parties have omitted to fill in box 19 stating the late payment interest rate, the official discount rate on bills of exchange as valid at the place of payment, plus 3 per cent, shall apply.

Clause 6: Itinerary

"(a) The schedule of the itinerary as specified in Box 17 shall be advised to the Charterers as early as possible together with prompt advice of any amendments thereto.

(b) The Owners shall be entitled to exercise the liberty to deviate as provided in the Hague-Visby Rules at any time without notice to the Charterers. However, if during the course of a voyage the Vessel should deviate in circumstances which are not permitted by a bill of lading or other contract of carriage covering Goods for which the Charterers have used a Slot, the Owners shall indemnify the Charterers for any liability thereby incurred, unless the Owners have given at least 48 hours prior notice to the Charterers of such intended deviation, in which case this indemnity shall not operate."

In order for the slot charterers to plan their shipments of goods and containers the owners shall as per sub-clause (a) of this clause, provide the slot charterers with the schedule of the vessel's itinerary as early as possible together with details of all amendments thereto as they are made.

Clause 7: Opening Containers

"The Owners shall be entitled at any time to open any Container or package and to inspect the contents. Any Container opened must be re-sealed and the Charterers advised accordingly."

This clause is self-explanatory.

Clause 8: Stowaways

> "Any costs incurred in respect of stowaways shall be for the Owners' account, unless it can be established that the means by which the stowaways gained access to the Vessel was by secreting away in the Charterers' Goods and/or Containers prior to loading, in which case all such costs shall be for the Charterers' account."

Stowaways have become one of the problems of our time. In particular the container trade has become the target for an increasing number of stowaway attempts despite measures taken by shipowners to prevent stowaways getting access to their vessels.

Considering that the slot charterers are responsible for the packing and sealing of containers and that stowaways may gain access to the vessel by hiding away in good and/or containers prior to their being received for shipment from the slot charterers, it is reasonable that not all costs incurred as a result of stowaways shall rest solely with the owners and that slot charterers should be responsible for costs incurred as a result of stowaways gaining access to the vessel via the slot charterers' goods and containers.

Clause 9: Drugs

> "In the event that contraband and/or unmanifested drugs or goods are found to have been shipped as part of the Charterers' Goods and/or in the Charterers' Containers on board the Vessel, any fines or imposts levied and legal and all other costs incurred, including but not limited to, loss of time for the Vessel shall be for the Charterers' account and the Charterers shall, on demand, provide the security required to enable the Vessel to sail. However, if it can be established that the presence of contraband and/or unmanifested drugs or goods was due solely to the act, neglect or default by the Owners, their servants, agents or Sub-contractors, such fines or imposts levied and legal and other costs incurred shall be for the Owners' account."

The increasing smuggling of narcotic drugs is another problem which has burdened the shipping industry during recent years. Many owners have been confronted with the unpleasant surprise of having unmanifested narcotic drugs on board, which have in some instances proved to be a costly experience, not least when the trading limits have involved the United States. As in the matter of stowaways, the slot charterers may be responsible, albeit unknowingly, for narcotic drugs coming abroad the vessel. Accordingly, in accordance with this clause, slot charterers have to absorb liabilities incurred in the event that unmanifested narcotic drugs are found to have been shipped as part of the slot charterers' goods and/or in the slot charterers' containers.

Clause 10: Repairs

"The Owners shall have liberty to take the Vessel out of service for maintenance and repairs, with reasonable notice to the Charterers."

This clause is self-explanatory.

Clause 11: Owners' Obligations

"(a) The Owners shall arrange for the loading onto, securing and discharging from the Vessel of the Charterers' Goods and Containers as agent for, and for the account of, the Charterers.

(b) If required by the Charterers, the Owners shall sign a receipt for the tally of Goods and Containers loaded on board the Vessel at each port of loading. In the absence of such receipt, both parties agree to accept terminal tallies as conclusive evidence of the tally of Goods and Containers loaded and discharged.

(c) During the voyage, the Master and Engineer shall keep full and correct logs and adequate records concerning the care and condition of the Goods and Containers and all such logs and records shall be accessible to the Charterers or their agents."

Attention is drawn to sub-clause (a) of this clause, according to which the owners shall arrange for the loading, securing and discharging of the slot charterers' goods and containers. As will be seen, the "SLOTHIRE" standard slot charter party is based on Free In and Out Stowed (FIOS) terms. However, in accordance with usual commercial practice within slot chartering, it is the owners who will be contracting with the stevedores as agents for the slot charterers regarding the loading and discharging of the containers received from the slot charterers. It is noteworthy that "security" for the purpose of this clause is meant to include the lashing of containers.

Clause 12: Charterers' Obligations

"(a) The Charterers shall provide such information and/or documentation and comply with the Owners' procedures in relation to any Goods and Containers under this Slot Charter Party as the Owners may reasonably require and the Charterers warrant that such information and/or documentation shall be complete, accurate and in time for loading/discharging operations to be planned.

(b) The Charterers shall undertake that all Goods and Containers within the Charterers' allocation shall be delivered at the loading terminal at least 24 hours before the arrival of the Vessel."

It is crucial that the slot charterers provide complete, accurate and timely documentation regarding the goods and/or containers to be loaded on board the vessel. This, in particular, applies to those items mentioned in clause 4 (Permitted Cargoes) and which require the owners' prior approval in order to be shipped.

In order to secure the prompt loading of the slot charterers' goods and containers, sub-clause (b) provides that the slot charterers must ensure that goods and containers within their allocation must be delivered latest 24 hours before the arrival of the vessel.

Clause 13: Indemnity and Agency

"(a) The Charterers undertake that no claim or allegation shall be made against the Owners or any servant, agent or Sub-contractor of the Owners by any person whomsoever, other than the Charterers, which imposes or attempts to impose upon the Owners or any such servant, agent or Sub-contractor or any Vessel owned by any of them, any liability whatsoever in connection with Goods and Containers, or their carriage, (even if such liability arises wholly or in part by reason of the act, neglect or default of the Owners or of such servant, agent or Sub-contractor), and in the event of any such claim or allegation nevertheless being made, the Charterers shall indemnify the Owners and such servant, agent or Sub-contractor against all consequences whatsoever thereof.

The Charterers further undertake that bills of lading issued for the Charterers' Goods and Containers carried under this Slot Charter Party shall contain:

(i) **No** Identity of Carrier Clause which purports to establish a contractual relationship between the Owners and the cargo interests of the Charterers.

(ii) A Clause Paramount applying the Hague or Hague-Visby Rules as enacted in the country of shipment.

(iii) A Himalaya Clause or Circular Indemnity Clause giving the Owners the benefit of the bill of lading terms and conditions and/or protection from tortious claims by third parties.

If, despite the provisions of (i) above, a contractual relationship between the Owners and the Charterers' cargo interests is construed, the Charterers shall indemnify the Owners against all consequences thereof.

(b) The Charterers shall not make any claim or allegation against any servant, agent or Sub-contractor of the Owners which imposes or attempts to impose on any such servant, agent or Sub-contractor any liability whatsoever in connection with Goods and Containers, or their carriage, (even if such liability arises wholly or in part by reason of the act, neglect or default of the Owners or of such servant, agent or Sub-contractor), and, in the event of any such claim or allegation nevertheless being made, the provisions of sub-clause 13(a) shall apply as if such claim or allegation had been made by persons other than the Charterers.

(c) Without prejudice to sub-clause 13(a) the Owners authorise and empower the Charterers to act as the Owners' agents and/or trustees to stipulate for the Owners to have as against other persons the benefit of any immunities, exemptions or liberties regarding the Goods and Containers, or their carriage, but the Charterers shall have no authority to make any contract imposing any obligations upon the Owners in connection with the Goods and Containers or their carriage.

(d) Nothing in this Clause shall preclude any claim made by the owners of any property on board the Vessel for a General Average contribution in accordance with the York-Antwerp Rules 1974, as amended 1990, or any subsequent modification thereof.

(e) If the Owners are not the actual owners of the Vessel, the provisions of sub-clauses 13(a), (b) and (c) shall also apply to the actual owners of the Vessel, their servants, agents and Sub-contractors in the same manner as they apply to the Owners, their servants, agents and Sub-contractors.”

Whilst a slot charter party governs the relationship between the owners and the slot charterers, there is no contractual relationship between the owners and any third parties such as the slot charterers’ customers. Sub-clause (a) recognises that, despite contractual provisions to the contrary, claims may well be made against the owners or any of their servants, agents or sub-contractors by third parties. However, in the event of such a claim being made, this sub-clause provides that the slot charterers shall indemnify the owners, their servants, agents or sub-contractors for the consequences thereof.

As the owners are not the party preparing the bills of lading with the owners of the goods and containers shipped under the “SLOTHIRE” charter party, the owners may wish to be assured that the slot charterers’ bills of lading with their customers contain the usual protective clauses. Accordingly, the second paragraph of sub-clause (a) lists a few protective clauses which must always form part of the slot charterers’ bills of lading. Another requirement of the owners must be that no identity of carrier clause, which purports to put the owners in a direct contractual relationship with the cargo interests, should form part of the slot charterers’ bills of lading.

Sub-clause (b) seems similar to the first paragraph of sub-clause (a), however, whilst sub-clause (a) concerns claims made by third parties against the owners or any of their servants, agents or sub-contractors this sub-clause concerns claims made against the owners’ servants, agents or sub-contractors by the slot charterers themselves, thereby limiting the slot charterers’ claims to the owners only. Thus, only the slot charterers may claim and they can claim only against the owners.

Sub-clause 13(c) is a general agency appointment provision whereby the owners appoint the charterers as their agent, so that the slot charterers stipulate for the owners to have the benefits from any immunities, exceptions or liberties in the slot charterers’ bill of lading terms and conditions. This is to give the owners the benefit of the Himalaya or circular indemnity clause in the slot charterers’ bill of lading.

Clause 14: Owners’ Responsibilities and Liabilities

“Except as otherwise provided elsewhere in this Slot Charter Party, the responsibilities and liabilities of the Owners shall be as follows:

(a) The Owners shall be responsible for the seaworthiness of the Vessel in accordance with Article III Rule 1 and Article IV Rule 1 of the Hague-Visby Rules and for all purposes in connection with this Slot Charter Party they shall be entitled to the rights and immunities set out in Article IV Rules 2, 4 and 6 of the said Hague-Visby Rules.

(b) Subject to sub-clause 14(a), the Owners shall be responsible for the proper and careful carriage, custody and care of the Goods and Containers whilst on board the Vessel, and for discharging, handling and storing Goods and Containers discharged solely in order to be re-loaded or in order to load or discharge other goods and containers, and for re-loading and re-stowing the same.

(c) The Owners shall provide electrical power to integral refrigerated unit Containers and to refrigeration clip-on units attached to insulated Containers shipped on the Vessel. The Owners shall use all reasonable endeavours to monitor and record the performance of all such units whilst on board, and, at the expense of the Charterers, to repair and rectify any breakdown, fault or deficiency which may occur in respect of such units, using the resources on board the Vessel.

If such resources are insufficient, the Owners, at the expense of the Charterers, shall use all reasonable endeavours promptly to obtain any required spares or specialised repair facilities.

Except as provided above, the Owners shall not be liable for malfunctioning of integral refrigerated Containers and power packs put on board by the Charterers.

(d) The liability of the Owners under this Clause shall be subject to Article III Rule 6 (including 6bis) of the Hague-Visby Rules.

(e) In respect of loss of or damage to Containers owned or hired by the Charterers, the quantum of liability of the Owners shall not in any event exceed the lesser of the reasonable cost of repair or market value of the Container, however, the Charterers shall make no claim for damage to any Container of less than USD 500 on any one voyage.

(f) In respect of loss of or damage to Goods, the quantum of liability of the Owners shall be determined as follows:

(i) If the port of loading is in a country which is a party to the Hague-Visby Rules the quantum of liability of the Owners to the Charterers shall be determined by the relevant legislation of that country as if this Slot Charter Party were a Bill of Lading with no declaration of value.

(ii) If the port of loading is in a country which is a party to the Hague Rules, the quantum of liability of the Owners to the Charterers shall be determined by the relevant legislation of that country as if this Slot Charter Party were a Bill of Lading with no declaration of value.

(iii) In all other cases the quantum of liability of the Owners to the Charterers shall be determined by reference to the Hague Rules Articles I-VIII only as if this Slot Charter Party were a Bill of Lading with no declaration of value, save that the limitation sum for the purposes of Article IV Rule 5 of the Hague Rules shall be GBP 100 sterling.

(iv) If quantum limitation is calculated by reference to packages, the quantum of liability of the Owners to the Charterers shall be calculated by reference to the same tally as is applicable between the Charterers and their customer.

(v) In addition to the liability as outlined in (i) to (iv) above, the Owners will reimburse the Charterers for reasonable legal and other costs necessarily incurred in connection with claims for which the Owners are liable under this Slot Charter Party.

(g) The Owners shall indemnify the Charterers against any claims for personal injury incurred on or about the Vessel unless caused by the negligence of the Charterers, their servants, agents or Sub-contractors or any defect in the Charterers' Goods and/or Containers."

This clause is a very important clause to which great attention should be paid.

As will be seen, the Hague-Visby Rules, as a widely accepted liability regime, have been applied in determining the owners' responsibilities and liabilities vis-à-vis the slot charterers under this charter party.

However, whilst it was hoped that the Hague-Visby Rules could be applied *in extenso*, this attractively simple approach did not appear to be a viable solution in the "SLOTHIRE" charter party. For instance, Article III, Rule 2 of the Hague-Visby Rules provides that the carrier shall properly and carefully load, handle, stow, carry, keep, care for, and discharge the goods to be carried. Recognising that the "SLOTHIRE" charter party is based on FIOS terms, it would not be appropriate to make reference to this Article of the Hague-Visby Rules.

Also, the drafting committee considered it appropriate to include separate limitation of liability provisions not provided for in the Hague-Visby Rules.

The approach adopted in the "SLOTHIRE" charter party is to provide full indemnity to the slot charterers for claims they have to pay to their customers but for which the owners are ultimately liable in accordance with the terms of the "SLOTHIRE" charter party. Accordingly, if the slot charterers, having issued a bill of lading to their customers to which the Hague or Hague-Visby Rules are mandatorily applicable, are obliged to settle a claim with their customers for damage caused to goods in the containers but for which the owners are liable, the owners must reimburse the slot charterers on the basis of the Hague or Hague-Visby Rules limits, whichever is mandatorily applicable. There is one notable exception to this rule.

In the event that the slot charterers, if no mandatory law applies, *contractually* apply the Hague Rules *in extenso* in their bills of lading with their customers, there have been court decisions in the United Kingdom, and also in other jurisdictions, which have interpreted Article IX (the gold clause) of the Hague Rules as applying the gold value of GBP100 Sterling leading to a package limitation of more than GBP6,000 Sterling (now over GBP8,000). Slot charterers can carefully avoid this situation by incorporating Articles I to VIII of the Hague Rules only, when contractually applied. However, some slot charterers may not be careful enough to avoid this situation. Therefore, in order to safeguard the owners against a back-to-back recovery being made by the slot charterers under these circumstances, sub-clause 14(f)(iii) provides that the limitation sum for the purpose of Article IV Rule 5 of the Hague Rules shall be GBP100 sterling in these circumstances (if Hague Rules are mandatorily applicable then the relevant law provides for the limitation sum).

Clause 15: Charterers'Responsibilities and Liabilities

"(a) Whilst the Charterers are responsible for all costs incurred prior to placing into stow in the Vessel and after removal from stow in the Vessel, the Owners acting as the Charterers' agents to arrange such services (see Clause 11(a)), the Charterers shall only be liable to the Owners for any loss of or damage to the Vessel or to other goods and containers caused by stevedores during such services to the extent that a recovery is made from the stevedores. This recovery right is herewith assigned to the Owners which assignment is accepted by the Owners.

(b) The Charterers shall be reasponsible for the proper and careful loading, stowage, lashing and securing of the Goods in the Containers offered by them for shipment and shall be liable for all loss or damage (including loss of or damage to the Vessel) caused to the Owners as a result of improper or careless performance of such operations.

(c) The Charterers shall indemnify the Owners against any expenses, liabilities, losses, damages, claims or demands which the Owners may incur or suffer by reason of any failure to comply with any relevant laws, regulations, directions or notices of Customs, port and any other authorities, or by reason of any infestation, contamination or condemnation of Goods and/or Containers, insofar as such failure, infestation, contamination or condemnation arises from any act, neglect or default of the Charterers, the consignors or consignees of their Goods and/or Containers, or their servants, agents or Sub-contractors.

(d) Whenever possible, the Charterers shall give all reasonable facilities to the Owners for inspecting damaged Goods and Containers for which they intend to seek reimbursement from the Owners.

(e) The Charterers shall make no payment in excess of the amount as stated in Box 20 in settlement of a claim for which they will seek recovery from the Owners without prior notice to the Owners. The Owners authorise the Charterers to grant extensions of time in respect of such claims provided the Charterers give the Owners immediate notice thereof.

(f) In any event, the Charterers shall be discharged from all liabilities arising under this Slot Charter Party unless suit is brought within 15 months of the occurrence of the incident giving rise to the liability or the date upon which the Owners became aware of such occurence."

Just as in clause 14, this is a very important clause to which careful attention should be paid.

Sub-clause (a) of this clause concerns damage caused by the stevedores to the vessel or to other goods and containers and for which the slot charterers shall be liable. However, recognising the practice within slot chartering that it is the owners who will be contracting with the stevedores and that the slot charterers have no control over the stevedores during the loading and discharging operations, the slot charterers shall not be liable to reimburse the owners for stevedore damage unrecovered from the stevedores.

According to sub-clause (b) the slot charterers shall, however, be fully responsible for damage caused to other goods and/or containers or to the vessel as a result of improper stowage, lashing and securing of goods inside the containers.

Sub-clause (c) merely provides that if the slot charterers' goods and containers, or any inaccurate or incomplete documentation relating to such goods and containers, result in any fines or costs etc. to the owners then the slot charterers must indemnify the owners for such fines and costs.

In a liner service, where a wide range of small claims can arise, the slot charterers need a degree of flexibility to handle claims arising from their customers. At the same time the owners want to control such matters and ensure that they get the earliest advice of claims so that they can advise their P & I club to avoid a claim being rejected by reason of late notification. Sub-clause (e) attempts to satisfy this requirement in a reasonable manner.

Sub-clause (f) provides that the owners must progress any claim they may have against the slot charterers within 15 months of occurrence of the incident giving rise to the liability or the date when the owners became aware of such occurrence or be time barred.

Clause 16: Mutual Exemption Clause

"(a) Neither the Owners nor the Charterers shall be responsible for any loss or damage or delay or failure in performance under this Slot Charter Party resulting from Act of God, war, civil commotion, quarantine, strikes, lock-outs, arrest or restraint of princes, rulers and peoples or any other event whatsoever which cannot be avoided or guarded against.

(b) Except as elsewhere provided, neither the Owners nor the Charterers shall be responsible for any indirect or consequential loss, including but not limited to damage or decline in the market value of the Vessel or Goods during delays, loss of profit or loss of business opportunities in respect of any claim that the one may have against the other."

Sub-clause (a) contains the usual provisions as regards mutual exemption.

Sub-clause (b) provides for the usual provisions relating to indirect or consequential loss.

Clause 17: Lien

"The Owners shall have a lien, including after discharge, upon the Charterers' Goods and Containers for all sums due to the Owners from the Charterers, their servants, agents, Sub-contractors or principals in respect of services provided by the Owners to the Charterers under the terms of this Slot Charter Party."

This is self-explanatory.

Clause 18: Dues, Charges and Taxes

"(a) The Owners shall pay all dues, charges and taxes customarily levied on the Vessel, howsoever the amount thereof may be assessed.

(b) The Charterers shall pay all dues, charges, duties and taxes customarily levied on the Goods and/or Containers, howsoever the amount thereof may be assessed."

This clause provides for a reasonable sharing of dues, charges and taxes customarily levied on the vessel, goods and containers as the case may be.

Clause 19: General Average

"General Average shall be adjusted at the place as indicated in Box 21 according to the York-Antwerp Rules 1974, as amended 1990, or any subsequent modification thereof. Slot Charter Hire shall not contribute to General Average. The Owners authorise and empower the Charterers to act as the agents of the Owners in the collection of General Average security. The Charterers shall guarantee the contributions properly due to the Owners in respect of:

(a) Goods for which the Charterers are the contracting carrier unless such Goods are delivered to the Charterers prior to notice being given by the Owners to the Charterers that General Average security is required; and

(b) Containers shipped by the Charterers under this Slot Charter Party"

Similar to time charter hire and bareboat charter hire, slot charter hire shall not contribute in general average. Provision is made for the slot charterers to guarantee contribution to the owners in respect of goods and containers in defined circumstances. This facilitates early release to the slot charterers in the event of a general average.

Clause 20: Salvage

"In the event of the Vessel needing to engage salvage services and in order to secure the release of Goods and/or Containers for on-carriage, the Owners shall be required to give any undertaking to salvors to assist in the collection of security and not to release Goods and/or Containers until acceptable salvage security has been provided. The Charterers shall guarantee to the Owners that the requirements of such undertaking will be met in respect of Goods, for which the Charterers are the contracting carrier and Containers shipped by the Charterers under this Slot Charter Party, provided that these requirements are notified to the Charterers prior to the delivery of the Goods and/or Containers to the Charterers."

This clause addresses the situation which arises if the vessel needs to engage salvage services from a third party. If the owners are required to give any undertaking to the salvors to assist in the collection of security and not to release goods and containers, before acceptable security has been provided, slot charterers undertake to exercise a lien until security is provided in order to secure early release of goods and containers for oncarriage to final destination, thereby reducing delay.

Clause 21: Deck Carriage

> “Goods and Containers may be carried on deck and shall contribute in General Average whether carried on or under deck.”

This clause is self-explanatory.

Clause 22: Sub-letting

> “The Charterers shall not assign this Slot Charter Party and shall not sub-let the Slots without the prior approval of the Owners.”

This clause is self-explanatory.

Clause 23: Law and Arbitration

“*) (a) This Slot Charter Party shall be governed by and construed in accordance with English law and any dispute arising out of this Slot Charter Party shall be referred to arbitration in London in accordance with the Arbitration Acts 1950 and 1979 or any statutory modification or re-enactment thereof for the time being in force, one arbitrator being appointed by each party. On the receipt by one party of the nomination in writing of the other party’s arbitrator, that party shall appoint their arbitrator within fourteen days, failing which the decision of the single Arbitrator appointed shall apply. If two Arbitrators properly appointed shall not agree they shall appoint an umpire whose decision shall be final. The Arbitrators shall be commercial men engaged in shipping.

*) (b) This Slot Charter Party shall be governed by and construed in accordance with Title 9 of the United States Code and the Maritime Law of the United States and should any dispute arise out of this Slot Charter Party, the matter in dispute shall be referred to three persons at New York, one to be appointed by each of the parties hereto, and the third by the two so chosen; their decision or that of any two of them shall be final, and for purpose of enforcing any award, this agreement may be made a rule of the Court. The Arbitrators shall be commercial men engaged in shipping.

*) (c) Any dispute arising out of this Slot Charter Party shall be referred to arbitration at the place indicated in Box 23, subject to the procedures applicable there. The laws of the place indicated in Box 23 shall govern this Slot Charter Party.

(d) If Box 23 in Part I is not filled in, sub-clause (a) of this Clause shall apply.

*) *(a), (b), (c) are alternatives; indicate alternative agreed in Box 23.*”

In a standard charter party intended for use on a worldwide basis, it has not been considered reasonable to let the charter party be governed by one law system only or to fix only one venue of arbitration which may restrict the use of the charter party in practice.

It has therefore been found reasonable to let clause 23 provide for optional law systems and venues of arbitration by leaving it to the parties to make their own choice in each individual case and to fill in box 23 accordingly.

As follows from sub-clause 23(d), if box 23 is not filled in, sub-clause (a) of this clause (i.e. English law and arbitration in London) will automatically apply.

(4) Feedership charter parties

It is a sad fact but, as inspection of any major combined transport operator's P & I claims record will show (if only you could get a look at it!), the majority of catastrophes occur, not whilst on that operator's own top-class container-ships, but whilst on board second rate chartered vessels and smaller feeder services. Accordingly it is primarily at such times that the casualty invoking the LLMC global limitation provision is likely to occur.

Two bases of limitation are available to carriers of goods by sea. Firstly, what is usually called the package limitation (although a weight-based alternative is incorporated), under the Hague/Hague-Visby Rules, where limitation is available to the contracting carrier: the issuer of the bill of lading. Secondly, what is usually called global limitation (LLMC: Limitation of Liability for Maritime Claims) is available to "Owners, Owners' Managers and Charterers" only, because this was drafted in 1976 before extensive hub and spoke style of operation and consortium arrangements were in common operation and fully understood by those drafting such conventions. This second limitation is based on a formula by reference to the registered tonnage of the vessel.

In an effort to persuade the courts that interpretation of the LLMC Convention needs to take account of changes and developments since the convention was drafted, P&O Nedlloyd incorporated a global limitation of liability clause in their bill of lading (*see* Chapter 6). Whether this clause will succeed or not will depend upon what the judge had for breakfast, but carriers clearly need to put themselves in the best position to give themselves the maximum opportunity to succeed in this area.

If a casualty occurs to cargo, for which a CTO is principal carrier, on a vessel not owned or operated by that CTO, he is clearly in a better position to claim global limitation if he is a slot charterer than if he was a bill of lading holder, as is often the case with feeder vessels to and from hub ports. Accordingly, there is a need to procure a relationship with feeder operators that is technically governed by a slot charter party rather than a bill of lading.

To facilitate this a simple slot charter party has been prepared. It has been kept simple to avoid frightening feeder operators, who may be suspicious of reasons for change and, in effect, the slot charter party largely follows the contracts of carriage set out in the feeder operators' bills of lading. However an opportunity to ensure that the terms of that bill of lading do not contain any "nasties" has been taken by incorporating provisions "outlawing" demise clauses and any provisions contrary to the Hague-Visby Rules.

As some encouragement has been given in two recent English judgments, indicating that the judiciary are prepared to interpret the law sensibly to cope with circumstances which were not envisaged when it was drafted, it would seem that there is hope for combined transport operators in this area. The first of these cases (*The Aegean Sea* [1998] 2 Lloyd's Rep. 39) produced a useful item of *obiter* that charterers should be entitled to limit where they incur liability under bills of lading issued by them in place of the shipowner. In an even more recent decision (*The Tychy* [1999] 2 Lloyd's Rep. 11) the judge asserted that charterers meant all charterers and concluded that slot charterers were also included within the term charterers. In the circumstances combined transport operators would be well advised to ensure that their relationships with their feeder operators are governed by slot charters and not bills of lading. The format of a suitable wording for such a charter is as follows:

"Feeder Slot Charterparty

It is agreed

this _____ day of _______________

Between

_______________ (*the Charterer*) and
_______________ (*the Operator*)

in respect of the feeder service offered by the Operator between the ports of _______________, _______________, _______________ and _______________ using vessels for which the Operator is owner or disponent owner (charterer) as follows:

In consideration of the Charterer agreeing to use the services of the Operator on a non-exclusive basis, it is hereby agreed that, whenever the Charterer does so, carriage of the Charterer's containers and goods shall be effected upon the terms of this Slot Charter party.

The terms of the contract of carriage shall be the terms and conditions of the Operator's Bill of Lading as attached hereto always, where appropriate, amended by the following provisions. In the event of conflict between the terms and conditions of the Operator's Bill of Lading and this Slot Charter party, the latter shall be paramount and prevail.

(1) The Operator undertakes primary responsibility for the carriage of the Charterer's containers and goods and acts as the contracting carrier throughout carriage. Any Demise or Identity of Carrier provision in the Operator's Bill of Lading contract is hereby declared null and void.
(2) The Charterer's containers and goods shall be carried subject to the provisions of the Hague-Visby Rules and any provision in the Operator's Bill of Lading contract which conflicts with the said Rules is hereby declared null and void.
(3) Any dispute arising under this Slot Charter party shall be resolved according to the laws of _______________ in the courts of said country. However nothing herein shall preclude dispute resolution by reference to arbitration in a forum acceptable to both parties if both parties so agree.

(4) Remuneration shall be upon terms from time to time agreed by the parties and shall be fair and reasonable."

Note that the above draft leaves the law and jurisdiction provision open. Clearly English law and jurisdiction would be preferable to many charterers but this cannot be insisted upon on all occasions. What must be avoided is courts with long delays (India), courts known to take a nationalistic view according to the nationality of the plaintiff/defendant (too many to mention) and courts known to lack the requisite expertise (again a large number to choose from).

Need for action along these lines has been frequently demonstrated. In one recent example an Indian trade coaster sank with a full cargo of cashew nuts valued at (and Hague-Visby limit at) +US$3 million. The limitation fund of the coaster was –US$1 million, a shortfall of US$2 million between the CTO's bill of lading liability and his recourse to his feeder operator sub-contractor. Thus appropriate action in this area is well worthwhile.

One final point worth making is that this charter applies Hague-Visby Rules. This protects the CTO where his liability is Hague-Visby based as a carry over from the deep-sea leg liability. However, if the feeder is operating into/out of a Hamburg Rules country, suitable amendment is recommended.

Slot charters are essentially for use with containerised cargo, with which they are synonymous, but they do have their equivalents in conventional shipping in the space charters, which large shippers used to arrange with some carriers to guarantee them space on every sailing at a time when there was a scarcity of space during a trade boom and cargo was chasing shipping space, instead of vice versa like today. With space charters the charterers were usually merchants and the charter merely reserved space, with the bill of lading remaining as the contract of carriage. With slot charters, the charterer is usually another contracting carrier himself and the charter provides the terms of the contract of carriage.

CHAPTER 4

CONTAINER AND CONTAINERSPACE HIRING AGREEMENTS (CONSORTIUM OPERATIONS)

INTRODUCTION

Good container management is the key to profitability in any combined transport operation. Having the right number of the right type of containers in the right place at the right time with minimum empty moves is a valuable art to any operator as MT (empty) moves are expensive and earn nothing.

There are a variety of procedures which may be open to a combined transport operator in pursuit of this goal, all of which are affected by a variety of factors like:

- what trades the CTO operates in (opportunities for triangulation movements to overcome imbalances of trade);
- size of container fleet (the larger, the more options that are usually available);
- the number of "specials" (i.e. tanks, integral or port-hole reefers, ventilated containers etc.) needed in a trade (often one way only) and whether these can be utilised on the return journey or must be returned empty);
- seasonal variations in demand (meat, fruit and primary produce etc.).

In some consortia pools are created, so that, when a member needs a container, he takes the next one, regardless of ownership, always assuming that he has made a contribution to the pool sufficient to cover his trade share. In such circumstances there is need of a CHA (Container Hiring Agreement) to cover inter-line liabilities.

Containerspace Hiring Agreements come in handy in a consortium operation to minimise the number of part-full LCL containers moving and consolidate them, so as to use the minimum number of containers needed to carry the cargo concerned. So, to take an example, if several consortium members each have some small "sweep up" LCL consignments at Birmingham Containerbase consigned to Singapore, they are all put into the same container, instead of each member utilising a container for his consignments. In this way one container is used instead of three or four with consequent cost savings. A CSHA (containerspace hiring agreement) governs inter-line relationships and lines take it in turn to provide and operate the container used for this purpose.

CONTAINER HIRING AGREEMENT (CHA)

This is essentially a consortium operating contract, rather than an arm's-length one, and incorporates the usual waiver approach to liability, to minimise inter-line claims, found in consortium contracts where there is mutuality. It is frequently included in consortium agreements to apply whenever one member uses another member's container. This may occur:

- because the consortium operates a pool;
- because there is an arrangement that, if any member is short of any particular type of container in any location and another member has one available, the member who has a spare will hire it to the member needing it at a rate to be agreed but on the terms of the CHA.

In the same way that the operating agreement may provide for the automatic implementation and signature of a cross charter party, it may also provide the same for a container hiring agreement.

A typical container hiring agreement may contain the following terms:

"Dated
Between
(1) ________________(*the Owner*) and
(2) ________________(*the Hirer*)
It is agreed:

1. Scope of Agreement

(1) The period of this Agreement shall be from the date hereof until terminated by either party giving written notice.
(2) The terms hereof shall apply whenever the Owner hires one or more of its containers to the Hirer for the carriage of goods in a (*name of consortium*) service and the hiring commences during the period of this Agreement."

This clause is self-explanatory.

2. Remuneration

"The Owner shall be remunerated in accordance with the provisions from time to time separately agreed by or on behalf of the parties or in default of agreement shall receive such remuneration as shall be fair and reasonable."

This clause ensures that consideration is adequately covered in the contract to ensure that all three constituents of a contract, offer, acceptance and consideration, are present.

3. Owner's Responsibilities

"3.1 The Owner shall be liable to the Hirer for any loss or damage which the Hirer suffers arising as a result of a container to which this Agreement relates failing to be:

(a) physically compatible with the Vessels;
(b) of such specifications as may be determined from time to time by or on behalf of the parties;
(c) constructed to the specifications of any recognised classification society acceptable by or on behalf of the parties and operated within an approved scheme under the International Convention for Safe Containers and in date on its CSC plating;
(d) properly maintained;
(e) in compliance with the relevant port and other regulations (including quarantine regulations);
(f) constructed of taint-free materials; and
(g) free from defect, whether manifest or latent, in construction.

Provided that:

(i) The liability of the Owner to the Hirer for any failure to comply with this sub-clause, insofar as it relates to latent defects, shall not in any event exceed the amount (if any) recoverable by the Owner from any third party in connection with such liability, but the Owner shall take all reasonable steps (short of court action) to recover such amount and shall account therefor to the Hirer. For this purpose the Owner's insurers shall not be considered as third parties.
(ii) The Owner shall, upon the written request from the Hirer, allow the Hirer to take over all conduct of any enforcement of any rights which the Owner may have against any third party to enable the Hirer to exercise such rights in the Owner's name but at the Hirer's expense. The Owner shall co-operate as much as is reasonably possible to assist the Hirer to exercise such rights which the Owner may have against the third party.
(iii) If the Owner should not be willing to transfer to the Hirer all conduct of any enforcement of rights and to co-operate as required above in assisting the Hirer, the provisions of sub-clause (i) of this proviso shall be null and void. The Owner shall be deemed to have shown unwillingness to transfer if he has not given the necessary authority in writing to the Hirer to proceed within 30 days of receipt of a written request so to do.

3.2 Subject to sub-clause 3.1 above, the Owner shall be under no liability whatsoever to the Hirer for any loss or damage arising out of any circumstances relating to the condition of the container rendering it unsuitable for any purpose, even if arising as a result of the act, neglect or default of the Owner, its servants, agents or sub-contractors."

3.1: This sub-clause provides that, whilst the owner is liable to the hirer for the consequences of supplying a container that does not comply with the requirements of this sub-clause generally, the latent defect requirement is subject to the mutual waiver provision. (Note how on this occasion the *Smith and Anor.* v. *South Wales Switchgear* clause is not included because the indemnity should not apply in the event of negligence on the part of the owner.)

In all other respects the owner is liable for ensuring that containers, the subject of the CHA, meet the minimum requirements listed therein.

3.2: This sub-clause protects the owner from claims not outlined in sub-clause 3.1, so that, in the event of an accident involving a third party, the owner would only incur liability if he were in breach of sub-clause 3.1.

4. Indemnity and Agency

"4.1 The Hirer undertakes that no claim or allegation shall be made against the Owner or any servant, agent or sub-contractor of the Owner by any person whomsoever, other

than the Hirer, which imposes or attempts to impose upon the Owner or any such servant, agent or sub-contractor any liability whatsoever in respect of such loss or damage as is mentioned in Clause 3 above, or in respect of any injury to persons or damage to property arising or caused by or in connection with the container or its use during the time it is hired to the Hirer (even if such liability arises wholly or in part by reason of the act, neglect or default of the Owner or of such servant, agent or sub-contractor) and, in the event of any such claim or allegation nevertheless being made, the Hirer shall indemnify the Owner and such servant, agent and sub-contractor against all consequences whatsoever thereof.
4.2 The Hirer shall not make any claim or allegation against any servant, agent or sub-contractor of the Owner which imposes or attempts to impose on any such servant, agent or sub-contractor any liability whatsoever in respect of such loss or damage as is mentioned in Clause 3 above, or in respect of any injury to persons or damage to property arising or caused by or in connection with the container or its use during the time it is hired to the Hirer (even if such liability arises wholly or in part by reason of the act, neglect or default of the Owner or of such servant, agent or sub-contractor) and, in the event of any such claim or allegation nevertheless being made, the provisions of sub-clause 4.1 above shall apply as if such claim or allegation has been made by a person other than the Hirer.
4.3 Without prejudice to sub-clause 4.1 above the Owner authorises and empowers the Hirer to act as the Owner's agent and/or trustee to stipulate for the Owner to have as against other persons the benefit of any immunities, exemptions or liberties regarding the container the subject of this Agreement, but the Hirer shall have no authority to make any contract imposing any obligations upon the Owner in connection with the container.
4.4 Where the Owner is not the actual owner of the container the provisions of sub-clauses 4.1, 4.2 and 4.3 above shall also apply to the actual owner of the container, its servants, agents and sub-contractors in the same manner as they apply to the Owner, its servants, agents and sub-contractors."

These four sub-clauses equate to sub-clauses 9.1, 9.2, 9.3 and 9.5 of the cross charter party with the hirer in the position of the charterers and the owner in the position of the owners. They protect the owner from direct action in tort by a third party, attempting to avoid any protection in a contract with the hirer, by providing an indemnity from the hirer in the event of a circuitous action of this nature.

5. Hirer's Responsibilities

"5.1 Subject only to the Owner's liabilities to the Hirer mentioned in Clause 3 above, the Hirer shall be liable for all injury to persons or damage to property (including the container) whenever occurring, arising or caused by or in connection with the container or its use during the time it is hired to the Hirer whether as a result of the act, neglect or default of the Hirer, its servants, agents or sub-contractors or otherwise.
5.2 The Hirer shall comply with any restriction imposed by the Owner which the parties have separately agreed on the use of any container for particular classes of goods. If the Hirer shall fail so to comply it shall indemnify the Owner against all consequences thereof.
5.3 The Hirer shall be under no liability under sub-clauses 5.1 or 5.2 above unless the loss or damage exceeds US$500 for any one incident. Where damage, repair and/or cleaning costs exceed US$500 per incident, the Hirer shall be liable to Owners for the reasonable cost of repair and cleaning or the replacement of the container(s) in full at

the line's depreciated value, whichever is the lesser, unless the Hirer can show that the Owner was in breach of his obligations in sub-clause 3.1 above or that loss or damage did not arise during the currency of this Agreement.
5.4 For the avoidance of doubt, it is recorded that the Hirer shall be liable for General Average contributions and salvage charges in respect of the container during the period of hire."

5.1: This sub-clause makes it absolutely clear that, except for the owner's liability to the hirer under clause 3, the hirer is responsible for all liabilities incurred whilst the container is on hire to him, as well as for damage to the container.

5.2: This sub-clause provides for any restrictions as to use which the owner may place upon the hirer of the container (e.g. no wet salted hides) so far as the types of cargo to be carried and provides an indemnity for any breach thereof.

5.3: This sub-clause provides for the hirer to be liable to the owner for container damage/cleaning costs above US$500 per incident, unless he can show that the owner breached clause 3.1 or that loss or damage did not occur whilst on hire. The hirer is not liable to the owner for claims below US$500 in order to obviate small claims where the administration costs would make the amount concerned not worth pursuing.

5.4: Any GA contributions incurred during hire are for the hirer's account.

The contract usually finishes with a suitable law and arbitration clause following the model in the other consortium contracts (operating agreement and cross charter party) and a definitions clause defining sub-contractors similar to that in clause 12 of the cross charter party.

The mutual waiver provision in this contract assumes that, over a period, lines are hirer and owner on a similar number of occasions. If any line were a constant underprovider of containers there would be imperfect mutuality and an agreement in these terms would be inequitable.

CONTAINERSPACE HIRING AGREEMENT (CSHA)

CSHAs are designed to prevent numerous containers with individual carriers' small consignments of LCL cargo, moving from the same place to the same place, when it is clearly more economical to rationalise and consolidate all into one container (all other things, like compatibility of cargoes, being equal). It is not usual for freight to change hands in such an arrangement as participants take it in turn to provide and operate the "sweep up" container, thereby ensuring equity. This means that, on any given sailing, one (or more) carriers may be collecting freight from their customers without incurring the cost of carriage. Accordingly, it is clearly equitable that, if a container owner is receiving no freight from a consortium partner for carrying that partner's cargo, he should do so on no liability terms.

A typical hiring agreement may contain the following terms:

"Dated ______________
Between
(1) ______________ (*the Owner*)
and
(2) ______________ (*The hirer*)
It is agreed:

1. Scope of Agreement

1.1 The period of this Agreement shall be from the date hereof until terminated by either party giving written notice.
1.2 The terms hereof shall apply wherever the Owner hires space in one of his containers (whether owned leased or hired) to the Hirer for the carriage of the Hirer's goods in the (*name of consortium*) service and the hiring commences during the period of this Agreement. For the purpose of this Agreement, Hirers goods means goods owned by the Hirer or in respect of which the Hirer, acting as a Principal Carrier, has issued a bill of lading or other contract of carriage to a merchant."

Like Clause 1 of the CHA, this clause is self-explanatory.

2. Owner's Responsibilities

"2.1 The Owner shall carry the Hirer's goods from the agreed place of receipt to the agreed place of delivery upon the terms of this Agreement.
2.2 (a) The liability of the Owner to the Hirer for loss, damage, delay or expense of whatsoever nature and howsoever arising in connection with this Agreement (even if such liability arises wholly or in part by reason of the act, neglect or default of the Owner or of his servants, agents or sub-contractors) shall not in any event exceed the amount (if any) recoverable by the Owner from any third party in connection with such liability, but the Owner shall take all reasonable steps (short of court action) to recover such amount and shall account therefor to the Hirer. For this purpose the Owner's insurers shall not be considered as third parties.
(b) The Owner shall, upon the written request from the Hirer, allow the Hirer to take over all conduct of any enforcement of any rights which the Owner may have against any third party to enable the Hirer to exercise such rights in the Owner's name but at the Hirer's expense. The Owner shall co-operate as much as is reasonably possible to assist the Hirer to exercise such rights which the Owner may have against the third party.
(c) If the Owner should not be willing to transfer to the Hirer all conduct of any enforcement of rights and to co-operate as required above in assisting the Hirer, the provisions of sub-clause (a) shall be null and void. The Owner shall be deemed to have shown unwillingness to transfer if he has not given the necessary authority in writing to the Hirer to proceed within 30 days of receipt of a written request so to do."

2.1: This is a self-explanatory basic statement of intent.

2.2: This is the full mutual waiver from the hirer in favour of the owner in respect of all liability of the owner to the hirer. The principle of the mutual waiver is explained exhaustively in Chapter 2.

3. Indemnity and Agency

"3.1 The Hirer undertakes that no claim or allegation shall be made against the Owner or any servant, agent or sub-contractor of the Owner by any person whomsoever other than the Hirer, which imposes or attempts to impose upon the Owner or any such servant, agent or sub-contractor any liability whatsoever in respect of loss, damage, delay or expense to or in connection with the Hirer's goods carried in the Owner's container (even if such liability arises wholly or in part by reason of the act, neglect or default of the Owner or of such servant, agent or sub-contractor) and, in the event of any such claim or allegation nevertheless being made, the Hirer shall indemnify the Owner and such servant, agent or sub-contractor against all consequences whatsoever thereof.

3.2 The Hirer shall not make any claim or allegation against any servant, agent or sub-contractor of the Owner which imposes or attempts to impose on any such servant, agent or sub-contractor any liability whatsoever in respect of loss, damage, delay or expense to or in connection with the Hirer's goods carried in the Owner's container (even if such liability arises wholly or in part by reason of the act, neglect or default of the Owner or of such servant, agent or sub-contractor) and, in the event of any such claim or allegation nevertheless being made, the provision of sub-clause 3.1 shall apply as if such claim or allegation had been made by a person other than the Hirer.

3.3 Without prejudice to sub-clause 3.1 the Owner authorises and empowers the Hirer to act as the Owner's agent to stipulate for the Owner to have as against other persons the benefit of any immunities, exemptions or liberties regarding the Hirer's goods, but the Hirer shall have no authority to make any contract imposing any obligations upon the Owner in connection with the Hirer's goods or their carriage.

3.4 Where the Owner is not the actual owner of the container, the provisions of sub-clauses 3.1, 3.2 and 3.3 above shall also apply to the actual owner of the container, his servants, agents and sub-contractors in the same manner as they apply to the Owner, his servants, agents and sub-contractors."

These four sub-clauses equate to sub-clauses 9.1, 9.2, 9.3 and 9.5 of the cross charter party (with the hirer in the position of the charterers and the owner in the position of the owners) and clause 4 of the container hiring agreement. They protect the owner from direct action in tort by a third party, in order to avoid any protection in a contract with the hirer, by providing an indemnity from the hirer in the event of a circuitous action of this nature.

4. Hirer's Responsibilities

"4.1 (a) The liability of the Hirer to the Owner for loss, damage, delay or expense of whatsoever nature and howsoever arising in connection with this Agreement, other than a liability under sub-clause 4.2 below (even if such liability arises wholly or in part by reason of the act, neglect, or default of the Hirer or his servants, agents or sub-contractors) shall not in any event exceed the amount (if any) recoverable by the Hirer from any third party in connection with such liability, but the Hirer shall take all reasonable steps (short of court action) to recover such amount and shall account therefor to the Owner. For this purpose the Hirer's insurers shall not be considered as third parties.

(b) The Hirer shall, upon the written request from the Owner, allow the Owner to take over all conduct of any enforcement of any rights which the Hirer may have against any third party to enable the Owner to exercise such rights in the Hirer's name but at the Owner's expense. The Hirer shall co-operate as much as is reasonably possible to assist the Owner to exercise such rights which the Hirer may have against the third party.

(c) If the Hirer should not be willing to transfer to the Owner all conduct of any enforcement of rights and to co-operate as required above in assisting the Owner, the provisions of sub-clause (a) shall be null and void. The Hirer shall be deemed to have shown unwillingness to transfer if he has not given the necessary authority in writing to the Owner to proceed within 30 days of receipt of a written request so to do.

4.2 The liability (if any) of the Hirer to the Owner under this Agreement in respect of loss of or damage to the container in which the Hirer's goods are carried shall be limited to whichever is the lesser of the cost of repair or replacement of the container, plus in each case any amount in excess of such cost which may be recoverable from any third party; provided always that the Hirer shall be under no liability for such loss or damage unless such costs exceed US$500."

4.1: This sub-clause is the converse of sub-clause 2.2 and provides a mutual waiver from the owner to the hirer, except for damage caused to the owner's container. This puts the hirer in the same position as he would have encountered if he had carried the cargo in his own container, in which case his container would have been damaged/lost.

Note that the waiver only covers claims from the owner and not any third party/co-charterer, which matters are left to the operating agreement. Also there is no equivalent in this agreement in favour of the hirer from the owner of the indemnity in clause 3 in favour of the owner from the hirer.

4.2: This clause provides the quantum for the liability of the hirer for container loss/damage excluded in the mutual waiver in sub-clause 4.1 and incorporates the usual minimum claim of US$500 to remove uneconomic claims.

5. Payments

"The Owner shall be remunerated in accordance with provisions from time to time to be separately agreed by or on behalf of the parties or, in default of agreement, shall receive such remuneration as shall be fair and reasonable. Such remuneration shall cover all costs of providing the space, including but not limited to inland haulage charges, Slot Charter fees, stuffing and stripping charges and normal cleaning before and after use."

As mentioned above, it is not usual practice for the owner to levy any charges for freight on the hirer, consideration being present in the reciprocal arrangement whereby the hirer applies the same approach when roles are reversed and the lines each take their turn to provide the container. This is the basis of payment "from time to time to be separately agreed by or on behalf of the parties". Accordingly this clause is included merely to provide visible evidence of consideration in the contract.

Like the container hiring agreement, the contract usually finishes with a suitable law and arbitration clause, following the model in the other consortium contracts, and a definitions clause defining sub-contractors, similar to that in clause 12 of the cross charter party.

CHAPTER 5

CONTAINER LEASING AND EQUIPMENT HANDOVER AGREEMENTS (GENERAL OPERATION)

Outside of consortium operations a plethora of individual contracts operate to govern the owner/hirer relationship in the container leasing industry. Most of the major container leasing companies have their own individual contracts specifically constructed to dovetail into their own particular operation and requirements. Inevitably such contracts tend to be lessor friendly because, although they are usually signed by the lessee and are thus not contracts of adhesion, they are drafted by the lessor and are thus subject to the *contra proferentem* doctrine, which construes any ambiguity narrowly against the drafter.

In this chapter I will consider three contracts of this nature:

- CONLEASE: the BIMCO standard container leasing contract published in 1997;
- a typical leasing agreement of the type used by my erstwhile employers for leasing outside of the consortium arrangement;
- equipment handover agreement: the record of the condition of a container when released to a customer/third party (e.g. for customer to take away to premises to load/unload and return) and when received back incorporating a short contract, principally covering liability and operational matters during the period that the container is out of the hands of the CTO.

CONLEASE

In 1997 BIMCO published a standard container leasing agreement called CONLEASE and in their BIMCO Bulletin they published a very adequate résumé of the circumstances leading up to this publication as well as brief explanatory notes of the clauses therein. As these notes are perfectly adequate, I reproduce them here with BIMCO's kind permission for the benefit of readers of this book:

As container shipping became a mature industry and developed its own methods of operation, a growing need was felt for tailor-made documents to cover the various activities in this field. In response to this development

1. Reference number	**STANDARD CONTAINER LEASE AGREEMENT** **CODENAME: "CONLEASE"** **(Issued 1997)** PART I
2. Effective date of agreement (Cl. 2 (a))	
3. Lessor (Name, Address)	4. Lessee (Name, Address)

5. Equipment

Type	Quantity	Depreciated Value (Cl 5 (b), 13(a), 14 (a)(1))	Per diem rate (Cl. 7 (a))	Per diem after build-down period (Cl. 10)

6. Commencement date of lease (Cl. 2 (b))	7. Earliest termination date (Cl. 2 (b))	8. Direct Interchange fee (Cl. 4 (c))	9. No. of days notice for repairs (Cl. 5 (b), Cl. 7 (d))

10. Pick-up locations (Cl. 6 (b))	11. Other charges (Cl. 7 (a))
12. Lessee's billing address (Cl. 7 (b))	13. Lessor's bank account (Cl. 7 (c))
14. No. of days for payment (Cl. 7 (c)) / 15. Notice of termination (Cl. 9 (a))	16. Early termination dates and per diems (Cl. 9 (c)) Date / Per Diem
17. Build-down period (Cl. 10)	
18. Minimum limit of general liability insurance (Cl. 14 (a)(ii), 14 (b)(i))	19. Law and Arbitration (state a. London, b. New York or c. alternative place) (Cl. 15 (a), (b), (c))
20. Maximum amount for small claims/shortened arbitration procedure (Cl. 15 (a), (b))	

21. Additional clauses agreed

It is agreed that this Contract shall be performed subject to the terms and conditions of Part I, including additional clauses if any agreed and stated in Box 21and of Part II. In the event of a conflict of conditions, the provisions of Part I shall prevail over those of Part II to the extent of such conflict but no further.

Signature Lessor	Signature Lessee

Printed and sold by Fr. G. Knudtzons Bogtrykkeri A/S, Vallensbaekvej 61, Box 128, DK-2625 Vallensbaek, Denmark, Telefax +45 4366 0708
by authority of The Baltic and International Maritime Council (BIMCO), Copenhagen

Figure 3: Standard Container Lease Agreement: "CONLEASE"

BIMCO in 1990 issued a specialised time charter called "Boxtime", followed three years later by "Slothire" which covers the hiring of space on vessels for the carriage of containers between two ports.

It was therefore not surprising that a requirement was also felt to standardise the various lease agreements which had come into use and which often presented the Lessees with extremely complicated terms and conditions.

An earlier attempt by the International Chamber of Shipping (ICS) to negotiate a standard lease agreement with the Institute of International Container Lessors (IICL) had failed. However, the demand by BIMCO members for a standard lease agreement continued and this led to a decision by the Documentary Committee to develop such a document. A sub-committee commenced work in early 1994, basing itself on the last draft which had been produced by the ICS working group.

It was the intention that when a suitable draft had been produced this would form the basis of discussions with IICL representing the vast majority of Lessors. However, after having initially shown interest in the project, IICL at a later stage declined to participate in discussions or even to offer comments on the draft.

All efforts to get IICL into negotiations having been in vain the Documentary Committee finally decided at its meeting in June 1997 to issue "CONLEASE" as a recommended BIMCO form without the endorsement of Lessors. As such it can therefore be used as a pro forma agreement to be used by Lessees as a basis for negotiations with container Lessors.

In designing the document BIMCO has aimed at producing a balanced and simple document without too much of the legalistic ballast which has made many of the current Lessors' contracts almost unreadable even to their own sales staff. The aim has also been to produce a single document which can be used for Master Leases as well as Term Leases. Finally it was decided at this stage not to make provisions for specials such as reefers, in view of the complications involved.

This being a new document the Secretariat is of course very interested to receive feedback from users in order to gauge the degree of usage and the problems which are encountered in negotiating it with Lessors. Users are therefore encouraged to advise the Secretariat of their experiences in order that adjustments might be made in due course.

Special observations

In accordance with standard BIMCO practice the Agreement is laid out in two parts. Part I is in a box layout and contains all the variable information, whilst Part II contains the standard terms and conditions. Part I forms the actual Contract and in the event of any conflict in conditions between the two parts the conditions of Part I will prevail.

The main idea behind this division is that it is made convenient for the users to do all the filling in, amendments and special provisions in Part I leaving the printed text of Part II unaltered. In this context it should be emphasised that a standard contract constitutes an integrated whole and that any changes to one or more of the clauses may upset the intended balance of the contract as a whole. This fact should never be lost sight of when attempting to introduce changes or amendments to the standard clauses in Part II which have been carefully drafted to take care of the contractual and legal aspects.

Part I

All variable details pertaining to the particular contract are to be entered in the boxes provided. Each box contains a short description of the intended contents and a cross-reference to the relevant clause or clauses in the printed body of Part II.

Although some of the boxes in Part I may call for special comments in these Notes, it has been considered more practical to make such comments when dealing with the relevant clauses in Part II.

Part II

Preamble

"Subject to the terms and conditions of this Agreement with reference number specified in Box 1, the Lessor named in Box 3 hereby agrees to lease to the Lessee named in Box 4 and the Lessee hereby agrees to lease from the Lessor the Equipment more particularly described in Box 5."

Part II starts with a number of definitions most of which for obvious reasons are self-explanatory.

Definitions

Equipment means freight containers as defined by the International Standards Organisation (ISO).

Master Lease means a lease agreement between Lessors and Lessees whereby Equipment is leased at fixed rates and conditions, but with a variable term and quantity and variable (re)delivery depots.

Term Lease means a lease agreement between Lessors and Lessees whereby Equipment is leased at fixed rates and conditions with a predetermined delivery schedule and for a fixed period of time.

Sub-lease means a contract by which the Lessee gives the use of Equipment to a third party for a specified period of time, but whereby the Lessee remains responsible for the Equipment under the terms and conditions of its Lease Agreement with the Lessors.

Direct Interchange means the transfer of leased Equipment between two parties both having a Lease Agreement with the same Lessor whereby at the time of transfer the receiving party assumes the responsibility for such transferred Equipment under its own Lease Agreement with the Lessor.

Replacement Value means the purchase of new Equipment of the same type on the date of replacement.

Depreciated Value means the amount agreed to be paid by the Lessee to the Lessor as replacement for Equipment lost or damaged beyond repair and which amount is determined by depreciating the agreed replacement value of the Equipment at an agreed rate per annum to an agreed residual value commencing from the date that the Equipment was manufactured as stated on the CSC plate.

Latent Defect means any defect that is not, or was not, apparent at the time of on-hire of the Equipment, arising from any event occurring before on-hire, including but not limited to, design, material, manufacture, workmanship, modification or maintenance.

Wear and Tear occurs through normal operational use in an industry pattern due to inevitable, continuous deterioration not reasonably avoidable by the user and may affect the cosmetic appearance of the Equipment and by accumulation or degree may eventually affect the integrity of the Equipment. Wear and tear shall include, but not be limited to:

(i) Corrosion of metal components not due to contact with foreign substances;
(ii) Delamination or rot of wooden components, such as general deterioration of floor, including expansion, shrinkage or warping arising our of normal use;
(iii) Colour fading or adhesion failure of decals;
(iv) Loose or missing parts or marking, except those that are normally removable, in the absence of evidence of accompanying damage;
(v) General paint failure or fading not due to contamination;
(vi) General wear and deterioration at corner fittings;
(vii) General deterioration at door gasket and fitting, including loose and corroded fittings or loose fittings arising from normal deterioration of doors;
(viii) Scratches to metal.”

The most difficult term to define appeared to be the concept of Wear and Tear and in the end it was decided to use the “definition” from the IICL 5 Repair Standards where a number of examples illustrate the concept.

Clause 1: Marginal Headings

“The marginal headings of this Agreement are for identification only and shall not be deemed to be part hereof or be taken into consideration in the interpretation or construction of this Agreement.”

This clause is self-explanatory

Clause 2: Term of the Agreement

“(a) All terms and conditions of this Agreement shall take effect from the date stated in Box 2 and shall remain in force until all Equipment covered by this Agreement has been redelivered.

(b) The period of lease for the full amount of Equipment stated in Box 5 shall commence on the date stated in Box 6 and shall continue at least until the date stated in Box 7.”

Sub-clause (a) states that the Agreement is effective from the date that the first container, the subject of this Agreement, is taken on hire until the last container has been redelivered.

The intention of sub-clause (b) is, in the case of a Term Lease, to define the period commencing after a certain build-up period, when the agreed number of containers has been on-hired and which ends when the build-down period described in Clause 10 commences. In the case of a Master Lease, although containers are continuously picked up and redelivered, it is nevertheless common that a certain minimum number of boxes during a certain period is agreed upon.

Clause 3: Condition of Equipment on Delivery

"(a) The Lessors warrant that at the time of delivery the Equipment shall be in a good and serviceable condition and shall have been designed, manufactured, tested and maintained in compliance with the standards detailed hereinafter:

(i) International Standards Organisation (ISO);

(ii) International Convention for Safe Containers (CSC) of 1972 or any amendment thereof;

(iii) Customs Convention on Containers of 1956 and 1972 or any amendment thereof;

(iv) Australian Quarantine Regulations in respect of Timber Component Treatment;

(v) Current IICL Standards for Repair and Cleaning.

(b) The Lessor warrants that the Equipment is delivered free from all liens and encumbrances.

(c) The Lessor warrants that the period of validity of the CSC Safety Approval Plate is 30 months from the date of on-hire, unless the Equipment is CSC controlled under an Approved Continuous Examination Programme (ACEP).

(d) The Lessee may appoint a surveyor to inspect any Equipment prior to on-hire. The Lessor will make the Equipment available for this inspection. The surveyor will apply the standards set out in the latest edition of the IICL Container Inspection and Repair Manuals. The surveyor's report of the condition of the Equipment at on-hire shall be prima facie evidence of the condition of the Equipment taken on hire."

This clause requires a warranty from the Lessors that the containers are in a good and serviceable conditions when delivered. It also sets out the most important standards to which the containers must be designed, manufactured, tested and maintained. It seems that a number of leasing companies object to giving such a warranty, but in BIMCO's opinion Lessees can be quite firm on this requirement. Sub-clause (c) ensures that unless the container is under an Approved Continuous Examination Programme (ACEP), the validity of the CSC Plate will be at least 30 months from on-hire.

On the financial side the Lessor is required in sub-clause (b) to warrant that the container on delivery is free from all liens and encumbrances.

Clause 4: Title to Equipment, Sub-lease and Direct Interchange

"(a) The Equipment shall at all times remain the property of the Lessor, and the Lessee shall acquire no title to Equipment by virtue of paying rents, costs oftransportationorrepairs,registrationorlicensingfees,taxes(propertyexcise or any other governmental fees or charges) or any other expenses or charges related to or assessed against such Equipment or its operation during the period of this Agreement.

(b) The Lessee shall not, without the Lessor's prior written consent, which shall not be unreasonably withheld, assign any right or interest in or to this Agreement or the Equipment, nor sub-lease Equipment except to a company which is directly or indirectly associated with the Lessee. In case of such assignment or sub-lease, the Lessee will remain responsible for all obligations in accordance with this Agreement.

(c) The Lessee may transfer Equipment to a third party in a Direct Interchange, but only with the Lessor's written consent, which shall not be unreasonably withheld. When the third party has confirmed to the Lessor its agreement with such a transfer, the Lessee's objections to pay rental shall cease and a Direct Interchange fee as stated in Box 8 shall be paid by the Lessee to the Lessor.

(d) The Equipment shall have the Lessor's serial numbers and other identifying marks affixed thereto, which shall not be obliterated, altered, concealed or otherwise changed or hidden from view by the Lessee so as to prevent or block access to such numbers or marks without prior written agreement from the Lessor. The Lessee has the option to have its own company logo applied on the Equipment provided that same is to be removed for the Lessee's account upon redelivery of the Equipment."

It is established in this clause that the equipment at all times remains the property of the Lessor whatever the Lessee may have paid as rent, repair costs, fees or any other expenses or charges. This implies that in case of a total loss the wreck remains the property of the Lessor even though the Lessee has paid for the replacement or depreciated value. It was considered that the burden of disposal of the wreck including possible liabilities was not compensated by any residual value the wreck might have.

Sub-clause (b) allows for sub-leasing under certain conditions and will mainly be used between Lessees which are in some way associated with another. It can have certain advantages but the original Lessor remains responsible for the container and for its eventual redelivery.

Sub-clause (c) allows for Direct Interchanges, an often used method for correcting imbalances as opposed to sub-leasing. The advantage with Direct Interchange is that the original Lessee can remove the container from his system and does not need to reposition the box, but it requires that the new user has an existing lease agreement with the Lessor. Normally an administration fee is charged for this service.

Clause 5: Condition of Equipment on Redelivery

"(a) The Equipment shall be redelivered in like condition to the condition at on-hire, normal Wear and Tear excepted and unless advised by the Lessor to the contrary in accordance with sub-clause 5(b), the Lessee may assume that the Equipment has been redelivered in undamaged condition.

(b) In the event that Equipment is redelivered in a damaged condition, excepting all normal Wear and Tear, the Lessor shall within the number of working days stated in Box 9 give notice to the Lessee providing a detailed estimate of repairs. If the Lessee does not respond to the Lessor within the number of working days stated in Box 9 of receiving the detailed estimate of repairs, the Lessor shall be entitled to assume that the Lessee agrees with the estimate of repairs and will pay for the said repairs, excepting all normal Wear and Tear, at the amount specified in the estimate, on presentation of an invoice.

If the Lessee disagrees with the estimate of repair costs and/or disagrees that any item therein should be for the Lessee's account, he shall detail his objections by notice to the Lessor within the period provided in Box 9.

In the event of a continuing dispute the parties shall within 14 days of the date of the Lessee's notice appoint a joint surveyor who will survey the Equipment and review the estimate of repairs. The parties agree to be bound by the decision of the joint surveyor as to the extent of the repairs payable by the Lessee and the reasonable cost thereof and to share the cost of the survey.

All damages will be defined in accordance with the current IICL Inspection Standards and all repairs will be performed in accordance with the current IICL Standards for Repair and Cleaning.

In the event that an agreed estimate of repairs exceeds the depreciated value of the Equipment as stated in Box 5, the Lessee will pay to the Lessor the Depreciated Value of the Equipment."

Sub-clause (a) stipulates that the container must be redelivered in the same good and serviceable condition as when picked up, normal wear and tear excepted. This not only relates to the container's physical condition but also to its cleanliness and general cargo-worthiness.

The rest of the clause describes the procedure to be followed in case the container is redelivered in damaged condition and is self-explanatory.

Clause 6: Pick-ups and Drop-offs

"(a) Master Lease: The Lessee may pick up Equipment at any of the Lessor's depots as may from time be mutually agreed. The Lessor shall not unreasonably withhold Equipment from the Lessee and shall use his best endeavours to fulfill the requirementss of the Lessee.

(b) Term Lease: The Lessee may pick up Equipment in the minimum quantities per period of time indicated at each of the Lessor's depots stated in Box 10.

Save for the provisions of Clauses 9 and 10 such Equipment shall remain on hire for at least the period stipulated in Clause 2(b).

(c) Subject to the terms of this Agreement, the Lessee may redeliver any of the Equipment, to any of the Lessor's depots designated in Annex A which may contain permissible redelivery quota and drop-off charges, or as may from time to time be mutually agreed. Redelivery will terminate this Lease Agreement insofar as it relates to the redelivered Equipment.

(a) and (b) are alternatives. Delete whichever is not applicable."

It is in the area of pick-ups and drop-off that the main distinction between Term Leases and Master Leases appears and it is therefore in this clause that one of two alternatives may be chosen. In sub-clause (a) the Master Lease option allows the Lessee to pick up containers at the Lessor's depots in quantities and at costs which are from time to time agreed. Redelivery under this alternative takes place in accordance with sub-clause (c) which may also apply to redeliveries under the second alternative, Term Lease. Pick-ups under this second alternative often take place in batches from a limited number of depots or other locations such as factories. A delivery schedule may be inserted in Box 10.

Clause 7: Rental and other Charges, Payment

"(a) In consideration for leasing the Equipment from the Lessor, the Lessee shall, as from the pick-up date, be liable to pay to the Lessor, as rent, the per diem leasing rate specified in Box 5, as well as any other charges which may be agreed upon and enumerated in Box 11. The Lessee's obligations to pay rental will cease on the day after redelivery into any of the Lessor's designated depots.

(b) An invoice shall be sent to the Lessee's billing address as stated in Box 12.

(c) Payment shall be made by the Lessee to the Lessor's bank account as stated in Box 13, within the number of working days stated in Box 14 of the date of the Lessor's invoice.

(d) The Lessee shall, within the number of days stated in Box 9, give written notice to the Lessor of any disputed items on the Lessor's invoice. The Lessor will reconcile disputed items within the number of days stated in Box 9 by either providing supporting documents for such items or by issuing an appropriate adjustment of the invoice. Notification of disputed items shall not prejudice the obligation of the Lessee to pay the undisputed portion of any invoice within the number of days stated in Box 14 after receipt."

The provisions concerning the payment of rental and other charges are fairly straightforward and perhaps somewhat oversimplified, only laying down the basic principles. It should in this respect be noted that the Agreement is silent on matters such as financial leases, payment schedules, self-billing schemes etc., leaving it to the parties to agree on these separately.

Clause 8: Taxes, Fees and Fines

"The Lessee shall pay all taxes, dues and charges levied on or against the Equipment arising out of or in connection with the use of the Equipment.

Upon the return of any Equipment to the Lessor, and provided it is a permissible return under the conditions of this Lease Agreement, the Lessor shall indemnifty the Lessee from any import duties or taxes whatsoever that may be imposed from the time the Equipment was returned to the Lessor provided that the Equipment is redelivered within 60 days of the importation date. The Lessee shall, to the best of its ability, and at the Lessor's request, assist the Lessor to avoid any import duties or taxes by co-operating to the fullest extent in requesting extension of the same as local regulations permit.

The Lessor shall pay all taxes, dues and charges levied on or against the Equipment arising out of or in connection with the ownership of the Equipment."

This clause attempts to strike a balance between Lessors and Lessees as far the payment of taxes, fees and fines is concerned. All such payments arising out of the operation of the container are for account of the Lessee, whilst those arising out of ownership are for Lessor's account.

In various countries import duties are assessed if a container remains there longer than a certain period of time. As long as the container is on hire with the Lessee this import duty will be his responsibility. Should he have redelivered the box to the Lessor then the latter becomes responsible for any import duties from the time of redelivery, provided this takes place within 60 days of importation. The Lessee is, however, required to assist the Lessor in avoiding import duty by requesting extension of stay wherever possible.

Clause 9: Termination of Agreement

"(a) Either party may terminate this Agreement by giving the other party written notice of termination at least the number of working days stated in Box 15 prior to the date stated in Box 7 or any later date agreed to by the parties.

(b) The Lessee may upon written notice cancel this Agreement with immediate effect insofar as it relates to any Equipment

(i) the use of which shall have been curtailed or obstructed by any legislation or regulation of any Government or statutory body of any country where the Lessee wishes to use said Equipment; or

(ii) which is shown to have latent defects such that it is unsafe or unsuitable for continued use.

Such Equipment shall be returned to the Lessor as soon as is practicable in accordance with Clause 6(c).

(c) Notwithstanding the stipulations of Clause 2 and sub-clause 6(b) and by giving the number of working days advance notice as stipulated in Box 15, the Lessee shall have the option of terminating the Agreement on any of the dates stated in Box 16. In such case the hire shall be retroactively adjusted in accordance with the appropriate per diem rates entered behind the dates in Box 16."

Apart from the possibility of termination by either party upon giving written notice, there is a further possibility for the Lessee to terminate if for some reason the containers cannot be operated in certain countries or if latent defects are found.

In order to give the Lessee some flexibility to adjust his stock of leased containers to changing market conditions sub-clause (c) allows earlier termination at certain dates but against payment of a penalty in the form of higher rental, retroactively applied.

Clause 10: Build-down Period

"On the date of termination as stipulated in Clause 2(b) a build-down period shall commence, during which time all the Equipment shall be redelivered to the Lessor. The length and redelivery schedule of the build-down period shall be as set out in Box 17.

Equipment still on lease after the build-down period will be charged the per diem rental stated in Box 5 until finally redelivered to the Lessor."

It is obvious that with any sizeable quantity of containers spread out geographically timely redelivery becomes a logistical problem. It is therefore common that a certain build-down period is agreed during which the containers may be redelivered and are on hire at the agreement rate. In order to induce redelivery within the build-down period it is common that the rate rises sharply at the end of this period.

Clause 11: Insolvency

"(a) Both the Lessee and the Lessor shall be entitled to terminate this Agreement in the event of an order being made or resolution passed for the winding up, dissolution, liquidation or bankruptcy of the other party (otherwise than for the purpose of reconstruction or amalgamation) or if a receiver is appointed, or if the other party suspends payment, ceases to carry on business or makes any special arrangement with their creditors.

(b) If the Lessor terminates this Agreement according to sub-clause 11(a), the Lessor shall have the right to take immediate possession of all empty Equipment leased to the Lessee under this Agreement.

(c) Should the Lessor obtain the right to immediate possession of any empty Equipment covered by this Agreement, then the Lessee must, upon written notice from the Lessor, immediately insofar as he is able to do so, notify the Lessor of the exact location of all Equipment leased to it under this Agreement and promptly redeliver all such empty Equipment to the nearest Lessor's depot unless otherwise mutually agreed."

This clause provides for termination by either party in the event of insolvency of the other. If it is the Lessor who terminates he shall have the right of immediate repossession of his equipment provided it is empty. The reason for this condition is an attempt to protect cargo owners against becoming hostages to the situation. It should in this connection be borne in mind that it is the Lessee who has the contractual duty towards the cargo owners to deliver their cargo whilst there is no such duty on the part of the Lessor.

Clause 12: Maritime Lien

"The Equipment is supplied for the purpose of intermodal operations in international trade and may be used for the carriage of lawful goods by sea as well as in inland transport including the handling at terminals and inland depots and freight stations. The Equipment is not designated for use on any particular Vessel and consequently no maritime lien securing the obligations under this Agreement may be attached to any Vessel connected in any way with the Lessee.

The Lessor is relying solely upon the credit of the Lessee in supplying containers under this lease."

This is one of the most controversial clauses in the Agreement and it is very likely that Lessors will insist on having it deleted. Nevertheless the sub-committee has decided to maintain the clause mainly to pre-empt inclusion by the Lessors of a specific clause allowing the arrest of any vessel which might carry the containers in question, irrespective of whether the Owners of the vessel were in default towards the Lessor or not. However, in a number of cases in the recent past where container shipping lines have gone bankrupt, Lessors have suffered considerable losses due to their equipment being non-recoverable. This has hardened their attitude in respect of having the right of lien.

Clause 13: Liabilities and Indemnity

"(a) The Lessee shall be liable to the Lessor for the actual or constructive total loss of, or damage, normal Wear and Tear excepted, to any Equipment occurring during the period of this Agreement.

The Lessee shall immediately notify the Lessor in writing of any actual or constructive total loss of any Equipment and upon such notice the Lessee's obligations to pay rental shall cease. In the event that such actual or constructive total loss occurs, the Lessee shall be promptly invoiced therefor and pay to the Lessor the agreed Depreciated Value of such Equipment. Should the Lessee later determine that Equipment previously declared lost has been recovered, the Lessor will, at the request of the Lessee, reimburse any previously paid Replacement Value/Depreciated Value less any rental accrued from the date the Equipment was declared lost.

(b) The Lessee shall defend, indemnify and hold the Lessor harmless for any and all claims, losses, expenses, costs or damages (including without limitation all reasonable expenses in defending any claim or suit or enforcing this indemnity, such as court costs, attorney's fees, and other expenses) arising or alleged to arise directly or indirectly or incidentally out of:

(i) any failure of the Lessee to comply with its obligations under this Agreement;

(ii) any claim, whether private or governmental, for bodily injury or death to persons (including employees of the Lessor) and for loss of or damage to property, cargo and/or vessels and/or means of transport, arising out of or incident to the possession, leasing, operation, control or use of the Equipment by the Lessee.

(c) The Lessor shall defend, indemnify and hold the Lessee harmless for any and all claims, losses, expenses, costs or damages (including without limitation all reasonable expenses in defending any claim or suit such as court costs, attorney's fees, and other expenses) arising or alleged to arise directly or indirectly or incidentally out of:

(i) any failure of the Lessor to comply with its obligations under this Agreement;

(ii) any claim, whether private or governmental, for bodily injury or death to persons (including employees of the Lessee) and for loss of or damage to property, cargo and/or vessels and/or means of transport, arising out of or incident to the ownership, manufacture, design or supply of the Equipment.

(d) Each party undertakes to give to the other party immediate notice of claims or actions arising under this Clause, and to assist in the handling of any and all such claims or actions."

Sub-clause (a) places liability for damage or total loss of the equipment on the Lessee. In case of actual or constructive total loss the Lessor shall be immediately notified upon which hire ceases and the Lessee becomes liable to pay the agreed Depreciated Value. Some leasing companies insist on a requirement to prove a total loss before agreeing to the described procedure. However, this is not a realistic demand as in many cases of an actual total loss the container simply vanishes, either overboard or stolen, or is otherwise untraceable. This is also the reason that a provision is made in sub-clause (a) allowing the process of declaring total loss to be reversed in case the container turns up after all.

Sub-clause (b) and (c) provide that each party shall defend, indemnify and hold the other harmless for any claims, loss or damage arising out of their respective responsibilities. In the case of the Lessee this is incident to the possession, leasing, operation, control or use of the equipment, whilst in the case of the Lessor it is incident to the ownership, manufacture, design or supply of the equipment.

Clause 14: Insurance

"(a) The Lessee agrees to procure and maintain in full force and effect during the term of this Agreement, at its sole cost and expense, the following insurances:

(i) Insurance to cover physical loss or damage to the Equipment for not less than the full Depreciated Value stipulated in Box 5.

(ii) General liability insurance to a minimum limit as stipulated in Box 18 for any one occurrence, to cover third party bodily injury and property damage. Such insurance shall be primary insurance.

Any and all deductibles under the terms of the foregoing insurances shall be for the Lessee's account. On request, the Lessee will provide the Lessor with evidence of the insurances.

(b) The Lessor agrees to procure and maintain in full force and effect during the term of this Agreement, at its sole cost and expense the following insurance:

(i) General liability insurance to a minimum limit as stipulated in Box 18 for any one occurrence, to cover third party bodily injury and property damage.

Any and all deductibles under the terms of the foregoing insurance shall be for the Lessor's account. On request, the lessors will provide the Lessee with evidence of the insurance.

Should a party fail to procure or maintain any of the required insurances, or by act or omission vitiate or invalidate any of such insurance, that party shall indemnify the other party to the extent the other party suffers or incurs loss, damage, liability or expense as a consequence of such failure, act or omission."

This clause sets out which insurances both parties are required to procure and maintain and is self-explanatory.

Clause 15: Law and Arbitration

"* (a) This Lease Agreement shall be governed by and construed in accordance with English law and any dispute arising out of this Lease Agreement shall be referred to arbitration in London in accordance with the Arbitration Act 1996 or any statutory modification or re-enactment thereof for the time being in force. Unless the parties agree upon a sole arbitrator, one arbitrator shall be appointed by each party and the arbitrators so appointed shall appoint a third arbitrator, the decision of the three-man tribunal thus constituted or any two of them, shall be final. On the receipt by one party of the nomination in writing of the other party's arbitrator, that party shall appoint their arbitrator within fourteen days, failing which the decision of the single arbitrator appointed shall be final.

For disputes where the total amount claimed by either party does not exceed the amount stated in Box 20** the arbitration shall be conducted in accordance with the Small Claims Procedure of the London Maritime Arbitrators Association.

* (b) This Lease Agreement shall be governed by and construed in accordance with Title 9 of the United States Code as well as by the maritime law of the United States, or if this Lease Agreement is not deemed to be a maritime contract, then by the law of the State of New York and should any dispute arise out of this Lease Agreement, the matter in dispute shall be referred to three persons at New York, one to be appointed by each of the parties hereto, and the third by the two so chosen; their decision or that of any two of them shall be final, and for purpose of enforcing any award, this agreement may be made a rule of the Court. The proceedings shall be conducted in accordance with the rules of the Society of Maritime Arbitrators, Inc.

For disputes where the total amount claimed by either party does not exceed the amount stated in Box 20** the arbitration shall be conducted in accordance with the Shortened Arbitration Procedure of the Society of Maritime Arbitrators, Inc.

* (c) Any dispute arising out of this Lease Agreement shall be referred to arbitration at the place indicated in Box 19, subject to the procedures applicable there. The laws of the place indicated in Box 19 shall govern this Lease Agreement.

(d) If Box 19 in Part I is not filled in, sub-clause (a) of this Clause shall apply.

* *(a), (b) and (c) are alternatives; indicate alternative agreed in Box 19.*

** *Where no figure is supplied in Box 20 in Part I, this provision only shall be void but the other provisions of this clause shall have full force and remain in effect.*"

The Standard BIMCO Law and Arbitration Clause has been inserted which provides for arbitration in London, New York or any other agreed place. It should be noted that if nothing is entered in box 19, London is the preferred alternative. In practice the larger leasing companies being based in the US will insist on jurisdiction in their home State.

Clause 16: Notices

"Any notice or notification or advice or communication of any kind to be served or given hereunder and/or any extension, variation, amendment, cancellation or deletion of any of the terms hereof shall (save in emergency) be in writing and sent or delivered to the registered office for the time being of the Lessor or the Lessee (as the case may be).

At the request of the Lessee the Lessor shall provide relevant information in electronic format."

This clause is self-explanatory. Reflecting the high degree of EDI application in container operations, the second paragraph requires Lessors, at the request of Lessees, to provide all relevant information in electronic format.

Clause 17: Overriding Agreement

"The terms and conditions set forth in this Agreement and attached exhibits shall constitute the only and total Agreement between the Lessor and the Lessee."

This clause is self-explanatory.

LEASING AGREEMENT

This is the sort of contract which my erstwhile employers used to use for leasing out containers outside of the consortium arrangement where a container hiring agreement would be appropriate if there were mutuality so that waivers could be considered (*see* Chapter 4).

Face

The BIMCO approach of grouping all individual data on the first page of a contract and presenting the standard contract wording as a separate item on the reverse thereafter is now widely adopted in many operational contracts. As can be seen from the specimen of the face of this lease agreement, this provides for recording the necessary individual data when a lessee takes a container (or number of containers) on hire.

Terms and Conditions

1. Use

"Container(s) leased under the terms and conditions of this Lease Agreement shall be used solely in international trade.
The Lessee may use the Container(s) for any purpose incidental to its business as a carrier of goods in containers, save that the Lessee shall not use the Container(s) for the carriage of dangerous or obnoxious goods which are likely to damage or contaminate the Container(s) or for the carriage of prohibited goods, such that the Container(s) would be liable to be seized by Customs or other authorities. The Lessee shall comply with all loading limitations as stated on the Container(s) and any other reasonable limitation which may be prescribed by the Lessor in writing and shall prevent excessive impact and concentrated loads.
The Container(s) shall at all times remain the property of the Lessor and the Lessee shall acquire no option to purchase or ownership right nor shall the Lessee sell, let or otherwise dispose of the Container(s)."

This clause, designed to control the uses to which the lessee may put the hired container, is mostly self-explanatory and the restrictions are mostly obvious and reasonable. "Prevent excessive impact" is primarily aimed at things like loading heavy scrap into an open top container using magnet loading and dropping the scrap into the container.

In the interests of safety of handling it is important that containers' loads are evenly spread and that a heavy item is not loaded to one side or end of the container, otherwise it might tip when lifted, particularly if lifted by side-loader. Irregular heavy loads should have their weight spread over the container floor by the use of dunnage. This is what is meant by "concentrated loads".

For the avoidance of doubt it is made quite clear that the lease carries no right of purchase or title.

AGREEMENT NO.

LEASE AGREEMENT

Name of Lessee:	Invoice Address if different:

, hereinafter referred to as the LESSOR, hereby leases to the party designated as the LESSEE, and hereinafter referred to as the LESSEE, and said LESSEE hereby leases from the LESSOR the following Container(s) as per Equipment Handover Agreement, upon the terms and conditions set forth on the reverse side hereof.

TERM: This lease will commence on:	and expire on:

QUANTITY AND DESCRIPTION OF EQUIPMENT:

RENTAL:	REPLACEMENT VALUE:

DELIVERY LOCATIONS:	CHARGES:	
	HANDLING:	PICK UP:

REDELIVERY LOCATIONS:	CHARGES:	
	HANDLING:	DROP OFF:

OTHER TERMS AND CONDITIONS:

SIGNED FOR LESSEE:	DATE:	SIGNED FOR LESSOR:	DATE:

Figure 4: Lease agreement

2. Responsibility

"(a) The Lessee shall be liable for the cost of repair or replacement, whichever is the lesser, in respect of all loss or damage to the Container(s) during the currency of this Lease Agreement (between Delivery-Clause 6 and Redelivery-Clause 7), unless said loss or damage is shown to have been caused by normal wear and tear or latent defect. The Lessee agrees to sign container interchange receipts/inspection reports at Delivery and Redelivery, which documents shall be conclusive evidence of the condition of the Container(s) at those times and form an integral part of this Leasing Agreement.

(b) The Lessor makes no warranty of the condition of the Container(s) or their suitability for use with any specific cargo.

(c) Between Delivery and Redelivery neither the Lessor nor any servant, agent or sub-contractor of the Lessor shall be liable for any:
 (i) loss of, or damage to cargo or property (belonging to the Lessee or any third party), or
 (ii) death or injury of any kind whatsoever to whomsoever
arising out of the leasing of the Container(s), howsoever caused and whether or not arising out of negligence on the part of the Lessor, his servants, agents or sub-contractors.

(d) In the event of any default by the Lessee in performance of his obligations under this Leasing Agreement the Lessor shall be entitled forthwith to repossess any Container(s) and the Lessee shall be responsible for any costs and expenses incidental thereto."

(a) Naturally the lessee is responsible for all loss or damage to the container(s) whilst on hire. Whether a container on hire has been damaged will be determined by comparing interchange receipts compiled at the time of on hire/off hire (frequently on an exception only basis: i.e. undamaged-no report, report compiled only if there is damage to record which is serious enough to lead to the container being rejected by the lessee). An Equipment Handover Agreement (EHA) is often used as an interchange receipt (*see* below) and these receipts are incorporated into and form part of the contract.

(b) This sub-clause makes it clear that it is the lessee's responsibility to examine the container to satisfy himself that it is undamaged and fit for the used to which he intends to put it (or if it is not to reject it and refuse to take it on hire). This equates to the approach in the shipper-packed container clause in the bill of lading (clause 8) where the FCL shipper has similar responsibilities.

(c) The responsibilities of the lessee in sub-clauses (a) and (b) above lead to this clause, in which liabilities incurred by the container whilst on hire are for the account of the lessee, even if traceable to negligence of the lessor etc. because, under (b), it was the responsibility of the lessee to inspect the container and satisfy himself that it was fit for use in the first place.

(d) This sub-clause gives the lessor the right of repossession in the event of breach by the lessee of any of his responsibilities under the contract.

3. Insurance

"The Lessee shall insure all Containers for the time being in his possession or control for their full replacement value with a reputable insurance company against those risks for which the Lessee is responsible and shall, if requested by the Lessor, provide a copy of the policy."

It is a requirement of the lease agreement that the lessee effects insurance on the container "with a reputable insurance company against those risks for which the Lessee is responsible". This means loss or damage to the container and any liability which might be incurred in its operation. The lessor may inspect the policy.

4. Duties of Lessee

"The Lessee agrees to make such spot checks on current location as may be requested by the Lessor.
The Lessee agrees to keep full records of container inspection and of any maintenance or repairs to the Container(s) and to make these available to the Lessor on redelivery.
The Lessee agrees to the following equipment handover conditions:

(a) The Lessee acknowledges receipt of the Container(s) in apparent good order and condition, except as may be indicated on the container interchange receipt/report which shall be signed by both parties hereto.

(b) The Container(s) are leased to the Lessee on the following conditions:

  (i) Any vehicle or railcar used for the transport of the Container(s) is suitable for the weight and other characteristics of the load involved and that the Container(s) are firmly secured thereto either by twistlocks or other methods agreed with the Lessor.

  (ii) The Container(s) are to be redelivered in a clean and cargoworthy condition (as defined in Clause 8). The Lessee will reimburse the Lessor for any cleaning costs and any other expenses whatsoever incurred by his failure so to do."

This clause lists the duties of the lessee:

- to make spot checks on current location as may be requested by the lessor (he may wish to repossess under clause 2(d));
- whilst a container is on hire, the lessee is responsible for CSC checks and repairs etc. This is necessary as many leases are long term and it would be impractical to redeliver containers to the lessor for these purposes.

(a) As mentioned in respect of sub-clause 2(a) above, interchange receipts/reports are frequently completed on an exception basis only and this sub-clause provides for no report to be an indication of delivery/redelivery in an undamaged condition.

(b)(i) Containers must be transported on suitable means of transport, purpose built to carry containers with twistlock fittings (in the absence of any agreement to the contrary by the lessor).

(b)(ii) This sub-clause is equivalent to bill of lading sub-clause 12(5), in which the user is responsible for returning any container to its owner in good condition and ready for reuse.

5. Convention for Safe Containers

"The Lessor shall ensure that the Container(s) which its supplies to the Lessee directly from one of its depots/terminals will comply with the provisions of the International Convention for Safe Containers (CSC) in force at the time.

Notwithstanding the above it shall be the Lessee's responsibility to ensure that all Container(s) taken on lease by the Lessee as the result of a Lease transfer comply with all relevant regulations.
During the term of the Lease and until Redelivery of each Container in accordance with the terms and conditions of the Lease, it shall be the responsibility of the Lessee to repair and maintain the Container(s) as necessary to a standard acceptable to the Lessor and to ensure that all necessary re-examinations and record keeping are properly carried out in accordance with requirements of the UK Freight Container (Safety Convention) Regulations 1984, or any local equivalent thereof which have been approved by a contracting party to the CSC."

The lessor is responsible for ensuring that, if he supplies a container to the lessee directly from one of his depots or terminals, the container's CSC rating is in force at the time. However, it is the lessee's responsibility to check containers as they are taken on hire to ensure that they do comply with "all relevant regulations". If a container is offered which does not comply with the regulations, it is the lessee's responsibility to reject it. It is necessary to put this responsibility on the lessee because there may be triangulation movements (lease transfers) with container hiring in the same way as with import/export deliveries, in which case a container may go directly from one lessee to another without going through the lessor's hands to give him an opportunity to check the condition of it.

The last paragraph of this clause links in with clause 4 above to make it clear that repairs and CSC inspections to containers whilst on hire are the lessee's responsibility.

6. Delivery

"The Lessor will tender the Container(s) to the Lessee at the agreed place(s) of delivery."

7. Redelivery

"The Lessee must advise the Lessor or his local agent of his intention to redeliver Container(s) a minimum of seven days prior to the date of Redelivery. The Lessee must redeliver Container(s) to the Lessor at premises indicated by the Lessor at the location of Redelivery.
Upon Redelivery of the Container(s) this Agreement shall terminate in respect of the individual Container, save that either party shall be at liberty to prosecute and defend any claim right or remedy arising out of this Agreement on that individual Container."

Clause 6 is self-explanatory.
Clause 7 is a bit more specific and provides for the lessee to give notice of redelivery to the lessor and to redeliver at the contracted point (often left to be agreed). Redelivery terminates the contract in respect of the container redelivered but the contract remains in force to apply to any subsequent claims which may arise.

8. Damage Repairs

"Should a container be returned to the Lessor in a damaged condition, as defined by the Lessor's Container Damage and Inspection Criteria (copies of which are available on request from the Lessor), the Lessor will provide the Lessee with an estimate of repair costs within seven working days from the date of Redelivery. Within seven working days of receipt of such repair estimate the Lessee must either:
(a) accept the repair costs as advised or,
(b) arrange a joint survey and subsequently reach agreement with the Lessor over repair costs.
If the Lessee fails to agree the repair estimate or fails to exercise his right to attend a joint survey within the stipulated time period, the Lessor will proceed to repair the Container without notice to the Lessee to a standard the Lessor thinks fit and the Lessee shall pay such repair costs. Until such time as the Container has been repaired, the Lessee shall continue to pay all hire charges as described herein."

This clause covers the situation if a container is redelivered damaged (as defined by the lessor's handbook). It provides for the lessor to submit a prompt repair estimate and for the lessee to make a prompt response to accept that estimate or arrange a joint survey to agree repair costs. Failure by the lessee to do so allows the lessor to proceed at the lessee's expense. As a damaged container cannot be used until repaired, the contract provides for the lessee to continue to pay hire until repairs are completed, thus prompt repairs and a system to promote them are as much in the lessee's interests as the lessor's.

9. Taxes and Charges

"The Lessee shall pay all taxes and charges arising out of, or incidental to, the use of the Container(s) until redelivered to the Lessor at the agreed location(s)."

10. Payment

"The Lessee shall pay all fees, taxes and charges within 30 days of the date of invoice. Should the Lessee fail to pay all aforesaid fees, taxes and charges within this period then, in addition, he shall pay interest at the rate of _____ per cent above the _______________ bank lending rate with a minimum rate of_____ per cent from the date of the invoice."

Clause 9 provides for the lessee to pay all expenses incurred in respect of the use of the container whilst on hire.

Clause 10 provides for prompt payment by the lessee of the lessor's invoices. An incentive is introduced by adding interest for late payment. The amount of the surcharge and the name of the chosen bank need to be inserted in the text.

11. Documentation

"All documentation relating to the hire of Container(s) hereunder, including the container interchange receipt/inspection report (but disregarding any conditions set out on the reverse thereof) shall form part of this Agreement. In the case of any conflict between the provisions of such documentation and these terms and conditions, these terms and conditions shall prevail."

12. Variation

"These terms and conditions can only be varied with the agreement of the Lessor in writing signed by a person duly authorised by the Lessor."

13. Law and Jurisdiction

"This Agreement shall be governed by and construed in accordance with the laws of England and the Lessor and the Lessee hereby submit to the jurisdiction of the English courts."

Clause 11 incorporates all documentation relating to the hire of the container into the contract. In the case of the EHA, the terms and conditions on the reverse are specifically excluded and, in any event, the terms in the lease agreement shall always be regarded as paramount and prevail in the event of conflict.

Clause 12 provides that any variation to these terms must be in writing and signed by the lessor.

Finally, clause 13 provides for English law and jurisdiction.

General

This is quite a short and simple contract which appears fair to both sides but one which inevitably places greater emphasis on the protection of the lessor's position to counteract the *contra proferentem* doctrine.

EQUIPMENT HANDOVER AGREEMENT (EHA)

The prime purpose of this contract is to cover the situation where a CTO allows a customer to take possession of one of his containers for some reason, usually to take away to load/unload. It can, however, be used in any situation where a CTO allows a container temporarily out of his care (e.g. to a haulier etc.) where it is thought necessary to record the condition thereof prior to removal and upon redelivery. As containers in such circumstances are frequently on the CTO's trailers, the EHA provides for them as well. As the usual use of an EHA is for a short period it does not incorporate the usual responsibilities on the customer for repairs, maintenance and CSC plating found in most leasing agreements.

Face

The face provides two sets of basic diagrams showing all aspects of the container with space to record details of any damage as well as indicating its position by marking with an X on the diagram. It records container and trailer details and details of the vehicle taking the container away/returning it. It also provides for whether a lift is required, as would be the case where the haulier had his own trailer. It has to be signed by the CTO's representative and the haulier concerned.

Terms and Conditions

1. Definitions

"Customer means the Shipper, Consignee or Lessee of Equipment who, or on whose behalf this Agreement is signed.
Company means_______________.
Equipment means any container and/or trailer and/or any associated and/or ancillary equipment the subject of this Agreement."

This clause is self-explanatory.

2. Clause Paramount

"The Equipment is loaned to the Customer on the terms of the Company's applicable Bill of Lading and Tariff for the relevant trade in force at the time of the loan and on the following conditions."

3. Receipt

"The Customer acknowledges receipt of the Equipment detailed overleaf in apparent good order and condition, except as indicated overleaf."

Clause 2 applies the bill of lading contract and tariff to this period, even though the contract of carriage under that contract may not have commenced (e.g. if a haulier, who is the shipper's sub-contractor, has collected an empty container to take away for loading, so that the contract to carriage only starts when the CTO receives the loaded container back at his depot) in addition to the terms incorporated herein.

Clause 3 binds the details on the face into the contract and provides for the customer's acknowledgement thereof.

4. Customer's Responsibility

"(a) The Customer is responsible for the cost of repair or replacement (whichever is the lesser) in respect of any damage or loss to the Equipment evidenced by the difference between the "out" and "in" receipts detailed overleaf, howsoever caused, whether occurring in the care of the Customer or that of his servant, agent or sub-contractor. Failure to return Equipment when called upon to do so shall entitle the Company to treat that Equipment as a loss and claim against the Customer for the cost of replacement in accordance with this clause.

(b) The Customer is responsible for all claims for loss, damage and/or injury and/or death caused by the Equipment whilst in his care. Whilst the Company will take reasonable care to ensure that all Equipment is serviceable and in good order and condition at the time of delivery to the Customer or his servant, agent or sub-

EQUIPMENT HANDOVER AGREEMENT

Between the Company and:	Party to be charged if different:

Handover to: (Customer Representative)	Reg. No:	CTO Office:	Place of Handover:	CTO Signature:

OUT

Container Number	C'Base Imp FCL	C'Base MT	20'	40'	For Freightliners F'liner Origin	For Freightliners Berth	For Freightliners Gross Weight	Trailer No.	20'	40'

Lift Required YES/NO

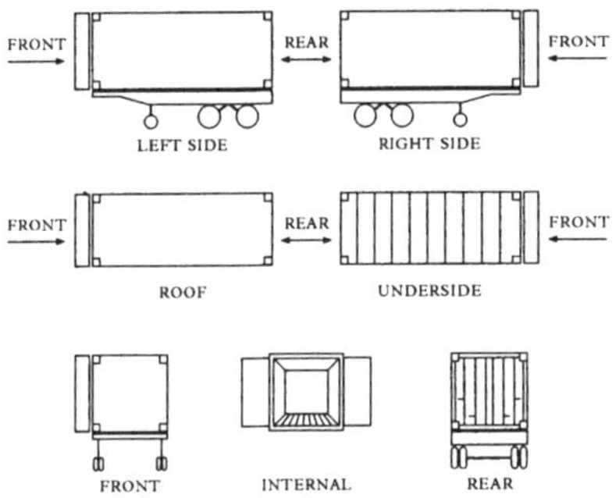

DAMAGE: List all details of damage and mark on the appropriate plan. If no damage enter "none"

Date/Time Out

The condition of the Equipment is as indicated above:

For the Company

The Equipment above is received in good order except where noted:

For Customer

Received From:	Reg. No.	Place of Handover	Freightliner Signature for Equipment

IN

Container (status below) and trailer as above YES/NO

Container Number	Exp FCL	MT	20'	40'	Voy.	Dest	Gross Weight	Berth	Dest. Port	Haz/Special	Trailer No.	20'	40'

TO
Remain on Trailer
Be off Loaded to Stack
Be off Loaded to Trailer(s)

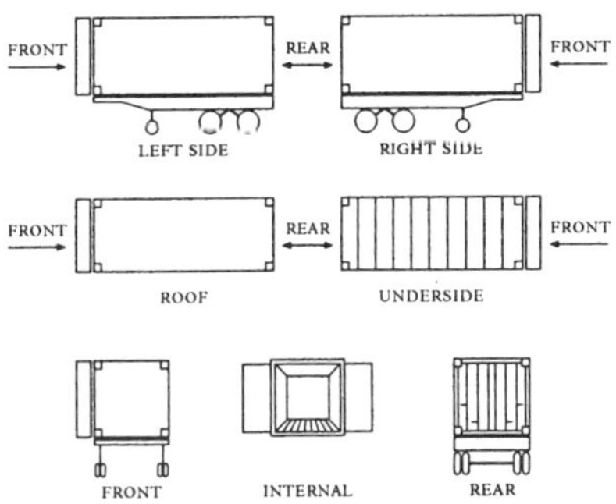

DAMAGE: List all details of damage and mark on the appropriate plan. If no damage enter "None"

Date/Time In

The condition of the Equipment indicated above:

For Customer

The Equipment above is received in good order and condition

For the Company

TO BE RETAINED BY CTO OR AGENT

Figure 5: Equipment Handover Agreement

contractor, it is the responsibility of the Customer to satisfy himself that the Equipment is what he requires and is in all respects fit to be used and taken onto a public highway before accepting it, rejecting any which he considers unsuitable/unfit.

(c) The Customer is responsible for any loss and/or damage to any goods carried by the Equipment whilst it is in his care, howsoever caused.

(d) The Customer shall supply to the driver such information as he requires in accordance with Clause 7(c).

(e) For the purpose of this contract the Customer's responsibilities are deemed to include responsibility for the actions of his servants, agents and sub-contractors in carrying out those matters for which the Customer is responsible and Equipment in the care of a Customer's servants, agents or sub-contractors is deemed to be in the care of the Customer."

This clause outlines the responsibilities of the customer in this contract. Note the definition of customer in clause 1, so it is the merchant who requests to be allowed to remove the container from the CTO's control who is the customer, not the haulier who he engages to collect and redeliver it. It is the customer to whom the CTO will look for reimbursement, not the haulier.

(a) This sub-clause makes the customer liable for damage or loss to the container/trailer evidenced by the difference between the out and in reports on the face of the agreement, howsoever caused. It is not necessary for there to be negligence on the part of the customer, his servant, agent or sub-contractor. So, if the haulier is an innocent party in a road accident, the customer is still liable to the company.

Additionally the customer must return the container when called upon to do so by the CTO. If he fails to do so, the CTO may treat the container as lost and claim accordingly.

(b) This sub-clause closely follows sub-clause 2(c) of the lease agreement in making the customer responsible for all liabilities incurred in respect of the container (and trailer) whilst in the care of the customer, his servants, agents or sub-contractors. Sub-clause (a) covers damage/loss to the container trailer, sub-clause (b) covers liabilities to third parties. It puts the onus on the customer (via the haulier) to satisfy himself that the container and trailer are fit to take onto a public highway before doing so and to reject them if they are not. This may sound quite harsh but it is in line with the haulier's responsibilities under the Road Traffic Act.

(c) This sub-clause covers goods in the container and puts the responsibility for any damage to these during the period of the agreement onto the customer, howsoever caused.

(d) Sometimes a driver under contract to the CTO may take a container (and trailer) to a customer's premises and leave it there to be collected later. If this is to be for a long period an EHA may be completed. When a driver goes to collect such container he has responsibilities under the Road Traffic Act to satisfy himself that the load is safe before taking it on to the public highway and, for this purpose, he may require certain information from the customer. This sub-clause provides for the customer to supply this information.

(e) This sub-clause makes it clear that the customer is responsible for the actions of his servants, agents and sub-contractors and that equipment in their care is deemed, for the purposes of this agreement, to be in the care of the customer.

5. Indemnity

"The Customer undertakes that no claim or allegation shall be made against the Company, its servants, agents or sub-contractors which imposes or attempts to impose upon any of them any liability whatsoever in connection with the Equipment whilst on loan to the Customer, whether or not arising out of negligence on the part of any of them and, if any such claim or allegation should nevertheless be made, to indemnify the Company, its servants, agents and sub-contractors (as the case may be) against all consequences thereof. In entering into this Agreement the Company does so, not only on its own behalf, but also as agent and trustee on behalf of its servants, agents and sub-contractors.
If the Company is not the owner of the Equipment the actual owner thereof shall come within the definition of servants, agents and sub-contractors for the purpose of this indemnity."

The responsibilities of the customer in clause 4 are reinforced in this clause 5 by an indemnity in favour of the CTO, his servants, agents and sub-contractors in respect of "any liability in connection with the Equipment whilst on loan to the Customer" (note use of the word loan rather than lease which demonstrates the nature of this contract). In case the container is hired by the CTO, the benefit of the indemnity is extended to the actual owner to cover the indemnity which the CTO has almost certainly given in his leasing contract with the actual owner.

6. Customer's Driver's Responsibilities

"If the driver is the servant, agent or sub-contractor of the Customer, his responsibilities will include the following, for the performance of which the Customer shall be vicariously responsible.

(a) The driver must ensure that the linking of the Equipment is compatible with his prime-mover and/or Trailer (as the case may be).
(b) The driver must ensure that the linking of the Equipment to his prime-mover and/or Trailer (as the case may be) is properly effected.
(c) The driver must ensure that his vehicle plus Equipment is thoroughly roadworthy before proceeding, in particular the driver is responsible for ensuring compliance with the Road Traffic Acts currently in force.
(d) The driver must be authorised to commit the Customer by completion and signature on this Agreement."

7. Company's Driver's Responsibilities/Authority

"(a) If the driver is the servant, agent or sub-contractor of the Company, save for completing and signing this Agreement as evidence of the condition of the Equipment at the time of delivery, he shall have no authority to commit the Company in any way whatsoever.

(b) The driver is under no obligation to assist the Customer in any way with the loading or unloading of goods to or from the Equipment or in any way preparing the Equipment for the Customer to do so. Should any driver elect to do so, he does so entirely on his own behalf and not as servant, agent or sub-contractor of the Company, who accept no responsibility whatsoever for his actions in this context and, vis-à-vis the Company, he is considered as the Customer's servant at such times.

(c) The driver is responsible for ensuring that his load is roadworthy and safe to be taken on to the public highway before proceeding from the Customer's premises (or those of his servants, agents or sub-contractors) and it is the responsibility of the Customer to supply the driver with such information as he may require to satisfy himself in this matter."

Clauses 6 and 7 cover the responsibilities of the drivers taking containers, the subject of EHAs, from the CTO's depot to the customer and vice versa. Clause 6 covers a situation where the haulier is the customer's servant and provides for the customer to be vicariously responsible for the haulier undertaking the following:

(a) ensuring that linking of equipment to his prime mover (tug unit of a lorry for towing a trailer) is compatible;
(b) ensuring that linking is properly effected;
(c) ensuring vehicle and equipment are roadworthy before proceeding and in compliance with Road Traffic Act requirements;
(d) authorised to sign EHA on behalf of the customer.

Clause 7 covers the situation where the haulier is the CTO's servant and provides as follows:

(a) driver authorised to sign EHA on behalf of CTO but cannot commit CTO in any other matter;
(b) driver not authorised to assist customer with loading or unloading. If he does so it is a matter directly between the customer and the driver in which the CTO is uninvolved. This is important as the CTO's tariff is on the basis that FCL is loaded/ unloaded by the customer. If goods are damaged on account of negligence in stowing/unstowing by the driver the CTO does not want to have any vicarious liability arising from the driver gratuitously undertaking tasks which are not his responsibility.
(c) this sub-clause had already been explained in commenting upon sub-clause 4(d) above.

8. Customer's Undertaking

"The Customer undertakes to observe the following Company requirements whilst the Equipment is on loan.

(a) In no circumstances may any Container be removed from its Trailer or other carrying vehicle without the prior permission of the Company and then only in a manner previously approved by the Company.

(b) Containers must at all times be firmly secured to their Trailer or other carrying vehicle either by twistlocks or some alternative method which the Company has approved prior to use.

(c) Equipment loaned by the Company must not be used for the carriage or storage of goods which have not been booked with the Company.
(d) In any case where the prime-mover, Trailer or other carrying vehicle is not supplied by or on behalf of the Company, the vehicle used must be suitable for the weight, size and other characteristics of the load involved.
(e) A Customer taking delivery of goods in a Container is responsible for returning the empty Container with the interior brushed and clean. Failure so to do will result in the Customer being debited with cleaning costs and other expenses (demurrage included) thereby incurred. In the case of a tank Container the Customer is responsible for returning the tank not only clean but gas free with a certificate to that effect. The Company may inspect any tank prior to accepting redelivery and refuse any which does not meet these requirements in which case demurrage shall accrue."

In this clause the CTO sets out his requirements which the customer must observe during the loan period.

(a) Containers must be handled only with purpose built equipment using a spreader to lift vertically from the four twistlock holes in the four top corner castings of the container. Four hooks and chains to a central point put unacceptable stresses upon a container which it is not designed to withstand, particularly if it has a heavy load at the time. For this reason CTOs require that containers not be removed from trailers to facilitate loading or discharge, except with prior permission of the CTO using equipment approved by the CTO.

(b) Containers must be secured to their trailers by twistlocks (or some other approved method) at all times. Unless a container is to be lifted off, there is no need to unlock a container from a trailer and to do so creates the danger of it inadvertently being moved in an unsecured state causing an accident.

(c) The use of containers on loan is restricted to goods which are the subject of a contract to carriage with the CTO.

(d) If the prime mover is not the CTO's, it is the responsibility of the Customer to ensure that it is suitable and powerful enough for the task in hand.

(e) This sub-clause reflects sub-clause 12(5) of the contract of carriage in providing that empty containers must be returned clean or the customer will be billed with the cost of cleaning. Special provisions are made for tank containers (used for the carriage of liquids in bulk). Failure to comply with this sub-clause will lead to a bill for cleaning, demurrage etc.

9. Leasing

"If Equipment is leased from the Company, the Customer agrees that the terms and conditions set out in the Company's Lease Agreement shall apply as if the Customer were Lessee and the Company were Lessor."

10. Law and Jurisdiction

"Any dispute under this contract shall be determined according to English law by the High Court of Justice in London, to the exclusion of the jurisdiction of the courts of any other country or, if the plaintiff to the claim or dispute so elects, by the court of the place where the defendant is domiciled and then in accordance with the law of that court."

Clause 9 incorporates the terms of the company's lease agreement if the equipment is leased and the EHA is being used as a condition report (*see* clause 11 of lease agreement) only.

Clause 10 is the usual law and jurisdiction clause. As there is not much mandatory law relating to contracts of this nature, a specific provision regarding law and jurisdiction is more likely to be upheld than in a contract of carriage, although that is not to say that some court will not agree to hear the case despite the law and jurisdiction clause asking them not to. If the company is the plaintiff and the customer the defendant there is not much point taking action against the customer outside of a jurisdiction where the customer has assets to attach to satisfy any judgment. Hence the provision to vary the English law and jurisdiction if the plaintiff elects to apply to an alternative court.

CHAPTER 6

CONTRACTS OF CARRIAGE

INTRODUCTION

Having procured tonnage to operate and a fleet of containers (both as either owned or chartered/hired) and then entered into a consortium arrangement with other carriers, to facilitate a frequent regular service, our CTO is now in a position to consider the terms and conditions of his contract of carriage (affreightment) with his customers (his bill of lading contract).

Our CTO has firstly to decide what sort of operator he wants to be. Will he be a CTO in which he offers a multimodal service under the terms of the offered contract, in which he acts as a principal throughout, regardless of whether or not he uses sub-contractors for part of the carriage? Alternatively, will he be a TTO (Through Transport Operator) in which he acts as an agent only, except for the sea leg, binding his customers into direct contracts with his sub-contractors? In the case of the latter, if he is using chartered tonnage and includes a demise clause in his contract, in theory he is agent throughout and not directly liable for anything. However, such an approach would be impractical, to say the least, in a combined transport operation within a consortium because:

(1) How does one cover "hidden damage", that is to say damage/loss where it cannot be shown during which period of the carriage it occurred?
(2) How does one cover loss due to container defect (e.g. refrigerated container breakdown)?
(3) Many consortium agreements forbid the use of demise clauses or any clauses purporting to put the consortium partners in direct contract with anyone who is a third party to them.

For these reasons and because it is desirable and competitive to offer customers an all-inclusive service, most blue-chip operators are CTOs, so it is this type of contract which we will consider, commenting appropriately where alternatives may be used by TTOs and different types of CTO.

BASIC PHILOSOPHY

Outside the sea leg, where the Hague/Hague-Visby Rules (and possibly even the Hamburg Rules) are frequently mandatory, there is generally freedom of contract during the land legs (excepting where these involve international land carriage in Europe, where CMR(road) and CIM(rail) may apply). The USA is contemplating a revision to its COGSA 1936 which would operate on a door-to-door basis and become the first effective national combined transport legislation (of which more later).

At present all regulation is discretionary only, so CTOs can choose which one to adopt or adopt none and use their own approach.

The rules presently available for guidance/adoption are:

ICC Rules for a Combined Transport Document (ICC Brochure No. 298)

These rules appear to be the basis for most blue-chip operators' contracts, although few, if any, comply with them fully and merely adopt the general philosophy of the rules as the format for their contracts. First published in 1975, these rules provide a basic fault and negligence approach to liability, applying any mandatory law which would apply in a unimodal movement if a certain document were issued (e.g. CMR/CIM) and deeming the CT document to be that document.

The "menu" approach to liability in these rules is attractive to carriers, who are familiar with this approach in the Hague/Hague-Visby Rules. The BIMCO COMBICONBILL adopts the ICC rules approach.

UNCTAD/ICC Rules for Multimodal Transport Documents (ICC Brochure No. 481)

As part of their continuing campaign to promote the Hamburg Rules and the UNCTAD/MMO Convention, UNCTAD sought the co-operation of the ICC to review and update the ICC Rules for a Combined Transport Document. The ICC Rules were in need of neither revision nor update and their general basic application worldwide attested to their acceptability to the parties concerned. Surprisingly the ICC were persuaded to join UNCTAD in this matter, possibly on the basis that a workable compromise, which would appease UNCTAD, might be achieved.

The working party constituted under Professor Jan Ramberg to review these rules was given a clear mandate to base its draft on the Hague-Visby Rules. They claim to have done so but to claim to provide rules based on the Hague-Visby Rules without incorporating the Article IV Rule 2 tariff of exceptions is untenable. Merely adding back the nautical fault and fire exclusions to a rule based on Hamburg Rules Article 5 does not equate to Hague-Visby Rules, as any judge will confirm. Professor Ramberg claims that a bill of lading issued subject to these rules could still list the Hague-Visby Rules Article IV Rule 2 exceptions without contravening these rules. This is stretching credulity too far. If the Article IV Rule 2 tariff of exceptions is acceptable, why not retain it in the rules and retain the certainty and wealth of case law based thereon, rather than introduce the ambiguous wording of Article 5 of the Hamburg Rules?

Accordingly there are few carriers prepared to be persuaded to adopt these rules voluntarily instead of the ICC Rules, which most likely will remain the basis for most combined transport contracts for the foreseeable future.

The only notable documents applying these rules are BIMCO MULTIDOC 95 (which appears to be little used in comparison to COMBICONBILL) and the FIATA Multimodal Transport bill of lading, where there is a hidden agenda in the decision to adopt these rules. Up to 1994 the FIATA bill of lading had always been mentioned in the ICC Uniform Customs and Practice for Documentary Credits (UCP) as an approved NVOCC document and thus authorised to carry the ICC logo. For reasons that are irrelevant here, the ICC working party preparing UCP500 to replace UCP400 declined to mention the FIATA bill or authorise use of the ICC logo on the FIATA bill to signify an approved document. Clearly the use of the ICC logo had important promotional implications to FIATA, who discovered that, what they could not achieve via UCP500, they could obtain by adopting the UNCTAD/ICC Rules, which UNCTAD and ICC were keen to promote. The FIATA members clearly thought that the cost of adopting the UNCTAD/ICC Rules was worthwhile in order to retain use of the ICC logo on their documents. The cost is the difference between their liability to their customers under their contract of carriage and their recourse under their cover bills with the actual carriers, which in most cases are based on the earlier rules.

Optional bill lading for combined transport shipment or port-to-port shipment

Thirty years ago, when combined transport was in its infancy, every trade had (at least) one separate bill of lading contract (which was often a conference document, as we are talking about a time when conferences were all powerful and exercised strong control over their members). Negotiating the terms of the conference bill was a nightmare which amply demonstrated the old adage that the speed of decision of any committee is in an inverse ratio to the number of members of that committee. Clearly the most efficient committee is a committee of one but conference politics would not permit that at this stage.

Added to this, one now had to prepare a contract to cover all possible liabilities on a door-to-door basis, instead of just port-to-port, where the Hague/Hague-Visby Rules were more or less universally applied.

A glance at any of the conference bills operating at the end of the 1960s evidenced a long-standing policy of always add more words and never delete anything. To say that such contracts were unreadable and a lawyer's charter to print money would be an understatement. Clearly the first requirement was for a blank sheet of paper for a fresh start (*see* comments in Chapter 1, Section 1 which are equally applicable here).

Conference bills continued for a few years more but, as conferences gradually became weaker, the possibility of achieving what would have been unthinkable only a few years previously manifested itself: a universal bill of lading to cover all trades. This was the "Holy Grail" after which I strove as I encouraged my employer's trade managers to secure amendment to their conference rules to permit each carrier to draft his own bill of lading and, as they did so, I achieved my goal of the committee of one: me!

To produce a contract of carriage that would give carriers appropriate protection in the courts of any country of the world, applying its national law to a claim, is a tall order and one which is impossible to accomplish totally in all circumstances. Nevertheless, it is vital to know an outline of the law and its interpretation in the courts of any country to which you trade, in order to know your exposure and this is a matter where P & I clubs can assist via their local correspondents. One cannot merely stipulate English law and jurisdiction and expect all courts worldwide to honour that, particularly countries with Supreme Court Acts (or similar) specifically forbidding such provisions and taking to themselves the right to hear any case they choose, particularly if it affects one of their nationals. As I have said before, transport may be international but law is national.

Thus there were difficulties and drawbacks to a universal bill of lading but, if it could be achieved, there were overwhelming advantages, not the least of which was simplification for claims handlers, only needing to adjust against one contract instead of a variety and for commercial staff, who only needed to load one batch of stationery onto the printer without the need for continual changes.

Having rid myself of the conference shackles and urged on by my commercial colleagues, I set to work to try to produce a single worldwide contract devoid of local clauses, without the need to refer to local rules and legislation but which would not run foul of local law. I found that, in most cases, this was possible. Many local acts applying the Hague or Hague-Visby Rules have a clause saying "you will mention our act in all Bills for exports from our country" (necessary if the law there applies the Rules to exports—as per the usual requirement in the Hague and Hague-Visby Rules—to ensure contractual application in the foreign importing country where the exporting country's laws are not mandatorily applicable) but provide no penalty for non-compliance and merely apply the law if the case is referred to one of their courts. In other words these laws are what I called "paper tigers" as they have no teeth! We do not seek to avoid mandatory law but merely to cover all mandatory law by one all-embracing reference to cover all areas. All areas, that is except the USA, where the law has teeth and says "if you do not comply with our requirements you will be denied the benefit of any of the protection in the act" (the fundamental breach concept). Thus, whilst most national act references are avoidable, that of the USA is not, so it is the only local clause needed in a universal bill of lading.

Such was the joint reputation of my company and myself that I soon found many of my colleagues in other carriers "breaching our copyright" by imitation (which is, of course, the sincerest form of flattery). In the intervening years I have made a point of keeping a close watch on claims and cases involving combined transport contracts of carriage and periodically updated our contract to take account of such points. In this way I have treated the contract as a living thing and kept it up to date to meet the ever-changing panorama of combined transport and any chinks in our armour discovered during operations. To use yet another metaphor, one horse may bolt but thereafter there is no excuse for leaving the stable door open!

After development over a number of years in consultation with my P & I club advisers, I feel that I have now developed an ideal model base for an optional contract of carriage for port-to-port and combined transport operation, according to how the data in it is shown. (Of course this contract is ideal only if the philosophy of the reader is identical to mine, that is to say full combined transport in a consortium operation.)

One thing which has to be emphasised in putting this contract forward is that there is little direct legal precedent for much of its contents. This is because combined transport and the way it operates is so different from break-bulk port-to-port operation as to make the wealth of case law on the latter inapplicable to or difficult to interpret when considering the former (the law on deviation is just one example of this). Added to this, the cost of legal action to create new precedents is so high that compromises out of court are common and only the occasional large claim comes to trial to create new case law. Thus there is a dearth of case law guidance on combined transport. Therefore, the most that one can say in most cases is that, having given due consideration to the matter, the proffered wording is the best available and, if that does not achieve the desired effect, it is unlikely that any alternative wording will succeed (short of an Act of Parliament) in doing so. On this basis the following is recommended for consideration to see whether or not it meets the philosophy and requirements of the party concerned.

To me a bill of lading has a "face" and a "back", the face being where the individual detail is shown and the back being the contract of carriage. This approach is by no means universally recognised and there are bills where terms and conditions are clearly marked "page 1" and the individual detail "page 2", presumably to enable the carrier to hold that you must read page 1 (and thereby be charged with a knowledge of the terms of the contract of carriage) before proceeding to page 2. BIMCO's CONLINEBILL and CONGENBILL are examples of this approach.

FACE

Different CTOs favour different layouts but the two shown and explained here are the two most commonly encountered. The first uses the Chamber of

Shipping recommended format, which is in widespread use worldwide outside the USA and the second is the USA version, which is in general use in the shipping industry there.

CHAMBER OF SHIPPING FORMAT

This bill of lading is an optional document which can be used as a port-to-port or combined transport bill of lading according to how it is completed (*see* definitions of port-to-port shipment and combined transport in clause 1). It has further flexibility to mix port-to-port at one end with combined transport at the other (*see* clause 6(3)).

The identities of the carrier and the agent signing on his behalf are clear from the signature clause. Thus the bill complies fully with the requirements of UCP500 on signature clauses.

Shipper

This space must be completed with the name of the party with whom the contract of carriage has been concluded by the carrier. It may show the actual shipper or the shipper's freight forwarder, either as a principal or as a disclosed or undisclosed agent (*see* clause 3).

Consignee or Order

This space may be completed, either with the name of the consignee or the words "to order", in which case the shipper becomes the consignee as well and delivery is made in accordance with his instructions. These instructions may be given:

- by specific endorsement on the bill of lading: "Deliver to John Smith and Co. (stamp and signature of shipper)";
- by attaching authorised delivery instructions on the shipper's stationery: a delivery order from the shipper to the consignee;
- by means of a blank endorsement on the bill of lading and passing the document to the consignee: shipper's stamp and signature with no qualification.

Note: a blank endorsed "Order" bill of lading is a bearer document and the carrier must make delivery to whoever presents it (unless he has reason to suspect fraud).

Thus it will be seen that, like a bearer cheque, a blank endorsed "Order" bill is a dangerous document. However, it is a much-used document on account of the requirements of banks advancing to funds against documents to finance foreign trade.

A bill contains indemnities to the carrier which impose liabilities upon the merchant. A bank advancing funds requires the security of documents of title,

Bill of Lading for Combined Transport shipment or Port to Port shipment

Shipper

B/L No.:

Reference

P&O Nedlloyd

Consignee or Order (for U.S. Trade only: Not negotiable unless consigned "To Order")

Notify Party/Address (It is agreed that no responsibility shall attach to the Carrier or his Agents for failure to notify (see clause 20 on reverse))

Place of Receipt (Applicable only when this document is used as a Combined Transport Bill of Lading)

Vessel and Voy. No.

Place of Delivery (Applicable only when this document is used as a Combined Transport Bill of Lading)

Port of Loading

Port of Discharge

Undermentioned particulars as declared by Shipper, but not acknowledged by the Carrier (see clause 11)

Marks and Nos; Container Nos;	Number and kind of Packages; Description of Goods	Gross Weight (kg)	Measurement (cbm)

CANCELLED - SPECIMEN COPY

*Total No. of Containers/Packages received by the Carrier	Movement	Freight payable at

Received by the Carrier from the Shipper in apparent good order and condition (unless otherwise noted herein) the total number or quantity of Containers or other packages or units indicated in the box above entitled "*Total No. of Containers/Packages received by the Carrier" for Carriage subject to all the terms and conditions hereof (INCLUDING THE TERMS AND CONDITIONS ON THE REVERSE HEREOF AND THE TERMS AND CONDITIONS OF THE CARRIER'S APPLICABLE TARIFF) from the Place of Receipt or the Port of Loading, whichever is applicable, to the Port of Discharge or the Place of Delivery, whichever is applicable. If the acknowledged tally is of Containers, this indicates that the Container has been packed and sealed by the Merchant at his premises without the Carrier being represented and able to check or verify either the tally of Goods or the stowage, which are consequently unknown to him (See Clause 8). The Merchant accepts that, except by special arrangement or pursuant to Clause 9 hereof, Containers are not weighed by the Carrier at any time. If the Carrier so requires, before he arranges delivery of the Goods one original Bill of Lading, duly endorsed, must be surrendered by the Merchant to the Carrier at the Port of Discharge or at some other location acceptable to the Carrier. In accepting this Bill of Lading the Merchant expressly accepts and agrees to all its terms and conditions whether printed, stamped or written, or otherwise incorporated, notwithstanding the non-signing of this Bill of Lading by the Merchant. Without prejudice to the generality of this reference, attention is drawn, inter alia, to Clauses 12 (Shipper's/Merchant's Responsibility), 19 (Dangerous Goods) and 24 (Law & Jurisdiction).

Number of Original Bills of Lading	Place and Date of Issue	IN WITNESS of the contract herein contained the number of originals stated opposite has been issued, one of which being accomplished the other(s) to be void

EXCESS VALUATION: REFER TO CLAUSE 7(3) ON REVERSE SIDE (U.S. TRADE ONLY)...... **ORIGINAL**

FOR P&O NEDLLOYD LTD, AS CARRIER:*

P&O Nedlloyd

2/DRS B/L4 10/98

*OPERATING IN PARTNERSHIP WITH P&O NEDLLOYD BV

Figure 6: P&O Nedlloyd Bill of Lading for Combined Transport Shipment or Port-to-Port Shipment

which it can use to foreclose on the goods if need arises, but does not wish to become a party to the contract of carriage, in case it thereby incurs any liabilities. Thus the bank can use the bill as a document of title to take delivery of the goods if it has to but, if it becomes aware of liabilities attaching to the goods, it can effectively conceal its interests and avoid them.

Hence blank endorsed "Order" bills of lading are the usual requirement in a documentary credit transaction, despite the dangers they represent.

Notify Party/Address

The name of the party to whom the carrier sends his arrival notification form advising of goods coming forward for delivery. This is done gratuitously to ensure smooth delivery but there is no obligation so to do and the responsibility to monitor transit and present himself to take delivery at the appropriate time rests with the merchant (*see* clause 20(1)). However, as this is now the normal method of operation, a court might well decide that it has become established practice and, applying the law of custom and usage, the court may regard any failure by a carrier to notify as a breach of contract.

Vessel and Voyage Number/Port of Loading/Port of Discharge

If the place of receipt/place of delivery boxes are blank, the bill is a port-to-port contract, so the ports of loading and discharge are the points of commencement and termination of the contract of carriage. Otherwise, if places of receipt and/or delivery are shown, they are commercial detail, usually necessary for documentary credits purposes, but with no more significance than any other item of data on the document. (Note the definition of these items in clause 1.)

Place of Receipt/Place of Delivery

Only used if combined transport is involved (*see* clause 6(3)), in which case they indicate where contract of carriage commences and terminates.

Undermentioned particulars as declared by Shipper but not acknowledged by the Carrier (*see* clause 11)

The main details shown in the bill of lading are commercial details provided and required by the shipper for commercial purposes, the accuracy of which the shipper warrants (clause 12(2) and (3)) and for which the carrier accepts no responsibility.

It is superfluous for the shipper to require the same full description of the goods here as is required in the commercial invoice. Certainly it is not required by the bank under the terms of the letter of credit, unless this credit specifically requires it.

Total Number of Containers/Packages received by the Carrier

This is the tally which the carrier acknowledges and for which he accepts responsibility. In the case of FCL goods, it will be one or a number of containers and, in the case of LCL goods, it will be a tally of pieces or packages (note cross-reference in incorporation clause and clause 11). In the case of multiple bill of lading FCLs it will be "one of . . . part cargoes in the container" (*see* clause 21(2)).

Some carriers do not incorporate this provision and link it in with their incorporation clause. They just show the tally provided by the shipper unqualified and rely upon showing that the container was FCL packed and the terms and conditions' provisions re FCLs to avoid claims from consignees for shortages from sealed containers. I consider it much safer to make it absolutely clear on the face of the bill what is acknowledged and what is not, hence this provision and the qualification to the shipper's details above it to make it clear that such details are not acknowledged by the carrier, who acknowledges only what appears in this box.

Movement

This information is incorporated to provide details of the movement at both ends of the sea transit.

Freight Payable at

This is an indication of where the shipper has told the carrier that he wishes the freight to be paid. It is not an undertaking by the carrier that freight is only payable at this place and if the carrier is unable to collect freight here he may exercise his lien for freight to refuse delivery until someone pays the freight or requires the shipper to pay it.

Incorporation Clause

This is the clause on the face of the bill of lading which links the terms and conditions on the reverse of the bill of lading and in the tariff with the detail set out on the face into one contract. This clause will be explained in greater detail later in conjunction with the explanation of the terms and conditions of the contract of carriage, of which it is an integral part.

Number of Original Bills of Lading

Bills of lading are usually issued in sets of two or three originals together with a number of non-negotiable copies for office/filing use. This dates from the days when various originals were sent by different means to destination to try and ensure that at least one arrived before or at the same time as the goods to facilitate delivery (*see* penultimate sentence in incorporation clause). As more than one original exists, any one of which carries title to the goods, the only way a buyer can be sure of title is to ensure that he has all the originals (not copies of originals, to say that would be a contradiction in terms) in his possession. For this reason all bills must state how many originals have been issued so that any buyer can check whether or not he had a full set of originals.

Place and Date of Issue

Place where the bill of lading was issued and date thereof. This date may be any date after the goods have been received for carriage but not before. In this respect the bill of lading is viewed as a receipt. By contrast the date of any "shipped on board" endorsement must reflect the precise date of shipment.

Signature Clause

Above the authenticating signature the provision in the incorporation clause that one original must be surrendered to secure delivery is reinforced with the provision that, after delivery has taken place against one original bill, all other originals of the same tenure become worthless. A full set of originals is not necessary to secure delivery, one only will do.

Note that the bill is signed "For P&O Nedlloyd Limited as Carrier" leaving no doubt as to the identity of the contracting carrier and the party who has signed the bill of lading, without the need to resort to the definitions clause. This complies with the requirements of UCP500 Articles 23–6 a(i).

FACE OF USA BILL OF LADING

This bill of lading is an optional document which can be used as a port-to-port or combined transport bill of lading according to how it is completed (*see* definitions of port-to-port shipment and combined transport in clause 1). It has further flexibility to mix port-to-port at one end with combined transport at the other (*see* clause 6(3)).

The identities of the carrier and the agent signing on his behalf are clear from the signature clause. Thus the bill complies fully with the requirements of UCP500 on signature clauses.

Shipper/Exporter

This space must be completed with the name of the party with whom the contract of carriage has been concluded by the carrier. It must show the actual shipper not merely a shipper's forwarding agent (*see* clause 3). The shipper number is assigned by the carrier for reference. An NVOCC is a shipper under

BILL OF LADING FOR COMBINED TRANSPORT OR PORT TO PORT SHIPMENT

P&O Nedlloyd

NOT NEGOTIABLE UNLESS CONSIGNED "TO ORDER"

North America Trade

SHIPPER/EXPORTER	BOOKING NUMBER	BILL OF LADING NO.	BROKERAGE
	EXPORT REFERENCES		
CONSIGNEE	FORWARDING AGENT - REFERENCES		
	POINT AND COUNTRY OF ORIGIN		
NOTIFY PARTY (It is agreed that no responsibility shall attach to the Carrier or his Agents for failure to notify of the arrival of the goods (see clause 20 on reverse))	ALSO NOTIFY / ROUTING / INSTRUCTIONS		

*PRECARRIAGE BY	*PLACE OF RECEIPT BY PRECARRIER	
EXPORTING CARRIER (VESSEL)	PORT OF LOADING	LOADING PIER/TERMINAL
PORT OF DISCHARGE	*PLACE OF DELIVERY BY ONCARRIER	TYPE OF MOVEMENT

PARTICULARS FURNISHED BY SHIPPER (but not acknowledged by the Carrier (see clause 11))

MARKS AND NUMBERS	NO. OF PKGS.	H M	DESCRIPTION OF PACKAGES AND GOODS	GROSS WEIGHT	MEASUREMENT

EXCESS VALUATION: REFER TO CLAUSE 7 (3) ON REVERSE SIDE | ITEM NUMBER

FREIGHT CHARGES PAYABLE AT: BY

**TOTAL NO. OF CONTAINERS/PACKAGES RECEIVED BY THE CARRIER

FREIGHT AND CHARGES		PREPAID		COLLECT
EXCESS VALUE CHARGE (SEE CLAUSE 7 (3))				
RESP. CODE / TOTAL CHARGES				

Received by the Carrier from the Shipper in apparent good order and condition (unless otherwise noted herein) the total number or quantity of Containers or other packages or units indicated in the box above entitled ***"Total No. of Containers/Packages received by the Carrier" for Carriage subject to all the terms and conditions hereof (INCLUDING THE TERMS AND CONDITIONS ON THE REVERSE HEREOF AND THE TERMS OF THE CARRIER'S APPLICABLE TARIFF) from the Place of Receipt or the Port of Loading, whichever is applicable, to the Port of Discharge or the Place of Delivery, whichever is applicable. If the Carrier so requires, before he arranges delivery of the Goods one original Bill of Lading, duly endorsed, must be surrendered by the Merchant to the Carrier at the Port of Discharge or at some other location acceptable to the Carrier. In accepting this Bill of Lading the Merchant expressly accepts and agrees to all its terms and conditions whether printed, stamped or written, or otherwise incorporated, notwithstanding the non-signing of this Bill of Lading by the Merchant.

IN WITNESS whereof original Bills of Lading (unless otherwise stated above) have been signed, one of which being accomplished, the others shall be void.

For P&O Nedlloyd Limited as Carrier

AS AGENT(S) ONLY

*APPLICATION FOR COMBINED TRANSPORT ONLY

B/L NO.	MO.	DAY	YEAR

Form - 51 Rev. 2/97

Figure 7: P&O Nedlloyd Bill of Lading for Combined Transport or Port-to-Port Shipment: North America Trade

US law but must indicate its status as an NVOCC to the carrier and maintain a tariff and bond with the Federal Maritime Commission (FMC).

Consignee

This space may be completed, either with the name of the consignee (in which case the bill is not negotiable), "to order (of a named Consignee)" or the words "to order" (unqualified), in which case the shipper becomes the consignee as well and delivery is made in accordance with his instructions. These instructions may be given:

- by specific endorsement on the bill of lading: "Deliver to John Smith and Co. (stamp and signature of shipper)";
- by attaching authorised delivery instructions on the shipper's stationery: a delivery order from the shipper to the consignee;
- by means of a blank endorsement on the bill of lading and passing the document to the consignee: shipper's stamp and signature with no qualification.

Note: a blank endorsed "Order" bill of lading is a bearer document and the carrier must make delivery to whoever presents it (unless he has reason to suspect fraud).

Thus it will be seen that, like a bearer cheque, a blank endorsed "Order" bill is a dangerous document. However, it is a much-used document on account of the requirements of banks advancing to funds against documents to finance foreign trade.

A bill contains indemnities to the carrier which impose liabilities upon the merchant. A bank advancing funds requires the security of documents of title, which it can use to foreclose on the goods if need arises, but does not wish to become a party to the contract of carriage, in case it thereby incurred any liabilities. Thus the bank can use the bill as a document of title to take delivery of the goods if it has to but, if it becomes aware of liabilities attaching to the goods, it can effectively conceal its interests and avoid them.

Hence blank endorsed "Order" bills of lading are the usual requirement in a documentary credit transaction, despite the dangers they represent.

The consignee number is assigned by the carrier for reference.

Notify Party

The name of the party to whom the carrier sends his arrival notification advising of goods coming forward for delivery. This is done gratuitously to ensure smooth delivery but there is no obligation so to do and the responsibility to monitor transit and present himself to take delivery at the appropriate time rests with the merchant (*see* clause 20(1)). However, as this is now the normal method of operation, a court might well decide that it has become established practice and, applying the law of custom and usage, the court may regard any failure by a carrier to notify as a breach of contract.

The notify number is assigned by the carrier for reference.

Precarriage by/Place of Receipt by Precarrier

If goods and containers are received from outports by feeder vessel for transhipment onto the deep-sea vessel, these spaces will be used to show the port at which the carrier received the goods and containers for carriage. If they have been received from an inland point, the place at which the carrier received the goods will be recorded here.

Exporting Carrier (Vessel)/Port of Loading/Port of Discharge

If the place of receipt/place of delivery boxes are blank, the bill is a port-to-port contract, so the ports of loading and discharge are the points of commencement and termination of the contract of carriage. Otherwise, if places of receipt and/or delivery are shown, they are commercial detail, usually necessary for documentary credits purposes, but with no more significance than any other item of data on the document. (Note the definition of these items in clause 1.)

Place of Delivery by Oncarrier

If combined transport is involved (*see* clause 6(3)), this space is used to indicate where contract of carriage terminates. It can also be used in the case of port-to-port carriage where a connecting carrier effects the final delivery after taking over the goods from the contracting carrier at a transhipment port.

Booking Number

This is a unique reference number allocated at the time of booking to identify the customer's order. It should be quoted in all subsequent dialogue and correspondence with the carrier to facilitate speedy reference to the correct data.

Brokerage

This should be completed with an N or a Y to indicate whether or not forwarding agent's commission has to be paid on the consignment in question.

Export References

This space is used by the shipper or his forwarder for bank or other references for his convenience.

Forwarding Agent—References/FMC Number

For shipments from the USA, only FMC licensed freight forwarders can receive commission/brokerage from the carrier for forwarding services. In order to do so the FMC licence number of the forwarder must be inserted in the space indicated and the forwarder's name etc. must be shown. Note that a freight forwarder is the merchant's agent whilst a freight broker is the agent of the carrier and does not perform forwarding services for the merchant.

Point and Country of Origin

If the CTO is not responsible for arranging the precarriage, the contract of carriage does not commence at the point of origin of the goods. As this is data often required by authorities, provision is made to record it here.

Also Notify/Routing/Instructions

A second notify party may be identified in this space or special routing requests may be recorded, which the CTO will endeavour to accommodate but which he does not guarantee to follow.

Loading Pier/Terminal

The identity of the place at which the carrier accepts the loaded container for carriage.

Type of Movement

This space will be used to indicate the type of service.

Particulars Furnished by Shipper (but not acknowledged by the Carrier (*see* Clause 11))

The main details shown in the bill of lading are commercial details provided and required by the shipper for commercial purposes, the accuracy of which the shipper warrants (clause 12(2) and (3)) and for which the carrier accepts no responsibility.

It is superfluous for a shipper to require the same full description of the goods here as is required in the commercial invoice. Certainly it is not required by the bank under the terms of the letter of credit unless the credit specifically requires it.

Excess Valuation

Unless this section is completed and additional freight paid, the limitations in clauses 6 and 27 will apply. This provision is incorporated following a US court decision that, unless the carrier gives the merchant the opportunity to declare value and pay *ad valorem* freight to obtain a higher level of recourse, he is denied the right to limit liability. (*American World Airways Inc.* v. *California Stevedores and Ballast Company* (1978) AMC 1834.)

Freight Charges Payable at

This is an indication of where the shipper has told the carrier that he wishes the freight to be paid. It is not an undertaking by the carrier that freight is only payable at this place and if the carrier is unable to collect freight here he may exercise his lien for freight to refuse delivery until someone pays the freight or require the shipper to pay it.

Item Number

This is the tariff code and item number to show what tariff freight rate has been applied.

Total Number of Containers/Packages Received by the Carrier

This is the tally which the carrier acknowledges and for which he accepts responsibility. In the case of FCL goods, it will be one or a number of containers and, in the case of LCL goods, it will be a tally of pieces or packages (note cross-reference in incorporation clause and clause 11). In the case of multiple bill of lading FCLs it will be "one of _____ part cargoes in the container" (*see* clause 21(2)).

Some carriers do not incorporate this provision and link it in with their incorporation clause. They just show the tally provided by the shipper unqualified and rely upon showing that the container was FCL packed and the terms and conditions' provisions re FCLs to avoid claims from consignees for shortages from sealed containers. I consider it much safer to make it absolutely clear on the face of the bill what is acknowledged and what is not, hence this provision and the qualification to the shipper's details above it to make it clear that such details are not acknowledged by the carrier, who acknowledges only what appears in this box.

Incorporation Clause

This is the clause on the face of the bill of lading which links the terms and conditions on the reverse of the bill of lading and in the tariff with the detail set out on the face into one contract. This clause will be explained in greater detail later in conjunction with the explanation of the terms and conditions of the contract of carriage, of which it is an integral part.

Number of Original Bills of Lading

Bills of lading are usually issued in sets of two or three originals together with a number of non-negotiable copies for office/filing use. This dates from the days when various originals were sent by different means to destination to try and ensure that at least one arrived before or at the same time as the goods to facilitate delivery (*see* penultimate sentence in incorporation clause). As more than one original exists, any one of which carries title to the goods, the only way a buyer can be sure of title is to ensure that he has all the originals (not copies of originals—to say that would be a contradiction in terms) in his possession. For this reason all bills must state how many originals have been issued so that any buyer can check whether or not he has a full set of originals.

Signature Clause

Above the authenticating signature the provision in the incorporation clause that one original must be surrendered to secure delivery is reinforced with the provision that, after delivery has taken place against one original bill, all other originals of the same tenure become worthless. A full set of originals is not necessary to secure delivery, one only will do.

Note that the bill is signed "For P&O Nedlloyd Limited as Carrier" leaving no doubt as to the identity of the contracting carrier and the party who has signed the bill of lading, without the need to resort to the definitions clause. This complies with the requirements of UCP500 Articles 23–6 a(i).

Bill of Lading number and Date of Issue

Note that the date shown here is the date of issue of the bill of lading and not the date of shipment on board.

Freight and Charges

Details of the freight and charges on the goods and whether they are to be pre-paid or are for collection at destination. These details are usually only shown on the non-negotiable copies of the bill, where they constitute an invoice, the space being left blank on the originals.

STRAIGHT BILLS OF LADING

A straight bill of lading is one in which the identity of the consignee is shown without any qualification, particularly important is the absence of any reference to "Order". A straight bill of lading is not a negotiable document and cannot be used to transfer title in the same way as a negotiable Order bill of lading. Whether it remains a document of title and must therefore be surrendered in order to secure delivery is something which is unclear in the courts of most countries but which has been clarified in the USA courts by reason of a piece of USA legislation call the Pomerene Act. This Act, which presently only applies to US exports and interstate traffic (it will be extended to US imports if and when their revised COGSA is enacted), provides that, if a bill of lading is a straight bill of lading, the carrier may deliver to the nominated consignee without surrender of any documents. In other words, this Act treats a straight bill of lading as if it were a waybill. The Pomerene Act also requires the bill to be marked "Not Negotiable" if delivery is to be made in this way and it is for this reason that bills of lading in the USA trades are almost all marked in the way which you will note at the top of the P&O Nedlloyd North American bill—not negotiable unless consigned "To Order". Thus marked a bill of lading becomes not negotiable if the consignee's name is shown in an unqualified way with no reference to the word "Order".

The straight bill of lading is an ideal example of the problems created for carriers by conflict of law in international trade. Here we have an American Act, only applying to American exports, directing delivery to be made beyond the jurisdiction of the American courts without surrender of any documents. The law in the country where delivery is effected is unclear as to whether this is permissible and the general consensus of opinion is that it is not. (In a private conversation with an English High Court judge I was assured that the court would always regard a bill of lading as a document of title and require its surrender prior to delivery.) This, then, is the dilemma of the carrier. Which law does he obey? If he delivers an American export in Europe an American exporter could sue him in a European court for breach of contract and it is questionable whether or not he could offer a defence that he was merely complying with American law.

TERMS AND CONDITIONS OF THE CONTRACT OF CARRIAGE

General

In drafting any contract the aim should always be absolute clarity, such that only one interpretation can be put on whatever is placed therein. Only in this way can exposure to court action be minimised.

One must always ensure that the contract is in compliance with any applicable law which, in view of the problems of the nature identified above in relation to straight bills of lading, is not always easy, especially when one has to cover the laws and the interpretations thereof in all countries to which the CTO trades.

The following assist in enhancing the readability and thus the clarity of a contract:

- *short sentences with simple wording:* easier said than done in an industry bedevilled by complicated law and jargon but a constant aim for which one must always strive;
- *tabulation, headings etc.:* it is always easier to read a contract set out in tabular form and clearly signposted;
- *a definitions clause:* a glance at a pre-1970s break-bulk conventional bill of lading will almost certainly reveal a continuous stream of words, regularly repeated in the text in an effort to be all-embracing. This is confusing. If one single word, used with the first letter as a capital, is defined to cover the entire list, use of that single word makes the sentence shorter, easier to read and thus more intelligible:
- *consistent language:* if the word "ship" is used in one place, "vessel" in another and "containership" elsewhere, you are inviting a judge to embark on a voyage of discovery to put different meanings on each word, the view being that if you use different words, you mean different things. So consistency of language is vital in drafting a contract and even more vital in drafting any additional clauses to be added on the face of the contract.

The bill of lading is a contract of adhesion, that is to say, it is a contract signed by one party only and not by both parties, which is the usual approach with contracts. In order to protect the party who does not sign the contract (the shipper), English law operates a doctrine of *contra proferentem*, which means to say that any provision in the contract will be construed narrowly against the carrier, because he is the party who has drafted the contract and it is therefore up to him to make any provision for his benefit absolutely clear if he wishes to enjoy that benefit. Furthermore, whilst it is always open to a carrier to waive any provision for his benefit in the contract, he cannot later enjoy the benefit of something for which he has not clearly provided in the contract. Thus, if he wishes to retain the initiative in a contract, he has to make sure that he has included absolutely everything for his benefit that he may later need in any circumstance whatsoever. For this reason a bill of lading may seem a very one-sided contract to any casual reader unfamiliar with the doctrines of English law.

Incorporation Clause

This is the clause on the face of the bill of lading which links the terms and conditions on the reverse of the bill of lading and in the tariff with the detail set out on the face into one contract. Furthermore it is the carrier's acknowledgement of the tally shown in the "Total Number of Containers/Packages received by the Carrier" box and provides for the acceptance of the terms and conditions of the contract by the merchant (*see* definition in clause 1) and the need to surrender one original to secure delivery at destination (*see* signature clause).

One of the great difficulties which carriers have is demonstrating to a court that the contract has been brought adequately to the attention of the other party. Courts have often sympathised with merchants who have failed to read the full contract on the back of a bill of lading and thus missed something shown there. For this reason, based on decisions and *obiter dicta* in the past, carriers often make particular reference to particularly important items on the face of the bill, so that they can plead that they have drawn the shipper's attention to that particular item. This is all part of the same problem which BIMCO and others have tried to overcome by making the terms and conditions on the back page 1 and the face of the bill page 2.

The incorporation clause on the front of the bill of lading reads as follows:

"Received by the Carrier from the Shipper in apparent good order and condition (unless otherwise noted herein) the total number or quantity of Containers or other packages or units indicated in the box opposite entitled 'Total Number of Containers/Packages received by the Carrier' for carriage subject to all the terms and conditions hereof (INCLUDING THE TERMS AND CONDITIONS ON THE REVERSE HEREOF AND THE TERMS AND CONDITIONS OF THE CARRIER'S APPLICABLE TARIFF) from the Place of Receipt or the Port of Loading, whichever is applicable, to the Port of Discharge or the Place of Delivery, whichever is applicable. If the acknowledged tally is of Containers, this indicates that the Container has been packed and sealed by the Merchant at his premises without the Carrier being represented and able to check or verify either the tally of Goods or the stowage, which are consequently unknown to him (see Clause 8). The Merchant accepts that, except by special arrangement or pursuant to Clause 9 hereof, Containers are not weighed by the Carrier at any time. If the Carrier so requires, before he arranges delivery of the Goods, one original bill of lading, duly endorsed, must be surrendered by the Merchant to the Carrier at the Port of Discharge or at some other location acceptable to the Carrier. In accepting this Bill of Lading the Merchant expressly accepts and agrees to all its terms and conditions, whether printed, stamped, written or otherwise incorporated, notwithstanding the non-signing of this Bill of Lading by the Merchant. Without prejudice to the generality of this reference, attention is drawn, *inter alia*, to Clauses 12 (Shipper's/Merchant's Responsibility), 19 (Dangerous Goods) and 24 (Law and Jurisdiction)."

This clause contains quite a lot of items in a relatively short space and needs extensive explanation. I will therefore take it a phrase at a time and explain the implications of it and the ideas behind it.

"Received by the Carrier from the Shipper": this clearly indicates that it is a received for shipment and not a shipped on board bill of lading, a separate endorsement on the face being necessary in order to convert it to the latter. Clearly a combined transport bill of lading has to be a received for shipment document as the contract of carriage starts well away from shipment at the terminal and, as a combined transport operator, the carrier is liable for the goods long before they reach the side of the ship.

"In apparent good order and condition (unless otherwise noted herein) the total number or quantity of Containers or other packages or units indicated in the box opposite entitled 'Total Number of Containers/Packages received by the Carrier' ": in the case of LCL goods, which are received by the carrier at a container freight station (CFS) for him to pack into the container, then clearly the receipt will be for a tally of packages and for the apparent condition of those packages (the carrier is not expected to open packages to ascertain the condition of the goods therein, so the receipt is in respect of apparent condition only). In the case of FCL goods, this is packed by the merchant, or some contractor acting on behalf of the merchant, so the receipt from the carrier can only evidence a tally of containers and any external apparent condition of the containers.

"for carriage subject to all the terms and conditions hereof (INCLUDING THE TERMS AND CONDITIONS ON THE REVERSE HEREOF AND THE TERMS AND CONDITIONS OF THE CARRIER'S APPLICABLE TARIFF)": this phrase incorporates all the terms of the contract printed on the back of the bill and in the tariff into the contract with the merchant. The tariff is not merely a schedule of rates but also includes some of the terms and conditions applicable to the contract of carriage. I am often asked what appears in the tariff and what appears in the bill. There is no hard and fast rule but the general approach is that the bill of lading, being a document of title which may be used to transfer title to goods to a third party, thereby binding that third party into the contract of carriage with the carrier, carries items relevant to the carriage of the goods, so that the carrier can demonstrate that the third party has had an opportunity to be aware of the terms of the contract into which he has entered by purchasing a bill of lading. This is necessary because the transaction between the consignee and the third party may take place in a location where the carrier does not have an office, thereby giving the third party an opportunity to say that he cannot be bound to a contract, the terms of which he has no means of knowing.

The terms and conditions relating to collection and delivery, which are relevant only to the shipper and the party taking delivery from the carrier at a final destination, are shown in the tariff. This is because, as these parties are in contact with the carrier to arrange collection or delivery, they are in a position to ask to see the tariff rules, which are incorporated as part of the contract of carriage, if they so wish. This is another example of the difficulty of overcoming the problem of ensuring that the terms and conditions of a contract of adhesion are brought properly to the attention of the party concerned.

"from the Place of Receipt or the Port of Loading, whichever is applicable, to the Port of Discharge or the Place of Delivery, whichever is applicable": being an optional contract of carriage, the carrier may take over the goods anywhere between the shipper's premises and the side of the vessel. He may equally effect delivery anywhere between the side of the vessel at a terminal in the port of discharge and the consignee's premises. In determining the parameters of the contract of carriage, account obviously has to be taken of this and, as we shall see later looking at clause 1 definitions, it is the way in which the bill of lading is completed which determines whether it is port-to-port or combined transport.

"If the acknowledged tally is of Containers, this indicates that the Container has been packed and sealed by the Merchant at his premises without the Carrier being represented and able to check or verify either the tally of Goods or the stowage, which are consequently unknown to him (see Clause 8)": although all of this is covered in greater detail in clause 8 on the reverse, it is considered prudent to take steps to bring to the attention of all parties concerned the fact that, in the case of an FCL packed container, the carrier accepts no liability for bad stowage of the goods within the container causing damage to the goods or any discrepancy in the tally if the container is delivered with seal intact to show that no entry to the container has been effected during transit. This links in with the clear indication of what the carrier acknowledges in the box referred to earlier in order to leave any party reading the contract in no doubt as to what the carrier acknowledges and the extent of his responsibilities in relation to the goods.

"The Merchant accepts that, except by special arrangement or pursuant to Clause 9 hereof, Containers are not weighed by the Carrier at any time": one of the ways in which merchants have sought to make recoveries from carriers for shortages from containers is by suggesting that the carrier has a duty to weigh containers prior to shipment, rather than just rely upon details provided by the shipper. Quite apart from all the extra work and cost involved in weighing containers, it is a fact that weighing facilities are rarely available at terminals and, if they are, they are frequently located in inconvenient areas and expensive. This sentence provides for the merchant's acceptance that the carrier will not weigh containers (unless specifically arranged to the contrary) and helps protect the carrier from attack using this approach in the event of large shortages from sealed containers.

"If the Carrier so requires, before he arranges delivery of the Goods, one original Bill of Lading, duly endorsed, must be surrendered by the Merchant to the Carrier at the Port of Discharge or at some other location acceptable to the Carrier": there are several important points to be noted here starting with the opening phrase: "If the Carrier so requires". As we shall see when considering sub-clause 20(7), this is an attempt to deal with the problem of a merchant requiring delivery against a straight bill of lading without surrender of documents. It purports to provide that a bill of lading needs to be surrendered in return for delivery of the goods only if the carrier so requires. The effectiveness of this provision cannot be guaranteed, because of the general custom that the bill of lading is always a document of title and must be surrendered to secure delivery. However, it does give the carrier some protection and at least a basis of argument for a compromise settlement according to the circumstances.

Note also at the end of the sentence the words "at the Port of Discharge or at some other location acceptable to the Carrier": traditionally the only requirement was for the surrender of one original bill of lading in return for the delivery of the goods. This was all well and good in port-to-port shipment, where delivery was made at ship's side, where the carrier had suitably experienced personnel to check the bill of lading before delivery was effected. However, with combined transport, where delivery is often made at the merchant's premises, if a merchant insisted that he would literally surrender the bill in return for delivery of the goods by giving it to the lorry driver when he arrived at his premises, few carriers would be happy to allow a lorry driver to check the bill to ensure that it was in order before delivery. Hence the requirement here to give the carrier control over where the bill of lading is surrendered in order to secure delivery.

"In accepting this Bill of Lading the Merchant expressly accepts and agrees to all its terms and conditions, whether printed, stamped, written, or otherwise incorporated, notwithstanding the non-signing of this Bill of Lading by the Merchant": this is an attempt by the carrier to overcome the problem of acceptance of the contract of carriage by the merchant as he does not sign it. It provides for acceptance of the bill to be equivalent to signature of it by the merchant. Different courts are known to take different views of this.

"Without prejudice to the generality of this reference, attention is drawn, *inter alia*, to Clauses 12 (Shipper's/Merchant's Responsibility), 19 (Dangerous Goods) and 24 (Law and Jurisdiction)": these are three clauses which experience has shown some courts require to be brought clearly to the attention of the merchant on the face of the document, if the carrier wishes to enjoy any of the benefits outlined therein.

Clause 1: Definitions

This is one of the most important clauses in the contract and anyone who tries to read the contract, without first taking account of this clause, will at best have an incomplete understanding of the contract and at worst a totally erroneous concept of it. This core clause is the key to the full meaning of every other clause in the contract and must be borne in mind when reading all other clauses. Not all of its implications are immediately obvious and are explained below.

"In this Bill of Lading the word:
'Carrier' means the party named in the Signature Box on the face hereof;
'Merchant' includes any Person who at any time has been or becomes the Shipper, Holder, Consignee, Receiver of the Goods, any Person who owns or is entitled to possession of the Goods or of this Bill of Lading and any Person acting on behalf of any such Person;
'Holder' means any Person for the time being in possession of (or entitled to the possession of) this Bill of Lading;
'Person' includes an individual, group, company or other entity;
'Sub-Contractor' includes (but is not limited to) owners and operators of any Vessels (other than the Carrier), stevedores, terminal and groupage operators, road, rail and air transport operators and any independent contractor employed by the Carrier in performance of the Carriage and any sub-sub-contractors thereof;

'indemnify' includes defend, indemnify and hold harmless whether or not the obligation to indemnify arises out of negligence or non-negligent acts or omissions of the Carrier, his servants, agents or Sub-Contractors;
'Goods' means the whole or any part of the cargo received from the Shipper and includes the packing and any equipment or Container not supplied by or on behalf of the Carrier;
'Container' includes any container, trailer, transportable tank, flat or pallet, or any similar article used to consolidate goods and any ancillary equipment;
'Carriage' means the whole or any part of the operations and services undertaken by the Carrier in respect of the Goods covered by this Bill of Lading;
'Port of Loading' means any port at which the Goods are loaded on board any Vessel (which may not necessarily be the Vessel named overleaf) for Carriage under this Bill of Lading;
'Port of Discharge' means any port at which the Goods are discharged from any Vessel (which may not necessarily be the Vessel named overleaf) after Carriage under this Bill of Lading;
'Vessel' means any waterborne craft used in the Carriage under this Bill of Lading which may be a feeder vessel or an ocean vessel;
'Combined Transport' arises if the Place of Receipt and/or the Place of Delivery are indicated on the face hereof in the relevant spaces;
'Port-to-Port' arises if the Carriage is not Combined Transport;
'Shipped on Board' relates only to the Container into which the Goods are manifested;
'Freight' includes all charges payable to the Carrier in accordance with the applicable Tariff and this Bill of Lading;
'Hague Rules' means that the provisions of the International Convention for the Unification of Certain Rules relating to Bills of Lading signed at Brussels on 25 August 1924 and includes the amendments by the Protocol signed at Brussels on 23 February 1968, but only if such amendments are compulsorily applicable to this Bill of Lading (it is expressly provided that nothing in this Bill of Lading shall be construed as contractually applying said Rules as amended by said Protocol)."

Let us now take these definitions one at a time and understand their precise meaning:

Carrier: this is a contract in which the party issuing the document, the contracting carrier, is the sole contracting party and, as we shall see later, steps are taken to prevent the merchant from dealing with any other parties who may be sub-contractors of the carrier. This clause makes it absolutely clear who the contracting carrier is. The wording shown is designed to be used by any carrier. This could be made even more simple by merely saying that "carrier means" and then naming the carrier.

Merchant: it will be noticed that the term merchant is given a very wide meaning to include virtually everyone who at any time has an involvement with the goods on behalf of the shipper or consignee, as opposed to the carrier. It is designed to create a situation where the contract is a simple one between carrier interests via the contracting carrier and cargo interests, who presumably will have contractual relationships between themselves defining their respective responsibilities (e.g. INCOTERMS). Where a shipper, against who the carrier wishes to make a claim for breach of contract, has "disappeared", the carrier could approach the consignee, although obviously he would approach the shipper first if this were possible.

As we come to read the clauses it will be noted that, even where initial responsibilities are placed on a specific person (for example, the responsibility of the shipper to provide information prior to shipment), all indemnities are taken from the merchant to give the carrier the widest possible target in the event of a need to enforce an indemnity.

Holder: this definition is self-explanatory and requires no further comment.

Person: a fairly obvious definition to make sure that all types of entities who enter into contract with the carrier are covered by a use of the word "Person".

Sub-Contractor: it should be sufficient to define sub-contractor merely in the terms of the last part of this definition, namely any independent contractor employed by the carrier. However, decisions in some courts have indicated the desirability of naming the types of sub-contractor involved. In doing so one has to beware of the English legal doctrine of *ejusdem generis* which would interpret the description sub-contractor narrowly to the examples quoted in this definition. This is an attempt to find the correct line between the all-embracing word and a list of every conceivable type of sub-contractor who may be used.

Indemnify: again an attempt to broaden out a term to avoid any nit-picking in the court. Note that indemnify covers situations when negligence is not involved as well as where negligence is involved. This follows the decision in *Smith and Anor.* v. *South Wales Switchgear* [1978] 1 W.L.R. 165 referred to in earlier chapters.

Goods: note that this definition includes the whole or any part of the cargo. It is insufficient merely to refer to the goods and expect that definition to cover all of it or part of it as the doctrine of *contra proferentem* would construe that narrowly against the carrier. If the carrier wishes to cover both then he must make it clear that he intends it to cover both.

Note also that the definition "Goods" covers a container supplied by or on behalf of the merchant. A merchant-supplied container would come within the definition of "Container" and "Goods", hence the use of a capital C for container when defining goods. Also within this definition is any other equipment or packing which the merchant may supply.

Container: there are many different types of container and this definition is designed to ensure that all are covered within that term. It goes even further to include pallets and any similar article used to consolidate goods and any ancillary equipment. Ancillary equipment would include such things as clip-on units on insulated port-hole containers.

Carriage: note again the use of the approach "the whole or any part of". This allows the carrier to cover the whole of the operation or any part of it (including such things as storage, handling etc.) within the term "Carriage".

The term even covers clerical tasks, in so far as these are part of the bill of lading contract (customs clearance would not come within this definition).

Port of loading/port of discharge: carriers frequently experience problems with merchants because merchants, even after 30 years of combined transport, have still to learn how to draft the applications for their letters of credit correctly to ask for combined transport and take account of the way in which it operates. Unfortunately the vast majority of letters of credit are still drafted calling for a marine ocean bill of lading on a port-to-port basis. They fail to take account of the fact that combined transport these days operates on a hub and spoke principle, with feeder vessels carrying goods from outlying ports to the ports of call of the main-line deep-sea vessels and with similar distribution at the other end. Merchants require their bills of lading immediately goods are loaded on board at their port and are unwilling to await shipment from the hub port before receiving the shipped on board bills of lading, that they demand to meet their letter of credit requirements in order to get paid. Some insist on having the name of the deep-sea vessel on the bill whilst others insist on the feeder vessel's name. All of this creates problems for a carrier trying to meet his customer's requirements without perjuring himself by putting incorrect data on a document of title. The very wide definitions of port of loading and port of discharge are to enable the carrier to meet his customer's requirements legitimately and not, as may appear on the face of it, to mislead by means of the data shown on the face of the bill of lading.

Vessel: a similarly wide definition of vessel is made for the same reason as the wide definitions of ports of loading and discharge. Note that the definition covers any waterborne craft so that river and canal craft are included as well as sea-going vessels.

Combined transport/port-to-port: as this is an optional bill of lading to cover both port-to-port and combined transport, there has to be a way in which it can be determined whether the document is a port-to-port or combined transport contract. This definition makes it clear that the completion or non-completion of the place of receipt and/or the place of delivery boxes on the face indicate the nature of the contract. If both of these boxes are blank, then it is a port-to-port shipment; if one of them is completed then the contract is for combined transport.

Shipped on board: once goods have been loaded into a container it is not possible to inspect their tally and condition until that container is opened, usually at destination. This means that the tally and condition can only be verified at the shipper's premises or the container freight station (according to whether it is an FCL or LCL) and not later alongside the vessel prior to loading. In some cases where goods have been damaged and the investigations of the carrier have shown that loss/damage occurred prior to loading on board and therefore the claim should be adjusted according to the land-basic portion of the contract, some claimants have sought to allege that the shipped on board endorsement indicates that the goods were shipped in a clean condition so that the doctrine of estoppel applies to prevent the carrier from showing that the goods were damaged prior to shipment. Such allegations may be made where a sea-based liability is more generous than that which applies on land. This clause seeks to redress that situation to permit evidence of where loss or damage occurred to determine the liability regime to be applied.

Freight: firstly, for some, it is necessary to point out that freight is the charge payable for carrying goods. It is a word often misused to refer to the goods themselves. In this contract freight is given a wide definition to include all charges and thus it would include demurrage, detention and any other charges levied in accordance with the bill of lading or applicable tariff.

Hague Rules: where used in this contract the term Hague Rules means both the Hague and Hague-Visby Rules. It only means the Hague-Visby Rules where such rules are mandatorily applicable to the shipment in question. On all other occasions it means the Hague Rules.

Notice that no mention is made anywhere of the Hamburg Rules, even though this bill of lading may be used for carriage to or from a nation which has ratified or acceded thereto. There are several reasons for this. Firstly, carriers do not wish to give the Hamburg Rules the oxygen of recognition and publicity, as they regard them as an unreasonable and unwarranted complication. Secondly, the Hamburg Rules are only mandatorily applicable in the courts of a few countries, a high percentage of which are land-locked and almost all of these countries are not generally recognised as major trading nations and claims are rarely dealt with within their jurisdiction. Thirdly, in any event, even if a claim was brought in the court of a signatory nation, all that would happen would be that they would mandatorily apply the Hamburg Rules. Many of the nations who have ratified or acceded to these rules have not passed the necessary domestic legislation to bring them into force in the courts of their own countries, so that the present situation with these rules is far from clear and they are best left to be dealt with on a case by case basis according to the circumstances. Furthermore, with those nations that are land-locked, it is possible to avoid Hamburg Rules, which are applicable only where either the port of loading or discharge is in a signatory nation or the bill of lading is issued in a signatory nation. If the nation is land-locked, neither the port of loading nor discharge can be in a signatory nation so, if the carrier avoids issuing the bill of lading in that nation, he can avoid the Hamburg Rules and there is nothing to prevent him from doing so. For example, Austria is a signatory nation and the carrier could issue any bills of lading for shipments from Austria in Switzerland, which is not a signatory nation.

Clause 2: Carrier's Tariff

"The terms and conditions of the Carrier's applicable Tariff are incorporated herein. Particular attention is drawn to the terms and conditions therein relating to Container and vehicle demurrage. Copies of the relevant provisions of the applicable Tariff are obtainable from the Carrier or his agents upon request. In the case of inconsistency between this bill of lading and the applicable Tariff, this bill of lading shall prevail."

This short clause merely incorporates the terms and conditions of the tariff for the trade concerned (the applicable tariff) into the contract of carriage and makes it clear that, in the event of any inconsistency between the tariff and the terms and conditions of the bill of lading, the bill of lading prevails and is paramount. Particular attention is drawn to the provisions in the tariff relating to container and vehicle demurrage, as these are the most frequent causes of dispute, and merchants are directed that, if they wish to see the tariff, they can obtain copies of the relevant provisions (the whole tariff is a rather large document) from the carrier or his agent on request.

Clause 3: Warranty

"The Merchant warrants that in agreeing to the terms and conditions hereof he is, or has the authority of, the Person entitled to the possession of the Goods and this Bill of Lading."

The carrier has no way of knowing whether or not a party contacting him to arrange for a contract carriage to carry goods from one place to another has authority to give instructions in relation to those goods, either because he owns them or is an agent for and acting on behalf of the owner. Goods could be contraband or stolen goods and the carrier needs to protect himself from becoming involved should disputes over the ownership of goods arise or the authorities discover contraband in the cargo.

Clause 4: Sub-contracting and Indemnity

This is the circular indemnity and Himalaya clause, which is the link in the chain of indemnity, to which extensive reference has already been made in discussion of the mutual waiver clause in the operating agreement and slot charter party. It consists of four sub-clauses. The first provides for the right to sub-contract. The second is the circular indemnity and Himalaya clause in favour of servants, agents and sub-contractors. The third extends the protection of the second sub-clause to co-charterers in the same consortium as the carrier, and the fourth is what I call my "Irene's Success" clause, to make absolutely certain that the bill of lading terms and conditions will apply to all claims.

"(1) The Carrier shall be entitled to sub-contract the Carriage on any terms whatsoever."

This clause merely makes it clear to the merchant that the carrier does not undertake all of the tasks involved in the contract of carriage himself and, on some occasions, uses sub-contractors. He is entitled to contract with the sub-contractors on any terms that he chooses, as he is not binding the merchant to these contracts. Any discrepancy between the terms of the bill of lading and the terms of his sub-contract, which leads to a shortfall in any recovery he may make for any liability which he may have to the merchant, is for his account.

Notice how the definition in clause 1 of the word "Carriage" enables one word to be used instead of "the carriage or any part thereof" or "any handling, stowing, transport, etc., etc., etc.".

"(2) The Merchant undertakes that no claim or allegation shall be made against any Person whomsoever by whom the Carriage is performed or undertaken (including all Sub-Contractors of the Carrier), other than the Carrier, which imposes or attempts to impose upon any such Person, or any vessel owned by any such Person, any liability whatsoever in connection with the Goods or the Carriage of the Goods, whether or not arising out of negligence on the part of such Person and, if any such claim or allegation should nevertheless be made, the Merchant will indemnify the Carrier against all consequences thereof. Without prejudice to the foregoing, every such Person or Vessel shall have the benefit of every right, defence, limitation and liberty of whatsoever nature herein contained or otherwise available to the Carrier (including, but not limited to, Clause 24 hereof) as if such provisions were expressly for his benefit and, in entering into this contract, the Carrier, to the extent of these provisions, does so not only on his own behalf but also as agent and trustee for such Persons or Vessel."

The only way to control somebody with whom you are not in contract is to require a third party, with whom you are in contract and who is in contract with the party you wish to control, to do so. In other words, you need to go through a chain of contracts in order to achieve the desired effect. This clause is an undertaking by the merchant that, not only will he not make any claims but that no claims will be made against anybody involved in the carriage, other than the carrier, via anybody else either. It is designed to prevent an action against an actual carrier instead of the contracting carrier, on a tort basis, in order to avoid any restrictions in the contract of carriage. As in certain circumstances in marine law vessels are legal entities, it is necessary to mention them as well as such parties as servants, agents and sub-contractors to have the benefit of such indemnity.

The usual reference to whether or not involving negligence is made to ensure that the indemnity has the widest application and then the clause, which has been in the nature of a circular indemnity clause so far, adopts the Himalaya clause approach to provide for the carrier to act as agent for these beneficiaries of the indemnity, in order to state for them to have such benefit. This benefit is to include the benefit of the law and jurisdiction clause (clause 24).

This clause has been found to be effective in cases in England and Australia. The leading case in England is usually referred to as the "Elbe Maru Injunction", given by Mr Justice (now Lord) Ackner (*Nippon Yusen Kaisha* v. *International Import and Export Co. Ltd.* [1978] 1 Lloyd's Rep. 206).

"(3) The provisions of Clause 4(2), including but not limited to the undertakings of the Merchant contained therein, shall extend to claims or allegation of whatsoever nature against other Persons chartering space on the carrying Vessel."

This sub-clause is to ensure that the same protection, as is given to servants, agents and sub-contractors in clause 4(2), is also available to the carrier's consortium partners who are co-charterers of space on the vessel.

"(4) The Merchant further undertakes that no claim or allegation in respect of the Goods shall be made against the Carrier by any Person, other than in accordance with the terms and conditions of this Bill of Lading, which imposes or attempts to impose upon the Carrier any liability whatsoever in connection with the Goods or the Carriage of the Goods, whether or not arising out of negligence on the part of the Carrier and, if any such claim or allegation should nevertheless be made, to indemnify the Carrier against all consequences thereof."

I refer to this as my "Irene's Success" clause as I drafted it to overcome a loophole identified in a case involving a vessel of that name (*Schiffahrt-und-Kohlen GmbH* v. *Chelsea Maritime Ltd.* [1981] 2 Lloyd's Rep. 635) in which the holder of a delivery order, who was not a party to the contract to carriage, successfully sued the carrier in tort, avoiding the defences and limitations in the contract of carriage. In English law this provision has since been overruled in the case of the *Aliakmon* (*Leigh and Sillivan Ltd.* v. *Aliakmon Shipping Company* [1986] 2 All E.R. 145) which was taken as far as the House of Lords for a final decision so that this could only be overruled by a new Act of Parliament. Nevertheless the situation might still operate in some other jurisdiction so the clause is retained to ensure maximum beneficial effect on an international basis.

So, whilst sub-clause (2) protects servants, agents and sub-contractors and sub-clause (3) protects co-charterers, sub-clause (4) protects the carrier from actions by anybody other than in accordance with the terms and conditions of the bill of lading and takes an indemnity from the merchant should this occur. (Note the definition of Merchant in clause 1 gives the carrier a wide choice of action should this indemnity need to be enforced.)

Clause 5: Carrier's Responsibility/Port-to-Port Shipment

All of the clauses in this optional port-to-port or combined transport contract of carriage apply to both options except for two. These are clauses 5 and 6. Clause 5 applies to port-to-port shipment only whereas clause 6 applies to combined transport.

"If Carriage is Port-to-Port, the liability (if any) of the Carrier for loss, damage or delay to the Goods occurring from and during loading onto any Vessel up to and during discharge from that Vessel or from another Vessel into which the Goods have been transhipped shall be determined in accordance with any national law making the Hague Rules compulsorily applicable to this Bill of Lading, or in any other case in accordance with the Hague Rules, Articles 1–8 inclusive only.

Unless Clause 25 applies, the Carrier shall be under no liability whatsoever for loss, damage or delay to the Goods, howsoever occurring, if such loss, damage or delay arises prior to loading onto or subsequent to discharge from a Vessel. Notwithstanding the above, in case and to the extent that any applicable law provides for any additional period of responsibility, the Carrier shall have the benefit of every right, defence, limitation and liberty in the Hague Rules as applied by this clause during that period, notwithstanding that the loss, damage or delay did not occur at sea.

In the event of the Goods being discharged at a port other than the Port of Discharge nominated in this Bill of Lading and forwarded to the nominated Port of Discharge by whatever means, the Hague Rules as referred to in paragraph 1 of this clause shall continue to apply until delivery at the nominated Port of Discharge (or elsewhere), notwithstanding that Carriage may not be by sea."

Now, taking this clause a paragraph at a time, let us examine the implications of the contents thereof.

Paragraph 1: note that reference is made to "loss, damage or delay". This is because there is increasing pressure these days for carriers to be liable for delay because of the "just-in-time" approach to stocktaking by many merchants. Some countries are starting to provide for the carrier to be liable for delay in their law but are not making appropriate provision as to what that liability should be. In order for a carrier to be in a position to control this as well as possible, he has first to recognise the potential of delay as a basis of liability. Hence the reference to delay, along with loss and damage as a head of claim in the liability clauses. However, the extent of liability for delay is covered later.

The traditional Hague Rules period for liability is from ship's rail at loading until ship's rail at discharge. However, as can be seen in later paragraphs, there are often local customs of the port which extend the carrier's liability beyond the ship's side in a way that cannot be avoided.

In reading this clause one needs to be a aware of the definition of Hague Rules in clause 1, which automatically applies the Hague-Visby Rules where mandatorily applicable. Where there is no mandatory law covering sea carriage the Hague Rules Articles 1 to 8 are applied. This is done deliberately to exclude Article 9, the "Gold Clause", which would bring about a level of liability of approximately £8,000 per package as the liability of GBP100 per package would be interpreted as 100 gold sovereigns, which are presently worth approximately that amount (*The Rosa S.* [1988] 2 Lloyd's Rep. 574). Provision is then made later in the contract for a limit of liability of sterling £100 as the limit of liability per package.

Paragraph 2: this paragraph starts by excluding application where the validity clause (which excludes anything that is invalid to the extent of its invalidity only) applies. It then goes on to provide that, in a port-to-port contract, the carrier has no liability prior to loading and after discharge. However, as local laws and customs of the port have frequently extended the carrier's liability beyond the ship's rail to ship's rail period, it is necessary to provide for a situation such as this, to ensure that the carrier continues to enjoy the protection of the Hague Rules where he continues to be liable away from the vessel. But for a provision at the bottom of this paragraph, which applies the Hague Rules (which are a sea-based basis of liability) even though loss, damage or delay did not occur at sea, a claimant might allege that, as the Hague Rules are only designed to cover sea-based liability, they cannot be applied to losses incurred on land and that the carrier is therefore liable in tort without the benefit of any defences or limitation in the contract.

Paragraph 3: this paragraph recognises the decision in *Mayhew Foods Ltd.* v. *OCL* [1984] 1 Lloyd's Rep. 317 in which it was held that, once goods are shipped and Hague Rules liability commences, liability continues to be subject to the Hague Rules until final discharge, even though the goods may have been on land in between during transhipment.

If for any reason a carrier discharges goods at a port other than that to which the goods are manifested, carriage on to the manifested port, whether by land or sea, will be subject to the Hague Rules. Although this is a port-to-port contract, it may be that the carrier and merchant will agree for goods to be delivered to an alternative port or place than the port of discharge to which the goods are manifested. In this case the oncarriage will continue to be subject to the Hague Rules, even though carriage may be by land and not by sea.

Clause 6: Carrier's Responsibility/Combined Transport

This clause is the combined transport clause. It is quite a long one so I will take it one section at a time.

"If Carriage is Combined Transport, the Carrier undertakes to perform and/or in his own name to procure performance of the Carriage from the Place of Receipt or the Port of Loading, whichever is applicable, to the Port of Discharge or the Place of Delivery, whichever is applicable, and, save as is otherwise provided for in this Bill of Lading, the Carrier shall be liable for loss, damage or delay occurring during the Carriage only to the extent set out below."

This preamble closely follows the provisions of Rule 5 in the ICC Uniform Rules for a Combined Transport Document (Brochure No. 298). It is an undertaking by the carrier that, if the carriage is combined transport, he will be personally responsible, under the terms of this contract and not some other unknown contracts of sub-contractors, to the merchant for carriage throughout the period of the contract. This may involve a combined transport at either end or both ends of the sea leg, hence the need to refer to place of receipt or port of loading and port of discharge or place of delivery, because one could have combined transport which started like a port-to-port shipment at the side of the ship that was combined transport because delivery was made inland at destination. Alternatively, it could be the other way round with combined transport prior to loading and delivery at ship's side at destination. Both of these would be combined transport by the definition in clause 1, as well as a full combined transport on a door-to-door basis.

The preamble finishes with a provision that the liability of the carrier shall be as set out in this clause, except to the extent as is otherwise provided in any other clauses in the bill of lading.

"(1) If the stage of the Carriage during which loss, damage or delay occurred is not known
(a) Exclusions
If the stage of the Carriage during which the loss, damage or delay occurred is not known, the Carrier shall be relieved of liability for any loss, damage or delay if such loss, damage or delay was caused by:
(i) an act or omission of the Merchant;
(ii) insufficiency of or defective condition of packing or marking;

(iii) handling, loading, stowage or unloading of the Goods by or on behalf of the Merchant (see Clause 8);
(iv) inherent vice of the Goods;
(v) strike, lock-out, stoppage or restraint of labour, from whatever cause, whether partial or general;
(vi) a nuclear incident;
(vii) any cause or event which the Carrier could not avoid and the consequences whereof he could not prevent by the exercise of reasonable diligence;
(viii) any act or omission of the Carrier the consequences of which he could not reasonably have foreseen;
(ix) compliance with the instructions of any Person entitled to give them."

This sub-clause covers the situation where it cannot be determined at which stage of carriage loss or damage arose in order to apply whichever basis of liability might be applicable at that particular time. This is known as "hidden damage". The menu approach of the exclusions is similar to that in Article IV Rule 2 of the Hague Rules, with which carriers are familiar and which is therefore an approach which is generally acceptable to them. It closely follows Rule 12 of the ICC Uniform Rules for a Combined Transport Document but has been extended where experience has shown this to be necessary. The list of exclusions is largely self-explanatory but the following comments may assist in identifying some points which might otherwise be missed.

Sub-clause (i): bearing in mind the definition of merchant, which is all embracing, this covers not only any act or omission of the merchant himself but also any of his servants, agents, sub-contractors or any other party with whom he is involved, except the carrier. It covers physical and documentary errors and covers things done, which are an act, and things which are omitted to be done, which are an omission, because, applying the doctrine of *contra proferentem*, act does not cover things which are not done, so one has to say act or omission.

Sub-clause (ii): in case law on the Hague Rules, it has been held that a similar defence to this in Article IV Rule 2 of the Hague Rules will only inure to the benefit of the carrier where such insufficiency or defective condition is not obvious so, if it is obvious, it is the responsibility of the carrier to reject the goods and insist that they are properly packed or to take extra care in the light of the insufficiency. Fortunately, in the case of FCL containers, the carrier can have no means of knowing whether the packing is insufficient or defective, so this defence is of greater value with containerised goods than with break-bulk goods. However, with LCL goods, the same situation applies as was the case with break-bulk goods and the carrier has to take care to ensure that the goods are properly packed and/or handled in a way which is commensurate with the level of packing.

Sub-clause (iii): this exclusion covers FCL goods (as the cross-reference to clause 8 demonstrates). Clearly the carrier cannot accept responsibility for loss or damage caused by the merchant or his sub-contractors loading/discharging containers etc.

Sub-clause (iv): inherent vice is the propensity of goods to damage themselves without being exposed to any negligence. Some goods naturally absorb water (deliquescent) whilst others dry out (efflorescent). If a merchant's goods have a property of this nature, it is his responsibility to prepare them for transit in such a way as to protect them against these natural properties, if he wishes them to arrive in good condition.

Sub-clause (v): the *contra proferentem* rule will come into play here so that only loss, damage or delay directly attributable to one of the activities named will be an adequate defence for the carrier. For example, goods damaged by becoming wet because they were left out in the open during a strike period would be deemed to have been damaged by failure to care for the goods, rather than the strike, and the former would be regarded as the proximate cause. Accordingly, in this case, the carrier would have a liability.

Sub-clause (vi): this exclusion needs no elaboration.

Sub-clause (vii): the problem with this exclusion is the need to use the word "reasonable", which is a subjective word, the interpretation of which will depend upon the point of view of the party concerned. This is the type of word which should be avoided wherever possible when drafting contracts like this but there are occasions when it cannot be avoided and is the only reasonable (!) approach.

In order to benefit from this exclusion, the carrier will necessarily need to show that he has been blameless, whatever the cause of loss, damage or delay, and has done everything possible to avoid or mitigate the effect.

Sub-clause (viii): another unavoidable use of the word "reasonably" designed to cover a situation where the carrier acts in good faith with the best intention of protecting the merchant's goods but where his actions, with the benefit of hindsight, are shown to have been the cause of loss, damage or delay.

Sub-clause (ix): the Persons envisaged in this exclusion will include state organisations, such as HM Customs and Excise, the insurers of the vessel (who may direct departure from a war risk area which will prevent completion of the advertised voyage) and parties of this nature. It does not cover instructions given by a carrier or his colleagues and other commercial parties for commercial reasons.

"(b) Burden of Proof
The burden of proof that the loss, damage or delay was due to one or more of the causes or events specified in this Clause 6(1) shall rest upon the Carrier, save that if the Carrier establishes that, in the circumstances of the case, the loss, damage or delay could be attributed to one or more of the causes or events specified in Clause 6(1)(a)(ii), (iii) or (iv), it shall be presumed that it was so caused. The Merchant shall, however, be entitled to prove that the loss, damage or delay was not, in fact, caused either wholly or partly by one or more of these causes or events."

The burden of proof can be an important factor in the negotiation of claims and, in most cases, this lies with the carrier, because he is the party with access to the evidence. In general the burden of proof is upon the merchant to prove that his goods are damaged, the extent of the damage, that he has taken appropriate steps to mitigate that damage and that such damage arose whilst in the care of the carrier. Thereafter it is for the carrier to show that either damage did not occur in his care or that he is protected by one of the exclusions of liability in the contract.

Clearly matters such as insufficiency of packing/marking, handling etc. by the merchant and inherent vice of the goods are matters where the merchant has the evidence so that, if the carrier pleads one of these exclusions as a defence, it is reasonable that responsibility should then be on the merchant to disprove these factors if he wishes to pursue his claim. In relation to all of the other exclusions listed, the carrier accepts that the burden of proof lies upon him to show that he is entitled to the benefit of the exclusion concerned.

"(c) Limitation of Liability
Except as provided in Clauses 7(2), 7(3), and 27, if Clause 6(1) operates total compensation for loss or damage shall in no circumstances whatsoever and howsoever arising exceed 2SDRs per kilo of the gross weight of the Goods lost or damaged. (SDR means Special Drawing Right as defined by the International Monetary Fund.) Limitation of liability for delay shall be as provided in the applicable international convention or national law, in the absence of which the Carrier accepts no liability whatsoever for delay, howsoever caused (see Clause 7(4))."

It must be borne in mind that we are still in a part of sub-clause 6(1) and thus talking about liability where the stage of carriage during which loss, damage or delay occurred is not known. In setting a limit to apply on these occasions (which, as we shall see later, can also apply on certain occasions where it is known when loss or damage occurred) an exception is made for where the Hague Rules are applied, an *ad valorem* bill of lading has been issued or the USA Clause Paramount applies. Those occasions excluded, a limit of liability is set at 2SDRs per kilo. A weight-based only liability regime.

Note that the limit of 2SDRs is applied only to "Goods lost or damaged" and not to delay. Delay is frequently a contentious matter which is often difficult to quantify and, where they can, carriers prefer to avoid liability under this heading. Accordingly, it is provided that they will only accept liability for delay where they are mandatorily required to do so and then in accordance with the appropriate international convention or national law which is being applied. Except on these occasions, the carrier accepts no liability for delay and draws attention to clause 7(4) in which this matter is covered in greater detail.

"(2) If the stage of the Carriage during which the loss, damage or delay occurred is known

Notwithstanding anything provided for in Clause 6(1) and subject to Clauses 15 and 16, if it is known during which stage of the Carriage the loss, damage or delay occurred, the liability of the Carrier in respect of such loss, damage or delay shall be determined:

(a) by the provisions contained in any international convention or national law which provisions:
   (i) cannot be departed from by private contract to the detriment of the Merchant; and
   (ii) would have applied if the Merchant had made a separate and direct contract with the Carrier in respect of the particular stage of the Carriage during which the loss, damage or delay occurred and received as evidence thereof any particular document which must be issued in order to make such international convention or national law applicable; or
(b) if no international convention or national law would apply by virtue of Clause 6(2)(a), by the Hague Rules, Articles 1–8 inclusive only if the loss, damage or delay is known to have occurred during waterborne Carriage; or
(c) by the provisions of Clause 6(1) if the provisions of Clause 6(2)(a) and (b) above do not apply.

For the purposes of Clause 6(2), references in the Hague Rules to carriage by sea shall be deemed to include references to all waterborne Carriage and the Hague Rules shall be construed accordingly."

This sub-clause is based on the requirements of Rule 13 of the ICC Uniform Rules for a Combined Transport Document. Clauses 15 and 16, to which this sub-clause is made subject, relate to the carriage of deck cargo and live animals (of which more later). Thereafter this sub-clause proceeds to provide:

(a) If in order for an appropriate convention or law to apply it is necessary for a certain document to be issued (a carnet or air waybill, for example), then the bill of lading is deemed to be that document in order to facilitate the application of the appropriate mandatory law.
(b) If no international convention or national law is mandatorily applicable in respect of carriage by waterborne transport (as could be the case if the shipment were from a nation with no mandatory law governing the carriage of goods by sea or if loss arose during carriage by an inland waterways craft) for the contractual application of Articles 1–8 of the Hague Rules in the event that loss, damage or delay arose during a waterborne carriage which is not mandatorily subject to the Hague Rules.
(c) If neither (a) nor (b) above apply then reference is made back to clause 6(1), which is applied to cover all situations where it is known the stage of the carriage during which the loss, damage or delay occurred but where there is no mandatory law covering that period and it is not a period of carriage by waterborne transport.

As the Hague Rules refer to carriage by sea, the final sentence in this sub-clause is to make it absolutely clear that it is intended to apply the Hague Rules to carriage by any form of waterborne transport, including river, canal and estuarial navigation.

"(3) If the Place of Receipt or Place of Delivery is not named on the face hereof.
Subject to Clauses 5 and 25:

(a) if the Place of Receipt is not named on the face hereof, the Carrier shall be under no liability whatsoever for loss, damage or delay to the Goods, howsoever occurring, if such loss, damage or delay arises prior to loading onto a Vessel.

(b) if the Place of Delivery is not named on the face hereof, the Carrier shall be under no liability whatsoever for loss, damage or delay to the Goods, howsoever occurring, if such loss, damage or delay arises subsequent to discharge from a Vessel."

Where either or both the place of receipt and/or place of delivery are shown on the face of the bill, the contract is, by definition, one for combined transport. If both boxes are completed this is a true door-to-door combined transport, with the carrier liable throughout from receipt through to delivery under the terms and conditions of the contract of carriage. However, if only one box is completed, the carrier will not be liable at the other end, either before or after (as the case may be) the ship's side. This sub-clause provides for the situation where only one box is completed and (a) provides for where this is the place of delivery for the carrier not to be liable prior to loading on board and (b) provides for where it is the place of receipt, in which case the carrier is not liable after discharge from the vessel. The sub-clause is made subject to clause 5 (the port-to-port clause) to and clause 25 (the validity clause).

"(4) Notice of Claim
Unless Clause 25 applies, the Carrier shall be deemed *prima facie* to have effected timely delivery of the Goods as described in this Bill of Lading unless notice of loss, damage or delay to the Goods, indicating the general nature of such loss, damage or delay, shall have been given in writing to the Carrier or to his representative at the Place of Delivery (or the Port of Discharge if no Place of Delivery is named on the face hereof) before or at the time of removal of the Goods into the custody of the Person entitled to delivery thereof under this Bill of Lading, or, if the loss or damage is not apparent at the time of delivery, within three working days thereafter.
(5) Time Bar
Unless Clause 25 applies, the Carrier shall be discharged of all liability whatsoever in respect of the Goods, unless suit is brought and notice thereof given to the Carrier within nine months after delivery of the Goods or, if the Goods are not delivered, ten months after the date of issue of this Bill of Lading."

I am dealing with sub-clauses (4) and (5) together because there is frequently confusion between notice of claim and time bar. In both cases the sub-clause is only applicable in the absence of the application of clause 25 (validity clause) so that, where there is a mandatory law with alternative provisions (such as the Hague Rules which has a notice period of three days—not necessarily working days—and a time bar of twelve months), these alternative mandatory provisions will naturally apply. Therefore it cannot be said that either of these clauses attempts to override a contrary mandatory law.

In sub-clause (4) note that the notice of claim provision applies to loss, damage *and delay*. Note also that notice has to be given in writing to the carrier or his representative, either at the time of removal of the goods into the custody of the person concerned or within three working days thereafter. As pointed out above, three working days is more generous than the unqualified three days provided in the Hague Rules.

The time bar of nine months is in line with the provisions in Rule 19 of the ICC Uniform Rules for a Combined Transport Document. In the event of a total loss, instead of trying to calculate when delivery should have taken place, in order to calculate the time bar period, an alternative of ten months from the issue of the bill is used for cases where the goods are, for some reason, never delivered.

Many people confuse the notice of claim and time bar. If a merchant allows the notice of claim period to expire without giving notice of loss, damage or delay to his goods, either by clausing his receipt to the carrier at the time of delivery or giving written notice within three working days, then there is a presumption that delivery has been effected in full and in apparent good order and condition. This does not preclude the merchant from later proving that this was not the case, but the onus of proof has changed from the carrier to the merchant. If notice is given within time, the onus is upon the carrier to show that loss or damage did not occur in his care or to bring himself within one of the exceptions. If timely notice is not given, then there is an onus on the merchant to show that loss or damage arose whilst in the care of the carrier and rebut the presumption of delivery in full and apparent good order and condition.

Notice of claim is not a time bar. The time bar comes much later after nine months and it is only then that the merchant loses his right to claim, unless he has obtained an extension of time or taken appropriate steps to protect his legal position.

Clause 7: Sundry Liability Provisions

As its name suggests, this clause is a collection of sundry liability provisions which may be applicable to either port-to-port or combined transport and cannot therefore be included in either clause 5 or 6, which are solely port-to-port or combined transport respectively.

"(1) Basis of Compensation
Unless Clause 25 applies, compensation shall be calculated by reference to the value of the Goods at the place and time they are delivered to the Merchant, or at the place and time they should have been delivered. For the purpose of determining the extent of the Carrier's liability for loss, damage or delay to the Goods, the sound value of the Goods is agreed to be the FOB/FCA invoice value plus freight and insurance if paid."

Again the carrier starts off by acknowledging that there may be some mandatory law, applicable on certain occasions, which will overrule the provisions of this clause and that, when this situation arises, the carrier naturally accepts that such mandatory law is paramount. Thereafter the carrier provides a formula for calculating the value of the goods for use in calculating the amount of the claim. It is the responsibility of the merchant to prove his loss and produce evidence of the value of the goods at the time when and place where they are delivered. With a commodity, where there is a market, this can be done but with manufactured goods, where there is not a market with published prices this can be difficult. To assist the merchant on such occasions the carrier, whilst starting off by accepting that the merchant is entitled to the value of the goods at the place and time they are delivered, suggests a method of calculating the sound value of the goods based on invoice value plus freight and insurance charges.

"(2) Hague Rules Limitation
If the Hague Rules are applicable by national law, the liability of the Carrier shall in no event exceed the limit provided in the applicable national law. If the Hague Rules are applicable otherwise than by national law, in determining the liability of the Carrier the liability shall in no event exceed £100 Sterling per package or unit."

This clause is fairly self-explanatory and starts by recognising the applicability of any limitation in any national law applying the Hague Rules (or Hague-Visby Rules, of course) and then goes on to provide for the situation where the Hague Rules are contractually applied on the basis of Articles 1–8 only. On such occasions the limit is set at that applied in the Hague Rules, namely £100 Sterling per package. This clause links up with earlier references in clauses 5 and 6 to the Hague Rules Articles 1–8 in order to avoid the gold clause.

"(3) *Ad Valorem*
The Merchant agrees and acknowledges that the Carrier has no knowledge of the value of the Goods, and that higher compensation than that provided for in this Bill of Lading may not be claimed unless, with the consent of the Carrier, the value of the Goods declared by the Shipper prior to the commencement of the carriage is stated in this Bill of Lading and extra freight paid, if required. In that case, the amount of the declared value shall be substituted for the limits laid down in this Bill of Lading. Any partial loss or damage shall be adjusted pro rata on the basis of such declared value."

An *ad valorem* bill of lading is one where the value of the goods is shown in the detail on the face of the bill of lading. This need not necessarily be just a statement of the total overall value of the goods and any statement which enables the value of the goods to be calculated (such as statements like 200 cartons, each 20 items and each item US dollars 2.50) can be regarded as making a bill of lading an *ad valorem* bill of lading. With an *ad valorem* bill of lading the liability of the carrier is the value shown on the face of the bill rather than any limitation which may be incorporated into the contract of carriage on the reverse. Accordingly, if an *ad valorem* bill of lading is required, the carrier usually requires additional freight to cover the increased liability, which he must insure separately as his P & I cover will not extend to cover goods carried on an *ad valorem* basis.

Because of the USA decision in *American World Airways Incorporated* v. *California Stevedores and Ballast Company* (1978) AMC 1834, in which it was held that, unless the merchant was given an opportunity to make an *ad valorem* declaration, the limitation provisions on the back of the bill of lading could not be relied upon, it is necessary on American bills of lading to make provision on the face of the bill of lading, however small, for an opportunity for the merchant to declare the value of the goods at the time of shipment.

Because being charged with knowledge of the value of the goods affects the carrier's liability, this clause commences with an acknowledgement by the merchant that the carrier has no knowledge of the value of the goods and the merchant cannot look for higher compensation than that provided in the contract unless, with the consent of the carrier, a value of the goods, declared by the shipper prior to the commencement of carriage, is stated in the bill of lading and extra freight paid. This acknowledgement that the carrier is not charged with knowledge of the value of the goods is extended in clause 11(3).

If *ad valorem* goods are partially lost or damaged, the resultant claim is adjusted pro rata on the basis of the declared value.

"(4) Delay

(a) Unless Clause 25 applies, the Carrier does not undertake that the Goods shall arrive at the Port of Discharge or Place of Delivery at any particular time or to meet any particular market or use and the Carrier shall in no circumstances whatsoever and howsoever arising be liable for direct, indirect or consequential loss or damage caused by delay.

(b) However, if Clause 25 applies, unless a latest date of delivery is shown on the face hereof and any required premium paid, timely delivery shall be considered to have been made if the Goods are made available to the Merchant at the Port of Discharge or Place of Delivery, as the case may be, within 60 days after the date published in the Carrier's inbound sailing schedule against the Port of Discharge nominated therein for the relevant ocean Vessel. The Carrier shall be entitled to all the defences, exceptions and limitations provided in the applicable international convention or national law and this bill of lading."

As previously mentioned, liability for delay is often a contentious matter and a situation which most carriers prefer to avoid if they possibly can. However, there is a need to provide for a growing tendency to incorporate a reference to liability for delay in the laws of some countries. Where this occurs the provisions are often unspecific and often refer to a reasonable time where no specific time or date is mentioned. In order to protect himself in such circumstances the carrier firstly needs to recognise his potential liability for delay in order to protect himself as best he can in such circumstances.

Accordingly, this sub-clause (a) provides that, unless clause 25 applies because there is some overriding mandatory law, the carrier makes no representations that the goods will arrive at any particular time or to meet any particular market or use and accepts no liability for delay. Then (b) addresses the situation where there is some mandatory law putting a liability on the carrier for delay. In most cases it is unlikely that merchants will pay a premium in order to get a specific date for delivery put on their bill of lading and the most likely scenario is that, if they incur a loss due to delay, they will then look at the bill of lading in the light of any applicable mandatory law to see if they can make any recovery from the carrier. In this sub-clause provision is made to define a timely delivery as being one made within 60 days of the published date of arrival of the vessel at the port of discharge. This avoids the ambiguity of subjective words like reasonable, which are often used in legislation and create problems when courts are asked to interpret what is reasonable.

"(5) Scope of Application
(a) The terms and conditions of this Bill of Lading shall, at all times, govern all responsibilities of the Carrier in connection with or arising out of the supply of a Container to the Merchant, not only during the Carriage, but also during the period prior to and/or subsequent to the Carriage.
(b) The rights, defences, limitations and liberties, of whatsoever nature, provided for in this Bill of Lading shall apply in any action against the Carrier for loss, damage or delay, howsoever occurring and whether the action be founded in contract or in tort and even if the loss, damage or delay arose as a result of unseaworthiness, negligence or breach of a fundamental term of this contract.
(c) Save as is otherwise provided for in this Bill of Lading, the Carrier shall, in no circumstances whatsoever and howsoever arising, be liable for direct or indirect or consequential loss or damage or loss of profit."

In (a) provision is made for the terms and conditions of the bill of lading to govern not only the carriage of the goods, but also the supply of the container. This needs to cover a wider period than the contract of carriage in circumstances where the carrier makes a container available to a merchant to take away to load or unload and it is made clear here that, whilst the contract of carriage may not have started or may have terminated, the terms and conditions will either start early or finish late in order to cover the supply of the container.

Sub-clause (b) seeks to ensure that the terms and conditions of the bill of lading shall apply at all times for the protection of the carrier. One of the tactics of recovery agents (where the circumstances may allow) is to allege that the carrier is in a fundamental breach of contract and cannot therefore rely upon the contract of carriage. In such circumstances the claim would be made in tort where the carrier's defences would be limited to act of God, Queen's enemies and inherent vice with no limitation provisions.

The approach of law to different concepts is constantly changing according to changes of circumstances and the persuasive influence of decisions in foreign courts, particularly where those foreign courts are the courts of countries whose law has a similar base to that of the court considering the case, as is the case with English law and decisions in the courts of Commonwealth countries, whose law has a common base with English law. Some years ago the concept of fundamental breach of contract was quite strong and it was frequently held that the actions of some carriers were so serious that they were, in effect, a repudiation of contract, which was effectively torn up, and the carrier could not rely upon any of the defences in the contract, so that the claim became one in tort. Deviation was a common basis of such claims and deviation then fell into two categories: physical deviation and technical deviation. Physical deviation is the actual deviation of the vessel from the advertised or most direct voyage and technical deviation is a serious breach, such as carriage of uncontainerised goods on deck against an unclaused bill of lading or delivery of goods without production of bill of lading.

Lately the courts have taken the other tack and have been reluctant to find fundamental breach of contract. This has been particularly so in the English and Australian courts, although the concept of fundamental breach appears still to be alive in the courts of the USA, although even this may change with the proposed amendment to the US COGSA to replace their 1936 Act. My favourite decision in this area is an Australian decision: the "Bunga Teratai" decided in the New South Wales Supreme Court of Appeal in April 1988. In the decision of Kirby P. the following unambiguous and uncompromising *obiter dicta* appear:

"there was no overt dispute that the flirtation of the common law with the so called 'doctrine' of 'fundamental breach' of contract is now over. That 'doctrine' had developed as a means of mollifying the apparently unacceptable consequences of very wide exemption or limitation clauses . . . Windeyer J. considered that the *Suisse Atlantique* decision had reinforced his view that there was no 'doctrine' of fundamental breach . . . In England, the coupe de grace to the 'doctrine' of fundamental breach, as a substantive rule of law was administered by the House of Lords in *Photo Production Ltd.* v. *Securicor Transport Ltd.* [1980] AC 827."

He went on to quote Lord Diplock:

"In commercial contracts negotiated between businessmen capable of looking after their own interests and of deciding how risks inherent in the performance of various kinds of contract can be most economically borne (generally by insurance), it is, in my view, wrong to place a strained construction on words in an exclusion clause which are clear and fairly susceptible of one meaning only even after due allowance has been made for the presumption in favour of the implied primary and secondary obligations."

Kirby P. continued with the following further obiter:

"If there is ambiguity, but only then, ambiguous words may be construed against the party which has proffered a written contract in standard form and in favour of the party to whom such a contract has been presented. But if the language of the written agreement clearly covers the eventualities which have occurred, that is an end to the matter . . . In the context of international transportation (including shipping) there are strong reasons of policy for seeking a consistent approach to the construction of common language in Bills of Lading (see *Riverstone Meats*). But there are equal reasons of policy for holding parties to the effect of the natural meaning of the language used in a written document, upon the basis of which parties may be advised (sometimes in languages other than English) and in relation to which they will make suitable arrangements for their own protection (including by insurance) . . . No court is authorised to bend and twist the language of such an agreement for the achievement of nationalistic, economic or other policies conceived to be desirable."

These are just a few of Kirby P.'s uncompromising comments in delivering that judgment which seems to have placed the concept of fundamental breach of contract much further the carrier's way than was the case some years ago. Carriers should see this as an invitation to draft their contracts of carriage in wordings which cannot be interpreted in any other way than the intended way and thus totally devoid of ambiguity. If this is done there would seem to be good reason to hope that the courts will enforce the terms of their contracts of carriage in the vast majority of cases. This sub-clause (b) provides, in the most unambiguous way possible, for the contract of carriage to apply to all dealings between the carrier and the merchant, whatever the circumstances. This sub-clause seeks to encourage the judiciary to follow Kirby P. in outlawing the concept of fundamental breach of contract.

Sub-clause (c) follows the policy outlined above in making the carrier's position absolutely clear. At first sight there may appear to be some duplication with sub-clause (4) but further inspection will show that sub-clause (4) relates to delay only whereas this sub-clause has wider application.

"(6) Inspection by Authorities
If by the order of the authorities at any place, a Container has to be opened for the Goods to be inspected, the Carrier will not be liable for any loss, damage or delay incurred as a result of any opening, unpacking, inspection or repacking. The Carrier shall be entitled to recover the cost of such opening, unpacking, inspection and repacking from the Merchant."

The carrier has absolutely no control whatsoever over Customs and other statutory authorities who take unto themselves within their own territories the right to open containers for any reason whatsoever, whether this be a search for narcotics and other illicit goods or in order to check declarations for duty purposes etc. It is possible that such inspections may take place at places and in circumstances which give rise to damage to the goods (particularly if the goods are refrigerated or have some other special protection). Not having any control over the circumstances on such occasions, the carrier accepts no responsibility for any loss, damage or delay thereby incurred and requires to recover the costs, that he incurs in complying with these instructions in relation to the merchant's goods, from the merchant.

Clause 8: Shipper-Packed Containers

This is a very important clause in respect of FCL containers packed by the shipper as it sets out the respective responsibilities on such occasions. It contains three sub-clauses which we shall take one at a time, having first noticed the preamble, which identifies those occasions when the provisions of the clause are applicable:

"If a Container has not been packed by or on behalf of the Carrier:
(1) The Carrier shall not be liable for loss, damage or delay to the Goods caused by matters beyond his control, including, *inter alia*, without prejudice to the generality of this exclusion:

(a) the manner in which the Container has been packed; or
(b) the unsuitability of the Goods for Carriage in the Container supplied; or
(c) the unsuitability or defective condition of the Container or the incorrect setting of any temperature controls thereof, provided that, if the Container has been supplied by or on behalf of the Carrier, this unsuitability, defective condition or incorrect setting could have been apparent upon inspection by the Merchant at or prior to the time when the Container was packed; or
(d) packing temperature controlled Goods that are not at the correct temperature for Carriage."

(1) Before launching into a list of reasons for which a carrier will not accept liability for loss or damage to FCL packed goods, the sub-clause makes a general provision that the carrier will not accept responsibility for matters beyond his control. The doctrines of *contra proferentem* and *ejusdem generis* will ensure that interpretation of what is beyond the control of the carrier will be restricted to a narrow interpretation and items of a similar nature to those listed. Those reasons specifically excluded are as follows:

(a) As the merchant or a sub-contractor acting on his behalf packs the container, it naturally follows that any damage caused by bad packing is for the merchant's account and not for the account of the carrier. In packing a container the merchant needs to bear in mind that he must make a tight stow to withstand the pitching and tossing and rolling if the vessel meets heavy weather. Clearly, a higher standard of packing is required for an international movement involving carriage by sea than for a lorry that is merely going up the motorway. In the event that goods outturn damaged, the dispute that is likely to arise and where a surveyor's opinion may be necessary, is whether the damage to the goods arose due to bad handling and packing of the goods into the container by the merchant or bad handling of the container by the carrier.
(b) As we shall see when we come to consider sub-clause 17(3), it is the merchant's responsibility to satisfy himself that the container which he requests for the carriage of his goods is one that is suitable for their safe carriage to destination. To take a ridiculous example, if the shipper is shipping refrigerated goods and a general purpose container is tendered for loading, then there is clearly a responsibility on the shipper to reject that container as being unsuitable and request a refrigerated container to be supplied at a higher cost. Obviously shippers wish to keep their freight rates as low as possible and will only ask for higher-priced special containers if they feel that they are absolutely necessary. This sub-clause, reinforced by sub-clause 17(3), puts the responsibility on the merchant to ensure that the container supplied is suitable for the goods to be carried.

(c) As pointed out in earlier chapters, the movement of empty containers is a costly business and, the more that carriers can reduce this expense, the more profitable their operation. If, for example, a carrier is delivering an FCL container to a consignee and there is a shipper requiring a container nearby, it makes sense to effect what is known as a triangulation, and send the loaded container out to the consignee for subsequent transfer to the shipper. As we shall see later, it is the consignee's responsibility to ensure that the container is clean once it has been discharged, but the carrier is in no position to ensure that he has done so. Nor is he in any position to inspect the container to ensure that it is undamaged (hole in roof etc.). Accordingly, although there is a responsibility on the consignee to return the container in a clean state, it is necessary to put a responsibility on the shipper to check the container before he commences to load it to make sure that it is both suitable for his goods and free from defects. The inspection required is that which a reasonable person would do, namely to ensure that it is clean and free of odours and that there is no obvious damage. A prudent shipper would enter the container and close the doors to see if there was any ingress of light, indicating the presence of a hole. This sub-clause puts the responsibility on the shipper to make such an inspection when the container is delivered to him for loading. If the container is a refrigerated container, the shipper is additionally expected to check to ensure that the setting of any temperature controls is in accordance with his requirements.

(d) Refrigerated containers are designed to maintain the temperature of the goods within them and not freeze them down. There are shippers who would use containers as a means of reducing the temperature of their goods to the required carrying temperature, when this is a responsibility that they should take upon themselves. Because containers are not designed as mobile freezing works, if the temperature of the goods is high at the time of loading, it will take some time to reduce the carriage temperature to an acceptable level and the goods may spoil in that period, as many refrigerated goods are very sensitive. Accordingly, the carrier makes a point of emphasising that, if goods spoil because they have not been presented for shipment at the correct temperature at which they are required to be carried, the carrier accepts no responsibility for such deterioration.

"(2) The Shipper is responsible for the packing and sealing of all Shipper-Packed Containers and, if a Shipper-Packed Container is delivered by the Carrier with its original seal as affixed by the Shipper intact, the Carrier shall not be liable for any shortage of Goods ascertained at delivery. If, nevertheless, a claim for shortage is made against the Carrier by any Person whomsoever, the Merchant agrees to indemnify the Carrier against the cost of any such claim plus any costs incurred in respect thereof."

This sub-clause provides for the shipper to be responsible for the loading and sealing of FCL containers, whether loaded at his premises or those of a sub-contractor or supplier. If such a container is delivered with the seal affixed by the shipper intact, then clearly any shortage has not occurred during the transit period and the carrier will not accept any responsibility for the discrepancy. Note that in this sub-clause reference is made only to shortage and not damage, as damage may have occurred due to bad packing by the shipper or bad handling of the container by the carrier. In the case of the former, sub-clause (1)(a) provides for the shipper to be responsible.

The sub-clause finishes with an indemnity in case a third party, with whom the carrier may not be in contract, brings a claim against the carrier. Note that the indemnity is from the merchant and not just the shipper, thereby giving the carrier a wider target at which to aim, in the event of need to enforce the indemnity and the shipper being elusive.

"(3) The Merchant shall indemnify the Carrier against any loss, damage, liability or expense whatsoever and howsoever arising caused by one or more of the matters referred to in Clause 8(1), save that, if the loss, damage, liability or expense was caused by a matter referred to in Clause 8(1)(c), the Merchant shall not be liable to indemnify the Carrier in respect thereof unless the proviso referred to in that Clause applies."

Sub-clause (1) provides a list of occasions where loss or damage or delay to the goods arises for which the carrier is not responsible. This sub-clause refers to the same menu and provides for an indemnity by the merchant to the carrier, if the carrier incurs any loss, damage, liability or expense on any of these occasions. It is emphasised that, in applying this indemnity to the circumstance outlined in sub-clause (1)(c), the indemnity will only apply if the proviso in that sub-clause (that the unsuitability, defective condition or incorrect setting could have been apparent upon inspection by the Merchant . . .) applies.

Clause 9: Inspection of Goods

"The Carrier or any Person to whom the Carrier has sub-contracted the Carriage or any Person authorised by the Carrier shall be entitled, but under no obligation, to open any Container or package at any time and to inspect, or weigh and/or measure the Goods and/or weigh the Container."

Clause 9 is mentioned in the incorporation clause as being an exception for the carrier not to weigh in the container. For a variety of reasons the carrier may wish to open a container and inspect it, or even weigh it and, if he wants this right, the carrier must ensure that he gives it to himself in the contract, otherwise the *contra proferentem* rule will prevent him from having such right. For the same reason he has to make it absolutely clear that, whilst he takes this right unto himself, he is not obliged to exercise that right on each and every occasion and may choose those occasions when he does so. He also has to make it clear who has this right, not just himself but his sub-contractors and anyone he authorises or instructs so to do.

Clause 10: Carriage affected by Condition of Goods

"If it appears at any time that, due to their condition, the Goods cannot safely or properly be carried or carried further, either at all or without incurring any additional expense or taking any measure in relation to the Container or the Goods, the Carrier may, without notice to the Merchant (but as his agent only), take any measure and/or incur any additional expense to carry or to continue the Carriage thereof, and/or sell or dispose of the Goods, and/or abandon the Carriage and/or store them ashore or afloat, undercover or in the open, at any place, whichever the Carrier, in his absolute discretion, considers most appropriate, which abandonment, storage, sale or disposal shall be deemed to constitute due delivery under this Bill of Lading. The Merchant shall indemnify the Carrier against any additional expense incurred."

This is a clause very much like one of the old-fashioned conventional clauses and amply demonstrates the problems which the *contra proferentem* approach to a contract of adhesion presents to the carrier. In insurance terms it could be referred to as a "Sue and Labour" clause and is, in fact, a clause designed to give the carrier the right to act as the agent of the merchant in what insurers would term a sue and labour situation. That is to say, a situation where goods are found to be discrepant during the voyage and the insurers agree that the merchant may incur expenses designed to prevent further damage and reduce the size of the claim for damage to the goods on arrival and insurers will pay these expenses in addition to any claim for damage to the goods up to the total insured value. The carrier has to try and consider every possible thing that he may have to do if some discrepancy is found in mid-voyage and give himself the right to do it, without consultation with the merchant if necessary, because it may not always be possible to contact the merchant, as the party with title (whoever holds the bill of lading) is not necessarily obvious from the manifest. Clearly a prudent carrier would consult the merchant if he could before taking any of the steps but he has to provide for a situation where this is not possible. He also has to provide to give himself the widest possible rights as to what action he takes; repair the goods, sell them before they deteriorate further, store them and invite the merchant to take delivery short of destination etc. The action which he adopts will be dictated by the individual circumstances on each occasion. The clause finishes with an indemnity from the merchant for all sue when labour charges incurred. Obviously the carrier will only seek to recover charges incurred as a result of damage for which he is not responsible, as otherwise the charges would merely form part of the claim against him from the merchant for delivery of the goods other than in the same apparent good order and condition in which they were received for carriage.

Clause 11: Description of Goods

This clause, as its title suggests, clarifies the liability of the carrier in respect of the description of the goods shown on the face of the bill of lading. It comprises three sub-clauses which we shall consider individually:

"(1) This Bill of Lading shall be *prima facie* evidence of the receipt by the Carrier from the Shipper in apparent good order and condition, except as otherwise noted, of the total number of Containers or other packages or units indicated in the box on the face hereof entitled 'Total Number of Containers/Packages received by the Carrier'."

This sub-clause merely reinforces the provisions made earlier in the incorporation clause to make it absolutely clear that the carrier only acknowledges the tally shown in the indicated box.

"(2) Except as provided in Clause 11(1), no representation is made by the Carrier as to the weight, contents, measure, quantity, quality, description, condition, marks, numbers or value of the Goods, and the Carrier shall be under no responsibility whatsoever in respect of such description or particulars, which are unknown to him.

It is agreed that, whilst he retains the right so to do at his sole discretion, the Carrier is not at any time under any obligation to weigh any Container or open any Container to make any check on the Goods therein or their stowage (see Clause 9)."

This sub-clause links closely with sub-clause (1) and is specifically designed to emphasise that the commercial detail shown in the main body of the bill of lading on the face is commercial detail provided by the shipper for his commercial purposes and that the carrier has no knowledge of that detail, so that he is unable to acknowledge the accuracy of it. Attention is drawn on the face of the bill in the main area to clause 11 by means of the sentence "Undermentioned Particulars as declared by Shipper, but not acknowledged by the Carrier (see Clause 11)".

The long list of details, which may be shown on the face a bill but for which the carrier accepts no responsibility, is another good example of the unreadability of clauses which could arise if the definitions in clause 1 were not provided.

The second paragraph of sub-clause (2) is added here to reinforce clause 9 and emphasise that the carrier is not responsible to take additional steps to ascertain the condition of goods other than to note their *apparent* condition as they are presented to him or his sub-contractor, so that he is not expected to weigh or open containers that have been packed on FCL terms in order to give a more detailed receipt.

"(3) If any particulars of any Letter of Credit and/or Import Licence and/or Sale Contract and/or Invoice or Order number and/or details of any contract to which the Carrier is not a party are shown on the face of this Bill of Lading, such particulars are included solely at the request of the Merchant for his convenience. The Merchant agrees that the inclusion of such particulars shall not be regarded as a declaration of value and in no way increases the Carrier's liability under this Bill of Lading. The Merchant further agrees to indemnify the Carrier against all consequences of including such particulars in this Bill of Lading. The Merchant acknowledges that, except when the provisions of Clause 7(3) apply, the value of the Goods is unknown to the Carrier."

Although drafted as a general provision, this is really a local clause covering those areas in the world (primarily Arab countries) which take the view that, if you show the letter of credit number or invoice number on a bill of lading, as these documents have details of the value of the goods in them, you are, in effect, incorporating details of the value of the goods into the contract to carriage, thereby making the bill of lading an *ad valorem* bill of lading, so that the carrier's liability is for the full value of the goods and the carrier cannot benefit from any limitation in the contract of carriage. This attitude in certain courts creates a problem, because the law in the countries concerned frequently also requires the letter of credit number to be shown on the bill of lading for Customs or exchange control purposes. This means that the shipper must have a bill of lading showing letter of credit details if he is to succeed in having his goods accepted for import, whilst the carrier is exposing himself to increased liability if he shows the letter of credit number on the bill.

Because this approach is the law of the country concerned, it is not possible to draft a clause to protect the carrier from having his liability calculated on an *ad valorem* basis. The only defence available is to incorporate in the contract of carriage an indemnity from the merchant, which can be enforced against the shipper, so that one is in effect saying to the shipper "if you require me to show details on the bill of lading which are nothing to do with the contract of carriage and, as a result thereof, my liability is affected, I will revert to you to recover the difference between what my liability was as calculated in the country concerned and what it would have been if my liability had been calculated in accordance with the terms and conditions of the bill of lading in a court in the exporting country". This is the only way in which the carrier can give the shipper what he wants and at the same time maintain a degree of protection against unreasonable claims in the event of loss, damage or delay. It is entirely up to the commercial and sales representatives in the carrier's organisation whether or not to enforce the indemnity in the event of such a claim being made. In this respect the draftsman is the ordnance operative and not the rifleman: he makes the bullets and it is up to others whether or not they are fired!

Clause 12: Shipper's/Merchant's Responsibility

"(1) All of the Persons coming within the definition of Merchant in Clause 1 shall be jointly and severally liable to the Carrier for the due fulfilment of all obligations undertaken by the Merchant in this Bill of Lading and remain so liable throughout Carriage, notwithstanding their having transferred this Bill of Lading and/or title to the Goods to another party."

This clause reinforces the definition of merchant in clause 1 and makes it clear that, once someone comes within the definition of merchant, they remain within the definition of merchant for the duration of that contract of carriage. Some merchants think that, once they have disposed of the bill of lading they have nothing further to do with that contract and that they cannot incur any liabilities to the carrier through one of the indemnities from the merchant thereafter. This is an erroneous view, as they remain responsible to the carrier under the terms of the bill of lading for the duration of the contract of carriage and, if it is not a matter for which they are personally responsible, then it is for them to resolve the matter with the party concerned under their contract of sale (or whatever), once they have settled the claim under the indemnity with the carrier.

"(2) The Shipper warrants to the Carrier that the particulars relating to the Goods as set out overleaf have been checked by the Shipper on receipt of this Bill of Lading and that such particulars, and any other particulars furnished by or on behalf of the Shipper, are adequate and correct. The Shipper also warrants that the Goods are lawful goods and contain no contraband. If the Container is not supplied by or on behalf of the Carrier, the Shipper further warrants that the Container meets all ISO and/or other international safety standards and is fit in all respects for Carriage by the Carrier."

This sub-clause contains three important undertakings by the shipper. Firstly, the shipper warrants to the carrier that the details of the goods, which he has supplied to the carrier, are adequate and accurate and, furthermore, that on receipt of the bill of lading he is responsible for checking the details shown therein to make sure that they are correct. Secondly, the shipper warrants that the goods are lawful goods and contain no contraband. Containers are ideal receptacles for the secretion of contraband and, particularly with FCL goods, the carrier has absolutely no knowledge of the nature of the goods inside the container. Thirdly, in the case of a container which the shipper himself supplies, the shipper warrants that the container meets the international safety standards and is, in all respects, fit for carriage by the carrier.

"(3) The Merchant shall indemnify the Carrier against all claims, losses, damages, fines and expenses arising or resulting from any breach of any of the warranties in Clause 12(2) hereof or from any other cause in connection with the Goods for which the Carrier is not responsible."

This is an indemnity from the merchant for any breach by the shipper of sub-clause (2) above. In addition to all claims, losses, damages, fines and expenses arising or resulting from breach of sub-clause (2), this indemnity is extended to cover similar costs incurred in connection with the goods for which the carrier is not responsible under this contract of carriage.

"(4) The Merchant shall comply with all regulations or requirements of Customs, port and other authorities, and shall bear and pay all duties, taxes, fines, imposts, expenses or losses (including without prejudice to the generality of the foregoing, Freight for any additional Carriage undertaken) incurred or suffered in respect of the Goods, and shall indemnify the Carrier in respect thereof."

This sub-clause makes it clear that it is the responsibility of the merchant to ensure that the goods meet with all regulations and requirements of the various statutory authorities likely to have an interest in them during the period of the contract of carriage. Accordingly, if there's a breach of any of these parties' regulations, the resultant costs must be for the merchant. Not having a defined term to use, it is necessary in this case to resort to a long string of potential costs in an effort to be all-embracing. Note that such costs include freight for any additional carriage undertaken. For example, it may be that some goods are refused landing at a port because the documentation supporting them is incorrect or inadequate and the goods have to be oncarried to a subsequent port and possibly even returned to their original port of shipment. In such cases the carrier would charge additional freight.

Although compliance with such regulations is the responsibility of the merchant, it often occurs that any fine etc. is levied on the carrier. In such cases the indemnity provides for the merchant to reimburse the carrier accordingly.

"(5) If Containers supplied by or on behalf of the Carrier are unpacked at the Merchant's premises, the Merchant is responsible for returning the empty Containers, free from labels etc., with interiors brushed, clean, odour free and in every respect fit for immediate re-use, to the point or place designated by the Carrier, his servants or agents, within the time prescribed. Should a Container not be returned as required above within the time prescribed, the Carrier is entitled to take such steps as he considers appropriate for the account of the Merchant and the Merchant shall be liable for any detention, loss or expense incurred as a result thereof."

This is the consignee's equivalent of the shipper's responsibilities (outlined in clause 8, particularly clause 8(1)(c)) which outlines the consignee's responsibilities necessary to facilitate a triangulation movement (explained in discussing clause 8(1)(c)). It puts upon the consignee a responsibility to return the container to the carrier free from labels etc. (e.g. any hazardous labels removed) and with interiors brushed, clean, and odour free and in every respect fit for immediate reuse. If the delivery has been made by a haulier who is a sub-contractor of the carrier, that is the end of it but, if the haulier is the sub-contractor of the consignee, then the consignee has a responsibility to return the container to the carrier at a point or place designated by the carrier or someone acting on his behalf. In both unpacking the container and either making it available to the carrier's haulier to take away or returning it to the carrier's designated point if the haulier is a sub-contractor of the consignee, breach of this time limit would make the consignee liable for detention charges.

If a consignee is in breach of the requirements of this sub-clause, the carrier takes unto himself the right to take appropriate action at the cost of the merchant. For example, if the consignee returned a container in a dirty condition and the carrier had to clean it before it could be used for the next export, the consignee could be charged with the cost of cleaning it plus detention charges whilst this is done.

"(6) Containers released into the care of the Merchant for packing, unpacking or any other purpose whatsoever are at the sole risk of the Merchant until redelivered to the Carrier. The Merchant shall indemnify the Carrier for all loss and/or damage to such Containers occurring during such period. The Merchant shall also indemnify the Carrier for any loss, damage, injury, fines or expenses caused or incurred by such Containers whilst in his control, whether or not caused by negligence on the part of the Merchant, his servants, agents or sub-contractors."

This sub-clause covers the liability of the merchant where he, or a sub-contracting haulier acting on his behalf, takes a container out of the possession of the carrier or one of his sub-contractors in order to take it away for loading or discharging etc. The sub-clause makes it absolutely clear that, at such times, the container is at the sole risk of the merchant until the carrier accepts the container back from the merchant or his sub-contractor. During such time the Merchant is responsible for all damage to the container and all liability incurred during its movement (e.g. in road accidents causing damage to third party property and injury etc.).

Clause 13: Freight

In reading this clause it is as well to bear in mind the wide definition of freight in clause 1.

"(1) Freight shall be deemed fully earned on receipt of the Goods by the Carrier and shall be paid and non-returnable in any event."

On the face of it, it may appear to be unreasonable that the carrier should earn his freight upon receipt of the goods rather than upon delivery of them. There is, however, good reason for arranging for freight to be earned at this point. Most goods moving are insured by shipper or consignee, usually on a basis which includes the cost of freight, so that the merchant, in effecting cargo insurance, is insuring the freight. If the freight were at the risk of the carrier until he delivered the goods, because this can be many millions of pounds at any one time on large vessels, the carrier would need to insure "Freight at Risk". The cost of the insurance plus the cost of administration to effect the insurance would form a charge against the freight earned and increase overall costs. The only party that would benefit from such an arrangement would be the Insurer, who would receive two premiums in respect of the freight, one as part of the cargo insurance from the merchant and the other to insure the freight from the carrier. In order to avoid a duplicity of cover, the carrier provides in the contract of carriage for freight to be earned on receipt of the goods rather than upon delivery, so that the risk of freight is insured as part of the cargo insurance and not for a second time as a separately identifiable item of freight at risk.

"(2) The Merchant's attention is drawn to the stipulations concerning currency in which the Freight is to be paid, rate of exchange, devaluation and other contingencies relative to Freight in the applicable Tariff."

As foreign currencies fluctuate against each other, it is necessary to decide upon a currency in which to calculate freight. US dollars is a popular choice. A date is usually set in relation to the voyage for the calculation of freight payable in other currencies instead of US dollars and an exchange rate set for each voyage from the tariff currency into whichever currency the carrier is willing to accept at different ports of call. In some cases a carrier may insist upon payment in a hard currency rather than accept the local currency, because of wide fluctuations in the exchange rate of that currency and difficulties in repatriating freight earned from countries which restrict the export of their currency. Some carriers publish what they call a CAF (Currency Adjustment Factor) for each voyage, which is used to deal with fluctuations in exchange rates. All of these matters are dealt with in the tariff rather than in the contract of carriage but it will be recalled that the tariff is incorporated into the contract of carriage by clause 2.

"(3) Freight has been calculated on the basis of particulars furnished by or on behalf of the Shipper. If the particulars furnished by or on behalf of the Shipper are incorrect, it is agreed that a sum equal to double the correct Freight less the Freight charged shall be payable as liquidated damages to the Carrier."

There are two kinds of freight: FAK (Freight All Kinds), where a set freight per container is charged, irrespective of the nature of the goods loaded therein, and tariff freight, where freight is charged according to the nature of the goods carried, with higher rates of freight being charged to higher valued and more delicate goods, which require greater care and have a greater propensity for loss or damage. Where freight is charged on a tariff basis, it is not unknown for a shipper deliberately to misdeclare the nature of the goods in order to achieve a lower freight rate than that which is correct for the goods concerned. Such shippers rely upon the fact that only a small percentage of containers can be inspected so that they are unlikely to be caught defrauding a carrier of his rightful freight.

On those occasions where the carrier makes an inspection and finds that there has been a misdeclaration, this sub-clause provides for the payment of an additional freight by the shipper. In English law penalties are unenforceable, unless they can be shown to be a genuine effort to pre-estimate the cost of the misdemeanour to the aggrieved party. Accordingly the word penalty is assiduously avoided and the formula provided to calculate the additional freight is justified on the basis that it is a genuine effort to pre-estimate the cost of operating the inspection service to discover those occasions where a fraud is being perpetrated. The sub-clause particularly provides that this is agreed liquidated damages and not a penalty for these reasons.

"(4) All Freight shall be paid without any set-off, counter-claim, deduction or stay of execution before delivery of the Goods."

The purpose of this sub-clause is to prevent merchants from withholding payment of freight due on the basis that they have just submitted a claim for damage to a previous consignment of goods and are offsetting that claim against the freight. This sub-clause is merely a statement of the situation which would apply in English law in the absence of such a clause because many people, with a poor knowledge of English law, will only believe what they read and not some explanation based on English law which is unknown to them. In effect this clause says that each case has to be dealt with separately without attempting to apply set-off or counterclaim as an excuse for non-payment of freight. Because the carrier has a lien for his freight, he will withhold delivery until it is paid (*see* clause 14).

Clause 14: Lien

"The Carrier shall have a lien on the Goods and any documents relating thereto for all sums payable to the Carrier under this contract. The Carrier shall also have a lien against the Merchant on the Goods and any documents relating thereto for all sums due from him to the Carrier under any other contract. The Carrier may exercise his lien at any time and at any place at his sole discretion, whether the contractual Carriage is completed or not. In any event any lien shall extend to cover the cost of recovering the sums due and for that purpose the Carrier shall have the right to sell the Goods by public auction or private treaty, without notice to the Merchant, at any time and at any place at the sole discretion of the Carrier."

A lien is a right to hold the property of another as security for the performance of an obligation, usually payment of a debt. There are several different types of lien and the law regarding liens does tend to differ from country to country. For instance, in some countries, whilst particular liens are legal, general liens are not. However, in England, both types are allowed.

The first sentence of this clause is a possessory, particular lien in favour of the carrier for any monies due to him from the merchant in relation to the consignment in question only. The second sentence is a possessory, general lien which enables the carrier to withhold delivery of the goods to a merchant, not only for debts due against that particular consignment, but also for earlier debts that remain unsatisfied.

Because of the function of the bill of lading as a document of title, which may be used to sell goods merely by the passage of the document, the carrier has to be careful to follow the correct procedure, if he wishes to have an effective lien. For example, if he issues a freight paid bill of lading and the cheque for freight bounces or he issues the bill as a freight paid bill, giving the shipper a period of credit, once the bill of lading is in the hands of an "innocent third party purchaser for value" the doctrine of estoppel applies to prevent the carrier from alleging that he has not received the freight and prevents him from exercising a lien on the goods for payment of the freight. This is because he has issued a receipt for the freight by issuing a freight paid bill of lading and the law protects the innocent third party purchaser, who relies upon the statement in the bill of lading that freight has been paid, by preventing the carrier from exercising a lien against him. The carrier may exercise a lien against the shipper who has not paid the freight if he is the party still in possession of the bill of lading but not against an innocent third party purchaser. Accordingly carriers need to be very wary as to who they allowed credit by the issue of freight paid bills of lading until freight has actually been paid (this does not just mean a cheque received but a cheque received and cleared).

The only way in which a carrier can exercise an effective lien is if he holds both goods and at least one original bill of lading covering the goods, thereby preventing further negotiation of the full set of bills of lading to an innocent third party. If the party against whom the carrier wishes to exercise a lien is an exporter, he should wait until the next consignment is presented for shipment and then refuse to issue the bill of lading until the debt is cleared, thereby exercising a lien against both goods and documents in his possession. If the party against whom the carrier wishes to exercise a lien is an importer, the carrier needs to wait until an original is surrendered to facilitate delivery and then exercise the lien with goods and documents in his possession.

Whilst not recognised everywhere, general liens are extremely valuable facilities on a variety of occasions, including where a consignee manages to persuade a naive clerk to deliver goods without presentation of an original bill of lading, duly endorsed. If the same consignee has other goods coming forward, one can await his surrender of a bill of lading for the next consignment and then exercise a lien on those goods and documents until he produces the original bill of lading for the earlier consignment.

The third sentence of the clause gives the carrier the right to exercise his lien at any time and at any place at his sole discretion, whether the contractual carriage is completed or not. It is necessary for the carrier to extend his rights in this way to cover situations which might arise in small outports to which goods may be transhipped (parts of Africa and Indonesia come to mind), where the security on the quay at a feeder port is negligible and consignees merely come down and help themselves to their goods without any documentation whatsoever. In such cases it behoves the carrier to hold the goods at the transhipment port, where he has control of them, and not arrange oncarriage by feeder vessel until the original bill of lading has been surrendered.

The fourth sentence provides for the lien to cover not only the cost of the debt, but also the cost of recovering the debt and gives the carrier the right to sell the goods by public auction or private treaty. Obviously a carrier would not dispose of goods in this way without prior consultation with the merchant concerned, if the merchant could be contacted and was prepared to act in a reasonable manner. However, in case the merchant cannot be contacted or is not prepared to be reasonable, the carrier must give himself the right to dispose of the goods without notice to the merchant and, for similar reasons to those outlined above, he has to give himself the right to dispose of them at any place at his sole discretion and not just at the place of delivery

Clause 15: Optional Stowage and Deck Cargo

"(1) The Goods may be packed by the Carrier in Containers and consolidated with other goods in Containers.
(2) Goods, whether or not packed in Containers, may be carried on deck or under deck, at the sole discretion of the Carrier, without notice to the Merchant. All such Goods, whether carried on deck or under deck, shall participate in General Average and shall be deemed to be within the definition of Goods for the purposes of the Hague Rules and shall be carried subject to those Rules.
(3) Notwithstanding Clause 15(2), in the case of Goods which are stated on the face hereof as being carried on deck and which are so carried, the Hague Rules shall not apply and the Carrier shall be under no liability whatsoever for loss, damage or delay,

howsoever arising, whether or not caused by negligence on the part of the Carrier his servants, agents or sub-contractors."

It is possible that someone might make a claim on the basis that damage was caused by goods being stowed in containers (condensation damage, for example). Accordingly, in sub-clause (1) the carrier takes to himself the right to stow goods in Containers. He also takes to himself the right to stow them with other goods, as would be the case with LCL cargo where several smaller consignments are consolidated at a Container Freight Station (CFS) into the one container. Obviously the other goods, with which the merchant's goods were stowed, would need to be compatible and not damage the merchant's goods in any way, otherwise the carrier would be negligent, as he is responsible for the stowage of LCL goods. Note the use of a small g for goods when talking about other goods as these are not goods as defined in clause 1.

In sub-clause (2) we are again concerned with the concept of fundamental breach of contract, which was discussed extensively when considering clause 7(5). At one time carriage of goods on deck without a clause in the bill of lading to notify the merchant that the goods were on deck was considered to be a fundamental breach of contract, which effectively denied the carrier the benefit of any exclusions or limitations in the Hague Rules. As previously discussed, this concept now appears to have been overtaken and there is a case which specifically addresses the point of limitation of liability in the case of the deck cargo where the bill of lading was not claused. This particular case concerned timber, where it could often be said that carriage on deck was in accordance with the custom of the trade. The case was the *Nea Tyhi* (*Parker Plywood Ltd.* v. *Nueva Fortuna Corporation of Liberia* [1982] 1 Lloyd's Rep. 606). Now that the major part of liner cargo is shipped in various types of containers on deck, one could also say that carriage of goods in any type of container is now a custom of the trade, including the carriage of things like heavy lift items on flat tracks etc.

The carrier gives the merchant the same recourse situation in respect of goods carried on deck as for goods carried under deck (unless the bill is claused: *see* sub-clause (3)). For this reason it is reasonable that he should provide to bring goods carried on deck, whether in containers or not, within the same parameters as goods carried under deck for the purposes of liability, general average etc. Sub-clause (2) provides for the carrier to be able to carry goods, whether or not packed in containers, on deck at his sole discretion and without notice to the merchant. It also provides for such goods to participate in general average and to come within the definition of goods for the purpose of the Hague Rules, which shall apply to their carriage whilst at sea. This is necessary because the Hague Rules specifically exclude deck cargo where the bill of lading is claused and live animals. Where this sub-clause operates, the bill of lading would not be claused but, to make it absolutely clear that it is the carrier's intention to apply the Hague Rules, provision is made to invoke them.

Sub-clause (3) is very rarely invoked as virtually no merchant is prepared to accept a bill of lading clause "Shipped on Deck (at Shippers Risk)". However, if a bill of lading is claused to indicate shipment on deck, the carrier invokes his right under the Hague Rules to carry them on a no liability basis.

Clause 16: Live Animals

"The Hague Rules shall not apply to the Carriage of live animals, which are carried at the sole risk of the Merchant. The Carrier shall be under no liability whatsoever for any injury, illness, death, delay or destruction to such live animals howsoever arising. Should the Master in his sole discretion consider that any live animal is likely to be injurious to any other live animal or any person or property on board or to cause the Vessel to be delayed or impeded in the prosecution of its voyage, such live animal may be destroyed and thrown overboard, without any liability attaching to the Carrier. The Merchant shall indemnify the Carrier against all and any extra costs incurred for any reason whatsoever in connection with the Carriage of any live animal."

The carriage of live animals is fraught with difficulties. They must be attended to, fed and protected from heat, spray etc. Unless a whole circus was being carried it would be impractical to carry a vet and many animals are notorious for becoming sick for no apparent reason. Many animals also have a propensity for being dangerous, so it is not just the animals that need to be considered but the crew, vessel and cargo as well. It is possible that the quarantine regulations at ports of call or at destination may change whilst the vessel is at sea, making it illegal to transit with or to land the animals, thereby creating a situation in which the vessel might be delayed. Charter hire on large containerships runs into several tens of thousands of dollars a day and delay caused by quarantine restrictions on a vessel is something which cannot be accepted.

All of these considerations mean that live animals are not a particularly attractive cargo to carriers but they are carried on occasions on a strictly no liability basis. This is allowed by the Hague Rules for the reasons outlined above. In view of these reasons it is unsurprising that carriers only accept live animals on terms which give them the widest possible discretion to react to any situation which may occur, on no liability terms and with a full indemnity.

Clause 17: Methods and Routes of Carriage

In this clause sub-clause (1) lists the liberties which the carrier takes unto himself in relation to the methods and routes of carriage. Sub-clause (2) then lists the reasons/occasions when the liberties set out in a sub-clause (1) may be exercised. Sub-clause (3) completes the clause by providing for carriage in a general purpose container to be acceptable to the merchant, unless the shipper specifically requests and pays for a special container.

"(1) The Carrier may at any time and without notice to the Merchant:

(a) use any means of carriage whatsoever;
(b) transfer the Goods from one conveyance to another, including but not limited to transhipping or carrying them on a Vessel other than that named on the face hereof;
(c) unpack and remove the Goods which have been packed into a Container and forward them in a Container or otherwise;
(d) proceed by any route in his discretion (whether or not the nearest or most direct or customary or advertised route), at any speed, and proceed to or stay at any place or port whatsoever, once or more often and in any order;
(e) load or unload the Goods at any place or port, whether or not such port is named overleaf as the Port of Loading or Port of Discharge and store the goods at any such place or port;
(f) comply with any orders or recommendations given by any government or authority, or any Person acting or purporting to act as or on behalf of such government or authority, or having under the terms of any insurance on any conveyance employed by the Carrier the right to give orders or directions;
(g) permit the Vessel to proceed with or without pilots, to tow or be towed and to be dry-docked, with or without Goods and/or Containers on board."

In considering the liberties outlined in this sub-clause, one must do so bearing in mind that they will be subject to the English law doctrines of *contra proferentem* and *ejusdem generis* and that they need to cover situations arising on land as well as at sea. It may be that a liberty in the list is contrary to the law of a country at sea but not on land, in which case clause 25 will invalidate that part which is contrary to law leaving the application which is not contrary to law intact.

Sub-paragraph (a) is a very sweeping statement but is in keeping with the concept of combined transport, in that the merchant should not be concerned as to the means of transport being used because he has a contract of carriage from door-to-door, which gives him appropriate recourse. Note that the word carriage is used here with a small c as it is not a defined term.

Sub-paragraph (b) provides the carrier with the necessary authority to tranship, which term here includes not just transferring from one ship to another, but substituting the vessel nominated on the face of the bill of lading with another vessel. The extent to which the court would allow this might depend upon the individual circumstances. In any event the carrier loses nothing by including the liberty designed to enable him to maintain the maximum flexibility in his operation to react to situations as he thinks best.

Sub-paragraph (c) provides for a situation where goods may not be carried through to final destination in a container. For example, LCL goods will be degrouped at a CFS and then delivered break-bulk. This clause puts the merchant on notice that his goods may not necessarily be carried throughout in a container from door-to-door.

Sub-paragraph (d) is primarily aimed at carriage by sea but is equally applicable to carriage by land. It purports to give the carrier the widest possible discretion as to route, speed etc. There is little modern case law on this type of thing with containerships and many people are of the view that the restrictive case law, which necessarily applied to break-bulk port-to-port shipment, is inapplicable in modern combined transport. Nevertheless a carrier would be well advised to exercise the liberties in this sub-paragraph in a prudent fashion and be able to justify his actions if they are questioned.

Sub-paragraph (e) is primarily aimed at situations where a strike at the intended port prevents the vessel from following the intended route and provides for the vessel to call instead at an alternative port, from which the goods will probably be forwarded to destination. This, again, is consistent with the concept of combined transport, where it is up to the carrier to arrange carriage door-to-door in the most efficient manner, according to changing circumstances.

Sub-paragraph (f) covers the situation where war or changing political circumstances prevent a carrier from carrying out his intended transport plan. The carrier has to comply with the instructions of sovereign states through whose waters he passes or over whose land he passes with goods, as well as instructions from war risks insurers not to enter waters which the insurers deem to have become too dangerous for normal commerce to continue.

Once all vessels over a certain size needed tugs in order to berth/unberth. This is not always the case today because larger vessels are frequently fitted with a bow and/or stern thruster to assist in berthing. It is also sometimes not possible to dry-dock a vessel (perhaps for emergency repairs to a casualty) without first discharging goods to lighten the vessel. This is a decision which the carrier and master have to take and sub-paragraph (g) gives them the necessary scope to act as they think best in deciding whether or not they need tugs and whether or not they need to lighten the vessel before dry-docking.

"(2) The liberties set out in Clause 17(1) may be invoked by the Carrier for any purpose whatsoever, whether or not connected with the Carriage of the Goods, including but not limited to loading or unloading other goods, bunkering, undergoing repairs, adjusting instruments, picking up or landing any persons, including but not limited to persons involved with the operation or maintenance of the Vessel and assisting vessels in all situations. Anything done in accordance with Clause 17(1) or any delay arising therefrom shall be deemed to be within the contract of carriage and shall not be a deviation home."

In trying to secure the widest possible liberties in a contract of adhesion, carriers face the perennial problem that, if they use words which are too general they will be rejected as inapplicable whilst, if they use a mixture of general and particular words the doctrine of *ejusdem generis* will only allow the general words to be interpreted to mean words of the same kind as the particular words. This rather puts them between a rock and a hard place and frequently leaves them at the mercy of the interpretation which the judge presiding chooses to put upon their form of wording. Accordingly carriers would be well advised to apply the liberties in this sub-clause sparingly and with good justification bearing the following points in mind. To be regarded as reasonable a deviation has to benefit the goods as well as the vessel. Deviations to bunker at a cheap but unadvertised port of call or to pick up some extra goods (or passengers), which have suddenly become available at an unadvertised wayport, may well be deemed a breach of contract in some courts. Whilst case law is binding, the problem is that it is only binding in so far as it applies to an equivalent operation and the nature of the operation today is so far removed from that when much of the case law was decided as to place a question-mark over its applicability. Accordingly carriers should continue to contract for maximum liberties but use the liberties sensibly and sparingly, if they do not wish to face the expense of having their contract tested in court.

"(3) By tendering Goods for Carriage without any written request for Carriage in a specialised Container, or for carriage otherwise than in a Container, the Merchant accepts that Carriage may be undertaken properly in a general purpose Container, carried on or under deck at the Carrier's sole discretion."

The purpose of this sub-clause is to make the merchant ask for a special container if he has special carriage requirements and pay accordingly. Unless the merchant does so, he is deemed to accept that stowage in a general purpose container (with neither ventilation nor temperature control) is suitable for his goods and that such container may be stowed on or under deck. This sub-clause is also useful on those occasions when recovery agents allege bad stowage by providing a general purpose container for the shipment of goods which require ventilation. This sub-clause puts the onus on the merchant to decide, for example, whether or not ventilation is required and, if it is, to request a special ventilated container, which is usually more expensive than an unventilated general purpose container. With FCL shipments it would be possible to defend claims by reference to clause 8, but with LCL shipments, in the absence of a provision like this, there could be problems.

Clause 18: Matters affecting Performance

In the days of conventional shipments of break-bulk goods, substantial problems would be caused if there were a strike at a port of call, as break-bulk goods are not easily moved to/from one port to another. In the event of a strike, a carrier has to consider whether or not he should abandon the goods short of destination at an adjacent port and there were several court cases at which the carrier's right to abandon was questioned; whether or not he should proceed to the port that was strike-bound in case the strike broke, how long he should wait before proceeding elsewhere to abandon etc. Probably the most famous of these cases was the "*Caspiana*" (*G.H. Renton & Co.* v. *Palmyra Trading* [1956] 2 Lloyd's Rep. 379) and this led to the drafting of a Caspiana clause, which was, in effect, an abandonment clause.

With the advent of combined transport, where carriers offered a unit-load door-to-door service and took to themselves the right to proceed by a variety of routes at their discretion, the situation changed. Having taken unto himself the right to go by a variety of routes, the carrier could not automatically abandon if the advertised route were blocked and was expected to seek alternative ways of completing his obligations under the contract of carriage to deliver at the nominated place of delivery. The break-bulk goods might have difficulty in finding warehouse space at an alternative port awaiting transhipment to final destination. Goods in containers are protected and can be stored in the open. Accordingly, much radical rethinking was needed to prepare an alternative clause for combined transport to the Caspiana clause for break-bulk shipping. Over a period of time the following provisions have proved attractive to the carrier, in allowing him to keep his options open and act as he thinks best, in the interests of all parties involved, given the circumstances, which are always different on every occasion.

The clause is quite a long one and follows a series of circumstances, in what is usually chronological order:

"If at any time the Carriage, the Vessel or other goods on board the Vessel are or are likely to be affected by any hindrance, risk, delay, difficulty or disadvantage of any kind whatsoever (other than the inability of the Goods, due to their condition, safely or properly to be carried or carried further) and howsoever arising (even though the circumstances giving rise to such hindrance, risk, delay, difficulty or disadvantage existed at the time this contract was entered into or the Goods were received for Carriage), the Carrier (whether or not the Carriage is commenced) may, without prior notice to the Merchant and at the sole discretion of the Carrier, either:"

This preamble sets the scene and needs to take quite a few points into account. As you will see, in the absence of a defined term, it is necessary to list all possible problems in the interest of completeness, on account of the *contra proferentem* doctrine. It is then necessary to provide that the problem may be one affecting the carriage of the merchant's goods, the vessel or somebody else's goods. Not all goods have the same priority. For example, perishable goods need a speedy transit and delay is an absolute anathema to such goods whereas some other goods, which are non-perishable, may not be so sensitive to delay and have a higher priority on being delivered at the correct place incurring the least charges.

It is also necessary to exclude problems arising from the condition of the goods, which is covered in clause 10, as otherwise there is a possibility of conflict between the two clauses. The threat of a strike or some action which may cause hindrance, risk, delay, difficulty or disadvantage is often made some time beforehand, prior to the commencement of the contract of carriage and is thus known at that time as a possible problem. To prevent a plaintiff alleging that, because the possibility of such a problem was known, either at the time of booking or at the time of receipt of the goods, the carrier should not have accepted the goods for shipment or, if he did, he did so with the knowledge of that problem, so that he had to bear the cost of overcoming it himself, it is necessary to provide that the carrier can exercise the liberties set out in this clause, even though there was knowledge of the possibility of such a problem prior to the contract of carriage being commenced or the goods being received for shipment. At that time it may have been known that a problem existed but it was uncertain whether or not the problem would manifest itself or be resolved by the time that it could affect the contract. If carriers had to stop shipping upon becoming aware of every threat of a problem en route, they would not move much cargo!

Note that the liberties set out in this clause may be invoked by the carrier without prior notice to the merchant and at the sole discretion of the carrier. At times when this clause is likely to be invoked, it will probably be virtually impossible to contact all merchants, although effort will probably be made to do so wherever possible. In any event, with order bills of lading, the carrier may not be aware of who has title at the time or the notify party may not respond. From a customer service point of view carriers will always endeavour to advise merchants what is happening and consult with them in case some mutually acceptable alternative solution can be agreed. For example, with refrigerated goods the delay caused by the alternative routing may be fatal and the consignee may prefer to take delivery of the goods at an earlier port for sale before their perishability renders them valueless.

The carrier has to retain the sole discretion in such matters, even though he will endeavour to meet individual merchant's wishes for a variety of reasons. For example, consider a container with several LCL consignments where some consignees wish their goods to be delivered at the interim port if the final port of discharge is strike-bound whereas others wish their goods to proceed by the alternative route. To meet the wishes of all consignees in a circumstance such as this would be impossible so the carrier has to retain to himself the right to decide how best to act in the circumstances in the best interests of the majority.

"(a) Carry the Goods to the contracted Port of Discharge or Place of Delivery, whichever is applicable, by an alternative route to that indicated in this Bill of Lading or that which is usual for Goods consigned to that Port of Discharge or Place of Delivery. If the Carrier elects to invoke the terms of this Clause 18(a) then, notwithstanding the provisions of Clause 17 hereof, he shall be entitled to charge such additional freight as the Carrier may determine.
or"

This is a first option which the flexibility of having the goods as unit loads gives to the carrier. For example, imagine that dockers at Genoa were on strike and other Italian ports would not handle Genoa goods. It might be possible to discharge Genoa goods at Marseilles and forward them, either to Genoa or, in the case of combined transport movements, to the inland destinations to which they were consigned, via Marseilles. It might also happen that a vessel homeward bound from the Far East was in the Indian Ocean when news was received of the blockage of the Suez Canal, due to a collision between two vessels at the entrance to the canal. The vessel could then deviate round the Cape of Good Hope, thereby incurring substantial extra costs in fuel and charter hire, all of which, under the terms of this sub-clause, could be recovered by means of a freight surcharge on the merchant. If delivering goods via Marseilles proved to be more expensive than via Genoa, the carrier would also be able to render a freight surcharge in that case, if he so chose.

The important point here is that the contract of carriage is flexible enough to enable the carrier to take whatever steps he considers to be in the best interests of all parties concerned, without having to go through the process of agreeing an amendment to the contract of carriage, as the flexibility to take that decision is written into the original contract of carriage. This clause will only be invoked at a time of crisis when everybody will be very busy and the very last thing that the carrier wants in such circumstances is staff tied up contacting merchants in order to amend contracts before additional freight can be charged for carrying goods by alternative means to destination, rather than exercising abandonment rights. Amending a contract means going through the same process as making a contract: offer, acceptance and consideration. This means that, if the carrier makes an offer to vary a contract to the merchant, he must obtain the merchant's agreement thereto before he can charge extra freight. This clause overcomes that problem by writing the right to take this decision and make the extra charge into the original contract of carriage.

Note the need to make it clear that the terms of this clause will apply, even though clause 17 gives the carrier the right to vary the route as a liberty. Even though clause 17 gives the carrier the right, within the existing contract of carriage, to vary the route, this is designed to cover minor things, like deviating to avoid bad weather etc. Clause 18 covers major problems which seriously disrupt the operation and, if the carrier elects to invoke clause 18, that is paramount over clause 17.

"(b) Suspend the Carriage of the Goods and store them ashore or afloat upon the terms of this Bill of Lading and endeavour to forward them as soon as possible, but the Carrier makes no representations as to the maximum period of such suspension of Carriage. If the Carrier elects to invoke the terms of this Clause 18(b) then, notwithstanding the provisions of Clause 17 hereof, he shall be entitled to charge such additional Freight as the Carrier may determine.
or"

It may be that it is not possible to carry the goods through to destination by an alternative route or it may be thought that the problem will be quickly solved, so that the original route can be adhered to by a short wait. In such circumstances the carrier may decide to discharge the goods at an alternative port to await oncarriage when the problem has been resolved, thereby allowing him to continue the voyage to the other ports of call in the interests of merchants who have goods on board for those other ports (the carrier must take into account the interests of all merchants with goods on board when deciding what to do to overcome problems of this nature, not just the interests of merchants with goods for the port or place where the problem is located). As with sub-clause (a), it is provided for this sub-clause to be paramount over clause 17 and for the carrier to be entitled to charge extra freight to cover landing, storage and reshipping etc.

"(c) Abandon the Carriage of the Goods and place them at the Merchant's disposal at any place or port which the Carrier may deem safe and convenient, whereupon the responsibility of the Carrier in respect of such Goods shall cease. The Carrier shall nevertheless be entitled to full Freight on the Goods received for Carriage, and the Merchant shall pay any additional cost of the Carriage to, and delivery and storage at, such place or port."

This sub-clause provides for the ultimate solution of abandonment if goods cannot be carried through to destination via an alternative route or by suspending carriage for a period until the problem is resolved. This ultimate solution might be adopted if a war were to break out in the destination area which looked to be likely to continue for some time. In such a case, the carrier would have no alternative but to abandon, as he would almost certainly be precluded from entering adjacent waters to the war area by his war risks insurers and, once on land, it is possible that he will not be insured for war risks on his containers (unless he is insured for war risk on containers with the TT Club or a some similar insurer, which is not always the case—many containers are not insured for war risks on land—WROL). Insurance of war risks on land is a very restricted market due to the potential concentration of risks at any one location, such as a terminal, CFS etc.

As the carrier has not insured his freight (*see* commentary on clause 13(1)) and as freight is deemed earned on shipment, it is provided here for full freight to be payable, even though the full contract of carriage has not been completed. The merchant has also to bear the additional costs incurred in taking delivery at the port of refuge.

Abandonment of goods in containers is easier said than done. In a situation where abandonment is desirable (to the carrier) it is most unlikely that there will be sufficient warehouse space available in which to put the goods or warehousekeepers prepared to accept goods with charges to goods. Accordingly the carrier may find that he is left with the goods stowed in his containers at the port of refuge until the merchant is prepared to or can arrange to take delivery. Accordingly abandonment will often take place over a period of time and it is not just a case of the carrier declaring abandonment, discharging the goods from his containers and leaving them on the quay. Until he can find someone to accept the goods on behalf of the merchant, he has a responsibility to care for them, which makes abandonment less than easy.

"If the Carrier elects to use an alternative route under Clause 18(a) or to suspend the Carriage under Clause 18(b) this shall not prejudice his right subsequently to abandon the Carriage."

The clause finishes with a sentence to make it absolutely clear that, whilst a carrier may elect in the first instance to carry by an alternative route or suspend carriage, this does not prevent him ultimately from abandoning the carriage, if circumstances become such that an alternative route or suspension are not viable.

Clause 19: Dangerous Goods

There is not very much remarkable about this clause, which is more or less in line with similar clauses found in all other bills of lading. Accordingly I reproduce the four sub-clauses individually with a brief commentary.

"(1) No Goods which are or may become dangerous, inflammable, damaging or injurious (including radioactive materials), or which are or may become liable to damage any property whatsoever or injure any person whomsoever, shall be tendered to the Carrier for Carriage without his express consent in writing and without the Container as well as the Goods themselves being distinctly marked on the outside so as to indicate the nature and character of any such Goods and so as to comply with any applicable laws, regulations or requirements. If any such Goods are delivered to the Carrier without such written consent and/or marking or if, in the opinion of the Carrier, the Goods are or are liable to become of a dangerous, inflammable, damaging or injurious nature, they may at any time be destroyed, disposed of, abandoned or rendered harmless without compensation to the Merchant."

The first thing to note is that the carrier does not have to wait until an accident has occurred before he can act. If in his opinion the goods may, at some future point in the carriage, become dangerous etc., he may take action then to prevent that accident and the list of actions which he is entitled to take is more or less exhaustive.

Both the goods and the container have to bear appropriate markings as required by the IMO IMDG Code and, if the goods are FCL packed, it is the responsibility of the shipper to make sure that these are in place, although it is the practice of the carrier to provide appropriate labels to the haulier taking the container for packing to give to the shipper. In the case of LCL goods it is the shipper's responsibility to make sure that the goods are labelled properly and declared to the carrier, who is then responsible for ensuring that non-compatible types of dangerous goods are not packed together and that the containers into which they are packed are properly labelled.

Although compliance with the IMO IMDG Code is mandatory, the clause is drafted wider than the requirements of this code so that, even if a certain consignment is not included in the IMO IMDG Code, if it has any propensity to cause damage or injury whatsoever, it is the responsibility of the shipper to comply with the requirements of this clause. Note that the carrier may act in the event of the shipper failing to obtain written consent to ship or failing properly to mark the goods and also if the shipper has complied with these requirements but the carrier is of the opinion that the goods are or may become of a dangerous etc. nature. These actions do not prejudice the carrier's right to freight, which is earned on receipt of the goods and non-returnable in any event.

"(2) The Merchant undertakes that such Goods are packed in a manner adequate to withstand the risks of Carriage, having regard to their nature and in compliance with all laws or regulations which may be applicable during the Carriage. In particular but without prejudice to the generality of this Clause 19(2), if the Goods are not packed into the Container by or on behalf of the Carrier, the Merchant undertakes that incompatible Goods are not packed in the same Container."

Many dangerous goods require special packing to prevent their dangerous nature causing an accident. In some cases this is a matter of common sense but in many cases it is a matter of complying with regulations in relation to the carriage of dangerous goods by whatever means of transport is being used. If dangerous goods are FCL packed (i.e. not packed into the container by or on behalf of the carrier), the merchant's responsibility is not only to make sure that the immediate packing of them is adequate to withstand the risks of carriage but also that the packing of the packages inside the container is effected with similar consideration. It is, of course, particularly important that different types of dangerous goods are not shipped together if they are incompatible (for instance, one must never ship goods with a low flash point with goods that produce oxygen to feed a fire). Note that, although it will be the shipper who needs to comply with these requirements, the undertaking that they will be complied with is made by the merchant, thereby giving the carrier a wider target in the event of non-compliance.

"(3) Whether or not the Merchant was aware of the nature of the Goods, the Merchant shall indemnify the Carrier against all claims, losses, damages or expenses arising in consequence of the Carriage of such Goods."

Ignorance by the shipper (merchant) of the nature of the goods is no defence to liability and this clause provides for a very full indemnity from the merchant to the carrier in respect of any claims, losses, damages or expenses which may arise *in consequence* of the carriage of such goods. Hence, negligence by the merchant is not necessary in order to invoke this indemnity, although, obviously, if there has been any breach of the contract by the carrier, which has in any way contributed to the claim etc., this will naturally be a defence for the merchant to any claim by the carrier.

"(4) Nothing contained in this Clause shall deprive the Carrier of any of his rights provided for elsewhere."

This is probably a fairly superfluous sub-clause but it is included to ensure that any defences in regulations or laws (such as the Hague Rules) relating to dangerous goods are not overruled by anything in this clause.

Clause 20: Notification and Delivery

Whilst it is not possible to draft a bill of lading entirely like a story, starting at the beginning and finishing at the end, an effort is made to try and present the terms and conditions, as far as possible, in some chronological order. We are now starting to get towards the end of the contract and have reached the point where we need to consider the obligations and liabilities of the parties at delivery. As this is a time when disputes may arise (for example, what are each party's obligations if the goods are damaged), it is important that the obligations of each party are clearly enunciated in this clause.

"(1) Any mention herein of parties to be notified of the arrival of the Goods is solely for the information of the Carrier and failure to give such notification shall not involve the Carrier in any liability nor relieve the Merchant of any obligation hereunder."

In the days of conventional break-bulk shipping it was the responsibility of the consignee to keep himself informed as to when the vessel was due to arrive from the shipping press etc. and present himself at the quayside at the appropriate time to take delivery, having first cleared the goods for Customs, paid any outstanding freight and surrendered the bill of lading to receive a delivery order etc. Not all conventional bills of lading provided for a notify party and if, as was usually the case, a bill of lading was an "Order" bill of lading, the identity of the consignee would be unknown to the carrier.

With the advent of combined transport offering a door-to-door service, where the carrier often effected delivery right through to the consignee's premises, there was a need for the carrier to be aware of the identity of the consignee in order to complete the contract of carriage and all combined transport bills of lading made provision for a notify party. It became the practice of the carrier to send out arrival notification forms advising the notify party of the arrival of the goods and requesting delivery instructions. In an effort to prevent this additional service giving rise to additional liability if, for some reason, notice failed to arrive at the notify party, this clause was included in an effort to preserve the conventional break-bulk situation from a liability point of view. However, as the giving of notice has now been common practice for 30 years, it is quite likely that it would be regarded as a custom of the trade and thus in conflict with the provisions of this sub-clause, which in consequence might be held to be null and void.

"(2) The Merchant shall take delivery of the Goods within the time provided in the Carriers applicable Tariff (see Clause 2). If the Merchant fails to do so the Carrier shall be entitled, without notice, to unpack the Goods, if packed in Containers, and/or to store the Goods ashore, afloat, in the open or under cover, at the sole risk of the Merchant. Such storage shall constitute due delivery hereunder and thereupon the liability of the Carrier in respect of the Goods stored as aforesaid shall wholly cease and the costs of such storage (if paid or payable by the Carrier or any agent or Sub-Contractor of the Carrier) shall forthwith upon demand be paid by the Merchant to the Carrier."

This sub-clause provides for the consignee to take delivery of the goods within the time provided in the carrier's applicable tariff. In order to take delivery the consignee must first complete all the necessary documentary and fiscal requirements of Customs, carrier and any other parties who may be in a position to prevent delivery.

The clause purports to give the carrier very wide rights in the event of the consignee failing to take delivery as required. It will be recalled that the point has been made previously that the carrier needs to give himself the right to do anything which he may need to do in any circumstance, howsoever arising, if he is to be able to do that in any given circumstance arising which makes that the most desirable course of action. Applying the *contra proferentem* doctrine in reading this clause, one can see that the removal of goods from a container for storage in the open could only be done if this could be done without exposing the goods to damage, that is to say goods which are unlikely to be damaged by weather or which are not liable to be pilfered. There will be occasion when goods can be safely stowed in the open and hence the clause needs to provide that right but that does not mean to say that that right can be exercised on all occasions for all goods.

In practice the ability of the carrier to exercise his rights under this sub-clause are likely to be severely limited by the lack of availability of warehouse space and the unwillingness of warehousekeepers to accept goods on the basis of charges to goods. Hence the clause needs to end with a provision for the situation where the carrier has to pay storage, if he unpacks the goods to release his container for further use, for the consignee (merchant) to reimburse the carrier accordingly. This might be an occasion when the carrier would exercise his lien and sell goods if the consignee refused to take up the goods within a reasonable period, but more of that in the next sub-clause.

"(3) If the Merchant fails to take delivery of the Goods within 30 days of delivery becoming due under Clause 20(2) or if, in the opinion of the Carrier, they are likely to deteriorate, decay, become worthless or incur charges, whether for storage or otherwise, in excess of their value, the Carrier may, without prejudice to any other rights which he may have against the Merchant, without notice and without any responsibility whatsoever attaching to him, sell, destroy or dispose of the Goods and apply any proceeds of sale in reduction of the sums due to the Carrier from the Merchant."

Whereas the previous sub-clause provided for the carrier to make an effective delivery by putting goods into a store at destination if the consignee did not take a prompt delivery, this sub-clause provides for the carrier to have wide rights to dispose of the goods in whichever way he considers appropriate, in the event of the consignee failing to take delivery. As previously noted, it may be difficult, if not impossible, to arrange for goods to be stored with charges to goods and a carrier's lien on them, so it is more likely that this sub-clause will be invoked than sub-clause (2).

According to what the goods are, the carrier may be able to realise some value by selling the goods but, if there is no market for them or they are damaged to the point where they have no commercial value, he will find himself incurring additional expenses disposing of them for destruction. In the latter case there is not much use in exercising a lien on the subject goods, although, of course, there is nothing to prevent the carrier from exercising a general lien on subsequent consignments in order to recover the costs incurred in relation to this consignment (*see* clause 14).

The circumstances which may give rise to the carrier having the right to sell, dispose etc. of the goods are as follows:

- the expiry of 30 days from delivery becoming due under clause 20(2);
- the likelihood (in the opinion of the carrier) of the goods deteriorating or decaying and becoming less valuable (possibly to the point of worthlessness);
- the goods incurring charges, whether for storage or otherwise, in excess of their perceived value.

Note that, in the event of the goods being sold, the proceeds of the sale (net proceeds that is—*see* clause 14) are applied in reduction of the sums due to the carrier from the merchant. If there is any surplus the carrier should hold this in an escrow account to hand to whoever surrenders an original bill of lading, duly endorsed. If the proceeds do not cover the debt due, then the lien in clause 14 can be enforced against any subsequent consignment or the carrier could take action for breach of contract against any party coming within the definition of merchant to recover the balance.

Again provision is made for all this to happen without prejudice to any other rights which the carrier may have against the merchant (for example, enforcement of a lien etc.), without notice to the merchant and without any responsibility attaching to the carrier. Obviously, no carrier would sell goods without notice to the merchant if a merchant could be identified and contacted, although, if there were a dispute, the sale would proceed without the merchant's prior approval. Carriers frequently give any party that they can identify who comes within the definition of merchant (shipper as well as consignee etc.) the opportunity to pay all charges incurred to date if they do not want goods sold but cannot yet take delivery for some reason. In this way the carrier avoids charges accruing in excess of the value of the goods, thereby preserving the value of his lien, whilst meeting the merchant's requirement not to dispose of them in accordance with the carrier's rights under this sub-clause.

"(4) Refusal by the Merchant to take delivery of the Goods in accordance with the terms of this Clause and/or to mitigate any loss or damage thereto shall constitute a waiver by the Merchant to the Carrier of any claim whatsoever relating to the Goods or the Carriage thereof."

A consignee has a legal responsibility to take delivery of any goods consigned to him, whether or not damaged, unless the damage is such that the specie of the goods has changed (e.g. cement which has turned to concrete as a result of contact with water). Except in this circumstance, the consignee has a legal obligation to take delivery and mitigate loss and, in the absence of any contractual provisions like this, his claim would be reduced by the extent that his refusal to take delivery leads to the goods becoming more damaged than they would have been if he had taken delivery in accordance with his obligations and mitigated loss. Where consignees act in this way the carrier's best course of action is to try to involve the cargo insurer, as both the insurer and the carrier have a common interest in preventing damaged goods becoming a total loss and squandering value by not taking prompt action, whoever has to meet the resultant costs.

This sub-clause is designed to persuade merchants, who are ignorant of their obligations to take delivery of goods, by holding over them the threat that their refusal to do so will constitute a waiver of claim against the carrier, which in turn will constitute a breach of their insurance contract, so that they will recover from neither. The sub-clause is primarily designed to be persuasive and literal application of its terms may not be enforceable in all courts. However, not all merchants would be aware of this and hopefully the drastic terms of the sub-clause would persuade them to act reasonably and in accordance with their legal obligation.

"(5) In the event of the Carrier agreeing to a request of the Merchant to amend the Place of Delivery stated herein without stipulating any particular terms and conditions to apply during said amended Carriage, to the extent provided by the applicable Tariff the terms and conditions of this Bill of Lading shall continue to apply, but only until the Goods are delivered by the Carrier to the Merchant at the amended Place of Delivery. Once the applicable Tariff ceases to provide for the continued application of the terms and conditions of the Bill of Lading or if the Carrier declines to extend the Bill of Lading terms to the amended Place of Delivery, then the Carrier shall act as agent only of the Merchant in arranging for delivery of the Goods to the amended Place of Delivery but shall then be under no liability whatsoever for loss, damage or delay to the Goods, howsoever arising for the period of amended Carriage.

If the Carrier agrees to make multiple point deliveries of an FCL Container, this contract terminates upon presentation of the sealed Container at the first place of delivery. Thereafter the Carrier acts as agent only to arrange any further deliveries."

Merchants frequently request carriers to amend the place of delivery shown on the bill of lading (or the port of discharge if it is a port-to-port bill of lading). An amended place of delivery may mean an amended port of discharge and, as the vessel will be stowed to discharge the container at the manifested port, this will lead to substantial additional costs. Accordingly the carrier will quote the merchant a cost for accepting amended instructions.

The question then arises as to the terms and conditions which will apply during the amended carriage. It is vital to the carrier that this situation is made clear, otherwise it may be held that he is operating on common law terms in the absence of a contract with no limitation and the only defences being act of God, Queen's enemies and inherent vice. The complication also arises that, in different trades, different rules may apply. For example, in one trade it may be permissible to offer a door-to-door service under the terms of the contract of carriage for LCL goods, whilst a conference rule in another trade may stipulate that all contracts of carriage under the terms of the bill of lading contract must cease at the CFS, in which case any delivery from the CFS by the carrier to the consignee's premises will have to be effected on alternative terms.

The first paragraph of this sub-clause provides for just such a situation and provides that, if a carrier agrees to an amended place of delivery and makes no stipulation about any amendment to the terms of the contract of carriage, he is deemed to have extended the existing contract of carriage up to delivery at the amended place of delivery, provided that there is nothing in the tariff which prevents this. If the tariff prevents it, then the carrier is deemed to act as agent only to arrange the amended delivery once the period of amended carriage commences.

The second paragraph of this sub-clause covers a situation where the carrier is asked to make a multiple drop-off of an FCL container. It may be that the consignee wishes the goods to be delivered to three or four different warehouses rather than take delivery of the entire consignment at one place. This creates a liability problem in respect of both shortage and damage as, with an FCL, the only receipt which is acceptable to the carrier is for one sealed container (contents unknown). Having received such a receipt from the first drop-off point, the liability of the carrier has to cease because he has no knowledge of the tally of goods in the container nor of how many packages the first consignee is removing. Added to this there is the problem that the first consignee will just take his goods and not "step the stow" of the remaining goods in the container or "tom it off" in any way so that, when the container is en-route to subsequent drop-off points, the unsupported stow will collapse, causing damage to the remaining goods. This sub-clause makes it absolutely clear that, in the case of multiple drop-offs, the carrier's liability ceases at the first drop-off point and the carrier acts as agent only thereafter to arrange the further deliveries.

"(6) If, at the place where the Carrier is entitled to call upon the Merchant to take delivery of the Goods under Clause 20(2), the Carrier is obliged to hand over the Goods into the custody of any Customs, port or other authority, such hand-over shall constitute due delivery to the Merchant under this Bill of Lading."

There are places and ports in the world where the carrier is prevented from delivering the goods directly to the consignee and, instead, has to deliver the goods to a local authority to take control of them for their purposes and subsequently deliver the goods to the consignee. This local authority, to whom delivery is made, is not the agent of the carrier and delivery is made to him by the carrier solely in order to comply with local law. If this local authority delivers the goods without surrender of a duly endorsed original bill of lading, loses or damages them, this is hardly the fault of the carrier. Accordingly, where the carrier is obliged to deliver to a statutory third party, it is reasonable for him to deem delivery to that third party in accordance with local law to be effective delivery of the goods, so that he is not responsible for any loss, damage, delay etc. subsequently caused.

"(7) This Bill of Lading shall not be a negotiable document of title unless consigned 'To Order', 'To the Order of . . . ', or 'To Bearer'. If not so consigned but instead consigned directly to a nominated party, this shall be a 'Straight' Bill of Lading and, at the sole discretion of the Carrier, delivery may be made to the nominated party only upon proof of identity, as if this Bill of Lading were a Waybill. Such delivery shall constitute due delivery hereunder."

Reference has already been made to this matter earlier in this chapter under the heading "Straight bills of lading" and when discussing the incorporation clause (the words "If the Carrier so requires"). The problem for the carrier arises on account of the difference between American law and the law in the rest of the world regarding a "Straight" bill of lading, where the law in the USA regards a straight bill of lading as equivalent to what is elsewhere called a waybill, whilst the law elsewhere appears to be uncertain as to the carrier's responsibility for delivery without surrender of any documentation against a straight bill of lading consignment but has a general consensus of opinion that, whilst it is not a negotiable instrument, it remains a document of title which must be surrendered in exchange for delivery of the goods. This puts the carrier in an invidious position with a conflict of law when dealing with merchants who wish to apply the American interpretation. Accordingly, in an attempt to give the carrier some protection and at least a basis upon which to formulate a defence, this sub-clause provides for a straight bill of lading not to be a document of title and for the carrier, at his sole discretion, to be able to effect delivery as if the document were a waybill.

Clearly the effectiveness of this clause has to be in question but this is the best protection that can be given to carriers who find themselves under commercial pressure to recognise American law and ignore the law elsewhere, even though the goods may not be within the jurisdiction of the American courts.

Clause 21: FCL Multiple Bills of Lading

A groupage agent who is packing several consignments into a container, which he will then offer to the carrier as an FCL, may find that his customers are not happy to accept his contract of carriage and, instead, prefer to have a contract of carriage directly from the carrier, with the groupage agent acting as an agent only and not as a contracting carrier. The problem is that, if the groupage agent has, say, six consignments, he needs six separate LCL style bills of lading. Because the container is being presented to him as an FCL, the carrier is only willing to issue bills of lading on an FCL basis. FCL multiple bills of lading are the solution to this problem in which the carrier issues however many bills of lading his customer (the groupage agent) requires (in this example six), showing the details declared by the shipper but not acknowledged by the carrier as required but only acknowledging in the appropriate box "One of six part cargoes in the Container".

This deals with the problem at the exporting end but then there are problems to be dealt with at the importing end. The groupage agent may wish the container to be delivered to his agent at destination but, before the carrier can do so, one of each of the original FCL multiple bills of lading must be surrendered to the carrier. In this clause, sub-clause (1) deals with the situation where the carrier delivers to the groupage agent's local agent at destination and what happens if not all bills of lading are surrendered, whilst sub-clause (2) deals with the situation where the carrier himself acts as the agent of the groupage agent to unpack the goods for LCL delivery and finds that the contents of the container do not necessarily tally with the manifest information supplied to him by the groupage agent.

"(1) Goods will be delivered in a Container to the Merchant only if all Bills of Lading in respect of the contents of the Container have been surrendered authorising delivery to a single Merchant at a single Place of Delivery. In the event that this requirement is not fulfilled, the Carrier may unpack the Container and, in respect of Goods for which Bills of Lading have been surrendered, deliver them to the Merchant on an LCL basis. Such delivery shall constitute due delivery hereunder but will be effected only against payment by the Merchant of LCL Service Charges and any charges appropriate to LCL Goods (as laid down in the Tariff) together with the actual costs incurred for any additional services rendered."

This sub-clause provides for the carrier to unpack containers containing goods covered by more than one bill of lading and to deliver the goods on an LCL basis against payment of the appropriate LCL service charges and any other charges incurred if all bills of lading in respect of the contents of the container are not surrendered to facilitate an FCL delivery.

"(2) If this is an FCL Multiple Bill of Lading (as evidence by the qualification of the tally acknowledged overleaf to the effect that it is 'One of _____ part cargoes in the Container'), then the Goods detailed overleaf are said to comprise part of the contents of the Container indicated. If the Carrier is required to deliver the Goods to more than one Merchant and if all or part of the total Goods within the Container consists of bulk Goods or unappropriated Goods, or is or becomes mixed or unmarked or unidentifiable, the Holders of Bills of Lading relating to Goods within the Container shall take delivery thereof (including any damaged portion) and bear any shortage in such proportions as the Carrier shall in his absolute discretion determine. Such a delivery shall constitute due delivery hereunder."

This sub-clause covers the situation where the carrier is obliged to unpack an FCL multiple bill of lading container, either because he has been requested to act as the agent of the shipper in doing so or because he has exercised his right under sub-clause (1) above to do so, in the absence of presentation of bills of lading covering all of the consignments. If the carrier unpacks a container which has been packed on FCL terms, provided that the seal has been intact throughout or the carrier can account for any change of seal, the liability of the carrier is determined according to the outturn tally produced by the carrier's agent at the CFS. The carrier will then be responsible for any discrepancy between that outturn tally and the receipt obtained by the CFS when the goods are delivered on behalf of the carrier to the consignee. If the outturn tally is not in accordance with the manifest or any goods are found to be damaged or wrongly marked etc., this sub-clause gives the carrier full discretion to determine what goods are delivered to whom against which FCL multiple bill of lading.

Clause 22: General Average and Salvage

The concept of general average has existed for over two millennia and was part of the Rhodian law in the time of the Phoenicians. It is an unwritten law and is not the subject of any international convention, although there are standard rules (the York-Antwerp Rules) which apply to its adjustment, but these need to be contractually incorporated into the contract of carriage if they are to apply.

Confusion sometimes occurs between general average and salvage, as both are adjusted, often together, as a casualty may give rise to both. The essential difference between general average and salvage is that general average involves a voluntary sacrifice or expense incurred by a party to the venture for the benefit of the whole venture, whereas salvage involves assistance by a third party, independent of contract, to the venture in order to save it (or part of it) in time of peril.

The institution of general average is presently under attack from cargo insurers who would prefer to abandon the concept, leaving the cost of general average to lie where it falls. As the majority of general average is usually either sacrifice or expense by the carrier, this would mean increased cost for the carrier which would not be popular with the carriers insurers (P & I clubs). Cargo insurers would then be left to bear the cost of such things as water damage to goods due to deliberate wetting to extinguish a fire. Due to the entrenched positions of the parties concerned, this is likely to be a lengthy debate and, therefore, for the time being, we have to deal with the subject of general average as it stands.

"(1) In the event of accident, danger, damage or disaster before or after the commencement of the voyage, resulting from any cause whatsoever, due to negligence or not, for which, or for the consequences of which, the Carrier is not responsible, by statute, contract or otherwise, the Merchant shall contribute with the Carrier in General Average to the payment of any sacrifices, losses or expenses of a General Average nature that may be made or incurred, and shall pay Salvage and special charges incurred in respect of the Goods."

This is known as the New Jason clause and is made necessary by the approach of American law, which does not give a carrier an automatic right to general average contribution unless he specifically provides for it. The New Jason clause is the agreement that permits the carrier to claim contribution in general average in situations where he is not at fault under the appropriate COGSA and is only necessary in respect of general average adjustments prepared according to American law.

"(2) Any General Average on a Vessel operated by the Carrier shall be adjusted according to the York-Antwerp Rules of 1994 or any subsequent amendment thereto authorised by the CMI at any port or place and in any currency at the option of and by an adjuster appointed by the Carrier, with the test of reasonableness in the Rule Paramount being made on the basis of what was known at the time of the General Average act and not subsequently with the benefit of hindsight. Any General Average on a Vessel not operated by the Carrier (whether a sea-going or inland waterways Vessel) shall be adjusted according to the requirements of the operator of that Vessel. In either case the Merchant shall give such cash deposit or other security as the Carrier may deem sufficient to cover the estimated General Average contribution of the Goods. Any security, other than cash deposits, must be given by a party acceptable to and with assets in a jurisdiction nominated by the Carrier. Such security must be provided before delivery if the Carrier so requires or, if the Carrier does not so require, within three months of the delivery of the Goods, whether or not at the time of delivery the Merchant had notice of the Carrier's lien. The Carrier shall be under no obligation to exercise any lien for General Average contribution due to the Merchant."

This is quite a long sub-clause which is probably best studied a sentence at a time.

The first sentence provides for the adjustment of any general average *on a vessel operated by the carrier* to be made in accordance with the York-Antwerp Rules of 1994 or any subsequent amendment authorised by the CMI (Comité Maritime International). (The CMI are the organisation that, from time to time, approve amendments to the York-Antwerp Rules in accordance with changes in practice and the requirements of the parties concerned. They are also responsible for the Hague Rules and several other sets of rules like the Uniform Rules for Sea Waybills and Rules for Electronic Bills of Lading.) In case the CMI should approve an amendment to the current 1994 York-Antwerp Rules, provision is made for the latest amendment to the Rules approved by the CMI to apply.

As previously mentioned, the York-Antwerp Rules are not mandatory law and have to be incorporated into the contract of carriage on a voluntary basis if they are to apply. This means that the carrier can incorporate amendments to the Rules if he so chooses. By and large I have felt that the York-Antwerp Rules are reasonable but I was unhappy at the lack of clarity, as I saw it, in the Rule Paramount regarding the test of reasonableness. I therefore incorporated my own clarification to avoid any problems in this area and to make it clear that such test had to be made on the basis of what was known at the time the decision was taken and not with the benefit of hindsight.

Whilst the first sentence covers the situation where the vessel concerned is operated by the carrier, the second sentence addresses the situation where the general average occurs on a vessel not operated by the carrier (perhaps a feeder vessel from a hub port and or even a river barge). The York-Antwerp Rules are not the only set of rules for the adjustment of general average. The Chinese have their own rules and the Rhine Rules are generally applied in the event of a general average on a Rhine barge. General average is usually (but not always—*see* last sentence of this sub-clause) declared by the owner of the vessel involved who, in a combined transport contract, is very likely not to be in contract with the owner of the goods. If the owner of the Vessel concerned decides to declare general average to be adjusted in accordance with a different set of rules than the York-Antwerp Rules, there is nothing that the CTO can do about it and the adjustment has to proceed in accordance with the requirements of the owner of that vessel. Accordingly, because the CTO cannot necessarily control how general average will be adjusted on every vessel on which the merchant's goods may travel, he has to provide for the appropriate rules to apply in situations which he cannot control.

The third sentence provides for the merchant to give a cash deposit or other security in respect of the general average contribution due from him whilst the precise amount of this is calculated by the average adjuster. Where goods are insured, it is usual for the cargo insurer to issue an average guarantee to support the general average bond supplied by the merchant but, if goods are uninsured, a cash deposit is usually required.

The fourth sentence provides for the situation where the security given is not cash and gives the carrier some control over the acceptability of that security. Because of the difficulty of repatriating funds from certain countries or enforcing judgments in their jurisdictions, a carrier may be reluctant to accept security in that jurisdiction and may stipulate that security has to be offered in an alternative jurisdiction of his choice and that the party giving the security has to be acceptable to him. In the event of salvage under Lloyd's open form, unless the salvor agrees otherwise, security has to be given in London by a party resident there.

Unless the CTO or owner of the vessel takes it upon himself to put up security for the goods to the salvor, it is possible that the merchant may be requested to put up two lots of security in the event of a casualty: security for general average to the owner of the vessel and security for salvage to the salvor.

In the vast majority of cases the carrier will require appropriate security from the merchant prior to delivery of the goods, but there may be occasions where he releases the goods before security is provided. The fifth sentence provides to allow the carrier to demand security before delivery but to retain a contractual right to general average contribution, independent of the possessory lien, which enables him to require security to be put up within three months of the delivery of the goods. This contractual right to contribution applies whether or not the merchant was given notice of the carrier's lien for general average contribution at the time of delivery.

Whilst it is the carrier or owner of the vessel who usually declares general average, this does not necessarily have to be the case and anyone who has made a general average sacrifice or incurred a general average expense can declare general average and require a contribution from the other interests involved in the venture but the carrier is clearly in the best position to do so. The last sentence of this sub-clause provides that there is no obligation on the carrier to declare general average and exercise a lien on the other goods to obtain contribution for the benefit of a merchant who has made a general average sacrifice or incurred a general average expense.

"(3) Conversion into the currency of the adjustment shall be calculated at the rate prevailing on the date of payment for disbursements and on the date of completion of discharge of the Vessel for allowances, contributory values, etc."

It is important to avoid disputes regarding the currency in which the adjustment is to be prepared and the exchange rates to be used to convert various disbursements and values etc. into that currency, as exchange rates vary on a daily basis. This sub-clause provides for the exchange rate on the date of payment for disbursements and the date of completion of discharge of the vessel for allowances, contributory values etc.

"(4) If a salving vessel is owned or operated by the Carrier, salvage shall be paid for as fully as if the salving vessel or vessels belonged to strangers."

This is a standard bill of lading clause known as the sister ship salvage clause. If a vessel receives salvage services from a sister ship then, in the normal way of things, it is not possible for that sister ship to claim salvage, because one cannot sue oneself. However, if this situation were allowed to obtain, the crew of the salving ship would be denied their right to a contribution from the salvage award that would normally be made if the vessel belonged to strangers. Accordingly the sister ship salvage clause provides for an arm's-length approach, in the event that a vessel receives salvage services from a sister ship.

"(5) In the event of the Master in his sole discretion or in consultation with owners considering that salvage services are needed, the Merchant agrees that the Master may act as his agent to procure such services to Goods and that the Carrier may act as his agent to settle salvage remuneration, without any prior consultation with the Merchant in both cases."

This is what I call my "*Choko Star*" clause, after the vessel on which the appropriate case was decided. Lawyers acting on behalf of goods and cargo insurers are frequently quick to allege that the carrier and master have no right to commit goods to contribution in salvage services without prior consultation with them, in cases where there is time to consult. I have been described as cynical but I have often thought that this is to prevent lawyers acting for both merchants and salvors being deprived of the opportunity to run up a substantial bill to travel to the location of the casualty to carry out a full investigation and then get involved in a long dispute with the carrier's lawyer over respective rights. Whether my cynicism is well placed or not I consider it desirable to take steps to prevent this type of dispute arising and accordingly have provided in this sub-clause for the master to have the right to engage salvage services without prior consultation with the merchant and, equally important, for the carrier to be able to commit the merchant in settlement of a salvage award, again without prior consultation where necessary. The latter would probably be most vehemently opposed by both merchant's and salvor's lawyers but it is a fact that shortly after the salvage is completed is often the best time to either settle the salvage claim or make an open offer. If an open offer is made and the subsequent award does not exceed that open offer, then the salvor has to pay both sides' costs from the date of the open offer, which are often substantial. Accordingly an open offer shortly after the conclusion of salvage services often concentrates the mind of salvor's solicitors and is therefore most unwelcome by them, so that they frequently resort to the most obscure reasons to try to persuade the arbitrator to set such offers aside. It therefore behoves the carrier to give himself the right to make such offers and commit merchants to their part of the contribution involved.

"(6) If the Merchant contests payment of contribution to General Average, salvage, salvage charges and/or special charges to Goods on any grounds whatsoever or fails to make payment of contribution within three months of the issue of the adjustment thereof, whether or not prior security had been provided, the Merchant shall pay interest for the period in excess of three months on the contribution due at two per cent per annum above the base lending rate of the central bank of the country in whose currency the adjustment is issued, in addition to the contribution due."

Comment has already been made concerning cargo insurers' attempts to remove general average completely from the shipping scene. Part of this campaign manifests itself in insurers' persistence in referring a large number of adjustments prepared by independent adjusters to a second adjuster to vet and comment upon. Cargo insurers lose no opportunity to contest general average on the slightest pretext. Even if they have to pay eventually, they use it as a means of deferring payment and improving their cash flow.

This sub-clause is my strike back on behalf of the carrier to such practices. The current York-Antwerp Rules allow the adjuster to add three months' interest from the date of the issue of the adjustment in favour of the party to whom contribution is due to cover the period during which contributions are collected by the adjuster for distribution to those due to be reimbursed in the adjustment. Accordingly this sub-clause provides for payment of a higher rate of interest than that obtaining in the jurisdiction of the adjustment, once the three month period of grace has expired, in the event that contribution is not paid on time. This is an incentive to pay timely and to prevent the carrier from being out of pocket in the event of a long delay in obtaining contribution from the party from whom it is due.

Clause 23: Variation of the Contract

"No servant or agent of the Carrier shall have the power to waive or vary any of the terms of this Bill of Lading, unless such waiver or variation is in writing and is specifically authorised or ratified in writing by the Carrier."

This clause is quite self-explanatory and requires little comment from me. The most usual way in which the standard contract might be varied on those rare occasions when the carrier agrees to make a variation, is by showing the agreed variation as a clause on the face of the bill of lading. Only in this way can one be sure that all parties, who acquire title to the goods through holding the bill of lading, become aware of the precise nature of the amendment to the standard contract.

Clause 24: Law and Jurisdiction

"(1) Unless Clause 25 or 27 applies, any claim against the Carrier under this Bill of Lading shall be determined only according to English law and exclusively in the High Court of Justice in London. The Merchant irrevocably submits to this jurisdiction.
(2) The Carrier shall be entitled to pursue any claim against the Merchant in London according to English law or in any jurisdiction in which the Merchant has assets but then in accordance with the local law of that jurisdiction.
(3) Nothing herein shall prevent the parties to any claim or dispute under this Bill of Lading from agreeing to submit the claim or dispute to arbitration by mutually acceptable arbitrator(s) on mutually acceptable terms at a mutually acceptable venue."

Sub-clause (1) provides for English law and jurisdiction, unless there is some law in a jurisdiction where a claim is made making this sub-clause invalid, as may be the case in a jurisdiction which has a Supreme Court Act preserving the right of local courts to hear such claims (this is quite a common occurrence, particularly in Commonwealth countries). There is a need to make reference to the US Clause Paramount in addition to the general sub-clause reference to where the clause may be invalid because, as we have learned earlier, the US Act does not just provide for its operation in the US courts, but provides that, if contractual provision is not made in the bill of lading for it to apply, the carrier is denied the benefit of any of the defences in the Act. Hence the sub-clause excludes clauses 25 and 27 from the application of sub-clause (1).

Whilst sub-clause (1) covers the situation where the claimant is the merchant claiming against the carrier, sub-clause (2) provides for the situation where the carrier is claiming against the merchant. Naturally the carrier would prefer to make such claims in the same court as that in which he would hope to defend any claim against him, but to take action against a defendant in a jurisdiction, in which that defendant had no assets to satisfy any judgment, could prove ineffective. Accordingly the carrier gives himself the option to pursue the merchant as a defendant in whichever court the carrier considers he is best likely to be able to obtain a judgment and satisfaction for the award once he had has obtained that judgment.

Finally in sub-clause (3) the carrier leaves the door open to arbitration, in the event that both parties to the dispute agree that this is the best way to resolve the matter. If the parties decide to proceed to arbitration, the clause leaves it open to them to agree the terms and the venue as part of the agreement to apply arbitration rather than proceed to court.

Clause 25: Validity

"In the event that anything herein contained is inconsistent with any applicable international convention or national law which cannot be departed from by private contract, the provisions hereof shall, to the extent of such inconsistency but no further, be null and void."

This clause provides that, if anything in the contract is contrary to any *mandatory* law then, to the extent of that inconsistency only, the contract is null and void but all other provisions of the contract remain in place. Note that we are here talking only of mandatory law and not rules which are provided for voluntary adoption, such as the York-Antwerp Rules or the ICC Rules for a Combined Transport Document etc.

A clause like this is designed to prevent any suggestion that the slightest breach of any law invalidates the whole contract, rather than just the small part of it which is invalid under the relevant mandatory law.

Clause 26: Limitation of Liability

"For the avoidance of doubt, it is hereby agreed by the Merchant that the Carrier qualifies and shall be regarded as a Person entitled to limit liability under the relevant Convention on the Limitation of Liability for Maritime Claims, notwithstanding that the Carrier may have procured space on board the Vessel concerned by means of a Slot Charter party, Bill of Lading or some other Contract of Carriage.
Except to the extent that mandatory law to the contrary applies in the appropriate jurisdiction (in which case said law shall apply), the size of the fund to which the Carrier may limit liability shall be identical to that proportion of the limitation fund by which the actual carrier is entitled to limit which is (or would be) available for the Carrier's claims against the actual carrier."

It will be remembered that, in discussing feedership charter parties in Chapter 3, reference was made to the problem which CTOs experience as a result of the current international convention on Limitation of Liability for Maritime Claims having been drafted prior to a full appreciation of the nature of their operation being available. The 1976 LLMC provides for the owner, charterer and manager to be able to benefit from limitation under the convention and the question arises as to whether or not a CTO, acting as a slot charterer or with a cover bill of lading for a feeder leg to/from a hub port, is entitled to limit by reference to this convention as well as under the terms and conditions of the bill of lading/Hague Rules. As a slot charterer or bill of lading holder had little control over the movements of the vessel in the way that an owner, charterer or manager might have, there was a feeling that LLMC limitation might be denied to CTOs and there was a discrepancy of views between different countries as to how this convention might be interpreted. The view amongst English lawyers was a pessimistic one initially but two recent decisions have changed this completely. The two decisions, to which references have been made in Chapter 3 when discussing feedership charter parties, are *The Aegean Sea* [1998] and *The Tychy* [1999] so it can be seen that these are two very much up-to-the-minute decisions. To encourage the judiciary to continue to follow this line and put all carrier interests on one side and all cargo interests on the other when dealing with cargo claims matters, a suitable clause is desirable in the bill of lading in order to persuade any wavering judges to adopt this approach.

The first paragraph of this clause provides for agreement by the merchant that the carrier qualifies under the LLMC as a party who can limit, whether or not he procured space on board the vessel concerned by means of a slot charter party, a bill of lading or some other contract to carriage. In the light of recent decisions the carrier may have a good chance of success if he procured space via a slot charter party but, if he procured a space by some other means, there obviously has to be a chance that he will not succeed in enforcing this contractual application of a convention which does not provide for limitation under bills of lading. This is why carriers are well advised to ensure that their feeder arrangements are made via feedership charter parties rather than cover bills of lading (*see* Chapter 3).

The second paragraph addresses the problem of calculating the size of the limitation fund which the carrier can apply and does so by reference to the size of the fund which the actual carrier can enforce against the contracting carrier. As the LLMC does not envisage slot chartering, it makes no provisions to calculate the size of the slot charterer's limitation fund and thus there is need for a provision of this nature.

Clause 27: USA Clause Paramount (if applicable)

We now come to the last clause in the contract of carriage and the most difficult one to deal with at this particular point. This is because the US is in the process of amending its Carriage of Goods by Sea Act and, at the time of writing, it is not known when this will happen nor is it certain as to the precise nature of the amendments until the Act passes through Congress. However, the general approach of the amendments is known and it is not expected that these will change greatly. Accordingly, I will provide a clause covering the present situation and then go on to suggest a clause that is likely to be appropriate when the new US Act comes into effect, although clearly when this happens there will be much liaison between carriers and their P & I clubs over the precise wording required.

To start with it may be as well to provide a little background to this subject. As has been commented previously, the US Act is probably the only one "with teeth" where one cannot avoid making direct reference to the US Act by merely referring generally to mandatory legislation, as is the case in most other places. Accordingly, if there is any chance of being a carrier in respect of goods transported to, from or through the US, it is vital to have a US clause paramount in the contract of carriage. As we shall see as we examine the present clause, much of its content has been necessitated by somewhat non-sensical decisions taken by the US judiciary over the years. The US Maritime Law Association, in drafting the revised COGSA, have attempted to write out the effect of these decisions and return the US approach to be similar to that which applies in most other countries. This means that the new US Act has to be somewhat complicated in order to simplify the overall effect and bring it into line.

Although the approach is changing, the US have a long history of legislation designed to prevent monopolies and protect the smaller operator to make sure that he can achieve the same deal as the bigger operator. When containerisation first started, anti-trust laws prevented carriers from operating as combined transport operators and issuing door-to-door bills of lading so the American market initially grew up expecting the land portion to be undertaken by a different operator and the furthest that the sea carrier went was to guarantee the performance of the land carrier. Accordingly, most container operators offered contracts reflecting this situation and, when the law changed to allow combined transport, as the customers were familiar with this approach, most carriers did not change their contracts of carriage but left things as they were. The new COGSA, when it comes in, will apply an amended form of Hague-Visby Rules on a door-to-door basis and be the first combined transport legislation in the world. Therefore carriers' liabilities in respect of goods to, from or through the US will change radically.

Present clause

"(1) If Carriage includes Carriage to, from or through a port in the United States of America, this Bill of Lading shall be subject to the United States Carriage of Goods by Sea Act 1936 (US COGSA), the terms of which are incorporated herein and shall be paramount throughout Carriage by sea and the entire time that the Goods are in the actual custody of the Carrier or his Sub-Contractor at the sea terminal in the United States of America before loading onto a Vessel or after discharge therefrom, as the case may be."

This is the clause paramount clause applying the present 1936 COGSA. Note that it applies in respect of goods whether carriage is "to, from or through a port in the USA" as, contrary to the intention of the Hague Rules (which are the rules applied by the 1936 Act in a slightly amended form), the US Act applies to imports as well as exports. Whilst the Hague Rules are designed to operate from ship's rail to ship's rail, this clause applies the Act to "the entire time that the goods are in the actual custody of the Carrier or his subcontractor at the sea terminal in the United States of America" as well as to the sea carriage portion of the contract.

"(2) The Carrier shall not be liable in any capacity whatsoever for loss, damage or delay to the Goods while the goods are in the United States of America away from the sea terminal and are not in the actual custody of the Carrier. At these times the Carrier acts as agent only to procure carriage by Persons (one or more) under the usual terms and conditions of those Persons. If, for any reason, the Carrier is denied the right to act as agent only at these times, his liability for loss, damage or delay to the Goods shall be determined in accordance with Clause 6 hereof."

This clause is designed to make the carrier a through transport operator instead of a combined transport operator whilst in America for reasons outlined above. That is to say his liability whilst the goods are not in his care shall be limited to whatever he is able to recover from the appropriate party.

However, as a backstop, in case a court should overrule this clause, there is a provision that, if the carrier is held liable, as there is no mandatory law governing carriage by land in the US, the provisions of clause 6 shall apply as they would elsewhere in the world.

"(3) If US COGSA applies the liability of the Carrier and/or the Vessel shall not exceed US$500 per package or customary freight unit (in accordance with Section 1304(5) thereof), unless the value of the Goods has been declared on the face hereof, in which case Clause 7(3) shall apply."

The provisions of this sub-clause are mostly included to comply with previous US decisions as to what data must be shown in a contract of carriage if the carrier wishes to enjoy the benefit of the US COGSA. As you can see there is a need to make reference to the amount of limitation and the appropriate section of US legislation which makes provision for this. Clause 7(3) is the *ad valorem* clause and reference to this links up with the facility to declare value on the face of the US bill of lading to provide for an *ad valorem* bill if the merchant requires it.

"(4) Notwithstanding the provisions of Clause 24, if Carriage includes Carriage to, from or through a port in the United States of America, the Merchant may refer any claim or dispute to the United States District Court for the Southern District of New York in accordance with the laws of the United States of America."

The concluding sub-clause of this clause is the law and jurisdiction provision which is a point upon which US law and lawyers are particularly sharp. It gives the merchant the option of US law and jurisdiction instead of the English law and jurisdiction as provided for in clause 24 on all shipments "to, from or through a port in the United States of America". The US judiciary is not arranged in the same way as that in the UK and most other places, where a collision case would be heard in an Admiralty court and a cargo claim in a commercial court in front of judges with specialist knowledge in those areas. In the US judges may hear a wide variety of cases, including those on which their knowledge may be sparse. It could be particularly calamitous to be sued in the court of some area where there was a judiciary with virtually no appreciation of maritime law, hence the provision in this clause for the Southern District of New York court, which is usually acceptable to US cargo interests as this is where the major insurance companies and the major firms of US lawyers have their main offices. It is also the area where one stands the best chance of a hearing in front of a judge with some degree of nautical knowledge.

Clause when new Act (US COGSA 2000/1?) in force

When the new US COGSA comes into effect, all carriers will need to change the US clause paramount in their contracts of carriage to take account of the fact. They will also need to take note that they will be liable on a door-to-door basis under the terms of the new Act. This will apply an amended form of Hague-Visby Rules on land as well as at sea. As the new Act has overruled some of the earlier US decisions, it would seem that a US clause paramount to give effect to the new US COGSA can be relatively simple, although I am sure that some judge will find good cause to prove otherwise given the opportunity! Also it is not just a US court that we need to take account of. I have been warned by an eminent US lawyer, who has been involved in the preparation of the revised US COGSA draft that, unless we are careful, a court outside the United States might interpret a simple clause merely incorporating the new US COGSA as an indication of intent by the parties to increase the carrier's liability by deleting the error of navigation or management defence. For this reason the second sentence of sub-clause (1) below is deemed necessary.

To start with, a clause along the following lines ought to prove sufficient but advice from the carriers' P & I clubs after consultation with New York lawyers is strongly recommended when this situation arises as, quite apart from any other considerations, there may be some last-minute alterations to the Act which this book cannot take into account at this stage.

"(1) If Carriage under this Bill of Lading includes Carriage to, from or through any port or place in the United States of America, this Bill of Lading shall be subject to the United States Carriage of Goods by Sea Act 2000 (US COGSA), the terms of which are incorporated herein and, notwithstanding any provisions to the contrary elsewhere in this Bill of Lading, shall be paramount throughout Carriage of the Goods. No provision of any Act, Statute or other law or rule will be incorporated contractually by reference into this Bill of Lading if its incorporation would increase the Carrier's liability above the provisions contained in the Hague Rules.
(2) Notwithstanding the provisions of Clause 24, if Carriage includes Carriage to, from or through a port or place in the United States of America, the Merchant has the option to refer any claim or dispute to the United States District Court for the Southern District of New York in accordance with the laws of the United States of America."

This, then, is a suggested contract of carriage for a combined transport operator.

Another piece of US legislation which should be noted is the US Shipping Reform Act of 1999 which changed the previous requirement that a carrier must offer the same deal to all shippers, large and small, according to rates, terms and conditions filed with the Federal Maritime Commission (FMC). Under this Act individual shippers are now allowed to negotiate shipping contracts with carriers at any rates and on any terms and conditions that they can negotiate. Some of the larger US shippers, suddenly released from these restrictions, are using their new found freedom, not only to negotiate lower rates with carriers, but also to require carriers to negotiate on the terms of their contracts of carriage, sometimes to a point where a full liability bill of lading (insured bill of lading) is required, so that the carrier has no defences or limitations and if goods are lost, damaged or delayed in his care he must pay, whatever the reason for the loss, damage or delay. Carriers are fighting this approach as best they can, as their P & I clubs are refusing to cover liabilities in excess of normal bill of lading liability, so that they will need to buy top-up cover elsewhere. However, with the amount of goods which some of the larger US shippers control, they are finding themselves between a rock and a hard place in what is a very competitive market.

In conclusion it may be appropriate to note one or two clauses, often found in conventional bills of lading, which are not included in and are inappropriate for combined transport.

Demise/identity of carrier clause

This is a clause by which an issuer of a bill of lading using a chartered vessel provides that he acts as agent only to make a contract between the owner of the vessel (actual carrier) and the merchant. Where several modes of transport are involved and it may not be possible to tell at which stage the loss or damage occurred, this is not an appropriate approach.

Transhipment clause

This is a clause by which the carrier provides that, if he tranships, he thereafter acts as agent only to arrange a contract with the oncarrier and the goods lie at the transhipment port at the merchant's risk. This again is clearly inappropriate in most combined transport contracts.

However, it may happen that a customer wants a combined transport bill through to an area where the carrier has neither representation nor control and where he is consequently unprepared to accept responsibility (delivery from ports like St. Petersburg through to Moscow comes to mind in view of the activities of the Russian Mafia). In such cases many carriers use a transhipment clause on the face of the bill of lading to provide for them to act as agent only during the period for which they are unprepared to accept responsibility but where the customer wants a combined transport bill of lading through to final destination. Such a clause might read:

> "The liability of the Carrier under the terms and conditions of this Bill of Lading ceases upon delivery to the oncarrier at ________________ . Thereafter the Carrier acts as agent only to arrange oncarriage and accepts no personal responsibility for the Goods."

It could happen that the customer wanted a combined transport bill of lading from an area where the carrier was unprepared to accept liability rather than to an area with this restriction. In such a case the clause would instead read as follows:

> "The liability of the Carrier under the terms and conditions of this Bill of Lading does not commence until receipt by the Carrier of the Goods at ________________ . Until such receipt the Carrier acts as agent only to arrange precarriage and accepts no personal responsibility for the Goods."

Lighterage clause

As the Hague and Hague-Visby Rules operate only from ship's side to ship's side, such a clause provides for any lighterage to be undertaken at the risk of the merchant. (Discharge overside other than onto a quay is unusual with containerships and, to the best of my knowledge, occurs only (to any extent) in sheltered waters in Hong Kong harbour.) A lighterage clause provides for lighterage to be undertaken at the risk of the merchant and for the liability of the carrier to cease as soon as the goods cross the ship's rail. This is another clause which was common with conventional break-bulk goods but which is rather out of place in a modern combined transport operation.

WAYBILLS

Once upon a time virtually all seaborne goods were carried under the cover of a bill of lading, except for a few odd consignments of personal effects and experimental shipments which were carried under non-negotiable receipts (NNRs). Carriers looked enviously at the relatively simple documentation which land and air carriers used, which was not a document of title with the consequent problems this brings. Even 30 years ago and with the beginning of computerised business documentation, businessmen involved in international trade were already beginning to try and get away from paper and discovered that one of the main stumbling blocks in their way was the fact that the bill of lading, which had become the cornerstone of international trade and documentary credits, had to be paper or some tangible object in order to be a document of title, thereby precluding the use of computerised communication where a bill of lading was concerned. Atlantic Container Line (ACL) developed a datafreight receipt with assistance from Professor Kurt Gronfors of Gothenburg University and this was an early attempt at what became the waybill. Where a document of title was not necessary in order to facilitate the sale of goods in transit or as security for payment in a documentary credit process, the use of waybills grew in those areas where there was no legislation requiring a bill of lading for Customs clearance or exchange control purposes. Accordingly, in considering contracts of carriage between carriers and customers, it is necessary to consider waybills and identify the ways in which they are similar to and different from bills of lading in order to decide when it is more appropriate to use one rather than the other.

In order to do this we need to consider the functions and properties of a waybill. A waybill is a receipt and evidence of the contract of carriage but it is not a document of title—rather like a straight bill of lading under US law, excepting that, not being a bill of lading, it is not mandatorily subject to the relevant Carriage of Goods by Sea Act (applying the Hague or Hague-Visby Rules which only apply to bills of lading and thus do apply to a straight bill but not a waybill). Not being a document of title a waybill cannot be used to pass title to goods merely by the passage of a set of pieces of paper with the appropriate endorsements where necessary. Accordingly it would be inappropriate to issue "Order" waybills and all waybills should have a nominated consignee. The obligation of the carrier where a waybill is issued is not to deliver against surrender of any documentation but to deliver to the nominated consignee upon production of evidence of identity (usually a delivery order on the consignee's headed stationery).

Although not mandatorily subject to the Hague or Hague-Visby Rules, which are clearly stated only to apply where a bill of lading or similar document of title is issued, carriers invariably apply the same contract of carriage terms where a waybill is issued as would have applied if a bill of lading were issued and do not take advantage of the opportunity to contract on lesser terms, which course is open to them on account of there being no overriding mandatory law. In 1990 at their Paris meeting, the Comité Maritime International (CMI) approved adoption of the CMI Uniform Rules for Sea Waybills. The title refers to sea waybills to differentiate from air waybills but the rules apply equally to combined transport waybills as well as sea waybills. *Inter alia* this admirably brief set of rules provides that, if a waybill is issued subject to these rules, then the contract of carriage which it evidences is in identical terms to that which would have applied if a bill of lading were issued. So it would seem that a waybill issued subject to the CMI Uniform Rules for Sea Waybills ought to meet the criteria for acceptability of parties looking for a bill of lading in order to be guaranteed the minimum recourse of the Hague or Hague-Visby Rules, which is available where a bill of lading is issued. If you look at the specimen P&O Nedlloyd Waybill at Figure 7, you will find at the base a note to the effect that "This Waybill is issued subject to the CMI Uniform Rules for Sea Waybills". Thus it is possible to make a waybill acceptable from a recourse point of view without the need for the party requiring reassurance to have to read the entire contract.

Another way in which the bill of lading differs from the waybill is that, in the United Kingdom under the Bill of Lading Act (which is now the Carriage of Goods by Sea Act 1992), because it is a document of title, the holder of a bill of lading with endorsements in order (rather like a cheque) can claim title to and control the goods. Once a shipper allows a bill of lading out of his hands he loses control of the goods, which passes to the new holder of the bill of lading, who now becomes a party to the contract of carriage with the carrier, so that he can sue the carrier in his own name without going through the shipper and equally be sued by the carrier in respect of the goods. Not being a document of title, possession of the waybill carries no right whatsoever and the contract of carriage is a personal contract between the carrier and the shipper with which (until COGSA 1992) the consignee was uninvolved. This means that, whereas a shipper under a bill of lading has very restricted rights of stoppage in transit, the shipper under a waybill retains control of the goods at all times through to delivery to the consignee. This was amended slightly by COGSA 1992 which gave a consignee the right to sue the carrier direct (and the exposure to be sued direct by the carrier) by becoming a party to the contract of carriage when he presented himself to the carrier to claim delivery. Note the difference between the bill of lading and the waybill. With the bill of lading the consignee becomes a party to the contract on taking up the documents but with the waybill, as no documents necessarily pass, this is not possible and the watershed is provided as the point at which the consignee presents himself to the carrier to claim delivery.

Another thing that follows from the fact that a waybill is essentially a personal contract between the carrier and the shipper is that, unless provision is made to the contrary in the waybill, the consignee has no right under the contract of carriage to make any claim against the carrier and, if the goods are discrepant in any way at the time of delivery, he must make his claim through the shipper who, having been paid, may regard the transaction as complete and be less than helpful. This situation is usually redressed in the waybill contract as it is in nobody's interest to prevent the most expedient way of dealing with claims applying, namely between the carrier and the consignee at destination.

Although some countries require the terms and conditions of the contract of carriage to be printed on the reverse of waybills issued there, by and large waybills are blank backed documents. This is because, not being documents of title (which can be used to sell goods to a third party who becomes a party to the contract of carriage and to whose attention the carrier has a need to bring the terms and conditions of the contract of carriage as is the case with a bill of lading), there is no need for the carrier to go to the trouble and expense of printing the contract of carriage on the back of the waybill as the contract is a personal contract with the shipper, who can ask to see the terms at the time of booking and, under COGSA 1992, the consignee who can ask to see the terms at the time of arranging delivery. The waybill therefore has a different incorporation clause on its face to that which appears on the bill of lading as it needs to make certain particular references and incorporate the terms and conditions of the bill of lading contract of carriage in an effective manner.

The following is recommended as a suitable incorporation clause for a waybill to apply the bill of lading terms and conditions outlined above:

"Received by the Carrier from the Shipper in apparent good order and condition (unless otherwise noted herein) the total number or quantity of Containers or other packages or units indicated in the box above entitled 'Total No. of Containers/Packages received by the Carrier' for Carriage from the Place of Receipt or the Port of Loading, whichever applicable, to the Port of Discharge or the Place of Delivery, whichever applicable, SUBJECT TO THE TERMS OF THE CARRIER'S STANDARD BILL OF LADING TERMS AND CONDITIONS AND TARIFF FOR THE RELEVANT TRADE WHICH ARE *MUTATIS MUTANDIS* APPLICABLE TO THIS WAYBILL (copies of which may be obtained from the Carrier or his agents). Except for live animals and goods which are stated herein to be carried on deck and are so carried, these terms and conditions are warranted by the Carrier in respect of the sea portion of Carriage to apply the Hague Rules or Hague-Visby Rules, whichever would have been applicable if this Waybill were a Bill of Lading. In either case the provisions of Article III Rule 4 of the Hague-Visby Rules are deemed to be incorporated herein.

Non-Negotiable Waybill for Combined Transport shipment or Port to Port shipment

Shipper

Waybill No.:

Reference

P&O Nedlloyd

Consignee (If the name shown in this space is a Bank, the Bank named is specifically excluded from the list of parties coming within the definition of Merchant in the Carrier's contract of carriage and incurs no liability to the Carrier under said contract unless applying for delivery in its own name.)

Notify Party/Address (It is agreed that no responsibility shall attach to the Carrier or his Agents for failure to notify.)

Place of Receipt (Applicable only when this document is used as a Combined Transport Waybill)

Vessel and Voy. No.

Place of Delivery (Applicable only when this document is used as a Combined Transport Waybill)

Port of Loading

Port of Discharge

Undermentioned particulars as declared by Shipper, but not acknowledged by the Carrier

Marks and Nos; Container Nos;	Number and kind of Packages; Description of Goods	Gross Weight (kg)	Measurement (cbm)

WAYBILL

*Total No. of Containers/Packages received by the Carrier	Movement	Freight payable at

Received by the Carrier from the Shipper in apparent good order and condition (unless otherwise noted herein) the total number or quantity of Containers or other packages or units indicated in the box above entitled "*Total No. of Containers/Packages received by the Carrier" for Carriage from the Place of Receipt or the Port of Loading, whichever applicable, to the Port of Discharge or the Place of Delivery, whichever applicable, SUBJECT TO THE TERMS OF THE CARRIER'S STANDARD BILL OF LADING TERMS AND CONDITIONS AND TARIFF FOR THE RELEVANT TRADE, WHICH ARE MUTATIS MUTANDIS APPLICABLE TO THIS WAYBILL (copies of which may be obtained from the Carrier or his agents). Except for live animals and Goods which are stated herein to be carried on deck and are so carried, these terms and conditions are warranted by the Carrier in respect of the sea portion of the Carriage to apply the Hague Rules or Hague Visby Rules, whichever would have been applicable if this Waybill were a Bill of Lading. In either case the provisions of Article III Rule 4 of the Hague Visby Rules are deemed to be incorporated herein. The contract evidenced by this Waybill is deemed to be a contract of carriage as defined in Article 1(b) of the Hague Rules and Hague Visby Rules. However this Waybill is not a document of title to the Goods.

Delivery will be made to the Consignee named, or his authorised agents, on production of proof of identity at the Port of Discharge or the Place of Delivery, whichever applicable. Should the Consignee require delivery to a party and/or premises other than as shown above in the "Consignee" box, then written instructions must be given by the Consignee to the Carrier or his agent. Unless the Shipper expressly waives his right to control the Goods until delivery by means of a clause on the face hereof, such instructions from the Consignee will be subject to any instructions to the contrary by the Shipper.

Unless instructed to the contrary by the Shipper prior to the commencement of Carriage and noted accordingly on the face hereof, the Carrier will, subject to the aforesaid terms and conditions, process cargo claims with the Consignee. Claims settlement, if any, shall be a complete discharge of the Carrier's liability to the Shipper. The Shipper accepts the said standard terms and conditions on his own behalf, on behalf of the Consignee and the Owner of the Goods, and authorises the Consignee to bring suit against the Carrier in his own name but as agent of the Shipper, and warrants that he has authority so to accept and authorise. The Shipper further undertakes that no claim or allegation in respect of the Goods shall be made against the Carrier by any person other than in accordance with the terms and conditions of this Waybill.

This Waybill is issued subject to the CMI Uniform Rules for Sea Waybills	Place and Date of Issue	IN WITNESS whereof this Waybill is signed.

FOR P&O NEDLLOYD LTD, AS CARRIER:*

P&O Nedlloyd

19/DRS W/B3 10/97 (8)

*OPERATING IN PARTNERSHIP WITH P&O NEDLLOYD B.V.

Figure 8: P&O Nedlloyd Non-Negotiable Waybill for Combined Transport Shipment or Port-to-Port Shipment

The contract evidenced by this Waybill is deemed to be a contract of carriage as defined in Article 1 (b) of the Hague Rules and Hague-Visby Rules. However this Waybill is not a document of title to the Goods.
Delivery will be made to the Consignee named, or his authorised agents, on production of proof of identity at the Port of Discharge or the Place of Delivery, whichever applicable. Should the Consignee require delivery to a party and/or premises other than as shown above in the 'Consignee' box, then a written instruction must be given by the Consignee to the Carrier or his agent. Unless the Shipper expressly waives his right to control Goods until delivery by means of a clause on the face hereof, such instruction from the Consignee will be subject to any instruction to the contrary by the Shipper.
Unless instructed to the contrary by the Shipper prior to the commencement of Carriage and noted accordingly on the face hereof, the Carrier will, subject to the aforesaid terms and conditions, process cargo claims with the Consignee. Claims settlement, if any, shall be a complete discharge of the Carrier's liability to the Shipper.
The Shipper accepts the said standard terms and conditions on his own behalf, on behalf of the Consignee and the owner of the Goods, and authorises the Consignee to bring suit against the Carrier in his own name but as agent of the Shipper, and warrants that he has authority so to accept and authorise. The Shipper further undertakes that no claim or allegation in respect of the Goods shall be made against the Carrier by any person other than in accordance with the terms and conditions of this Waybill."

Paragraph 1: The first sentence of this paragraph follows closely that in the incorporation clause in the bill of lading by acknowledging the tally shown in the appropriate box and indicating the parameters of the contract. It concludes (in capital letters to draw the attention of the merchant to it) by providing that the carriage is subject to the terms of the carrier's standard bill of lading and tariff. *Mutatis mutandis* means literally let that which must be changed be changed. Used here it means that, wherever in the bill of lading terms and conditions, which are incorporated herein, the term bill of lading is used, that word necessarily has to be changed to waybill in order to make appropriate sense. The sentence finishes with a provision in brackets to draw the attention of the merchant to the fact that, whilst the terms and conditions are not printed on the reverse, they are available on application to the carrier or his agents.

The second sentence is a warranty that the bill of lading terms and conditions, to which reference has been made, incorporate the Hague or Hague-Visby Rules, which are applicable, as if the waybill were a bill of lading, to all shipments except live animals and goods carried on deck against an appropriately claused waybill. The paragraph concludes with a provision incorporating Article III Rule 4 of the Hague-Visby Rules, which provides that the document shall be *prima facie* evidence of the receipt by the carrier of the goods as therein described therein.

Paragraph 2: This paragraph deems a waybill to come within the definition of contract of carriage in the Hague Rules as being a contract to which the rules will apply. In the rules the definition refers to "a bill of lading or any similar document of title" which would normally exclude a waybill but this sentence deems waybills to come within this definition so that the Hague/

Hague-Visby Rules shall be applicable. The second sentence makes it clear that the incorporation of the rules are relevant to liability only and do not go so far as to make the waybill a document of title. This is the main difference between the bill of lading and the waybill and is likely to be the difference which leads to the waybill supplanting the bill of lading in due course when the documentation of international trade finally transfers to electronic commerce.

Paragraph 3: This paragraph concerns delivery of the goods at destination. The first sentence provides that, in order to obtain delivery, the consignee only needs to produce proof of identity and does not need to surrender any documents. The second sentence provides for the consignee to give written notice to the carrier if he wishes delivery to be made to a person or place other than that shown on the waybill, whilst the third sentence makes it clear that, as he has control throughout until delivery, the shipper can step in and countermand such instructions, unless he has agreed to a clause on the face of the waybill depriving him of this right.

Paragraph 4: The first sentence of this paragraph is designed to overcome the requirement for the consignee to revert via the shipper in order to claim against the carrier and allows the carrier to settle claims with the consignee. The second sentence provides for any release that the carrier obtains from the consignee to be good as against the shipper in order to avoid double indemnity. The third sentence provides for the shipper to accept the bill of lading terms and conditions on his own behalf, on behalf of the consignee and (in case this party is a separate person) the owner of the goods. It concludes with an authorisation in favour of the consignee to bring suit against the carrier in his own name but as agent of the shipper and a warranty from the shipper that he has authority from the parties mentioned to agree to the terms and conditions and authority to authorise the consignee to sue the carrier direct. The paragraph concludes with a sentence in which the shipper undertakes that no one will claim against the carrier other than in accordance with the terms and conditions of the waybill, rather along the lines of bill of lading clause 4(4).

Whilst the bill of lading has been the cornerstone of international trade for many years by reason of its function as a document of title which has facilitated secure delivery and payment, the need for a paper document is now a substantial drawback as commerce becomes electronic. For this reason it would seem that the days of the paper bill of lading are numbered. That the bill of lading will be with us for some time yet is not disputed but, as electronic commerce spreads its tentacles, the bill of lading will be overtaken by the waybill, because a waybill can be an electronic message by reason of the fact that it is not a document of title and does not therefore need to be represented in some tangible form. The future therefore lies with the electronic waybill allied to a system not reliant upon a document of title to facilitate secure payment and transfers of title. Various schemes are presently being developed to facilitate this approach and only time will tell which of these will succeed. One thing is sure, however, whichever scheme succeeds, it will not be based on a paper bill of lading as a document of title but rather a waybill as an electronic contract of carriage and receipt.

CHAPTER 7

STANDARD TRADING CONDITIONS

INTRODUCTION

In the days of break-bulk, port-to-port carriage, carriers operated one contract only: the contract of carriage in the bill of lading as this covered all of their activities. With the advent of combined transport the contract of carriage had to be expanded to cover liability during land carriage as well as sea carriage and then gradually carriers started to offer additional services to their customers to create a "one stop shopping" approach by offering "value added services" which covered activities outside of the contract of carriage, such as Customs clearance, distribution, warehousing etc. in an effort to offer customers an all inclusive service and bind them into the carrier's services by taking over their entire distribution network, so that the customer could concentrate on manufacturing or retailing, whichever was his business.

Many of these activities fell outside of the contract of carriage in the bill of lading and it was therefore necessary for the combined transport operator to develop a set of terms and conditions to cover activities that were not covered by the bill of lading contract. These terms and conditions had to be dovetailed into the bill of lading terms and conditions so that it was clear which are applied to any particular activity. By and large terms and conditions similar to those of the British International Freight Association (BIFA) were the sort of thing required and, if the CTO was a member of BIFA, these conditions would be appropriate, provided that it could be made clear where the dividing line fell between the bill of lading terms and conditions and the BIFA terms and conditions. Many carriers preferred to develop their own standard trading conditions, which were usually heavily based on the BIFA conditions but adjusted to be complementary to their bill of lading terms and conditions. The following standard trading conditions are designed to dovetail with the bill of lading terms and conditions described in Chapter 6.

Any carrier who undertakes services over and above the contract of carriage, without adopting a set of standard trading conditions to cover those services, risks operating without the protection of a contract. In England he would be operating on common law terms, which means that he would have three defences: act of God, Queen's enemies and inherent vice but no limitation of liability. Accordingly the back-up of a set of standard trading conditions is vital to a combined transport operator.

CONDITIONS

Preamble

"The majority of services offered by the Company and its subsidiary organisations are covered by the contract of carriage, the terms of which appear in the Bill of Lading terms and conditions and Tariff for the trade in question. However some value added services are offered which fall outside the scope of the contract of carriage.
In order to formalise the relationship of the Company with its Customers on such occasions the following Standard Trading Conditions are published.
(The Customer's attention is drawn to the clauses herein which exclude or limit the Company's liability and those which require the Customer to indemnify the Company in certain circumstances)."

The preamble merely introduces the conditions and outlines briefly the reason for them and when they will apply. These are terms and conditions, rather like the bill of lading terms and conditions, where the company will always find difficulty in showing that the terms and conditions have been brought adequately to the attention of the customer and the third paragraph of the preamble is an attempt to warn a customer who does not read the whole conditions that there are provisions therein of which he should make himself aware.

1. Definitions

"In these conditions:
'The Company' means [..........].
'Customer' means any person to whom the Company provides any services.
'Person' includes individuals, groups, companies or any other legal entity.
'Owner' means the owner of the goods to or in respect of which the Company provides any services and any other Person who has or may acquire an interest in them.
'Goods' means all or any part of the goods (including any packaging, containers or equipment supplied by the Customer or Owner) which are the subject of any Services.
'Conditions' means the provisions of this contract.
'Instructions' means any statement of the Customer's requirements, whether verbal or written.
'Service(s)' means all or any business undertaken by the Company for the Customer including the provision of advice, information and any services whatsoever.
'Sub-Contractor' means direct and indirect sub-contractors and their respective servants, agents and sub-contractors.
Any reference in these Conditions to agreement in writing that varies these terms and conditions must be on the Company's stationery and signed by an authorised official of the Company."

Like the bill of lading terms and conditions, these conditions start with a series of definitions of important words, which are self-explanatory. The clause finishes with a provision that any variation of the terms and conditions has to be on the company's stationery and signed by an authorised official of the company.

2. Application

"Any Services provided by the Company, whether gratuitous or otherwise, shall be subject to these Conditions unless:

(A) The Company contracts in writing with the Customer on alternative terms and conditions, including, but not limited to, issuing Bills of Lading, Air or Sea Waybills or any other contract for carriage or any other Service to Goods, or

(B) Any Conditions herein are contrary to any mandatory applicable law relating to the Services undertaken by the Company on behalf of the Customer.

In which case the alternative terms and conditions or mandatory applicable law shall be paramount and prevail to the extent of any inconsistency with these Conditions (but no further). In case of (A) or (B) these Conditions shall continue to operate in respect of any Services to which the alternative terms and conditions or mandatory law do not apply or in respect of any matter upon which they are silent."

This clause provides for when the conditions shall apply by creating a formula as follows:

They apply to all Services provided by the company unless:

(a) that service is covered by a separate specific alternative contract agreed between the company and the customer or the bill of lading contract; or

(b) any of the conditions are contrary to applicable law.

In either of these cases the alternative terms specifically agreed, the bill of lading contract or the mandatory law overrides and is paramount, but only to the extent of such conflict and, if there is no provision in these contracts or law for anything which is covered in these conditions, then the provisions in these conditions apply.

3. Role

"(A) Unless specifically agreed in writing between the Customer and the Company prior to the commencement of the Service, the Company shall be at liberty to provide the Service as a principal or to procure it as an agent, in either case subject to the appropriate Conditions herein.

(B) The agreement of a price for the Service is not of itself an indication of whether the Company is acting as a principal or as an agent."

This clause provides for the carrier to be able to choose whether he acts as principal or agent, unless the customer and the company specifically agree in writing prior to the commencement of the service that the company will act in any particular agreed role. The mere fact that a price is agreed for a service is not an indication that the company is acting as a principal.

4. The Company's General Conditions

"(A) **Performance**: The Company will undertake the tasks necessary to provide the contracted Services to the Customer with a reasonable degree of care and skill and, subject to Clause 8(D), within a reasonable timescale."

An undertaking by the company to exercise a reasonable degree of care and skill and to perform services within a reasonable timescale (subject to the provisions regarding consequential loss and delay in clause 8(D)).

"(B) **Deviation from Customer's Instructions**: Whilst, subject to these Conditions, the Company will take reasonable steps to perform the Customer's Instructions, if at any time the Company, in its sole discretion, considers that there is good reason, in the Customer's interest, to depart from any of the Customer's Instructions, it shall be free to do so without prior notice to the Customer or incurring any additional liability as a result thereof."

In this sub-clause the company takes to itself the right to deviate from the customer's instructions if it considers it to be in the customer's best interest to do so. The sub-clause provides for this to be done without prior notice to the customer in case the customer cannot be contacted or there is not time to do so, but clearly any reasonable carrier would consult the customer beforehand if this were possible.

"(C) **Customer fails to take Delivery**: If Services provided involve the handling and/or carriage of Goods and the Customer, Consignee or Owner fails to take delivery thereof at the time and place when and where the Company is entitled to call upon such Person to take delivery thereof, the Company shall be entitled to store said Goods, at the sole risk of the Customer, whereupon the Company's liability (if any) for the Goods shall wholly cease. The cost of such storage, if paid or payable by the Company or any of its agents or Sub-Contractors, shall forthwith, upon demand, be paid by the Customer to the Company."

This sub-clause provides the company's rights in the event of the customer failing to take delivery of goods in the agreed manner, if the service provided is one involving the handling and/or carriage of goods. As with all contracts of this nature, it has to provide for a worst possible scenario and is not necessarily an indication of the action which the company would pursue initially in such a situation.

"(D) **Disposal of Goods**: If the Services provided involve the handling, storage and/or carriage of Goods and the Customer fails to take delivery thereof in accordance with Clause 4(C), the Company shall be entitled to dispose of the Goods, at the expense of the Customer, by sale or otherwise at the Company's sole discretion, after the Goods have been in the Company's control for 30 days.

The Company shall give 14 days notice in writing to the Customer of any intention to dispose of the Goods.

However, in respect of Goods that, in the sole opinion of the Company, are likely to deteriorate, decay, become worthless or incur charges in excess of their value, or Goods which may cause loss or damage to other Goods, injury to Persons or contravene any applicable laws or regulations, the Company may dispose of such Goods immediately without prior notice to the Customer.

The proceeds of sale, after deducting the cost of sale and any sums whatsoever due by the Customer to the Company for this or any earlier Services, shall be held by the Company to the credit of the Customer. The Customer shall forth-with upon demand remit any shortfall between the proceeds of sale and the sums owed by him to the Company."

This sub-clause follows clause 20(3) in the bill of lading, adapted to cover the different situation envisaged which might bring about its application. It starts by giving the company the right to dispose of the goods at the expense of the customer, however they think fit, if the customer fails to take delivery in accordance with sub-clause 4(C) after the goods have been in the company's control for 30 days. Unlike in the bill of lading, provision is made for the company to give fourteen days' notice in writing to the customer of any intention to dispose of the goods, unless this is impractical because the goods are deteriorating and, in the sole opinion of the company, likely to become worthless or incur charges in excess of their value in that time. There is then added a short note about dangerous goods along the lines of bill of lading clause 19(1).

The sub-clause concludes with a provision requiring the customer to remit any shortfall if the sale realises insufficient funds or for the company to hold any surplus to the credit of the customer.

"(E) **Separate Service to Goods**: Services to Goods may be undertaken in conjunction with goods of other customers or third parties, unless specifically agreed in writing prior to commencement of the Services."

Self-explanatory.

"(F) **Effecting Insurance**: No insurance will be effected, except upon express instructions given in writing by the Customer, and all insurances effected by the Company are subject to the usual exceptions and conditions of the policies of the insurance company or underwriters taking the risk. Unless otherwise agreed in writing, the Company shall not be under any obligation to effect a separate insurance on each consignment but may declare it on any open or general policy held by the Company.
Insofar as the Company agrees to arrange insurance, it acts solely as agent for the Customer to arrange such insurance."

This sub-clause provides as follows:

- insurance is not effected automatically, only upon the express instructions of the customer;
- when effected, insurance is subject to the usual exceptions and conditions of the policy upon which the insurance is placed;
- the company may effect insurance by means of making a declaration on their open cover and need not effect a separate cover;
- the company acts as agent only in effecting insurance.

"(G) **Declarations**: Except in accordance with Instructions in writing previously received and accepted by the Company, the Company shall not be obliged to make any declaration for the purpose of any statute, convention, contract or other requirement as to the nature or value of any Goods, any characteristic of any Goods or Services to any Goods."

The company will not make any declaration to any parties in respect of goods handled, except upon explicit instructions from the customer.

"(H) **Special Delivery Arrangements**: Except by prior written agreement or under the terms of a printed document signed by the Company, any Instructions relating to the delivery or release of Goods in specified circumstances only, such as (but without prejudice to the generality of this Clause) against payment or against surrender of a particular document, are accepted by the Company only as agents for the Customer if third Persons are engaged to effect compliance with the Instructions.
The Company shall not be under any liability in respect of such arrangements unless such arrangements are made in writing.
In any event, the Company's liability in respect of the performance of such Instructions shall not exceed that provided for in these Conditions in respect of loss of or damage to Goods."

This sub-clause covers a situation where the customer requests special delivery arrangements, such as cash on delivery. Such arrangements have to be agreed in writing by the company beforehand and, if the delivery is not effected by the company direct but by a sub-contractor, the company acts as an agent only. Any liability of the company arising from accepting such instructions is subject to the provisions elsewhere in these conditions covering loss of or damage to goods.

5. The Company as a Principal

In the same way as clauses 5 and 6 of the bill of lading were the only clauses that did not refer to both port-to-port and combined transport, so clauses 5 and 6 of the standard trading conditions are the only clauses which do not refer to the company acting both as a principal and as an agent. Clause 5 provides for where the company agrees to act as a principal (in accordance with clause 3) and provides for the standard trading conditions to apply, to the extent that a separate contract under agreed terms has not been signed between the parties. Except where this is the case, the following conditions apply specifically to where the company acts as a principal.

"If, in accordance with Clause 3 hereof, the Company agrees to act as a principal, then it will perform, or in its own name procure the performance of the Services contracted, subject to the provisions of any specific contract for Services which it may issue subject to Clause 2(A), failing which these Conditions in general and this Clause in particular shall apply.

(A) **Liberties**: The Company is not a common carrier and, except to the extent provided in Clause 2 hereof, contracts on the basis of these Conditions alone. The Company reserves to itself the liberties as to the means, routes and procedures to be followed in the handling, storage and carriage of Goods."

In this sub-clause the company provides that it is not a common carrier. This has different implications in different jurisdictions but, in an English jurisdiction, the most important point is that the company can refuse to accept goods for services and is not obliged to accept all goods offered to it. The sub-clause further reinforces that these conditions apply in respect of all services undertaken, unless specific terms are agreed and signed between the parties, and provides for the company to have discretion as to how it carries out the services for which it has contracted with the customer.

"(B) **Period of Responsibility**: If the Company contracts to provide Services as a principal, it accepts liability for loss of or damage to Goods occurring between the time when it takes the Goods into its charge and the time when it is entitled to call upon the Customer, Consignee or Owner to take delivery of the Goods. The Company shall be deemed to have taken the Goods into its charge when the Goods have been received by the Company or have been released or handed over by the Customer, or any Person acting on behalf of the Customer, to any Person acting on behalf of the Company in accordance with any directions of the Company for the performance of the Services. The Company shall be deemed to have delivered the Goods, either when they have been placed at the disposal of the Customer (or its nominee) and notice thereof has been given to the Customer (or its nominee) at the address provided by the Customer, following completion of the contracted Service(s), or following the implementation of Clause 4(B), (C) or (D)."

This sub-clause provides for the company to be responsible for goods, where it has agreed to act as a principal, from the time when it takes the goods into charge to the time when it is entitled to call upon the customer, consignee or owner to take delivery of the goods. It then proceeds to define more closely how to identify these particular times in order to avoid any confusion or misunderstanding.

"(C) **Liabilities**: The Company's liabilities will be as provided in Clause 8 hereof."

This sub-clause is self-explanatory.

6. The Company as an Agent

This sub-clause provides for where the Company acts as an agent.

"If, in accordance with Clause 3 hereof, the Company acts as an agent then, without prejudice to the general applicability of these Conditions, its responsibilities shall be as follows:

(A) **Agency**: The Company shall be entitled and the Customer hereby expressly authorises the Company, except in so far as has been otherwise specifically agreed between the Company and the Customer, to enter into contracts with third parties on behalf of the Customer for the Service required. (Third parties for the purpose of this Clause, includes the Company's parent, subsidiary and/or associated companies).

When acting as an agent the Company does not make, or purport to make, any contract with the Customer for Services, but acts solely on behalf of the Customer in establishing contracts with third party contractors for the Services required, so that a direct contractual relationship is established between the Customer and such third party contractor."

This sub-clause provides for the customer to authorise the company, when acting as an agent, to enter into contracts on behalf of the customer with third parties for the services required. ("Third parties" is defined to include any associated companies etc. of the company, in case the company is a conglomerate.) The sub-clause finishes with a provision which outlines the duties and responsibilities of an agent, which would have applied even in the absence of such a clause as this is the generally accepted definition of what an agent does.

"(B) **Contracting Terms with Third Parties**: If there is a choice of prices according to the extent or degree of the liability assumed by third party contractors, no declaration of value will be made, except under prior Instructions received in writing and accepted by the Company; nor shall the Company be under any liability to the Customer by reason of having entered into any contract on behalf of the Customer, whereby the extent or degree of the liability assumed by a third party contractor is in any respect excluded or limited, unless such contract is entered into contrary to prior written Instructions given by the Customer and accepted in writing by the Company."

This sub-clause gives the company the right to enter into contracts with third parties on behalf of the customer upon whichever terms the company considers appropriate, unless the customer gives prior specific written instructions to the contrary. This means that, if there is a choice of rates with the cheaper rate offering a lower level of recourse, the company may opt for the cheaper rate in the absence of specific instructions to the contrary.

"(C) **Evidence of Contract with Third Party Contractor**: The Company shall, on demand by the Customer, provide evidence of any contract entered into as agent for the Customer. Insofar as the Company may be in default of this obligation, it shall be deemed to have contracted with the Customer as a principal for the performance of the Customer's Instructions."

If the company wishes to be able to claim to act as an agent it must, upon demand by the customer, provide evidence of any contract entered into on behalf of the customer. If it fails to do so then it is deemed to act as a principal.

7. Customer's Warranties and Indemnities

This clause contains important warranties and indemnities to protect the company in respect of the services which it renders on behalf of the customer. Many of the warranties and indemnities found here are very similar to those found in the bill of lading.

"(A) **Goods**: The Customer warrants that, unless the Customer provides prior written notification to and obtains written agreement from the Company, the Customer will not tender for Services any Goods which are:

(a) **Hazardous/Obnoxious Goods**:

(i) classified by the IMO Dangerous Goods Code as being hazardous,

(ii) nevertheless of a dangerous, damaging or obnoxious nature, so as to be liable to cause damage to any other goods or to be a risk to property, life or health, or

(iii) likely to harbour or encourage vermin or other pests.

(b) **High Value Goods**: of a valuable nature (which description shall include but not be restricted to bullion, coin, precious stones, jewellery, works of art, antiques and valuables of all kinds).

(c) **Perishables**: perishable and require temperature controlled conditions or have a short shelf-life.

(d) **Packing/Marking**: not properly and sufficiently prepared, packed, stowed, labelled and/or marked for the Services for which they are being tendered, unless those Services include said tasks.

If the Goods are tendered in/on containers, trailers, flats, railway wagons, tanks, igloos, or any other unit load device specifically constructed for the carriage of goods by land, sea or air, (each hereafter individually referred to as 'transport unit') then, unless the Company has accepted Instructions as principal to load the transport unit, the Customer also warrants that:

(i) the Goods have been properly and competently loaded into/onto the transport unit;

(ii) the Goods are suitable for carriage in/on the transport unit being utilised, and

(iii) the transport unit is in a suitable condition to carry the Goods loaded therein/on,

and if nevertheless Goods which breach any of the warranties in this Clause 7(A) are tendered for Services, the Customer shall indemnify the Company, its servants, agents and Sub-Contractors against all penalties, claims, damages, costs and expenses of whatsoever nature and howsoever arising in connection with such Goods.

Unless prior arrangements have been made and prior written acceptance obtained from the Company, no liability whatsoever, howsoever arising, will be accepted by the Company in connection with such Goods and the Company, their servants, agents and/or Sub-Contractors may deal with such Goods as they, in their sole discretion, consider appropriate."

In this sub-clause the customer makes warranties in respect of any goods tendered for services. He warrants that, unless he provides prior written notification and obtains the written agreement of the company, he will not tender the following goods for service:

(a) hazardous/obnoxious goods;
(b) high-value goods;
(c) perishables;
(d) improperly packed or marked goods.

The customer also warrants that any goods tendered already packed in some way have been properly packed in a transport unit suitable for their carriage. Failure to comply with any of the requirements of this sub-clause leads to the customer having to indemnify the company, its servants, agents and sub-contractors against all consequences thereof. Also, if the customer fails to make prior arrangements with and obtain prior written agreement from the company before tendering such goods, the company reserves the right to deal with such goods as it considers appropriate, in its sole discretion.

"(B) **Details of Goods**: The Customer warrants that the description and particulars of the Goods furnished by or on behalf of the Customer or Owner are complete and accurate and include all data necessary to accomplish the required Services safely and effectively."

This sub-clause is self-explanatory.

"(C) **Authority**: The Customer warrants that he is either the Owner or has the authority of the Owner to contract with the Company for the Services."

This sub-clause is equivalent to bill of lading clause 3. As the company has no way of knowing whether or not the customer is entitled to contract with the company for the services, the company requires a warranty from the customer that he is entitled to do so.

"(D) **Circular Indemnity**: The Customer warrants that no claim or allegation shall be made by any Person against any parent, subsidiary or associate company, director, servant, agent, Sub-Contractor or employee of the Company (hereinafter referred to as 'such Persons') which imposes or attempts to impose upon any of such Persons any liability whatsoever in connection with any Services and/or Goods (whether or not arising out of negligence on the part of such Persons) unless the Company is acting as an agent only in accordance with Clause 6 and such Persons are independent contractors providing a Service to the Customer through the agency of the Company, in which case the Customer may proceed against such Persons under the terms of the contract procured on its behalf from such Persons by the Company acting as an agent only. Excepting for such instance, if any such claim or allegation should nevertheless be made, the Customer will indemnify the Company and such Persons against all consequences thereof.

Without prejudice to the foregoing, unless trading directly with the Customer under its own conditions through the agency of the Company, every such Person shall have the benefit of every right, defence, limitation and liberty of whatsoever nature herein contained or otherwise available to the Company as if such provisions were expressly for his benefit; and in entering into this contract the Company, to the extent of these provisions, does so not only on its own behalf but also as agent and trustee for such Persons.

The Customer further warrants that no claim or allegation in respect of any Services or Goods shall be made against the Company by any Person other than in accordance with these Conditions which imposes or attempts to impose upon the Company any liability whatsoever, whether or not arising out of negligence on the part of the Company and, if any such claim or allegation should nevertheless be made, to indemnify the Company against all consequences thereof."

This sub-clause is the equivalent of clause 4 of the bill of lading and is the link in the chain of indemnity in the standard trading conditions. However, as in these conditions the company may be acting as an agent, it is necessary to exclude this situation from the circular indemnity in order to allow the customer to proceed against any third party with whom the company may have contracted on behalf of the customer whilst acting as agent only. Accordingly the clause provides for the circular indemnity to operate only when the company acts as a principal.

"(E) **Acting on Customer's Instructions**: The Customer shall indemnify the Company against all liability, loss, damage, cost and expense whatsoever and howsoever arising as a result of the Company acting in accordance with the Customer's Instructions or arising from any breach by the Customer of any warranty contained in these Conditions or from the negligence of the Customer."

This is an indemnity to the company against the consequences of acting in accordance with the customer's instructions, arising from any breach by the customer of any warranty in these conditions or from the negligence of the customer.

"(F) **Duty, Fines, etc**: The Customer shall be liable for and shall indemnify the Company in respect of all duties, taxes, imposts, levies, deposits and outlays of whatsoever nature levied by any authority in relation to the Goods and for all payments, fines, costs expenses, loss or damage whatsoever and howsoever incurred or sustained by the Company in connection therewith."

This sub-clause is self-explanatory.

"(G) **General Average**: The Customer shall indemnify the Company in respect of any claims of a General Average or Salvage nature which may be made on it and shall provide such security as may be required by the Company in this connection on demand."

This sub-clause provides for the customer to be responsible for any general average or salvage costs incurred by goods during the period that the company is providing services on them.

"(H) **Information Indemnity**: Advice and information, in whatever form it may be given, is provided by the Company for the Customer only and the Customer shall indemnify the Company against any liability, claim, loss, damage, cost or expense arising out of any other Persons relying upon such advice or information. Except under special arrangements previously made in writing, advice and information which is not related to Instructions accepted by the Company is provided gratuitously and without liability."

This sub-clause refers to information or advice which the company may give to the customer relating to some matter in connection with instructions received by the company from the customer. It provides that such advice is for the customer's use only and, if the customer passes it on to another party who suffers any loss etc. as a result of relying upon it, the customer indemnifies the company if that other party brings any action against the company based on that advice.

If the company gives advice to the customer on matters not related to instructions to the company by the customer, such advice is provided gratuitously and without liability.

"(I) **EDI Transmission**: In the event of Instructions data being transmitted via electronic communication, the Customer accepts that the sender is responsible for the quality of such Instructions or data."

This sub-clause is self-explanatory.

8. Liability

"(A) **Time Bar**: Any claim by the Customer against the Company in respect of any Service must be made in writing without delay. In the event of delay in presentation of a claim causing prejudice to the Company's ability to investigate said claim or reserve its rights against its Sub-Contractors, the Company shall be relieved of any liability in respect of such claim.

In any event, the Company shall be discharged of all liability whatsoever and howsoever arising in respect of any Service provided for the Customer unless suit be brought and written notice thereof given to the Company within nine months from the date of any event or occurrence alleged to give rise to a cause of action against the Company."

This sub-clause provides the time bar in respect of any claims by the customer against the company. It provides for notice of any claim to be made in writing without delay and for a claim to be time barred if delay prejudices the company's ability to investigate the claim or reserve its rights against the contractor whom it engaged to undertake the service required. In any event any claim becomes time barred nine months after the date of any event or occurrence alleged to have given rise to a course of action against the company, unless the customer commences suit beforehand.

"(B) **Exclusions**: Whether the Company acts as agent or principal it shall be relieved of liability for loss, damage or expense if and to the extent that same was caused by:

(a) the act or omission of the Customer, or Person other than the Company acting on behalf of the Customer, Owner or of the Person from whom the Company took the Goods in charge;
(b) insufficiency of the packing and/or marks and/or labels and/or numbers unless the Company had undertaken to carry out the packing, application of marks or labelling or numbering of the Goods;
(c) handling, loading, stowage or unloading of the Goods by the Customer, Owner or any Person other than the Company acting on behalf of the Customer;
(d) inherent vice of the Goods;
(e) strike, lock out, stoppage or restraint of labour;
(f) a nuclear incident;
(g) any cause or event which the Company was unable to avoid and the consequences whereof the Company was unable to prevent by the exercise of reasonable diligence;
(h) any act or omission of the Company the consequences of which it could not reasonably have foreseen;
(i) compliance with the instructions of any Person entitled to give them.

The burden of proving that the loss or damage was due to one or more of the above causes or events shall rest upon the Company."

The exclusions listed in this sub-clause are comparable with those listed in clause 6(1) to the bill of lading and the comments made in Chapter 6 are equally applicable here.

"(C) **Limits of Liability**: Subject to Clause 2, unless the Company agrees in writing to accept alternative levels of liability (in which case such limits as agreed shall be substituted for those provided in this Clause), the Company's liability (if any and whether acting as principal or agent), howsoever arising, and notwithstanding that the cause of loss, damage or expense is unexplained, shall not exceed:

(a) in the case of claims for loss or damage to Goods:
  (i) the value of any Goods lost or damaged, or
  (ii) a sum at the rate of two Special Drawing Rights as defined by the International Monetary Fund, (hereinafter referred to as SDRs), per kilo of gross weight of any Goods lost or damaged,
 whichever shall be the lesser.

(b) in the case of all other claims:
  (i) the value of the Goods the subject of the relevant Service; or
  (ii) a sum at the rate of two SDRs per kilo of the gross weight of the Goods the subject of the said Service, or
  (iii) 75,000 SDRs in respect of any one Service,
 whichever shall be the lesser.

For the purposes of this Clause the value of the Goods shall be their value at the place and time they are delivered to the Consignee in accordance with the relevant Service or should have been so delivered. The exchange from SDRs to settlement currency shall be calculated at the rate applicable on the date when the claim is paid.

Details of the Company's additional charges for accepting increased liability will be provided on request."

Unless the customer agrees an alternative limit with the company in writing, the limits of liability as provided in this clause shall apply, whether the company be acting as a principal or as an agent. These limits will apply whether the cause of the loss etc. be obvious or unexplained.

In the event of claims for loss or damage to goods, liability is limited to the lesser of the value of the goods lost or damaged or 2 SDRs (special drawing rights) per kilo of the gross weight of any goods lost or damaged. In the case of all other claims limitation is the same but with the added maximum limit of any one service of 75,000 SDRs.

The value of goods for the purposes of claim is their value at the place and time when they are delivered or should have been delivered. The exchange from the currency of the claim into SDRs is calculated at the rate applicable on the date when the claim is paid.

The sub-clause finishes with an offer of details of the company's additional charges for accepting increased liability to be available on request to the company from the customer. The purpose of this provision is to make it clear that the customer has an alternative in order to protect these conditions against any claim of breach of the Unfair Contract Terms Act.

"(D) **Consequential Loss/Delay**: Except by prior written agreement, the Company shall not in any circumstances, whatsoever or howsoever arising, be liable for indirect or consequential loss, such as (but not limited to) loss of profits, loss of market or the consequences of delay or deviation howsoever caused.

However, if pursuant to Clause 4(B) the Company accepts any liability for delay, liability shall in no circumstances exceed a sum equal to twice the amount of the Company's charges in respect of the relevant Service.

The defences and limits of liability provided for in these Conditions shall apply in any action against the Company whatsoever, howsoever arising, whether the action be founded in contract, tort or otherwise."

This sub-clause provides that, except by prior written agreement, the company accepts no liability for consequential loss or delay. However, if the company does agree to accept liability for delay, such liability is limited to a sum equal to twice the amount of the company's charges in respect of the relevant service.

Postscript: The clause ends with a provision that the conditions apply in any action against the company, whether such action be founded in contract, tort or otherwise.

9. Payments, etc.

"(A) **Payment of the Company's Invoices**: The Customer shall pay to the Company in cash or as otherwise agreed all sums immediately when due, without reduction or deferment on account of any claim, counterclaim or set off. If any sum due is still unpaid 30 days after the date of the invoice, the Company shall be entitled to add interest at 2% above the minimum lending rate of the local national bank for any period in excess thereof."

This sub-clause provides for the company's invoices to be paid in cash (or as otherwise agreed) immediately when due. Claim, counterclaim or set-off is no excuse for delayed payment. Interest at two per cent above the minimum lending rate of the local national bank must be paid on any sums outstanding 30 days after the date of the invoice.

"(B) **Collecting Charges for Customer**: Despite the acceptance by the Company of Instructions to collect freight, duties, charges or other expenses from the Consignee or any other Person, the Customer shall remain responsible for such freight, duties, charges or expenses on receipt of evidence of proper demand and in the absence of evidence of payment (for whatever reason) by such Consignee or other Person when due."

Even though the company may accept instructions from the customer to collect freight, duties, charges or other expenses from the consignee, the customer remains responsible for such costs and must pay them on demand, unless he can produce evidence of payment by the consignee or some other person.

"(C) **Lien**:

(a) Subject to sub-clause (b), the Company shall have a general lien on all Goods and documents relating to Goods in its possession, custody or control for all sums due at any time from the Customer or Owner, in respect of Services to the Goods under lien or of any earlier Services on other Goods, and shall be entitled to sell or dispose of such Goods or documents as agent for and at the expense of the Customer and apply the proceeds in or towards the payment of such sums. Upon accounting to the Customer for any balance remaining after payment of any sum due to the Company and the costs of sale or disposal, the Company shall be discharged of any liability whatsoever in respect of the Goods or documents.

(b) If the Goods, in the sole opinion of the Company, are liable to perish or deteriorate, the Company's right to sell or dispose of the Goods shall arise immediately upon any sum becoming due to the Company, subject only to the Company taking reasonable steps to bring to the Customer's attention its intention of selling or disposing of the Goods before doing so."

Sub-clause (a) provides for the company to have a general lien on all goods and documents. That is to say a lien on any goods and documents held at that time, not only for any charges on those goods, but also for any unsatisfied charges on earlier consignments. Applying the lien the company may sell or dispose of the goods and documents as agent for and at the expense of the customer in order to realise funds towards the payment of the customer's outstanding liability to the company. After the sale the company will account to the customer for any balance remaining (or debit still outstanding) and thereafter the liability of the company in respect of those goods or documents shall be discharged.

In sub-clause (b) it is particularly provided that, if the company considers the goods are liable to perish or deteriorate, the lien arises immediately upon any sum becoming due and the right to sale in such circumstances is subject only to the company taking reasonable steps to inform the customer of its intention to sell or dispose of the goods before doing so.

"(D) **Brokerages, Commissions, etc**: The Company shall be entitled to be paid and retain all brokerages, commissions, allowances and other remunerations customarily retained by or paid to freight forwarders."

This sub-clause provides for the company to retain any brokerages or commissions earned in respect of services procured from third parties by the company, acting either as agent or principal, on behalf of the customer.

10. Law and Jurisdiction

"(A) **Law**: The Services undertaken pursuant to and the interpretation of these Conditions shall be governed by English Law.

(B) **Jurisdiction**: Any claim or dispute arising under these Conditions shall be referred to the High Court of Justice in London, to the exclusion of the jurisdictions of the courts or any other places, unless the Company appeals to the jurisdiction of any other place and voluntarily submits thereto.

(C) **Arbitration**: Nothing herein shall prevent the parties to any dispute under these Conditions agreeing to refer it to arbitration on mutually acceptable terms."

This clause provides for English law and jurisdiction and allows parties to agree to arbitration. According to where the services are provided, this can be varied according to the wishes of the company. (The provisions of this clause are very similar to clause 24 of the bill of lading.)

CHAPTER 8

INDEMNITIES

In a liability conscious world indemnities inevitably proliferate and are frequently regarded (often incorrectly) as the answer to every problem. Before offering an indemnity as a solution to a problem an indemnifyor should consider carefully the wording of the indemnity and the exposure to liability that this precipitates. Equally the indemnifyee should bear in mind that an indemnity is only as good as the person giving it and consider the difficulties that he is likely to have enforcing it if need arises. Overall consideration needs to be given to how the law looks at such matters, particularly regarding enforcement. It has been explained in earlier chapters that the English court will only enforce indemnities in the absence of negligence, unless the indemnity makes it quite clear that it is to operate even in the event of negligence. It also needs to be borne in mind that the law regards indemnities for the issue of clean bills of lading for discrepant goods as being tantamount to conspiracy between the carrier and the shipper to defraud a consignee who is entitled to rely upon the description of the goods shown on the bill of lading as being accurate at the time of the commencement of carriage. Accordingly the law would not enforce such indemnities as being illegal contracts and, if the shipper chose not to honour this indemnity, there would be nothing that the carrier could do about it.

Nevertheless indemnities of various types are frequently encountered in shipping and the combined transport industry. There are indemnities for allowing officers and crew to take their wives to sea, which indemnities are as much to bring vital instructions to the attention of the parties concerned as to act as an indemnity in respect of all medical expenses which the wife may incur and against which the wife is required to take out appropriate insurance. Similar indemnities are usually required from livestock shippers for allowing a handler to travel with any livestock. This indemnity is usually taken from the employer rather than the employee as, in English law, it may not always be enforceable against the employee under the Unfair Contract Terms Act because of the lack of parity in bargaining stature between the livestock handler and the carrier. However, the most frequently encountered indemnity is that for delivery of goods without production of bill of lading if the goods arrive ahead of the documents or the documents become lost. In such cases an indemnity in the form displayed on page 311 is recommended.

DELIVERY WITHOUT PRODUCTION OF BILL OF LADING

One of the first things to note in relation to this situation is that, in most circumstances, P & I cover does not operate to protect the carrier in respect of any claim arising out of delivery of goods without production of bill of lading. Clubs will advise on the wording of indemnities but this is one area where there is no cover. This is because it is a practice open to abuse and is one where there is not mutuality between club members, as some members would adopt this practice more frequently than others. Accordingly the only protection which a carrier who agrees to deliver goods without production of bill of lading has, is the indemnity which he takes in return for so doing. He is therefore usually reluctant to accept a personal indemnity from the merchant and requires the indemnity to be countersigned by a reputable bank to guarantee performance.

Let us examine the terms of a typical indemnity of this type (which is shown opposite) and see what provision it contains and why.

(1) This is the main indemnity clause in which the merchant indemnifies the carrier etc. against all consequences of complying with his request to deliver the goods to him without surrender of the appropriate documentation.

(2) Disputes involving delivery of goods without production of a bill of lading to the wrong party often drag on for a considerable period of time. Therefore the carrier makes provision for being put in funds from time to time if complying with the Merchant's request involves him in a court action with a third party.

(3) If a third party takes action against the carrier for wrongful delivery, he may reinforce this action and guarantee his recovery in the event of a successful court action by arresting one of the carrier's vessels or placing a Mareva injunction on some other asset. This clause provides for the carrier to take whatever action is necessary to remove the arrest or threat of arrest at the expense of the merchant. It is carefully worded to be an indemnity rather than a bail bond, under which the merchant would have to put up the necessary security to secure freedom from arrest, in order that the bank will countersign it, as most banks will not countersign bail bonds.

(4) Sometimes the merchant may approach the carrier to request a delivery order for goods that are still in transit without production of a bill of lading. In this case it is possible that additional charges may accrue and it is even possible for general average to occur prior to delivery. This clause covers this situation but, if the voyage is completed and there is no further possibility of additional charges or general average, the clause may be amended accordingly.

(5) This clause provides for the merchant to surrender an original bill of lading to the carrier as soon as it comes into his care. The merchant will probably do this very promptly in any event as he will wish to recover the bank supported indemnity from the carrier so that he can surrender it to his bank

INDEMNITY AND UNDERTAKING DELIVERY WITHOUT PRODUCTION OF BILL OF LADING

To: (name of carrier)

In consideration of your releasing for delivery to us or to our order the undermentioned goods of which we claim to be the rightful owners, without production of the relevant Bill(s) of Lading (not as yet in our possession) we hereby agree as follows:

1. Indemnify you, your principals, servants and agents (as the case may be) and to hold all of you harmless in respect of any liability, loss, damage or expense of whatsoever nature and howsoever arising which you may sustain by reason of delivering the goods in accordance with our request and to reimburse you forthwith on demand for all payments which you make or are called upon to make in respect of thereof.

2. In the event of any proceedings being commenced against you, your principal or any of your servants or agents in connection with the delivery of the goods as aforesaid, to provide you or them from time to time with sufficient funds to defend the same.

3. That if any vessel or other asset owned by you, your principals, servants or agents (as the case may be) or any person is arrested or threatened with arrest in connection with the delivery of the goods the subject of this Indemnity, you may take such steps as you in your sole discretion consider necessary, in the light of the prevailing local circumstances, to remove or avoid such arrest or remove or avoid the threat thereof, including (but not restricted to) immediate settlement of any claim in connection with the said goods, or the provision of security therefore and all the costs of such actions shall be for our account. At your sole discretion this action may be taken without prior consultation with us and we agree that our prior consent shall not be a condition precedent to indemnity.

4. Upon demand to pay any freight and / or General Average and / or charges due on goods aforesaid (it being expressly agreed and understood that all liens shall subsist and be unaffected by the same terms hereof).

5. As soon as any original Bills of Lading for the above goods shall have arrived and / or come into our possession, to produce and deliver the same to you properly endorsed whereupon our liability hereunder shall cease in respect of all future claims or expenses, but shall remain in force in respect of any already incurred by you even if not already paid.

6. The liability of each and every person under this Indemnity shall be joint and several and shall not be conditional upon your proceeding first against any person, whether or not such person is party to or liable under this Indemnity.

7. This Indemnity shall be construed in accordance with English law and each and every person liable under this Indemnity shall at your request submit to the jurisdiction of the High Court of Justice of England.

8. This Indemnity shall be unlimited in time and amount so far as we are concerned but shall be limited to two hundred percent (200%) of CIF value of the goods and three (3) years so far as the guarantee of the Bank is concerned, unless you give notice to the Bank within the three year period that a claim has been made for which indemnity is sought, in which case the guarantee of the Bank shall continue until said claim is resolved, plus one month.

CONSIGNEE	VESSEL & VOY. NO	DELIVERY ORDER TO BE ISSUED IN THE NAME OF:

BILL(S) OF LADING No(s):	QUANTITY AND DESCRIPTION OF GOODS	CONTAINER NO(S):

NOTE
INDEMNITIES LIMITING LIABILITY, INCORPORATING AN EXPIRY DATE OR BEARING ANY QUALIFYING REMARKS WHATSOEVER (EXCEPT AS PROVIDED HEREIN IN CLAUSE 8) CANNOT BE ACCEPTED.

For and on behalf of (Company) ....

Signed .... Date ....

We the Bank named opposite join the above indemnity and guarantee its performance, subject to the provisions of Clause 8 above

For and on behalf of (Bank) ....

....

Signed .... Date ....

Figure 9: Indemnity and undertaking delivery without production of bill of lading

and stop the accrual of interest which he is paying to secure the bank's countersignature to the indemnity. The Carrier needs to be wary of such occasions as delivering the goods without production of a bill of lading may have caused some third party to incur costs of which the carrier is unaware, so that there may be a claim forthcoming from a third party unbeknown to the carrier. He may also have incurred expenses, which he has not yet paid, that he will wish to recover from the merchant. For this reason he would be well advised to ask for a personal indemnity from the merchant (which the merchant should be quite happy to give if there is no hidden reason of which he is aware for it to need to be enforced) in return for the bank supported indemnity, so that the carrier still has an indemnity which he can enforce if the need arises. This is the thinking behind the last phrase in this clause.

(6) The point of this clause is to allow the carrier to proceed directly against the bank in the first instance without first having to show that he has proceeded without success against the merchant. If, unbeknown to the carrier, the merchant is engaged in questionable activities, he is frequently very difficult to locate and, even if located, often less than co-operative. Accordingly, the carrier prefers to proceed against the bank and leave the bank to sort out the problem with its customer.

(7) This draft indemnity applies English law and calls for the jurisdiction of the High Court of Justice of England. In some areas banks are averse to signing indemnities with foreign jurisdiction clauses and carriers may encounter resistance and have to compromise on the law and jurisdiction clause in indemnities. The extent to which they are willing to compromise will depend upon their view of the alternative law and court required by the bank. In this context it must be borne in mind that it is the carrier who is being asked to take the risk by delivering other than in accordance with normal commercial practice and he should therefore be allowed to require an indemnity in the terms of his choice.

(8) Once upon a time banks were prepared to countersign indemnities unlimited in both time and amount but, with increasing regulation by central banks which require the banks to deposit funds with them based on their dependent liabilities, there is increasing pressure on banks to quantify their outstanding liabilities. For this reason banks are increasingly resistant to signing unlimited indemnities. As a claim based on delivery of goods without production of a bill of lading will frequently include other expenses in addition to the value of the goods, it is not possible to agree to limit the indemnity to the value of the goods. Two hundred per cent of the value of the goods is the arbitrary figure commonly used as a reasonable maximum to apply. So far as time bars are concerned, with the possibility of the Hamburg Rules with a two year time bar being involved, this is set at three years in case of a last minute claim being made at the end of two years to give the carrier time to investigate and refer it on the indemnity.

This clause provides for the indemnity from the merchant to be unlimited in time and amount but limits the bank's countersignature to 200 per cent and three years in order to produce a finite guarantee, which banks find more acceptable for reasons outlined above.

Carriers would be well advised always to be on their guard whenever requested to deliver goods without production of a bill of lading, whether or not against a letter of indemnity as, amongst the genuine requests, there will be requests based on mischievous action. In most cases those "up to no good" will attempt to secure delivery without production of a bill of lading without an indemnity or against a personal indemnity pleading that the bill is coming tomorrow and will be surrendered then and the merchant wishes to avoid incurring the charges of the bank to secure the bank's countersignature. Instances have occurred (more than one!) of naive shipping clerks being taken in by glib merchants with this type of request, when the real reason behind the request is that the merchant has an outstanding dispute with his supplier over an earlier consignment (poor quality etc.) and thinks that, if he can get hold of the next consignment without paying for it (i.e. taking up the bill of lading at the bank), he has the upper hand in any dealings with his supplier over his claim on an earlier consignment. On such occasions a suspicious mind and an insistence on checking back with the shipper that he has been paid, before delivery is effected against a bank supported indemnity, is essential if grief is wished to be avoided.

CHAPTER 9

GENERAL AVERAGE AND SALVAGE (IN CONTAINER AND CONSORTIUM OPERATIONS)

General average is an unwritten international maritime law universally recognised and applied. It has been practised since time immemorial and is founded on the principle that vessel and cargo are parties to the same venture and share exposure to the same perils, which may require sacrifice or the incurring of extraordinary expense on the part of one party for the benefit of the whole venture.

General average may be either a sacrifice or an expenditure but in order to qualify as such it must satisfy ALL of the following criteria. It must be:

- extraordinary in nature (normal expense or damage is excluded);
- voluntarily;
- deliberately (accidental damage is excluded: that is particular average);
- and reasonably incurred;
- in time of general peril (the whole venture (i.e. vessel and cargo) must be threatened);
- for the common safety (expense aimed at saving only part of the venture is excluded);
- of a maritime venture (GA is peculiar to maritime ventures only);
- the danger must be real (imagined danger does not qualify);
- and imminent (expenses foreseeing and avoiding danger do not qualify (e.g. deviation to avoid a storm) as this is part of the carrier's normal expense/responsibility);
- and must succeed in saving some part of the venture (otherwise nothing is left to contribute!).

Each of these requirements is essential and, if one is missing, the sacrifice or expense involved is not allowable in general average. General average is then the process by which those parties to the venture, whose interests have been sacrificed or who have incurred extra expense, are proportionately recompensed by the contribution of those whose interests have been saved. Typical examples of general average sacrifice are jettison to lighten a grounded vessel in order to float off and water damage to cargo from attempts to extinguish a fire. General average expenses can be port of refuge expenses if a vessel puts into an unscheduled port for essential repairs to complete the voyage.

When a general average occurs, a specialist firm of average adjusters is appointed to assist with the initial problems and calculate the contributions due from each interest. Vessel, containers, goods and bunkers will contribute according to their salved value. The first problem is to obtain security for general average contribution from cargo interests, because the adjustment may take many months or even years before it is issued. This is achieved by obtaining the merchant's signature on an average bond (the promise to pay), which is backed up by either an average guarantee signed by a reputable insurer, or by a cash deposit based on the contributing value estimated by the average adjuster. Although the principle of general average is a generally accepted unwritten law, the practical application of it and the preparation of the adjustment could give rise to disagreement in the absence of written guidelines. In modern times the most usually applied rules are those provided by the Comité Maritime International (CMI), who publish rules governing general average known as the York-Antwerp Rules. Not being law, it is necessary to incorporate these rules into contracts of carriage by specific mention therein (*see* Chapter 6 the bill of lading clause 22). The rules are periodically reviewed and revised in the light of changing requirements and circumstances. The presently applicable version of the rules is the 1994 version.

In addition (or alternatively) to a vessel in distress incurring extraordinary expense or making deliberate sacrifice in the interest of the whole venture and declaring general average, it may occur that a vessel in distress receives assistance from a third party to save the adventure. Another vessel may tow a powerless vessel to a place of safety, assist in extinguishing a fire or render some other service valuable to the vessel and its cargo. In such circumstances that other vessel is entitled to claim salvage from the vessel and its cargo once it has completed the valuable service and redelivered vessel and cargo to its owners. It is entitled to exercise a lien on the vessel and cargo for its salvage reward. Salvage is usually (but not always) undertaken subject to Lloyd's Open Form of Salvage Agreement, which is a no cure–no pay arrangement under which the salvor only gets paid if he succeeds in saving the vessel and its cargo (or some part thereof). If Lloyd's Open Form is used, security for salvage (often in addition to separate security for general average) must be lodged with Lloyd's in London by a London-based acceptable security (usually a cargo insurer or his London agent) to secure the release of the cargo, unless the salvor agrees otherwise. If more than one salvor is involved, separate security for each salvor may be necessary.

Salvage is not necessarily rendered only by other vessels. For example, containers floating off a stricken vessel which come ashore may be salved by land-based salvors using land-based gear. In such a case the same principles apply and the salvors have a lien on whatever they have salved for an appropriate reward, but it is unlikely that a Lloyd's Open Form of Salvage Agreement will be used in such circumstances.

Salvage is usually assessed by an arbitrator in the absence of prior agreement between the parties and adjusted by an average adjuster in the same way as general average and very often in conjunction with a general average declared by the owners of the vessel.

The adjustment of general average and salvage is a complicated enough process at the best of times but when this occurs on a large deep-sea containership with hundreds, if not thousands of contracts of carriage involving a large number of interests, the matter becomes even more complicated. Where this happens in a consortium operation involving several principal carriers/slot charterers as contracting carriers in addition to the owner/operator of the vessel, this complication is exacerbated even further. General average and salvage inevitably occur at the time of a casualty when all departments within the respective carriers will be alerted and busy. The degree of involvement will vary according to whether or not the contracting carrier is the vessel operator or merely a slot charterer and the following notes are designed to give guidance as to the points that need to be addressed, according to the situation of the contracting carrier in any given circumstance.

With general average you are almost invariably dealing with the owner of the vessel via his average adjuster, who will exercise a lien on cargo, containers and bunkers (if the vessel is a chartered vessel and the bunkers belong to the charterers) for security in the form of a general average bond signed by the owners of the cargoes/containers and a general average guarantee signed by an acceptable insurer.

With salvage, if effected under Lloyd's Open Form, security must be put up in London by someone in London to the satisfaction of Lloyd's, unless salvors agree otherwise. Sometimes, particularly if the average adjuster is not London based, in order to simplify things and adjust the salvage with the inevitable general average that is almost always involved when a salvage occurs, the salvor agrees to security being put up to the average adjuster, wherever he is located, and does not insist on the London security to follow the almost inevitable London arbitration to decide the level of the salvage award (if not agreed between the parties). Sometimes, instead of salvage being effected under Lloyd's Open Form, a fixed price contract is agreed between the owner of the vessel and the salvor, in which case the owner has to pay the salvor in the first instance and then put the cost of the salvage into the adjustment as a general average expense.

TYPES OF GENERAL AVERAGE/SALVAGE SITUATIONS

In decreasing order of involvement by the carrier, the following are the types of general average and/or salvage situations that may be encountered:

(a) own vessels (operating in joint services);
(b) own vessels (on charter to third parties);
(c) chartered vessels (operating as the carrier's tonnage in a joint service);

(d) chartered vessels (operated by the carrier as a dedicated feeder with the cargo being 100 per cent carrier's own cargo);
(e) joint service partner's owned vessels;
(f) joint service partner's chartered vessels;
(g) common user feeders (and other vessels with just a few of the carrier's containers aboard).

Action required will differ according to which of the above categories the casualty falls into.

PARTIES LIKELY TO BE INVOLVED

Fleet manager: safety of the vessel;
Trade manager: policy;
Marketing/Commercial: liaise all with regional/overseas offices and customers;
Local operations: getting containers removed from lien for oncarriage;
TT club: put up security for containers;
P & I club: general assistance in providing temporary cargo security and the appointment of lawyers and surveyors;
Average adjuster: provide assistance in preparing initial estimates of costs and advice generally before preparing adjustment and collecting contributions;
Lawyer: if necessary to represent carrier's interests in any dispute regarding general average contribution and to represent carrier in any salvage arbitration;
Surveyor: to inspect vessel and also act as a GA surveyor for the general interest to inspect any damage to cargo and/or containers.

The roles of the above will vary according to the level of expertise in the carrier's organisation. If the carrier has personnel competent to control activities during the general average and salvage process, particularly the legal aspects thereof, then the carrier will act as the focal point to control and co-ordinate the activities of the above parties. If, however, the carrier does not have adequate expertise, the roles of the P & I club and lawyer in particular will extend to cover those areas which the carrier is not competent to cover.

INFORMATION LIKELY TO BE REQUIRED AS SOON AS POSSIBLE

- manifests of cargo on board at the time of the casualty;
- tally of containers on board by size and type;
- loading/discharging ports for cargo on board;
- details of vessel's itinerary;
- details of casualty—progress reports, particularly regarding estimates for revised itinerary after repairs;
- estimated salved value of vessel;

- estimated total cost of GA expenses and estimate of salvage award;
- estimated value of cargo, containers and bunkers on board.

The above information is the type of data that the average adjusters will be looking to accumulate to assist in their calculations as to the likely size of deposit required in the absence of an average guarantee. The carrier will also be looking to the average adjuster for an estimate of total costs involved in order to make the decision whether or not to declare general average. It may be that the size of the general average is within his GA waiver clause in his Hull and Machinery policy. If the decision as to whether or not to declare general average is borderline, the carrier may wish to discuss the matter with his consortium partners in order to decide whether or not they may be prepared to contribute in a truncated adjustment in respect of their cargo and containers to avoid the need to approach customers.

ROLE OF CARRIER'S INSURANCE AND CLAIMS DEPARTMENT

Assuming that the carrier's insurance and claims department has the necessary expertise to discharge these roles, the following are a list of the matters to which they will need to give attention.

(1) Act as the "spider at the middle of the web" to ensure effective liaison between all parties involved.
(2) With P & I club advice as necessary, monitor situation as it develops and keep Trade Division and Fleet Management Division advised, obtaining necessary decisions on action to be taken and communicating same to relevant parties.
(3) Liaise with average adjuster to obtain advice needed to take decisions required.
(4) Liaise with TT club to get necessary security put up to cover containers.
(5) Liaise with average adjusters (where vessel involved is not the carrier's own vessel) to secure release of the carrier's cargo and containers against a temporary personal security in order to keep the cargo moving.
(6) Liaise with carrier's operational staff regarding liens and the removal thereof.
(7) Liaise with Trade Division and Marketing/Commercial Division to draft notice to customers to be sent out with GA documentation.
(8) Get agents to keep note of costs incurred in GA matters for inclusion in the adjustment.
(9) Decide whether we need representation by lawyer (if so, who and from where—e.g. English? American? etc.) and/or surveyor. Liaise with P & I club re appointment.
(10) Make sure all necessary decisions are taken promptly and that there are no hold-ups.

Speed is of the essence in all areas so decisions need to be taken quickly. If the casualty involved is a major casualty then expert witnesses are likely to be called upon by a variety of parties, the carrier, slot charterers and cargo interests to name but a few. If the matter ends up in court it is important to have the right expert witness available and, in any given field, there are often one or two experts who are head-and-shoulders above the others in their field. It is important to strike early in order to secure the services of the best lawyer/surveyor/expert witness, otherwise he will be scooped up by the other party and, on occasions, this could mean the difference between winning or losing the case.

PROCEDURES FOR DIFFERENT SITUATIONS

1. Own Vessels Operating in Joint Services

(A) This is where you really are in the driving seat. Most of the decisions are down to the carrier and it is up to you to liaise with all parties concerned to ensure that the right decision is taken by the right person at the right time. You are the "master of ceremonies" and everyone will be on your back for information/advice/decisions. Stay calm and do not be rushed into moving faster than you are happy to move but, by the same token, do not let anyone hold you up by not coming up with the necessary data/decisions on time. Chase them unmercifully.

(B) The first advice of a casualty involving general average or salvage will invariably come from Fleet Management Division (often out of hours or on a Friday afternoon!) who have been advised by the master of the vessel concerned.

(C) If salvage is needed/involved then Fleet Management Division will deal with any negotiations with salvors but may need assistance from the P & I club or the company's admiralty lawyer. On such occasions time is of the essence and, whilst FMD/P & I club/lawyer may offer advice, at the end of the day the decision belongs to the master.

If the vessel is in imminent danger (e.g. engine stopped in bad weather), no time must be lost but, if danger is not imminent (grounded on soft bottom area in good weather with good forecast), a little more time can be taken in coming to a decision. In such circumstances it may be possible to arrange a fixed price contract (at favourable rates if there is competition for the job) rather than sign Lloyd's Open Form of Salvage Agreement.

Remember once you have agreed to accept salvage services under Lloyd's Open Form you are committed (even though you have yet to sign on the dotted line) and cannot change your mind and back off if a change of circumstances (weather!) indicates the possibility of salving yourself (i.e. refloating) without assistance.

(D) If salvage services, subject to Lloyd's Open Form, are agreed then, absent any agreement by the parties concerned to the contrary, salvage security must be provided in London by a local guarantor to the satisfaction of Lloyd's. It may be that Lloyd's will agree to remove the lien from the cargo and containers for salvage security if the salvor can be persuaded to accept a temporary blanket security from the carrier for all cargo for which the carrier is principal carrier, on the basis that such security reduces as you obtain individual security from cargo insurers and pass it on to Lloyd's. As this approach removes from the salvor the difficult task of collecting individual security from a large number of cargo interests, he is often inclined to agree to such approaches, provided that the carrier has a sufficiently good reputation.

(E) As the carrier's local agents are probably doing the salvor's job of collecting security, they are entitled to be remunerated in the adjustment, so all agents and head office staff must keep records of time and expenses expended on handling the matter, as the cost of doing so is a valid claim in the adjustment.

(F) Your "best of friends" on such occasions will be:

Lawyer: do not blow your nose without checking with him;

Average adjuster: he can guide you towards producing the all-important estimates provided you feed him the data that he needs;

P & I club: keep them informed—you may need their assistance quickly with guarantees, advice etc.

(G) By now everybody is screaming at you for information.

Trade division:

- what is going on?
- what is the salvage award likely to be?
- how soon can we get the lien on the vessel, cargo and containers removed?
- how badly is the vessel damaged?
- what repairs must be done immediately and what can be deferred?
- what delays are there likely to be?
- must we declare GA or can we absorb this under the GA waiver clause in Hull and Machinery policy?
- if we do declare GA what will any of our consortium partners do? (Be aware of any waiver provision in the operating agreement and whether or not any consortium partner has insurance for cargo's proportion of GA, in which case they are unlikely to declare GA to their customers if their insurance policy will cover it, thereby putting marketing pressure on you to do likewise.)

Consortium partners: will be asking similar questions to trade division.

Average adjusters: will want everybody's manifest and the latest news on the casualty. (Because of the commercial sensitivity of manifest information, the carrier has to arrange for each slot charterer to send his manifest direct to the average adjuster in return for an undertaking of confidentiality. This means that the adjuster produces a separate adjustment for each principal carrier in which individual consignments are identified, with the full adjustment carrying only a summary of each principal carrier's contribution details.)

Lawyers: will also want our manifest and copies of everything we have on file. (By now a lawyer and probably a surveyor with possibly someone from FMD has proceeded to the casualty to gather evidence for internal inquiry and to counter inevitable claims arising from the casualty. In so far as it is possible, the master should be instructed to give statements to no one and allow no one on board until this party arrives to advise him. This may not always be possible if authorities, in whose waters the casualty has occurred, proceed on board and make certain demands, probably under the excuse of needing to protect their coastline from possible pollution dangers.)

Cargo lawyers: will probably want to put a surveyor on board and take statements from the crew. They must be kept at bay with assistance from your lawyer until your enquiries have been completed. In some places (like the US) this may not be possible and there may be subpoenas to be satisfied. In this case it is essential that any inspection or statements are only made/taken with your lawyer present.

Consortium partners: will also want to gather evidence to deal with claims from customers, to whom they are principal carriers. They must be dealt with firmly but with tact, as the carrier will probably need to liaise with them later and get their co-operation to contest their customers' claims, which will necessitate providing them with the necessary information to do so. Alternatively, the carrier may offer to take over the conduct of the cargo claims under a claim settling agreement, so that all claims arising out of the same casualty are dealt with by one party.

(H) Somewhere along the way a decision will have to be taken whether or not general average expense or sacrifice and any salvage award is going to be absorbed or whether general average is going to be declared. If GA is to be declared, then all of the carrier's out-of-pocket expenses (port of refuge expenses, damage during salvage efforts etc.) are recoverable in the adjustment and steps must be taken to identify these and obtain the appropriate vouchers, as without these average adjusters cannot include them in the adjustment.

(I) Roughly in the following order (but not always) you will have done the following:

- appointed a lawyer.
- appointed an appropriate surveyor (fire surveyor if the casualty has been a fire, engineering surveyor if the casualty has involved a mechanical fault, naval architect if the structure of the vessel is involved and cargo surveyor if any damage to cargo has been involved).
- appointed average adjusters.
- established contact with salvor's lawyer/Lloyd's Salvage Department.

- provided bulletins to: trade division, consortium partners, commercial division (for customers), overseas offices (for customers) and public relations department at appropriate junctures.
- liaised with FMD/trade division over handling casualty, whether to declare GA or absorb etc.
- considered need to retain expert witness(es) if necessary.
- arranged for TT club to put up salvage security to secure release of containers.
- checked operating agreement to determine position vis-à-vis partners in event of GA and/or salvage.

It is now your job to act as liaison party between them all (P & I club included) and to ensure that they are all pulling in the same direction in the best interests of the carrier.

(J) If salvage is involved you will need to put up security for the vessel's salvage contribution. If the carrier is well known, you may succeed in persuading the salvor to accept the carrier's personal security (get your lawyer to draft or approve the draft if it is put up by salvors) otherwise this must be obtained from the P & I club or some other third party guarantor. Security will also need to cover the vessel's bunkers.

(K) If the casualty has arisen through a collision with a third party vessel who is in any way or proportion to blame, the thorny problem of security from the third party vessel for your claims and counter-security to the third party for their claims against you must be dealt with. Your own lawyer will need to be involved and, unless you can agree personal security, the P & I club or some other third party guarantor may be involved. Whatever you do, do not let your adversary in the casualty get away until you have got your security for your potential claim if you can possibly avoid it.

(L) If there is any problem involving pollution of the environment be particularly sensitive to the handling of such matters and involve the carrier's health and safety officer to ensure that appropriate action is taken to protect the environment and to protect the corporate image and avoid bad publicity.

(M) In the event of salvage, provided that all of the facts are clear, shortly after the salvage service is completed is a good time to consider an open offer of settlement to the salvor. As has been previously commented, this will not be appreciated by the salvor's lawyers, as they would much prefer to have this matter deferred until they have accrued a substantial amount of charges, which will have to be paid by the carrier in addition to the salvage award. The point of making an open offer at this point (a realistic not just a token one) is that, unless the salvor achieves an award in excess of the offer, all legal expenses (which are often considerable) from the date of the offer for both sides have to be paid by the salvor. Accordingly a realistic open offer at this stage concentrates the mind beautifully! No wonder the salvor's lawyers are at pains to try to persuade arbitrators to set aside such offers!

Each GA/salvage inevitably has a unique development that makes the writing of a manual impossible. This development has to be taken in your stride and dealt with according to the guiding principles outlined above, under guidance from the experts retained. Having retained experts, use them but apply your knowledge of the operation of the carrier, its personnel, systems, operations etc. to make sure that, before they advise you, they fully understand all the necessary aspects of your operation, as advice is only as good as the brief upon which it is based.

2. Own Vessels Chartered Out

(A) In most cases in this situation the matter is simplified by not having any marketing considerations to take into account, as the charterer is the principal carrier and issuer of the bills of lading, so that it is he that has the marketing worries. Accordingly you can concentrate on the technicalities of playing it "by the book", unless the charterer approaches you with a "deal" by which he puts up security to avoid upsetting his customers.

(B) With the exception of the marketing considerations, things will proceed almost identically as for 1 above excepting, of course, that instead of dealing with a trade division you will be dealing with a third party charterer, who will doubtless hassle you for information but who may not be quite so co-operative in making your life easy, because he will want to demonstrate to his customers that it is you who are putting them to this inconvenience not him! So watch him like a hawk and always expect the worst!

(C) If the charterer agrees to put up temporary security to secure the release of cargo and containers for oncarriage and delivery against counter-security, get your lawyer to agree the terms. Whatever you do watch your lien and that of any salvor.

(D) You will need to put up salvage security for the vessel but security for bunkers (which belong to charterers) is the responsibility of charterers.

3. Chartered Vessels Operating in Joint Services

(A) Now that we are talking about a vessel which we neither own nor operate, we are not in the driving seat and all the decisions that matter are going to be taken by the owner in conjunction with his lawyer and average adjuster. Probably your only contact with the owner will be, at best, second-hand through his shipbroker (to your shipbroker or chartering manager to you), lawyer or average adjuster and very often your best bet is the average adjuster, because he needs your help as much as you need his.

(B) The average adjuster invariably has all the latest information and, whilst not straying from the path of client confidentiality, is often less cagey than the lawyer. You may find yourself dealing with a small outfit in Hamburg, Rotterdam or a UK-based adjuster, sometimes acting as a local agent for the adjuster in the owner's country.

Adjusters are usually mines of information and quite helpful people if approached correctly, particularly once they realise that you can make their lives easier for them by the provision of manifest data for your own and joint service partner's cargo and containers, putting up temporary security to secure the oncarriage of cargo to preclude the need to exercise a lien (with all the attendant problems of cost and storage charges) and allowing them to use your extensive commercial network to collect security from cargo, a task they would find nigh-on impossible with a large containership without your co-operation.

(C) If salvage is involved, the same requirements apply as for an owned vessel, although very often the salvor agrees to allow the average adjuster to collect non-London-based security instead of insisting upon security at Lloyd's.

(D) Joint service agreements (operating agreements etc.) usually include provisions under which partner lines guarantee security for their cargo and containers, provided that you tell them of this requirement before delivering to them. Check the relevant agreement to establish the relationship with partner lines in the event of GA and/or salvage and make sure you have all the necessary undertakings in place from partners before releasing cargo and containers to them.

(E) If it is a large GA or salvage, you will almost certainly need the services of a lawyer and possibly a surveyor. You may need to use a different lawyer to joint service partners as there is not necessarily a commonality of interest. You have a charter party agreement with the owner but your partners have an operating agreement/slot charter party agreement with you. That is not to say you cannot co-operate but, with a potential conflict of interests, your lawyer would be well advised to act for you only.

(F) If the incident has been a large one, your lawyer and/or surveyor (or one appointed by the TT club) will by now be digging for evidence of any unseaworthiness of the vessel to be applied in support of refusal to contribute in general average and for indemnity for salvage (which must be paid anyway), together with any claim for indemnity in respect of any settlement you may have been obliged to make with cargo interests.

The ironic thing is that, all the time you are gathering evidence against the vessel you are interested in the comments of (and will probably exchange reports with) the owner's surveyor. It is his comments that you must initially submit in defence of any claim against you if you want indemnity from the owner.

Just occasionally one comes up against a sensible lawyer/P & I club acting for owners who recognises that, if cargo succeeds against you, you will succeed against him for a similar amount plus legal fees. In this case it is simpler and cheaper for him to take over handling of all claims (in your name but at his expense) so that only one lawyer is involved instead of two, three, four or more in the case of a large consortium. Provided claims are under subrogation from insurers and not from customers, who might be upset by owners who have no marketing angle to consider, this is the best approach.

4. Chartered Vessels-dedicated Feeders

(A) In many ways a smaller version of 3 but as vessels are invariably smaller with small amounts involved this may affect any considerations. In some cases trade divisions may prefer to absorb the GA/salvage to avoid bothering customers. In other cases it may be a case of putting up temporary blanket security to be replaced later by separate individual security collected by agents at destination (or port of shipment).

(B) Whatever the case, a close liaison with the average adjuster and TT club is required. The TT club will put up security to secure the release of containers. You must negotiate release of cargo for oncarriage, preferably against a personal indemnity (if they want you to renew the charter or else!). Again you are the conductor waiving the baton but commercial division does the work:

- distributing letters, bonds and guarantee forms;
- collecting completed forms;
- controlling agencies to make sure goods are only released when all procedures are completed: otherwise your indemnity (temporary) is at risk.

5. Joint Service Partners' Owned Vessels

(A) This is one where you can sit back and do the sniping instead of being sniped at! You will now be chasing your opposite number in your consortium partner's office for information, decisions etc. He (and his salvor if salvage is involved) will be chasing you for manifests for their average adjusters, without which they cannot estimate values and provide the rough estimate so vital in deciding whether to declare GA or not.

(B) Based on data supplied by you, trade division will be in dialogue with the joint service partner to decide whether or not to declare GA or for each principal carrier to bear his own estimated portion for his cargo and containers.

(C) Manifests are market sensitive information and, as such, are never made available to competitor lines, even if the competitor is also a joint service partner. However, they can be made available direct to the average adjuster against an undertaking by him to produce a separate adjustment for your cargo, shown only as a bulk amount with no detail on the full adjustment, together with a separate detailed adjustment for the carrier's cargo sent only to you, together with an undertaking to treat such information as confidential to himself.

(D) Apart from the above, the procedures to be followed by commercial division in collecting security or directing payment to Lloyd's are the same as previously described and again a record of costs must be kept for inclusion in the adjustment by way of reimbursement.

6. Joint Service Partners' Chartered Vessels

(A) The situation here is not unlike 3 above excepting that, instead of dealing directly with the owner of the vessel, you are one removed and are dealing with him through your joint service partner. The longer line of communication means that obtaining information becomes that much more difficult so that, once the identity of owner's average adjuster is known, it is often a good idea to establish a direct link with him for relevant matters. He will appreciate it as well, as direct dealing will give you both quicker communication.

(B) However, sight must not be lost of the fact that you have no direct contractual relationship with the owner, who has a charter party with your joint service partner, whilst you have your space via a slot charter party with your joint service partner and the terms of the two contracts are unlikely to be back-to-back. Hence, if lawyers need to be involved, whilst joint service partner slot charterers could share a lawyer, it is not a good idea for you to use the same lawyer as your time chartering joint service partner (who is your disponent owner) because of potential conflicts of interest.

(C) Be aware of any operating agreement/slot charter party provisions relating to GA and salvage, particularly any guarantees re security.

7. Common User Feeders

This should be the simplest of the lot, assuming that the carrier has only got a few containers on board.

(a) get the TT club to put up security for the containers;
(b) persuade the average adjusters to release containers to you against a temporary personal guarantee not to deliver without collecting required bond and guarantee from the consignee;
(c) provide data re container numbers and cargo manifest details to TT club and average adjuster. TT club will put up security for containers' contribution;
(d) if salvage involved, make similar arrangements with salvor/Lloyd's;
(e) get commercial division to undertake the necessary work, instructing and controlling agents to do above;
(f) sit back and wait for TT club to send you a debit note for reimbursement of containers' contribution below deductible (which they will have paid against the guarantee) but not before opening a file and agreeing an estimate with the TT club.

8. Average Bonds and Guarantees

In the event of a declaration of general average there is a need to collect average bonds and guarantees from all cargo interests. With so many different interests represented on board, this is quite a task and is one where the average adjuster is always most grateful for the assistance of the combined transport operator in undertaking this task on his behalf. Standard Lloyd's forms are available but these require a substantial amount of detail to be inserted on the forms and many combined transport operators prefer to assist their customers by producing pre-printed forms leaving the customer to insert a minimum amount of detail prior to authorisation.

It is possible to write a computer program which will produce such forms from the manifest. The program written needs to take account of the fact that containerships are rarely completely empty, as they load concurrent with discharge at most ports so that, at any one time, a vessel may have imports from one voyage together with exports for the next voyage on board. Accordingly, the program needs to be written so that, by inserting the names of the two ports between which the general average incident occurred, the appropriate detail is extracted from the manifests of the two voyages concerned, if the incident occurs during a discharging/loading sequence and not deep-sea during the main voyage.

Such bonds (for signature by the merchant) and guarantees (for signature by the merchant's insurer) will probably look something like the following proforma drafts, which would be produced with a third page giving all of the manifest detail to assist the customer in quick identification of the consignment involved.

As can be seen both documents incorporate a "Non Separation Agreement". This is an agreement necessary if goods are discharged at a port of refuge and forwarded on another vessel, rather than await repairs to the original vessel. It is an undertaking that GA will be paid, even if the goods are subsequently lost on the oncarrying vessel. As container cargoes are mostly time-sensitive these days, if a vessel is to be delayed for very long at a port of refuge, it is usual practice to forward goods by the next available vessel to meet the requirements of customers operating a "just in time" approach to inventory, something which is possible because of the unit load approach with containers which was not so easy with a break-bulk operation.

AVERAGE BOND

Date: .... Page: 1

B/Lading or W/Bill No: .... Vessel: .... Voyage Number: .... Casualty Date: ....

Place of Receipt: .... Port of Loading: ....
Place of Delivery: .... Port of Discharge: ....

We the undersigned agree, in consideration of the delivery of the goods represented by the above bill of lading/waybill to us or our order and payment of the freight payable on delivery (if any), to pay to the shipowner the proper and respective proportion of any salvage and/or general average and/or particular and/or other charges which may be chargeable upon this consignment or to which we may be liable to contribute in respect of damage, loss, sacrifice or expenditure (including making any payment on account of such sum as is duly certified by the average adjusters to be due from the goods). We further promise and agree forthwith to furnish to the shipowner a correct account and particulars of the value of the goods delivered to us in order that any such salvage and/or general average and/or particular and/or other charges may be ascertained and adjusted in the usual manner. We further agree that general average will be adjusted and settled according to York/Antwerp Rules 1994, or any subsequent amendment thereto, at a place designated by the shipowner, according to the law of that place.

Non Separation Agreement

It is agreed that in the event of the vessel's cargo or part thereof being forwarded to original destination by another vessel, vessels or conveyance, rights and liabilities in general average shall not be affected by such forwarding, it being the intention to place the parties concerned as nearly as possible in the same position in this respect as they would have been in the absence of such forwarding and with the adventure continuing by the original vessel for so long as justifiable under the law applicable or under the contract of carriage.

The basis of contribution to general average of the property involved shall be the values on delivery at original destination unless sold or otherwise disposed of short of that destination, but where none of her cargo is carried forward in the vessel, the vessel shall contribute on the basis of her actual value on the date she completes discharge of her cargo.

Signature of owner of cargo (or his authorised agent) ....

Owner of Cargo	Insurers of Cargo
Name	Name ....
Address	Address ....
....	....
....	....
Tel No .... Date ....../....../......	Tel No .... Policy No ....

C.I.F. or C.I.P. Value of Goods .... Ocean Freight US$ ....

Please return this page duly completed to the carrier's office or agent with whom you are arranging collection/delivery together with:

A) A copy of the commercial invoice for the goods (if available)
B) The average guarantee (see below) signed by (or on behalf of) your insurers (if obtainable without undue delay)

(Do not delay returning this bond (duly completed) if either A or B are not immediately available but send undertaking as soon as possible and forward other documents as soon as they are to hand).

*** WARNING ***

Please note that if delivery of cargo is prevented by delay in the provision of the required security, all costs incurred as a result thereof will be for the account of the owners of the cargo and must be paid before delivery can be effected.

Figure 10: Average Bond

AVERAGE GUARANTEE

Date .... Page 2

Important

This guarantee will only be accepted provided no additions, deletions or amendments are made to the wording by insurers.

B/Lading or W/Bill No: .... Vessel: .... Voyage Number: .... Casualty Date: ....

Place of Receipt: .... Port of Loading: ....
Place of Delivery: .... Port of Discharge: ....

In consideration of the delivery in due course to the consignees of the goods represented by the above bill of lading/waybill, without collection of a deposit on account of average, we, the undersigned underwriters, hereby guarantee to the shipowner on account of the concerned the payment of any contribution to general average and/or salvage and/or charges which may hereafter be ascertained to be due in respect of the said goods.

We further agree to make a prompt payment on account if required as soon as such payment may be certified by the average adjusters.

Non Separation Agreement

It is agreed that in the event of the vessel's cargo or part thereof being forwarded to original destination by another vessel, vessels or conveyance, rights and liabilities in general average shall not be affected by such forwarding, it being the intention to place the parties concerned as nearly as possible in the same position in this respect as they would have been in the absence of such forwarding and with the adventure continuing by the original vessel for so long as justifiable under the law applicable or under the contract of carriage.

The basis of contribution to general average of the property involved shall be the values on delivery at original destination unless sold or otherwise disposed of short of that destination: but where none of her cargo is carried forward in the vessel, the vessel shall contribute on the basis of her actual value on the date she completes discharge of her cargo.

Name of Insurers	Policy or Cert No ....
Address	Insured Value ....
....	Average Adjuster (Local Office):
....	Name ....
Tel No .... Fax No	Address ....
Name of Contact	....
	....
Insurers Signature	Tel No .... Telex No ....
Date	Fax No .... Contact ....

*** WARNING ***

Please note that if delivery of cargo is prevented by delay in the provision of the required security, all costs incurred as a result thereof will be for the account of the owners of the cargo and must be paid before delivery can be effected.

Figure 11: Average guarantee

In the event of salvage under Lloyd's Open Form the standard Lloyd's Salvage Guarantee will have to be used or, if the salvor requires an alternative guarantee, he will provide it. Thus, if the customer has to give a separate salvage guarantee because the carrier does not put up a full guarantee and collect in the general average adjustment, he will have to insert the necessary data.

APPENDICES

APPENDIX 1

BOXTIME CHARTER PARTY (PARTS I, II & III)

1. Shipbroker	THE BALTIC AND INTERNATIONAL MARITIME COUNCIL (BIMCO) UNIFORM TIME CHARTER PARTY FOR CONTAINER VESSELS CODE NAME: "BOXTIME" PART I 2. Place and Date
3 Owners/Disponent Owners & Place of Business, Telephone, Telex and Telefax Number	4. Charterers & Place of Business, Telephone, Telex and Telefax Number
5. Vessel's Name	6. Call Sign/Telex Number
7. GRT/NRT	8. DWT on Summer Freeboard	9 TEU Capacity (Maximum)
10. Class (Cl. 5)	11. Flag	12. Service Speed (See Part III)	13 Fuel Consumption (See Part III)
14 Type(s) of Fuel(s) (Cl 12 (d))	15 Maximum Bunker Capacity
16. Bunkers/Price on Delivery (Min.-Max.) (Cl. 12 (a) and (c))	17 Bunkers/Price on Redelivery (Min.-Max.) (Cl. 12 (a) and (c))
18. Place of Delivery (Cl. 1 (b))	19. Earliest Date of Delivery (local time) (Cl 1 (b))
20 Latest Date of Delivery (local time) (Cl 1 (b))	21. Place of Redelivery (Cl. 6 (m))
22. Trading Limits (Cl. 3 and Cl 5 (c))	
23. Period of Charter and Options if any (Cl 1 (a), Cl 6 (m) and Cl 7 (f))	24 State number of Days Options have to be declared after commencement of Charter Period (Cl. 1 (a))
25 Rate of Hire per Day and to whom payable (Cl 1 (a), Cl. 7 (a) and (b))	26 Quantity of Hazardous Goods allowed (Cl 4 (b))
27. Insured Value of Vessel (Cl. 18 (a))	28. Daily Rate for Supercargo (Cl. 13 (h)) 29. Victualling Rate per Meal for other Charterers' Servants etc (Cl. 13 (j))
30. Name of Owners' P & I Club (Cl. 18 (b))	31. Name of Charterers' P & I Club (Cl 18 (b))
32. Charterers' maximum Claim settlement authority (Cl. 16 (h))	33 General Average to be adjusted at (Cl 14 (c))
34 Law and Arbitration (state a, b, or c of Cl 20, as agreed, if c agreed also state Place of Arbitration) (Cl. 20)	35 Brokerage Commission and to whom payable (Cl. 21)
36. Number of Additional Clauses covering special Provisions	

It is mutually agreed between the party mentioned in Box 3 (hereinafter referred to as "the Owners") and the Party mentioned in Box 4 (hereinafter referred to as "the Charterers") that this Contract shall be performed in accordance with the conditions contained in Part I including additional clauses, if any agreed and stated in Box 36, and Part II as well as Part III. In the event of a conflict of conditions, the provisions of Part I and Part III shall prevail over those of Part II to the extent of such conflict but no further

Signature (Owners)	Signature (Chaterers)

Printed and sold by Fr G. Knudtzons Bogtrykkeri A/S, 55 Toldbodgade, DK-1253 Copenhagen K, Telefax +45 33 93 11 84, by authority of The Baltic and International Maritime Council (BIMCO), Copenhagen.

INDEX
"BOXTIME" Charter Party

CLAUSE NO.

1. **PERIOD OF CHARTER PARTY AND DELIVERY**

2. **OWNERS' UNDERTAKING**

3. **TRADING LIMITS**

4. **PERMITTED CARGOES**
    - a) Uncontainerised Goods
    - b) Hazardous Goods
    - c) Live Animals
    - d) Radioactive Goods
    - e) Arms & Ammunition

5. **OWNERS' OBLIGATIONS**
    Maintain in Class and efficient operation.
    - a) Container Lashings
    - b) Crew Assistance
    - c) Documentation
    - d) Insurance of the Vessel
    - e) Fumigation and/or Deratisation
    - f) Smuggling

6. **CHARTERERS' OBLIGATIONS**
    - a) Provision of Details
    - b) Instructions to the Master
    - c) Stevedoring
    - d) Charterers' Lashings
    - e) Condition of Containers
    - f) Stowage in Containers
    - g) Stowage Planning
    - h) Operating Expenses
    - j) Bunker Fuel
    - k) Agency Costs
    - l) Damage to Vessel
    - m) Redelivery
    - n) Additional Premiums
    - o) Advances to Master
    - p) Contraband

7. **HIRE**
    - a) Rate
    - b) Payment
    - c) Default
    - d) Redelivery Adjustment
    - e) Deductions
    - f) Extension

8. **OFF HIRE**
    - a) Unable to Comply with Instructions
    - b) Deviation
    - c) Blocking & Trapping
    - d) Requisitions
    - e) Loss of Time

9. **LOSS OF VESSEL**

10. **LASHINGS AND STEVEDORING**
    - a) Owners' Lashings
    - b) Charterers' Lashings
    - c) Stowage Planning
    - d) Stevedoring
    - e) Liability

11. **VESSEL'S GEAR**
    - a) Regulations
    - b) Condition
    - c) Suez and Panama Canal
    - d) Refrigeration
    - e) Lighting

12. **BUNKER FUEL**
    - a) Quantity at Delivery/Redelivery
    - b) Pre and Post Charter Bunkering
    - c) Purchase Price
    - d) Specification
    - e) Consumption
    - f) Bunkering

13. **CHARTERERS' REQUIREMENTS**
    - a) Plans
    - b) Flag, Funnel, Name and Configuration
    - c) Ballast Warranty
    - d) Weather Routing
    - e) Communications Facilities
    - f) Logs and Witnesses
    - g) Replacement of Master and Officers
    - h) Supercargo
    - j) Victualling
    - k) Sub-Letting
    - l) Inspections
    - m) Substitution and Sub-Contracting
    - n) Laid-Up Returns
    - o) Signing Bills of Lading

14. **OWNERS' REQUIREMENTS**
    - a) Maintenance
    - b) Bills of Lading
    - c) General Average
    - d) Salvage
    - e) Liens

15. **SUNDRY MATTERS**
    - a) Pilotage/Towage
    - b) Watchmen
    - c) Stowaways
    - d) On/Off Hire Surveys
    - e) Sub-Contractors

16. **CHARTERERS' RESPONSIBILITIES/LIABILITIES**
    - a) Charterers' Responsibilities
    - b) Claims Handling
    - c) General Indemnity
    - d) Fines etc.. Indemnity
    - e) Time Limit
    - f) Agency
    - g) General Average Exclusion
    - h) Claims Authority

17. **OWNERS' RESPONSIBILITIES/LIABILITIES**
    - a) For Goods and Containers
    - b) For Refrigerated Goods
    - c) Limitation of Liability
    - d) Time Limit
    - e) For Personal Injury
    - f) Limitation Proceedings
    - g) Consequential Loss

18. **INSURANCES**
    - a) Hull and Machinery
    - b) Protection and Indemnity (P & I)
    - c) War Risks

19. **WAR**

20. **LAW AND ARBITRATION**
    - a) London
    - b) New York
    - c) Alternative

21. **COMMISSION**

22. **NOTICES**

PART II
"BOXTIME" Charter Party

It is agreed on the date shown in Box 2 between the party named in Box 3 as the Owners of the Vessel named in Box 5 and the party named in Box 4 as the Charterers as follows:

1. Period of Charter Party and Delivery

(a) In consideration of the hire detailed in Box 25 the Owners let and the Charterers hire the Vessel for the period together with any optional extension(s) thereto as indicated in Box 23. Such options, always at the Charterers' discretion, must be declared to the Owners within the period as indicated in Box 24.

(b) The Owners shall deliver the Vessel to the Charterers at the Place of Delivery as indicated in Box 18. Unless agreed by the Charterers to the contrary, delivery shall take place no earlier than the time/date as indicated in Box 19 and no later than the time/date as indicated in Box 20.

If prior to delivery the Owners give notice to the Charterers that the Vessel will not be ready for delivery by the time/date as indicated in Box 20, the Charterers shall declare within 48 hours after receiving notice thereof from the Owners whether they cancel or will take delivery of the Vessel but without prejudice to the Charterers' right to claim proved damages.

(c) If the Owners are unable to deliver the Vessel at the Place of Delivery as indicated in Box 18 for any reason beyond the control of the Owners, delivery shall take place at the nearest point to the nominated Place of Delivery to which the Vessel may safely and reasonably proceed.

The Owners shall give notice of readiness to deliver to the Charterers and/or the Charterers' local agents when in position to come on hire.

(d) Delivery shall be effected at any time, day or night, Saturdays, Sundays and holidays included.

(e) At the time of delivery the Vessel shall be clean and in all respects fit to receive goods and ISO standard containers.

(f) The Charterers' acceptance of delivery of the Vessel shall not prejudice their rights against the Owners under this Charter Party.

2. Owners' Undertaking

The Owners undertake that, at delivery, the Vessel shall be of the description set out in Parts I and III hereof.

3. Trading Limits

The Vessel shall be employed in lawful trades within Institute Warranty Limits (IWL) and within the Trading Limits as indicated in Box 22 for the carriage of lawful goods between safe ports or places where she can safely lie always afloat. The Vessel shall not be obliged to force ice nor to follow icebreakers.

The Owners warrant that, at the time of signing this Charter Party, the Vessel has not traded to any countries which would make the Vessel unacceptable for calls at ports within the Trading Limits as indicated in Box 22. The Charterers shall provide a list of such countries

4. Permitted Cargoes

Except as provided below, the Vessel shall be used exclusively for the carriage of goods in ISO standard containers complying with the International Convention for Safe Containers

(a) *Uncontainerised Goods:* Uncontainerised goods may be carried only with the prior consent of the Owners and the Master provided that they are suitably prepared for carriage.

(b) *Hazardous Goods:* The Owners agree that the Charterers may carry the maximum quantity as indicated in Box 26 of hazardous goods in containers, provided same are loaded, stowed, discharged and documented in accordance with IMO regulations, any mandatory local requirements and regulations of the flag state

(c) *Live Animals:* Live animals may be carried only with the prior consent of the Owners and the Master.

(d) *Radioactive Goods:* Radioactive goods other than isotopes shall be excluded Radioactive isotopes may be carried only with the prior consent of the Owners and the Master and provided that they are of such a category as not to invalidate the Vessel's P & I cover.

(e) *Arms & Ammunition.* Arms and ammunition may be carried only with the prior consent of the Owners and the Master.

5. Owners' Obligations

Except as provided elsewhere in this Charter Party, the Owners shall, at their expense, maintain the Vessel in the Class as indicated in Box 10, in a thoroughly efficient state of hull and machinery and in every way fitted for the service throughout the currency of this Charter Party.

The Owners shall, inter alia, provide and pay the cost of the following:

(a) *Container Lashings:* (See Clause 10 (a)).

(b) *Crew Assistance* with inter alia:-

(i) preparing the Vessel's cranes, derricks, winches and/or cargo handling gear for use,
(ii) opening and closing any hatches (other than pontoon type hatches), ramps and other means of access to goods and containers,
(iii) docking, undocking and shifting operations in port,
(iv) bunkering,
(v) maintaining power during loading and discharging operations,
(vi) instructing crane drivers and winchmen in use of Vessel's gear,
(vii) supervising stevedores lashing and unlashing goods and containers and the regular checking of lashings at sea when weather conditions permit (See Clause 10 (d)(ii)),
(viii) monitoring, recording performances and, when available, supplying labour for the repairing of the Charterers' refrigeration machinery, weather permitting (See Clause 17 (b)).

The above services shall be rendered by the crew if required, provided port and local labour regulations permit, and except when repairing the Charterers' refrigeration machinery any overtime incurred shall be for the account of the Owners.

(c) *Documentation:* Any documentation relating to the Vessel that may be required to permit the Vessel to trade within the limits as indicated in Box 22, including, but not limited to, certificates of financial responsibility for oil pollution, provided such oil pollution certificates are obtainable from the Owners' P & I club or some other available source, valid international tonnage certificate, Suez and Panama tonnage certificates, valid certificate of registry and certificates relating to the strength and/or serviceability of the Vessel's gear (See Clause 11 (a)).

(d) *Insurance of the Vessel:* (See Clause 18).

(e) *Fumigation and/or deratisation:* The provision of certificates thereof at the commencement of the Charter Party and the renewal thereof throughout the Charter Party, except if this is required as a result of the Charterers' goods and containers carried under this Charter Party, in which case these expenses shall be for the account of the Charterers.

(f) *Smuggling:* In the event of smuggling by the Master, Officers and/or crew, the Owners shall bear the cost of any fines, taxes or imposts levied and the Vessel shall be off hire for any time lost as a result thereof (See Clause 6 (p)).

6. Charterers' Obligations

Except as provided elsewhere in this Charter Party, the Charterers shall provide and pay the costs of the following throughout the currency of this Charter Party:

(a) *Provision of Details:* The provision of full and accurate details of goods and containers (including any documentation required at any ports of call), their weights and stowage positions to the Master as early as possible but not later than upon arrival at the port of loading, with regular updating thereof and the provision of a full and accurate plan of the stowage of all goods and containers actually loaded prior to sailing. Such details shall include:-

(i) gross weights of containers,
(ii) any feature of the goods requiring attention by the crew during the voyage, including, but not limited to, any hazardous or other dangerous feature and/or the need for carriage within a specified temperature range.

(b) *Instructions to the Master:* The Master, although appointed by the Owners, shall at all times during the currency of this Charter Party be under the orders and directions of the Charterers as regards employment and agency. The Charterers shall be obliged at all times to furnish the Master with full and timely instructions.

(c) *Stevedoring:* (See Clause 10 (d)(i)).

(d) *Charterers' Lashings:* (See Clause 10 (b)).

(e) *Condition of Containers:* The Charterers warrant that all containers carried pursuant to this Charter Party have been constructed to a design approved by a Classification Society and are properly maintained.

(f) *Stowage in Containers:* The correct stowage and safe securing of all goods within containers (including securing to flat rack containers) to withstand the rigours of the voyage

(g) *Stowage Planning:* (See Clause 10 (c)).

(h) *Operating Expenses:* All port charges, light and canal dues, pilotage, towage, consular charges, and all other charges and expenses relating to the operation of the Vessel not otherwise provided for in this Charter Party, other than charges or expenses relating to the crew.

(j) *Bunker Fuel:* (See Clause 12).

(k) *Agency Costs:* All agency fees and expenses for normal ship's husbandry at all ports or places of call.

(l) *Damage to Vessel:* Any damage to the Vessel or loss or damage to its equipment caused by stevedores during the currency of this Charter Party shall be reported by the Master to the Charterers or their agents, in writing, within 24 hours of the occurrence or as soon as possible thereafter but latest when the loss or damage could have been discovered by the exercise of due diligence. The Master shall endeavour to obtain written acknowledgment by the party causing loss or damage unless it is made good in the meantime. The Charterers shall pay for stevedore damage whether or not payment has been made by stevedores to the Charterers.

Damage for which the Charterers are responsible affecting seaworthiness, or the proper working of the Vessel and/or her equipment, shall be repaired without delay to the Vessel after each occurrence in the Charterers' time and shall be paid for by the Charterers. Other repairs to damage for which the Charterers are responsible shall also be carried out in the Charterers' time but, if this is not possible, such repairs shall be carried out whilst the Vessel is in drydock in the Owners' time provided this does not interfere with the Owners' repair work, or by the Vessel's crew at the Owners' convenience. All costs of such repairs shall be for the Charterers' account.

(m) *Redelivery:* Redelivery of the Vessel at the Place of Redelivery as indicated in Box 21, unless agreed by the Owners or provided elsewhere to the contrary, in the same condition to that pertaining when the Vessel was delivered, fair wear and tear excepted, at the end of the period as indicated in Box 23. The Charterers shall give the Owners one month notice of expected date and Place of Redelivery, which advice shall be updated 10, 5 and 2 days prior to expected redelivery.

At the time of redelivery the Vessel shall be clean and fit to load goods and ISO standard containers. If the Charterers have changed the configuration of the Vessel to carry different size ISO standard containers or non ISO standard containers, they shall, in their time and at their cost, prior to redelivery, return the Vessel to its previous configuration, unless the Owners agree to waive this requirement, in which case the Charterers shall return the Vessel to its previous configuration, at their cost, after redelivery at such time and place stipulated by the Owners but in the Owners' time. Without prejudice to any other claim the Owners may have under this Charter Party the Owners shall not be obliged to accept redelivery of the Vessel before it is returned to its previous configuration.

(n) *Additional Premiums:* All additional premiums for hull and machinery, war risks, including blocking and trapping, or protection and indemnity insurance incurred by the Owners over and above the premiums payable by the Owners. The Owners shall allow the Charterers to arrange these additional covers on their behalf if the Charterers so request and if the proposed insurers and terms are acceptable to the Owners. If the Charterers arrange such insurance the Charterers' insurers shall confirm cover latest 24 hours before the Vessel is due to be exposed to the risk so insured (See Clause 18)

(o) *Advances to Master:* The Charterers shall procure that their local agents at all ports of call shall, upon request by the Master, make funds available to him for disbursements, which advances the Charterers may recoup from the Owners by deduction from the hire payments in accordance with Clause 7(e).

(p) *Contraband:* In the event that contraband and/or unmanifested drugs or goods are found to have been shipped as part of the goods and/or in containers on board, any fines, taxes or imposts levied shall be for the Charterers' account, and the Vessel shall remain on hire during any time lost as a result thereof, unless it can be established that the Master, Officers and/or crew are involved in smuggling (See Clause 5 (f)). In this event any security required shall be provided by the Charterers.

7. Hire

(a) *Rate:* The Charterers shall pay hire at the rate stated in Box 25, per day or pro rata for part of a day, from the time the Vessel is delivered to the Charterers until her redelivery to the Owners. All calculation of hire shall be made by reference to Universal Time Co-ordinated (U.T.C.).

(b) *Payment:* Payment of hire shall be made in cash in full and without discount, semi-monthly in advance. If hire or any instalment thereof is not paid as aforesaid, the Charterers shall pay interest at the rate of 0.1 per cent per day on the amount outstanding from and including the due date until the date of payment.

(c) *Default:* In default of punctual and regular payment as herein specified, the Owners may require the Charterers to make payment of the amount due within 96 running hours of receipt of notification from the Owners, failing which the Owners will have the right to withdraw the Vessel without prejudice to any claim the Owners may have against the Charterers under this Charter Party. Further, so long as the hire remains unpaid, the Owners shall be entitled to suspend the performance of any and all of their obligations hereunder and shall have no responsibility whatsoever for any consequences thereof in respect of which the Charterers hereby indemnify the Owners. Hire shall continue to accrue and any extra expenses resulting from such suspension shall be for the Charterers' account.

(d) *Redelivery Adjustment:* Should the Vessel be on her voyage towards the Place of Redelivery at the time payment of hire becomes due, said payment shall be made for the estimated time necessary to complete the voyage, less disbursements made by the Charterers for the Owners' account, including the estimated value of bunker fuel on board at redelivery. When the Vessel is redelivered to the Owners any difference shall be refunded to or paid by the Charterers as appropriate, but not later than three months after redelivery of the Vessel.

(e) *Deductions:* On production of supporting vouchers the Charterers shall be entitled to deduct from payments of hire any expenditure incurred on behalf of the Owners which may be payable by the Owners under this Charter Party. If such expenditure is incurred in a currency other than that in which hire is payable, conversion into such currency for the purpose of deduction shall be effected at the rate of exchange at the place of the bank where hire is paid prevailing on the date when the expenditure was incurred.

(f) *Extension:* The Charterers shall arrange the Vessel's trading so as to permit redelivery at the place and in the period as indicated in Boxes 21 and 23, respectively. If the Vessel is not chartered for a minimum/maximum period and the Vessel is sent on a final voyage reasonably calculated to allow redelivery within such period at the Place of Redelivery as provided under this Charter Party, and the voyage is prolonged for reasons beyond the Charterers' control, the Charterers shall have the use of the Vessel at the rate and on the conditions of this Charter Party for such extended time as may be required for completion of said voyage and redelivery as aforesaid.

8. Off Hire

After delivery in accordance with Clause 1 hereof, the Vessel shall remain on hire until redelivered in accordance with Clause 6(m), except for the following periods:

(a) *Unable to Comply with Instructions:* If the Vessel is unable to comply with the instructions of the Charterers on account of:-

(i) any damage, defect, breakdown, or deficiency of the Vessel's hull, machinery, equipment or repairs or maintenance thereto, including dry-docking, excepting those occasions when Clause 6 (l) applies,

(ii) any deficiency of the Master, Officers and/or crew, including the failure, refusal or inability of the Master, Officers and/or crew to perform service immediately required, whether or not within the control of the Owners,

(iii) arrest of the Vessel at the suit of a party where a claim is not caused by the Charterers, their servants, agents or sub-contractors (See Clause 5(f)),

(iv) any delay occasioned by any breach by the Owners of any obligation or warranty in this Charter Party.

If any of the above incidents affect the full use of the Vessel, it shall be off hire. If they partially affect the use of the Vessel, it shall be off hire to the extent such incidents affect the Charterers' use of the Vessel (See also Clause 11(b)).

(b) *Deviation:* In the event of the Vessel deviating (which expression includes putting back, or putting into any port or place other than that to which she is bound under the instructions of the Charterers) other than to save life or property, hire shall cease to be payable from the commencement of such deviation until the time when the Vessel is again ready to resume her service from a position not less favourable to the Charterers than that at which the deviation commenced, provided always that due allowance shall be given for any distance made good towards the Vessel's destination and any bunkers saved. However, should the Vessel alter course to avoid bad weather or be driven into port or anchorage by stress of weather, the Vessel shall remain on hire and all costs thereby incurred shall be for the Charterers' account

(c) *Blocking and Trapping:* If during the currency of this Charter Party the Vessel is blocked or trapped in circumstances where Clause 19 (b) applies, the Vessel shall be off hire for the period blocked or trapped. If the Vessel is blocked or trapped for a period of 365 days this Charter Party shall be terminated.

(d) *Requisitions:* Should the Vessel be requisitioned by any government or governmental authority during the period of this Charter Party, it shall be off hire during the period of such requisition and any hire or other compensation paid by any government or governmental authority in respect of such requisition shall be paid to the Owners However, the Charterers shall have the option of cancelling the balance period of this Charter Party, provided this option is exercised within 14 days of receipt of notice of requisition.

(e) *Loss of Time:* In the event of loss of time for which the Owners are responsible, including but not limited to terms of employment of Master, Officers and/or crew, the Vessel shall be off hire for the time thereby lost.

Any time during which the Vessel is off hire under this Charter Party may be added to the charter period, at the option of the Charterers. Such option shall be declared not less than two months before expected redelivery, or latest two weeks after the event if less than two months before expected redelivery.

9. Loss of Vessel

Should the Vessel be lost, or become a constructive total loss, hire shall cease at noon on the day of her loss or constructive total loss, and if missing, from noon on the date when last heard of, and any hire paid in advance and not earned shall be returned to the Charterers and payment of any hire due shall be suspended until the Vessel is reported safe.

10. Lashings and Stevedoring

(a) *Owners' Lashings:* The Owners shall supply and maintain in good working order throughout the currency of this Charter Party sufficient lashing and securing equipment to facilitate the proper lashing and securing in accordance with the plan supplied by the Owners of the maximum number of ISO standard containers which may be carried in accordance with the details provided in Part III hereto. The Owners further warrant that both the strength of the lashings and the design of the lashing pattern are adequate for the stowage in accordance with Part III hereto and that these have been approved by the Vessel's Classification Society.

(b) *Charterers' Lashings:* Should any additional or alternative lashings to those supplied by the Owners be required, these shall be supplied by the Charterers at their expense. Should the Charterers supply gear, equipment or stores, the Master shall keep a record of it and care for it. Such gear, equipment or stores shall be redelivered to the Charterers at the time required by the Charterers in the same condition as supplied fair wear and tear excepted.

(c) *Stowage Planning:* The Charterers shall ensure that stowage is effected in accordance with the requirements of this Charter Party and of the Vessel's stability including, inter alia, that stack and tier weights are not exceeded and that heavy containers are not stowed over light containers on or under deck, except with the Master's prior approval.

(d) *Stevedoring:*

(i) The Charterers shall provide and pay for the cost of all stevedoring operations during the currency of this Charter Party including, inter alia, receipt, loading, handling, stowing, lashing, securing, unsecuring, unlashing, unstowing, discharging, tallying and delivering of all uncontainerised goods and containers and shall be liable to the Owners for all loss or damage caused to the Vessel by the improper or careless performance of such operations.

(ii) The Master shall supervise stevedores undertaking the tasks outlined in Clause 10 (d) (i) to ensure that these are done correctly and to his satisfaction. The Master shall ensure that all lashings are regularly checked whilst at sea, weather permitting.

(e) *Liability:* Except in respect of the failure of any lashing supplied by the Charterers, the Owners shall be responsible, subject to the provisions of Clause 17, for the consequences of the failure of any lashings or lashing pattern design or execution or the failure to properly service lashings during the voyage.

11. Vessel's Gear

(a) *Regulations:* The Vessel's cargo gear if any, and any other equipment shall comply with the regulations of the countries to which the Vessel will be employed and the Owners shall ensure that the Vessel is at all times during the currency of this Charter Party in possession of valid certificates of efficiency to comply with such regulations. If stevedores are not permitted to work due to failure of the Master and/or the Owners and/or the Owners' agents to comply with the aforementioned regulations or because the Vessel is not in possession of such valid certificates of efficiency, then the Charterers may suspend hire for the time lost thereby and the Owners shall pay all expenses incurred incidental to and resulting from such failure (see Clause 5 (c)).

(b) *Condition:* All cargo handling gear, including derrick(s), crane(s) and winch(es) if any, shall be kept in good working order and the Owners shall maintain, repair and/or replace such gear whenever necessary. In the event of loss of time due to a breakdown of derrick(s), crane(s) or winch(es) for any period by reason of disablement or insufficient power, hire shall be reduced pro rata for the period of such inefficiency in relation to the number of hatches affected, unless caused by mishandling by the Charterers or their servants. If the Charterers continue working by using shore-crane(s) the Owners shall pay such cranage but not exceeding the hire payable for such period, in which case the Vessel shall not be off hire pro rata as stipulated above. The Vessel shall, however, be pro-rata off hire if shore-cranes are not available during stoppages of derrick(s), crane(s) or winch(es) and all other unavoidable expenses thereby incurred shall be for the Owners' account.

(c) *Suez and Panama Canal:* The Vessel shall be maintained during the currency of this Charter Party with all necessary fittings for Suez and Panama Canal transit in good working order.

(d) *Refrigeration:* The Owners shall ensure that all refrigeration facilities as described in PART III are maintained in good working order throughout the currency of this Charter Party.

(e) *Lighting:* The Owners shall ensure that the Vessel will supply sufficient lighting to deck and holds to permit 24 hour working free of expense to the Charterers and that such lighting will comply with the port regulations at all ports of call throughout the currency of this Charter Party.

12. Bunker Fuel

(a) *Quantity at Delivery/Redelivery:* The Vessel shall be delivered with approximately the quantity of fuel as indicated in Box 16 and, unless indicated to the contrary in Box 17, the Vessel shall be redelivered with an approximately similar quantity, provided that the quantity of fuel at redelivery is at least sufficient to allow the Vessel to reach safely the nearest port at which fuel of the required type is available.

(b) *Pre and Post Charter Bunkering:* Provided that it can be accomplished without hindrance to the operation of the Vessel, the Owners shall allow the Charterers to bunker for the account of the Charterers prior to delivery and the Charterers shall allow the Owners to bunker for the account of the Owners prior to redelivery, in both cases by prior arrangement between the parties.

(c) *Purchase Price:* Unless otherwise stated in Boxes 16 and 17, the Charterers shall purchase the fuel on board at delivery and the Owners shall purchase the fuel on board at redelivery at the Platts Oil Gram mean prices at the ports and dates of delivery and redelivery, respectively, or the nearest bunkering port thereto

(d) *Specification:* The Charterers shall supply fuel of the B.S.M.A. 100:1989 specification or any amendment thereto as indicated in Box 14.

(e) *Consumption:* The Vessel's fuel consumption in port and at sea shall not exceed the amounts shown in PART III, at all times for port consumption and in smooth water with winds not exceeding Beaufort Scale 4 for consumption at sea.

(f) *Bunkering:* The Chief Engineer shall co-operate with the Charterers' bunkering agents and fuel suppliers and comply with their requirements during bunkering, including, but not limited to, checking, verifying and acknowledging readings or soundings, meters etc before, during and/or after delivery of fuel.

Three (3) samples of all fuel shall be taken during delivery, sealed and signed by suppliers, Chief Engineer and the Charterers' agent, each of whom should retain one sample. If any claim should arise in respect of the quality or specification of the fuel supplied, the Owners and the Charterers agree to have samples of the fuel analysed by a mutually agreed qualified analyst.

13. Charterers' Requirements

(a) *Plans:* On signing this Charter Party the Owners shall, if the Charterers so request, furnish the Charterers with the following documents in English:

(i) General Arrangement Plan
(ii) Capacity Plan
(iii) Container Stowage Plan
(iv) Plan of Deck and (where the Vessel not cellular) Under-Deck Container Lashing Plan approved by the Vessel's Classification Society.
(v) Trim and Stability Book
(vi) Hydrostatic Curves Plan
(vii) Loading Scale
(viii) Tank Plan

and any other operational documents that the Charterers may reasonably request and which are necessary for the safe and efficient operation of the Vessel. All documents received by the Charterers shall be returned to the Owners on redelivery.

(b) *Flag, Funnel, Name and Configuration:* The Charterers, if required, shall be allowed to fly their house flag, paint the funnel in the Charterers' colours and/or the name of the Line on the Vessel's side, change the Vessel's name, subject to the authorities' approval, and/or change the Vessel's container stowage configuration to carry different sized containers, all during the currency of this Charter Party. If the Charterers elect to exercise any or all of these options all alterations necessary shall be effected during the Charterers' time and at the Charterers' expense. Unless the Owners elect to waive this requirement or enter into an alternative agreement with the Charterers, the Vessel shall be returned to its condition prior to the commencement of the Charter Party at the Charterers' expense before redelivery.

(c) *Ballast Warranty:* The Owners warrant that the Vessel is capable of operating under this Charter Party in ballast without requiring any solid ballast and using fuel and water ballast only.

(d) *Weather Routing:* The Charterers may supply the Master with weather routing information during the currency of this Charter Party. In this event the Master shall comply with the reporting procedure of the Charterers' weather routing service.

(e) *Communications Facilities:* The Owners shall permit the Charterers use of the Vessel's communication facilities at cost during the currency of this Charter Party.

(f) *Logs and Witnesses:* The Owners shall maintain full deck, engine room and, where appropriate, refrigeration logs during the currency of this Charter Party and the Charterers shall have full access to all the Vessel's logs, rough and official, covering this period. The Owners undertake to produce all such documentation promptly upon request of the Charterers.

The Owners also undertake to endeavour to assist the Charterers by producing or assisting the Charterers to trace the Vessel's witnesses as may be requested by the Charterers to give testimony in connection with matters arising in relation to this Charter Party and such expenses as may be incurred shall be for the Charterers' account.

(g) *Replacement of Master and Officers:* If the Charterers shall have reason to be dissatisfied with the conduct of the Master or Officers, the Owners shall, on receiving particulars of the complaint, investigate same and, if confirmed, replace the offending party(ies) at the Owners' expense.

(h) *Supercargo:* The Owners shall provide and maintain a clean and adequate room for the Charterers' supercargo if any, furnished to the same standard as officers' accommodation Supercargo shall be victualled with the Vessel's officers The Charterers shall pay for accommodation and victualling of any supercargo at the daily rate as indicated in Box 28.

(j) *Victualling:* The Owners, when requested and authorised by the Charterers or their agents, shall victual other officials and servants of the Charterers at the rate per person per meal as indicated in Box 29.

(k) *Sub-Letting:* The Charterers shall have the right to sub-let all or part of the Vessel with the prior consent of the Owners, which shall not be unreasonably withheld, whilst still remaining responsible to the Owners for the performance of this Charter Party.

(l) *Inspections:* The Owners shall co-operate with the Charterers to facilitate the Charterers' inspection of the Vessel at any time, upon receipt of reasonable notice, in the Charterers' time

(m) *Substitution and Sub-Contracting:* Unless the Charterers' prior consent be obtained in writing, which shall not be unreasonably withheld, the Owners may not:-

(i) substitute any other vessel for that named herein, even though it might be of identical specification, before, at the beginning of or throughout the currency of this Charter Party or,
(ii) sub-contract any of their obligations including the management of the Vessel In the event of any sub-contracting the Owners shall remain responsible for the performance of this Charter Party or,
(iii) change the flag of the Vessel.

(n) *Laid-Up Returns:* The Charterers shall have the right to order the laying-up of the Vessel at any time and for any period of time at a safe berth or place and in the event of such laying-up the Owners shall promptly take steps to effect all the economies in operating costs, including insurance, which may be possible and give prompt credit to the Charterers in respect of all such economies. At the request of the Charterers, the Owners shall at any time provide an estimate of the economies which would be possible in the event of the laying-up of the Vessel. The laying-up port or place shall be at the Charterers' option but shall always be safe and acceptable to the Owners' insurers. Should the Charterers in liaison with the Owners decide that the Master, Officers and crew should be paid off, then the cost of repatriation and, later, cost of rejoining, including laying-up preparation and reactivation cost, and all expenses incurred shall be for the Charterers' account. The Charterers shall give sufficient notice of their intention in this respect to enable the Owners to make necessary arrangements for decommissioning and recommissioning

Any returns of premium or calls payable to the Owners by reason of the Vessel remaining within the confines of any port area in excess of any minimum period provided for in the Owners' insurance policies shall be remitted to the Charterers upon receipt by the Owners, provided the Vessel was on hire for the full period, otherwise such return shall be shared pro rata between the Owners and the Charterers according to the proportion of qualifying time on and off hire.

(o) *Signing Bills of Lading:* If required, the Master shall sign bills of lading as presented by the Charterers. If required, the Charterers and/or their agents are hereby authorised by the Owners to sign bills of lading on the Owners' and/or the Master's behalf (See Clauses 16 (a), (b) and (c)). The Charterers shall indemnify the Owners and the Master against all consequences or liabilities arising therefrom.

14. Owners' Requirements

(a) *Maintenance:* The Owners shall have the right to take the Vessel out of service for emergency repairs at any time and for routine maintenance by prior arrangement with the Charterers. The Owners shall endeavour to accommodate the Charterers' requirements in determining the timing of such maintenance and the Charterers shall endeavour to accommodate the Owners' choice of location for maintenance (See Clause 8(a)(i)).

(b) *Bills of Lading:* The Charterers warrant that bills of lading issued in respect of the carriage of goods and containers under this Charter Party shall contain the following clauses:

(i) A clause paramount applying the Hague or Hague-Visby Rules or a carriage of goods by sea statute making either of these mandatorily applicable, in either case according to the practice prevalent at the port(s) of loading.
(ii) A "New Jason" clause.
(iii) A "General Average" clause providing for adjustment at a port or place at the option of the Carrier according to the York-Antwerp Rules 1974 or any amendment thereto.
(iv) A "Himalaya" or "Circular Indemnity" clause giving the Owners the benefit of the bill of lading terms and conditions and/or protection from tortious claims by third parties.
(v) A "Sister Ship Salvage" clause.
(vi) A "Both-to-Blame Collision" clause.

(c) *General Average:* General average shall be adjusted at the place as indicated in Box 33 according to the York-Antwerp Rules 1974 or any amendment thereto by an adjuster appointed by the Owners. In the event of general average or salvage, the Charterers shall provide an acceptable temporary security covering all goods and containers to avoid delay and secure their release so that transit/delivery may continue. The Owners agree that the Charterers temporary guarantee may be exchanged in due course for a full set of securities from the appropriate interested parties covering all goods and containers. The Charterers agree to co-operate with the Owners and the Owners' appointed adjusters, to assist by supplying manifest and other information and, where required, to endeavour to secure the assistance of the Charterers' local agents in the collection of security, at the Owners' expense.

All goods and containers shall contribute in general average, whether shipped on or under deck. Charter hire shall not contribute.

General average shall be adjusted in any currency at the sole option of the Owners. Exchange into the currency of adjustment shall be calculated at the rate prevailing on the date of payment for disbursements and on the date of completion of discharge of the Vessel for allowances, contributory values, etc

(d) *Salvage:* All time lost and all legal and other expenses (excluding any damage to the Vessel) incurred in saving or attempting to save life or property shall be borne equally by the Owners and the Charterers. All salvage and proceeds from derelicts shall be divided equally between the Owners and the Charterers after deducting the Master's, Officers' and crew's share The Charterers shall be bound by all measures taken by the Owners in order to secure payment of salvage and to settle its amount.

(e) *Liens:* The Charterers warrant that they will not suffer, nor permit to be continued, any lien or encumbrance incurred by them or their agents, which might have priority over the title and interest of the Owners in the Vessel. In no event shall the Charterers procure, nor permit to be procured, for the Vessel any supplies, necessaries or services without previously obtaining a statement, signed by an authorised representative of the furnisher thereof, acknowledging that such supplies, necessaries or services are being furnished on the credit of the Charterers and not on the credit of the Vessel or of the Owners and that the furnisher claims no maritime lien on the Vessel therefor.

The Owners shall have a lien on the Charterers' goods and containers and upon all sub-freights and/or sub-hire for unpaid charter hire, unreimbursed Charterers' expenses initially paid by the Owners and contributions in general average properly due.

15. Sundry Matters

(a) *Pilotage/Towage:* Although engaged by the Charterers or their agents and paid by the Charterers, all pilotage, towage and other such services to the Vessel to assist with navigation shall be engaged as agents of the Owners who, for the purposes of this Charter Party, shall remain responsible for the due performance thereof. Nothing contained in this Charter Party shall be construed as a demise of the Vessel to the Charterers and the Owners remain responsible for the navigation thereof at all times.

(b) *Watchmen:* The cost of compulsory shore gangway watchmen shall be borne equally between the Owners and the Charterers throughout the currency of this Charter Party.

(c) *Stowaways:* Any costs incurred in respect of stowaways shall be for the Owners' account, unless it can be established that the means by which the stowaway gained access to the Vessel was by secreting away in the Charterers' goods and containers prior to loading, in which case all such costs shall be for the Charterers' account.

(d) *On/Off Hire Surveys:* Joint on and off hire surveys shall be conducted by mutually acceptable surveyors at the Places of Delivery and Redelivery, respectively. The on hire survey shall be conducted in the Owners' time unless the Vessel has commenced loading. The off hire survey shall be conducted in the Charterers' time.

Both surveys shall cover condition of the Vessel and amounts of fuel on board and the Owners shall procure that the Master, Chief Engineer, Officers and crew shall co-operate with the surveyors in conducting such surveys.

(e) *Sub-Contractors:* In this Charter Party the term "sub-contractor" shall include sub-contractors and their respective servants, agents and sub-contractors.

16. Charterers' Responsibilities/Liabilities

(a) *Charterers' Responsibilities:* Except as elsewhere provided in this Charter Party and without prejudice to the Charterers' right to initiate recovery against the Owners under Clause 17, the Charterers shall be responsible for all claims in respect of any liability or expense whatsoever or howsoever arising in connection with the goods and containers carried pursuant to this Charter Party or their carriage (even if such liability arises wholly or in part by reason of the act, neglect or default of the Owners or of such servant, agent or sub-contractor).

(b) *Claims Handling:* If any such claim or allegation as described in Clause 16(a) shall be made against the Owners or against any vessel owned by any of them, the Charterers will:-

(i) take over the conduct and defence of such claim or allegation and settle same at their own expense obtaining, where appropriate, releases in joint names or, should the Owners so request,
(ii) put the Owners in funds to meet legal fees, witness and third party expenses and settlement funds, excluding the Owners' own office expenses, to deal with such claim or allegation themselves.

(c) *General Indemnity:* If in spite of Clause 16(a) any claims as therein described are nevertheless made, the Charterers shall indemnify the Owners and such servant, agent or sub-contractor against all consequences whatsoever thereof, without prejudice to the Charterers' right subsequently to initiate action against the Owners.

(d) *Fines etc.. Indemnity:* The Charterers shall indemnify the Owners against any expenses, fines, liabilities, losses, damages, claims or demands which the Owners may incur or suffer by reason of any failure of the goods or containers or the documentation relating thereto to comply with any relevant laws, regulations, directions or notices of customs, port and other authorities, or by reasons of any infestation, contamination or condemnation of goods or containers or infestation, damage or contamination of the Vessel by the Charterers' goods or containers.

(e) *Time Limit:* The Charterers shall be discharged from all liability under this Charter Party unless notice of arbitration in accordance with Clause 20 is given within 15 months of redelivery.

(f) *Agency:* Without prejudice to sub-clause 16 (a) the Owners authorise and empower the Charterers to act as the Owners' agents and/or trustees to stipulate for the Owners to have as against other persons the benefit of any immunities, exemptions or liberties regarding the goods and containers the subject of this Charter Party or their carriage but the Charterers shall have no authority to make any contracts imposing any obligations upon the Owners in connection with the goods and containers or their carriage.

(g) *General Average Exclusion:* Nothing in this Clause 16 shall apply to preclude any claim made by the owners of any property on board the Vessel for general average contribution in accordance with the York-Antwerp Rules 1974 or any amendment thereto.

(h) *Claims Authority:* The Charterers shall make no payment in excess of the amount as stated in Box 32 in settlement of a claim for which they intend to seek recovery from the Owners without prior consultation with the Owners. The Owners authorise the Charterers to grant extensions of time in respect of such claims provided the Charterers give the Owners immediate notice thereof.

17. Owners' Responsibilities/Liabilities

Except as elsewhere provided in this Charter Party, the responsibilities and liabilities of the Owners shall be as follows:

(a) *For Goods and Containers.* The Owners shall be liable for loss, damage or expense in respect of goods and containers arising or resulting from:-

(i) lack of due diligence on their part before and at the beginning of each voyage to make the Vessel seaworthy and to properly man, equip and supply it and make all parts of the Vessel in which goods and containers are carried fit and safe for their reception, carriage and preservation, unless the Charterers consent to load containers in parts of the Vessel which the Master considers to be unfit, in which case the Charterers shall indemnify the Owners.

(ii) failure on their part properly and carefully to carry, keep and care for the goods and containers while on board, or

(iii) unreasonable deviation from the voyage ordered or approved by the Charterers.

(b) *For Refrigerated Goods:* In respect of blown-air containers, the Owners shall be responsible only to maintain the supply of air at the required temperature to the containers, provided proper instructions are given to the Master by the Charterers and the containers are presented at the carriage temperatures.

In respect of integral refrigerated containers or blown-air containers with a marine refrigeration clip-on unit attached or any containers with any machinery for temperature/atmosphere control containing goods, the Owners shall be responsible for the provision of electrical power only. The Owners shall endeavour to monitor and record the performance of all such units whilst on board in accordance with the Charterers' instructions and to repair and rectify any breakdown, fault or deficiency which may occur in respect of such units, using the resources on board the Vessel. If repair works are performed, all additional expenses incurred by the Owners, including spare parts, shall be for the account of the Charterers and the Vessel's crew shall always be considered the Charterers servants. If such resources are insufficient, the Owners shall immediately notify the Charterers so they may take action to obtain any required spares or specialised repair facilities.

Except as provided above, the Owners shall not be liable for malfunctioning of integral refrigerated containers and power packs put on board by the Charterers.

The Owners shall be entitled to reject and require the Charterers to discharge any container loaded at a temperature not within the required carriage temperature range. If, at the Charterers' request, the Owners consent to receive and carry such container(s), the Charterers shall indemnify the Owners against all consequences thereof.

(c) *Limitation of Liability:* The liability of the Owners to the Charterers for loss, damage or expense in respect of goods and containers as herein provided shall be limited as follows:

(i) In respect of goods liability shall be on the same basis as applicable under mandatory law between the Charterers and a third party by reason of the Charterers having issued a bill of lading or similar contract of carriage, provided that such Bill of Lading contains no declaration of value. Where no mandatory law so applies, liability shall be limited to GB Pounds 100 per package

(ii) In respect of containers, liability shall be the reasonable cost of repair or the value of the container at the time of such loss or damage, whichever is the lesser. The value of a leased container is the value stated in the lease agreement and for an owned container it is its market value. For the purpose of this Charter Party containers not owned or leased by the Charterers shall be regarded as goods for liability purposes.

(d) *Time Limit:* Except as provided in Clause 16(h), the Owners shall be discharged from all liability under this Charter Party in respect of claims for which extensions of time have not been sought and obtained by the Charterers unless notice of arbitration in accordance with Clause 20 is given within 15 months of the delivery of goods, if the claim relates to goods, or the date when the Charterers become aware of the incident giving rise to the claim for all other claims.

(e) *For Personal Injury:* The Owners shall indemnify the Charterers against any claims for personal injury incurred on or about the Vessel unless caused by the negligence of the Charterers, their servants, agents or subcontractors or any defect in the Charterers' goods and/or containers.

(f) *Limitation Proceedings:* The Owners shall have the control and conduct of any limitation proceedings on the joint behalf of the Owners and the Charterers If successful, any unrecovered costs of such proceedings shall be borne equally between the Owners and the Charterers. If unsuccessful, the costs shall be borne by the party responsible under the terms of this Charter Party for the factor which caused the proceedings to fail. If more than one factor contributed and the Owners and the Charterers were each responsible for at least one factor the costs shall be borne equally.

(g) *Consequential Loss:* Under no circumstances shall the Owners be responsible for any indirect or consequential loss arising from loss, damage or delay to goods and containers, howsoever caused.

18. Insurances

(a) *Hull and Machinery:* The Owners warrant that the Vessel is insured under Institute Time Clauses or similar clauses for IWL trading against loss, damage and collision liabilities for the value as indicated in Box 27 which cover will be maintained throughout the currency of this Charter Party. Upon 10 days notice to the Charterers, the Owners shall be entitled to effect any reasonable change to this value. The Owners agree that their insured value for the purpose of this Clause shall represent the Charterers maximum liability to the Owners for damage to the Vessel in accordance with Clause 6 (l), including time spent on repairs.

(b) *Protection and Indemnity (P & I):* The Owners and the Charterers warrant that the Vessel is entered on full terms with their respective P & I Clubs as indicated in Boxes 30 and 31 and that such entries will be maintained with all calls paid up to date throughout the currency of this Charter Party.

(c) *War Risks:* The Owners warrant that the Vessel is insured against loss of the Vessel by War Risks and War P & I Risks for IWL trading excluding additional premium/restricted/ prohibited areas, which cover will be maintained throughout the currency of this Charter Party.

19. War

(a) Unless the consent of the Owners be first obtained, the Vessel shall not be ordered to nor obliged to:-

(i) remain in or pass through any area which is dangerous or is likely to become dangerous as a result of war, hostilities, warlike action or piracy, actual or threatened, nor

(ii) call at any port where there is any revolution, civil war, civil commotion or any threat thereof, nor

(iii) carry any goods that may in any way expose her to any risk of seizure, capture or detention.

(b) However, should the Owners consent to allowing the Vessel to proceed, notwithstanding the existence or threat of the danger(s) outlined in Clause 19 (a), the Owners agree that the Vessel proceeds at their own risk in consideration of the Charterers agreeing that the Owners may effect the following insurances for which the Charterers will reimburse the Owners the net cost of premium/calls therefor: (See Clause 6 (n))

(i) Reinstatement of the War Risks cover on Hull and P & I for trading to the required area.

(ii) Any further additional premia necessary to maintain Hull cover whilst blocked or trapped pending release of the Vessel, acceptance of constructive total loss by insurers or trapped for 365 consecutive days, whichever shall first occur.

(iii) Insurance of hire on the Vessel for not exceeding 365 days.

(c) In the event of the wages of the Master, Officers and/or crew and/or other of the Vessel's operating expenses are affected by any of the factors mentioned in (a) above, the amount of any increase shall be added to the hire due upon production of the Owners' account therefor together with appropriate receipts and paid by the Charterers to the Owners with the next hire payment.

(d) The Vessel shall have the liberty to comply with any orders or directions of whatsoever nature given by the government of the nation where the Owners are domiciled or whose flag the Vessel flies or any other government or person or body acting, or purporting to act, with the authority of such government or by any party having, under the terms of the war risk insurance on the Vessel, the right to give such orders or directions.

(e) In the event of the outbreak of war, whether there be a declaration of war or not, between any two or more of the following countries or involving the nation where the Owners are domiciled or whose flag the Vessel flies:-

People's Republic of China, France, Federal Republic of Germany, United States of America, United Kingdom, Union of Soviet Socialist Republics,

either the Owners or the Charterers may cancel this Charter Party and, unless otherwise agreed, the Vessel shall be redelivered to the Owners at the port of destination or, if debarred under this Clause from reaching or entering it, at a near open and safe port at the Owners' option after discharge of any goods and containers on board.

(f) If in compliance with the provisions of this Clause anything is done or is not done, such shall not be deemed a deviation.

20. Law and Arbitration

*) (a) *London:* This Charter Party shall be governed by English law and any dispute arising out of this Charter Party shall be referred to arbitration in London, one arbitrator being appointed by each party, in accordance with the Arbitration Acts 1950 and 1979 or any statutory modification or re-enactment thereof for the time being in force. On the receipt by one party of the nomination in writing of the other party's arbitrator, that party shall appoint their arbitrator within fourteen days, failing which the decision of the single Arbitrator appointed shall apply If two Arbitrators properly appointed shall not agree they shall appoint an umpire whose decision shall be final.

*) (b) *New York:* Should any dispute arise out of this Charter Party, the matter in dispute shall be referred to three persons in New York, one to be appointed by each of the parties hereto, and the third by the two so chosen; their decision or that of any two of them shall be final, and for the purpose of enforcing any award. this agreement may be made a rule of the Court The arbitrators shall be members of the Society of Maritime Arbitrators, Inc. of New York and the proceedings shall be conducted in accordance with the rules of the Society.

*) (c) *Alternative:* Any dispute arising out of this Charter Party shall be referred to arbitration at the place indicated in Box 34, subject to the law and procedures applicable there.

If Box 34 in Part I is not filled in, sub-clause (a) of this Clause shall apply.

*) *(a), (b) and (c) are alternatives; indicate alternative agreed in Box 34.*

21. Commission

The Owners shall pay a commission at the rate stated in Box 35 to the party mentioned in Box 35 on any hire paid under this Charter Party but in no case less than is necessary to cover the actual expenses of the Brokers. If the full hire is not paid owing to breach of Charter Party by either of the parties the party liable therefor shall indemnify the Brokers against their loss of commission.

Should the parties agree to cancel this Charter Party, the Owners shall indemnify the Brokers against any loss of commission but in such case the commission shall not exceed the brokerage on one year's hire.

22. Notices

Any notice to the Owners shall be sent to the address as indicated in Box 3. Any notice to the Charterers shall be sent to the address as indicated in Box 4.

PART III

"BOXTIME" Charter Party

VESSEL'S SPECIFICATION

Built:
Official No.:
Hull & Machinery value:
Type: (cellular, non-cellular, self-sustained, gearless etc.):
DWT at design draft
DWT at summer draft

Tonnage:

	GRT	NRT
International:		
Suez:		
Panama:		

Main Dimensions:

Length overall:
Breadth:
Draft fully laden on SF:
Max. height:

Container Capacity TEU (20' x 8' x 8'6"):

General distribution:	in holds	TEU
	on deck	TEU
	Total:	

Below deck: _____ units stowed as follows:

Hold No. 1	units _____/_____/_____/_____/_____/_____ units in 1st/ 2nd/ 3rd/ 4th/ 5th/ 6th	tier
Hold No. 2	units _____/_____/_____/_____/_____/_____ units in 1st/ 2nd/ 3rd/ 4th/ 5th/ 6th	tier
Hold No. 3	units _____/_____/_____/_____/_____/_____ units in 1st/ 2nd/ 3rd/ 4th/ 5th/ 6th	tier
Hold No. 4	units _____/_____/_____/_____/_____/_____ units in 1st/ 2nd/ 3rd/ 4th/ 5th/ 6th	tier

PART III

"BOXTIME" Charter Party

On deck: _____ units stowed as follows:

Hatch No. 1	units ____/	____/	____/	____/	____/	____ units		
	in	1st/	2nd/	3rd/	4th/	5th/	6th	tier
Hatch No. 2	units ____/	____/	____/	____/	____/	____ units		
	in	1st/	2nd/	3rd/	4th/	5th/	6th	tier
Hatch No. 3	units ____/	____/	____/	____/	____/	____ units		
	in	1st/	2nd/	3rd/	4th/	5th/	6th	tier
Hatch No. 4	units ____/	____/	____/	____/	____/	____ units		
	in	1st/	2nd/	3rd/	4th/	5th/	6th	tier

Container Capacity FEU (40' x 8' x 8'6"):

General distribution:	in holds	**FEU**
	on deck	**FEU**
	Total:	

Below deck: _____ units stowed as follows:

Hold No. 1	units ____/	____/	____/	____/	____/	____ units		
	in	1st/	2nd/	3rd/	4th/	5th/	6th	tier
Hold No. 2	units ____/	____/	____/	____/	____/	____ units		
	in	1st/	2nd/	3rd/	4th/	5th/	6th	tier
Hold No. 3	units ____/	____/	____/	____/	____/	____ units		
	in	1st/	2nd/	3rd/	4th/	5th/	6th	tier
Hold No. 4	units ____/	____/	____/	____/	____/	____ units		
	in	1st/	2nd/	3rd/	4th/	5th/	6th	tier

On deck: _____ units stowed as follows:

Hatch No. 1	units ____/	____/	____/	____/	____/	____ units		
	in	1st/	2nd/	3rd/	4th/	5th/	6th	tier
Hatch No. 2	units ____/	____/	____/	____/	____/	____ units		
	in	1st/	2nd/	3rd/	4th/	5th/	6th	tier
Hatch No. 3	units ____/	____/	____/	____/	____/	____ units		
	in	1st/	2nd/	3rd/	4th/	5th/	6th	tier
Hatch No. 4	units ____/	____/	____/	____/	____/	____ units		
	in	1st/	2nd/	3rd/	4th/	5th/	6th	tier

Stability cases bases 20' x 8 x 8'6":

Basis 14 tons homogeneous weight:
15 tons homogeneous weight:
16 tons homogeneous weight:

PART III
"BOXTIME" Charter Party

Reefer Container Capacity:

On deck:

Number and type of plugs:
Power supply:

Under deck:

Reefer capacity:	blown air
	integral

Maximum Permissible Stack Weight:

Tanktop:
Weather deck:

Type of Hatch Covers:

Hatch Dimensions:

Cranes/Gear:

Vessel equipped with Spreader:

Type:

Main Engine and Types:

Bunker fuel specification:

PART III

"BOXTIME" Charter Party

Type of propellers: (controllable pitch or fixed)

Auxiliary Engines and types:

Bunker fuel specification:

Shaft generator:

Bow thruster:

Generator sets:

Turbo alternators:

Speed/Consumption:

in smooth water and with winds not exceeding Beaufort Scale 4

Consumption: Pilotage/River/Shallow Waters Manouvering:

Port Consumption:

Waiting at anchor or waiting at berth without any commercial operations:

Working (gearless):

With cranes/gear working (geared):

Reefer containers:

Donkey boilers:

Bunker Capacity:

Ballast Capacity:

APPENDIX 2

CROSS CHARTERPARTY

dated _____
Between
1. _______________(Disponent) owners (hereinafter called "the Owners") of the Containership_______________and
2. _______________(hereinafter called "the Charterers").
It is agreed

1. Space Allocation and Period

The Owners let and the Charterers hire for the carriage of goods and containers _____ per cent of the container carrying capacity of the Containership by reference to TEU capacity and deadweight, whichever is reached first, (or more or less as may be agreed for each voyage) from _______________ until _______________ and thereafter unless and until terminated by either party giving _____ months' notice in writing.

2. Employment

2.1 The Containership shall be employed only in lawful trades within the Institute Warranty Limits for the carriage of lawful goods, properly packed and stowed in seaworthy containers of standard sizes and specifications, as may be mutually agreed, between good and safe ports, where it can safely lie always afloat, save that uncontainerised and out of gauge goods may be carried, but only with the prior consent of the Owners. If accepted, such items shall be carried under the terms of this Charter party but subject to such additional conditions as the Owners may require.
Goods which are of a dangerous, inflammable, radio-active, obnoxious or damaging nature shall not be shipped unless:

(a) prior written notice of their nature has been given to the Owners by or on behalf of the Charterers (including particulars of the characteristics of the goods, the flash point (if any), the type of packing of the goods and any other information which the Owners may reasonably require); and
(b) the Owners have consented, after receipt of such notice, to accept those goods for shipment; and
(c) all the relevant requirements and recommendations of the International Maritime Organisation and the law and regulations in force in the country of registration of the Containership, the port of shipment, the port of discharge, any area through which the Containership may pass and any scheduled port of call have been complied with; and
(d) the goods shall have been packed, labelled and stowed within the containers and the containers have been labelled in accordance with such law, regulations, requirements or recommendations and, in any event, so as to avoid such goods

causing damage, injury or material discomfort to the Containership, crew and other goods and to any other property or person.

Live animals shall not be shipped, except by special arrangement with the Owners and then on no liability terms.

2.2 If the requirements of sub-clause 2.1 are not complied with, the Charterers shall, to the extent provided in sub-clause 10.9, indemnify the Owners against all loss, damage or expense arising out of the goods being tendered for shipment or being handled or carried by the Owners.

2.3 Goods which, in the opinion of the Owners, are or may at any time become dangerous, inflammable, radio-active, obnoxious, damaging or injurious may, at any time or place, be unloaded, destroyed, or rendered harmless, without compensation to the Charterers and without liability to make any general average contribution in respect of such goods.

3. Remuneration

The Owners shall be remunerated in accordance with the provisions from time to time separately agreed or, in default of agreement, shall receive such remuneration as shall be fair and reasonable.

4. Owners' Expenses

Save as provided in sub-clause 10.7, the Owners shall pay all wages, insurance premiums, charges, dues, taxes, agencies, commissions, fees and all other expenses whatsoever incurred in connection with the operation of the Containership.

5. Voyage and Destination

5.1 The itinerary of each voyage shall be mutually agreed between the Owners and the Charterers.

5.2 The Owners shall be entitled to exercise the liberties to deviate provided in the Hague Rules at any time without prior notice to the Charterers. However, if during the course of a voyage the Owners should deviate in circumstances which under English law does not permit the Charterers to deviate under the Hague Rules, the Owners shall indemnify the Charterers for any liability thereby incurred, unless the Owners shall have obtained the prior consent of the Charterers to such deviation, in which case this indemnity shall not operate. Any deviation agreed by the line's representatives in the Operating Committee shall be deemed to have the prior consent of the Charterers.

5.3 Subject as may be otherwise agreed, the Owners shall have the liberty to take the Containership out of service for maintenance and repairs. In arranging such periods the Owners will take account of the Charterers' requirements so far as is possible.

6. Opening Containers

The Owners shall be entitled, at any time (but under no obligation), to open any container or package and to inspect the contents at the Owners' expense and shall promptly notify the Charterers if they do so.

Containers opened must be properly closed and sealed and records maintained, which must be available to the Charterers. The Owners must advise the Charterers promptly in writing of the replacement seal number.

7. Access to Logs

The Master and Engineer shall keep full and correct logs and adequate records concerning the care and condition of the containers and the goods and all the logs and records relevant to the voyage, the containers and the goods shall be accessible to the Charterers.
The Owners will co-operate with the Charterers to assist them to identify witnesses and obtain statements in respect of any incident during the currency of this Charterparty which gives rise to a claim against the Charterers.

8. Charterers Obligations

8.1 The Charterers shall provide such information in relation to any goods shipped under this Charterparty as the Owners may reasonably require in connection with this Charterparty, and the Charterers warrant such information shall be complete and accurate.
8.2 The Charterers shall comply with the directions of the Master or other persons responsible for the stowage on behalf of the Owners as to when and where containers are to be stowed. The Charterers shall, in their capacity as such, be under no liability in respect of the consequences of complying with such directions, notwithstanding the provisions of sub-clause 10.7, and the Owners shall indemnify the Charterers against the same.
8.3 Any liability of the Charterers arising from their obligations under this clause 8 shall be subject to sub-clause 10.9.

9. Indemnity and Agency

9.1 The Charterers undertake that no claim or allegation shall be made against the Owners or any servant, agent or sub-contractor of the Owners by any person whomsoever, other than the Charterers, which imposes or attempts to impose upon the Owners, or any such servant, agent or sub-contractor or any Containership owned by any of them, any liability whatsoever in connection with the goods and containers the subject of this Charterparty (even if such liability arises wholly or in part by reason of the act, neglect or default of the Owners or of such servant, agent or sub-contractor) and, in the event of any such claim or allegation nevertheless being made, the Charterers shall (to the extent provided in sub-clause 10.9) indemnify the Owners and such servant, agent and sub-contractor against all consequences whatsoever thereof.
9.2 The Charterers shall not make any claim or allegation against any servant, agent or sub-contractor of the Owners which imposes or attempts to impose on any such servant, agent or sub-contractor any liability whatsoever in connection with the goods and containers the subject of this Charterparty (even if such liability arises wholly or in part by reason of the act, neglect or default of the Owners or such servant, agent or sub-contractor) and, in the event of any such claim or allegation nevertheless being made, the provisions of sub-clause 9.1 shall apply as if such claim or allegation had been made by a person other than the Charterers.
9.3 Without prejudice to sub-clause 9.1, the Owners authorise and empower the Charterers to act as the Owners' agent and/or trustees to stipulate for the Owners to have, as against other persons, the benefit of any immunities, exemptions or liberties regarding the goods and containers the subject of this Charterparty or their carriage, but the Charterers shall have no authority to make any contracts imposing any obligations upon the Owners in connection with the goods and containers or their carriage.

9.4 Sub-clauses 9.1 and 9.2 shall not apply to or preclude any claim made by the owners of any property on board the Containership for a General Average contribution in accordance with the York-Antwerp Rules 1994, unless any subsequent modification thereto is approved by the CMI, in which case the latter shall apply.
9.5 If the Owners are not the actual owners of the Containership, the provisions of sub-clauses 9.1, 9.2 and 9.3 shall also apply to the actual owners of the Containership, their servants, agents and sub-contractors in the same manner as they apply to the Owners, their servants, agents and sub-contractors.

10. Responsibilities, Liabilities and Exemptions

Without prejudice to the provisions of clauses 2, 8 and 9 hereof, as between the Owners and the Charterers, the responsibilities arising out of and in connection with this Charterparty shall be borne and divided as follows:
10.1 The Owners will be responsible for the seaworthiness of the Containership in accordance with Article III, Rule 1 and Article IV, Rule 1 of the Hague Rules as scheduled to the Carriage of Goods by Sea Act 1924 and for all purposes in connection with this Charterparty shall be entitled to the rights and immunities set out in Article IV, Rules 2, 4 and 6 of said Hague Rules.
10.2 Subject to sub-clause 10.1, the Owners will be responsible for the proper and careful carriage, custody and care of the containers and goods whilst on board the Containership, and for discharging, handling and storing containers and goods discharged solely in order to be reloaded or in order to load or discharge other containers and goods, and for reloading and restowing the same.
10.3 Subject to sub-clause 10.1, the Owners shall be responsible for the provision of:
(a) electrical power;
(b) a supply of refrigerant gas; and
(c) a supply of the recommended lubricating oil;
(d) plugging in or unplugging
to integral refrigerated containers, insulated containers with marine clip-on units fitted and ventilated containers (hereinafter in this clause 'mechanical containers') containing goods shipped on the Containership.
The Owners shall use all reasonable endeavours to monitor and record the performance of all such units whilst on board and to repair and rectify any breakdown, fault or deficiency which may occur in respect of such units, using the resources on board the Containership. If such resources are insufficient the Owners, at the expense of the Charterers, shall use all reasonable endeavours promptly to obtain any required spares or specialised repair facilities. The Owners shall be liable for any loss of or damage to a mechanical container or the goods therein arising out of any breakdown, fault or deficiency of its machinery, only to the extent that such loss or damage was caused by the failure of the Owners to comply with the terms of this sub-clause. Save as expressly provided, nothing in the sub-clause shall reduce or limit the liability of the Owners to the Charterers under this Charterparty.
10.4 The liabilities of the Owners under sub-clauses 10.1, 10.2 and 10.3 shall be time barred absolutely 18 months after discharge of the goods from the Containership. If the Charterers receive a claim for which they intend to pursue recourse against the Owners, the Charterers shall give prompt notice thereof with full details to the Owners. Requests for extensions of time shall not be unreasonably refused.
10.5 The liability of the Owners for any loss, damage or delay to or in connection with the goods, including containers not owned or hired by the Charterers, shall be subject to Article IV Rule 5 of the said Hague Rules, but as if no declaration as to value is made, provided always that:

(a) the liability of the Owners to the Charterers as aforesaid shall in no event exceed the liability (if any) of the Charterers to the persons interested in such goods in respect of such loss or damage;

(b) where the liability of the Owners to the Charterers and the liability of the Charterers to any other person(s) in respect of such goods are both subject to Article IV Rule 5 of the said Hague Rules, those goods shall be deemed, as between that the Owners and the Charterers and for the purposes of the said Rule 5, to consist of the number of packages or units which is applicable for the purposes of the said Rule 5 as between the Charterers and such other person(s).

(c) where, by operation of law, the liability of the Charterers to any other person is subject to Article IV Rule 5 of the Hague Rules as amended by the Carriage of Goods by Sea Act 1971 or similar legislation (the Hague-Visby Rules), the Owners' liability to the Charterers shall be subject to Article IV Rule 5 as so amended.

(d) notwithstanding the provisions of this Charterparty elsewhere, if the liability of the Charterers to any other party for loss, damage, delay or expense to the goods and containers is governed by some other mandatory law, then the liability of the Owners to the Charterers shall be determined according to that mandatory law.

(e) in addition to liability for the claim in accordance with the provisions of this sub-clause, the Owners shall be liable for and shall reimburse the Charterers for reasonable legal and other expenses incurred by the Charterers in defending/settling claims for which the Owners are liable under the terms of this Charter party.

Except in cases of emergency, the Charterers shall consult with and obtain the Owners' prior approval to expenses which will form a part of a claim against the Owners under the provisions of this sub-clause.

(f) the Charterers do not contractually incorporate Article IX of the 1924 Hague Rules into their contracts of carriage with their cargo interests and, where such Rules are contractually applied, they limit liability to GBP 100 Sterling per package or equivalent national Hague Rules limit.

10.6 The liability of the Owners and the Containership for any loss of or damage to or in connection with a container owned or hired by the Charterers shall not in any event exceed the cost of repair or the market value of the container at the time of such loss or damage, whichever is the lesser, and the Owners and the Containership shall not in any event be liable for any damage to a container which does not exceed US$500 on any one voyage.

10.7 Subject as aforesaid and subject to sub-clause 10.9, the Charterers will be responsible for the proper and careful receipt, loading, handling, stowage/securing of goods inside containers, discharge and delivery of the goods and containers and shall pay all sums relating to such operations and shall be liable for all loss, damage (including loss of or damage to the Containership) or expense caused to the Owners by the improper or careless performance of such operations.

10.8 The Charterers shall, to the extent provided in sub-clause 10.9, indemnify the Owners against any expenses, liabilities, losses, damages, claims or demands which the Owners may incur or suffer by reason of any failure to comply with any relevant laws, regulations, directions or notices of Customs, port and any other authorities, or by reason of any infestation, contamination or condemnation or damage or loss arising from any act, neglect or default of the consignors or consignees of any goods or containers, the subject of this Charterparty, their servants or agents.

The indemnity provided in this sub-clause shall extend to any loss suffered by the Owners in procuring, by whatever means the Owners consider appropriate, the release of the Containership where the Containership has been arrested either:

(a) by virtue of any act done or omitted to be done by the Charterers, or

(b) in circumstances where, but for the fact that the Containership was chartered to the Charterers, such arrest would not have occurred.

Unless the arrest follows from an event for which the Owners are responsible under this Charter party or otherwise.

10.9

(a) The liability of the Charterers for loss, damage or delay of whatsoever nature and howsoever arising in connection with this Charterparty (even if such liability arises wholly or in part by reason of the act, neglect, or default of the Charterers or their servants, agents or sub-contractors) shall not in any event exceed the amount (if any) recoverable by the Charterers from any third party in connection with such liability, but the Charterers shall take all reasonable steps (short of court action) to recover such amount and shall account therefor to the Owners. For this purpose the Charterers' insurers shall not be considered as third parties.

(b) The Charterers shall, upon the written request from the Owners, allow the Owners to take over all conduct of any enforcement of any rights which the Charterers may have against any third party to enable the Owners to exercise such rights in the Charterer's name but at the Owner's expense. The Charterers shall co-operate as much as is reasonably possible to assist the Owners to exercise such rights which the Charterers may have against the third party.

(c) If the Charterers should not be willing to transfer to the Owners all conduct of any enforcement of rights and to co-operate as required above in assisting the Owners, the provisions of sub-clause (a) shall be null and void. The Charterers shall be deemed to have shown unwillingness to transfer if they have not given the necessary authority in writing to the Owners to proceed within 30 days of receipt of a written request so to do.

Notwithstanding the above, the provisions of this sub-clause shall not operate in respect of the indemnities under sub-clause 9.1 and 10.8 where fines or other penalties have been imposed by any Customs, port or other authorities in respect of a failure to comply with the regulations relating to declaration of goods or documentation of cargo or other infringement of the law or regulations of any Customs, port or other authority. The provisions of this sub-clause shall also not operate in respect of the indemnity in sub-clause 10.8 relating to the arrest of the Containership.

10.10 The Owners undertake that no claim or allegation shall be made against the Charterers by any person other than the Owners which imposes or attempts to impose upon the Charterers any liability whatsoever arising from loss or damage to the Containership, whether for actual loss or consequential loss and whether or not arising as a result of negligence on the part of the Charterers, their servants, agents or sub-contractors and, if any such claim or allegation should nevertheless be made, to indemnify the Charterers, their servants, agents or sub-contractors against all consequences thereof.

10.11 Nothing in this Charter party shall prejudice or deprive the Owners of their rights of limitation or exclusion of liability under any applicable or relevant law.

10.12 The Owner shall maintain the Containership's class and container carrying capacity throughout the period of this Charterparty, unless otherwise mutually agreed.

11. Bill of Lading, etc.

11.1 The Charterers shall issue bills of lading and other contracts of carriage in their own regular forms for all goods occupying slots (space) hereby chartered. All such contracts shall contain the Paramount Clause incorporating Hague or Hague-Visby Rules legislation for the sea transportation period, the New Jason Clause, the Both-

to-Blame Collision Clause and a full Circular Indemnity/Himalaya Clause in favour of both the Owners and Co-charterers.
11.2 Such contracts shall provide for General Average to be adjusted and settled at any port or place in the option of the Owners according to York-Antwerp Rules 1994 (unless any subsequent modification thereto is approved by the CMI, in which case the latter shall apply). All such contracts shall mention that the rules governing responsibility and provision for General Average apply to containers and goods loaded either on deck or under deck.
11.3 It is hereby agreed that no such contracts of carriage will be issued by the Charterers whereby a contractual relationship is established between cargo interests and the Master or Owners respectively.
11.4 Issuers of such contracts of carriage are to process all claims lodged under their respective contracts/bills of lading.

12. Sub-contractors

In this Charter party the expression 'sub-contractor' shall include direct and indirect sub-contractors and their respective servants and agents.

13. General Average and Salvage Services Received

13.1 General Average shall be settled according to the York-Antwerp Rules 1994 (unless any subsequent modification thereto is approved by the CMI, in which case the latter shall apply). The Owners remuneration shall not contribute to General Average. The Owners authorise and empower the Charterers to act as the agents of the Owners in the collection of General Average securities. The Charterers shall guarantee the contributions properly due to the Owners in respect of:
(a) goods for which the Charterers are principal carrier under a Bill of Lading or contract of carriage unless delivered to the consignees prior to notice being given by the Owners to the Charterers that General Average security is required; and
(b) containers owned or hired by the Charterers.
13.2 In the event of the Containership needing to engage salvage services and, in order to secure the release of goods and containers for on-carriage, the Owners are required to give any undertaking to salvors to assist in the collection of security and not to release goods and containers until acceptable salvage security has been provided, the Charterers shall guarantee to the Owners that the requirements of such undertaking will be met in respect of the goods for which the Charterers are the contracting carrier and containers owned, hired or operated by the Charterers, provided that these requirements are notified to the Charterers prior to the delivery of the goods and containers to the Charterers.
13.3
(a) The Owners undertake not to declare General Average or seek contribution in salvage from the Charterers unless they are also doing so from their own cargo interests, to whom they have issued Bills of Lading, Waybills or similar contracts of carriage, provided always that, where the Owners are prepared to absorb cargoes' proportion of General Average or salvage for goods for which they are principal carrier, the Charterers are willing to do likewise in respect of goods for which they are principal carrier.
(b) The Owners undertake that their demands for General Average security and counter security for salvage (where sub-clause 13.2 applies) shall be reasonable in the light of what is readily available at the destination port/place of delivery. If the Owners are unprepared to accept security offered, they will accept any storage costs which the Charterers, despite best endeavours, are unable to recover from their cargo interests.

(c) In the event of a General Average situation arising at a port of refuge, the Owners and the Charterers shall consult on the desirability and practicability of on-carriage under a non-separation agreement. Unless agreed to the contrary, the arrangement and cost of on-carriage shall be for the account of the Charterers.

14. Salvage

The Charterers shall be entitled to the percentage, as agreed for the voyage under Clause 1, of all Salvage and assistance to other vessels, after deducting the Master's and crew's proportion and all legal and other expenses, including a reasonable sum for the time lost in salvage and the cost of repairing damage incurred in the salvage, to the extent not recoverable from Hull insurers. The Charterers shall be bound by all measures taken by the Owners in order to secure payment of salvage and to fix its amount.

15. Stowaways

Any fines, costs and losses incurred in respect of stowaways shall be for the Owners' account, unless it can be proved that the means by which the stowaway gained access to the Containership was by hiding in the Charterers' goods and/or containers prior to loading, in which case all such fines, costs and losses shall be for the Charterers' account, except to the extent that such fines, costs and losses have arisen as a result of unlawful conduct by the Master officers or crew.

16. Deck Carriage

Goods and containers may be carried on deck and shall contribute in General Average whether carried on or under deck.
Goods not in containers and goods stowed on flat tracks may be carried on deck only with the prior approval of the Charterers.

17. Non-Assignment

The Charterers shall not assign this Charterparty. The Charterers shall not sub-let any space or part thereof unless otherwise agreed.

18. Law and Arbitration

18.1 This Cross Charterparty shall be governed by and construed in accordance with the laws of England and each line hereby submits to the jurisdiction of the English courts.
18.2 All disputes or differences arising under this Cross Charterparty, which cannot be amicably resolved, shall be referred to arbitration in England in accordance with the Arbitration Act 1996, together with the LMAA (London Maritime Arbitration Association) terms.
18.3 The lines agree to appoint a single/sole arbitrator, having appropriate commercial and consortia experience, within 21 days of any line seeking an appointment. If any line should so request, a panel of three arbitrators shall be appointed. Should there be no agreement on the appointment within the said 21 days, then the LMAA president will appoint a single/sole arbitrator (or a panel of three arbitrators as appropriate) at the request of any line.
18.4 The lines further agree that, where the amount in dispute is US$200,000 or less, the arbitration will proceed on a document and written submission basis only. However, oral evidence will be allowed exceptionally and at the discretion of the arbitrator(s).

APPENDIX 3

SLOTHIRE (SLOT CHARTERPARTY)

1 Shipbroker	THE BALTIC AND INTERNATIONAL MARITIME COUNCIL (BIMCO) STANDARD SLOT CHARTER PARTY CODE NAME: "SLOTHIRE" PART I 2 Place and date
3 Owners/Address	4. Charterers/Address
5 Vessel	6 Call Sign
7 Slot Allocation (state no of TEUs) (Cl. 1)	8 Weight Allocation (state maximum total weight of Containers) (Cl 1)
9 State no of Containers to be connected to Vessel's refrigerating machinery/ power supply (Cl 1)	10. Vessel's Itinerary (Cl 6)
11. Commencement Date and Place (Cl. 2)	
12. Termination (state period of notice of termination) (Cl 2)	
13. Notice (state earliest date on which notice of termination may be given) (Cl 2)	
14. State port and date, or scheduled period (Cl 2)	
15 Slot Charter Hire (FIOS) per voyage (Cl 5)	16 Additional amount (per day) payable for each Container receiving a supply of power from the Vessel (Cl. 5)
	17 Place of payment, also state beneficiary and bank account (Cl. 5)
18 Latest payment date (Cl 5)	19 Interest rate per annum (Cl 5)
20. Charterers' maximum claim settlement authority (Cl. 15(d))	
21. General Average to be adjusted at (Cl. 19)	22 Brokerage commission and to whom payable
23 Law and Arbitration (state (a), (b) or (c) of Cl. 23; if (c) agreed also state Place of Arbitration) (Cl 23)	24 Number of additional clauses covering special provisions

It is mutually agreed that this Contract shall be performed in accordance with the conditions in PART I including additional clauses, if any agreed and stated in Box 23, and PART II. In the event of a conflict of conditions, the provisions of PART I shall prevail over those of PART II to the extent of such conflict but no further

Signature (Owners)	Signature (Charterers)

Issued by
The Documentary Committee of
The Baltic and International Maritime Council (BIMCO), Copenhagen

Printed and sold by Fr. G. Knudtzons Bogtrykkeri A/S, 55 Toldbodgade, DK-1253 Copenhagen K, Telefax +45 33 93 11 84,
by authority of The Baltic and International Maritime Council (BIMCO), Copenhagen

Part II: "SLOTHIRE" Standard Slot Charter Party

It is agreed on the date as indicated in Box 2 between the party named in Box 3 (hereinafter referred to as "the Owners") of the Vessel named in Box 5 and with the call sign as stated in Box 6, and the party named in Box 4 (hereinafter referred to as "the Charterers") as follows:

Definitions

In this Slot Charter Party, the following words shall have the meanings hereby assigned to them:
"TEU" means a Twenty Foot Equivalent Unit.
"Slot" means the space on board the Vessel necessary to accommodate one TEU.
"Container" means any Standard ISO Container.
"Goods" means the whole or any part of the cargo received from the Charterers and includes any Container not owned or hired by the Charterers.
"Sub-contractor" shall include direct and/or indirect sub-contractors and/or their respective servants and agents.

1. Slot and Weight Allocation

(a) The Owners shall let and the Charterers shall hire the number of Slots as agreed in Box 7 for the carriage of Goods and Containers, of which the number of Containers as indicated in Box 9 may be connected to the Vessel's refrigerating machinery and/or power supply, provided that the total weight of said Goods and Containers does not exceed the weight shown in Box 8.

(b) Slots shall be available to the Charterers on a voyage basis as specified in Box 15 and may be used by the Charterers for the carriage of Goods and Containers between all the specified ports.

(c) The Owners shall have free use of any Slot or weight allocation unused by the Charterers on any voyage leg, provided that such Slot or weight allocation is available to the Charterers at the next port at which the Charterers are entitled to load.

2. Period

This Slot Charter Party shall commence on the date and at the place shown in Box 11 and shall terminate upon either party giving notice in writing as agreed in Box 12, which notice shall not be given before the date agreed in Box 13. Alternatively, the parties may agree that the termination of this Slot Charter Party shall be effected upon discharge at a port and on a scheduled date or within a scheduled period as agreed in Box. 14.

3. Trading Limits

The Vessel shall be employed in lawful trades within the Institute Warranty Limits for the carriage of lawful merchandise.

4. Permitted Cargoes

Except as provided below, the Slots shall be used exclusively for the carriage of Goods properly packed and stowed in Containers complying with the International Convention for Safe Containers. The following items may only be shipped with the prior approval of the Owners (see also Clause 12):

(a) Uncontainerised Goods

(b) Containers of Non-Standard Sizes and Specifications

(c) Live Animals

(d) Hazardous Goods, provided also that such Goods are loaded, stowed, discharged and documented in accordance with IMO Regulations

(e) Radioactive Materials

provided that

(i) previous written full particulars of such Goods have been given to the Owners by or on behalf of the Charterers and;

(ii) all the relevant requirements and recommendations and the law in force in the port of loading and discharge and any intermediate scheduled port of call as well as the law of the country in which the Vessel is registered, have been complied with

(iii) the carriage of such Goods is not excluded under the Onwers' P&I cover.

5. Slot Charter Hire

Slot Charter Hire at the rate shown in Box 15 and an additional amount (per day) indicated in Box 16 for each Container receiving a supply of power from the Vessel, if any, shall be payable at the place indicated in Box 17, within the number of days shown in Box 18 after commencement of the voyage. Such Slot Charter Hire and additional amount, if any, shall be deemed earned upon the commencement of the voyage, irrespective of the number of Slots used, and shall be non-returnable in any event.

Late payment shall entitle the Owners to an interest rate per annum as agreed in Box 19. If Box 19 has not been filled in, the official discount rate on bills of exchange as valid at the place of payment indicated in Box 17, increased by 3 per cent., shall apply.

6. Itinerary

(a) The schedule of the itinerary as specified in Box 17 shall be advised to the Charterers as early as possible together with prompt advice of any amendments thereto.

(b) The Owners shall be entitled to exercise the liberty to deviate as provided in the Hague-Visby Rules at any time without notice to the Charterers. However, if during the course of a voyage the Vessel should deviate in circumstances which are not permitted by a bill of lading or other contract of carriage covering Goods for which the Charterers have used a Slot, the Owners shall indemnify the Charterers for any liability thereby incurred, unless the Owners have given at least 48 hours prior notice to the Charterers of such intended deviation, in which case this indemnity shall not operate.

7. Opening Containers

The Owners shall be entitled at any time to open any Container or package and to inspect the contents. Any Container opened must be re-sealed and the Charterers advised accordingly.

8. Stowaways

Any costs incurred in respect of stowaways shall be for the Owners' account, unless it can be established that the means by which the stowaways gained access to the Vessel was by secreting away in the Charterers' Goods and/or Containers prior to loading, in which case all such costs shall be for the Charterers' account.

9. Drugs

In the event that contraband and/or unmanifested drugs or goods are found to have been shipped as part of the Charterers' Goods and/or in the Charterers' Containers on board the Vessel, any fines or imposts levied and legal and all other costs incurred, including but not limited to, loss of time for the Vessel shall be for the Charterers' account and the Charterers shall, on demand, provide the security required to enable the Vessel to sail. However, if it can be established that the presence of contraband and/or unmanifested drugs or goods was due solely to the act, neglect or default by the Owners, their servants, agents or Sub-contractors, such fines or imposts levied and legal and other costs incurred shall be for the Owners' account.

10. Repairs

The Owners shall have liberty to take the Vessel out of service for maintenance and repairs, with reasonable notice to the Charterers.

11. Owners' Obligations

(a) The Owners shall arrange for the loading onto, securing and discharging from the Vessel of the Charterers' Goods and Containers as agent for, and for the account of, the Charterers.

(b) If required by the Charterers, the Owners shall sign a receipt for the tally of Goods and Containers loaded on board the Vessel at each port of loading. In the absence of such receipt, both parties agree to accept terminal tallies as conclusive evidence of the tally of Goods and Containers loaded and discharged.

(c) During the voyage, the Master and Engineer shall keep full and correct logs and adequate records concerning the care and condition of the Goods and Containers and all such logs and records shall be accessible to the Charterers or their agents.

12. Charterers' Obligations

(a) The Charterers shall provide such information and/or documentation and comply with the Owners' procedures in relation to any Goods and Containers under this Slot Charter Party as the Owners may reasonably require and the Charterers warrant that such information and/or documentation shall be complete, accurate and in time for loading/discharging operations to be planned.

(b) The Charterers shall undertake that all Goods and Containers within the Charterers' allocation shall be delivered at the loading terminal at least 24 hours before the arrival of the Vessel.

13. Indemnity and Agency

(a) The Charterers undertake that no claim or allegation shall be made against the Owners or any servant, agent or Sub-contractor of the Owners by any person whomsoever, other than the Charterers, which imposes or attempts to impose upon the Owners or any such servant, agent or Sub-contractor or any Vessel owned by any of them, any liability whatsoever in connection with Goods and Containers, or their carriage, (even if such liability arises wholly or in part by reason of the act, neglect or default of the Owners or of such servant, agent or Sub-contractor), and in the event of any such claim or allegation nevertheless being made, the Charterers shall indemnify the Owners and such servant, agent or Sub-contractor against all consequences whatsoever thereof.

The Charterers further undertake that bills of lading issued for the Charterers' Goods and Containers carried under this Slot Charter Party shall contain:

(i) No Identity of Carrier Clause which purports to establish a contractual relationship between the Owners and the cargo interests of the Charterers.

(ii) A Clause Paramount applying the Hague or Hague-Visby Rules as enacted in the country of shipment.

(iii) A Himalaya Clause or Circular Indemnity Clause giving the Owners the benefit of the bill of lading terms and conditions and/or protection from tortious claims by third parties.

If, despite the provisions of (i) above, a contractual relationship between the Owners and the Charterers' cargo interests is construed, the Charterers shall indemnify the Owners against all consequences thereof,

(b) The Charterers shall not make any claim or allegation against any servant, agent or Sub-contractor of the Owners which imposes or attempts to impose on any such servant, agent or Sub-contractor any liability whatsoever in connection with Goods and Containers, or their carriage, (even if such liability arises wholly or in part by reason of the act, neglect or default of the Owners or of such servant, agent or Sub-contractor), and, in the event of any such claim or allegation nevertheless being made, the provisions of sub-clause 13(a) shall apply as if such claim or allegation had been made by persons other than the Charterers.

(c) Without prejudice to sub-clause 13(a) the Owners authorise and empower the Charterers to act as the Owners' agents and/or trustees to stipulate for the Owners to have as against other persons the benefit of any immunities, exemptions or liberties regarding the Goods and Containers, or their carriage, but the Charterers shall have no authority to make any contract imposing any obligations upon the Owners in connection with the Goods and Containers or their carriage.

(d) Nothing in this Clause shall preclude any claim made by the owners of any property on board the Vessel for a General Average contribution in accordance with the York-Antwerp Rules 1974, as amended 1990, or any subsequent modification thereof.

(e) If the Owners are not the actual owners of the Vessel, the provisions of sub-clauses 13(a), (b) and (c) shall also apply to the actual owners of the Vessel, their servants, agents and Sub-contractors in the same manner as they apply to the Owners, their servants, agents and Sub-contractors.

14. Owners' Responsibilities and Liabilities

Except as otherwise provided elsewhere in this Slot Charter Party, the responsibilities and liabilities of the Owners shall be as follows:

(a) The Owners shall be responsible for the seaworthiness of the Vessel in accordance with Article III Rule 1 and Article IV Rule 1 of the Hague-Visby Rules and for all purposes in connection with this Slot Charter Party they shall be entitled to the rights and immunities set out in Article IV Rules 2, 4 and 6 of the said Hague-Visby Rules.

(b) Subject to sub-clause 14(a), the Owners shall be responsible for the proper and careful carriage, custody and care of the Goods and Containers whilst on board the Vessel, and for discharging, handling and storing Goods and Containers discharged solely in order to be re-loaded or in order to load or discharge other goods and containers, and for re-loading and re-stowing the same.

(c) The Owners shall provide electrical power to integral refrigerated unit Containers and to refrigeration clip-on units attached to insulated Containers shipped on the Vessel The Owners shall use all reasonable endeavours to monitor and record the performance of all such units whilst on board, and, at the expense of the Charterers, to repair and rectify any breakdown, fault or deficiency which may occur in respect of such units, using the resources on board the Vessel.

If such resources are insufficient, the Owners, at the expense of the Charterers, shall use all reasonable endeavours promptly to obtain any required spares or specialised repair facilities.

Except as provided above, the Owners shall not be liable for malfunctioning of integral refrigerated Containers and power packs put on board by the Charterers.

(d) The liability of the Owners under this Clause shall be subject to Article III Rule 6 (including 6bis) of the Hague-Visby Rules.

(e) In respect of loss of or damage to Containers owned or hired by the Charterers, the quantum of liability of the Owners shall not in any event exceed the lesser of the reasonable cost of repair or market value of the Container, however, the Charterers shall make no claim for damage to any Container of less than USD 500 on any one voyage.

(f) In respect of loss of or damage to Goods, the quantum of liability of the Owners shall be determined as follows:

(i) If the port of loading is in a country which is a party to the Hague-Visby Rules the quantum of liability of the Owners to the Charterers shall be determined by the relevant legislation of that country as if this Slot Charter Party were a Bill of Lading with no declaration of value.

(ii) If the port of loading is in a country which is a party to the Hague Rules, the quantum of liability of the Owners to the Charterers shall be determined by the relevant legislation of that country as if this Slot Charter Party were a Bill of Lading with no declaration of value.

(iii) In all other cases the quantum of liability of the Owners to the Charterers shall be determined by reference to the Hague Rules Articles I-VIII only as if this Slot Charter Party were a Bill of Lading with no declaration of value, save that the limitation sum for the purposes of Article IV Rule 5 of the Hague Rules shall be GBP 100 sterling.

(iv) If quantum limitation is calculated by reference to packages, the quantum of liability of the Owners to the Charterers shall be calculated by reference to the same tally as is applicable between the Charterers and their customer.

(v) In addition to the liability as outlined in (i) to (iv) above, the Owners will reimburse the Charterers for reasonable legal and other costs necessarily incurred in connection with claims for which the Owners are liable under this Slot Charter Party.

(g) The Owners shall indemnify the Charterers against any claims for personal injury incurred on or about the Vessel unless caused by the negligence of the Charterers, their servants, agents or Sub-contractors or any defect in the Charterers' Goods and/or Containers.

15. Charterers' Responsibilities and Liabilities

(a) Whilst the Charterers are responsible for all costs incurred prior to placing into stow in the Vessel and after removal from stow in the Vessel, the Owners acting as the Charterers' agents to arrange such services (see Clause 11(a)), the Charterers shall only be liable to the Owners for any loss of or damage to the Vessel or to other goods and containers caused by stevedores during such services to the extent that a recovery is made from the stevedores. This recovery right is herewith assigned to the Owners which assignment is accepted by the Owners.

(b) The Charterers shall be reasponsible for the proper and careful loading, stowage, lashing and securing of the Goods in the Containers offered by them for shipment and shall be liable for all loss or damage (including loss of or damage to the Vessel) caused to the Owners as a result of improper or careless performance of such operations.

(c) The Charterers shall indemnify the Owners against any expenses, liabilities, losses, damages, claims or demands which the Owners may incur or suffer by reason of any failure to comply with any relevant laws, regulations, directions or notices of Customs, port and any other authorities, or by reason of any infestation, contamination or condemnation of Goods and/or Containers, insofar as such failure, infestation, contamination or condemnation arises from any act, neglect or default of the Charterers, the consignors or consignees of their Goods and/or Containers, or their servants, agents or Sub-contractors.

(d) Whenever possible, the Charterers shall give all reasonable facilities to the Owners for inspecting damaged Goods and Containers for which they intend to seek reimbursement from the Owners.

(e) The Charterers shall make no payment in excess of the amount as stated in Box 20 in settlement of a claim for which they will seek recovery from the Owners without prior notice to the Owners. The Owners authorise the Charterers to grant extensions of time in respect of such claims provided the Charterers give the Owners immediate notice thereof.

(f) In any event, the Charterers shall be discharged from all liabilities arising under this Slot Charter Party unless suit is brought within 15 months of the occurrence of the incident giving rise to the liability or the date upon which the Owners became aware of such occurence.

16. Mutual Exemption Clause

(a) Neither the Owners nor the Charterers shall be responsible for any loss or damage or delay or failure in performance under this Slot Charter Party resulting from Act of God, war, civil commotion, quarantine, strikes, lock-outs, arrest or restraint of princes, rulers and peoples or any other event whatsoever which cannot be avoided or guarded against.

(b) Except as elsewhere provided, neither the Owners nor the Charterers shall be responsible for any indirect or consequential loss, including but not limited to damage or decline in the market value of the Vessel or Goods during delays, loss of profit or loss of business opportunities in respect of any claim that the one may have against the other.

17. Lien

The Owners shall have a lien, including after discharge, upon the Charterers' Goods and Containers for all sums due to the Owners from the Charterers, their servants, agents, Sub-contractors or principals in respect of services provided by the Owners to the Charterers under the terms of this Slot Charter Party.

18. Dues, Charges and Taxes

(a) The Owners shall pay all dues, charges and taxes customarily levied on the Vessel, howsoever the amount thereof may be assessed.

(b) The Charterers shall pay all dues, charges, duties and taxes customarily levied on the Goods and/or Containers, howsoever the amount thereof may be assessed.

19. General Average

General Average shall be adjusted at the place as indicated in Box 21 according to the York-Antwerp Rules 1974, as amended 1990, or any subsequent modification thereof. Slot Charter Hire shall not contribute to General Average. The Owners authorise and empower the Charterers to act as the agents of the Owners in the collection of General Average security. The Charterers shall guarantee the contributions properly due to the Owners in respect of:

(a) Goods for which the Charterers are the contracting carrier unless such Goods are delivered to the Charterers prior to notice being given by the Owners to the Charterers that General Average security is required; and

(b) Containers shipped by the Charterers under this Slot Charter Party.

20. Salvage

In the event of the Vessel needing to engage salvage services and in order to secure the release of Goods and/or Containers for on-carriage, the Owners shall be required to give any undertaking to salvors to assist in the collection of security and not to release Goods and/or Containers until acceptable salvage security has been provided. The Charterers shall guarantee to the Owners that the requirements of such undertaking will be met in respect of Goods, for which the Charterers are the contracting carrier and Containers shipped by the Charterers under this Slot Charter Party, provided that these requirements are notified to the Charterers prior to the delivery of the Goods and/or Containers to the Charterers.

21. Deck Carriage

Goods and Containers may be carried on deck and shall contribute in General Average whether carried on or under deck.

22. Sub-letting

The Charterers shall not assign this Slot Charter Party and shall not sub-let the Slots without the prior approval of the Owners.

23. Law and Arbitration

*) (a) This Slot Charter Party shall be governed by and construed in accordance with English law and any dispute arising out of this Slot Charter Party shall be referred to arbitration in London in accordance with the Arbitration Acts 1950 and 1979 or any statutory modification or re-enactment thereof for the time being in force, one arbitrator being appointed by each party. On the receipt by one party of the nomination in writing of the other party's arbitrator, that party shall appoint their arbitrator within fourteen days, failing which the decision of the single Arbitrator appointed shall apply. If two Arbitrators properly appointed shall not agree they shall appoint an umpire whose decision shall be final. The Arbitrators shall be commercial men engaged in shipping.

*) (b) This Slot Charter Party shall be governed by and construed in accordance with Title 9 of the United States Code and the Maritime Law of the United States and should any dispute arise out of this Slot Charter Party, the matter in dispute shall be referred to three persons at New York, one to be appointed by each of the parties hereto, and the third by the two so chosen; their decision or that of any two of them shall be final, and for purpose of enforcing any award, this agreement may be made a rule of the Court. The Arbitrators shall be commercial men engaged in shipping.

*) (c) Any dispute arising out of this Slot Charter Party shall be referred to arbitration at the place indicated in Box 23, subject to the procedures applicable there. The laws of the place indicated in Box 23 shall govern this Slot Charter Party.

(d) If Box 23 in Part I is not filled in, sub-clause (a) of this Clause shall apply.

*) *(a), (b), (c) are alternatives; indicate alternative agreed in Box 23.*

APPENDIX 4

FEEDER SLOT CHARTERPARTY

Feeder Slot Charterparty

It is agreed

this _____ day of _______________

Between

_______________ (*the Charterer*) and
_______________ (*the Operator*)

in respect of the feeder service offered by the Operator between the ports of _______________, _______________, _______________ and _______________ using vessels for which the Operator is owner or disponent owner (charterer) as follows:

In consideration of the Charterer agreeing to use the services of the Operator on a non-exclusive basis, it is hereby agreed that, whenever the Charterer does so, carriage of the Charterer's containers and goods shall be effected upon the terms of this Slot Charter party.

The terms of the contract of carriage shall be the terms and conditions of the Operator's Bill of Lading as attached hereto always, where appropriate, amended by the following provisions. In the event of conflict between the terms and conditions of the Operator's Bill of Lading and this Slot Charter party, the latter shall be paramount and prevail.

(1) The Operator undertakes primary responsibility for the carriage of the Charterer's containers and goods and acts as the contracting carrier throughout carriage. Any Demise or Identity of Carrier provision in the Operator's Bill of Lading contract is hereby declared null and void.

(2) The Charterer's containers and goods shall be carried subject to the provisions of the Hague-Visby Rules and any provision in the Operator's Bill of Lading contract which conflicts with the said Rules is hereby declared null and void.

(3) Any dispute arising under this Slot Charter party shall be resolved according to the laws of _______________ in the courts of said country. However nothing herein shall preclude dispute resolution by reference to arbitration in a forum acceptable to both parties if both parties so agree.

(4) Remuneration shall be upon terms from time to time agreed by the parties and shall be fair and reasonable.

APPENDIX 5

CONTAINER HIRING AGREEMENT

Dated
Between
(1) ______________ (*the Owner*) and
(2) ______________ (*the Hirer*)
It is agreed:

1. Scope of Agreement

(1) The period of this Agreement shall be from the date hereof until terminated by either party giving written notice.
(2) The terms hereof shall apply whenever the Owner hires one or more of its containers to the Hirer for the carriage of goods in a (*name of consortium*) service and the hiring commences during the period of this Agreement.

2. Remuneration

The Owner shall be remunerated in accordance with the provisions from time to time separately agreed by or on behalf of the parties or in default of agreement shall receive such remuneration as shall be fair and reasonable.

3. Owner's Responsibilities

3.1 The Owner shall be liable to the Hirer for any loss or damage which the Hirer suffers arising as a result of a container to which this Agreement relates failing to be:
(a) physically compatible with the Vessels;
(b) of such specifications as may be determined from time to time by or on behalf of the parties;
(c) constructed to the specifications of any recognised classification society acceptable by or on behalf of the parties and operated within an approved scheme under the International Convention for Safe Containers and in date on its CSC plating;
(d) properly maintained;
(e) in compliance with the relevant port and other regulations (including quarantine regulations);
(f) constructed of taint-free materials; and
(g) free from defect, whether manifest or latent, in construction.
Provided that:
(i) The liability of the Owner to the Hirer for any failure to comply with this sub-clause, insofar as it relates to latent defects, shall not in any event exceed

the amount (if any) recoverable by the Owner from any third party in connection with such liability, but the Owner shall take all reasonable steps (short of court action) to recover such amount and shall account therefor to the Hirer. For this purpose the Owner's insurers shall not be considered as third parties.

(ii) The Owner shall, upon the written request from the Hirer, allow the Hirer to take over all conduct of any enforcement of any rights which the Owner may have against any third party to enable the Hirer to exercise such rights in the Owner's name but at the Hirer's expense. The Owner shall co-operate as much as is reasonably possible to assist the Hirer to exercise such rights which the Owner may have against the third party.

(iii) If the Owner should not be willing to transfer to the Hirer all conduct of any enforcement of rights and to co-operate as required above in assisting the Hirer, the provisions of sub-clause (i) of this proviso shall be null and void. The Owner shall be deemed to have shown unwillingness to transfer if he has not given the necessary authority in writing to the Hirer to proceed within 30 days of receipt of a written request so to do.

3.2 Subject to sub-clause 3.1 above, the Owner shall be under no liability whatsoever to the Hirer for any loss or damage arising out of any circumstances relating to the condition of the container rendering it unsuitable for any purpose, even if arising as a result of the act, neglect or default of the Owner, its servants, agents or sub-contractors.

4. Indemnity and Agency

4.1 The Hirer undertakes that no claim or allegation shall be made against the Owner or any servant, agent or sub-contractor of the Owner by any person whomsoever, other than the Hirer, which imposes or attempts to impose upon the Owner or any such servant, agent or sub-contractor any liability whatsoever in respect of such loss or damage as is mentioned in Clause 3 above, or in respect of any injury to persons or damage to property arising or caused by or in connection with the container or its use during the time it is hired to the Hirer (even if such liability arises wholly or in part by reason of the act, neglect or default of the Owner or of such servant, agent or sub-contractor) and, in the event of any such claim or allegation nevertheless being made, the Hirer shall indemnify the Owner and such servant, agent and sub-contractor against all consequences whatsoever thereof.

4.2 The Hirer shall not make any claim or allegation against any servant, agent or sub-contractor of the Owner which imposes or attempts to impose on any such servant, agent or sub-contractor any liability whatsoever in respect of such loss or damage as is mentioned in Clause 3 above, or in respect of any injury to persons or damage to property arising or caused by or in connection with the container or its use during the time it is hired to the Hirer (even if such liability arises wholly or in part by reason of the act, neglect or default of the Owner or of such servant, agent or sub-contractor) and, in the event of any such claim or allegation nevertheless being made, the provisions of sub-clause 4.1 above shall apply as if such claim or allegation has been made by a person other than the Hirer.

4.3 Without prejudice to sub-clause 4.1 above the Owner authorises and empowers the Hirer to act as the Owner's agent and/or trustee to stipulate for the Owner to have as against other persons the benefit of any immunities, exemptions or liberties regarding the container the subject of this Agreement, but the Hirer shall have no authority to make any contract imposing any obligations upon the Owner in connection with the container.

4.4 Where the Owner is not the actual owner of the container the provisions of sub-clauses 4.1, 4.2 and 4.3 above shall also apply to the actual owner of the container, its servants, agents and sub-contractors in the same manner as they apply to the Owner, its servants, agents and sub-contractors.

5. Hirer's Responsibilities

5.1 Subject only to the Owner's liabilities to the Hirer mentioned in Clause 3 above, the Hirer shall be liable for all injury to persons or damage to property (including the container) whenever occurring, arising or caused by or in connection with the container or its use during the time it is hired to the Hirer whether as a result of the act, neglect or default of the Hirer, its servants, agents or sub-contractors or otherwise.
5.2 The Hirer shall comply with any restriction imposed by the Owner which the parties have separately agreed on the use of any container for particular classes of goods. If the Hirer shall fail so to comply it shall indemnify the Owner against all consequences thereof.
5.3 The Hirer shall be under no liability under sub-clauses 5.1 or 5.2 above unless the loss or damage exceeds US$500 for any one incident. Where damage, repair and/or cleaning costs exceed US$500 per incident, the Hirer shall be liable to Owners for the reasonable cost of repair and cleaning or the replacement of the container(s) in full at the line's depreciated value, whichever is the lesser, unless the Hirer can show that the Owner was in breach of his obligations in sub-clause 3.1 above or that loss or damage did not arise during the currency of this Agreement.
5.4 For the avoidance of doubt, it is recorded that the Hirer shall be liable for General Average contributions and salvage charges in respect of the container during the period of hire.

APPENDIX 6

CONTAINERSPACE HIRING AGREEMENT

Dated ______________
Between
(1) ______________ (*the Owner*)
and
(2) ______________ (*the Hirer*)
It is agreed:

1. Scope of Agreement

1.1 The period of this Agreement shall be from the date hereof until terminated by either party giving written notice.
1.2 The terms hereof shall apply wherever the Owner hires space in one of his containers (whether owned leased or hired) to the Hirer for the carriage of the Hirer's goods in the (*name of consortium*) service and the hiring commences during the period of this Agreement. For the purpose of this Agreement, Hirers goods means goods owned by the Hirer or in respect of which the Hirer, acting as a Principal Carrier, has issued a bill of lading or other contract of carriage to a merchant.

2. Owner's Responsibilities

2.1 The Owner shall carry the Hirer's goods from the agreed place of receipt to the agreed place of delivery upon the terms of this Agreement.

2.2 (a) The liability of the Owner to the Hirer for loss, damage, delay or expense of whatsoever nature and howsoever arising in connection with this Agreement (even if such liability arises wholly or in part by reason of the act, neglect or default of the Owner or of his servants, agents or sub-contractors) shall not in any event exceed the amount (if any) recoverable by the Owner from any third party in connection with such liability, but the Owner shall take all reasonable steps (short of court action) to recover such amount and shall account therefor to the Hirer. For this purpose the Owner's insurers shall not be considered as third parties.

(b) The Owner shall, upon the written request from the Hirer, allow the Hirer to take over all conduct of any enforcement of any rights which the Owner may have against any third party to enable the Hirer to exercise such rights in the Owner's name but at the Hirer's expense. The Owner shall co-operate as much as is reasonably possible to assist the Hirer to exercise such rights which the Owner may have against the third party.

(c) If the Owner should not be willing to transfer to the Hirer all conduct of any enforcement of rights and to co-operate as required above in assisting the Hirer, the provisions of sub-clause (a) shall be null and void. The Owner shall be deemed to have shown unwillingness to transfer if he has not given the necessary authority in writing to the Hirer to proceed within 30 days of receipt of a written request so to do.

3. Indemnity and Agency

3.1 The Hirer undertakes that no claim or allegation shall be made against the Owner or any servant, agent or sub-contractor of the Owner by any person whomsoever other than the Hirer, which imposes or attempts to impose upon the Owner or any such servant, agent or sub-contractor any liability whatsoever in respect of loss, damage, delay or expense to or in connection with the Hirer's goods carried in the Owner's container (even if such liability arises wholly or in part by reason of the act, neglect or default of the Owner or of such servant, agent or sub-contractor) and, in the event of any such claim or allegation nevertheless being made, the Hirer shall indemnify the Owner and such servant, agent or sub-contractor against all consequences whatsoever thereof.

3.2 The Hirer shall not make any claim or allegation against any servant, agent or sub-contractor of the Owner which imposes or attempts to impose on any such servant, agent or sub-contractor any liability whatsoever in respect of loss, damage, delay or expense to or in connection with the Hirer's goods carried in the Owner's container (even if such liability arises wholly or in part by reason of the act, neglect or default of the Owner or of such servant, agent or sub-contractor) and, in the event of any such claim or allegation nevertheless being made, the provision of sub-clause 3.1 shall apply as if such claim or allegation had been made by a person other than the Hirer.

3.3 Without prejudice to sub-clause 3.1 the Owner authorises and empowers the Hirer to act as the Owner's agent to stipulate for the Owner to have as against other persons the benefit of any immunities, exemptions or liberties regarding the Hirer's goods, but the Hirer shall have no authority to make any contract imposing any obligations upon the Owner in connection with the Hirer's goods or their carriage.

3.4 Where the Owner is not the actual owner of the container, the provisions of sub-clauses 3.1, 3.2 and 3.3 above shall also apply to the actual owner of the container, his servants, agents and sub-contractors in the same manner as they apply to the Owner, his servants, agents and sub-contractors.

4. Hirer's Responsibilities

4.1 (a) The liability of the Hirer to the Owner for loss, damage, delay or expense of whatsoever nature and howsoever arising in connection with this Agreement, other than a liability under sub-clause 4.2 below (even if such liability arises wholly or in part by reason of the act, neglect, or default of the Hirer or his servants, agents or sub-contractors) shall not in any event exceed the amount (if any) recoverable by the Hirer from any third party in connection with such liability, but the Hirer shall take all reasonable steps (short of court action) to recover such amount and shall account therefor to the Owner. For this purpose the Hirer's insurers shall not be considered as third parties.

(b) The Hirer shall, upon the written request from the Owner, allow the Owner to take over all conduct of any enforcement of any rights which the Hirer may have against any third party to enable the Owner to exercise such rights in the Hirer's name but at the Owner's expense. The Hirer shall co-operate as much as is reasonably possible to assist the Owner to exercise such rights which the Hirer may have against the third party.

(c) If the Hirer should not be willing to transfer to the Owner all conduct of any enforcement of rights and to co-operate as required above in assisting the Owner, the provisions of sub-clause (a) shall be null and void. The Hirer shall be deemed to have shown unwillingness to transfer if he has not given the necessary authority in writing to the Owner to proceed within 30 days of receipt of a written request so to do.

4.2 The liability (if any) of the Hirer to the Owner under this Agreement in respect of loss of or damage to the container in which the Hirer's goods are carried shall be limited to whichever is the lesser of the cost of repair or replacement of the container, plus in each case any amount in excess of such cost which may be recoverable from any third party; provided always that the Hirer shall be under no liability for such loss or damage unless such costs exceed US$500.

5 Payments

The Owner shall be remunerated in accordance with provisions from time to time to be separately agreed by or on behalf of the parties or, in default of agreement, shall receive such remuneration as shall be fair and reasonable. Such remuneration shall cover all costs of providing the space, including but not limited to inland haulage charges, Slot Charter fees, stuffing and stripping charges and normal cleaning before and after use.

APPENDIX 7

CONLEASE—CONTAINER LEASE AGREEMENT

STANDARD CONTAINER LEASE AGREEMENT
CODENAME: "CONLEASE"
(Issued 1997)

PART I

1. Reference number

2. Effective date of agreement (Cl. 2 (a))

3. Lessor (Name, Address)

4. Lessee (Name, Address)

5. Equipment

Type	Quantity	Depreciated Value (Cl. 5 (b), 13(a), 14 (a)(1))	Per diem rate (Cl. 7 (a))	Per diem after build-down period (Cl 10)

6. Commencement date of lease (Cl. 2 (b))

7. Earliest termination date (Cl. 2 (b))

8. Direct Interchange fee (Cl. 4 (c))

9. No. of days notice for repairs (Cl. 5 (b), Cl. 7 (d))

10. Pick-up locations (Cl. 6 (b))

11. Other charges (Cl. 7 (a))

12. Lessee's billing address (Cl. 7 (b))

13. Lessor's bank account (Cl. 7 (c))

14. No. of days for payment (Cl. 7 (c))

15. Notice of termination (Cl. 9 (a))

16. Early termination dates and per diems (Cl. 9 (c))

Date   Per Diem

17. Build-down period (Cl. 10)

18. Minimum limit of general liability insurance (Cl. 14 (a)(ii), 14 (b)(i))

19. Law and Arbitration (state a. London, b. New York or c. alternative place) (Cl. 15 (a), (b), (c))

20. Maximum amount for small claims/shortened arbitration procedure (Cl. 15 (a), (b))

21. Additional clauses agreed

It is agreed that this Contract shall be performed subject to the terms and conditions of Part I, including additional clauses if any agreed and stated in Box 21and of Part II. In the event of a conflict of conditions, the provisions of Part I shall prevail over those of Part II to the extent of such conflict but no further.

Signature Lessor

Signature Lessee

Printed and sold by Fr. G. Knudtzons Bogtrykkeri A/S, Vallensbaekvej 61, Box 128, DK-2625 Vallensbaek, Denmark, Telefax +45 4366 0708
by authority of The Baltic and International Maritime Council (BIMCO), Copenhagen

1. **Marginal Headings**

The marginal headings of this Agreement are for identification only and shall not be deemed to be part hereof or be taken into consideration in the interpretation or construction of this Agreement.

2. **Term of the Agreement**

(a) All terms and conditions of this Agreement shall take effect from the date stated in Box 2 and shall remain in force until all Equipment covered by this Agreement has been redelivered.

(b) The period of lease for the full amount of Equipment stated in Box 5 shall commence on the date stated in Box 6 and shall continue at least until the date stated in Box 7.

3. **Condition of Equipment on Delivery**

(a) The Lessors warrant that at the time of delivery the Equipment shall be in a good and serviceable condition and shall have been designed, manufactured, tested and maintained in compliance with the standards detailed hereinafter:

(i) International Standards Organisation (ISO);

(ii) International Convention for Safe Containers (CSC) of 1972 or any amendment thereof;

(iii) Customs Convention on Containers of 1956 and 1972 or any amendment thereof;

(iv) Australian Quarantine Regulations in respect of Timber Component Treatment;

(v) Current IICL Standards for Repair and Cleaning.

(b) The Lessor warrants that the Equipment is delivered free from all liens and encumbrances.

(c) The Lessor warrants that the period of validity of the CSC Safety Approval Plate is 30 months from the date of on-hire, unless the Equipment is CSC controlled under an Approved Continuous Examination Programme (ACEP).

(d) The Lessee may appoint a surveyor to inspect any Equipment prior to on-hire. The Lessor will make the Equipment available for this inspection. The surveyor will apply the standards set out in the latest edition of the IICL Container Inspection and Repair Manuals. The surveyor's report of the condition of the Equipment at on-hire shall be prima facie evidence of the condition of the Equipment taken on hire.

4. **Title to Equipment, Sub-lease and Direct Interchange**

(a) The Equipment shall at all times remain the property of the Lessor, and the Lessee shall acquire no title to Equipment by virtue of paying rents, costs of transportation or repairs, registration or licensing fees, taxes (property excise or any other governmental fees or charges) or any other expenses or charges related to or assessed against such Equipment or its operation during the period of this Agreement.

(b) The Lessee shall not, without the Lessor's prior written consent, which shall not be unreasonably withheld, assign any right or interest in or to this Agreement or the Equipment, nor sub-lease Equipment except to a company which is directly or indirectly associated with the Lessee. In case of such assignment or sub-lease, the Lessee will remain responsible for all obligations in accordance with this Agreement.

(c) The Lessee may transfer Equipment to a third party in a Direct interchange, but only with the Lessor's written consent, which shall not be unreasonably withheld. When the third party has confirmed to the Lessor its agreement with such a transfer, the Lessee's objections to pay rental shall cease and a Direct Interchange fee as stated in Box 8 shall be paid by the Lessee to the Lessor

(d) The Equipment shall have the Lessor's serial numbers and other identifying marks affixed thereto, which shall not be obliterated, altered, concealed or otherwise changed or hidden from view by the Lessee so as to prevent or block access to such numbers or marks without prior written agreement from the Lessor. The Lessee has the option to have its own company logo applied on the Equipment provided that same is to be removed for the Lessee's account upon redelivery of the Equipment.

5. **Condition of Equipment on Redelivery**

(a) The Equipment shall be redelivered in like condition to the condition at on-hire, normal Wear and Tear excepted and unless advised by the Lessor to the contrary in accordance with sub-clause 5(b), the Lessee may assume that the Equipment has been redelivered in undamaged condition.

(b) In the event that Equipment is redelivered in a damaged condition, excepting all normal Wear and Tear, the Lessor shall within the number of working days stated in Box 9 give notice to the Lessee providing a detailed estimate of repairs. If the Lessee does not respond to the Lessor within the number of working days stated in Box 9 of receiving the detailed estimate of repairs, the Lessor shall be entitled to assume that the Lessee agrees with the estimate of repairs and will pay for the said repairs, excepting all normal Wear and Tear, at the amount specified in the estimate, on presentation of an invoice.

If the Lessee disagrees with the estimate of repair costs and/or disagrees that any item therein should be for the Lessee's account, he shall detail his objections by notice to the Lessor within the period provided in Box 9.

In the event of a continuing dispute the parties shall within 14 days of the date of the Lessee's notice appoint a joint surveyor who will survey the Equipment and review the estimate of repairs. The parties agree to be bound by the decision of the joint surveyor as to the extent of the repairs payable by the Lessee and the reasonable cost thereof and to share the cost of the survey.

All damages will be defined in accordance with the current IICL Inspection Standards and all repairs will be performed in accordance with the current IICL Standards for Repair and Cleaning.

In the event that an agreed estimate of repairs exceeds the depreciated value of the Equipment as stated in Box 5, the Lessee will pay to the Lessor the Depreciated Value of the Equipment.

6. **Pick-ups and Drop-offs**

(a) Master Lease: The Lessee may pick up Equipment at any of the Lessor's depots as may from time be mutually agreed. The Lessor shall not unreasonably withhold Equipment from the Lessee and shall use his best endeavours to fulfill the requirementss of the Lessee.

(b) Term Lease: The Lessee may pick up Equipment in the minimum quantities per period of time indicated at each of the Lessor's depot stated in Box 10.

Save for the provisions of Clauses 9 and 10 such Equipment shall remain on hire for at least the period stipulated in Clause 2(b).

(c) Subject to the terms of this Agreement, the Lessee may redeliver any of the Equipment, to any of the Lessor's depots designated in Annex A which may contain permissible redelivery quota and drop-off charges, or as may from time to time be mutually agreed. Redelivery will terminate this Lease Agreement insofar as it relates to the redelivered Equipment.

(a) and (b) are alternatives. Delete whichever is not applicable.

7. **Rental and other Charges, Payment**

(a) In consideration for leasing the Equipment from the Lessor, the Lessee shall, as from the pick-up date, be liable to pay to the Lessor, as rent, the per diem leasing rate specified in Box 5, as well as any other charges which may be agreed upon and enumerated in Box 11. The Lessee's obligations to pay rental will cease on the day after redelivery into any of the Lessor's designated depots.

(b) An invoice shall be sent to the Lessee's billing address as stated in Box 12.

(c) Payment shall be made by the Lessee to the Lessor's bank account as stated in Box 13, within the number of working days stated in Box 14 of the date of the Lessor's invoice.

(d) The Lessee shall, within the number of days stated in Box 9, give written notice to the Lessor of any disputed items on the Lessor's invoice. The Lessor will reconcile disputed items within the number of days stated in Box 9 by either providing supporting documents for such items or by issuing an appropriate adjustment of the invoice. Notification of disputed items shall not prejudice the obligation of the Lessee to pay the undisputed portion of any invoice within the number of days stated in Box 14 after receipt.

8. **Taxes, Fees and Fines**

The Lessee shall pay all taxes, dues and charges levied on or against the Equipment arising out of or in connection with the use of the Equipment.

Upon the return of any Equipment to the Lessor, and provided it is a permissible return under the conditions of this Lease Agreement, the Lessor shall indemnifty the Lessee from any import duties or taxes whatsoever that may be imposed from the time the Equipment was returned to the Lessor provided that the Equipment is redelivered within 60 days of the importation date. The Lessee shall, to the best of its ability, and at the Lessor's request, assist the Lessor to avoid any import duties or taxes by co-operating to the fullest extent in requesting extension of the same as local regulations permit.

The Lessor shall pay all taxes, dues and charges levied on or against the Equipment arising out of or in connection with the ownership of the Equipment.

9. **Termination of Agreement**

(a) Either party may terminate this Agreement by giving the other party written notice of termination at least the number of working days stated in Box 15 prior to the date stated in Box 7 or any later date agreed to by the parties.

(b) The Lessee may upon written notice cancel this Agreement with immediate effect insofar as it relates to any Equipment

(i) the use of which shall have been curtailed or obstructed by any legislation or regulation of any Government or statutory body of any country where the Lessee wishes to use said Equipment; or

(ii) which is shown to have latent defects such that it is unsafe or unsuitable for continued use.

Such Equipment shall be returned to the Lessor as soon as is practicable in accordance with Clause 6(c).

(c) Notwithstanding the stipulations of Clause 2 and sub-clause 6(b) and by giving the number of working days advance notice as stipulated in Box 15, the Lessee shall have the option of terminating the Agreement on any of the dates stated in Box 16. In such case the hire shall be retroactively adjusted in accordance with the appropriate per diem rates entered behind the dates in Box 16.

10. **Build-down Period**

On the date of termination as stipulated in Clause 2(b) a build-down period shall commence, during which time all the Equipment shall be redelivered to the Lessor. The length and redelivery schedule of the build-down period shall be as set out in Box 17.

Equipment still on lease after the build-down period will be charged the per diem rental stated in Box 5 until finally redelivered to the Lessor.

11. Insolvency

(a) Both the Lessee and the Lessor shall be entitled to terminate this Agreement in the event of an order being made or resolution passed for the winding up, dissolution, liquidation or bankruptcy of the other party (otherwise than for the purpose of reconstruction or amalgamation) or if a receiver is appointed, or if the other party suspends payment, ceases to carry on business or makes any special arrangement with their creditors.

(b) If the Lessor terminates this Agreement according to sub-clause 11(a), the Lessor shall have the right to take immediate possession of all empty Equipment leased to the Lessee under this Agreement.

(c) Should the Lessor obtain the right to immediate possession of any empty Equipment covered by this Agreement, then the Lessee must, upon written notice from the Lessor, immediately insofar as he is able to do so, notify the Lessor of the exact location of all Equipment leased to it under this Agreement and promptly redeliver all such empty Equipment to the nearest Lessor's depot unless otherwise mutually agreed.

12. Maritime Lien

The Equipment is supplied for the purpose of intermodal operations in international trade and may be used for the carriage of lawful goods by sea as well as in inland transport including the handling at terminals and inland depots and freight stations. The Equipment is not designated for use on any particular Vessel and consequently no maritime lien securing the obligations under this Agreement may be attached to any Vessel connected in any way with the Lessee.

The Lessor is relying solely upon the credit of the Lessee in supplying containers under this lease.

13. Liabilities and Indemnity

(a) The Lessee shall be liable to the Lessor for the actual or constructive total loss of, or damage, normal Wear and Tear excepted, to any Equipment occurring during the period of this Agreement.

The Lessee shall immediately notify the Lessor in writing of any actual or constructive total loss of any Equipment and upon such notice the Lessee's obligations to pay rental shall cease. In the event that such actual or constructive total loss occurs, the Lessee shall be promptly invoiced therefor and pay to the Lessor the agreed Depreciated Value of such Equipment.

Should the Lessee later determine that Equipment previously declared lost has been recovered, the Lessor will, at the request of the Lessee, reimburse any previously paid Replacement Value/Depreciated Value less any rental accrued from the date the Equipment was declared lost.

(b) The Lessee shall defend, indemnify and hold the Lessor harmless for any and all claims, losses, expenses, costs or damages (including without limitation all reasonable expenses in defending any claim or suit or enforcing this indemnity, such as court costs, attorney's fees, and other expenses) arising or alleged to arise directly or indirectly or incidentally out of:

(i) any failure of the Lessee to comply with its obligations under this Agreement;

(ii) any claim, whether private or governmental, for bodily injury or death to persons (including employees of the Lessor) and for loss of or damage to property, cargo and/or vessels and/or means of transport, arising out of or incident to the possession, leasing, operation, control or use of the Equipment by the Lessee.

(c) The Lessor shall defend, indemnify and hold the Lessee harmless for any and all claims, losses, expenses, costs or damages (including without limitation all reasonable expenses in defending any claim or suit such as court costs, attorney's fees, and other expenses) arising or alleged to arise directly or indirectly or incidentally out of:

(i) any failure of the Lessor to comply with its obligations under this Agreement;

(ii) any claim, whether private or governmental, for bodily injury or death to persons (including employees of the Lessee) and for loss of or damage to property, cargo and/or vessels and/or means of transport, arising out of or incident to the ownership, manufacture, design or supply of the Equipment.

(d) Each party undertakes to give to the other party immediate notice of claims or actions arising under this Clause, and to assist in the handling of any and all such claims or actions.

14. Insurance

(a) The Lessee agrees to procure and maintain in full force and effect during the term of this Agreement, at its sole cost and expense, the following insurances:

(i) Insurance to cover physical loss or damage to the Equipment for not less than the full Depreciated Value stipulated in Box 5.

(ii) General liability insurance to a minimum limit as stipulated in Box 18 for any one occurrence, to cover third party bodily injury and property damage. Such insurance shall be primary insurance.

Any and all deductibles under the terms of the foregoing insurances shall be for the Lessee's account On request, the Lessee will provide the Lessor with evidence of the insurances.

(b) The Lessor agrees to procure and maintain in full force and effect during the term of this Agreement, at its sole cost and expense the following insurance:

(i) General liability insurance to a minimum limit as stipulated in Box 18 for any one occurrence, to cover third party bodily injury and property damage.

Any and all deductibles under the terms of the foregoing insurance shall be for the Lessor's account. On request, the lessors will provide the Lessee with evidence of the insurance.

Should a party fail to procure or maintain any of the required insurances, or by act or omission vitiate or invalidate any of such insurance, that party shall indemnify the other party to the extent the other party suffers or incurs loss, damage, liability or expense as a consequence of such failure, act or omission.

15. Law and Arbitration

* (a) This Lease Agreement shall be governed by and construed in accordance with English law and any dispute arising out of this Lease Agreement shall be referred to arbitration in London in accordance with the Arbitration Act 1996 or any statutory modification or re-enactment thereof for the time being in force. Unless the parties agree upon a sole arbitrator, one arbitrator shall be appointed by each party and the arbitrators so appointed shall appoint a third arbitrator, the decision of the three-man tribunal thus constituted or any two of them, shall be final. On the receipt by one party of the nomination in writing of the other party's arbitrator, that party shall appoint their arbitrator within fourteen days, failing which the decision of the single arbitrator appointed shall be final.

For disputes where the total amount claimed by either party does not exceed the amount stated in Box 20** the arbitration shall be conducted in accordance with the Small Claims Procedure of the London Maritime Arbitrators Association.

* (b) This Lease Agreement shall be governed by and construed in accordance with Title 9 of the United States Code as well as by the maritime law of the United States, or if this Lease Agreement is not deemed to be a maritime contract, then by the law of the State of New York and should any dispute arise out of this Lease Agreement, the matter in dispute shall be referred to three persons at New York, one to be appointed by each of the parties hereto, and the third by the two so chosen; their decision or that of any two of them shall be final, and for purpose of enforcing any award, this agreement may be made a rule of the Court. The proceedings shall be conducted in accordance with the rules of the Society of Maritime Arbitrators, Inc.

For disputes where the total amount claimed by either party does not exceed the amount stated in Box 20** the arbitration shall be conducted in accordance with the Shortened Arbitration Procedure of the Society of Maritime Arbitrators, Inc.

* (c) Any dispute arising out of this Lease Agreement shall be referred to arbitration at the place indicated in Box 19, subject to the procedures applicable there. The laws of the place indicated in Box 19 shall govern this Lease Agreement.

(d) If Box 19 in Part I is not filled in, sub-clause (a) of this Clause shall apply.

* *(a), (b) and (c) are alternatives; indicate alternative agreed in Box 19.*

** *Where no figure is supplied in Box 20 in Part I, this provision only shall be void but the other provisions of this clause shall have full force and remain in effect.*

16. Notices

Any notice or notification or advice or communication of any kind to be served or given hereunder and/or any extension, variation, amendment, cancellation or deletion of any of the terms hereof shall (save in emergency) be in writing and sent or delivered to the registered office for the time being of the Lessor or the Lessee (as the case may be).

At the request of the Lessee the Lessor shall provide relevant information in electronic format.

17. Overriding Agreement

The terms and conditions set forth in this Agreement and attached exhibits shall constitute the only and total Agreement between the Lessor and the Lessee.

APPENDIX 8

LEASING AGREEMENT

AGREEMENT NO.

LEASE AGREEMENT

Name of Lessee:

Invoice Address if different:

, hereinafter referred to as the LESSOR, hereby leases to the party designated as the LESSEE, and hereinafter referred to as the LESSEE, and said LESSEE hereby leases from the LESSOR the following Container(s) as per Equipment Handover Agreement, upon the terms and conditions set forth on the reverse side hereof.

TERM: This lease will commence on: and expire on:

QUANTITY AND DESCRIPTION OF EQUIPMENT:

RENTAL:

REPLACEMENT VALUE:

DELIVERY LOCATIONS:

CHARGES:

HANDLING:

PICK UP:

REDELIVERY LOCATIONS:

CHARGES:

HANDLING:

DROP OFF:

OTHER TERMS AND CONDITIONS:

SIGNED FOR LESSEE:	DATE:	SIGNED FOR LESSOR:	DATE:

1. Use

Container(s) leased under the terms and conditions of this Lease Agreement shall be used solely in international trade.
The Lessee may use the Container(s) for any purpose incidental to its business as a carrier of goods in containers, save that the Lessee shall not use the Container(s) for the carriage of dangerous or obnoxious goods which are likely to damage or contaminate the Container(s) or for the carriage of prohibited goods, such that the Container(s) would be liable to be seized by Customs or other authorities. The Lessee shall comply with all loading limitations as stated on the Container(s) and any other reasonable limitation which may be prescribed by the Lessor in writing and shall prevent excessive impact and concentrated loads.
The Container(s) shall at all times remain the property of the Lessor and the Lessee shall acquire no option to purchase or ownership right nor shall the Lessee sell, let or otherwise dispose of the Container(s).

2. Responsibility

(a) The Lessee shall be liable for the cost of repair or replacement, whichever is the lesser, in respect of all loss or damage to the Container(s) during the currency of this Lease Agreement (between Delivery-Clause 6 and Redelivery-Clause 7), unless said loss or damage is shown to have been caused by normal wear and tear or latent defect. The Lessee agrees to sign container interchange receipts/inspection reports at Delivery and Redelivery, which documents shall be conclusive evidence of the condition of the Container(s) at those times and form an integral part of this Leasing Agreement.

(b) The Lessor makes no warranty of the condition of the Container(s) or their suitability for use with any specific cargo.

(c) Between Delivery and Redelivery neither the Lessor nor any servant, agent or sub-contractor of the Lessor shall be liable for any:
   (i) loss of, or damage to cargo or property (belonging to the Lessee or any third party), or
   (ii) death or injury of any kind whatsoever to whomsoever

   arising out of the leasing of the Container(s), howsoever caused and whether or not arising out of negligence on the part of the Lessor, his servants, agents or sub-contractors.

(d) In the event of any default by the Lessee in performance of his obligations under this Leasing Agreement the Lessor shall be entitled forthwith to repossess any Container(s) and the Lessee shall be responsible for any costs and expenses incidental thereto.

3. Insurance

The Lessee shall insure all Containers for the time being in his possession or control for their full replacement value with a reputable insurance company against those risks for which the Lessee is responsible and shall, if requested by the Lessor, provide a copy of the policy.

4. Duties of Lessee

The Lessee agrees to make such spot checks on current location as may be requested by the Lessor.

The Lessee agrees to keep full records of container inspection and of any maintenance or repairs to the Container(s) and to make these available to the Lessor on redelivery.
The Lessee agrees to the following equipment handover conditions:

(a) The Lessee acknowledges receipt of the Container(s) in apparent good order and condition, except as may be indicated on the container interchange receipt/report which shall be signed by both parties hereto.
(b) The Container(s) are leased to the Lessee on the following conditions:
    (i) Any vehicle or railcar used for the transport of the Container(s) is suitable for the weight and other characteristics of the load involved and that the Container(s) are firmly secured thereto either by twistlocks or other methods agreed with the Lessor.
    (ii) The Container(s) are to be redelivered in a clean and cargoworthy condition (as defined in Clause 8). The Lessee will reimburse the Lessor for any cleaning costs and any other expenses whatsoever incurred by his failure so to do.

5. Convention for Safe Containers

The Lessor shall ensure that the Container(s) which its supplies to the Lessee directly from one of its depots/terminals will comply with the provisions of the International Convention for Safe Containers (CSC) in force at the time.
Notwithstanding the above it shall be the Lessee's responsibility to ensure that all Container(s) taken on lease by the Lessee as the result of a Lease transfer comply with all relevant regulations.
During the term of the Lease and until Redelivery of each Container in accordance with the terms and conditions of the Lease, it shall be the responsibility of the Lessee to repair and maintain the Container(s) as necessary to a standard acceptable to the Lessor and to ensure that all necessary re-examinations and record keeping are properly carried out in accordance with requirements of the UK Freight Container (Safety Convention) Regulations 1984, or any local equivalent thereof which have been approved by a contracting party to the CSC.

6. Delivery

The Lessor will tender the Container(s) to the Lessee at the agreed place(s) of delivery.

7. Redelivery

The Lessee must advise the Lessor or his local agent of his intention to redeliver Container(s) a minimum of seven days prior to the date of Redelivery. The Lessee must redeliver Container(s) to the Lessor at premises indicated by the Lessor at the location of Redelivery.
Upon Redelivery of the Container(s) this Agreement shall terminate in respect of the individual Container, save that either party shall be at liberty to prosecute and defend any claim right or remedy arising out of this Agreement on that individual Container.

8. Damage Repairs

Should a container be returned to the Lessor in a damaged condition, as defined by the Lessor's Container Damage and Inspection Criteria (copies of which are available on request from the Lessor), the Lessor will provide the Lessee with an estimate of repair costs within seven working days from the date of Redelivery. Within seven working days of receipt of such repair estimate the Lessee must either:

(a) accept the repair costs as advised or,

(b) arrange a joint survey and subsequently reach agreement with the Lessor over repair costs.

If the Lessee fails to agree the repair estimate or fails to exercise his right to attend a joint survey within the stipulated time period, the Lessor will proceed to repair the Container without notice to the Lessee to a standard the Lessor thinks fit and the Lessee shall pay such repair costs. Until such time as the Container has been repaired, the Lessee shall continue to pay all hire charges as described herein.

9. Taxes and Charges

The Lessee shall pay all taxes and charges arising out of, or incidental to, the use of the Container(s) until redelivered to the Lessor at the agreed location(s).

10. Payment

The Lessee shall pay all fees, taxes and charges within 30 days of the date of invoice. Should the Lessee fail to pay all aforesaid fees, taxes and charges within this period then, in addition, he shall pay interest at the rate of _____ per cent above the _______________ bank lending rate with a minimum rate of_____ per cent from the date of the invoice.

11. Documentation

All documentation relating to the hire of Container(s) hereunder, including the container interchange receipt/inspection report (but disregarding any conditions set out on the reverse thereof) shall form part of this Agreement. In the case of any conflict between the provisions of such documentation and these terms and conditions, these terms and conditions shall prevail.

12. Variation

These terms and conditions can only be varied with the agreement of the Lessor in writing signed by a person duly authorised by the Lessor.

13. Law and Jurisdiction

This Agreement shall be governed by and construed in accordance with the laws of England and the Lessor and the Lessee hereby submit to the jurisdiction of the English courts.

APPENDIX 9

EQUIPMENT HANDOVER AGREEMENT

EQUIPMENT HANDOVER AGREEMENT

Between the Company and:	Party to be charged if different:

Handover to: (Customer Representative)	Reg. No:	CTO Office:	Place of Handover:	CTO Signature:

OUT

Container Number	C'Base Imp FCL	C'Base MT	20'	40'	For Freightliners F'liner Origin	For Freightliners Berth	For Freightliners Gross Weight	Trailer No.	20'	40'

Lift Required YES/NO

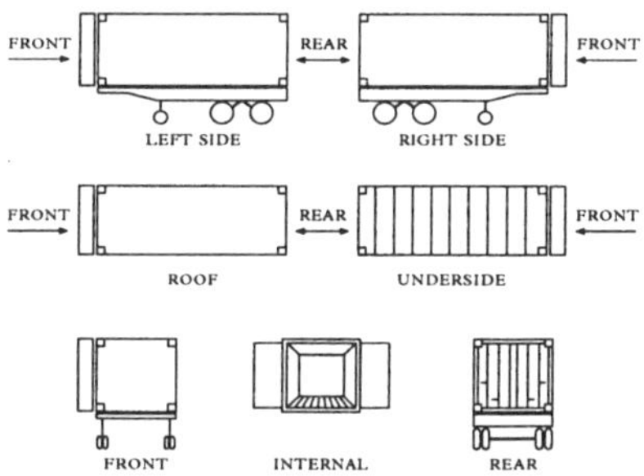

DAMAGE: List all details of damage and mark on the appropriate plan.
If no damage enter "none"

Date/Time Out

The condition of the Equipment is as indicated above:

For the Company

The Equipment above is received in good order except where noted:

For Customer

Received From:	Reg. No.	Place of Handover	Freightliner Signature for Equipment

IN

Container (status below) and trailer as above YES/NO

Container Number	Exp FCL	MT	20'	40'	Voy.	Dest	Gross Weight	Berth	Dest. Port	Haz/Special	Trailer No.	20'	40'

TO
Remain on Trailer
Be off Loaded to Stack
Be off Loaded to Trailer(s)

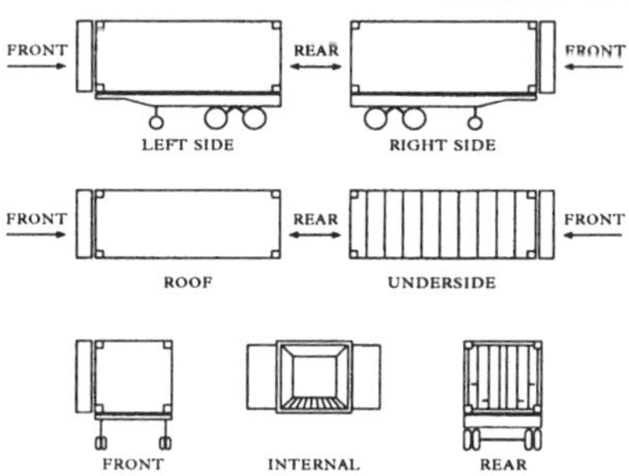

DAMAGE: List all details of damage and mark on the appropriate plan.
If no damage enter "None"

Date/Time In

The condition of the Equipment indicated above:

For Customer

The Equipment above is received in good order and condition

For the Company

TO BE RETAINED BY CTO OR AGENT

1. Definitions

Customer means the Shipper, Consignee or Lessee of Equipment who, or on whose behalf this Agreement is signed.
Company means_______________.
Equipment means any container and/or trailer and/or any associated and/or ancillary equipment the subject of this Agreement.

This clause is self-explanatory.

2. Clause Paramount

The Equipment is loaned to the Customer on the terms of the Company's applicable Bill of Lading and Tariff for the relevant trade in force at the time of the loan and on the following conditions.

3. Receipt

The Customer acknowledges receipt of the Equipment detailed overleaf in apparent good order and condition, except as indicated overleaf.

4. Customer's Responsibility

(a) The Customer is responsible for the cost of repair or replacement (whichever is the lesser) in respect of any damage or loss to the Equipment evidenced by the difference between the "out" and "in" receipts detailed overleaf, howsoever caused, whether occurring in the care of the Customer or that of his servant, agent or sub-contractor. Failure to return Equipment when called upon to do so shall entitle the Company to treat that Equipment as a loss and claim against the Customer for the cost of replacement in accordance with this clause.
(b) The Customer is responsible for all claims for loss, damage and/or injury and/or death caused by the Equipment whilst in his care. Whilst the Company will take reasonable care to ensure that all Equipment is serviceable and in good order and condition at the time of delivery to the Customer or his servant, agent or sub-contractor, it is the responsibility of the Customer to satisfy himself that the Equipment is what he requires and is in all respects fit to be used and taken onto a public highway before accepting it, rejecting any which he considers unsuitable/unfit.
(c) The Customer is responsible for any loss and/or damage to any goods carried by the Equipment whilst it is in his care, howsoever caused.
(d) The Customer shall supply to the driver such information as he requires in accordance with Clause 7(c).
(e) For the purpose of this contract the Customer's responsibilities are deemed to include responsibility for the actions of his servants, agents and sub-contractors in carrying out those matters for which the Customer is responsible and Equipment in the care of a Customer's servants, agents or sub-contractors is deemed to be in the care of the Customer.

5. Indemnity

The Customer undertakes that no claim or allegation shall be made against the Company, its servants, agents or sub-contractors which imposes or attempts to impose

upon any of them any liability whatsoever in connection with the Equipment whilst on loan to the Customer, whether or not arising out of negligence on the part of any of them and, if any such claim or allegation should nevertheless be made, to indemnify the Company, its servants, agents and sub-contractors (as the case may be) against all consequences thereof. In entering into this Agreement the Company does so, not only on its own behalf, but also as agent and trustee on behalf of its servants, agents and sub-contractors.
If the Company is not the owner of the Equipment the actual owner thereof shall come within the definition of servants, agents and sub-contractors for the purpose of this indemnity.

6. Customer's Driver's Responsibilities

If the driver is the servant, agent or sub-contractor of the Customer, his responsibilities will include the following, for the performance of which the Customer shall be vicariously responsible.

(a) The driver must ensure that the linking of the Equipment is compatible with his prime-mover and/or Trailer (as the case may be).
(b) The driver must ensure that the linking of the Equipment to his prime-mover and/or Trailer (as the case may be) is properly effected.
(c) The driver must ensure that his vehicle plus Equipment is thoroughly roadworthy before proceeding, in particular the driver is responsible for ensuring compliance with the Road Traffic Acts currently in force.
(d) The driver must be authorised to commit the Customer by completion and signature on this Agreement.

7. Company's Driver's Responsibilities/Authority

(a) If the driver is the servant, agent or sub-contractor of the Company, save for completing and signing this Agreement as evidence of the condition of the Equipment at the time of delivery, he shall have no authority to commit the Company in any way whatsoever.
(b) The driver is under no obligation to assist the Customer in any way with the loading or unloading of goods to or from the Equipment or in any way preparing the Equipment for the Customer to do so. Should any driver elect to do so, he does so entirely on his own behalf and not as servant, agent or sub-contractor of the Company, who accept no responsibility whatsoever for his actions in this context and, vis-à-vis the Company, he is considered as the Customer's servant at such times.
(c) The driver is responsible for ensuring that his load is roadworthy and safe to be taken on to the public highway before proceeding from the Customer's premises (or those of his servants, agents or sub-contractors) and it is the responsibility of the Customer to supply the driver with such information as he may require to satisfy himself in this matter.

8. Customer's Undertaking

The Customer undertakes to observe the following Company requirements whilst the Equipment is on loan.

(a) In no circumstances may any Container be removed from its Trailer or other carrying vehicle without the prior permission of the Company and then only in a manner previously approved by the Company.

(b) Containers must at all times be firmly secured to their Trailer or other carrying vehicle either by twistlocks or some alternative method which the Company has approved prior to use.

(c) Equipment loaned by the Company must not be used for the carriage or storage of goods which have not been booked with the Company.

(d) In any case where the prime-mover, Trailer or other carrying vehicle is not supplied by or on behalf of the Company, the vehicle used must be suitable for the weight, size and other characteristics of the load involved.

(e) A Customer taking delivery of goods in a Container is responsible for returning the empty Container with the interior brushed and clean. Failure so to do will result in the Customer being debited with cleaning costs and other expenses (demurrage included) thereby incurred. In the case of a tank Container the Customer is responsible for returning the tank not only clean but gas free with a certificate to that effect. The Company may inspect any tank prior to accepting redelivery and refuse any which does not meet these requirements in which case demurrage shall accrue.

9. Leasing

If Equipment is leased from the Company, the Customer agrees that the terms and conditions set out in the Company's Lease Agreement shall apply as if the Customer were Lessee and the Company were Lessor.

10. Law and Jurisdiction

Any dispute under this contract shall be determined according to English law by the High Court of Justice in London, to the exclusion of the jurisdiction of the courts of any other country or, if the plaintiff to the claim or dispute so elects, by the court of the place where the defendant is domiciled and then in accordance with the law of that court.

APPENDIX 10

BILL OF LADING—CONTRACT OF CARRIAGE

1. Definitions

In this Bill of Lading the word:
'Carrier' means the party named in the Signature Box on the face hereof;
'Merchant' includes any Person who at any time has been or becomes the Shipper, Holder, Consignee, Receiver of the Goods, any Person who owns or is entitled to possession of the Goods or of this Bill of Lading and any Person acting on behalf of any such Person;
'Holder' means any Person for the time being in possession of (or entitled to the possession of) this Bill of Lading;
'Person' includes an individual, group, company or other entity;
'Sub-Contractor' includes (but is not limited to) owners and operators of any Vessels (other than the Carrier), stevedores, terminal and groupage operators, road, rail and air transport operators and any independent contractor employed by the Carrier in performance of the Carriage and any sub-sub-contractors thereof;
'indemnify' includes defend, indemnify and hold harmless whether or not the obligation to indemnify arises out of negligence or non-negligent acts or omissions of the Carrier, his servants, agents or Sub-Contractors;
'Goods' means the whole or any part of the cargo received from the Shipper and includes the packing and any equipment or Container not supplied by or on behalf of the Carrier;
'Container' includes any container, trailer, transportable tank, flat or pallet, or any similar article used to consolidate goods and any ancillary equipment;
'Carriage' means the whole or any part of the operations and services undertaken by the Carrier in respect of the Goods covered by this Bill of Lading;
'Port of Loading' means any port at which the Goods are loaded on board any Vessel (which may not necessarily be the Vessel named overleaf) for Carriage under this Bill of Lading;
'Port of Discharge' means any port at which the Goods are discharged from any Vessel (which may not necessarily be the Vessel named overleaf) after Carriage under this Bill of Lading;
'Vessel' means any waterborne craft used in the Carriage under this Bill of Lading which may be a feeder vessel or an ocean vessel;
'Combined Transport' arises if the Place of Receipt and/or the Place of Delivery are indicated on the face hereof in the relevant spaces;
'Port-to-Port' arises if the Carriage is not Combined Transport;
'Shipped on Board' relates only to the Container into which the Goods are manifested;

'Freight' includes all charges payable to the Carrier in accordance with the applicable Tariff and this Bill of Lading;
'Hague Rules' means that the provisions of the International Convention for the Unification of Certain Rules relating to Bills of Lading signed at Brussels on 25 August 1924 and includes the amendments by the Protocol signed at Brussels on 23 February 1968, but only if such amendments are compulsorily applicable to this Bill of Lading (it is expressly provided that nothing in this Bill of Lading shall be construed as contractually applying said Rules as amended by said Protocol).

2. Carrier's Tariff

The terms and conditions of the Carrier's applicable Tariff are incorporated herein. Particular attention is drawn to the terms and conditions therein relating to Container and vehicle demurrage. Copies of the relevant provisions of the applicable Tariff are obtainable from the Carrier or his agents upon request. In the case of inconsistency between this bill of lading and the applicable Tariff, this bill of lading shall prevail.

3. Warranty

The Merchant warrants that in agreeing to the terms and conditions hereof he is, or has the authority of, the Person entitled to the possession of the Goods and this Bill of Lading.

4. Sub-contracting and Indemnity

(1) The Carrier shall be entitled to sub-contract the Carriage on any terms whatsoever.
(2) The Merchant undertakes that no claim or allegation shall be made against any Person whomsoever by whom the Carriage is performed or undertaken (including all Sub-Contractors of the Carrier), other than the Carrier, which imposes or attempts to impose upon any such Person, or any vessel owned by any such Person, any liability whatsoever in connection with the Goods or the Carriage of the Goods, whether or not arising out of negligence on the part of such Person and, if any such claim or allegation should nevertheless be made, the Merchant will indemnify the Carrier against all consequences thereof. Without prejudice to the foregoing, every such Person or Vessel shall have the benefit of every right, defence, limitation and liberty of whatsoever nature herein contained or otherwise available to the Carrier (including, but not limited to, Clause 24 hereof) as if such provisions were expressly for his benefit and, in entering into this contract, the Carrier, to the extent of these provisions, does so not only on his own behalf but also as agent and trustee for such Persons or Vessel.
(3). The provisions of Clause 4(2), including but not limited to the undertakings of the Merchant contained therein, shall extend to claims or allegation of whatsoever nature against other Persons chartering space on the carrying Vessel.
(4) The Merchant further undertakes that no claim or allegation in respect of the Goods shall be made against the Carrier by any Person, other than in accordance with the terms and conditions of this Bill of Lading, which imposes or attempts to impose upon the Carrier any liability whatsoever in connection with the Goods or the Carriage of the Goods, whether or not arising out of negligence on the part of the Carrier and, if any such claim or allegation should nevertheless be made, to indemnify the Carrier against all consequences thereof.

5. Carrier's Responsibility/Port-to-Port Shipment

If Carriage is Port-to-Port, the liability (if any) of the Carrier for loss, damage or delay to the Goods occurring from and during loading onto any Vessel up to and during discharge from that Vessel or from another Vessel into which the Goods have been transhipped shall be determined in accordance with any national law making the Hague Rules compulsorily applicable to this Bill of Lading, or in any other case in accordance with the Hague Rules, Articles 1–8 inclusive only.

Unless Clause 25 applies, the Carrier shall be under no liability whatsoever for loss, damage or delay to the Goods, howsoever occurring, if such loss, damage or delay arises prior to loading onto or subsequent to discharge from a Vessel. Notwithstanding the above, in case and to the extent that any applicable law provides for any additional period of responsibility, the Carrier shall have the benefit of every right, defence, limitation and liberty in the Hague Rules as applied by this clause during that period, notwithstanding that the loss, damage or delay did not occur at sea.

In the event of the Goods being discharged at a port other than the Port of Discharge nominated in this Bill of Lading and forwarded to the nominated Port of Discharge by whatever means, the Hague Rules as referred to in paragraph 1 of this clause shall continue to apply until delivery at the nominated Port of Discharge (or elsewhere), notwithstanding that Carriage may not be by sea.

6. Carrier's Responsibility/Combined Transport

If Carriage is Combined Transport, the Carrier undertakes to perform and/or in his own name to procure performance of the Carriage from the Place of Receipt or the Port of Loading, whichever is applicable, to the Port of Discharge or the Place of Delivery, whichever is applicable, and, save as is otherwise provided for in this Bill of Lading, the Carrier shall be liable for loss, damage or delay occurring during the Carriage only to the extent set out below.

(1) If the stage of the Carriage during which loss, damage or delay occurred is not known

(a) Exclusions

If the stage of the Carriage during which the loss, damage or delay occurred is not known, the Carrier shall be relieved of liability for any loss, damage or delay if such loss, damage or delay was caused by:

(i) an act or omission of the Merchant;
(ii) insufficiency of or defective condition of packing or marking;
(iii) handling, loading, stowage or unloading of the Goods by or on behalf of the Merchant (see Clause 8);
(iv) inherent vice of the Goods;
(v) strike, lock-out, stoppage or restraint of labour, from whatever cause, whether partial or general;
(vi) a nuclear incident;
(vii) any cause or event which the Carrier could not avoid and the consequences whereof he could not prevent by the exercise of reasonable diligence;
(viii) any act or omission of the Carrier the consequences of which he could not reasonably have foreseen;
(ix) compliance with the instructions of any Person entitled to give them.

(b) Burden of Proof

The burden of proof that the loss, damage or delay was due to one or more of the causes or events specified in this Clause 6(1) shall rest upon the Carrier, save that if the Carrier establishes that, in the circumstances of the case, the loss, damage or delay could be attributed to one or more of the causes or events specified in Clause

6(1)(a)(ii), (iii) or (iv), it shall be presumed that it was so caused. The Merchant shall, however, be entitled to prove that the loss, damage or delay was not, in fact, caused either wholly or partly by one or more of these causes or events.

(c) Limitation of Liability

Except as provided in Clauses 7(2), 7(3), and 27, if Clause 6(1) operates total compensation for loss or damage shall in no circumstances whatsoever and howsoever arising exceed 2SDRs per kilo of the gross weight of the Goods lost or damaged. (SDR means Special Drawing Right as defined by the International Monetary Fund.) Limitation of liability for delay shall be as provided in the applicable international convention or national law, in the absence of which the Carrier accepts no liability whatsoever for delay, howsoever caused (see Clause 7(4)).

(2) If the stage of the Carriage during which the loss, damage or delay occurred is known

Notwithstanding anything provided for in Clause 6(1) and subject to Clauses 15 and 16, if it is known during which stage of the Carriage the loss, damage or delay occurred, the liability of the Carrier in respect of such loss, damage or delay shall be determined:

(a) by the provisions contained in any international convention or national law which provisions:
   (i) cannot be departed from by private contract to the detriment of the Merchant; and
   (ii) would have applied if the Merchant had made a separate and direct contract with the Carrier in respect of the particular stage of the Carriage during which the loss, damage or delay occurred and received as evidence thereof any particular document which must be issued in order to make such international convention or national law applicable; or

(b) if no international convention or national law would apply by virtue of Clause 6(2)(a), by the Hague Rules, Articles 1–8 inclusive only if the loss, damage or delay is known to have occurred during waterborne Carriage; or

(c) by the provisions of Clause 6(1) if the provisions of Clause 6(2)(a) and (b) above do not apply.

For the purposes of Clause 6(2), references in the Hague Rules to carriage by sea shall be deemed to include references to all waterborne Carriage and the Hague Rules shall be construed accordingly.

(3) If the Place of Receipt or Place of Delivery is not named on the face hereof.

Subject to Clauses 5 and 25:

(a) if the Place of Receipt is not named on the face hereof, the Carrier shall be under no liability whatsoever for loss, damage or delay to the Goods, howsoever occurring, if such loss, damage or delay arises prior to loading onto a Vessel.

(b) if the Place of Delivery is not named on the face hereof, the Carrier shall be under no liability whatsoever for loss, damage or delay to the Goods, howsoever occurring, if such loss, damage or delay arises subsequent to discharge from a Vessel.

(4) Notice of Claim

Unless Clause 25 applies, the Carrier shall be deemed *prima facie* to have effected timely delivery of the Goods as described in this Bill of Lading unless notice of loss, damage or delay to the Goods, indicating the general nature of such loss, damage or delay, shall have been given in writing to the Carrier or to his representative at the Place of Delivery (or the Port of Discharge if no Place of Delivery is named on the face hereof) before or at the time of removal of the Goods into the custody of the Person entitled to delivery thereof under this Bill of Lading, or, if the loss or damage is not apparent at the time of delivery, within three working days thereafter.

(5) Time Bar
Unless Clause 25 applies, the Carrier shall be discharged of all liability whatsoever in respect of the Goods, unless suit is brought and notice thereof given to the Carrier within nine months after delivery of the Goods or, if the Goods are not delivered, ten months after the date of issue of this Bill of Lading.

7. Sundry Liability Provisions

(1) Basis of Compensation
Unless Clause 25 applies, compensation shall be calculated by reference to the value of the Goods at the place and time they are delivered to the Merchant, or at the place and time they should have been delivered. For the purpose of determining the extent of the Carrier's liability for loss, damage or delay to the Goods, the sound value of the Goods is agreed to be the FOB/FCA invoice value plus freight and insurance if paid.
(2) Hague Rules Limitation
If the Hague Rules are applicable by national law, the liability of the Carrier shall in no event exceed the limit provided in the applicable national law. If the Hague Rules are applicable otherwise than by national law, in determining the liability of the Carrier the liability shall in no event exceed £100 Sterling per package or unit.
(3) *Ad Valorem*
The Merchant agrees and acknowledges that the Carrier has no knowledge of the value of the Goods, and that higher compensation than that provided for in this Bill of Lading may not be claimed unless, with the consent of the Carrier, the value of the Goods declared by the Shipper prior to the commencement of the carriage is stated in this Bill of Lading and extra freight paid, if required. In that case, the amount of the declared value shall be substituted for the limits laid down in this Bill of Lading. Any partial loss or damage shall be adjusted pro rata on the basis of such declared value.
(4) Delay
(a) Unless Clause 25 applies, the Carrier does not undertake that the Goods shall arrive at the Port of Discharge or Place of Delivery at any particular time or to meet any particular market or use and the Carrier shall in no circumstances whatsoever and howsoever arising be liable for direct, indirect or consequential loss or damage caused by delay.
(b) However, if Clause 25 applies, unless a latest date of delivery is shown on the face hereof and any required premium paid, timely delivery shall be considered to have been made if the Goods are made available to the Merchant at the Port of Discharge or Place of Delivery, as the case may be, within 60 days after the date published in the Carrier's inbound sailing schedule against the Port of Discharge nominated therein for the relevant ocean Vessel. The Carrier shall be entitled to all the defences, exceptions and limitations provided in the applicable international convention or national law and this bill of lading.
(5) Scope of Application
(a) The terms and conditions of this Bill of Lading shall, at all times, govern all responsibilities of the Carrier in connection with or arising out of the supply of a Container to the Merchant, not only during the Carriage, but also during the period prior to and/or subsequent to the Carriage.
(b) The rights, defences, limitations and liberties, of whatsoever nature, provided for in this Bill of Lading shall apply in any action against the Carrier for loss, damage or delay, howsoever occurring and whether the action be founded in contract or in tort and even if the loss, damage or delay arose as a result of unseaworthiness, negligence or breach of a fundamental term of this contract.
(c) Save as is otherwise provided for in this Bill of Lading, the Carrier shall, in no circumstances whatsoever and howsoever arising, be liable for direct or indirect or consequential loss or damage or loss of profit.

(6) Inspection by Authorities
If by the order of the authorities at any place, a Container has to be opened for the Goods to be inspected, the Carrier will not be liable for any loss, damage or delay incurred as a result of any opening, unpacking, inspection or repacking. The Carrier shall be entitled to recover the cost of such opening, unpacking, inspection and repacking from the Merchant.

8. Shipper-Packed Containers

If a Container has not been packed by or on behalf of the Carrier:
(1) The Carrier shall not be liable for loss, damage or delay to the Goods caused by matters beyond his control, including, *inter alia*, without prejudice to the generality of this exclusion:
(a) the manner in which the Container has been packed; or
(b) the unsuitability of the Goods for Carriage in the Container supplied; or
(c) the unsuitability or defective condition of the Container or the incorrect setting of any temperature controls thereof, provided that, if the Container has been supplied by or on behalf of the Carrier, this unsuitability, defective condition or incorrect setting could have been apparent upon inspection by the Merchant at or prior to the time when the Container was packed; or
(d) packing temperature controlled Goods that are not at the correct temperature for Carriage.
(2) The Shipper is responsible for the packing and sealing of all Shipper-Packed Containers and, if a Shipper-Packed Container is delivered by the Carrier with its original seal as affixed by the Shipper intact, the Carrier shall not be liable for any shortage of Goods ascertained at delivery. If, nevertheless, a claim for shortage is made against the Carrier by any Person whomsoever, the Merchant agrees to indemnify the Carrier against the cost of any such claim plus any costs incurred in respect thereof.
(3) The Merchant shall indemnify the Carrier against any loss, damage, liability or expense whatsoever and howsoever arising caused by one or more of the matters referred to in Clause 8(1), save that, if the loss, damage, liability or expense was caused by a matter referred to in Clause 8(1)(c), the Merchant shall not be liable to indemnify the Carrier in respect thereof unless the proviso referred to in that Clause applies.

9. Inspection of Goods

The Carrier or any Person to whom the Carrier has sub-contracted the Carriage or any Person authorised by the Carrier shall be entitled, but under no obligation, to open any Container or package at any time and to inspect, or weigh and/or measure the Goods and/or weigh the Container.

10. Carriage affected by Condition of Goods

If it appears at any time that, due to their condition, the Goods cannot safely or properly be carried or carried further, either at all or without incurring any additional expense or taking any measure in relation to the Container or the Goods, the Carrier may, without notice to the Merchant (but as his agent only), take any measure and/or incur any additional expense to carry or to continue the Carriage thereof, and/or sell or dispose of the Goods, and/or abandon the Carriage and/or store them ashore or afloat, undercover or in the open, at any place, whichever the Carrier, in his absolute discretion, considers most appropriate, which abandonment, storage, sale or disposal shall be deemed to constitute due delivery under this Bill of Lading. The Merchant shall indemnify the Carrier against any additional expense incurred.

11. Description of Goods

(1) This Bill of Lading shall be *prima facie* evidence of the receipt by the Carrier from the Shipper in apparent good order and condition, except as otherwise noted, of the total number of Containers or other packages or units indicated in the box on the face hereof entitled 'Total Number of Containers/Packages received by the Carrier'.
(2) Except as provided in Clause 11(1), no representation is made by the Carrier as to the weight, contents, measure, quantity, quality, description, condition, marks, numbers or value of the Goods, and the Carrier shall be under no responsibility whatsoever in respect of such description or particulars, which are unknown to him.
It is agreed that, whilst he retains the right so to do at his sole discretion, the Carrier is not at any time under any obligation to weigh any Container or open any Container to make any check on the Goods therein or their stowage (see Clause 9).
(3) If any particulars of any Letter of Credit and/or Import Licence and/or Sale Contract and/or Invoice or Order number and/or details of any contract to which the Carrier is not a party are shown on the face of this Bill of Lading, such particulars are included solely at the request of the Merchant for his convenience. The Merchant agrees that the inclusion of such particulars shall not be regarded as a declaration of value and in no way increases the Carrier's liability under this Bill of Lading. The Merchant further agrees to indemnify the Carrier against all consequences of including such particulars in this Bill of Lading. The Merchant acknowledges that, except when the provisions of Clause 7(3) apply, the value of the Goods is unknown to the Carrier.

12. Shipper's/Merchant's Responsibility

(1) All of the Persons coming within the definition of Merchant in Clause 1 shall be jointly and severally liable to the Carrier for the due fulfilment of all obligations undertaken by the Merchant in this Bill of Lading and remain so liable throughout Carriage, notwithstanding their having transferred this Bill of Lading and/or title to the Goods to another party.
(2) The Shipper warrants to the Carrier that the particulars relating to the Goods as set out overleaf have been checked by the Shipper on receipt of this Bill of Lading and that such particulars, and any other particulars furnished by or on behalf of the Shipper, are adequate and correct. The Shipper also warrants that the Goods are lawful goods and contain no contraband. If the Container is not supplied by or on behalf of the Carrier, the Shipper further warrants that the Container meets all ISO and/or other international safety standards and is fit in all respects for Carriage by the Carrier.
(3) The Merchant shall indemnify the Carrier against all claims, losses, damages, fines and expenses arising or resulting from any breach of any of the warranties in Clause 12(2) hereof or from any other cause in connection with the Goods for which the Carrier is not responsible.
(4) The Merchant shall comply with all regulations or requirements of Customs, port and other authorities, and shall bear and pay all duties, taxes, fines, imposts, expenses or losses (including without prejudice to the generality of the foregoing, Freight for any additional Carriage undertaken) incurred or suffered in respect of the Goods, and shall indemnify the Carrier in respect thereof.
(5) If Containers supplied by or on behalf of the Carrier are unpacked at the Merchant's premises, the Merchant is responsible for returning the empty Containers, free from labels etc., with interiors brushed, clean, odour free and in every respect fit for immediate re-use, to the point or place designated by the Carrier, his servants or agents, within the time prescribed. Should a Container not be returned as required above within the time prescribed, the Carrier is entitled to take such steps as he

considers appropriate for the account of the Merchant and the Merchant shall be liable for any detention, loss or expense incurred as a result thereof.
(6) Containers released into the care of the Merchant for packing, unpacking or any other purpose whatsoever are at the sole risk of the Merchant until redelivered to the Carrier. The Merchant shall indemnify the Carrier for all loss and/or damage to such Containers occurring during such period. The Merchant shall also indemnify the Carrier for any loss, damage, injury, fines or expenses caused or incurred by such Containers whilst in his control, whether or not caused by negligence on the part of the Merchant, his servants, agents or sub-contractors.

13. Freight

(1) Freight shall be deemed fully earned on receipt of the Goods by the Carrier and shall be paid and non-returnable in any event.
(2) The Merchant's attention is drawn to the stipulations concerning currency in which the Freight is to be paid, rate of exchange, devaluation and other contingencies relative to Freight in the applicable Tariff.
(3) Freight has been calculated on the basis of particulars furnished by or on behalf of the Shipper. If the particulars furnished by or on behalf of the Shipper are incorrect, it is agreed that a sum equal to double the correct Freight less the Freight charged shall be payable as liquidated damages to the Carrier.
(4) All Freight shall be paid without any set-off, counter-claim, deduction or stay of execution before delivery of the Goods.

14. Lien

The Carrier shall have a lien on the Goods and any documents relating thereto for all sums payable to the Carrier under this contract. The Carrier shall also have a lien against the Merchant on the Goods and any documents relating thereto for all sums due from him to the Carrier under any other contract. The Carrier may exercise his lien at any time and at any place at his sole discretion, whether the contractual Carriage is completed or not. In any event any lien shall extend to cover the cost of recovering the sums due and for that purpose the Carrier shall have the right to sell the Goods by public auction or private treaty, without notice to the Merchant, at any time and at any place at the sole discretion of the Carrier.

15. Optional Stowage and Deck Cargo

(1) The Goods may be packed by the Carrier in Containers and consolidated with other goods in Containers.
(2) Goods, whether or not packed in Containers, may be carried on deck or under deck, at the sole discretion of the Carrier, without notice to the Merchant. All such Goods, whether carried on deck or under deck, shall participate in General Average and shall be deemed to be within the definition of Goods for the purposes of the Hague Rules and shall be carried subject to those Rules.
(3) Notwithstanding Clause 15(2), in the case of Goods which are stated on the face hereof as being carried on deck and which are so carried, the Hague Rules shall not apply and the Carrier shall be under no liability whatsoever for loss, damage or delay, howsoever arising, whether or not caused by negligence on the part of the Carrier his servants, agents or sub-contractors.

16. Live Animals

The Hague Rules shall not apply to the Carriage of live animals, which are carried at the sole risk of the Merchant. The Carrier shall be under no liability whatsoever for any injury, illness, death, delay or destruction to such live animals howsoever arising. Should the Master in his sole discretion consider that any live animal is likely to be injurious to any other live animal or any person or property on board or to cause the Vessel to be delayed or impeded in the prosecution of its voyage, such live animal may be destroyed and thrown overboard, without any liability attaching to the Carrier. The Merchant shall indemnify the Carrier against all and any extra costs incurred for any reason whatsoever in connection with the Carriage of any live animal.

17. Methods and Routes of Carriage

(1) The Carrier may at any time and without notice to the Merchant:
(a) use any means of carriage whatsoever;
(b) transfer the Goods from one conveyance to another, including but not limited to transhipping or carrying them on a Vessel other than that named on the face hereof;
(c) unpack and remove the Goods which have been packed into a Container and forward them in a Container or otherwise;
(d) proceed by any route in his discretion (whether or not the nearest or most direct or customary or advertised route), at any speed, and proceed to or stay at any place or port whatsoever, once or more often and in any order;
(e) load or unload the Goods at any place or port, whether or not such port is named overleaf as the Port of Loading or Port of Discharge and store the goods at any such place or port;
(f) comply with any orders or recommendations given by any government or authority, or any Person acting or purporting to act as or on behalf of such government or authority, or having under the terms of any insurance on any conveyance employed by the Carrier the right to give orders or directions;
(g) permit the Vessel to proceed with or without pilots, to tow or be towed and to be dry-docked, with or without Goods and/or Containers on board.

(2) The liberties set out in Clause 17(1) may be invoked by the Carrier for any purpose whatsoever, whether or not connected with the Carriage of the Goods, including but not limited to loading or unloading other goods, bunkering, undergoing repairs, adjusting instruments, picking up or landing any persons, including but not limited to persons involved with the operation or maintenance of the Vessel and assisting vessels in all situations. Anything done in accordance with Clause 17(1) or any delay arising therefrom shall be deemed to be within the contract of carriage and shall not be a deviation home.

(3) By tendering Goods for Carriage without any written request for Carriage in a specialised Container, or for carriage otherwise than in a Container, the Merchant accepts that Carriage may be undertaken properly in a general purpose Container, carried on or under deck at the Carrier's sole discretion.

18. Matters Affecting Performance

If at any time the Carriage, the Vessel or other goods on board the Vessel are or are likely to be affected by any hindrance, risk, delay, difficulty or disadvantage of any kind whatsoever (other than the inability of the Goods, due to their condition, safely or properly to be carried or carried further) and howsoever arising (even though the circumstances giving rise to such hindrance, risk, delay, difficulty or disadvantage existed at the time this contract was entered into or the Goods were received for Carriage), the Carrier (whether or not the Carriage is commenced) may, without prior notice to the Merchant and at the sole discretion of the Carrier, either:

(a) Carry the Goods to the contracted Port of Discharge or Place of Delivery, whichever is applicable, by an alternative route to that indicated in this Bill of Lading or that which is usual for Goods consigned to that Port of Discharge or Place of Delivery. If the Carrier elects to invoke the terms of this Clause 18(a) then, notwithstanding the provisions of Clause 17 hereof, he shall be entitled to charge such additional freight as the Carrier may determine.

or

(b) Suspend the Carriage of the Goods and store them ashore or afloat upon the terms of this Bill of Lading and endeavour to forward them as soon as possible, but the Carrier makes no representations as to the maximum period of such suspension of Carriage. If the Carrier elects to invoke the terms of this Clause 18(b) then, notwithstanding the provisions of Clause 17 hereof, he shall be entitled to charge such additional Freight as the Carrier may determine.

or

(c) Abandon the Carriage of the Goods and place them at the Merchant's disposal at any place or port which the Carrier may deem safe and convenient, whereupon the responsibility of the Carrier in respect of such Goods shall cease. The Carrier shall nevertheless be entitled to full Freight on the Goods received for Carriage, and the Merchant shall pay any additional cost of the Carriage to, and delivery and storage at, such place or port.

If the Carrier elects to use an alternative route under Clause 18(a) or to suspend the Carriage under Clause 18(b) this shall not prejudice his right subsequently to abandon the Carriage.

19. Dangerous Goods

(1) No Goods which are or may become dangerous, inflammable, damaging or injurious (including radioactive materials), or which are or may become liable to damage any property whatsoever or injure any person whomsoever, shall be tendered to the Carrier for Carriage without his express consent in writing and without the Container as well as the Goods themselves being distinctly marked on the outside so as to indicate the nature and character of any such Goods and so as to comply with any applicable laws, regulations or requirements. If any such Goods are delivered to the Carrier without such written consent and/or marking or if, in the opinion of the Carrier, the Goods are or are liable to become of a dangerous, inflammable, damaging or injurious nature, they may at any time be destroyed, disposed of, abandoned or rendered harmless without compensation to the Merchant.

(2) The Merchant undertakes that such Goods are packed in a manner adequate to withstand the risks of Carriage, having regard to their nature and in compliance with all laws or regulations which may be applicable during the Carriage. In particular but without prejudice to the generality of this Clause 19(2), if the Goods are not packed into the Container by or on behalf of the Carrier, the Merchant undertakes that incompatible Goods are not packed in the same Container.

(3) Whether or not the Merchant was aware of the nature of the Goods, the Merchant shall indemnify the Carrier against all claims, losses, damages or expenses arising in consequence of the Carriage of such Goods.

(4) Nothing contained in this Clause shall deprive the Carrier of any of his rights provided for elsewhere.

20. Notification and Delivery

(1) Any mention herein of parties to be notified of the arrival of the Goods is solely for the information of the Carrier and failure to give such notification shall not involve the Carrier in any liability nor relieve the Merchant of any obligation hereunder.
(2) The Merchant shall take delivery of the Goods within the time provided in the Carriers applicable Tariff (see Clause 2). If the Merchant fails to do so the Carrier shall be entitled, without notice, to unpack the Goods, if packed in Containers, and/or to store the Goods ashore, afloat, in the open or under cover, at the sole risk of the Merchant. Such storage shall constitute due delivery hereunder and thereupon the liability of the Carrier in respect of the Goods stored as aforesaid shall wholly cease and the costs of such storage (if paid or payable by the Carrier or any agent or Sub-Contractor of the Carrier) shall forthwith upon demand be paid by the Merchant to the Carrier.
(3) If the Merchant fails to take delivery of the Goods within 30 days of delivery becoming due under Clause 20(2) or if, in the opinion of the Carrier, they are likely to deteriorate, decay, become worthless or incur charges, whether for storage or otherwise, in excess of their value, the Carrier may, without prejudice to any other rights which he may have against the Merchant, without notice and without any responsibility whatsoever attaching to him, sell, destroy or dispose of the Goods and apply any proceeds of sale in reduction of the sums due to the Carrier from the Merchant.
(4) Refusal by the Merchant to take delivery of the Goods in accordance with the terms of this Clause and/or to mitigate any loss or damage thereto shall constitute a waiver by the Merchant to the Carrier of any claim whatsoever relating to the Goods or the Carriage thereof.
(5) In the event of the Carrier agreeing to a request of the Merchant to amend the Place of Delivery stated herein without stipulating any particular terms and conditions to apply during said amended Carriage, to the extent provided by the applicable Tariff the terms and conditions of this Bill of Lading shall continue to apply, but only until the Goods are delivered by the Carrier to the Merchant at the amended Place of Delivery. Once the applicable Tariff ceases to provide for the continued application of the terms and conditions of the Bill of Lading or if the Carrier declines to extend the Bill of Lading terms to the amended Place of Delivery, then the Carrier shall act as agent only of the Merchant in arranging for delivery of the Goods to the amended Place of Delivery but shall then be under no liability whatsoever for loss, damage or delay to the Goods, howsoever arising for the period of amended Carriage.
If the Carrier agrees to make multiple point deliveries of an FCL Container, this contract terminates upon presentation of the sealed Container at the first place of delivery. Thereafter the Carrier acts as agent only to arrange any further deliveries.
(6) If, at the place where the Carrier is entitled to call upon the Merchant to take delivery of the Goods under Clause 20(2), the Carrier is obliged to hand over the Goods into the custody of any Customs, port or other authority, such hand-over shall constitute due delivery to the Merchant under this Bill of Lading.
(7) This Bill of Lading shall not be a negotiable document of title unless consigned 'To Order', 'To the Order of . . . ', or 'To Bearer'. If not so consigned but instead consigned directly to a nominated party, this shall be a 'Straight' Bill of Lading and, at the sole discretion of the Carrier, delivery may be made to the nominated party only upon proof of identity, as if this Bill of Lading were a Waybill. Such delivery shall constitute due delivery hereunder.

21. FCL Multiple Bills of Lading

(1) Goods will be delivered in a Container to the Merchant only if all Bills of Lading in respect of the contents of the Container have been surrendered authorising delivery

to a single Merchant at a single Place of Delivery. In the event that this requirement is not fulfilled, the Carrier may unpack the Container and, in respect of Goods for which Bills of Lading have been surrendered, deliver them to the Merchant on an LCL basis. Such delivery shall constitute due delivery hereunder but will be effected only against payment by the Merchant of LCL Service Charges and any charges appropriate to LCL Goods (as laid down in the Tariff) together with the actual costs incurred for any additional services rendered.
(2) If this is an FCL Multiple Bill of Lading (as evidence by the qualification of the tally acknowledged overleaf to the effect that it is 'One of _____ part cargoes in the Container'), then the Goods detailed overleaf are said to comprise part of the contents of the Container indicated. If the Carrier is required to deliver the Goods to more than one Merchant and if all or part of the total Goods within the Container consists of bulk Goods or unappropriated Goods, or is or becomes mixed or unmarked or unidentifiable, the Holders of Bills of Lading relating to Goods within the Container shall take delivery thereof (including any damaged portion) and bear any shortage in such proportions as the Carrier shall in his absolute discretion determine. Such a delivery shall constitute due delivery hereunder.

22. General Average and Salvage

(1) In the event of accident, danger, damage or disaster before or after the commencement of the voyage, resulting from any cause whatsoever, due to negligence or not, for which, or for the consequences of which, the Carrier is not responsible, by statute, contract or otherwise, the Merchant shall contribute with the Carrier in General Average to the payment of any sacrifices, losses or expenses of a General Average nature that may be made or incurred, and shall pay Salvage and special charges incurred in respect of the Goods.
(2) Any General Average on a Vessel operated by the Carrier shall be adjusted according to the York-Antwerp Rules of 1994 or any subsequent amendment thereto authorised by the CMI at any port or place and in any currency at the option of and by an adjuster appointed by the Carrier, with the test of reasonableness in the Rule Paramount being made on the basis of what was known at the time of the General Average act and not subsequently with the benefit of hindsight. Any General Average on a Vessel not operated by the Carrier (whether a sea-going or inland waterways Vessel) shall be adjusted according to the requirements of the operator of that Vessel. In either case the Merchant shall give such cash deposit or other security as the Carrier may deem sufficient to cover the estimated General Average contribution of the Goods. Any security, other than cash deposits, must be given by a party acceptable to and with assets in a jurisdiction nominated by the Carrier. Such security must be provided before delivery if the Carrier so requires or, if the Carrier does not so require, within three months of the delivery of the Goods, whether or not at the time of delivery the Merchant had notice of the Carrier's lien. The Carrier shall be under no obligation to exercise any lien for General Average contribution due to the Merchant.
(3) Conversion into the currency of the adjustment shall be calculated at the rate prevailing on the date of payment for disbursements and on the date of completion of discharge of the Vessel for allowances, contributory values, etc.
(4) If a salving vessel is owned or operated by the Carrier, salvage shall be paid for as fully as if the salving vessel or vessels belonged to strangers.
(5) In the event of the Master in his sole discretion or in consultation with owners considering that salvage services are needed, the Merchant agrees that the Master may act as his agent to procure such services to Goods and that the Carrier may act as his agent to settle salvage remuneration, without any prior consultation with the Merchant in both cases.

(6) If the Merchant contests payment of contribution to General Average, salvage, salvage charges and/or special charges to Goods on any grounds whatsoever or fails to make payment of contribution within three months of the issue of the adjustment thereof, whether or not prior security had been provided, the Merchant shall pay interest for the period in excess of three months on the contribution due at two per cent per annum above the base lending rate of the central bank of the country in whose currency the adjustment is issued, in addition to the contribution due.

23. Variation of the Contract

No servant or agent of the Carrier shall have the power to waive or vary any of the terms of this Bill of Lading, unless such waiver or variation is in writing and is specifically authorised or ratified in writing by the Carrier.

24. Law and Jurisdiction

(1) Unless Clause 25 or 27 applies, any claim against the Carrier under this Bill of Lading shall be determined only according to English law and exclusively in the High Court of Justice in London. The Merchant irrevocably submits to this jurisdiction.
(2) The Carrier shall be entitled to pursue any claim against the Merchant in London according to English law or in any jurisdiction in which the Merchant has assets but then in accordance with the local law of that jurisdiction.
(3) Nothing herein shall prevent the parties to any claim or dispute under this Bill of Lading from agreeing to submit the claim or dispute to arbitration by mutually acceptable arbitrator(s) on mutually acceptable terms at a mutually acceptable venue.

25. Validity

In the event that anything herein contained is inconsistent with any applicable international convention or national law which cannot be departed from by private contract, the provisions hereof shall, to the extent of such inconsistency but no further, be null and void.

26. Limitation of Liability

For the avoidance of doubt, it is hereby agreed by the Merchant that the Carrier qualifies and shall be regarded as a Person entitled to limit liability under the relevant Convention on the Limitation of Liability for Maritime Claims, notwithstanding that the Carrier may have procured space on board the Vessel concerned by means of a Slot Charter party, Bill of Lading or some other Contract of Carriage.

Except to the extent that mandatory law to the contrary applies in the appropriate jurisdiction (in which case said law shall apply), the size of the fund to which the Carrier may limit liability shall be identical to that proportion of the limitation fund by which the actual carrier is entitled to limit which is (or would be) available for the Carrier's claims against the actual carrier.

27. USA Clause Paramount (if applicable)

Present clause

(1) If Carriage includes Carriage to, from or through a port in the United States of America, this Bill of Lading shall be subject to the United States Carriage of Goods by

Sea Act 1936 (US COGSA), the terms of which are incorporated herein and shall be paramount throughout Carriage by sea and the entire time that the Goods are in the actual custody of the Carrier or his Sub-Contractor at the sea terminal in the United States of America before loading onto a Vessel or after discharge therefrom, as the case may be.
(2) The Carrier shall not be liable in any capacity whatsoever for loss, damage or delay to the Goods while the goods are in the United States of America away from the sea terminal and are not in the actual custody of the Carrier. At these times the Carrier acts as agent only to procure carriage by Persons (one or more) under the usual terms and conditions of those Persons. If, for any reason, the Carrier is denied the right to act as agent only at these times, his liability for loss, damage or delay to the Goods shall be determined in accordance with Clause 6 hereof.
(3) If US COGSA applies the liability of the Carrier and/or the Vessel shall not exceed US$500 per package or customary freight unit (in accordance with Section 1304(5) thereof), unless the value of the Goods has been declared on the face hereof, in which case Clause 7(3) shall apply.
(4) Notwithstanding the provisions of Clause 24, if Carriage includes Carriage to, from or through a port in the United States of America, the Merchant may refer any claim or dispute to the United States District Court for the Southern District of New York in accordance with the laws of the United States of America.

Clause when new Act (US COGSA 2000/1?) in force

(1) If Carriage under this Bill of Lading includes Carriage to, from or through any port or place in the United States of America, this Bill of Lading shall be subject to the United States Carriage of Goods by Sea Act 2000 (US COGSA), the terms of which are incorporated herein and, notwithstanding any provisions to the contrary elsewhere in this Bill of Lading, shall be paramount throughout Carriage of the Goods. No provision of any Act, Statute or other law or rule will be incorporated contractually by reference into this Bill of Lading if its incorporation would increase the Carrier's liability above the provisions contained in the Hague Rules.
(2) Notwithstanding the provisions of Clause 24, if Carriage includes Carriage to, from or through a port or place in the United States of America, the Merchant has the option to refer any claim or dispute to the United States District Court for the Southern District of New York in accordance with the laws of the United States of America.

APPENDIX 11

WAYBILL—INCORPORATION CLAUSE

Non-Negotiable Waybill for Combined Transport shipment or Port to Port shipment

Shipper	Waybill No.: Reference P&O Nedlloyd
Consignee (If the name shown in this space is a Bank, the Bank named is specifically excluded from the list of parties coming within the definition of Merchant in the Carrier's contract of carriage and incurs no liability to the Carrier under said contract unless applying for delivery in its own name.)	
Notify Party/Address (It is agreed that no responsibility shall attach to the Carrier or his Agents for failure to notify.)	Place of Receipt (Applicable only when this document is used as a Combined Transport Waybill)
Vessel and Voy. No.	Place of Delivery (Applicable only when this document is used as a Combined Transport Waybill)
Port of Loading / Port of Discharge	

Undermentioned particulars as declared by Shipper, but not acknowledged by the Carrier

Marks and Nos; Container Nos;	Number and kind of Packages; Description of Goods	Gross Weight (kg)	Measurement (cbm)

WAYBILL

*Total No. of Containers/Packages received by the Carrier	Movement	Freight payable at

Received by the Carrier from the Shipper in apparent good order and condition (unless otherwise noted herein) the total number or quantity of Containers or other packages or units indicated in the box above entitled "*Total No. of Containers/Packages received by the Carrier" for Carriage from the Place of Receipt or the Port of Loading, whichever applicable, to the Port of Discharge or the Place of Delivery, whichever applicable. SUBJECT TO THE TERMS OF THE CARRIER'S STANDARD BILL OF LADING TERMS AND CONDITIONS AND TARIFF FOR THE RELEVANT TRADE, WHICH ARE MUTATIS MUTANDIS APPLICABLE TO THIS WAYBILL (copies of which may be obtained from the Carrier or his agents). Except for live animals and Goods which are stated herein to be carried on deck and are so carried, these terms and conditions are warranted by the Carrier in respect of the sea portion of the Carriage to apply the Hague Rules or Hague Visby Rules, whichever would have been applicable if this Waybill were a Bill of Lading. In either case the provisions of Article III Rule 4 of the Hague Visby Rules are deemed to be incorporated herein.
The contract evidenced by this Waybill is deemed to be a contract of carriage as defined in Article 1(b) of the Hague Rules and Hague Visby Rules. However this Waybill is not a document of title to the Goods.
Delivery will be made to the Consignee named, or his authorised agents, on production of proof of identity at the Port of Discharge or the Place of Delivery, whichever applicable. Should the Consignee require delivery to a party and/or premises other than as shown above in the "Consignee" box, then written instructions must be given by the Consignee to the Carrier or his agent. Unless the Shipper expressly waives his right to control the Goods until delivery by means of a clause on the face hereof, such instructions from the Consignee will be subject to any instructions to the contrary by the Shipper.
Unless instructed to the contrary by the Shipper prior to the commencement of Carriage and noted accordingly on the face hereof, the Carrier will, subject to the aforesaid terms and conditions, process cargo claims with the Consignee. Claims settlement, if any, shall be a complete discharge of the Carrier's liability to the Shipper. The Shipper accepts the said standard terms and conditions on his own behalf, on behalf of the Consignee and the Owner of the Goods, and authorises the Consignee to bring suit against the Carrier in his own name but as agent of the Shipper, and warrants that he has authority so to accept and authorise. The Shipper further undertakes that no claim or allegation in respect of the Goods shall be made against the Carrier by any person other than in accordance with the terms and conditions of this Waybill.

This Waybill is issued subject to the CMI Uniform Rules for Sea Waybills	Place and Date of Issue	IN WITNESS whereof this Waybill is signed. FOR P&O NEDLLOYD LTD, AS CARRIER:* P&O Nedlloyd

19/DRS W/B3 10/97 (8)

*OPERATING IN PARTNERSHIP WITH P&O NEDLLOYD B.V.

Received by the Carrier from the Shipper in apparent good order and condition (unless otherwise noted herein) the total number or quantity of Containers or other packages or units indicated in the box above entitled 'Total No. of Containers/Packages received by the Carrier' for Carriage from the Place of Receipt or the Port of Loading, whichever applicable, to the Port of Discharge or the Place of Delivery, whichever applicable, SUBJECT TO THE TERMS OF THE CARRIER'S STANDARD BILL OF LADING TERMS AND CONDITIONS AND TARIFF FOR THE RELEVANT TRADE WHICH ARE *MUTATIS MUTANDIS* APPLICABLE TO THIS WAYBILL (copies of which may be obtained from the Carrier or his agents). Except for live animals and goods which are stated herein to be carried on deck and are so carried, these terms and conditions are warranted by the Carrier in respect of the sea portion of Carriage to apply the Hague Rules or Hague-Visby Rules, whichever would have been applicable if this Waybill were a Bill of Lading. In either case the provisions of Article III Rule 4 of the Hague-Visby Rules are deemed to be incorporated herein.

The contract evidenced by this Waybill is deemed to be a contract of carriage as defined in Article 1(b) of the Hague Rules and Hague-Visby Rules. However this Waybill is not a document of title to the Goods.

Delivery will be made to the Consignee named, or his authorised agents, on production of proof of identity at the Port of Discharge or the Place of Delivery, whichever applicable. Should the Consignee require delivery to a party and/or premises other than as shown above in the 'Consignee' box, then a written instruction must be given by the Consignee to the Carrier or his agent. Unless the Shipper expressly waives his right to control Goods until delivery by means of a clause on the face hereof, such instruction from the Consignee will be subject to any instruction to the contrary by the Shipper.

Unless instructed to the contrary by the Shipper prior to the commencement of Carriage and noted accordingly on the face hereof, the Carrier will, subject to the aforesaid terms and conditions, process cargo claims with the Consignee. Claims settlement, if any, shall be a complete discharge of the Carrier's liability to the Shipper. The Shipper accepts the said standard terms and conditions on his own behalf, on behalf of the Consignee and the owner of the Goods, and authorises the Consignee to bring suit against the Carrier in his own name but as agent of the Shipper, and warrants that he has authority so to accept and authorise. The Shipper further undertakes that no claim or allegation in respect of the Goods shall be made against the Carrier by any person other than in accordance with the terms and conditions of this Waybill.

APPENDIX 12

STANDARD TRADING CONDITIONS

The majority of services offered by the Company and its subsidiary organisations are covered by the contract of carriage, the terms of which appear in the Bill of Lading terms and conditions and Tariff for the trade in question. However some value added services are offered which fall outside the scope of the contract of carriage.
In order to formalise the relationship of the Company with its Customers on such occasions the following Standard Trading Conditions are published.
(The Customer's attention is drawn to the clauses herein which exclude or limit the Company's liability and those which require the Customer to indemnify the Company in certain circumstances).

1. Definitions

In these conditions:
'The Company' means [..........].
'Customer' means any person to whom the Company provides any services.
'Person' includes individuals, groups, companies or any other legal entity.
'Owner' means the owner of the goods to or in respect of which the Company provides any services and any other Person who has or may acquire an interest in them.
'Goods' means all or any part of the goods (including any packaging, containers or equipment supplied by the Customer or Owner) which are the subject of any Services.
'Conditions' means the provisions of this contract.
'Instructions' means any statement of the Customer's requirements, whether verbal or written.
'Service(s)' means all or any business undertaken by the Company for the Customer including the provision of advice, information and any services whatsoever.
'Sub-Contractor' means direct and indirect sub-contractors and their respective servants, agents and sub-contractors.
Any reference in these Conditions to agreement in writing that varies these terms and conditions must be on the Company's stationery and signed by an authorised official of the Company.

2. Application

Any Services provided by the Company, whether gratuitous or otherwise, shall be subject to these Conditions unless:
(A) The Company contracts in writing with the Customer on alternative terms and conditions, including, but not limited to, issuing Bills of Lading, Air or Sea Waybills or any other contract for carriage or any other Service to Goods, or

(B) Any Conditions herein are contrary to any mandatory applicable law relating to the Services undertaken by the Company on behalf of the Customer.

In which case the alternative terms and conditions or mandatory applicable law shall be paramount and prevail to the extent of any inconsistency with these Conditions (but no further). In case of (A) or (B) these Conditions shall continue to operate in respect of any Services to which the alternative terms and conditions or mandatory law do not apply or in respect of any matter upon which they are silent.

3. Role

(A) Unless specifically agreed in writing between the Customer and the Company prior to the commencement of the Service, the Company shall be at liberty to provide the Service as a principal or to procure it as an agent, in either case subject to the appropriate Conditions herein.

(B) The agreement of a price for the Service is not of itself an indication of whether the Company is acting as a principal or as an agent.

4. The Company's General Conditions

(A) **Performance**: The Company will undertake the tasks necessary to provide the contracted Services to the Customer with a reasonable degree of care and skill and, subject to Clause 8(D), within a reasonable timescale.

(B) **Deviation from Customer's Instructions**: Whilst, subject to these Conditions, the Company will take reasonable steps to perform the Customer's Instructions, if at any time the Company, in its sole discretion, considers that there is good reason, in the Customer's interest, to depart from any of the Customer's Instructions, it shall be free to do so without prior notice to the Customer or incurring any additional liability as a result thereof.

(C) **Customer fails to take Delivery**: If Services provided involve the handling and/or carriage of Goods and the Customer, Consignee or Owner fails to take delivery thereof at the time and place when and where the Company is entitled to call upon such Person to take delivery thereof, the Company shall be entitled to store said Goods, at the sole risk of the Customer, whereupon the Company's liability (if any) for the Goods shall wholly cease. The cost of such storage, if paid or payable by the Company or any of its agents or Sub-Contractors, shall forthwith, upon demand, be paid by the Customer to the Company.

(D) **Disposal of Goods**: If the Services provided involve the handling, storage and/or carriage of Goods and the Customer fails to take delivery thereof in accordance with Clause 4(C), the Company shall be entitled to dispose of the Goods, at the expense of the Customer, by sale or otherwise at the Company's sole discretion, after the Goods have been in the Company's control for 30 days.

The Company shall give 14 days notice in writing to the Customer of any intention to dispose of the Goods.

However, in respect of Goods that, in the sole opinion of the Company, are likely to deteriorate, decay, become worthless or incur charges in excess of their value, or Goods which may cause loss or damage to other Goods, injury to Persons or contravene any applicable laws or regulations, the Company may dispose of such Goods immediately without prior notice to the Customer.

The proceeds of sale, after deducting the cost of sale and any sums whatsoever due by the Customer to the Company for this or any earlier Services, shall be held by the Company to the credit of the Customer. The Customer shall forth-with upon demand remit any shortfall between the proceeds of sale and the sums owed by him to the Company.

(E) **Separate Service to Goods**: Services to Goods may be undertaken in conjunction with goods of other customers or third parties, unless specifically agreed in writing prior to commencement of the Services.

(F) **Effecting Insurance**: No insurance will be effected, except upon express instructions given in writing by the Customer, and all insurances effected by the Company are subject to the usual exceptions and conditions of the policies of the insurance company or underwriters taking the risk. Unless otherwise agreed in writing, the Company shall not be under any obligation to effect a separate insurance on each consignment but may declare it on any open or general policy held by the Company.

Insofar as the Company agrees to arrange insurance, it acts solely as agent for the Customer to arrange such insurance.

(G) **Declarations**: Except in accordance with Instructions in writing previously received and accepted by the Company, the Company shall not be obliged to make any declaration for the purpose of any statute, convention, contract or other requirement as to the nature or value of any Goods, any characteristic of any Goods or Services to any Goods.

(H) **Special Delivery Arrangements**: Except by prior written agreement or under the terms of a printed document signed by the Company, any Instructions relating to the delivery or release of Goods in specified circumstances only, such as (but without prejudice to the generality of this Clause) against payment or against surrender of a particular document, are accepted by the Company only as agents for the Customer if third Persons are engaged to effect compliance with the Instructions.

The Company shall not be under any liability in respect of such arrangements unless such arrangements are made in writing.

In any event, the Company's liability in respect of the performance of such Instructions shall not exceed that provided for in these Conditions in respect of loss of or damage to Goods.

5. The Company as a Principal

If, in accordance with Clause 3 hereof, the Company agrees to act as a principal, then it will perform, or in its own name procure the performance of the Services contracted, subject to the provisions of any specific contract for Services which it may issue subject to Clause 2(A), failing which these Conditions in general and this Clause in particular shall apply.

(A) **Liberties**: The Company is not a common carrier and, except to the extent provided in Clause 2 hereof, contracts on the basis of these Conditions alone. The Company reserves to itself the liberties as to the means, routes and procedures to be followed in the handling, storage and carriage of Goods.

(B) **Period of Responsibility**: If the Company contracts to provide Services as a principal, it accepts liability for loss of or damage to Goods occurring between the time when it takes the Goods into its charge and the time when it is entitled to call upon the Customer, Consignee or Owner to take delivery of the Goods. The Company shall be deemed to have taken the Goods into its charge when the Goods have been received by the Company or have been released or handed over by the Customer, or any Person acting on behalf of the Customer, to any Person acting on behalf of the Company in accordance with any directions of the Company for the performance of the Services. The Company shall be deemed to have delivered the Goods, either when they have been placed at the disposal of the Customer (or its nominee) and notice thereof has been given to the Customer (or its nominee) at the address provided by the Customer, following completion of the contracted Service(s), or following the implementation of Clause 4(B), (C) or (D).

(C) **Liabilities**: The Company's liabilities will be as provided in Clause 8 hereof.

6. The Company as an Agent

If, in accordance with Clause 3 hereof, the Company acts as an agent then, without prejudice to the general applicability of these Conditions, its responsibilities shall be as follows:

(A) **Agency**: The Company shall be entitled and the Customer hereby expressly authorises the Company, except in so far as has been otherwise specifically agreed between the Company and the Customer, to enter into contracts with third parties on behalf of the Customer for the Service required. (Third parties for the purpose of this Clause, includes the Company's parent, subsidiary and/or associated companies).

When acting as an agent the Company does not make, or purport to make, any contract with the Customer for Services, but acts solely on behalf of the Customer in establishing contracts with third party contractors for the Services required, so that a direct contractual relationship is established between the Customer and such third party contractor.

(B) **Contracting Terms with Third Parties**: If there is a choice of prices according to the extent or degree of the liability assumed by third party contractors, no declaration of value will be made, except under prior Instructions received in writing and accepted by the Company; nor shall the Company be under any liability to the Customer by reason of having entered into any contract on behalf of the Customer, whereby the extent or degree of the liability assumed by a third party contractor is in any respect excluded or limited, unless such contract is entered into contrary to prior written Instructions given by the Customer and accepted in writing by the Company.

(C) **Evidence of Contract with Third Party Contractor**: The Company shall, on demand by the Customer, provide evidence of any contract entered into as agent for the Customer. Insofar as the Company may be in default of this obligation, it shall be deemed to have contracted with the Customer as a principal for the performance of the Customer's Instructions.

7. Customer's Warranties and Indemnities

(A) **Goods**: The Customer warrants that, unless the Customer provides prior written notification to and obtains written agreement from the Company, the Customer will not tender for Services any Goods which are:

(a) **Hazardous/Obnoxious Goods**:

(i) classified by the IMO Dangerous Goods Code as being hazardous,

(ii) nevertheless of a dangerous, damaging or obnoxious nature, so as to be liable to cause damage to any other goods or to be a risk to property, life or health, or

(iii) likely to harbour or encourage vermin or other pests.

(b) **High Value Goods**: of a valuable nature (which description shall include but not be restricted to bullion, coin, precious stones, jewellery, works of art, antiques and valuables of all kinds).

(c) **Perishables**: perishable and require temperature controlled conditions or have a short shelf-life.

(d) **Packing/Marking**: not properly and sufficiently prepared, packed, stowed, labelled and/or marked for the Services for which they are being tendered, unless those Services include said tasks.

If the Goods are tendered in/on containers, trailers, flats, railway wagons, tanks, igloos, or any other unit load device specifically constructed for the carriage of goods by land, sea or air, (each hereafter individually referred to as 'transport unit') then, unless the Company has accepted Instructions as principal to load the transport unit, the Customer also warrants that:

(i) the Goods have been properly and competently loaded into/onto the transport unit;

(ii) the Goods are suitable for carriage in/on the transport unit being utilised, and

(iii) the transport unit is in a suitable condition to carry the Goods loaded therein/on,

and if nevertheless Goods which breach any of the warranties in this Clause 7(A) are tendered for Services, the Customer shall indemnify the Company, its servants, agents and Sub-Contractors against all penalties, claims, damages, costs and expenses of whatsoever nature and howsoever arising in connection with such Goods.

Unless prior arrangements have been made and prior written acceptance obtained from the Company, no liability whatsoever, howsoever arising, will be accepted by the Company in connection with such Goods and the Company, their servants, agents and/or Sub-Contractors may deal with such Goods as they, in their sole discretion, consider appropriate.

(B) **Details of Goods**: The Customer warrants that the description and particulars of the Goods furnished by or on behalf of the Customer or Owner are complete and accurate and include all data necessary to accomplish the required Services safely and effectively.

(C) **Authority**: The Customer warrants that he is either the Owner or has the authority of the Owner to contract with the Company for the Services.

(D) **Circular Indemnity**: The Customer warrants that no claim or allegation shall be made by any Person against any parent, subsidiary or associate company, director, servant, agent, Sub-Contractor or employee of the Company (hereinafter referred to as 'such Persons') which imposes or attempts to impose upon any of such Persons any liability whatsoever in connection with any Services and/or Goods (whether or not arising out of negligence on the part of such Persons) unless the Company is acting as an agent only in accordance with Clause 6 and such Persons are independent contractors providing a Service to the Customer through the agency of the Company, in which case the Customer may proceed against such Persons under the terms of the contract procured on its behalf from such Persons by the Company acting as an agent only. Excepting for such instance, if any such claim or allegation should nevertheless be made, the Customer will indemnify the Company and such Persons against all consequences thereof.

Without prejudice to the foregoing, unless trading directly with the Customer under its own conditions through the agency of the Company, every such Person shall have the benefit of every right, defence, limitation and liberty of whatsoever nature herein contained or otherwise available to the Company as if such provisions were expressly for his benefit; and in entering into this contract the Company, to the extent of these provisions, does so not only on its own behalf but also as agent and trustee for such Persons.

The Customer further warrants that no claim or allegation in respect of any Services or Goods shall be made against the Company by any Person other than in accordance with these Conditions which imposes or attempts to impose upon the Company any liability whatsoever, whether or not arising out of negligence on the part of the Company and, if any such claim or allegation should nevertheless be made, to indemnify the Company against all consequences thereof.

(E) **Acting on Customer's Instructions**: The Customer shall indemnify the Company against all liability, loss, damage, cost and expense whatsoever and howsoever arising as a result of the Company acting in accordance with the Customer's Instructions or arising from any breach by the Customer of any warranty contained in these Conditions or from the negligence of the Customer.

(F) **Duty, Fines, etc**: The Customer shall be liable for and shall indemnify the Company in respect of all duties, taxes, imposts, levies, deposits and outlays of whatsoever nature levied by any authority in relation to the Goods and for all payments, fines, costs expenses, loss or damage whatsoever and howsoever incurred or sustained by the Company in connection therewith.

(G) **General Average**: The Customer shall indemnify the Company in respect of any claims of a General Average or Salvage nature which may be made on it and shall provide such security as may be required by the Company in this connection on demand.

(H) **Information Indemnity**: Advice and information, in whatever form it may be given, is provided by the Company for the Customer only and the Customer shall indemnify the Company against any liability, claim, loss, damage, cost or expense arising out of any other Persons relying upon such advice or information. Except under special arrangements previously made in writing, advice and information which is not related to Instructions accepted by the Company is provided gratuitously and without liability.

(I) **EDI Transmission**: In the event of Instructions data being transmitted via electronic communication, the Customer accepts that the sender is responsible for the quality of such Instructions or data.

8. Liability

(A) **Time Bar**: Any claim by the Customer against the Company in respect of any Service must be made in writing without delay. In the event of delay in presentation of a claim causing prejudice to the Company's ability to investigate said claim or reserve its rights against its Sub-Contractors, the Company shall be relieved of any liability in respect of such claim.

In any event, the Company shall be discharged of all liability whatsoever and howsoever arising in respect of any Service provided for the Customer unless suit be brought and written notice thereof given to the Company within nine months from the date of any event or occurrence alleged to give rise to a cause of action against the Company.

(B) **Exclusions**: Whether the Company acts as agent or principal it shall be relieved of liability for loss, damage or expense if and to the extent that same was caused by:

(a) the act or omission of the Customer, or Person other than the Company acting on behalf of the Customer, Owner or of the Person from whom the Company took the Goods in charge;

(b) insufficiency of the packing and/or marks and/or labels and/or numbers unless the Company had undertaken to carry out the packing, application of marks or labelling or numbering of the Goods;

(c) handling, loading, stowage or unloading of the Goods by the Customer, Owner or any Person other than the Company acting on behalf of the Customer;

(d) inherent vice of the Goods;

(e) strike, lock out, stoppage or restraint of labour;
(f) a nuclear incident;
(g) any cause or event which the Company was unable to avoid and the consequences whereof the Company was unable to prevent by the exercise of reasonable diligence;
(h) any act or omission of the Company the consequences of which it could not reasonably have foreseen;
(i) compliance with the instructions of any Person entitled to give them.

The burden of proving that the loss or damage was due to one or more of the above causes or events shall rest upon the Company.

(C) **Limits of Liability**: Subject to Clause 2, unless the Company agrees in writing to accept alternative levels of liability (in which case such limits as agreed shall be substituted for those provided in this Clause), the Company's liability (if any and whether acting as principal or agent), howsoever arising, and notwithstanding that the cause of loss, damage or expense is unexplained, shall not exceed:

(a) in the case of claims for loss or damage to Goods:
  (i) the value of any Goods lost or damaged, or
  (ii) a sum at the rate of two Special Drawing Rights as defined by the International Monetary Fund, (hereinafter referred to as SDRs), per kilo of gross weight of any Goods lost or damaged,

whichever shall be the lesser.

(b) in the case of all other claims:
  (i) the value of the Goods the subject of the relevant Service; or
  (ii) a sum at the rate of two SDRs per kilo of the gross weight of the Goods the subject of the said Service, or
  (iii) 75,000 SDRs in respect of any one Service,

whichever shall be the lesser.

For the purposes of this Clause the value of the Goods shall be their value at the place and time they are delivered to the Consignee in accordance with the relevant Service or should have been so delivered. The exchange from SDRs to settlement currency shall be calculated at the rate applicable on the date when the claim is paid.

Details of the Company's additional charges for accepting increased liability will be provided on request.

(D) **Consequential Loss/Delay**: Except by prior written agreement, the Company shall not in any circumstances, whatsoever or howsoever arising, be liable for indirect or consequential loss, such as (but not limited to) loss of profits, loss of market or the consequences of delay or deviation howsoever caused.

However, if pursuant to Clause 4(B) the Company accepts any liability for delay, liability shall in no circumstances exceed a sum equal to twice the amount of the Company's charges in respect of the relevant Service.

The defences and limits of liability provided for in these Conditions shall apply in any action against the Company whatsoever, howsoever arising, whether the action be founded in contract, tort or otherwise.

9. Payments, etc.

(A) **Payment of the Company's Invoices**: The Customer shall pay to the Company in cash or as otherwise agreed all sums immediately when due, without reduction or deferment on account of any claim, counterclaim or set off. If any sum due is still unpaid 30 days after the date of the invoice, the Company shall be entitled to add interest at 2% above the minimum lending rate of the local national bank for any period in excess thereof.

(B) **Collecting Charges for Customer**: Despite the acceptance by the Company of Instructions to collect freight, duties, charges or other expenses from the Consignee or any other Person, the Customer shall remain responsible for such freight, duties, charges or expenses on receipt of evidence of proper demand and in the absence of evidence of payment (for whatever reason) by such Consignee or other Person when due.

(C) **Lien**:

(a) Subject to sub-clause (b), the Company shall have a general lien on all Goods and documents relating to Goods in its possession, custody or control for all sums due at any time from the Customer or Owner, in respect of Services to the Goods under lien or of any earlier Services on other Goods, and shall be entitled to sell or dispose of such Goods or documents as agent for and at the expense of the Customer and apply the proceeds in or towards the payment of such sums. Upon accounting to the Customer for any balance remaining after payment of any sum due to the Company and the costs of sale or disposal, the Company shall be discharged of any liability whatsoever in respect of the Goods or documents.

(b) If the Goods, in the sole opinion of the Company, are liable to perish or deteriorate, the Company's right to sell or dispose of the Goods shall arise immediately upon any sum becoming due to the Company, subject only to the Company taking reasonable steps to bring to the Customer's attention its intention of selling or disposing of the Goods before doing so.

(D) **Brokerages, Commissions, etc**: The Company shall be entitled to be paid and retain all brokerages, commissions, allowances and other remunerations customarily retained by or paid to freight forwarders.

10. Law and Jurisdiction

(A) **Law**: The Services undertaken pursuant to and the interpretation of these Conditions shall be governed by English Law.

(B) **Jurisdiction**: Any claim or dispute arising under these Conditions shall be referred to the High Court of Justice in London, to the exclusion of the jurisdictions of the courts or any other places, unless the Company appeals to the jurisdiction of any other place and voluntarily submits thereto.

(C) **Arbitration**: Nothing herein shall prevent the parties to any dispute under these Conditions agreeing to refer it to arbitration on mutually acceptable terms.

APPENDIX 13

LETTER OF INDEMNITY (DELIVERY OF GOODS WITHOUT BILL OF LADING)

In consideration of your releasing for delivery to us or to our order the undermentioned goods of which we claim to be the rightful owners, without production of the relevant Bill(s) of Lading (not as yet in our possession) we hereby agree as follows:

1. Indemnify you, your principals, servants and agents (as the case may be) and to hold all of you harmless in respect of any liability, loss, damage or expense of whatsoever nature and howsoever arising which you may sustain by reason of delivering the goods in accordance with our request and to reimburse you forthwith on demand for all payments which you make or are called upon to make in respect of thereof.

2. In the event of any proceedings being commenced against you, your principal or any of your servants or agents in connection with the delivery of the goods as aforesaid, to provide you or them from time to time with sufficient funds to defend the same.

3. That if any vessel or other asset owned by you, your principals, servants or agents (as the case may be) or any person is arrested or threatened with arrest in connection with the delivery of the goods the subject of this Indemnity, you may take such steps as you in your sole discretion consider necessary, in the light of the prevailing local circumstances, to remove or avoid such arrest or remove or avoid the threat thereof, including (but not restricted to) immediate settlement of any claim in connection with the said goods, or the provision of security therefore and all the costs of such actions shall be for our account. At your sole discretion this action may be taken without prior consultation with us and we agree that our prior consent shall not be a condition precedent to indemnity.

4. Upon demand to pay any freight and / or General Average and / or charges due on goods aforesaid (it being expressly agreed and understood that all liens shall subsist and be unaffected by the same terms hereof).

5. As soon as any original Bills of Lading for the above goods shall have arrived and / or come into our possession, to produce and deliver the same to you properly endorsed whereupon our liability hereunder shall cease in respect of all future claims or expenses, but shall remain in force in respect of any already incurred by you even if not already paid.

6. The liability of each and every person under this Indemnity shall be joint and several and shall not be conditional upon your proceeding first against any person, whether or not such person is party to or liable under this Indemnity.

7. This Indemnity shall be construed in accordance with English law and each and every person liable under this Indemnity shall at your request submit to the jurisdiction of the High Court of Justice of England.

8. This Indemnity shall be unlimited in time and amount so far as we are concerned but shall be limited to two hundred percent (200%) of CIF value of the goods and three (3) years so far as the guarantee of the Bank is concerned, unless you give notice to the Bank within the three year period that a claim has been made for which indemnity is sought, in which case the guarantee of the Bank shall continue until said claim is resolved, plus one month.

CONSIGNEE	VESSEL & VOY. NO	DELIVERY ORDER TO BE ISSUED IN THE NAME OF:

BILL(S) OF LADING No(s):	QUANTITY AND DESCRIPTION OF GOODS	CONTAINER NO(S):

NOTE
INDEMNITIES LIMITING LIABILITY, INCORPORATING AN EXPIRY DATE OR BEARING ANY QUALIFYING REMARKS WHATSOEVER (EXCEPT AS PROVIDED HEREIN IN CLAUSE 8) CANNOT BE ACCEPTED.

For and on behalf of (Company) ....

Signed .... Date ....

We the Bank named opposite join the above indemnity and guarantee its performance, subject to the provisions of Clause 8 above

For and on behalf of (Bank) ....

....

Signed .... Date ....

AVERAGE BOND

Date: .... Page: 1

B/Lading or W/Bill No: .... Vessel: .... Voyage Number: .... Casualty Date: ....

Place of Receipt: .... Port of Loading: ....
Place of Delivery: .... Port of Discharge: ....

We the undersigned agree, in consideration of the delivery of the goods represented by the above bill of lading/waybill to us or our order and payment of the freight payable on delivery (if any), to pay to the shipowner the proper and respective proportion of any salvage and/or general average and/or particular and/ or other charges which may be chargeable upon this consignment or to which we may be liable to contribute in respect of damage, loss, sacrifice or expenditure (including making any payment on account of such sum as is duly certified by the average adjusters to be due from the goods). We further promise and agree forthwith to furnish to the shipowner a correct account and particulars of the value of the goods delivered to us in order that any such salvage and/or general average and/or particular and/or other charges may be ascertained and adjusted in the usual manner. We further agree that general average will be adjusted and settled according to York/Antwerp Rules 1994, or any subsequent amendment thereto, at a place designated by the shipowner, according to the law of that place.

Non Separation Agreement

It is agreed that in the event of the vessel's cargo or part thereof being forwarded to original destination by another vessel, vessels or conveyance, rights and liabilities in general average shall not be affected by such forwarding, it being the intention to place the parties concerned as nearly as possible in the same position in this respect as they would have been in the absence of such forwarding and with the adventure continuing by the original vessel for so long as justifiable under the law applicable or under the contract of carriage.

The basis of contribution to general average of the property involved shall be the values on delivery at original destination unless sold or otherwise disposed of short of that destination, but where none of her cargo is carried forward in the vessel, the vessel shall contribute on the basis of her actual value on the date she completes discharge of her cargo.

Signature of owner of cargo (or his authorised agent) ....

Owner of Cargo	Insurers of Cargo
Name	Name ....
Address	Address ....
....	....
....	....
Tel No .... Date ....../....../......	Tel No .... Policy No ....
C.I.F. or C.I.P. Value of Goods	Ocean Freight US$ ....

Please return this page duly completed to the carrier's office or agent with whom you are arranging collection/delivery together with:

A) A copy of the commercial invoice for the goods (if available)
B) The average guarantee (see below) signed by (or on behalf of) your insurers (if obtainable without undue delay)

(Do not delay returning this bond (duly completed) if either A or B are not immediately available but send undertaking as soon as possible and forward other documents as soon as they are to hand).

*** WARNING ***

Please note that if delivery of cargo is prevented by delay in the provision of the required security, all costs incurred as a result thereof will be for the account of the owners of the cargo and must be paid before delivery can be effected.

APPENDIX 15

AVERAGE GUARANTEE

Date .... Page 2

Important

This guarantee will only be accepted provided no additions, deletions or amendments are made to the wording by insurers.

B/Lading or W/Bill No: .... Vessel: .... Voyage Number: .... Casualty Date: ....

Place of Receipt: .... Port of Loading: ....
Place of delivery: .... Port of Discharge: ....

In consideration of the delivery in due course to the consignees of the goods represented by the above bill of lading/waybill, without collection of a deposit on account of average, we, the undersigned underwriters, hereby guarantee to the shipowner on account of the concerned the payment of any contribution to general average and/or salvage and/or charges which may hereafter be ascertained to be due in respect of the said goods.

We further agree to make a prompt payment on account if required as soon as such payment may be certified by the average adjusters.

Non Separation Agreement

It is agreed that in the event of the vessel's cargo or part thereof being forwarded to original destination by another vessel, vessels or conveyance, rights and liabilities in general average shall not be affected by such forwarding, it being the intention to place the parties concerned as nearly as possible in the same position in this respect as they would have been in the absence of such forwarding and with the adventure continuing by the original vessel for so long as justifiable under the law applicable or under the contract of carriage.

The basis of contribution to general average of the property involved shall be the values on delivery at original destination unless sold or otherwise disposed of short of that destination: but where none of her cargo is carried forward in the vessel, the vessel shall contribute on the basis of her actual value on the date she completes discharge of her cargo.

Name of Insurers ....

Address ....

....

....

Tel No .... Fax No ....

Name of Contact ....

Insurers Signature ....

Date ....

Policy or Cert No ....

Insured Value ....

Average Adjuster (Local Office):

Name ....

Address ....

....

....

Tel No .... Telex No ....

Fax No .... Contact ....

*** WARNING ***

Please note that if delivery of cargo is prevented by delay in the provision of the required security, all costs incurred as a result thereof will be for the account of the owners of the cargo and must be paid before delivery can be effected.

GLOSSARY OF USEFUL TERMS AND ABBREVIATIONS

ADR	Accord European Nation du transport international des marchandise Dangereux par Route	A European dangerous goods classification.
ATA Carnet (Europe)	Admission Temporaire—Temporary Admission	An ATA Carnet makes the Customs clearance of certain temporary importations and exportations easier.
Ad Valorem	(literally) "according to the value"	An Ad Valorem freight rate is one where freight is based on the value of the goods. An Ad Valorem Bill of Lading is one where the value of the goods is shown on the face of the document, which value becomes the Carrier's limit of liability, in return for the payment of a freight surcharge.
Athens Convention		International convention governing Carrier's liability for Passengers and their baggage.
Average Bond		Undertaking by Merchant to pay G.A. contribution (*see* Chapter 9).

Average Guarantee		Guarantee from Cargo Insurer that G.A. contribution will be paid (*see* Chapter 9).
BAF	Bunker Adjustment Factor	Freight adjustment factor to reflect current cost of bunkers
B/E	Bill of Exchange	A forward dated undertaking to pay prepared by the debtor and signed by the creditor to acknowledge debt and date payment due. Used in Documentary Credits to allow period of credit
BIFA	British International Freight Association	Trade Association of British Freight Forwarders
BIMCO	Baltic and International Maritime Council	A Danish based organisation to which many shipowners belong that represents their interests and assists by preparing standard charter parties and other shipping documents and providing other advisory services
B/L	Bill of Lading	Acts as a receipt for goods, contains the terms of the contract of carriage and is usually a document of title to the goods
B/L Ton	Bill of Lading Ton	The greater of weight or measurement of goods where 1 ton is either 1000 kilos or 1 cubic metre (also called Freight Ton)

BMLA	British Maritime Law Association	
BSC	British Shippers Council	
BSI	British Standards Institution	The authorised body for the preparation of national standards in the UK
Blank Endorsement		The unqualified stamp and signature on a Bill of Lading by the Shipper that converts an "Order" Bill into a Bearer document
Blanket Guarantee		Temporary guarantee to Salvor for all cargo and containers to secure release for oncarriage
Bolero		An "Electronic" Bill of Lading project
Box		Colloquial name for container
Boxtime		A standard BIMCO time charter for containerships
Break-Bulk Cargo		Goods shipped loose in the vessel's hold and not in a container
Bunkers		Fuel for vessel's engines
CABAF	Currency and Bunker Adjustment Factor	A combination of CAF and BAF
CAF	Currency Adjustment Factor	Freight adjustment factor to reflect currency exchange fluctuations
CAP (Europe)	Common Agricultural Policy	EU Policy relating to agricultural produce

C/B	Containerbase	One of a group of UK Container Freight Stations
CCC	Customs Co-operation Council	The forum for international co-operation between Customs authorities in an attempt to provide harmony and uniformity of approach
CCP	Cross Charter Party (*see* Chapter 3)	
C&D	Collection and Delivery	Carriage from/to Customer's premises to/ from CFS
C&E (UK)	Customs and Excise	
CEFIC	European Chemical Industry Council	The party who prepares Trem Cards
CENSA	Council of European & Japanese National Shipowners' Associations	
C&F	Cost and Freight	A conventional/port-to-port INCOTERM term of sale. (More correctly known as CFR)
CFS	Container Freight Station	Place for packing and unpacking LCL consignments. Variously known as C/Bs (in UK), Depots (Australia), and ICDs (UK and the Indian Subcontinent)
CFR	Cost and Freight	A conventional/port-to-port only INCOTERM term of sale. (More popularly referred to as C&F)

CHA	Container Hiring Agreement (*see* Chapter 4).	
CHIEF (UK)	Customs Handling of Import and Export Freight	Customs computer system to handle clearance procedures
CIF	Cost Insurance Freight	A conventional port-to-port only INCOTERM term of sale
CIM (Europe)	Convention Internationale concernant le transport des Marchandises par chemin de fer	International convention on Carriage of Goods by Rail (Part of COTIF)
CIP	Carriage and Insurance paid to	A new Combined Transport INCOTERM replacing CIF where CT is involved but applicable to all modes of transport. Particularly appropriate for Combined Transport
CISG	Convention on the International Sale of Goods 1980 (Vienna Convention)	
CMI	Comite Maritime International	An international committee of maritime lawyers
CMR (Europe)	Conventional relative au contrat transport international des Marchandises par Route	International convention on carriage of Goods by Road

COGSA	Carriage of Goods by Sea Act	
(UK)	COGSA 1971= Hague-Visby Rules COGSA 1992 = Rights of Suit against Carrier – replaced 1855 Bill of Lading Act	
(US)	COGSA 1936 = Hague Rules	
COT (UK)	Customer's Own Transport	Customer collects from/ delivers to CFS/CY
COTIF (Europe)	Convention Concerning International Carriage by Rail (includes CIM)	
COU	Clip on Unit or Central Operating Unit	Portable refrigeration units. Body set up to co-ordinate consortium operations in a trade
CPT	Carriage Paid to	A new Combined Transport INCOTERM replacing CFR where CT is involved but applicable to all modes of transport Particularly appropriate for Combined Transport
CRN (UK)	Customs Registered Number	A number allocated by C&E to an exporter or agent (Freight Forwarder) for use when exports are to be entered under the SCP
CSC	Container Safety Convention	International convention for safe containers

CSHA	Containerspace Hiring Agreement (*see* Chapter 4)	
CT	Combined Transport	Carriage by more than one mode of transport against one contract of carriage
CTD	Combined Transport Document	The CTO's Bill of Lading.
CTO	Combined Transport Operator	A Carrier who contracts as a principal to perform a CT operation
CWE	Cleared Without Examination	Cleared by Customs without inspection
CY	Container Yard	Collection and Distribution point for loaded FCL and empty containers
Certificate of Compliance		Document issued by regulatory body certifying compliance with ISM Code
Certificate of Origin		Document certifying the country of origin of goods which is normally issued or signed by a Chamber of Commerce or Embassy.
Cellular		Term used to describe hold configuration of purpose built containerships equipped with cell guides into which containers fit
Circular Indemnity		Chain of Indemnity clause in Bill of Lading (*see* Chapter 6—Clause 4)

Classification Clause	ICC Insurance clause listing criteria for vessels on which automatic cargo insurance cover applies at standard rates
Clean B/L	One bearing no qualification re tally or condition of goods or packing
Closing Date	Last date on which export goods can be accepted for a nominated sailing
Co-Charterer	Fellow consortium member chartering slots on same vessel
Conference	Organisation of a group of lines operating in one trade who agree to operate a common tariff
Conlease	A standard BIMCO lease for containers
Consignee	Importer
Consortium	A group of CTOs who agree to rationalise sailings in a trade and carry each other's containers
Container Service Charge	(*see* THC)
Contingency Cover	Cargo insurance by Shipper in case Consignee does not take up documents
Contracting Carrier	(*see* Principal Carrier)

Contra Proferentem		English legal doctrine applying least favourable interpretation against party proferring contract
Controlled Atmosphere		Container in which mixture of gases is controlled to retard ripening
Customs 2000		A paperless simplified clearance procedure
DAF	Delivery at Frontier	An INCOTERM term of sale applicable to all modes of transport
DAN (UK)	Deferment Approval Number	An account held by a trader with HMC&E to which duty and VAT are debited direct
DDP	Delivery Duty Paid	An INCOTERM term of sale applicable to all modes of transport
DDU	Delivered Duty Unpaid	An INCOTERM term of sale applicable to all modes of transport
DEQ	Delivered Ex Quay	A conventional/port-to-port INCOTERM term of sale. (Used to be EXQ)
DES	Delivered Ex Ship	A conventional/port-to-port INCOTERM term of sale. (Used to be EXS)
DETR	Department of the Environment, Transport and the Regions	
DGN (UK)	Dangerous Goods Note	

DTI (UK)	Department of Trade and Industry	Government Department with responsibility for trade matters
DTI (UK)	Direct Trade Input	Procedure for Customs entry Clearance
DataFreight Receipt		An electronic Waybill system developed by Atlantic Container Line
Data Logger		Electronic temperature recording device for refrigerated containers
Delivery Order		A document authorising delivery to a nominated party of goods in the care of a third party. Can be issued by a Carrier on surrender of a Bill of Lading and then used by Merchant to transfer title by endorsement
Demise Clause		An identity of carrier clause used by issuer of B/L (who does not own vessel) providing to act as agent only to create contract between vessel owner and cargo owner
Demurrage		Charge raised for detaining FCL container/trailer at a CFS for longer period than provided in Tariff. (Do not confuse with Detention)
Depot		A CFS
Designated Person		Person in ship operating company nominated to be responsible for compliance with ISM Code

Detention		Charge raised for detaining container/trailer at Customer's premises for longer period than provided in Tariff. (Do not confuse with Demurrage)
Disponent Owner		Charterer of a vessel acting like an owner to make space available to other parties
Doc. Credit	Documentary Credit	The basis of international trade by means of which payment is made to the Shipper against surrender of specified documents to a bank acting on behalf of Consignee
Document of Title		Function of Bill of Lading that makes it a cheque for the goods represented on its face
Dock Receipt (US)		Acknowledgement of receipt of goods/container at Pier incorporating Bill of Lading terms from time of receipt
Drawback		Repayment of duty upon re-exportation of goods previously imported
EC		European Community
ECG (UK)	Export Credits Guarantee	Insurance on goods shipped against non-payment by reason of commercial and/or political risks as arranged

ECP	Electronic Commerce Project	An ICC initiative on electronic commerce relative to Documentary Credits
ECSA	European Community Shipowners Association	
EDI	Electronic Data Interchange	The transfer of structured data from one computer system to another
EDIFACT	EDI For Administration Commerce and Transport	Organisation responsible to UN ECE for the development of standard EDI messages for Administration, Commerce and Transport
EDISHIP		An organisation to develop systems for exchanging data between major Carriers and Merchants by electronic means
EDP	Electronic Data Processing	Computer processing of Data
EHA	Equipment Handover Agreement	Agreement acknowledging condition signed when taking over Carrier's equipment and returning it, which incorporates terms of contract under which equipment is taken over
EPU (UK)	Entry Processing Unit	Customs office that processes Customs entries
ESC	European National Shippers Councils	

ETA	Estimated Time of Arrival	
ETD	Estimated Time of Departure	
EU	European Union (now more usually referred to as the EC)	
EXW	Ex Works	An INCOTERM term of sale applicable to all modes of transport
Ejusdem Generis		English law doctrine restricting interpretation of general words used after specific words to words similar to the specific words
Electronic Commerce (or E-commerce)		The presently preferred term for trading with EDI
Estoppel		English law doctrine precluding party from denying the truth of a statement previously made
Export Declaration		US Customs Service Form No. 75-25-V
Export Licence		Governmental document authorising export of restricted goods
FAK	Freight All Kinds	System whereby freight is charged per container, irrespective of nature of goods, and not according to a Tariff
FAS	Free Alongside Ship	A conventional/port-to-port only INCOTERM term of sale

FCA	Free Carrier (named place)	A new Combined Transport INCOTERM replacing FOB where CT is involved, but applicable to all modes of transport. Particularly appropriate for Combined Transport
FCL	Full Container Load	Arrangements whereby Shipper utilises all the space in a container which he packs himself.
FEU	Forty-Foot Equivalent Unit	
FIATA	International Federation of Freight Forwarders Associations	(Federation Internationales des Associations de Transitaires et Assimiles.)
FILO	Free In Liner Out	Freight includes cost of discharge but not loading
FFI	For Further Instructions	Used in Place of Delivery box in Bill of Lading if final destination uncertain at time of shipment, e.g. Barking Containerbase FFI
FIOS	Free In Out + Stow	Shipper pays for loading, stowing and discharging
FMC	Federal Maritime Commission	U.S. Federal Authority governing sea transport
FOB	Free On Board	A conventional/port-to-port only INCOTERM term of sale
Fantainer		Container with built-in forced ventilation.

Feeder Vessel		A short-sea vessel used to fetch and carry goods and containers to and from deep sea vessels
Flat Rack		A container consisting of a base and two ends but no sides or roof
Flexitank		Polythene bag to allow bulk liquids and powders to be carried in GPs
Force Majeure		Circumstances beyond the control of either party to a contract
Freight		The amount payable for the carriage of goods. Sometimes also used to describe the goods themselves which are better described as cargo in marine transportation
Freight Broker		The Carrier's Agent
Freight Forwarder		The Merchant's Agent
Freight Ton		The tonnage on which freight is charged (also called B/L Ton)
GA	General Average (*see* Chapter 9).	
GATT	General Agreement on Tariffs and Trade	An international multilateral agreement embodying a code of practice for fair trading in international commerce

GBP	Pounds Sterling	
GO (US)	General Order	Issued by US Customs as notice of intention to seize goods
GP	General Purpose container	
Gold Clause	Hague Rules Article IX (*see* Chapters 3 & 6—B/L Clause 7(3))	
Groupage		Consolidation of several LCL consignments into a container
Groupage Agent		One who consolidates LCL consignments to offer to a Carrier as an FCL
H/C	High Cube	Containers 9ft 6ins high instead of usual 8ft 6ins
H/H	Half Height	An OT container only 4ft 3ins high
H/L	Heavy Lift	
H&M	Hull & Machinery	
HMC (UK)	Her Majesty's Customs	
HMC&E (UK)	Her Majesty's Customs & Excise	
HNS	Hazardous & Noxious Substances	An international convention governing the carriage of these substances which was agreed at a diplomatic conference in 1996
Hague Rules		1924 International Convention on Carriage of Goods by Sea

Hague-Visby Rules		1968 Revision of Hague Rules
Hamburg Rules		1978 UNCITRAL alternative to the Hague Rules
Haulier (UK)		A road transport operator (a trucker in US)
Himalaya Clause		B/L clause extending protection of B/L to servants, agents and sub-contractors
Hub & Spoke		The way of describing modern containerised operations whereby large containerships call at a restricted number of major (hub) ports to or from whence containers are carried to/from minor ports by feeder services (spokes)
IBAP	Intervention Board for Agricultural Produce	Authority monitoring application of EC CAP policy
ICC (Europe)	International Chamber of Commerce	A Paris-based international forum that aims to facilitate trade
ICC (US)	Interstate Commerce Commission	The US governmental body to regulate interstate trade
ICC (Ins)	Institute Cargo Clauses	The International Underwriting Association standard clauses for cargo insurance
ICD	Inland Clearance Depot	A CFS with Customs Clearance Facilities

ILU	Institute of London Underwriters	London Marine Insurers governing body. Now renamed: International Underwriting Association (IUA)
IMDG Code	International Maritime Dangerous Goods Code	The IMO recommendations for the carriage of dangerous goods by sea
IMO	International Maritime Organisation	The UN Body charged with the duty of making safety and anti-pollution conventions and recommendations concerning sea transport
INCOTERMS	International Rules for the Interpretation of Trade Terms	A list (currently 13) of standard terms for foreign trade contracts compiled by ICC. Current edition is 2000
ISM Code	International Safety Management Code	
ISO	International Standards Organisation	International Organisation of National Standard Bodies responsible, *inter alia*, for setting standards for container construction
IUA	International Underwriting Association New name for ILU (*see* ILU)	
IWL	Institute Warranty Limits	Parameters of navigation covered by normal cargo insurance
Indemnifyee		He who is indemnified

Indemnifyor		He who indemnifies
Inherent Vice		Those properties of certain goods which lead to their arrival in damaged condition without accident or negligence, e.g. unprotected steel will "*weather*", bales of rubber stick together, copra is almost invariably infested.
Integral		Refrigerated container with own machinery
Jettison		Throw overboard (to lighten the vessel)
JIT	Just in Time.	Stockholding process by which minimum stocks are maintained and reliance placed on frequent regular deliveries
L&A	Law & Arbitration	
L/C	Letter of Credit	The document in which the terms of a Documentary Credit transaction are set out
LCL	Less than Container Load	A parcel of goods too small to fill a container which is grouped by the Carrier at a CFS with other compatible goods for the same destination
LEC (UK)	Local Export Control	A system of clearing export containers at Exporter's premises

L/I	Letter of Indemnity	Sometimes used to allow Consignee to take delivery of goods without surrendering B/L which has been delayed or become lost
LIC (UK)	Local Import Control	A system of clearing import containers at Importer's premises
LIFO	Liner In Free Out	Freight includes the cost of loading but not discharging
L&J	Law & Jurisdiction	
LLMC	International Convention on Limitation of Liability for Maritime Claims	A 1976 limitation convention enacted in the UK by the Merchant Shipping Act 1979
LMAA	London Maritime Arbitration Association	
LOF	Lloyds Open Form	A standard form of salvage agreement
LO-LO	Lift-On/Lift Off	A containership onto which and from which containers are lifted by crane (as opposed to Ro-Ro)
Latent Defect		A defect not obvious from cursory inspection
Lessee		Party taking property under lease
Lessor		Party letting out property under lease

Lien		A right to retain goods and documents against payment of charges etc. due but unpaid
Liner		Vessel plying a regular trade/defined route against a published sailing schedule
Liner Terms		Freight includes the cost of loading onto and discharging from the vessel
Log		Vessel's official record
MAFF		Minister of Agriculture, Fisheries & Food
MLA	Maritime Law Association	
MMO	Multi Modal Operator	
MSA	Merchant Shipping Act	
MT	Empty or Multimodal Transport	An empty container
MTD	Multimodal Transport Document	
MTO	Multimodal Transport Operator (Same as MMO)	
Manifest		List of goods (or passengers) on a vessel
Measurement Ton		1 cubic metre One of the alternative bases of Freight Tariff

Multimodal Transport		The UNCTAD preferred term for what we call Combined Transport
Mutatis mutandis		The necessary changes being made (*see* Chapter 6—Waybills)
Mutual Waiver		Liability philosophy in Consortium Operating Agreements (*see* Chapter 2)
NAWK	National Association of Warehouse Keepers	
NVO(C)C	Non Vessel-Owning/ Operating (Common) Carrier	A Carrier issuing Bs/L for carriage of goods on vessels which he neither owns nor operates
New Jason Clause	A B/L GA clause for US adjustments	
Non-Separation Agreement		A GA Bond/Guarantee clause covering oncarriage on another vessel (*see* Chapter 9)
O/H	Overheight	A container/flat rack with goods protruding above the top of the corner posts
OOG	Out of Gauge	Goods whose dimensions exceed those of the container/flat rack in which they are packed
OPA 90	Oil Pollution Act 1990	A US Act with very onerous provisions covering all vessels trading to/from USA

O, S&D Report	Over, Short and Damage Report	Outturn report from a break-bulk vessel
O/T	Open Top	A container with tarpaulin covered open roof
O/W	Overwidth	A container with goods protruding beyond the sides of the container/flat rack onto which they are packed
Op. Ag.	Operating Agreement	A consortium contract (*see* Chapter 2)
PA	Particular Average	Partial accidental loss or damage (as opposed to Total Loss or General Average)
PHA	Port Health Authority	
P & I Club	Protection and Indemnity Association	Carrier's mutual liability insurer
POA	Place of Acceptance	Where the goods are received for transit and Carrier's liability commences. Now more usually called a POR.
POD	Place of Delivery	Where goods are delivered and Carrier's liability ceases or Proof of Delivery A signed receipt acknowledging delivery
POR	Place of Receipt (*see* POA above).	

P to P	(UK)	Port to Port	
	(US)	Pier to Pier	
Paramount Clause			A clause which takes precedence over all others—usually applying COGSA
Particular Charges			Also known as Special Charges. Sue & labour type charges
Partlow Chart			Paper disc recording chart for refrigeration temperatures
Poincare Franc			Fictitious gold franc originally used amongst other things to assess Carrier's liability in an inflation-proofed manner in Hague-Visby Rules. Now largely replaced by SDRs
Pomerene Act			The US Bill of Lading Act
Porthole			Insulated container relying on external source of cold air
Port Service Charge			(*see* THC).
Principal Carrier			The Carrier issuing a CTD (regardless of whether or not goods are carried on his own, a third party's or a consortium member's vessel)
RFS		Received for Shipment	

RN	Release Note	Receipt signed by Customer acknowledging delivery of goods
RO-RO	Roll On-Roll Off	A ferry type vessel onto which goods and containers can be driven, usually via a ramp
Reefer	Refrigerated	
Removal Note (UK)	Indicates goods clear of Customs	
SAD (UK)	Single Administrative Document	Customs Declaration Form for both import and export cargo
SCOPIC Clause	Special Compensation P&I Clause	Amendment to LOF agreed between Salvors & P & I Clubs
SCP (UK)	Simplified Clearance Procedure	A simplified clearance procedure, under which Exporters of goods not requiring special control may submit an abbreviated Customs pre-entry or an approved commercial document at the time of export and provide the full statistical information after the goods are exported
	or Slot Charter Party	
SDR	Special Drawing Rights	The mean of a basket of currencies designed to "iron out" currency exchange fluctuations in international valuations. (Now used to express limitation in the Hague-Visby Rules and MSA Limitation Convention etc.)

SITPRO	Simpler Trade Procedures Board	
SMS	Safety Management System	Safe vessel operating procedure required by ISM Code
SOB	Shipped On Board	Endorsement on a Bill of Lading confirming loading on vessel
SOL	Shipowners' Liability	A marine liability insurance to cover carriers' liabilities outside P & I cover
SOLAS	Safety of Life at Sea	An IMO Convention governing the safe operation of vessels
SSN (UK)	Standard Shipping Note	
STC	Said to Contain or Standard Trading Conditions	
STCW 95	Standards of Training, Certification and Watchkeeping Convention	
SWIFT	Society for Worldwide Interbank Financial Telecommunications	
Salvage		Assistance by 3rd Party independent of contract to vessel in distress
Salvor		One who renders salvage services

Shipper	The person tendering goods for carriage Not to be confused with the party issuing the B/L or the vessel operator who is the Carrier
Shut-out	Goods not carried on intended vessel
Sister-ship Salvage Clause	B/L clause covering situation where salvage services are rendered by a sistership (*see* Chapter 6—B/L Clause 22(4))
Slot	Space on board a vessel occupied by a container
Slothire	A standard BIMCO slot charter for containerships
Special Charges	Also known as Particular Charges. Sue & labour type charges
Standard Trading Conditions	The terms under which a Carrier contracts for any services to Customers not covered by the Bill of Lading (*see* Chapter 7)
Straight Bill of Lading	A term for a non-negotiable Bill of Lading. In the U.S. the Pomerene Act governs its operation (*see* Chapter 6)
Stuffing/ Stripping	The action of packing/ unpacking a container
Sue & Labour Charges	Charges incurred short of destination to prevent damaged goods deteriorating further

Supercargo		The Charterer's representative on board a chartered vessel
TEU	Twenty-foot Equivalent Unit.	e.g. 1 ′ 40ft = 2 TEU 1 ′ 20ft = 1 TEU
THC	Terminal Handling Charge	A charge for handling FCLs at port terminals. Also known as a Container/Port Service Charge
TIR (Europe)	Transports International Routiers	A system involving the issue of a carnet to road hauliers which allows loaded vehicles to cross national frontiers with minimum Customs formalities
TIR (US)	Trailer Interchange Receipt	Receipt to Shipper delivering a loaded export container to a terminal
T/S	Transhipment	Transfer from one vessel to another for oncarriage
TT Club	Through Transport Club	Mutual insurer in the container/combined transport industry
TTD	Through Transport Document	The TTO's Bill of Lading
TTO	Through Transport Operator	A Carrier who contracts to carry goods (only part of which carriage he undertakes himself) on the basis that he is a principal whilst the goods are in his personal care and an agent only whilst they are not

Tanktainer		Container for bulk liquids
Tariff		Terms, conditions and scale of charges
Terminal		Port at which containers are loaded/unloaded onto/ from container vessels
Third Party		Any party other than the parties to a contract
Ton		2,240 lbs
Tonne		1,000 kilos
Tort		A civil breach of common law
Trem Card	Transport Emergencies Card	Essential details which must accompany all movements of dangerous goods in Europe
Triangulation		Movement of a discharged import container directly to an exporter to load
Trucker (US)		A road transport operator (a haulier in the UK)
Trunking		Movement of containers between Terminals and CFS's/CYs
Twistlocks		Devices to lock containers together
UCC (US)	Uniform Commercial Code	

UCP	Uniform Customs and Practice for Documentary Credits	The "*Bankers Bible*" on Documentary Credit interpretation issued by the ICC (Brochure no. 500 operating from 1st January 1994)
UN	United Nations	
UNCITRAL	United Nations Commission on International Trade and Law	
UNCON	Uncontainerised Goods	Goods which, because of their dimensions, cannot be containerised and which are therefore carried other than in a container
UNCTAD	United Nations Conference on Trade and Development	
UNCTAD MMO	UNCTAD Multi Modal Transport Convention	
UN ECE	United Nations Economic Commission for Europe	
VAT	Value Added Tax	An EU tax on goods and services
Vienna Convention		The United Nations Convention on Contracts for the International Sale of Goods (Vienna 1980)
Waybill		Acts as a receipt for the goods and evidence of the contract of carriage, but is not a document of title
York/Antwerp Rules		Rules relating to the adjustment of GA Present draft is 1994

INDEX

[All references are to page number]